Easy Object Programming for Windows™ Using Visual C++™

Richard O. Parker

PRENTICE HALL, Englewood Cliffs, New Jersey 07632

Library of Congress Cataloging-in-Publication Data

```
Parker, Richard O.
    Easy Object Programming for Windows Using Visual C.. / Richard O.
  Parker.
        p.   cm.
    Includes index.
    ISBN 0-13-291337-2
    1. Object-oriented programming (Computer science)  2. Microsoft
  Visual C++.  3. Microsoft Windows (Computer file)  I. Title.
  QA76.64.P37  1995
  005.265--dc20
```

                                                                94-26679
                                                                    CIP

Publisher: Alan Apt
Production Editor: Bayani Mendoza de Leon
Copy Editor: Brenda Melissaratos
Cover Designer: Ray Lundgren Graphics
Production Coordinator: Linda Behrens
Editorial Assistant: Shirley McGuire

ISBN 0-13-291337-2

Prentice-Hall International (UK) Limited, *London*
Prentice-Hall of Australia Pty. Limited, *Sydney*
Prentice-Hall Canada, Inc., *Toronto*
Prentice-Hall Hispanoamericana, S.A., *Mexico*
Prentice-Hall of India Private Limited, *New Delhi*
Prentice-Hall of Japan, Inc., *Tokyo*
Simon & Schuster Asia Pte. Ltd, *Singapore*
Editora Prentice-Hall do Brasil, Ltda., *Rio de Janeiro*

In this period in the history of the information age,
when the predictions of Alvin Toffler have come into being,
and the "electronic highway" is almost a reality,
I find myself an enthusiastic member of the new
"electronic cottage" community.

As such, I value most highly my "electronic friends,"
without whose daily communications I would be
little more than a hermit in my own
"electronic castle."

To Henry, Anne, Bob, Dan, John,
Doug, Dave, Mike, and many others.
This book is dedicated to you.

Table of Contents

Chapter 3

Designing the Primary Form 43

Chapter 4

Chapter 7

Adding Support for Reports 233

Chapter 8

Chapter 9

Adding Custom Report Features 331

Chapter 10

Chapter 11

Adding Support for Charts

Preface

This book is about object-oriented programming for the Windows™ operating system, using Microsoft's Visual C++™ and Microsoft Foundation Class Library (MFC) software development tools. Visual C++ offers a treasure house of visual development tools, including the "wizards" which make the development of new programs so effortless and easy to accomplish. No other tools are required to recreate the application that is featured in this text. Although we are using version 1.5 of the Visual C++ product, with MFC version 2.0, in this book, the tutorials and code apply equally well to version 1.0 of the product, with few differences.

This book describes the evolutionary development of a complex small business accounting application, which supports the definition of multiple accounts of various types, direct entry of new transactions into a custom account view, and the preparation of various reports and graphs for display or hard copy printout—all within the context of a multiple document interface (MDI) Windows application. The application provides for the creation of a data file whose contents can be saved and then loaded at a future date.

The application, called Keepit, is implemented in stages. During each stage of its construction, the book contains detailed tutorials for the construction of windows, dialogs, menus, and other user interface objects. The use of the Visual C++ AppWizard, ClassWizard, and App Studio tools is featured in the tutorials. Following the addition of each new user interface feature, the book describes the code that is created by the ClassWizard tool. The descriptions provide detailed information on how the wizard-created code relates to the application as a whole and also how it relates to the Microsoft Foundation Class library in particular.

Following the description of the wizard-created code, the newly designed features are implemented fully, with the addition of custom code, and each section of that code is described in detail. Thus, each new addition to the application is covered in a pair of chapters. The first chapter describes how the user interface of the feature is created and then describes the wizard-created code. The second chapter describes the custom code that implements the new feature. Each stage of the application's development ment culminates in a fully operational version of the program, which can be compiled and run either within the Visual C++ environment, or as a stand-alone Windows application.

During the course of the application's development, you will be exposed to many features of both the MFC and the Windows application programming interface (API). Some of the features which highlight the development of the Keepit application are as follows:

❖ Automatic creation of the initial skeleton application without writing a single line of code.

❖ Creation of a custom owner-draw list box with support for direct text entry and tabbing between fields in each entry of a special implementation of the Account view.

❖ Creation of multiple document templates for use with a single text file, for viewing the document's data in various ways.

❖ A tutorial for creating a *super* browser for use in debugging and browsing through Visual C++ applications and the MFC library.

❖ Creation of a custom "form frame" window which eliminates the maximize, minimize, and resizing features of standard MDI frame windows.

❖ Creation of custom dialogs for setting account options and the definition and management of transaction categories.

❖ Custom code for creating new account commands in the menu bar, code to enable the newly added commands, and code to dispatch the commands and create their corresponding account views when the commands are chosen.

❖ Descriptions of how reports are generated from the basic transaction data, including a description of how the MM_TEXT mapping mode is used to provide a device-independent display, print preview, and hard copy printout of the report data.

❖ Creation of dynamically-modified dialogs for the specification of report options, with each set of options being unique to a specified report type. A very useful technique of using the App Studio dialog editor to prototype dynamic dialog options is presented.

❖ Creation of vertical bar and line plots of the transaction data, in the form of a summarized Net Worth Chart. Special chart options, created dynamically while the dialog is running, provide the ability to specify colors for various properties of the chart. Print preview and hard copy printout of the charts are provided, in addition to the on-screen display.

The foregoing features are only a few highlights of what is presented in a step by step, evolutionary manner. The development process emphasizes the power of the Visual C++ environment for developing a complex application, one step at a time. At the end of each phase of the development, the application can be compiled and executed with the features that it has at that point. Great care is taken to refrain from discarding code which has already been written. Instead, the existing code is modified, where necessary, and new code is written to implement the newly added features.

In short, this book, above all else, presents a development strategy for the creation of large and complex applications. While the Keepit application is only moderately complex, it is a microcosm of the features and capabilities of most real world applications.

Acknowledgments

The creation of this book would not have been possible without having the fine Visual C++ development environment, which the Microsoft engineers have crafted so carefully. I'd like to thank each and every one of the engineers who contributed to the development of the Visual C++ product and its very capable Microsoft Foundation Class library.

I'd also like to personally thank Kay McKenzie for encouraging me to launch a new career as a developer and writer so many years ago. Her support has led me to this point.

It would be remiss of me to leave out Dan Shafer, who was my mentor when it came time to begin writing technical books. Dan offered a wealth of information about the writing and publishing process and it is with a great deal of personal regard that I thank him for all of his help.

My publisher, Alan Apt, his very capable staff, and with special mention of Shirley McGuire, are responsible for much of the quality of this work. I thank them all.

And to the reviewers of this manuscript, I offer my heartfelt thanks. I appreciate your candid comments and for helping to keep my use of the nomenclature consistent.

Last, but certainly not least, I thank my agent, Carole McClendon, who has worked with me to create books which will appeal to the greatest number of people possible. Her continued efforts on my behalf are gratefully acknowledged.

Notation Used in This Book

In order to make the book easier to read and to stress certain elements in the text, we have used a number of different typefaces for various purposes. These are as follows:

❖ Class and member function names are written using the Adobe Garamond™ body text typeface and as defined in the code. For example, we will talk about the CKeepitDoc class and its AddAcctMenu member function.

❖ References to variable names in the text are in the Courier typeface. A variable name might be written in the form `m_szTitle`, to indicate that it is a member variable and that it is a zero-terminated string. We use Microsoft-defined "Hungarian" notation, whenever possible.

❖ Many of the messages and control identifiers in the application are defined with all uppercase letters. For these, we will use small capitals, so that these words do not impair the readability of the text. So, you will find many such words expressed as ID_RPT_CASH_FLOW, instead of using large capital letters. Also, common acronyms such as ASCII, or constant values such as FALSE and NULL will also be written with small capitals.

❖ File names are shown in boldface type. So, you will see **keepdoc.h**, for example, as the name of the header file for the CKeepitDoc class.

❖ All code examples are written using the Courier typeface.

❖ Modified statements in the code examples have associated "change bars," as is shown for this paragraph. Newly added code will not contain change bars, but will be specified as having been newly added.

How to Use This Book

This book is tutorial in nature, so if you are learning how to develop Windows applications using Microsoft's Visual C++ product, you may wish to recreate the Keepit application, using the step by step instructions and code examples in the book. Another approach would be to use the code contained on the accompanying disk (instructions on how to install this code will be given shortly) and then build the various versions of the application while referring to the explanations in the book.

The Table of Contents provides a glimpse of the various features in each version of the application, so you may wish to jump directly to a particular page in the book when one of the topics is of interest.

The index has been compiled to be especially helpful. When you are unsure of how to create a particular feature that is included in the Keepit application, you will find a list of "Techniques" in the index, to which you can refer for creating some of the application's "special" features.

All of the classes and their member functions are indexed, so that referencing the code for a particular class or member function will be as easy as possible. Member functions are indexed within their class names.

Finally, you may wish simply to read the book, learning how the various features were designed and implemented. The text of the book is a continuous "story," from beginning to end. It chronicles the development of the application in detailed terms, using illustrations and screen shots whenever these would be helpful in understanding or recreating the application. Although the text may not be as exciting as a mystery novel, it is not without its surprises and exciting developments.

Installing the Included Source Code

The source code enclosed with the book is held on a 3.5" floppy disk. When installed, the code is stored in six directories, corresponding to the six stages of development of the Keepit Application. The directory for each section is named according to the chapters which describe the code contained in that directory. For example, the directory for the code described in Chapters 5 and 6 is named **CH05-06**. The code in each directory reflects the completed version of the application, including the custom code, at each stage of development.

You can install the source code onto your hard disk as follows:

1. Make sure that you are in the DOS environment, with the DOS prompt on your screen (e.g., `C:\>`).

2. Navigate to a directory in which you want all of the chapter directories to be stored. Create a new directory, if desired. For example, you might create a directory with a path name of `C:\SRC\KEEPIT`.

3. Change to the foregoing directory using the `CHDIR` command.

4. Place the disk in either your A or B drive and execute the command:

       ```
       A:INSTALL
       ```

   This will cause the source files to be copied from the floppy disk (substitute `B:` for `A:` in the foregoing, if necessary) to your hard disk, in the current directory (e.g., `C:\SRC\KEEPIT`).

5. At the beginning of the installation process, the install batch file will give you the opportunity to verify that the current directory is

where you wish for the source files to be installed. Type a Control-C character to terminate the installation or type any other key to continue the installation When the installation is complete, the install file will display "Installation Complete!"

6. If the foregoing steps have been completed satisfactorily, you should have six new directories in the current directory, named **CH01-02**, **CH03-04**, **CH05-06**, **CH07-08**, **CH09-10**, and **CH11-12**.

7. You can now remove the disk from your A or B drive and put it in a safe place, in case you want to reinstall the code.

Just to verify further that you have installed the files properly, make sure that each of the foregoing chapter directories contains a subdirectory named **RES**. This directory contains files that are needed to recreate the compiled resources for the application.

Author's Final Note

Creating and then writing about the Keepit application gave me the rare opportunity to look closely at the Windows application programming interface through the vehicle of the Microsoft Foundation Classes. In doing so, I was constantly amazed by the degree to which the creation of programs is greatly eased, compared to when we needed to write directly to the Windows API.

Even so, although the Keepit application has its shortcomings and is not yet a "finished" product, it is well along the way to being so. When you are working with the sources, if you decide to create the application in Debug mode, you should compile it using the Large memory model.This will allow space for the extra code generated to aid the debugging effort. If you are going to build it for release, you can do so using the Medium memory model, as the final program is relatively small.

I would like to urge you strongly to create the *super* browser described in Chapter 3. Doing so will permit you to browse through the source files of the MFC. You will also be able to put the cursor on the name of one of the MFC member functions and jump directly to its source code by using the Shift-F11 keyboard shortcut. It is quite educational to see how some of the (otherwise hidden) features of the MFC are implemented.

Richard O. Parker

Chapter 1

Learning to Use the Tools

Microsoft Visual C++ is much more than a language. It is a complete development environment. It contains a skeleton application code generator called AppWizard, a visual resource editor called App Studio, a code generator for adding new classes, message handlers, and member variables called ClassWizard, a robust C++ compiler, code editor, debugger, project management tools, and a source code browser, all in an integrated environment.

This chapter begins the process of teaching you how to write programs for Microsoft® Windows™ easily, by illustrating the construction of the first phase of a nontrivial application using Microsoft Visual C++. The application that we will be using for this tutorial and all those that follow is a typical example of a real-world program. In this case, it is an accounting application. It keeps records of transactions associated with one or more accounts, loads and saves data files, prints reports of various types, and displays charts that illustrate relationships between various data in the stored accounts. The intention is to include as many typical program features as possible in an application that is worthwhile to save and use when you are finished with the book.

In this chapter we will show you how to build a skeleton multiple document interface (MDI) application for windows. In the chapter that follows, we will describe the skeleton code, tell you what it does, and show how Microsoft Visual C++™ greatly eases the task of creating complex programs with a few clicks of the mouse.

Creating the Application Skeleton

No doubt you're ready to see how easy it is to use Visual C++, so we will get started right away by describing how to create an initial skeleton application. We are going to call this application Keepit. When it is complete, it will be a useful tool for your own home or office record keeping. To begin the creation process, we must first launch Visual C++ by double clicking on its icon as shown in Figure 1-1.

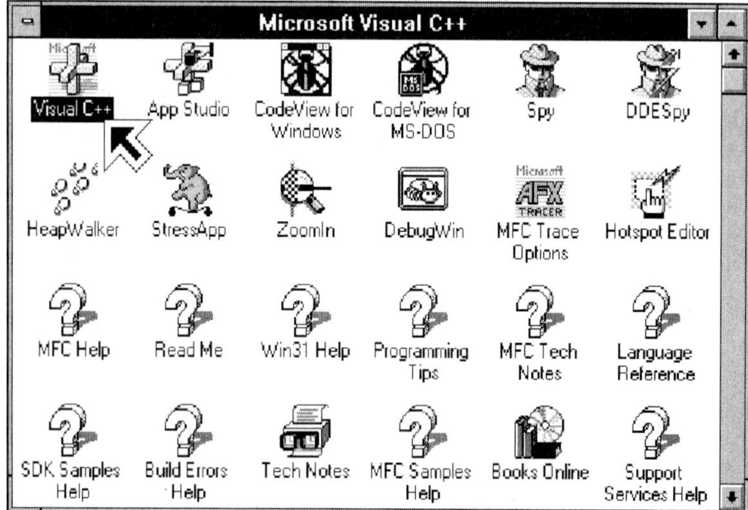

Figure 1-1
Launching Visual C++

When the Visual C++ application is first launched, no project files should be open. If this is not the case, close the current project by pulling down the Project menu and choosing the Close command. In addition, make sure that no windows are currently open by pulling down the Windows menu and choosing the Close All command.

Now that we have established the proper initial conditions, pull down the Project menu and choose the AppWizard command, as shown in Figure 1-2. This causes the AppWizard application to be launched.

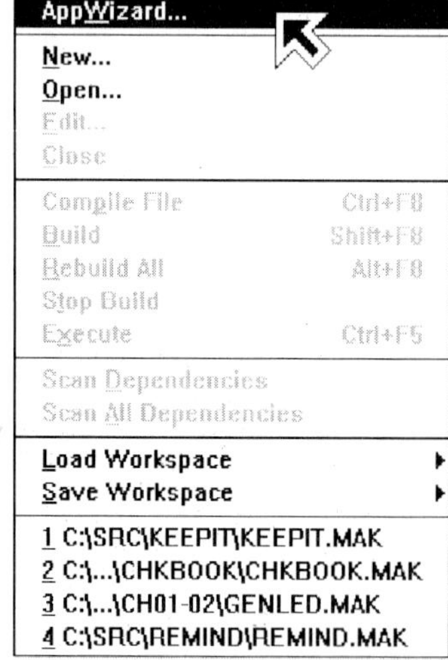

Figure 1-2
Launching AppWizard

AppWizard is used only once in the course of developing a new application. It creates an initial set of files that, when compiled, form the basis of your application. Depending upon the initially selected set of options, AppWizard will create a single document interface (SDI) or multiple document interface (MDI) application. In either case, you can elect for the generated code to include support for various user interface features, including a toolbar, printing and print preview capabilities, support for Visual Basic™ custom controls (VBX support), and context-sensitive help, as well as database and OLE support. When AppWizard is first launched, it will display a dialog that gives you an opportunity to name your application and choose a directory in which the generated source files will be stored. If the directory does not already exist, AppWizard will create it for you. In addition to allowing you to name the project (we've used the name **keepit**), the dialog contains two buttons (named Options and Classes) that when clicked allow you to customize the type of application to be generated and customize the names of the classes and files to be generated, respectively. The dialog is shown in Figure 1-3.

Figure 1-3
Creating a new application using AppWizard

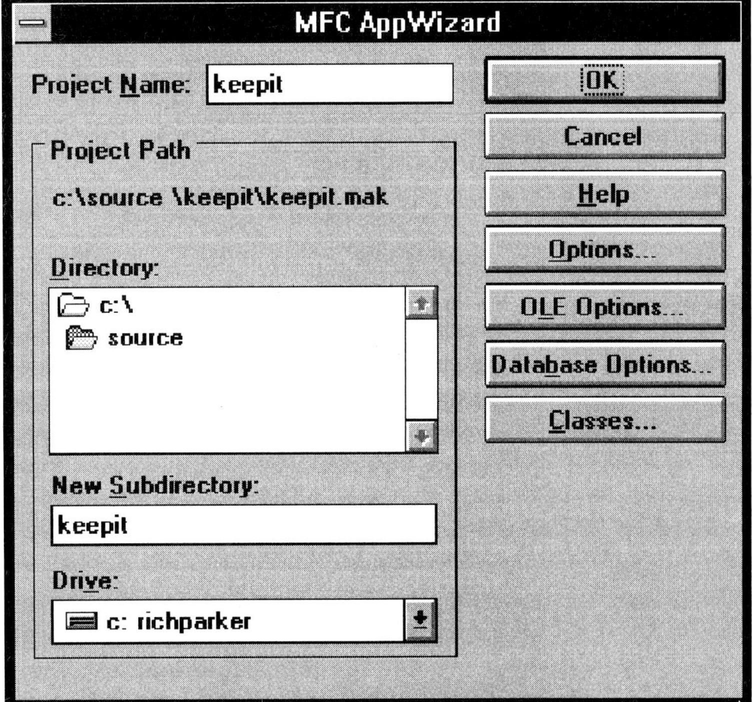

Type the name **keepit** into the box, as shown, then click the Options button to display the options dialog pictured in Figure 1-4. In this case, we have chosen for the application to contain code which supports the multiple document interface, printing and print preview code, and comments interspersed in the source code. This last option is especially helpful because the generated comments indicate where you need to add

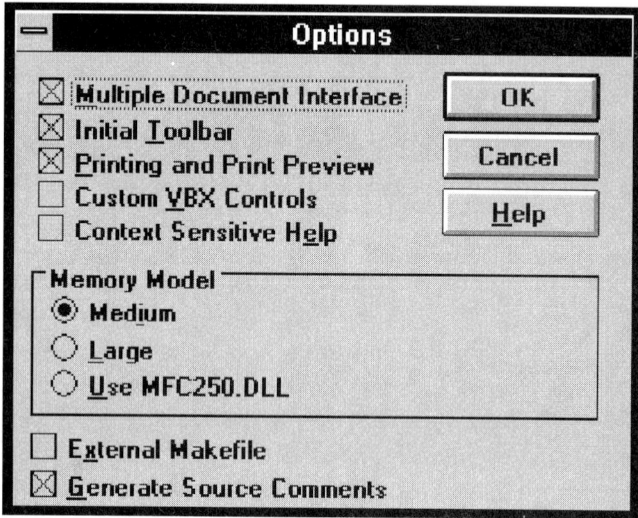

custom code to complete your application. We won't be adding context-sensitive help because doing so requires that you have an application that can edit files in Rich Text Format (RTF), such as Word for Windows. It is our intention to work with the facilities available only in the Visual C++ product environment.

After you have chosen the indicated options, click the OK button to dismiss the dialog. Then click the Classes button to allow you to modify the default class and file names that AppWizard proposes to use in generating the initial skeleton code. The dialog, shown in Figure 1-5 indicates the changes we made to the source file names AppWizard has proposed to use for the CKeepitDoc class. Also note that we have specified that the file extension for our source files will be **kpd** and that the document type name is **Keepit**. Make sure that your version of the dialog reflects these same settings, so that your source files and classes will correspond to what is shown in the remainder of the tutorial.

Figure 1-6 shows the changes we have made to the file names that App-Wizard has proposed to use for the CKeepitView class. Once again, make sure that your settings match what is shown in the figure. We have changed only the file names for the CKeepitDoc and CKeepitView classes. All other names proposed by the AppWizard are fine.

When you have completed making the changes shown in the figure, you can click the OK button in the dialog to dismiss it (we will not be using database or OLE features in this application). At this point, you have completed making all of the selections necessary for the generation of your skeleton program. If you need help with any of the choices, you can

Figure 1-5
Changing the file names
for the CKeepitDoc class

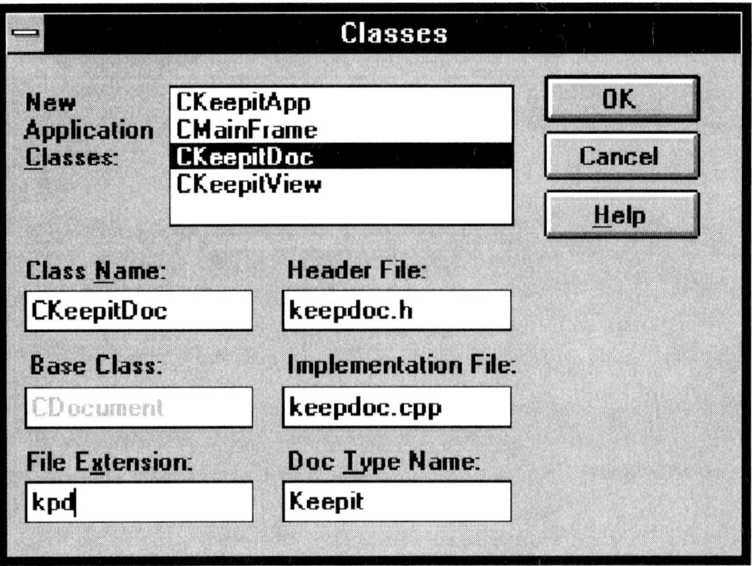

Figure 1-6
Changing the file names
for the CKeepitView
class

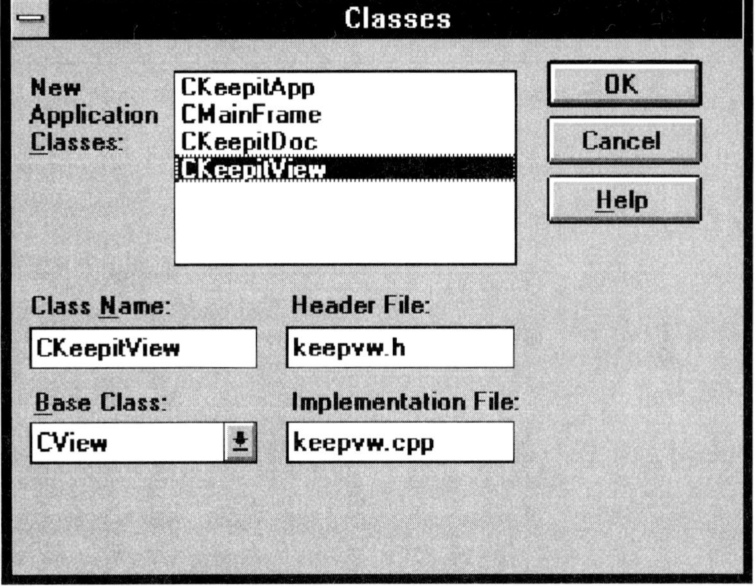

click the Help button shown in Figure 1-3. To continue the generation
process, click the OK button shown in Figure 1-3.

After you have clicked the OK button to dismiss the AppWizard dialog,
another dialog will be displayed, which indicates what AppWizard proposes to generate for your skeleton application. This dialog is shown in
Figure 1-7. As you can see, in this case, AppWizard proposes to create a

Figure 1-7
Proposed contents of the
AppWizard-generated
skeleton application

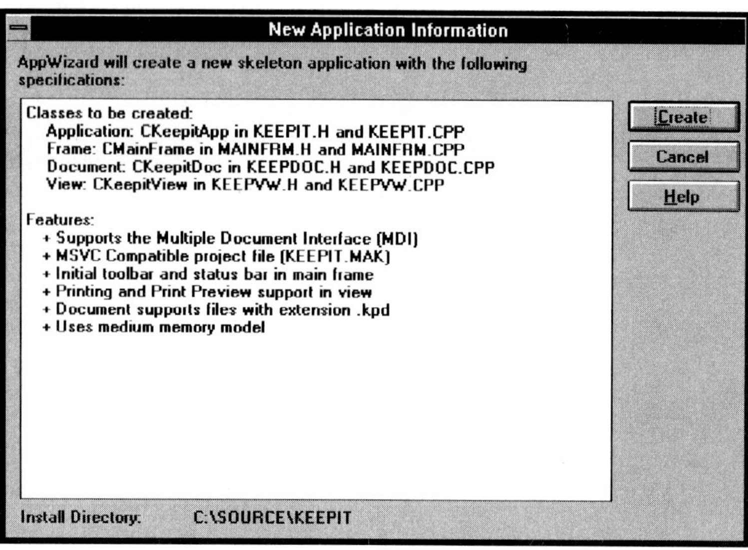

number of classes, indicating the names of the files in which they will be written, and it also specifies the features it intends to include in the skeleton application. These features are the ones that we chose in the dialog shown in Figure 1-4. If you agree with the proposed code generation plan, then you should click the Create button to allow AppWizard to proceed. If you need help, click the Help button. If you disagree with any of the information, you can click the Cancel button, AppWizard will lead you back to the dialog shown in Figure 1-3. You can then click the Options button to change the features included in the skeleton application, or click the Classes button to change the class or file names to be generated. When you click the Create button shown in Figure 1-7, AppWizard will momentarily display a dialog indicating that it is creating the necessary files. When generation of the skeleton application is complete, the title bar of the Visual Workbench window will indicate that your **keepit.mak** project file has been opened and the development environment is ready to accept further commands.

Now that the creation of the skeleton application code is complete, you will want to choose the Rebuild All command from the Project menu, as shown in Figure 1-8, to compile and link the code. This step will result in an executable application. Choosing Rebuild All isn't strictly necessary the first time you compile. Choosing Build KEEPIT.EXE from the Project menu would have resulted in compilation of all of the files because none had been compiled previously.

When you choose to rebuild the program from scratch, the Rebuild All command is used. If you desire to build only the portions of the application whose files (or those on which it is dependent) have changed, then

Figure 1-8
Building the **Keepit**
program initially

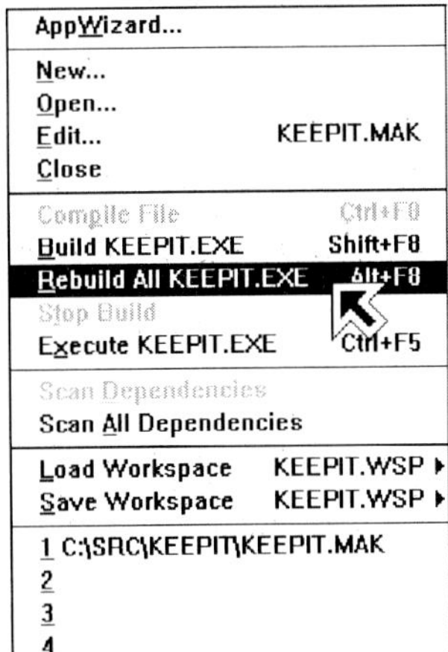

you can choose the Build command instead. In this case, either choice will cause the entire application to be built. No errors should be encountered in this initial build process, mainly because all of the code has been generated automatically.

When the build operation is complete, to execute the skeleton version of the application, pull down the Project menu and choose the Execute KEEPIT.EXE command, as shown in Figure 1-9.

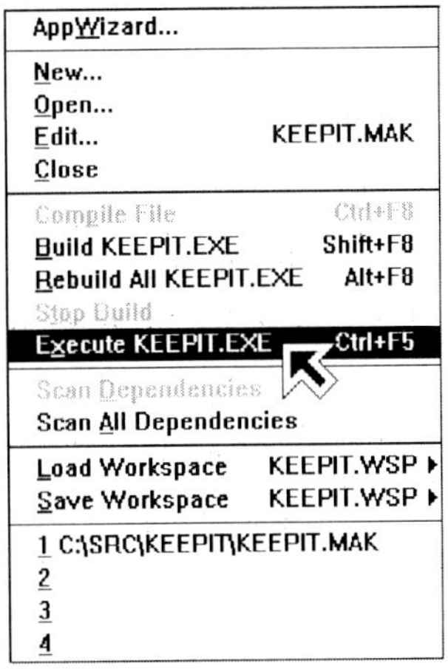

Figure 1-9
Executing the compiled
skeleton application

Upon choosing to execute the Keepit application, you should see the main frame window, containing a single MDI child window, as shown in Figure 1-10.

If you pull down the File, Edit, View, Window, and Help menus in the executing application, you will see that the commands in many of these are already implemented. For example, the New command, when chosen, will create another MDI child window, with a new title of **Keepit2**.

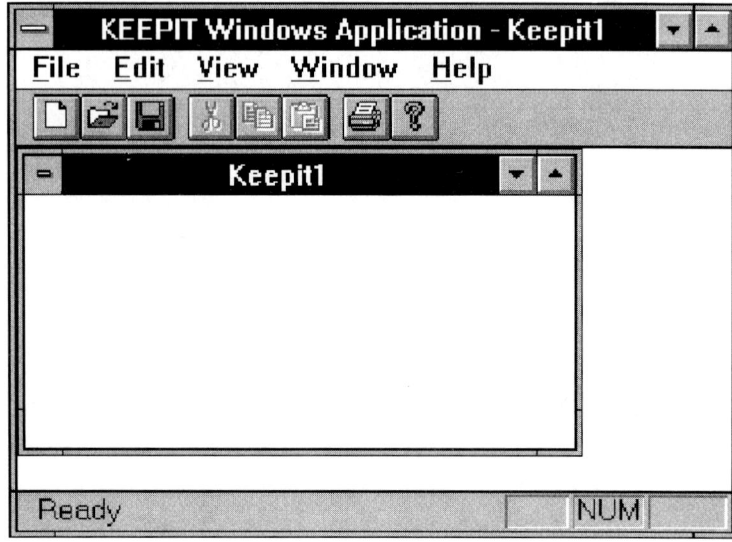

Figure 1-10
The appearance of the **Keepit** application when executed initially

The Help menu contains only the About command, which displays a dialog containing information concerning the Keepit application. We will be adding custom code to implement the various menu commands in a later chapter.

When you have finished trying the various menu commands and wish to quit executing the application, pull down the File menu and choose the Exit command. Doing so will bring you back to the Visual Workbench environment. Note that AppWizard has generated all the files pertaining to the Keepit application into a separate directory. In addition, if you look into that directory, you will also see a subdirectory named RES, which contains the compiled resources used in the application.

In addition to the source files, whose extensions are **cpp**, and header files, whose extensions are **h**, you will see other file types that are pertinent to the application or the use of the Visual Workbench environment for the application. For example, you will see a file with the extension **clw** that is used by the ClassWizard, and the make file, whose extension is **mak**.

Of particular interest is the file named **readme.txt**, which describes the files generated by AppWizard for this application. Take a few moments to read this file. It can be opened by the text editor within the Visual Workbench or by any ASCII text editor, such as the Windows Notebook application. You will notice that this file lists each of the files that have been generated, and then describes, in general terms, the purpose of the file. You may wish to print this file for future reference.

Exercises

This book contains exercises at the end of each chapter. Some of the exercises are quite easy and will be simple to perform. Others will require much more work. The latter are identified by a comment in the exercise or a footnote. A few of the exercises propose that you engage in a significant development effort. These exercises could be assigned as extra-credit projects by the instructor. Even if you are not a student, you may gain a new understanding of a particular topic or procedure by working through the exercise.

1. Define the difference between SDI and MDI applications in the Windows environment. What application form lends itself to which kind of projects?

2. Try creating several types of projects using the AppWizard and describe the differences and similarities in the generated code.

3. Examine the AppWizard-created files, in preparation for the discussions of this code in the next chapter.

4. After examining the wizard-created code, have you formed an opinion on how it compares with what you would need to write manually, to create similar functionality? Describe your impressions.pp

Chapter 2

Examining the Skeleton Code

In this chapter, we are going to examine the wizard-created code, which was produced by the AppWizard module of the Visual C++ environment after you completed the tutorial in Chapter 1.

Before jumping right into the code, it will be instructive to examine the overall structure of the generated application, how the pieces relate, and how they interface with the Microsoft Windows application programming interface (API). The initial dynamic structure of the Keepit application is shown in Figure 2-1. The Windows API is shown as a black oval with white lettering. Classes and functions in the Microsoft Foundation Class (MFC) library are shown in shaded ovals, while user-defined classes are shown in white ovals. In general, the names of member function calls are shown near the lines that connect the ovals. The direction of the member function call is indicated by an arrowhead at the destination class oval. So, for example, referring to Figure 2-1, the WinMain function in the MFC calls the InitInstance member function of the CKeepitApp class, and then calls the Run function, which happens to be inherited from the CWinApp class and is executed in that code.

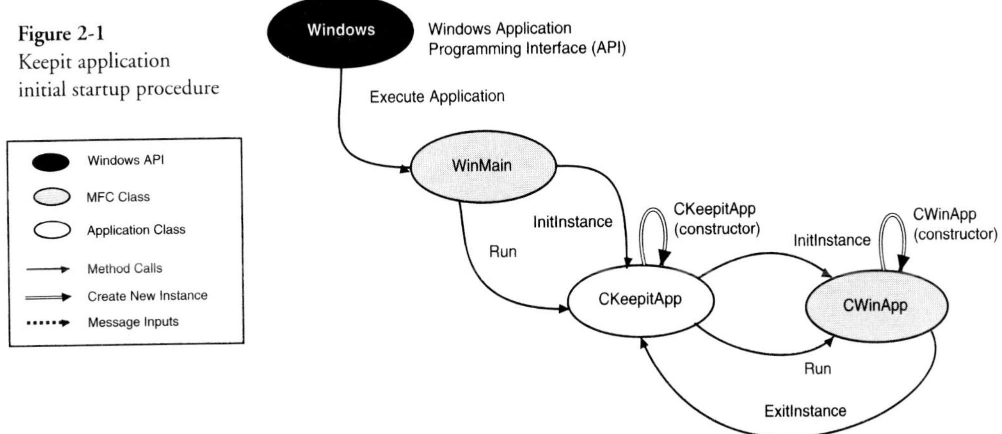

Figure 2-1
Keepit application
initial startup procedure

Analyzing the CKeepitApp Code

Figure 2-1 shows that an object of the CKeepitApp class is created, but not how it occurs. This is accomplished by the declaration of an object of that class in the **keepit.cpp** file (i.e., `CKeepitApp NEAR theApp;`). Once declared in this fashion, the CWinApp's constructor is invoked and then the CKeepitApp's constructor is invoked. (Execution of constructors takes place from the earliest ancestor to the latest descendent, except in circumstances where multiple inheritance is specified, in which case, the execution order for constructors is modified somewhat.) In the case of our Keepit application, the CKeepitApp constructor is the last to be invoked. The code for this constructor is empty in the wizard-created code. After the CKeepitApp constructor is invoked, the WinMain procedure (supplied by the MFC framework) calls the InitInstance member function in the CKeepitApp object. This is the member function in which most of the initialization for the application is performed. After the InitInstance member function's execution is complete, the WinMain procedure calls the CWinApp's Run member function. The Run member function is responsible for accessing the message queue and dispatching each message as it is extracted from the queue. The Run member function retains control throughout the execution of the program, causing message handler functions to be called to handle the various message types. When the Run member function determines that termination of the application has been requested, it calls the ExitInstance member function and returns control to WinMain. Upon receiving control from the Run member function, WinMain returns control to the Windows operating system, terminating execution of the application.

Because most of the processing in an application is conditioned upon receipt of an appropriate message, understanding how messages are generated and processed is of particular importance.

The Message Loop

Messages can be generated in various ways. Choosing a menu command, clicking a button on a toolbar, striking a key on the keyboard—all of these generate messages, which the Windows operating system accepts and places into the message queue. The handling of these messages by a running application is shown in Figure 2-2. Message processing begins in the CWinApp::Run member function, which first calls the OnIdle member function to ascertain whether idle processing is necessary at the time, giving the application an opportunity to perform idle tasks that may be needed. When all idle time processing is complete, the CWinApp::Run member function calls the PumpMessage member function in the application object. This member function accesses the next message in the

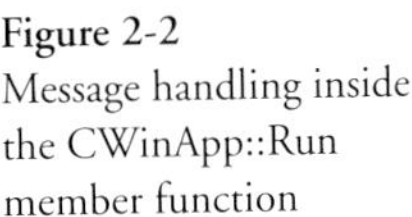

Figure 2-2
Message handling inside
the CWinApp::Run
member function

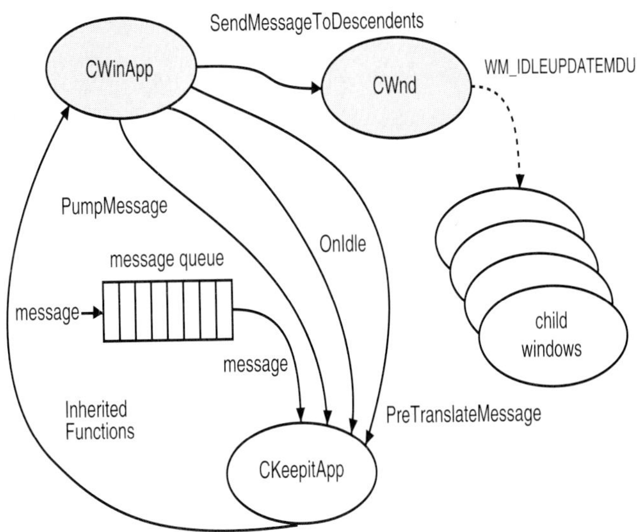

message queue and calls the PreTranslateMessage member function to handle the message. Figure 2-2 shows that the OnIdle, PumpMessage, and PreTranslateMessage member functions are sent to the CKeepitApp object. It is important to point out that there is but a single application object and all of the member functions and member variables of the CWinApp class are inherited by the CKeepitApp class. CWinApp is shown only to indicate that the member functions that comprise the core-level message loop are contained in that MFC class. We will continue to show the *base class* ovals in these diagrams; however, you should bear in mind that they do not exist as separate objects.

Of even more importance is the fact that the CKeepitApp object has the ability to override any of the member functions in its MFC base class, CWinApp. Should we wish to write our own PumpMessage member function to acquire messages from the message queue, we would be able to do so. The same privilege exists for the PreTranslateMessage and On-Idle member functions shown in the figure. Because code for these is not generated into the CKeepitApp class, the corresponding member functions inherited from the CWinApp class are called. We will not be over-riding any of these member functions.

We will cover messages and the various means for handling these later, after we discuss the various classes in the source code that rely upon the receipt of messages to provide the application's features.

The wizard-created code for the CKeepitApp class is contained in two files. It is the practice of the AppWizard, and is also our own coding practice, to keep the class declaration in a header file, whose name is de-rived from the class name, with an extension of **h**. In a similar fashion, we keep the source code definitions for the member functions contained within the class in a separate file, whose name is derived from the class name, with an extension of **cpp**.

CKeepitApp Header File

The declaration for the CKeepitApp class is generated into the **keepit.h** file and is as follows:

```
//
// keepit.h : main header file for the KEEPIT application
//

#ifndef __AFXWIN_H__
    #error include 'stdafx.h' before including this file for PCH
#endif

#include "resource.h"  // main symbols

/////////////////////////////////////////////////////////////////
// CKeepitApp:
// See keepit.cpp for the implementation of this class
//

class CKeepitApp : public CWinApp
{
public:
    CKeepitApp();

// Overrides
    virtual BOOL InitInstance();

// Implementation

    //{{AFX_MSG(CKeepitApp)
    afx_msg void OnAppAbout();
        // NOTE - the ClassWizard will add and remove
        //   member functions here.
        // DO NOT EDIT what you see in these blocks of
        //   generated code !
    //}}AFX_MSG
    DECLARE_MESSAGE_MAP()
};
```

The foregoing code was generated entirely by AppWizard. The important section of this code is contained within the CKeepitApp class declaration. The wizard-created code specifies a public constructor for the class and an override of the InitInstance member function, described earlier, in connection with Figure 2-1.

Note that AppWizard has also generated a declaration for the message handler, OnAppAbout, which is called when the user chooses the About KEEPIT command from the automatically provided Help menu.

The `DECLARE_MESSAGE_MAP()` macro is required for any class that contains message handlers. The macro declaration is included automatically by AppWizard in each of the wizard-created header files, and also by ClassWizard when new classes are created. AppWizard encloses the generated message handler declarations within special comments, which should be preserved in order for the ClassWizard to be able to interpret these as we enhance the application's abilities in the chapters that follow.

CKeepitApp Source File

The source code file for the CKeepitApp class is named **keepit.cpp**. The code is presented in several sections, as follows:

```cpp
//
// keepit.cpp : Defines the class behaviors for the
// application.
//

#include "stdafx.h"
#include "keepit.h"

#include "mainfrm.h"
#include "keepdoc.h"
#include "keepvw.h"

#ifdef _DEBUG
#undef THIS_FILE
static char BASED_CODE THIS_FILE[] = __FILE__;
#endif

/////////////////////////////////////////////////////////////////
// CKeepitApp

BEGIN_MESSAGE_MAP(CKeepitApp, CWinApp)
    //{{AFX_MSG_MAP(CKeepitApp)
    ON_COMMAND(ID_APP_ABOUT, OnAppAbout)
        // NOTE - the ClassWizard will add and remove mapping
        //   macros here.
        // DO NOT EDIT what you see in these blocks of
        //   generated code !
    //}}AFX_MSG_MAP
    // Standard file based document commands
    ON_COMMAND(ID_FILE_NEW, CWinApp::OnFileNew)
    ON_COMMAND(ID_FILE_OPEN, CWinApp::OnFileOpen)
    // Standard print setup command
    ON_COMMAND(ID_FILE_PRINT_SETUP,
CWinApp::OnFilePrintSetup)
END_MESSAGE_MAP()
```

The first section of the wizard-created code for the CKeepitApp class specifies the other header files to be included in the compilation,. The **stdafx.h** file includes, in turn, the declarations for standard Windows components (such as the `ON_COMMAND` macro) that are referenced by the generated code. The **keepit.h** file has been shown previously (see page 14). The **mainfrm.h**, **keepdoc.h**, and **keepvw.h** files will be described shortly.

The main attraction of this first section of code is the message map, which defines which messages will be handled by the CKeepitApp class, and where the handlers for the messages are located. The message map begins with the macro BEGIN_MESSAGE_MAP and is concluded with the macro END_MESSAGE_MAP. The un-commented lines between these two macros define the various messages to be handled. If you are familiar with programming Windows using C or Pascal, you may recall that Command Messages, such as WM_COMMAND, are generated from user interface objects such as menus, toolbars, and accelerator keys. When the user chooses the Open command from the File menu, a WM_COMMAND message, that contains a value specifying the ID_FILE_OPEN action, is sent to the application object. The message map for the CKeepitApp class includes an entry that directs the MFC to call the CWinApp::OnFileOpen handler when this message is received. Additional entries are provided for the ID_FILE_NEW and ID_PRINT_SETUP messages. The very first entry in the message map directs the ID_APP_ABOUT message to the OnAppAbout handler contained in the CKeepitApp class's code.

CKeepitApp Constructor

The next section of the wizard-created code in the **keepit.cpp** file contains the constructor function for the class. The code is as follows:

```
/////////////////////////////////////////////////////////////////////
// CKeepitApp construction

CKeepitApp::CKeepitApp()
{
    // TODO: add construction code here,
    // Place all significant initialization in InitInstance
}

/////////////////////////////////////////////////////////////////////
// The one and only CKeepitApp object

CKeepitApp NEAR theApp;
```

In the foregoing code, the constructor function for the CKeepitApp instance is empty. If there is any one-time initialization to be performed, it can be included in this member function; however, bear in mind that no windows have been constructed at the point when this constructor is invoked. The usual place for placing application-wide initialization code is in the InitInstance member function. A default version of the InitInstance member function can be found in the CWinApp class, which simply returns a TRUE result.

The MFC expects that you will override the InitInstance member function, in order to perform any necessary first-time initialization of the application instance. Note that at the time the InitInstance member function is called, no windows have been created, so it is not possible to perform initialization that depends upon the existence of windows.

(As an aside, the WinMain function also calls a member function named InitApplication, prior to calling the InitInstance member function, but only if no previous instance of the application has been created. It is very rare to override this member function; however, if you need to perform initialization tasks that are global to all instances of the application, the InitApplication member function is the one to override.)

InitInstance Member Function

The InitInstance member function is called once for each instance of the application. The code for the override of this member function is as follows:

```
/////////////////////////////////////////////////////////////
// CKeepitApp initialization
BOOL CKeepitApp::InitInstance()
{
    // Standard initialization
    // If you are not using these features and wish to
    /  reduce the size of your final executable, you should
    // remove from the following the specific initialization
    // routines you do not need.

    SetDialogBkColor();  // set dialog background color to gray
    LoadStdProfileSettings();  // Load standard INI file options
                            // (including MRU)

    // Register the application's document templates.
    // Document templates serve as the connection between
    // documents, frame windows and views.
    AddDocTemplate(new CMultiDocTemplate(IDR_KEEPITTYPE,
        RUNTIME_CLASS(CKeepitDoc),
        RUNTIME_CLASS(CMDIChildWnd),// standard MDI child
        RUNTIME_CLASS(CKeepitView)));

    // create main MDI Frame window
    CMainFrame* pMainFrame = new CMainFrame;
    if (!pMainFrame->LoadFrame(IDR_MAINFRAME)) return FALSE;
    m_pMainWnd = pMainFrame;

    // enable file manager drag/drop and DDE Execute open
    EnableShellOpen();
    RegisterShellFileTypes();

    // simple command line parsing
    if (m_lpCmdLine[0] == '\0')
    {
        // create a new (empty) document
        OnFileNew();
    }
```

```
        else
        {
           // open an existing document
           OpenDocumentFile(m_lpCmdLine);
        }

        m_pMainWnd->DragAcceptFiles();

        // The main window has been initialized,
        // so show and update it
        pMainFrame->ShowWindow(m_nCmdShow);
        pMainFrame->UpdateWindow();

        return TRUE;
}
```

The foregoing InitInstance code was generated entirely by AppWizard. You will notice that the comments at the beginning of the code indicate that you can delete portions of the following code if you do not require the features it provides. Specifically, the comments refer to the function that sets the dialog background color (SetDialogBkColor) and the function to load any standard **ini** file options (LoadStdProfileSettings) that may apply to this application, including the most recently used file names.

Following these optional initialization actions, the InitInstance member function adds a new document template to the list of document templates maintained by the application. The contents of the template, in this case, is a new instance of CMultiDocTemplate, which requires arguments identifying the document type (IDR_KEEPITTYPE), and RUNTIME_CLASS declarations, which identify the document class (CKeepitDoc), the child window class (CMDIChildWnd), and the view class (CKeepitView). This information (stored in the document template) will be used when the InitInstance member function creates the document, MDI child window, and the initial view.

It is important to point out that the Microsoft Foundation Classes establish a standard structure for applications that use the library. It is expected that all applications will contain one or more documents (each of which relates to a physical file), one or more views of that document, and a main frame window (in a single document interface [SDI] application, the document window is also the main frame window), within which the views are displayed. The view object is the window on the data managed by the document object.

Figure 2-3 illustrates the structure of the skeleton application, as well as the ability for the structure to expand to include new elements. The CKeepitApp application object is shown at the top. This object creates a document template object, which in turn creates the CKeepitDoc document object, the CMDIChildWnd object, and its associated CKeepit-

View view object. A view is intended to contain a unique representation of a portion or all of the document's data. These elements are shown on the left side of the figure. The right side of Figure 2-3 illustrates how the application structure can be expanded by creating a new document template, specifying the reuse of the CKeepitDoc document object, but including a new child window and its associated view. We will be enhancing the Keepit application in this manner, later.

Figure 2-3
Application structure and potential for expansion

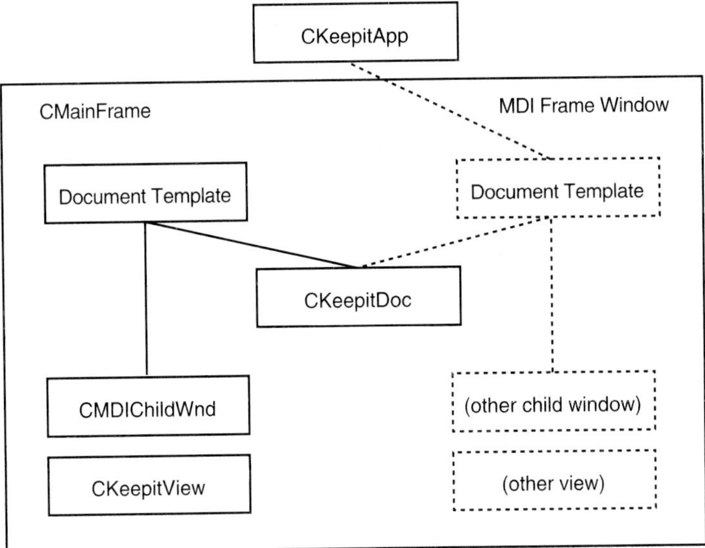

Following the construction of the document template and its addition to the application's list, the wizard-created code contains an instance of the CMainFrame class, which was generated by AppWizard as a derived class of the MDIFrameWnd class in the MFC. This object will serve as the main frame window for our application. The characteristics of the main frame window are stored in a resource named IDR_MAINFRAME. These characteristics are loaded, establishing the features in the main frame window, by calling the LoadFrame member function (which is inherited from the CMDIFrameWnd class). After the main frame window has been loaded, its pointer is stored in the `m_pMainFrame` member variable, from which it can be referenced later.

The InitInstance member function continues by calling two member functions that enable drag and drop, as well as dynamic data exchange (DDE) execute and open procedures.

Following this, the InitInstance member function determines whether the command line associated with the application is empty or if it contains at least one file name. In the case where the command line is empty, the member function calls the OnFileNew member function to create a new, empty document. In the case where a command line is given, a pointer to the command line is passed to the OpenDocumentFile member function, which attempts to open the first file specified in the command line.

The final section of the InitInstance member function calls the DragAcceptFiles member function to indicate that the application will accept dropped files from the Windows File Manager. In addition, the ShowWindow and UpdateWindow member functions are called to display the main frame window, making it and its contents visible to the user.

The InitInstance member function completes its execution by returning a result of TRUE to the WinMain function.

CWinApp OnFileNew Member Function

The OnFileNew member function is inherited from the CWinApp class. Its default features provide the necessary functionality for our initial application. The OnFileNew member function checks whether multiple document templates have been added to the application's list and displays a dialog, requesting the user to choose a particular document type, if so. If but a single document template exists (as is the case with our wizard-created code), the member function accesses the template and calls its OpenDocumentFile member function, with a parameter value of NULL, indicating that an empty document, with a default document name, is to be created. In the course of creating the document, an MDI child window and its corresponding view (taken from the document template) are also created. The source code for the member functions that implement this behavior is provided with the Visual C++ product.

CAboutDlg Class Declaration

The **keepit.cpp** file contains the class declaration for the "ABOUT KEEPIT" command in the application's Help menu. The wizard-created code for this class declaration is as follows:

```
/////////////////////////////////////////////////////////////////
// CAboutDlg dialog used for App About

class CAboutDlg : public CDialog
{
public:
    CAboutDlg();

// Dialog Data
    //{{AFX_DATA(CAboutDlg)
    enum { IDD = IDD_ABOUTBOX };
    //}}AFX_DATA

// Implementation
protected:
    virtual void DoDataExchange(CDataExchange* pDX);// DDX/
```

```
DDV support
   //{{AFX_MSG(CAboutDlg)
      // No message handlers
   //}}AFX_MSG
   DECLARE_MESSAGE_MAP()
};
```

While we don't completely agree with AppWizard's policy of generating this code into the **keepit.cpp** source file, the small amount of code necessary to completely specify and handle the "About" dialog makes this a reasonable exception to our rule. We would like to stress that the best practice is to create a separate header file for each new class declaration and a separate source file for to contain the member functions of the class. This is the methodology we follow in the code that we write.

CAboutDlg Source File

The source code for the constructor, DoDataExchange member function, message map, and OnAppAbout handler in the CAboutDlg class is as follows:

```
CAboutDlg::CAboutDlg()  : CDialog(CAboutDlg::IDD)
{
   //{{AFX_DATA_INIT(CAboutDlg)
   //}}AFX_DATA_INIT
}

void CAboutDlg::DoDataExchange(CDataExchange* pDX)
{
   CDialog::DoDataExchange(pDX);
   //{{AFX_DATA_MAP(CAboutDlg)
   //}}AFX_DATA_MAP
}

BEGIN_MESSAGE_MAP(CAboutDlg, CDialog)
   //{{AFX_MSG_MAP(CAboutDlg)
      // No message handlers
   //}}AFX_MSG_MAP
END_MESSAGE_MAP()

// App command to run the dialog
void CKeepitApp::OnAppAbout()
{
   CAboutDlg aboutDlg;
   aboutDlg.DoModal();
}
```

In the foregoing code, the CAboutDlg constructor, although empty, illustrates the special comments placed into the source code by AppWizard so that data can be exchanged between the object that invokes the dialog and the dialog object itself. Although no data are exchanged in this case, the AFX_DATA_MAP comments provide a placeholder for later inclusion of data exchange entries by the ClassWizard tool. When the constructor is invoked, it, in turn, calls its ancestor CDialog with the identifier of the dialog resource that describes the contents of that user interface element (CAboutDlg ::IDD). The constructor for the CDialog object will create the dialog and its contents according to the specifications in the corresponding resource (the IDD symbol has been equated, via an enumerator in the header file, to IDD_ABOUTBOX). By examining that dialog resource using the App Studio tool, you will see what elements it contains and how it will appear on the screen, when invoked.

The DoDataExchange member function for the CAboutDlg class is also empty. It is called by the UpdateData member function to exchange data between the dialog and the object from which it has been invoked. In this case, no data are exchanged.

The message map for this dialog is also empty. In more elaborate dialogs, the map might contain quite a number of message handler entries. None are needed for the CAboutDlg class.

The code for the OnAppAbout handler, which was mentioned in the message map for the CKeepitApp object (see page 15), is the last to be shown. Note that the handler is a member function of the CKeepitApp class, rather than that of the CAboutDlg class. When the user chooses the ABOUT KEEPIT command from the Help menu, the message map for the application object is searched, the ID_APP_ABOUT entry is found, and the OnAppAbout handler is called. The code for this member function is very simple. It creates an object of the CAboutDlg class on the stack (called `aboutDlg`) and then calls its DoModal member function. This causes the dialog to be displayed on the screen. When the user clicks the OK buttons the dialog is dismissed, the DoModal member function returns, and the OnAppAbout member function completes execution, returning control to the message loop in the Run member function of CWinApp.

Many dialogs will be much more complex than the simple about box that the foregoing code implements. Note, however, that the code to implement this feature was generated entirely by AppWizard, with no additional coding needed to make it operational.

CKeepitApp Command Handler Placeholder

The wizard-created code in the **keepit.cpp** class concludes with some comments which indicate that additional command handlers can be added at that point in the code. In fact, when we customize the code for the application, we will be using the ClassWizard to install handlers for newly defined commands. In the meantime, the comments stand alone at the end of the file, as follows:

```
/////////////////////////////////////////////////////////////////
// CKeepitApp commands
```

Analyzing the CMainFrame Code

When the InitInstance member function of the CKeepitApp object is called, an instance of the CMainFrame class is created. This object inherits most of its features from the CMDIFrameWnd class, which implements the main frame window (in this case, an MDI window) that encloses the MDI child window associated with the application's document. If multiple instances of the application are created, a single instance of the CMainFrame class is created for each of these. The components of the main frame window and its relationship to the MDI child document window are shown in Figure 2-4.

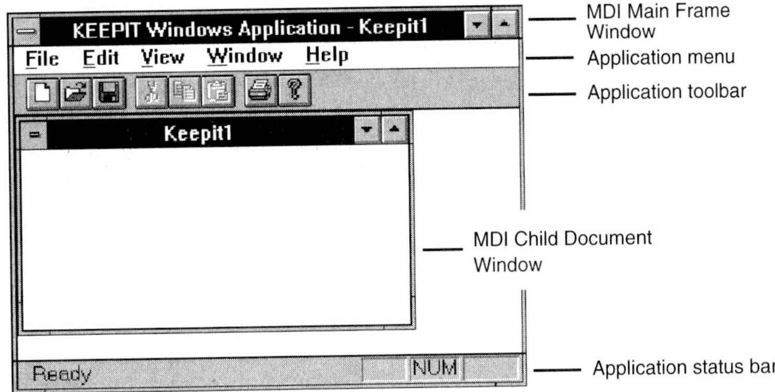

Figure 2-4
Main frame window and its enclosed MDI child windows

The wizard-created code for the CMainFrame class and its member functions is contained in the **mainfrm.h** header file and its corresponding **mainfrm.cpp** source file. The CMainFrame object fits into the application's structure by enclosing the application object's document and its corresponding MDI child window, as shown in Figure 2-4.

CMainFrame Header File

The code that embodies the declarations for the CMainFrame class was generated by AppWizard and is as follows:

```
//
// mainfrm.h : interface of the CMainFrame class
//
/////////////////////////////////////////////////////////////////

class CMainFrame : public CMDIFrameWnd
```

```cpp
{
    DECLARE_DYNAMIC(CMainFrame)
public:
    CMainFrame();

// Attributes
public:

// Operations
public:
// Implementation
public:
    virtual ~CMainFrame();
#ifdef _DEBUG
    virtual void AssertValid() const;
    virtual void Dump(CDumpContext& dc) const;
#endif

protected:      // control bar embedded members
    CStatusBar    m_wndStatusBar;
    CToolBar      m_wndToolBar;

// Generated message map functions
protected:
    //{{AFX_MSG(CMainFrame)
    afx_msg int OnCreate(LPCREATESTRUCT lpCreateStruct);
        // NOTE - the ClassWizard will add and remove member
        //    functions here.
        // DO NOT EDIT what you see in these blocks of
generated
        //    code !
    //}}AFX_MSG
    DECLARE_MESSAGE_MAP()
};
```

The class declaration for CMainFrame begins with a line that declares the object to be capable of being dynamically created at run time. This is indicated by the `DECLARE_DYNAMIC(CMainFrame)` macro. This macro expands into a set of declarations, which are then used by an `IMPLEMENT_DYNAMIC` macro in the source code for the class. Placeholder comments for attributes and operations follow in the header file. The constructor for the class is the next to be declared, followed by a declaration of the destructor. You will also notice that AppWizard has generated declarations for AssertValid and Dump member functions, which are compiled if the application is being built with debugging mode turned on (it is presumed that after the application has been debugged completely, these functions will no longer be necessary).

Because we have elected for the application's main frame window to contain a toolbar and status bar (see the selected options in Figure 1-6 and the appearance of these elements in Figure 2-4), AppWizard has generated declarations for two member variables, called `m_wndStatusBar` and `m_wndToolBar`. These member variables are objects of the CStatusBar and CToolBar classes, respectively. When the CMainFrame object is constructed, these objects will be constructed also.

Finally, the header file contains the ClassWizard-compatible message map handler declarations, followed by the DECLARE_MESSAGE_MAP() macro. The only message handler in the wizard-created code is the one for the WM_CREATE message (OnCreate). Additional handlers can be added later by using ClassWizard to create new entries.

CMainFrame Source File

The wizard-created source code for the CMainFrame object is contained in the **mainfrm.cpp** file. This file contains several sections of code, each of which will be presented separately. The presentation is sequential for easy reference. Although AppWizard has generated quite a bit of code automatically, we will be adding new code to this class in later versions of the program.

Initial CMainFrame Code

The first section in the **mainfrm.cpp** file contains directives to include various header files, whose declarations are referenced in the current class, as well as declarations to be compiled if we are building a debug version of the application. The first section of code is as follows:

```
// mainfrm.cpp : implementation of the CMainFrame class
//

#include "stdafx.h"
#include "keepit.h"

#include "mainfrm.h"

#ifdef _DEBUG
#undef THIS_FILE
static char BASED_CODE THIS_FILE[] = __FILE__;
#endif
```

As is usual, AppWizard has generated a #include "stdafx.h" directive so that the declarations common to all Windows applications will be available to be referenced. In addition, both the main application header file (**keepit.h**) and the main frame's header file (**mainfrm.h**) are included. If we build a debugging version of the application, a definition of a static character string for the symbol THIS_FILE is generated. Visual C++ supports several standard predefined macros, among which is the __FILE__ macro, which expands to the name of the current source file enclosed by quotation marks (i.e., in this case, **"mainfrm.cpp"**).

CMainFrame's Message Map

The message map for the CMainFrame object follows next in the wizard-created code. It starts with the `BEGIN_MESSAGE_MAP` macro and is complete when the `END_MESSAGE_MAP` macro is expanded. The name of the current class and its base class are generated inside the parentheses that follow the `BEGIN_MESSAGE_MAP` macro. The body of the message map contains but a single entry, for the `ON_WM_CREATE` message. This declaration expands to the standard MFC message handler, OnCreate. Special comments are generated for the future use of the ClassWizard tool. Message handlers are defined inside these comments. The code that comprises the message map definition is as follows:

```
/////////////////////////////////////////////////////////////////
// CMainFrame

IMPLEMENT_DYNAMIC(CMainFrame, CMDIFrameWnd)

BEGIN_MESSAGE_MAP(CMainFrame, CMDIFrameWnd)
   //{{AFX_MSG_MAP(CMainFrame)
      // NOTE - the ClassWizard will add and remove mapping
      //   macros here.
      // DO NOT EDIT what you see in these blocks of
      //   generated code !
      ON_WM_CREATE()
   //}}AFX_MSG_MAP
END_MESSAGE_MAP()
```

The content of the message map is a reference to a single handler, On-Create, via the message `ON_WM_CREATE`, which will be described shortly.

Toolbar and Status Bar Definitions

We have specified (see Figure 1-6) that both a toolbar and status bar are to be included in the main frame window (Figure 2-4 shows these as they appear on screen). In order to make provision for the buttons in the toolbar and the various sections of the status window, AppWizard has generated arrays of initialized data into the code, which are used by the application to implement these visual elements. The code to define these arrays is as follows:

```
/////////////////////////////////////////////////////////////////
// arrays of IDs used to initialize control bars

// toolbar buttons - IDs are command buttons
static UINT BASED_CODE buttons[] =
{
   // same order as in the bitmap 'toolbar.bmp'
   ID_FILE_NEW,
   ID_FILE_OPEN,
   ID_FILE_SAVE,
      ID_SEPARATOR,
```

```
    ID_EDIT_CUT,
    ID_EDIT_COPY,
    ID_EDIT_PASTE,
        ID_SEPARATOR,
    ID_FILE_PRINT,
    ID_APP_ABOUT,
};

static UINT BASED_CODE indicators[] =
{
    ID_SEPARATOR,           // status line indicator
    ID_INDICATOR_CAPS,
    ID_INDICATOR_NUM,
    ID_INDICATOR_SCRL,
};
```

Each of the elements in the two arrays refers to a resource that is referenced by the OnCreate member function of the CMainFrame object. The resources can also be manipulated by the App Studio resource editor. We will be using the App Studio resource editor to create new resources when constructing new user interface features in the Keepit application.

CMainFrame's Constructor and Destructor Code

The constructor and destructor code for the CMainFrame object are both empty; however, if we need to add initialization code for future member variables, we can do so in the constructor. If we allocate any memory in the constructor, we must dispose of it in the destructor. The code for these is as follows:

```
///////////////////////////////////////////////////////////////
// CMainFrame construction/destruction

CMainFrame::CMainFrame()
{
    // TODO: add member initialization code here
}

CMainFrame::~CMainFrame()
{
}
```

CMainFrame's OnCreate Handler

The most important section of code in the **mainfrm.cpp** file is that which handles the construction of the main frame window, the toolbar, and the status bar. The code is as follows:

```
int CMainFrame::OnCreate(LPCREATESTRUCT lpCreateStruct)
{
    if (CMDIFrameWnd::OnCreate(lpCreateStruct) == -1)
      return -1;
```

```cpp
    if (!m_wndToolBar.Create(this) ||
      !m_wndToolBar.LoadBitmap(IDR_MAINFRAME) ||
      !m_wndToolBar.SetButtons(buttons,
        sizeof(buttons)/sizeof(UINT)))
    {
      TRACE("Failed to create toolbar\n");
      return -1;// fail to create
    }
    if (!m_wndStatusBar.Create(this) ||
      !m_wndStatusBar.SetIndicators(indicators,
        sizeof(indicators)/sizeof(UINT)))
    {
      TRACE("Failed to create status bar\n");
      return -1;// fail to create
    }
    return 0;
}
```

The first action of the OnCreate handler is to call its CMDIFrameWnd base class member function and test the result returned by that function. If the return value is -1, then it is assumed that construction of the main frame window was unsuccessful, in which case, the handler returns a -1 as its result. After it has been determined that the creation of the main frame window was successful, the OnCreate handler installs the CToolbar object into the client portion of its window. This is a process of several steps, each of which returns a boolean result (i.e., TRUE or FALSE), and which results are combined with a logical-OR operator to ascertain the combined result, as follows:

1. Although the CToolbar object has been created as a result of executing the constructor for its `m_wndToolBar` member variable, the Create member function must be called for this object, to establish the main frame window as the enclosure for the new child window to hold the toolbar object.

2. The bitmap resource (IDR_MAINFRAME) is loaded. This resource contains icons that represent the functions of each of the toolbar's buttons.

3. The SetButtons member function is called for the CToolbar object, causing command identifiers (specified in the **buttons** array) to be assigned to the corresponding buttons in the toolbar.

If the logical addition of the return values from the foregoing steps effects a TRUE result, then the toolbar has been constructed properly and the handler continues execution; otherwise, the handler generates an error and returns a value of -1, indicating that construction of the main frame window is incomplete.

Construction of the status bar is similar to the process for the toolbar, but is handled by a two-step process, as follows:

1. The Create member function is called for the m_wndStatusBar member variable, which is an object of the CStatusBar class. This constructs the child window that displays the status information.

2. The SetIndicators member function of the CStatusBar class associates the identifiers in the **indicators** array with the various sections of the status bar window.

If the logical addition of the return values from the foregoing steps effects a TRUE result, the handler continues execution; otherwise, the handler generates an error and returns a value of -1, indicating its failure to complete construction of the main frame window.

CMainFrame Diagnostic Code

In addition to the code that implements the primary features of the main frame window, AppWizard generates diagnostic code that is optionally included in the compiled application, depending upon whether a debug version of the application is being built. If so, then code to implement both the AssertValid and Dump member functions are compiled. The code for these member functions is as follows:

```
/////////////////////////////////////////////////////////////////
// CMainFrame diagnostics

#ifdef _DEBUG
void CMainFrame::AssertValid() const
{
    CMDIFrameWnd::AssertValid();
}

void CMainFrame::Dump(CDumpContext& dc) const
{
    CMDIFrameWnd::Dump(dc);
}

#endif //_DEBUG
```

CMainFrame Handler Placeholder

The final section of code in the **mainfrm.cpp** file is a comment block that provides a placeholder for the addition of new message handlers for the CMainFrame object, in the future. The ClassWizard will generate new handler member functions, following these comments, should we choose for the main frame window to handle additional messages. The comments are as follows:

```
/////////////////////////////////////////////////////////////////
// CMainFrame message handlers
```

Analyzing the CKeepitDoc Code

The relationship of the document object to the rest of the application's features is shown in Figure 2-3 and is discussed on page 19. It is important to note that the MFC is structured around the concept of a frame, document, and view being intimately related. Each MDI (or SDI) frame window requires an attached document and one or more views. Although it is possible to defeat this intended organization, you will find that it will meet most of your application's needs.

At this point, it is appropriate to make you aware of where the development of the Keepit application is heading. What we foresee is a single document that holds all of the data for a number of different home or business accounts. Each account is to be displayed in a view, and each view is shown in its own MDI child window. We also intend to create new MDI child windows to hold reports, which are additional views of the data. Also, we intend to show charts that display properties of the data, and these will be contained in separate MDI child windows. Now that you know where we are heading, let's look at the document object in the wizard-created code.

The document is intended to be both the repository for data associated with a single file and the encapsulation of member functions that read, write, accept, and furnish these data to other objects in the application. It is the so-called *data server* for the application model. The wizard-created code contains a number of member functions that aid the document object in providing these services.

CKeepitDoc Header File

The wizard-created declarations for the CKeepitDoc class are contained in the **keepitdoc.h** header file. The code is as follows:

```
// keepdoc.h : interface of the CKeepitDoc class
//
/////////////////////////////////////////////////////////////////

class CKeepitDoc : public CDocument
{
protected: // create from serialization only
    CKeepitDoc();
    DECLARE_DYNCREATE(CKeepitDoc)

// Attributes
public:

// Operations
public:

// Implementation
```

```
public:
  virtual ~CKeepitDoc();
  virtual void Serialize(CArchive& ar);// overridden for
                                       // document i/o
#ifdef _DEBUG
  virtual void AssertValid() const;
  virtual void Dump(CDumpContext& dc) const;
#endif
protected:
  virtual BOOL OnNewDocument();

// Generated message map functions
protected:
  //{{AFX_MSG(CKeepitDoc)
     // NOTE - the ClassWizard will add and remove member
     //   functions here.DO NOT EDIT what you see in these
     //   blocks of generated code !
  //}}AFX_MSG
  DECLARE_MESSAGE_MAP()
};
```

The foregoing declarations specify the member functions and message map constituents of the CKeepitDoc class. The constructor for the class has been declared to be "protected," so that descendents and friends of the class will be allowed to call it. In fact, the CKeepitDoc object is created at the time the document template is referenced in the OnFileNew member function, which was described briefly on page 20. The DECLARE_DYNCREATE macro allows the document object to be created dynamically at run time, as needed.

Although the CKeepitDoc class declaration has no member variables in the wizard-created code, we will be adding variables at a later stage of the Keepit application's development.

The class does contain public member functions for both the destructor of the object and a Serialize member function for reading or writing the contents to the document from/to the disk.

As is usual, AppWizard has generated optionally compiled debugging member functions called AssertValid and Dump. We will not be making use of these in this application, but they are there to aid in debugging the code. The functions will not be contained in a release version of the application (i.e., when the _DEBUG variable is undefined).

One of the primary member functions in the foregoing class declaration is OnNewDocument, which is called by the framework each time a new document object is created.

The message map declarations for this class are empty, but AppWizard has provided placeholders for ClassWizard to add message handlers, should the need arise. We will be adding message handlers to this class in a future version of the Keepit application.

CKeepitDoc Source File

The source code for the CKeepitDoc class is in the **keepitdoc.cpp** file. The code is presented in several sections, as follows:

Initial CKeepitDoc Code

```
//
// keepdoc.cpp : implementation of the CKeepitDoc class
//

#include "stdafx.h"
#include "keepit.h"

#include "keepdoc.h"
#ifdef _DEBUG
#undef THIS_FILE
static char BASED_CODE THIS_FILE[] = __FILE__;
#endif
```

As is usual, AppWizard has generated preprocessor directives to include the standard Windows definitions in the **stdafx.h** file, and has also included the main application and document header files. If a debug version of the application is being built, a string constant is defined, which will contain the name of the current source file (**"keepdoc.cpp"**).

The Message Map

The message map is the next to be defined. Although it is empty in the wizard-created code, it is in the proper form for the ClassWizard tool to add new message handlers should we need to do so in the future. The message map code is as follows:

```
/////////////////////////////////////////////////////////////////////
// CKeepitDoc

IMPLEMENT_DYNCREATE(CKeepitDoc, CDocument)

BEGIN_MESSAGE_MAP(CKeepitDoc, CDocument)
  //{{AFX_MSG_MAP(CKeepitDoc)
    // NOTE - the ClassWizard will add and remove mapping
    //   macros here. DO NOT EDIT what you see in these
    //   blocks of generated code !
  //}}AFX_MSG_MAP
END_MESSAGE_MAP()
```

CKeepitDoc Constructor and Destructor

The wizard-created code for the document's constructor and destructor follow in the source code file. These are both empty at the present time;

however we can add one-time initialization code in the constructor, as indicated by the comment, if we wish.

```
/////////////////////////////////////////////////////////////
// CKeepitDoc construction/destruction

CKeepitDoc::CKeepitDoc()
{
   // TODO: add one-time construction code here
}

CKeepitDoc::~CKeepitDoc()
{
}
```

OnNewDocument Member Function

The OnNewDocument member function is called by the MFC framework each time a new document object is created. This member function is provided to allow you to initialize any data structures used by the document. (As an aside, in an SDI application, this member function is called, instead of the constructor, when a File New command is chosen. It is therefore important to place initialization code in this member function, rather than the document's constructor.)

As we add new functionality to the Keepit application, we will be adding initialization code to the OnNewDocument member function. The wizard-created code for this member function is as follows:

```
BOOL CKeepitDoc::OnNewDocument()
{
   if (!CDocument::OnNewDocument())
     return FALSE;
   // TODO: add reinitialization code here
   // (SDI documents will reuse this document)
   return TRUE;
}
```

As is evident from the foregoing code, the OnNewCommand member function merely calls its ancestor member function, inherited from the CDocument class. If the ancestor member function returns a FALSE result, this member function will, in turn, return a FALSE result to the framework's OpenDocumentFile caller.

Serialize Member Function

The Serialize member function is common to all objects inherited from the framework's CObject class. It provides the means to read from and write to a standard file, which has previously been opened for this purpose during the OnFileNew or OnFileOpen member functions (default versions of which are included in the MFC framework). The code for Serialize is as follows:

```
/////////////////////////////////////////////////////////////
// CKeepitDoc serialization

void CKeepitDoc::Serialize(CArchive& ar)
{
   if (ar.IsStoring())
   {
      // TODO: add storing code here
   }
   else
   {
      // TODO: add loading code here
   }
}
```

The CArchive object is passed as a single argument to the Serialize member function. The IsStoring member function of the CArchive object returns TRUE if the user has chosen to save the contents of the document, and FALSE if the file is to be read into the document. The wizard-created code is empty; however, it includes the necessary structure and associated comments to aid you in adding code to store or load the document's contents.

Diagnostic Member Functions

AppWizard has also generated diagnostic routines into the CKeepitDoc source code. While we will not use these member functions in our application, the author has found them to be valuable when attempting to find especially elusive bugs. The code is not compiled if you are building a release version of the application. The wizard-created code for these member functions is as follows:

```
/////////////////////////////////////////////////////////////
// CKeepitDoc diagnostics

#ifdef _DEBUG
void CKeepitDoc::AssertValid() const
{
   CDocument::AssertValid();
}

void CKeepitDoc::Dump(CDumpContext& dc) const
{
   CDocument::Dump(dc);
}

#endif //_DEBUG
```

In the case of the AssertValid member function, the ancestor member function in the CDocument class is called to verify that all of the views associated with the document are valid objects. The Dump member function is called with a device context object from the CDumpContext class. By calling the ancestor member function in the CDocument class, various features of the current document context, including the document's title, file pathname, status of the `m_bModified` member variable, information concerning the current document template, and data concerning each active view, are written to the dump file.

Command Handler Placeholder

As is usual, AppWizard has generated code to act as a placeholder for future command handler member functions. The ClassWizard tool will add new handlers following these comments:

```
/////////////////////////////////////////////////////////////////
// CKeepitDoc commands
```

Analyzing the CKeepitView Code

In addition to the foregoing classes, AppWizard has also generated a single view class, whose code is intended to provide the basis for continued development of our application.

We will not be using most of this code; however, it is instructive to show it here. Version 1.5 (and later) of the Visual C++ product offers the ability to derive the AppWizard-created view code from a selection of base classes, including the CFormView class, which we will eventually be using. We decided to let the AppWizard generate its view code based upon the CView class, mainly because this is compatible with earlier versions of the product and because the code is easily replaced by newly generated code when we build the CFormView-based view. When we generate the new code, we will be reusing the code for the GetDocument member function from this file. Instructions for modifying the new CAccount view to include the GetDocument function are included in the next chapter, beginning on page 54.

The CKeepitView object is created at the same time the document template is used to create the document and MDI child windows. The view is intended to serve as a single window on the document, and although a view can be attached to one document only, a document can manage multiple views. In fact, several views can share a single child window, as in the case with splitter windows, or multiple views can be displayed in individual child frame windows.

CKeepitView Header File

The declarations for the CKeepitView class are generated into a file named **keepvw.h**. The code in this file is as follows:

```
// keepvw.h : interface of the CKeepitView class
//
/////////////////////////////////////////////////////////////////

class CKeepitView : public CView
{
protected: // create from serialization only
   CKeepitView();
   DECLARE_DYNCREATE(CKeepitView)

// Attributes
public:
   CKeepitDoc* GetDocument();

// Operations
public:

// Implementation
public:
   virtual ~CKeepitView();
   virtual void OnDraw(CDC* pDC); // overridden to draw this view
#ifdef _DEBUC
   virtual void AssertValid() const;
   virtual void Dump(CDumpContext& dc) const;
#endif

   // Printing support
protected:
   virtual BOOL OnPreparePrinting(CPrintInfo* pInfo);
   virtual void OnBeginPrinting(CDC* pDC, CPrintInfo*
pInfo);
   virtual void OnEndPrinting(CDC* pDC, CPrintInfo* pInfo);
// Generated message map functions
protected:
   //{{AFX_MSG(CKeepitView)
      // NOTE - the ClassWizard will add and remove member
      //   functions here. DO NOT EDIT what you see in these
      //   blocks of generated code !
   //}}AFX_MSG
   DECLARE_MESSAGE_MAP()
};

#ifndef _DEBUG// debug version in keepvw.cpp
inline CKeepitDoc* CKeepitView::GetDocument()
   { return (CKeepitDoc*) m_pDocument; }
#endif
```

The foregoing class begins with the declaration of a protected constructor member function, as well as the DECLARE_DYNCREATE macro, which permits the object to be created at run time, dynamically.

The GetDocument member function, declared in the "Attributes" section of the header file, permits us to access the current document from within the current view. You will see an implementation of this function at the bottom of the header file, which is compiled only if a nondebug version of the application is being built. In the debug version, the definition of the GetDocument member function is contained in the **keepvw.cpp** source file's code. The reason for this distinction is that inline functions (as is the case with the nondebug version) cannot be debugged, whereas normal member functions can be.

Public member functions for the destructor and OnDraw member functions are declared. The OnDraw member function is where all of the drawing code specific to this view is contained. Declarations for the AssertValid and Dump member functions are optionally included in the compiled application, depending upon whether a debug version is being built. In addition to the OnDraw member function, which is called to render the contents of the view onto the selected output device, AppWizard has generated declarations for member functions to support printing the contents of the view. The OnPreparePrinting, OnBeginPrinting, and OnEndPrinting member functions provide the view with the ability to control various aspects of the printing process.

Finally, the message map declarations (although empty) are included in the wizard-created code. Note also that the aforementioned in-line definition of the GetDocument member function is written into this file, between conditional statements that allow it to be compiled only if a nondebug version of the application is being built.

CKeepitView Source File

The source file containing the definition of the CKeepitView member functions is named **keepvw.cpp**. This file contains several categories of code, each of which will be presented separately in the paragraphs that follow.

Initial CKeepitView Code

The initial section of code in the **keepvw.cpp** file contains the standard `#include` statements and the definition of the current file name. The code is as follows:

```
// keepvw.cpp : implementation of the CKeepitView class
//

#include "stdafx.h"
#include "keepit.h"

#include "keepdoc.h"
#include "keepvw.h"
```

```
#ifdef _DEBUG
#undef THIS_FILE
static char BASED_CODE THIS_FILE[] = __FILE__;
#endif
```

As is usual, the declarations for standard Windows objects can be referenced by including the **stdafx.h** file. In addition, the main application header file, **keepit.h**, the header file for the document, **keepdoc.h**, and the header file for the CKeepitView class, **keepvw.h**, are included. If a debug version of the application is being built, a string constant containing the current file name (**"keepvw.cpp"**) is also defined.

CKeepitView Message Map

Just above the message map definition is the IMPLEMENT_DYNCREATE macro, which permits the object to be dynamically created at run time. The arguments in the macro specify the current view class and its immediate ancestor (CView).

The wizard-created code for the CKeepitView class contains a message map that supports handlers for the Print and Print Preview features of a standard Windows application. These handlers are invoked when the view receives a File Print or File Print Preview command. The code for these features is as follows:

```
/////////////////////////////////////////////////////////////////
// CKeepitView
IMPLEMENT_DYNCREATE(CKeepitView, CView)

BEGIN_MESSAGE_MAP(CKeepitView, CView)
  //{{AFX_MSG_MAP(CKeepitView)
    // NOTE - the ClassWizard will add and remove mapping
    //   macros here. DO NOT EDIT what you see in these
    //   blocks of generated code !
  //}}AFX_MSG_MAP
  // Standard printing commands
  ON_COMMAND(ID_FILE_PRINT, CView::OnFilePrint)
  ON_COMMAND(ID_FILE_PRINT_PREVIEW,
CView::OnFilePrintPreview)
END_MESSAGE_MAP()
```

CKeepitView Constructor and Destructor

The constructor and destructor for the CKeepitView class are empty in the wizard-created code. As is usual, the code contains comments that indicate that it is appropriate to add code into both the constructor and destructor functions, as needed. We will rarely add code to the constructors, as Windows often requires that an initialization function be called to perform this task. The wizard-created code is as follows:

```
///////////////////////////////////////////////////////////////
// CKeepitView construction/destruction

CKeepitView::CKeepitView()
{
    // TODO: add construction code here
}

CKeepitView::~CKeepitView()
{
}
```

OnDraw Member Function

All drawing of the visible contents of the view is accomplished in the OnDraw member function. This member function is called by the framework when it has determined that an image of the document must be redrawn. Never call the OnDraw member function directly. Instead, depend upon the framework to recognize that the document's contents have changed or the visible region of the view has changed. If necessary use the Invalidate, InvalidateRect, or InvalidateRgn member functions to force the framework to generate the WM_PAINT message that causes OnDraw to be called. The code for the OnDraw member function is as follows:

```
///////////////////////////////////////////////////////////////
// CKeepitView drawing

void CKeepitView::OnDraw(CDC* pDC)
{
    CKeepitDoc* pDoc = GetDocument();

    // TODO: add draw code here
}
```

Printing Support Member Functions

AppWizard has generated three member functions that can be expanded to support printing the contents of the current view on the document.

The OnDraw member function is used to draw the data into a printer device context (as well as the screen device context) that the framework supplies in its pDC argument; however, device settings and other initilization specific to the document or the device are handled by these member functions. The wizard-created code provides us with the means to interact with the user when a hardcopy output has been requested. The functions that support these features are as follows:

```
/////////////////////////////////////////////////////////////////
// CKeepitView printing

BOOL CKeepitView::OnPreparePrinting(CPrintInfo* pInfo)
{
   // default preparation
   return DoPreparePrinting(pInfo);
}

void CKeepitView::OnBeginPrinting(CDC* /*pDC*/,
   CPrintInfo* /*pInfo*/)
{
   // TODO: add extra initialization before printing
}

void CKeepitView::OnEndPrinting(CDC* /*pDC*/,
   CPrintInfo* /*pInfo*/)
{
   // TODO: add cleanup after printing
}
```

OnPreparePrinting is called by the framework when a document is about to be printed. You can change the default values in the print dialog by using this function. OnBeginPrinting is called by the framework after OnPreparePrinting has returned. OnBeginPrinting provides the means for you to make changes that depend upon the settings the user has selected in the print dialog box (e.g., if the page size has been changed, the number of pages to print will also change). The OnEndPrinting member function is called by the framework when the print operation is complete. You can override this member function to free any Graphic Device Interface (GDI) resources you allocated in the OnBeginPrinting member function.

Diagnostic Member Functions

The wizard-created code for the AssertValid and Dump member functions are compiled only if a debug version of the application is being built. The code is as follows:

```
/////////////////////////////////////////////////////////////////
// CKeepitView diagnostics

#ifdef _DEBUG
void CKeepitView::AssertValid() const
{
   CView::AssertValid();
}

void CKeepitView::Dump(CDumpContext& dc) const
{
   CView::Dump(dc);
}
```

GetDocument Member Function

The nondebug version of the GetDocument member function is generated as in line code. The GetDocument member function included in the **keepvw.cpp** source file is compiled if a debug version of the application is being built. The code is as follows:

```
CKeepitDoc* CKeepitView::GetDocument() // non-debug is inline
{
   ASSERT(m_pDocument->IsKindOf(RUNTIME_CLASS(CKeepitDoc)));
   return (CKeepitDoc*) m_pDocument;
}

#endif //_DEBUG
```

Note that the final directive in the foregoing code ends the section that is compiled if a debug version of the application is being built. In the case of a production version of the code, the AssertValid, Dump, and GetDocument member functions presented in the foregoing sections will not be compiled into the executable application. However, the in line version of the GetDocument member function will be used.

CKeepitView Message Handler Placeholder

AppWizard has generated a placeholder, in the form of a set of comments, which indicates where future message handler member functions should be placed. The AppWizard tool will generate new message handlers in this position of the file. The comments are as follows:

```
/////////////////////////////////////////////////////////////////
// CKeepitView message handlers
```

Exercises

The following exercises are intended to help you understand the structure of a standard Windows application, as built by the AppWizard tool, by requiring you to do some investigation into the MFC source code, as well as the code we have already presented.

1. Define the major class types included in a standard MFC application. How does each of these relate to the corresponding class or classes in the MFC framework? Explain your answer.

2. Describe the startup process for an application. How does execution begin and in what order does it proceed?

3. Describe the difference between an "old style" procedural application and a "new style" event-driven application. List the advantages and disadvantages of each of these application structures.

4. Define the term "message handler" and how this term applies to applications written for use in the Windows execution environment. Contrast the use of the term "event handler" with the term "message handler" and how these may differ in practice. (*Hint:* The term "event handler" is used in preference to "message handler" on other execution platforms.)

5. Clarify the intent of the AssertValid and Dump functions. Describe why they are included within conditional compilation directives and in what circumstances these functions would be used.

Chapter 3
Designing the Primary Form

In this chapter, we are going to create a new view to serve as the primary form (or account register) for the Keepit application. Making the necessary changes will involve discarding most of the code contained in the current **keepvw.cpp** and **keepvw.h** files, described in the previous chapter. Instead, we will implement a new view that is based upon the CFormView class and is constructed using the App Studio tool as a dialog box. When construction of the dialog is complete, we will make changes to the view class included in the document template creation (shown in the InitInstance member function on page 17). This will allow the new view to be created. We will also remove the old view's files from the project and add new classes that add functionality to the new view. Chapter 4 will show the custom code to implement fully the features of the new view.

The new view is that of an account register. Its main feature is a list of entries, which will be managed by a new class, based upon the CListBox class in the MFC. The CListBox-based class will be implemented in an "owner draw" style, and will require that we furnish the necessary code to draw the contents of each of its entries. That code will be shown in Chapter 4.

In this chapter, we will also be adding support for a dynamically created CEdit object, which we will use to allow the user to type information into the custom list box fields. The following sections contain tutorials for creating the new view class and its layout, for creating new classes, modifying existing classes, and editing the project and other support files, in preparation for adding the custom code to make the initial version of the Keepit application fully operational.

Designing the New View

We will be using the App Studio tool to create a new view that contains controls similar to those found in a dialog box. The dialog created with App Studio will be based upon the CFormView class, which supports this type of view. In going through the tutorial for creating the Account view, you may wish to refer to Figure 3-11, which shows the completed appearance of the view. The steps to create the new view are as follows:

1. Launch Visual C++ and load in the current project file, **keepit.mak**.

2. Pull down the Tools menu and choose the App Studio command, as shown in Figure 3-1.

Figure 3-1
Choosing App Studio from the Tools menu

3. Click Dialog in the Type column, on the left side of the view. App Studio should display a single existing dialog in the Resources column, named `IDD_ABOUTBOX`. Pull down the Resource menu and choose the New command as shown in Figure 3-2.

Figure 3-2
Choosing to create a new resource

4. App Studio will display a new dialog, requesting that you choose the type of resource to be created. Choose Dialog, as shown in Figure 3-3, and then click OK.

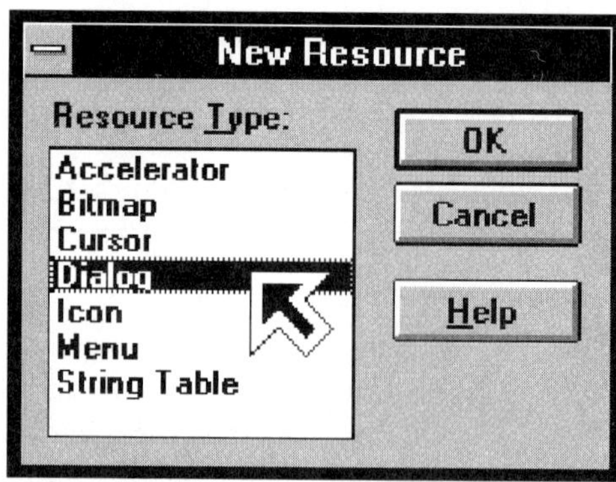

Figure 3-3
Choosing to create a Dialog resource

5. App Studio will create a standard dialog window containing OK and Cancel buttons. Click on the Cancel button and press the delete key, deleting that button. It will not be used.

6. Resize the dialog by positioning your mouse in its bottom right corner and, holding down the left mouse button, drag the lower right corner until the dimensions of the dialog (shown in the lower right corner of the Status Bar) indicate 245x172, and then release the mouse button.

   (*Note:* In this and other tutorials, when numeric coordinates or dimensions are given, it is not necessary to be exactly precise when you duplicate this work. However, if you use the arrow keys when an item is selected, you can often move the selected item in single-unit increments in the direction corresponding to the key being pressed. If you also hold down the Shift key when using the arrow keys, you can resize the selected element in the direction corresponding to the key being pressed.)

   Make sure the dialog window is still selected, pull down the Resource menu and choose the Properties command (or double click on the dialog window). Change the General properties to match those shown in Figure 3-4, including changing the ID to IDD_ACCOUNT.

<table>
<tr><td>

Figure 3-4
General properties of
the IDD_ACCOUNT
dialog

</td></tr>
</table>

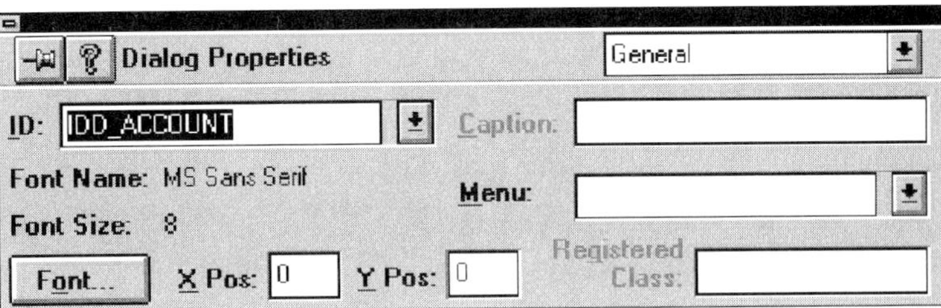

Figure 3-4
General properties of the IDD_ACCOUNT dialog

7. Without dismissing the properties window, click the combo box's arrow at the top right of the window to display the Styles choice. Select Styles and the window's contents will change. Make the necessary changes to the styles so that they are the same as shown in Figure 3-5.

Figure 3-5
Styles properties of the IDD_ACCOUNT dialog

Make certain that the Style is Child, and that the Border combo box contains the word None. Make sure that the Titlebar checkbox is not checked, and that the Visible checkbox is also not checked. (While you are placing the various elements in the dialog, you may want to change the dialog to have a Thin border; however, you must change it to none before you leave App Studio, so that the form is displayed correctly by the code.)

8. Click on the OK button in the dialog and move the button to a position toward the bottom left corner of the window. Its coordinates should be 15,156 in the Status Bar box to the left of its dimensions, which are 50x14.

9. Click the mouse button on the List Box element in the floating control palette (it's the fifth tool in the right column—the one to its immediate left is a combo box). Hold down the mouse button and drag the list box's outline onto the dialog window. Position and resize the list box by clicking and dragging its lower right corner until its dimensions are 245x127, as shown in the lower right corner of the Status Bar. Its coordinates, shown in the box to the left of its dimensions should be 0,21. Now, double click the list box (or choose the Properties command from the Resource menu) and set its general properties to match those shown in Figure 3-6. Note that the ID has been changed to IDC_ACCT_LIST.

<table>
<tr><td>

Figure 3-6

General properties of the list box resource

</td><td>

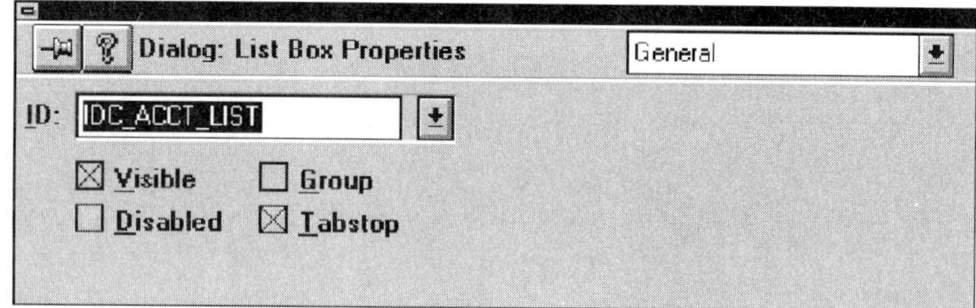

</td></tr>
</table>

10. Click on the combo box arrow at the top right of the properties window and select the Styles option. Change the styles to match those shown in Figure 3-7. Note that the Selection type is Single, and the Owner Draw style is Fixed. The List Box has only a vertical scrollbar. The Border, Sort, and Notify checkboxes are checked.

11. Double click on the OK button to show its properties and change the Caption field to the word "Save." The ID field should continue to contain IDOK and the Default Button, Tabstop, and Visible checkboxes should be checked, as shown in Figure 3-8. By making the Save button retain the IDOK identifier and remain the default button, we can choose for the Return (or Enter) key to save the contents of an entry.

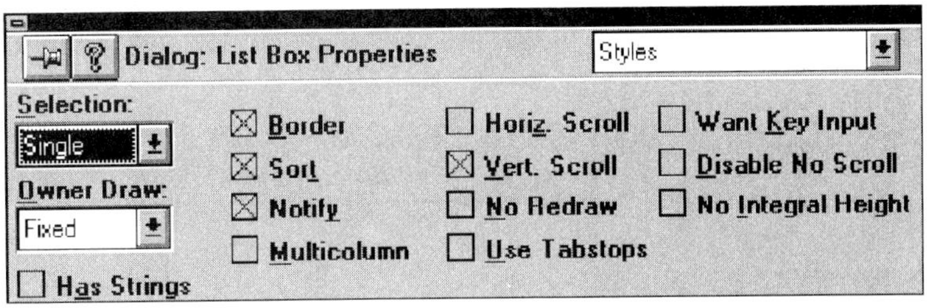

Figure 3-7
Style properties of the list box resource

Figure 3-8
Properties of the new Save button

12. Click on the Static Text tool in the floating control palette (the second one in the left column, which displays an 'A') and drag the outline of a static text field to the coordinates 127,156. Double click on the field and change its ID to IDC_BAL_LABEL and its Caption to "Current Balance," as shown in Figure 3-9.

Figure 3-9
Properties of the Account Balance static text field

13. Choose the Static Text tool once again and drag a new field onto the dialog, at coordinates of 195,156. Double click on this field, and change its properties to reflect those in Figure 3-10. The ID should be changed to IDC_BALANCE and its Caption should contain the string "$10,249.23."

Figure 3-10
Properties of the IDC_BALANCE static text field

When the foregoing steps are complete, the form view should have the general appearance shown in Figure 3-11.

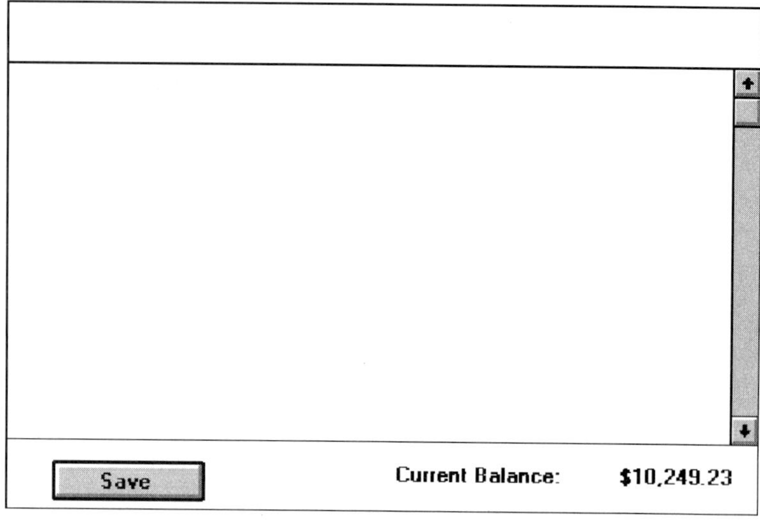

Figure 3-11
Appearance of Account form view (with border shown)

Note in Figure 3-11 that a border is shown for the form view. This border was included in the screen shot to give you an idea of the relative positions of the various elements with respect to the view's boundaries. The border should be removed when construction of the form is complete, by changing the Border property in the dialog's Style settings to None.

The next series of steps concerns the creation of code for a new view class, which will display the newly created form view. You should still have App Studio running, with the IDD_ACCOUNT form view showing on the screen. The steps to create the new view class are as follows:

1. Pull Down App Studio's Resource menu and choose the ClassWizard command, as shown in Figure 3-12.

Figure 3-12
Choosing the ClassWizard command

2. The ClassWizard tool will display a New Class dialog. Fill in the fields in this dialog, as shown in Figure 3-13, making sure to change the contents of the Class Type field to CFormView by selecting that class from the list in the combo box.

Figure 3-13
Add Class dialog filled in
for new CAccount class

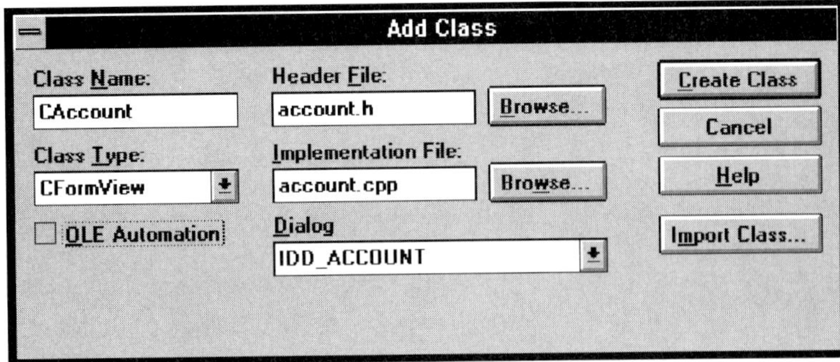

3. When the Add Class dialog has been filled in as shown, click the Create Class button. This will allow ClassWizard to create new header and source files for the CAccount class. After creating the code, the ClassWizard will display the dialog shown in Figure 3-14. This dialog contains a list of the Object IDs, a list of their corresponding Messages, and a list of Member Functions. The figure shows that the IDC_ACCT_LIST object has been selected, and that its LBN_SELCHANGE message has also been selected.

Figure 3-14
CAccount class with
messages for the
IDC_ACCT_LIST
control shown

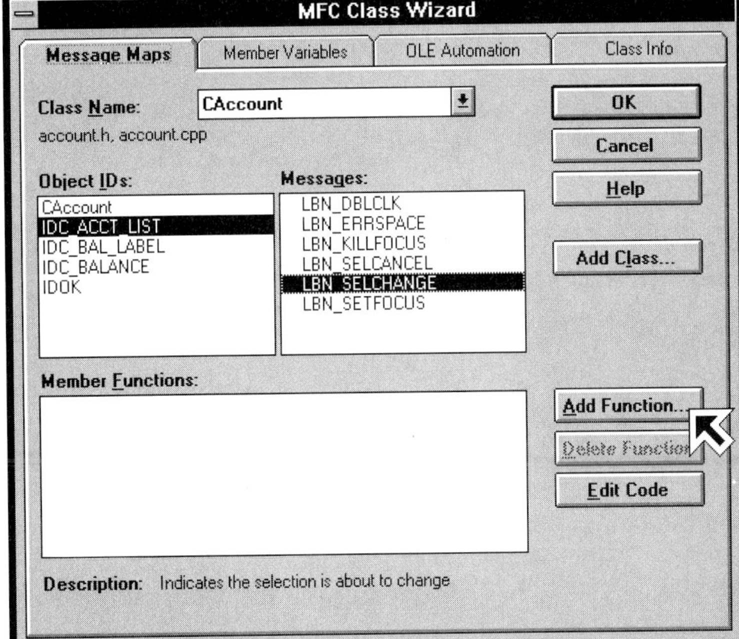

4. After selecting the IDC_ACCT_LIST object (the list box) and then selecting the LBN_SELCHANGE message in the scrolling list of messages, click the Add Function button. ClassWizard will display a new dialog that allows you to specify the member function name to be called when a new selection is chosen from the list box by the user. The member function name should be entered in the dialog, as shown in Figure 3-15, and then click OK.

Figure 3-15
Specifying the member function name for the LBN_SELCHANGE message

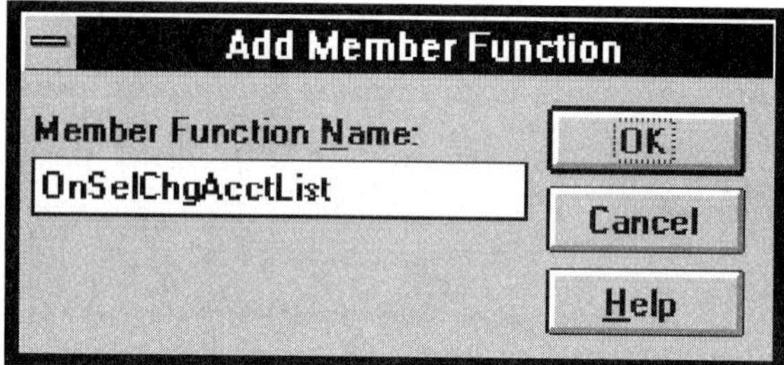

5. Select the IDOK Object ID and then select the BN_CLICKED message, as is shown in Figure 3-16. After making these selections, click the Add Function button and change the member function name to OnSave, as shown in the figure.

Figure 3-16
Selecting the BN_CLICKED message for the IDOK control

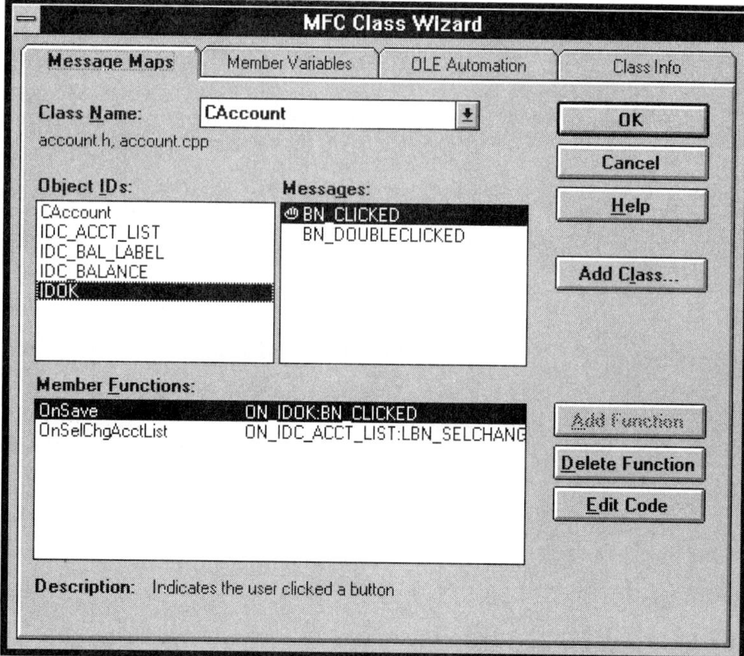

6. After the foregoing steps are complete, the screen should still contain the dialog shown in Figure 3-16. Click the Add Class button in the dialog. This will cause ClassWizard to show the Add Class dia-

log, which should be filled in as shown in Figure 3-17. Note that we have selected generic CWnd for the Class Type in this dialog. We will change this later to be a descendent of CListBox; however, for the time being, leave it as it is and click the Create Class button.

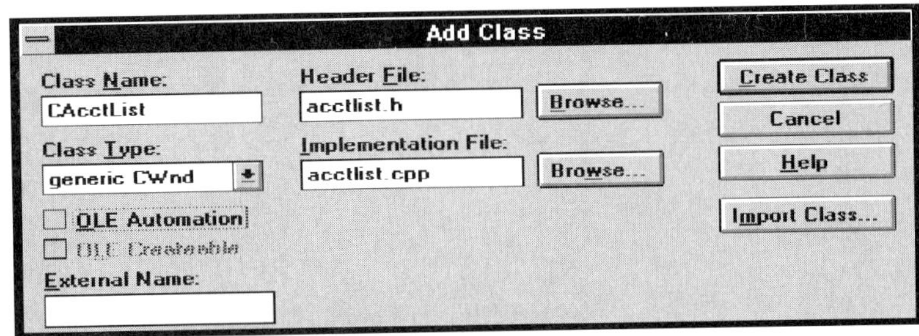

Figure 3-17
Adding the CAcctList class

7. After the CAcctList class has been created, you should see a dialog similar to Figure 3-16, but for the CAcctList class, on your screen. You will not be adding any message handlers for that class. Click the Add Class button and fill in the dialog as shown in Figure 3-18. When you have completed the dialog, click the Create Class button.

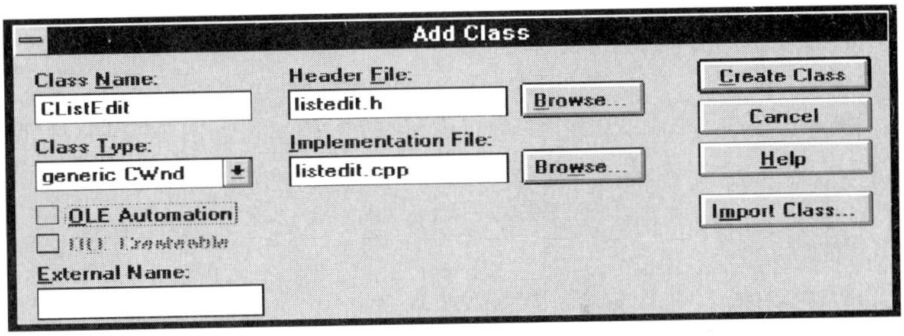

Figure 3-18
Creating the CListEdit class

8. After the CListEdit class has been created, ClassWizard will display the dialog shown in Figure 3-19. Select the indicated messages for the CListEdit object (OnChar for the ON_WM_CHAR message, OnGetDlgCode for the ON_WM_GETDLGCODE message, and OnKeyDown for the ON_WM_KEYDOWN message).

9. After assigning the member functions to these classes, click the OK button to terminate execution of the ClassWizard tool.

At this point, three new classes have been created. CAccount was created to manage the IDD_ACCOUNT dialog. The new CAcctList class was created, based upon the CListBox class, and to provide member functions for handling the "owner draw" characteristics of the list in our CFormView derived class. Finally, the CListEdit class was created, based upon the CEdit class, which contains member functions to override the keyboard-related messages that will be generated when the user enters information into the new CAccount view, when it is implemented fully.

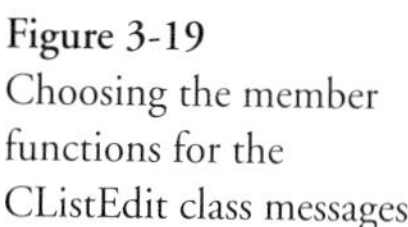

Figure 3-19
Choosing the member
functions for the
CListEdit class messages

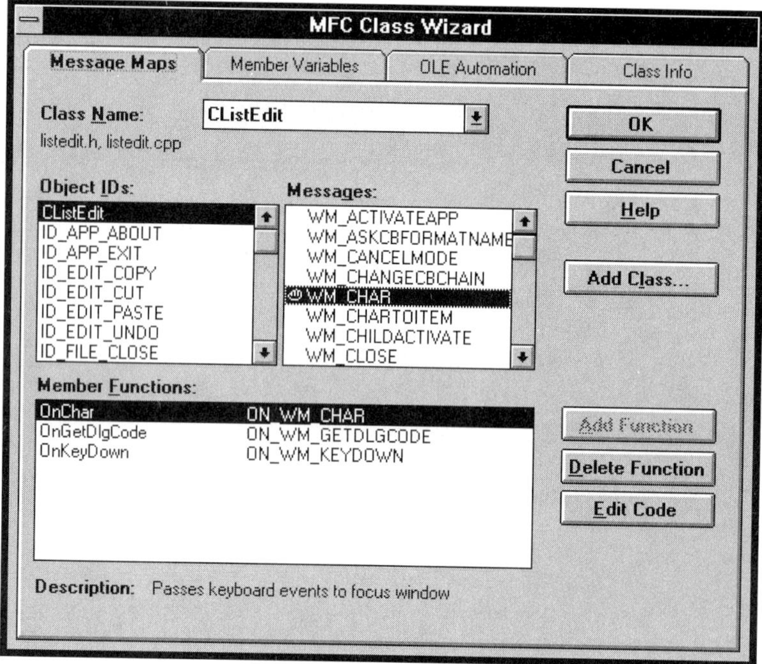

When the ClassWizard is exited, the Account view will still be showing on your screen, as it was designed using the App Studio tool. You can exit App Studio by first choosing the Save command from the File menu and then choosing the Exit command from the File menu.

Changes to the CAcctList Class

In the code listings that follow, changes will be indicated by the use of "change bars" at the left side of the affected statements. Newly added code will not be so marked, but will be accompanied by a heading or comment that indicates this fact.

In order to associate the CAcctList class with its appropriate ancestor, we need to change the **acctlist.h** header file to reflect the new class hierarchy. in the project.

(*Note*: In the case of this application, we chose to let the AppWizard tool create a standard view class as its default view. Doing so was necessary with Visual C++ version 1.0. In version 1.5 of Visual C++, the initial view class can be changed to be a descendent of the CFormView class. While you may wish to create such a class as your initial view—and we recommend doing so if you are using the later version of the Visual C++ product—we elected to create the view as it would have been done with version 1.0 of the product, not only to show how to change this decision

at a later time, but also to postpone the tutorial for creating the Account
dialog until this chapter. Had you elected to create the initial view as a
descendent of the CFormView class, then the initial view would have
been displayed on the screen with an onscreen comment indicating that
form controls need to be added to the dialog.)

Because version 1.0 of Visual C++ does not offer the ability for a new
class to be a descendent of CListBox, we chose to make it a descendent
of the generic CWnd class. The following code shows how the header
file is modified to change the ancestry of this class. The modified code
for the CAcctList class declaration is as follows:

```
// acctlist.h : header file
//
/////////////////////////////////////////////////////////////////
// CAcctList window

class CAcctList : public CListBox
{
// Construction
public:
   CAcctList();

// Attributes
public:

// Operations
public:

// Implementation
public:
   virtual ~CAcctList();

   // Generated message map functions
protected:
   //{{AFX_MSG(CAcctList)
      // NOTE - the ClassWizard will add and remove member
      //    functions here.
   //}}AFX_MSG
   DECLARE_MESSAGE_MAP()
};
```

In the foregoing, we have changed only the CWnd ancestor to CListBox
in the first line of the class declaration. This effectively makes the CAcct-
List class an immediate derived class of the CListBox class, which is what
we want. It is not necessary to make any changes in the **acctlist.cpp**
source file at this time. We will be adding quite a bit of new functionality
to this class in the next chapter.

Changes to the CListEdit Class

We also need to change the ancestry of the CListEdit class so that the revised header file, **listedit.h**, contains the proper ancestor declaration, as
follows:

```
// listedit.h : header file
//
////////////////////////////////////////////////////////////
// CListEdit window

class CListEdit : public CEdit
{
// Construction
public:
   CListEdit();

// Attributes
public:

// Operations
public:

// Implementation
public:
   virtual ~CListEdit();

   // Generated message map functions
protected:
   //{{AFX_MSG(CListEdit)
   afx_msg UINT OnGetDlgCode();
   afx_msg void OnKeyDown(UINT nChar, UINT nRepCnt, UINT
      nFlags);
   afx_msg void OnChar(UINT nChar, UINT nRepCnt, UINT
nFlags);
   //}}AFX_MSG
   DECLARE_MESSAGE_MAP()
};
```

In the foregoing code, by making the CEdit class the immediate ancestor
of the CListEdit class, the latter will be able to inherit and specialize the
behavior of the CEdit class. Note that the CListEdit class has message
map declarations for the member functions we have added. It will not be
necessary to modify the **listedit.cpp** source file at this time. We will be
adding functionality to this class in the next chapter.

Changes to the CAccount Class

In order for the new CAccount class to assume the role as the new default view, we need to add a few changes to the code generated by the
ClassWizard. The CAccount class object is created by the CKeepitApp
application object when the document template is processed. The
changes to this class include code cut and pasted from the original Keep-
itView class for accessing the document from within the view. The modified code in the **account.h** file is as follows:

```
// account.h : header file
//

class  CKeepitDoc;  // added forward class reference
```

```
///////////////////////////////////////////////////////////////
// CAccount form view

#ifndef __AFXEXT_H__
#include <afxext.h>
#endif

class CAccount : public CFormView
{
   DECLARE_DYNCREATE(CAccount)
protected:
   CAccount();// protected constructor used by dynamic creation
// Form Data
public:
   //{{AFX_DATA(CAccount)
   enum { IDD = IDD_ACCOUNT };
      // NOTE: the ClassWizard will add data members here
   //}}AFX_DATA

// Attributes
public:
   CKeepitDoc* GetDocument();

// Operations
public:

// Implementation
protected:
   virtual ~CAccount();
   virtual void DoDataExchange(CDataExchange* pDX);// DDX/
DDV support
   // Generated message map functions
   //{{AFX_MSG(CAccount)
   afx_msg void OnSelChgAcctList();
   afx_msg void OnSave();
   //}}AFX_MSG
   DECLARE_MESSAGE_MAP()
};

#ifndef _DEBUG// debug version in keepvw.cpp
inline CKeepitDoc* CAccount::GetDocument()
   { return (CKeepitDoc*) m_pDocument; }
#endif
```

Adding the foregoing statements to the **account.h** header file must also be accompanied by the addition of the GetDocument member function to the source file. The modified **account.cpp** source file is as follows:

```
// account.cpp : implementation file
//

#include "stdafx.h"
#include "keepit.h"
#include "keepdoc.h"    // added reference to document header
#include "account.h"
#ifdef _DEBUG
#undef THIS_FILE
static char BASED_CODE THIS_FILE[] = __FILE__;
#endif

///////////////////////////////////////////////////////////////
// CAccount
```

```
IMPLEMENT_DYNCREATE(CAccount, CFormView)

CAccount::CAccount()
   : CFormView(CAccount::IDD)
{
   //{{AFX_DATA_INIT(CAccount)
      // NOTE: the ClassWizard will add member
      //    initialization here
   //}}AFX_DATA_INIT
}

CAccount::~CAccount()
{
}

void CAccount::DoDataExchange(CDataExchange* pDX)
{
   CFormView::DoDataExchange(pDX);
   //{{AFX_DATA_MAP(CAccount)
      // NOTE: the ClassWizard will add DDX and DDV calls
here
   //}}AFX_DATA_MAP
}

BEGIN_MESSAGE_MAP(CAccount, CFormView)
   //{{AFX_MSG_MAP(CAccount)
   ON_LBN_SELCHANGE(IDC_ACCT_LIST, OnSelChgAcctList)
   ON_BN_CLICKED(IDOK, OnSave)
   //}}AFX_MSG_MAP
END_MESSAGE_MAP()

#ifdef _DEBUG
CKeepitDoc* CAccount::GetDocument() // non-debug version is
inline
{
   ASSERT(m_pDocument->IsKindOf(RUNTIME_CLASS(CKeepitDoc)));
   return (CKeepitDoc*) m_pDocument;
}
#endif //_DEBUG

/////////////////////////////////////////////////////////////
// CAccount message handlers

void CAccount::OnSelChgAcctList()
{
   // TODO: Add your control notification handler code here

}

void CAccount::OnSave()
{
   // TODO: Add your control notification handler code here

}
```

Changes to the CKeepitApp Class

In order to substitute the CAccount class for the previously used CKeep-itView class as the primary view, it is necessary to make a few changes in the **keepit.cpp** source file. The modified version of this source file is as follows:

```cpp
// keepit.cpp : Defines the class behaviors for the application.
//

#include "stdafx.h"
#include "keepit.h"

#include "mainfrm.h"
#include "keepdoc.h"
#include "account.h"   // changed to refer to CAccount

#ifdef _DEBUG
#undef THIS_FILE
static char BASED_CODE THIS_FILE[] = __FILE__;
#endif

/////////////////////////////////////////////////////////////////////
// CKeepitApp

BEGIN_MESSAGE_MAP(CKeepitApp, CWinApp)
   //{{AFX_MSG_MAP(CKeepitApp)
   ON_COMMAND(ID_APP_ABOUT, OnAppAbout)
      // NOTE - the ClassWizard will add and remove mapping
      //   macros here. DO NOT EDIT what you see in these
      //   blocks of generated code !
   //}}AFX_MSG_MAP
   // Standard file based document commands
   ON_COMMAND(ID_FILE_NEW, CWinApp::OnFileNew)
   ON_COMMAND(ID_FILE_OPEN, CWinApp::OnFileOpen)
   // Standard print setup command
   ON_COMMAND(ID_FILE_PRINT_SETUP,
CWinApp::OnFilePrintSetup)
END_MESSAGE_MAP()

/////////////////////////////////////////////////////////////////////
// CKeepitApp construction

CKeepitApp::CKeepitApp()
{
   // TODO: add construction code here,
   // Place all significant initialization in InitInstance
}

/////////////////////////////////////////////////////////////////////
// The one and only CKeepitApp object

CKeepitApp NEAR theApp;

/////////////////////////////////////////////////////////////////////
// CKeepitApp initialization

BOOL CKeepitApp::InitInstance()
{
   // Standard initialization
   // If you are not using these features and wish to
   // reduce the size of your final executable, you should
   // remove from the following the specific initialization
   // routines you do not need.

   SetDialogBkColor(); // set dialog background color to gray
   LoadStdProfileSettings();  // Load standard INI file options
                        //    (including MRU)

   // Register the application's document templates.
   // Document templates serve as the connection between
   // documents, frame windows and views.
```

```cpp
      AddDocTemplate(new CMultiDocTemplate(IDR_KEEPITTYPE,
          RUNTIME_CLASS(CKeepitDoc),
          RUNTIME_CLASS(CMDIChildWnd), // standard MDI child
          RUNTIME_CLASS(CAccount)));

   // create main MDI Frame window
   CMainFrame* pMainFrame = new CMainFrame;
   if (!pMainFrame->LoadFrame(IDR_MAINFRAME))
      return FALSE;
   m_pMainWnd = pMainFrame;

   // enable file manager drag/drop and DDE Execute open
   EnableShellOpen();
   RegisterShellFileTypes();

   // simple command line parsing
   if (m_lpCmdLine[0] == '\0')
   {
      // create a new (empty) document
      OnFileNew();
   }
   else
   {
      // open an existing document
      OpenDocumentFile(m_lpCmdLine);
   }

   m_pMainWnd->DragAcceptFiles();
   // the main window has been initialized,
   // so show and update it
   pMainFrame->ShowWindow(m_nCmdShow);
   pMainFrame->UpdateWindow();

   return TRUE;
}

/////////////////////////////////////////////////////////////////////
// CAboutDlg dialog used for App About

class CAboutDlg : public CDialog
{
public:
   CAboutDlg();

// Dialog Data
   //{{AFX_DATA(CAboutDlg)
   enum { IDD = IDD_ABOUTBOX };
   //}}AFX_DATA

// Implementation
protected:
   virtual void DoDataExchange(CDataExchange* pDX);
   //{{AFX_MSG(CAboutDlg)
      // No message handlers
   //}}AFX_MSG
   DECLARE_MESSAGE_MAP()
};

CAboutDlg::CAboutDlg() : CDialog(CAboutDlg::IDD)
{
   //{{AFX_DATA_INIT(CAboutDlg)
   //}}AFX_DATA_INIT
}

void CAboutDlg::DoDataExchange(CDataExchange* pDX)
{
```

```
    CDialog::DoDataExchange(pDX);
    //{{AFX_DATA_MAP(CAboutDlg)
    //}}AFX_DATA_MAP
}

BEGIN_MESSAGE_MAP(CAboutDlg, CDialog)
    //{{AFX_MSG_MAP(CAboutDlg)
        // No message handlers
    //}}AFX_MSG_MAP
END_MESSAGE_MAP()

// App command to run the dialog
void CKeepitApp::OnAppAbout()
{
   CAboutDlg aboutDlg;
   aboutDlg.DoModal();
}


/////////////////////////////////////////////////////////////
// CKeepitApp commands
```

Updating the Project Directory and Class Wizard Database

After the foregoing header and source file changes have been made, it is necessary to delete the **keepvw.h** header and **keepvw.cpp** source files from the project directory. In addition, delete the file named **keepit.clw**. This is the Class Wizard database. It is no longer valid because we have changed the ancestry of two of the classes that it generated. You can use the Windows File Manager to delete these files. The ClassWizard database (in **keepit.clw**) will be rebuilt shortly.

In addition to deleting the old view's files (**keepvw.h** and **keepvw.cpp**) from the project directory, it is also necessary to delete them from the project file itself. To do this, make sure that Visual C++ is running and that the Keepit project is loaded; then choose the Edit command from the Project menu. This will cause a dialog that contains the names of all of the files in the project to be displayed. The bottom section of the dialog holds the files that currently exist in the project. To remove the old view files, select the **keepvw.cpp** file in the list and click the Delete button, as shown in Figure 3-20.

After the old view files have been removed from the project directory, the application can be compiled and executed. The appearance of the new view is shown in Figure 3-21.

Although we specified that the list box should have a vertical scroll bar, it is not visible in Figure 3-21 because the list is empty. In order for the scroll bar to become visible, we must add enough entries to cause it to activate. Other than the absence of the scroll bar in the list, the new view contains all of the elements that we have specified.

Figure 3-20
Deleting the old view
files from the project

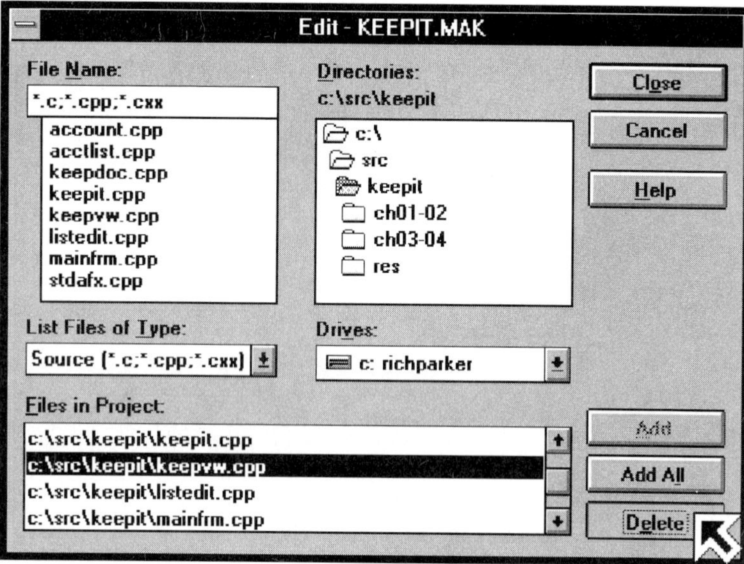

Figure 3-21
Appearance of new view
while Keepit application
is executing

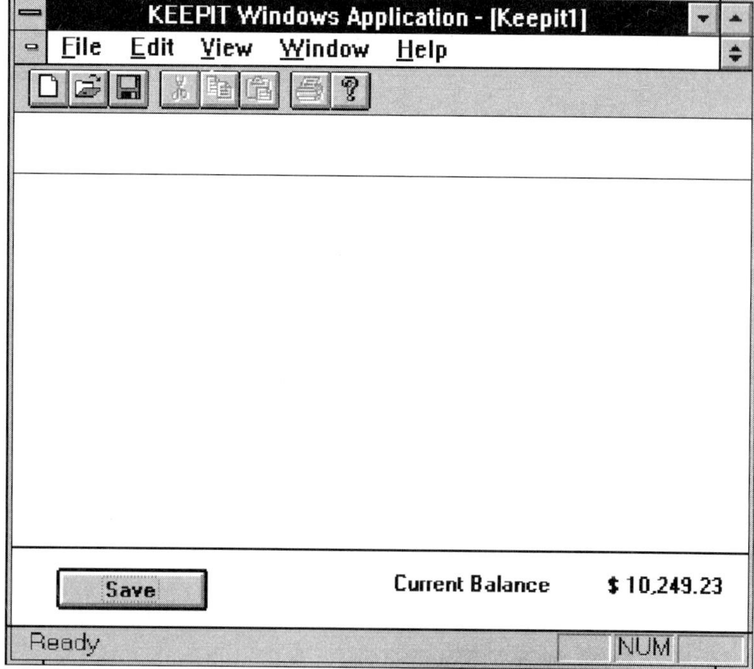

Rebuilding the ClassWizard Database

To rebuild the ClassWizard database, which is stored in the **keepit.clw**
file that you deleted previously, perform the following steps:

1. With Visual C++ running and the Make file for the Keepit application loaded (**keepit.mak**), pull down the Tools menu and choose the App Studio command. This will launch the App Studio product.

2. With App Studio in execution, pull down its Resource menu and choose the ClassWizard command.

3. When ClassWizard is launched, it will discover that the **keepit.clw** file doesn't exist and will display a dialog, offering to rebuild the file from your project's source files. Click Yes in this dialog to rebuild the database.

4. When you perform the foregoing step, ClassWizard will display the project dialog, listing all of the files that make up the project. If you need to add or delete any source files from the project at this time, do so before clicking the OK button in this dialog. You should not have to do so, as the necessary files that make up your project have been specified previously (see Figure 3-20). Click the OK button in the dialog.

5. ClassWizard will rebuild the database and display its standard class information dialog (see Figure 3-19). You may find that the dialog is blank; however, if you click the combo box arrow, to the immediate right of the Class Name title, you will see a list of the classes that are currently included in the project.

6. Select the CAcctList class from the combo box and click the Class Info button in the ClassWizard dialog. You will see that the base class for this class has now been changed to CListBox. Click the Close box in the information dialog.

7. Select the CListEdit class in the ClassWizard combo box and then click the Class Info button. Notice that the base class has been changed to CEdit. Click the Close Box in the information dialog, and then click OK in the ClassWizard dialog to terminate execution of that tool.

App Studio should still be running at this time. Pull down its File menu and choose the Quit command to terminate its execution. The rebuilding process is now complete.

Creating a *Super* Browser

In the course of building the Keepit application, Visual C++ has also, by default, created a browser database. Unfortunately, this database includes entries only for the files directly included in the project, and not the MFC source files, in which many of the member functions used in most Visual

C++ applications reside. After building what we call a *Super* Browser, you can place the cursor on almost *any* type name, Windows interface function, or member function in the MFC, press function-key F11, and be shown the definition of that entity. We feel that it is important to have such a universal browser available. In order for you to construct such a browser, you will need close to a megabyte of available disk space to contain the browser database files for the MFC. You should also be aware that the following procedure creates a set of browser files for only one memory model—the large model in this case. The steps are as follows:

1. The first part of the process to construct browser files requires that you execute some commands in the DOS environment. It may be best for you to shut down Windows for the first few steps.

2. Create two new directories on your disk, one inside the other. The name we have assigned to the first directory is C:\MFCSBRS. This name was chosen to indicate that it will contain SBR files for the MFC. Create a second directory, inside the first, with a name corresponding to the library for which memory model the browser is being built. In our case, we used the name LAFXCWD to match the name associated with the corresponding large model library.

3. After the foregoing directories have been created, navigate to the MFC source file directory, which, by default, will be at the following location on your disk: C:\MSVC\MFC\SRC. If you have located the files for Visual C++ in some other directory, move to the corresponding subdirectory holding the MFC source files.

4. Enter the following command at the DOS prompt:

```
NMAKE MODEL=L TARGET=W DEBUG=1 "OPT=FRc:\MFCSBRS\LAFXCWD\ /Zn"
```

   This command will cause the NMAKE utility to create large model browser files for all of the MFC source classes and place these files in the directory you created in the foregoing step. The same process applies to other memory models, by using a different parameter in the MODEL= specification.

5. You can now launch Windows and load your project, for example, the Keepit project with which we have been working. You will need to change the project options for the Debug version of the project, as follows:

   a. Choose Project from the Options menu.

   b. Make sure that Debug is selected as the Build Mode and click the Compiler button in the Customize Build Options group.

c. Select the Listing Files entry in the Category list and uncheck the Include Local Variables and Browser Information selections in their respective checkboxes.

d. Select the Custom Options entry in the Category list and add the following to the end of the Other Options field: "`/Fr.\`", making sure that there is a space separating the `/Fr` from the previous options, if any. Don't enter the quotation marks.

e. Click on the OK button to dismiss the Compiler Options dialog and then click the OK button to dismiss the Project Options dialog.

6. The foregoing step has disabled the generation of browser information for your project. To create browser information that will include the files in your project and also the files in the newly generated SBR files for the MFC, you will need to add a new command to the Tools menu in Visual C++. This is accomplished as follows:

a. Choose Tools from the Options menu.

b. Click the Add button in the dialog. This will bring up a standard file dialog, which you should use to navigate to the location of the BSCMAKE tool (which is used to create the browser database file). The standard path is: `C:\MSVC\BIN\BSCMAKE`.

c. In the succeeding dialog, modify the contents of the Menu Text field to something like "BSCMAKE with LAFXCWD," without the quotation marks.

d. Enter the following into the Arguments field:
```
/o$PROJ /n *.SBR C:\MFCSBRS\LAFXCWD\*.SBR
```

e. Click the OK button to dismiss the Tools dialog

This concludes the steps for creation of the tools necessary to build a browser database that includes the browser source files for both the current project and the MFC files. To build the database for your current project, pull down the Tools menu and choose the new command. This will launch the BSCMAKE utility, which will take a bit of time to complete its actions. When the browser database has been built, control will be returned to the Visual C++ Project Manager.

(*Note:* If you have difficulty running the BSCMAKE program from within the Visual C++ environment, then you may have to do so from within DOS. We have also noticed that if enough virtual memory is available, the build process is more likely to work properly inside the Visual C++ environment.)

When you rebuild your project in Debug mode, you will notice that the Building Browser Database message no longer appears. You will need to use the new command in the Tools menu to accomplish this purpose, but only for the current project. You need not rebuild the MFC browser source files for use in any new projects; however, you will need to change the Compiler Options for each new project, as specified on page 62, in the foregoing Step 5.

Having a full browser will greatly increase your ability to peruse the source files of the MFC, giving you better access to its member functions and making the development process much more efficient.

Exercises

1. Describe the features of the App Studio tool. What primary purpose does it serve? What is the full scope of its abilities?

2. Examine the features of the CFormView class in the Visual C++ documentation. List several important applications for views built upon this class. How do they differ from classes that inherit their behaviors directly from CView or CScrollView?

3. The Microsoft Foundation Classes have been designed to support a document-view architecture. What does this mean? Describe the characteristics of this architecture.

4. Examine the documentation for the CListBox class and describe why it is necessary to create a derived class of that class for owner draw styles. What member functions will need to be overridden?

5. Examine the appearance of the view depicted in Figure 3-22. Based upon your knowledge of owner draw list box elements, how do you think this appearance was achieved? Explain your answer.

6. In examining the documentation for the CListBox class, you will find that it is not possible to type directly into a selected list entry, nor is it possible to create an entry with varying width fields, in the multiple row style you see in Figure 3-22. With that knowledge and the results of the examination in the foregoing exercise, describe how you would create the variable-size fields shown in the figure.[1]

7. There is also the need to allow the user to enter data, directly into the fields shown in Figure 3-22. Knowing that the CListEdit class

---

[1] This exercise requires a great deal of study of the MFC library and its various classes to be answered. Although the answer to this exercise will be found in the next chapter, it is recommended that students and developers attempt to determine the right approach to the problems pointed out in the exercise text.

Figure 3-22
Keepit application with the new view fully implemented

has been created to be a derived class of the CEdit class in the MFC and that it has been provided with the ability to process certain messages, how would you implement what appears to be direct keyboard entries into the fields of the figure?[1] (*Hint*: An object of the CListEdit class can be created, sized, and positioned anywhere in the confines of the active view.)

8. If you own version 1.5 (or later) of the Visual C++ product, you may want to re-create the Keepit application from scratch, using the improved features in the AppWizard and ClassWizard tools. Doing so will provide you with experience in creating the initial view and its associated class in a more efficient manner. The process for accomplishing this is as follows:[2]

   a. When you create a new project, click the Classes button in the AppWizard dialog.

   b. In the Classes dialog, select the view class and then change its base class by dropping down the Base Class combo box and select the CFormView entry.

---

[1] This exercise also requires a great deal of study to be answered. Although the answer to this will be found in the next chapter, it is recommended that students and developers attempt to develop an approach to solving this problem.

[2] Re-creating the application at this early stage is not a very difficult task. It should be attempted only if version 1.5 (or later) of Visual C++ is available to the student. After regenerating the application, you will still need to modify the ClassWizard-generated code for the CAcctList and CListEntry classes, to change their base class ancestors, as indicated on pages 52–54; however, the main CAccount view class can be derived from CFormView and used, as is, as a basis for future versions of the application.

    c. Make sure that the names of the source and header files are what you want them to be, and then close the Classes dialog by clicking its OK button.

    d. Clicking OK in the AppWizard dialog will cause it to generate the initial skeleton code, using the newly chosen base classes.

Compare the two methodologies and use this information in the creation of future projects.

Chapter 4

Customizing the Primary Form's Code

In this chapter, we will describe how to customize the code to implement fully the custom form shown in Figure 4-1.

Figure 4-1
Final appearance of custom account form view

	KEEPIT1.KPD					
DATE	ITEM	DESCRIPTION		PAYMENT	DEPOSIT	BALANCE
		INFO	CATEGORY			
07/01		Opening Balance				
1993			Bal. Fwd		3500.00	3500.00
07/02		Hometown Mortgage Co.				
1993	1001	July	Mortgage	1923.10		1576.90
07/02		Hometown Gas & Electric				
1993	1002	Electric	Utilities	65.29		1511.61
07/05		Waste Disposal, Inc.				
1993	1003	Garbage	Utilities	25.00		1486.61
07/10		United Telephone				
1993	1004	Phone	Utilities	45.67		1440.94
07/10		Hometown Manufacturing				
1993		Paycheck	Income		1550.00	2990.94

Save   Current Balance: $ 2771.58

The foregoing figure illustrates the final appearance of the form when the code has been fully customized. In order to provide you with a better idea of both the concept and customization process, we will provide detailed descriptions of our concept and the result of implementing the concept in the context of the Keepit application.

The Account View Concept

Figure 4-1 shows the final result of executing the Keepit application to create a set of entries that provide a record of deposits and payments in a typical household checking account. We arrived at this result only after making quite a number of additions to the source and header files that were presented in the foregoing chapters. This figure, however, does not depict our ultimate goal. It is an intermediate result. But, even so, it is very useful because it illustrates many of the development techniques that you can use to create a host of other views in your Windows applications. In addition, the custom code for this section of the final application illustrates quite a few features of the MFC, as well as methods to specialize a number of its member functions to create custom results.

Our concept, from the beginning, was to create a fully functioning personal financial tool that would handle the bookkeeping tasks for a number of different accounts. In addition, we envisioned a tool that would provide reports on expenditures, income, tax-related information, and even charts of these data. We felt that being able to print the raw data, reports, and charts would provide us with a truly useful application.

In addition to the *features* and *functions* of the Keepit application, we wanted to create a paradigm of a typical, nontrivial Windows application so that we could present as many facets of the Microsoft Foundation Class library—and its use—as possible. It was particularly important to present the implementation details in the context of a real-world application development.

In order to achieve the preceding goals, we realized that we would need to accomplish the implementation in several stages. In the foregoing chapters, we presented the foundation for the what will follow. Because the application is going to begin to assume a recognizable identity in this chapter, we felt that it was important to provide you with a glimpse of our vision so that you will know where we are heading as each of the features in the Keepit application is added. The structure of the Keepit application, after we are finished with our customization in this chapter, is shown in Figure 4-2. The figure shows only the major object classes and from which other classes they are created. In addition, the important messages handled by each class is shown. The legend shows how to interpret the shading and line styles.

Creating the Custom View

The CAccount class is the basis for the new custom view. In Chapter 3 we showed how to construct the basic elements of the view and the wizard-created code to implement these features. In addition, we used the ClassWizard to create the CAcctList class to enable us to subclass the CListBox element and provide custom code to draw the list entries.

The most difficult chore in creating the result shown in Figure 4-1 is the implementation of the custom view, with heading labels that remain on top of the form and complex, multifield entries that scroll underneath the labels.

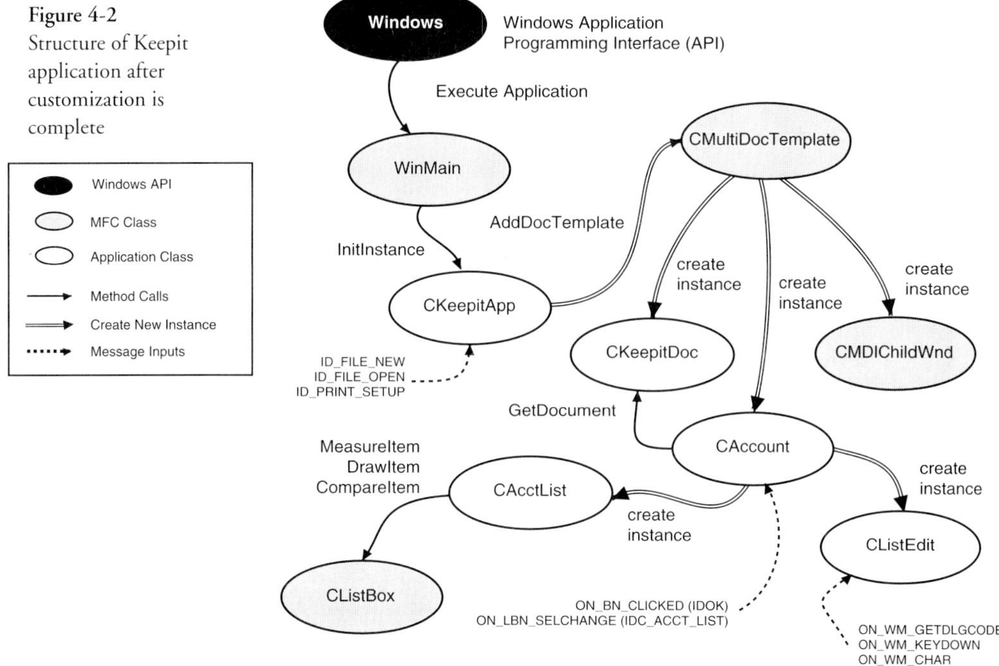

Figure 4-2
Structure of Keepit application after customization is complete

Creating the List of Entries

The custom view contains a series of list entries, each of which is stored initially in a newly created CObList object in the CKeepitDoc class (whose code is to be shown shortly).

A new class was created to contain the data declarations (member variables) and member functions for the list entries. By encapsulating the definition of a list entry in this way, we have more flexibility in making any necessary changes to either its contents or the way in which its fields are manipulated in the future.

Creating the CListEntry Header File

To create a new class while only the Visual Workbench is active, pull down the File menu and choose New. This will create a new file. Enter the following declarations into this file and save it as **listntry.h**, the new header file for list entry objects (note that no change bars are included in the source code for the following statements, as they are all newly added code, in a brand new file):

```
//////////////////////////////////////////////////////////////////////
// class CListEntry
#define    E_EMPTY        0
#define    E_SELECTED     1
#define    E_MODIFIED     2
#define    E_COMPLETE     3

class CListEntry : public CObject
{
protected:
   WORD       m_nStatus;          // entry status
   CTime      m_EntryDate;        // entry date
   CString    m_szItemNo;         // item number
   CString    m_szDescription;    // description
   CString    m_szInfo;           // info field
   CString    m_szCategory;       // category
   long       m_nPayment;         // payment amount
   long       m_nDeposit;         // deposit amount

   DECLARE_SERIAL (CListEntry)
public:
   CListEntry ( );   // public constructor
   void       Serialize (CArchive& ar);

   void       InitEntry (void);
   int        GetStatus(void);
   CTime      GetDate (void);
   CString    GetItem (void);
   CString    GetDescription (void);
   CString    GetInfo (void);
   CString    GetCategory (void);
   CString    GetPayment (void);
   long       GetPaymentValue (void);
   CString    GetDeposit (void);
   long       GetDepositValue (void);

   void       SetStatus (int status);
   void       SetDate (CTime aDate);
   void       SetItem (CString anItem);
   void       SetDescription (CString aDescription);
   void       SetInfo (CString info);
   void       SetCategory (CString category);
   BOOL       SetPayment (CString payment);
   BOOL       SetDeposit (CString deposit);
   BOOL       VerifyValue (CString& szS, long& value);
};
```

As is apparent in the foregoing code, the CListEntry class is created to
inherit behavior directly from the CObject class. The member variables
have been protected, so that we can modify and access them using only
the member functions provided for that purpose. The various member
variables that make up an entry are described as follows:

m_nStatus   Contains the current status of an entry. The allowable status codes are
E_EMPTY, E_SELECTED, E_MODIFIED, and E_COMPLETE. The meanings of
these will become clear when we discuss the entry-processing features of
the customized code.

m_nEntryDate	Contains the date that pertains to the entry, in the form of an object of the CTime class.
m_szItemNo	Contains a string, in the form of an object of the CString class, which was entered by the user in the ITEM field (usually a check number, but can be any other descriptive information).
m_szDescription	Contains the user-specified description of the transaction, in the form of an object of the CString class.
m_szInfo	Contains additional user-specified information pertaining to the transaction, in the form of an object of the CString class.
m_szCategory	Contains a string that specifies the category of the deposit or expenditure item in the form. This is also an object of class CString. It is anticipated that reports will use the category field for grouping information.
m_nPayment	Contains a long integer value that specifies (in pennies) the value in the payment field of the entry.
m_nDeposit	Contains a long integer value that specifies (in pennies) the value in the deposit field of the entry.

The header file also defines member functions that implement access to each of the foregoing member variables. Should we decide to modify the way in which these data are stored, only the access functions will need to be modified. In addition to the access member functions, a member function to verify whether an user-specified value is valid (VerifyValue) is also declared, as is a member function for serializing (either for input from or output to a file) the contents of each CListEntry object. All member functions have public access. The member variables are protected.

The source file for the CListEntry class is created in a fashion similar to that used to create the header file. Pull down the File menu in the Visual Workbench environment and choose the New command. Immediately save the file with the name **listntry.cpp**, and then add the code that implements the access member functions. The code is presented in several sections so that we can comment on its various member functions, in the order in which they appear in the listing. Once again, note that this is all newly added code and no change bars accompany the listing.

The Initial CListEntry Source Code

The first section of source code contains the `#include` directives that are necessary to resolve references to both the MFC and Windows support routine definitions. In addition, the `IMPLEMENT_SERIAL` directive, as shown generates C++ code for a class derived from the CObject class to provide access to its class name and position within the object hierarchy. This is necessary to support run-time serialization of an object's contents. A default constructor for the class is shown.

```
///////////////////////////////////////////////////////////////
// CListEntry member functions - listntry.cpp
//

#include "stdafx.h"
#include "ctype.h"// added
#include "listntry.h"

IMPLEMENT_SERIAL (CListEntry, CObject, 1)

CListEntry::CListEntry ( )
{
    // used both for explicit construction
    // and for serialization.
}
```

Initializing a CListEntry Object

The code to initialize a newly created CListEntry object with its default
contents is as follows:

```
void CListEntry::InitEntry ()
{
    CTime tim = CTime::GetCurrentTime();
    int year  = tim.GetYear();
    int month = tim.GetMonth();
    int day   = tim.GetDay();
    CTime date (year, month, day, 0, 0, 0);

    m_nStatus = E_EMPTY;
    CString szS = "";
    CString szN = "0.00";
    SetDate (date);
    SetItem (szS);
    SetDescription (szS);
    SetInfo (szS);
    SetCategory (szS);
    SetPayment (szN);
    SetDeposit (szN);
}
```

In the foregoing InitEntry member function, the m_EntryDate field is
set to the current date, but with the time portion of the date set to mid-
night (the beginning of the day). All of the string member variables are
set to empty strings and the numeric member variables are initialized
with zero string values.

Access Member Functions to Retrieve CListEntry Variables

The access member functions to retrieve the values of the various member variable fields in a CListEntry object return the what is stored in the
variable in most cases. Because the external interfaces require both the
numeric and string-equivalent values for the m_nPayment and

m_nDeposit numeric member variables, access member functions for both types of data are provided. The code is as follows:

```
int CListEntry::GetStatus (void)
{
   return m_nStatus;
}

CTime CListEntry::GetDate (void)
{
   return m_EntryDate;
}

CString CListEntry::GetItem (void)
{
   return m_szItemNo;
}

CString CListEntry::GetDescription (void)
{
   return m_szDescription;
}

CString CListEntry::GetInfo (void)
{
   return m_szInfo;
}

CString CListEntry::GetCategory (void)
{
   return m_szCategory;
}

CString CListEntry::GetPayment (void)
{
   CString aValue;
   long dollars, cents;

   dollars = m_nPayment/100;
   cents = m_nPayment - (dollars * 100);
   wsprintf (aValue.GetBuffer(14), "%ld.%02ld", dollars, cents);
   aValue.ReleaseBuffer();
   return aValue;
}

long CListEntry::GetPaymentValue (void)
{
   return m_nPayment;
}

CString CListEntry::GetDeposit (void)
{
   CString aValue;
   long dollars, cents;

   dollars = m_nDeposit/100;
   cents = m_nDeposit - (dollars * 100);
   wsprintf (aValue.GetBuffer(14), "%ld.%02ld", dollars, cents);
   aValue.ReleaseBuffer();
   return aValue;
}
```

```
long CListEntry::GetDepositValue (void)
{
   return m_nDeposit;
}
```

Access Member Functions to Store CListEntry Variables

The access member functions to store into the member variables are the
mirror image of the retrieval member functions. The code is as follows:

```
void CListEntry::SetStatus (int status)
{
   m_nStatus = status;
}

void CListEntry::SetDate (CTime aDate)
{
   m_EntryDate = aDate;
}

void CListEntry::SetItem (CString anItem)
{
   m_szItemNo = anItem;
}

void CListEntry::SetDescription (CString aDescription)
{
   m_szDescription = aDescription;
}

void CListEntry::SetInfo (CString info)
{
   m_szInfo = info;
}

void CListEntry::SetCategory (CString category)
{
   m_szCategory = category;
}

BOOL CListEntry::SetPayment (CString payment)
{
   long value;

   if (VerifyValue (payment, value))
   {
     m_nPayment = value;
     return TRUE;
   }
   else
   {
     AfxMessageBox ("Invalid Payment Item");
     return FALSE;
   }
}

BOOL CListEntry::SetDeposit (CString deposit)
{
   long value;
```

```
      if (VerifyValue (deposit, value))
      {
         m_nDeposit = value;
         return TRUE;
      }
      else
      {
         AfxMessageBox ("Invalid Deposit Item");
         return FALSE;
      }
}
```

VerifyValue Member Function Code

In the foregoing access member functions, when a value is to be stored into the numeric m_nPayment or m_nDeposit field, it is first verified to be valid before being converted from a string to a numeric value. The code for performing both the validation and conversion is as follows:

```
BOOL CListEntry::VerifyValue (CString& szS, long& value)
{
   char ch;
   int  index, length;
   long dollars, cents;
   BOOL bInt, bFrac;

   value = 0;
   length = szS.GetLength();
   if (length > 0)
   {
      bInt = bFrac = FALSE;
      dollars = cents = 0;
      for (index = 0; index < length; index++)
      {
         ch = szS.GetAt (index);
         if (isdigit (ch))
         {
            dollars *= 10;
            dollars += (ch - '0');
            bInt = TRUE;
         }
         else if (ch == '.')
         {
            while (++index < length)
            {
               ch = szS.GetAt (index);
               if(isdigit (ch))
               {
                  cents *= 10;
                  cents += (ch - '0');
                  bFrac = TRUE;
               }
               else
               {
                  value = 0;
                  return FALSE;
               }
            }
         }
```

```
               else
               {
                  value = 0;
                  return FALSE;
               }
           }
         value = (bInt)   ? dollars * 100  : 0;
         value = (bFrac)  ? value + cents  : value;
      }
      else
      {
         value = 0;
      }
      return TRUE;
}
```

In the foregoing validation member function, the input string must contain a positive numeric value in any of the following forms:

123
45.
6.56
.05

That is, the value may contain an integral value only, with or without a trailing decimal; an integral value, a decimal point, and two decimal digits; or a decimal point and two decimal digits.

Handling the CListEntry Objects

Ownership of the data pertaining to a file, and thus its associated document, is vested in the document class of the application (in our case this is CKeepitDoc). To support this principle, we have declared an object of the class CObList in the CKeepitDoc header file (**keepdoc.h**), as follows:

```
// Attributes
public:

    CObList   m_ListEntries; // list of entries
```

In addition to the addition of the m_ListEntries member variable, we have also added declarations for new member functions in the CKeepitDoc header file (**keepdoc.h**) for creating a new list entry, deleting a list entry, and adding an entry to the list. The code is as follows:

```
// Operations
public:

    CListEntry*  NewListEntry (void);
    void         DeleteListEntry (CListEntry* anEntry);
    void         AddListEntry (CListEntry* anEntry);
```

```
// Implementation
public:
   virtual void Serialize(CArchive& ar); // overridden for
                                         // document i/o
```

Modifications to existing files are shown with change bars, as in the foregoing statements. When the document object is created, the m_ListEntries member variable is also created. Objects of the CObList class are particularly useful because they maintain lists of other objects and support the serialization concept directly. When the document's Serialize member function is called by the framework, the override member function in our CKeepitDoc class handles the serialization task by calling the Serialize member function of the CListEntry class directly. The code for the Serialize member function in the CKeepitDoc source file (**keepdoc.cpp**) is modified as follows:

```
/////////////////////////////////////////////////////////////
// CKeepitDoc serialization

void CKeepitDoc::Serialize(CArchive& ar)
{
   int count;

   m_ListEntries.Serialize (ar);
   if (ar.IsLoading)
   {
       count = m_ListEntries.GetCount();
       if (count < 7)
       {
           //
           // if we didn't load enough entries to
           // cause the vertical scroll bar to activate,
           // do so.
           //
           for (int i=count-1; i < 7; i++)
           {
             CListEntry* pEntry = NewListEntry();
             AddListEntry (pEntry);
           }
       }
   }
}
```

In the foregoing code, the Serialize member function for the m_ListEntries CObList object is called first, followed by the code specific to the CKeepitDoc object. The Serialize member function for the m_ListEntries CObList object is supported by code embedded in the MFC, which determines the object type of each entry in the list, in turn, and calls its Serialize member function. In our case, all of the list entries are objects of the CListEntry class, so the Serialize member function for that class is called for each of the entries.

The remaining code in the document's Serialize member function makes sure that there are at least seven entries in the list. This is to support the member functions which load the entries into the list box in the CAccount view, which we shall describe shortly. It is useful for the `m_ListEntries` list to contain at least seven objects of the CListEntry class, even if some of these are empty, so that the scroll bar in the list box will always be active.

Access Member Functions for the CObList Object

Note in the foregoing code that we have called two new member functions that haven't been described previously. These are NewListEntry and AddListEntry. As is our custom, we have provided member functions in the document class to access the list, rather than write code that might possibly need to be modified if we later decide to implement the storage of the CListEntry objects in a different manner. The new member functions for interfacing with the `m_ListEntries` member variable are located in the source file for the CKeepitDoc class (**keepdoc.cpp**) and are as follows:

```
CListEntry* CKeepitDoc::NewListEntry (void)
{
    //
    // creates a new CListEntry object
    //
    CListEntry* anEntry = new CListEntry;
    anEntry->InitEntry ();
    return anEntry;
}

void CKeepitDoc::DeleteListEntry (CListEntry* anEntry)
{
    POSITION pos;

    ASSERT (anEntry != NULL);
    if ((pos = m_ListEntries.Find (anEntry)) == NULL)
    {
        AfxMessageBox ("Attempt to Delete Non-Existent List Entry");
        return;
    }
    m_ListEntries.RemoveAt (pos);
}

void CKeepitDoc::AddListEntry (CListEntry* anEntry)
{
    m_ListEntries.AddTail (anEntry);
}
```

In the foregoing, the NewListEntry member function creates a new object of the CListEntry class, calls the InitEntry member function to initialize the new object, and then returns the object to the caller. Both the DeleteListEntry and AddListEntry member functions take a pointer to a

CListEntry object and delete it from or add it to the `m_ListEntries` list, respectively.

OnNewDocument Member Function Code

The final member function associated with the creation of initial CList-Entry objects is OnNewDocument, which is called by the framework when the user chooses the New command from the File menu.

We have added an additional declaration to the CKeepitDoc header file (**keepdoc.h**) to allow us to override this function. The newly added declaration is as follows:

```
protected:
   virtual BOOL OnNewDocument();
```

In order to provide the CObList object with the requisite seven entries, the code in our override of the OnNewDocument member function creates seven initialized objects of the CListEntry class and adds these to the `m_ListEntries` list, as follows:

```
BOOL CKeepitDoc::OnNewDocument()
{
   if (!CDocument::OnNewDocument())
   {
      //
      // tell the framework we weren't successful
      //
      return FALSE;
   }

   //
   // for a new document, we need to generate enough
   // empty entries in the m_ListEntries list to force
   // the list box to activate its vertical scroll bar.
   //
   for (int i=0; i < 7; i++)
   {
      CListEntry* pEntry = NewListEntry();
      AddListEntry (pEntry);
   }
   return TRUE;
}
```

In the foregoing, as was previously stated, we are creating the empty entries so as to force the CAcctList list box object to activate its vertical scroll bar. This is an issue of appearance and will be described shortly.

Initializing the View

When the user chooses the New or Open commands from the File menu, the framework creates an instance of the child's frame window, the document, and also the view. We have already discussed the actions related to the document when either of these commands has been chosen. We will now begin the discussion of the process by which the view is created and initialized.

The document template, created by the application object, specifies the type of SDI or MDI frame window and its associated view. In the case of the Keepit application, we have specified that a standard MDI child window be created. In addition, we have indicated that the custom view specified by the CAccount class is to be associated with our document.

OnInitialUpdate Member Function Code

When the view is first created, the framework calls the OnInitialUpdate member function to perform one-time initialization for the view. It is in this member function that we have placed most of the code to create the initial appearance of the complete form. The exception to this is code that draws the contents of the individual list entries. That code is contained in the CAcctList class, which we will describe shortly. The OnInitialUpdate member function is described in several sections. It is necessary to break it up in order to separate and describe the various initialization functions that are included in the code. The OnInitialUpdate member function begins as follows:

```
void CAccount::OnInitialUpdate()
{
    int entryCount;
    POSITION pos;

    //
    // first, resize the parent frame to fit the formview
    //
    GetParentFrame()->RecalcLayout ();
    ResizeParentToFit (FALSE);
    ResizeParentToFit (TRUE);

    //
    // subclass the list box in the form view
    // and set the height of the items.
    //
    m_pAcctList = new CAcctList;
    VERIFY(m_pAcctList->SubclassDlgItem (IDC_ACCT_LIST, this));
    m_pAcctList->SetItemHeight (0, 33);
```

The foregoing code defines a couple of variables that will be used in later sections of the member function, and then it resizes the parent frame to fit the size of the view exactly. The ResizeParentToFit member function is called twice. Prior to the first call, the Windows-default size might include scroll bars, so the MDI child frame window is sized to account for the scroll bars. After this has been done, the member function is called the second time, with TRUE as the argument, to force the frame to shrink to exactly fit the size of the CFormView view. After this, an object of the CAcctList class is created. The SubclassDlgItem member function is called for the new object, causing the existing form's list box control to be associated with the object. This causes the framework to call the new CAcctList member functions for MeasureItem (used for sizing the individual list box entries), DrawItem (for drawing each item's contents), and CompareItem (for sorting the list box's items), instead of the built-in member functions for CListBox controls.

```
//
// fill the list box with all of the entries in the
// document's m_ListEntry list and then select the
// first entry in the list.
//
entryCount = GetDocument()->m_ListEntries.GetCount();
pos = GetDocument()->m_ListEntries.GetHeadPosition();
while (pos != NULL)
{
    CListEntry* pEntry;
    pEntry = (CListEntry *)GetDocument()->
        m_ListEntries.GetNext (pos);
    m_pAcctList->AddString ((LPCSTR)pEntry);
}
m_nCurSel = 0;
m_pAcctList->SetCurSel (m_nCurSel);
m_pCurEntry = (CListEntry *)m_pAcctList->
    GetItemDataPtr (m_nCurSel);
```

The foregoing section of the OnInitialUpdate member function accesses the CObList object in the document to obtain a count of the number of entries in the list and then stores a pointer to each object into the list box object. In this case, we are using the AddString member function in the CListBox class to insert each new entry in its appropriate position in the list, according to its date. When the AddString member function is used, the CompareItem member function in the CAcctList class is called to aid in sorting the items. When the entries have been stored, the m_nCurSel member variable is set to point to the first entry. The SetCurSel member function inherited from the CListBox class is called to select the entry referenced by the m_nCurSel variable and then the CListEntry object pointer for the entry is accessed by calling the CListBox's GetItem-DataPtr member function, storing the result in the m_pCurEntry member variable.

```
//
// create a derived class of a CEdit control and
// set its initial justification.
//
m_pListEdit = new CListEdit;
m_pListEdit->Create (WS_CHILD | WS_VISIBLE
   | ES_AUTOHSCROLL | ES_LEFT, fields[0], this, 99);
```

The foregoing code creates an initial object of the CListEdit class. If you recall, we created a derived class of the CEdit class in Chapter 3 using the ClassWizard to associate WM_GETDLGCODE, WM_KEYDOWN, and WM_CHAR messages with objects of that class. While the initial object of this class will be deleted shortly, we need to create it at this time. After constructing the object, we need to call its Create member function to specify the features of the child window so that it can be attached to the object. Recall that although the constructor of a CEdit object creates the object, it does not create the Windows HWND that points to the visible entity that the user sees.

```
//
// create the font to use for the edit control
//
m_pEditFont = new CFont;
ASSERT (m_pEditFont != NULL);
m_pEditFont->CreateFont (-10, 0, 0, 0, FW_NORMAL, 0, 0, 0,
   DEFAULT_CHARSET, OUT_DEFAULT_PRECIS,
   CLIP_DEFAULT_PRECIS, DEFAULT_QUALITY,
   DEFAULT_PITCH | FF_SWISS, "Arial");
m_pListEdit->SetFont (m_pEditFont);
```

In addition to creating an object of the CListEdit control and its associated window (HWND), we also construct a font that will be used when we provide code for the user to enter data into this control. The entry of user data will be covered shortly.

```
// create a child window to hold the
// item labels.
m_pAcctLabel = new CWnd;
CRect aRect(0, 1, 430, 32);
m_pAcctLabel->Create (NULL, NULL, WS_BORDER
   | WS_CHILD | WS_VISIBLE,
   aRect, this, IDC_ACCT_LABEL, NULL);
```

The foregoing code creates a new child window in which we intend to draw the labels for the list box entries. The size of the window was determined in somewhat a "cut and try" method. Although there is a function to map dialog units to screen units, this is unsatisfactory for dialogs that contain multiple fonts, as the conversion is based upon the "system font" used for all dialog text. We therefore copied down the overall dimensions of the dialog, as given in DLUs; then we set a breakpoint in the OnInitialUpdate member function and used the Watch capability to discover the overall size of the dialog in screen units. We could then calculate a conversion factor for translating the various sizes in DLUs to pixels. Therefore, although the size of the area reserved for the labels is seen to be approximately 245x21 DLUs (located at coordinates 0,0), this translates to approximately 430x32 pixels using our conversion factor for a standard VGA display adapter.

```
//
// create a new font for the child window.
//
m_pLabelFont = new CFont;
ASSERT (m_pLabelFont != NULL);
m_pLabelFont->CreateFont (-10, 0, 0, 0, FW_BOLD, 0, 0, 0,
    DEFAULT_CHARSET, OUT_DEFAULT_PRECIS,
    CLIP_DEFAULT_PRECIS, DEFAULT_QUALITY,
    DEFAULT_PITCH | FF_SWISS, "Arial");
```

In a similar fashion, we experimented with different font-height parameters until we found one that suited the available space that we had to spare in both the field labels and list entries. We chose Arial as the font for both the labels and list entries because it is standard for all Windows version 3.1 systems and we wanted to use something other than the standard system font, which is too bold in our judgment.

```
//
// initialize miscellaneous attributes
//
m_bFirstTime = TRUE;    // set first time switch.
m_nBalanceFwd = 0;      // set balance forward
}
```

The final section of the OnInitialUpdate member function initializes a first-time switch to TRUE and sets the balance forward member variable to zero, in preparation for computing the running balance in the account.

Drawing the Form's Heading

The heading is implemented by overriding the OnDraw member function for the CAccount view. Although the documentation for the MFC states that one should be careful not to interfere with the self-drawing controls in a view such as this, we have set aside space in the view to contain the heading block, and we therefore will not be in conflict with any of the other member functions. Take a look at Figure 3-11 and you'll see that the top of the list box is somewhat below the top of the form. This was arranged, purposely, so that we could draw the heading block immediately above the list.

OnDraw Member Function Code

The code for the OnDraw member function is as follows:

```
void CAccount::OnDraw(CDC* pDC)
{
   TEXTMETRIC aTM;
   int txHeight;
   CString szL1=
   "\tDATE\tITEM\tDESCRIPTION\tPAYMENT\tDEPOSIT\tBALANCE";
   CString szL2 = "\tINFO\tCATEGORY";
   int nTabsL1[] = {2, 41, 112, 223, 290, 360};
   int nTabsL2[] = {96, 152};

   //
   // on the first entry, create a new CListEdit
   // child window and select the first field for
   // keyboard input.
   //
   if (m_bFirstTime)
   {
      ASSERT (m_pCurEntry != NULL);
      m_bFirstTime = FALSE;
      m_pCurEntry->SetStatus (E_SELECTED);
      SetUpEditItem (0);
   }
```

The first section of the OnDraw member function defines a number of local variables, including two strings that contain the text for the two rows of the list label block. In addition, two corresponding arrays of tab settings are provided for placing each field label in the correct location. (We had to experiment a bit to find the appropriate positions for these tabs, but by using tabbed text and the arrays to specify where each substring was to begin, the process was relatively painless.)

If the OnDraw member function is being entered for the first time (which is conditioned on the value of the first time switch, m_bFirstTime), then we reset the switch, change the status of the current entry to E_SELECTED, and call a member function to set up the first edit item. If this isn't the first entry, the foregoing actions are not taken.

```
   //
   // draw the column labels for the form view
   //
   CClientDC aDC (m_pAcctLabel);
   CFont* oldFont = aDC.SelectObject (m_pLabelFont);
   if (!aDC.GetTextMetrics (&aTM))
   {
```

```
      AfxMessageBox ("Can't get label text metrics.");
      return;
   }
   txHeight = aTM.tmHeight;
   aDC.TabbedTextOut (0, 1, szL1, 46, 6, nTabsL1, 0);
   aDC.TabbedTextOut (0, txHeight+3, szL2, 14, 2, nTabsL2, 0);
   aDC.SelectObject (oldFont);
```

The foregoing code creates a device context object, using the pointer to the child window (m_pAcctLabel, created in the OnInitialUpdate member function, as shown on page 82), to use as the client area for subsequent calls to the GDI functions.

The code selects the label font that was created in the OnInitialUpdate member function (see page 83), accesses the text metrics to obtain the font height, and then calls the TabbedTextOut member function to draw both rows of the list header labels. After the labels have been drawn, the previous font is selected back into the device context.

```
   //
   // we also need to draw the separators
   // for the list labels.
   //
   CPen aPen (PS_SOLID, 0, RGB(192, 192, 192));
   CPen* oldPen = aDC.SelectObject (&aPen);
   CPoint aPoint (-1, 0); // -1 because of the frame width
   DrawLines (aPoint, &aDC);
   aDC.SelectObject (oldPen);
}
```

The foregoing code creates a CPen object whose color is solid gray, saves the old pen, selects the new pen, specifies a starting coordinate, and calls a member function that we have provided to draw the lines that separate the two rows of the list header and their respective fields. The old pen is reselected after the lines have been drawn.

DrawLines Member Function Code

The OnDraw member function calls the DrawLines member function to draw the separator lines between the fields in the list header label field. The DrawLines member function is also called by the DrawItem member function (to be described shortly), which also requires separator lines to be drawn for the list entries. The code for this member function is as follows:

```
void CAccount::DrawLines (CPoint p, CDC* pDC)
{
   pDC->MoveTo ( p.x+34,  p.y+0);
   pDC->LineTo ( p.x+34,  p.y+31);
   pDC->MoveTo ( p.x+75,  p.y+0);
   pDC->LineTo ( p.x+75,  p.y+31);
```

```
        pDC->MoveTo (p.x+141, p.y+16);
        pDC->LineTo (p.x+141, p.y+31);
        pDC->MoveTo (p.x+217,  p.y+0);
        pDC->LineTo (p.x+217, p.y+31);
        pDC->MoveTo (p.x+279,  p.y+0);
        pDC->LineTo (p.x+279, p.y+31);
        pDC->MoveTo (p.x+346,  p.y+0);
        pDC->LineTo (p.x+346, p.y+31);
        pDC->MoveTo (p.x+ 75, p.y+16);
        pDC->LineTo (p.x+429, p.y+16);
}
```

The foregoing code is very simple. It consists of a series of pen movements and line-drawing commands. After the pen is positioned at a new
location, a line is drawn from that position to a new position in the child
window. Figuring out where to draw the lines in the confines of the
header or list entries took a bit of experimentation.

We continue to mention the fact that experimentation has been necessary because we don't want you to think that there is some automatic
method to arrive at the exact position of labels or lines without trying
several settings and finally settling on a result that appeals to our eyes.
We got a general idea of how wide the label block needed to be by drawing a replica of it with a drawing program and then using the coordinate
values it displayed as a starting point in the iterative process of creating
the final result.

Drawing the Contents of the List Entries

Before getting into the realm of user input and what we have done to
customize the code to handle entry of data into the various *pseudo fields*
of the list entries, it will be instructive to discuss the code we have created for drawing the contents of the entries, when instructed to do so by
the framework. Whenever the framework detects that the document has
changed, it calls the OnDraw member function for the view. Although
most controls know how to draw themselves, we have specified the list
box to be an owner-draw control, and so we must supply the routines
that support that specification. In particular, we need to override the
MeasureItem, DrawItem, and CompareItem (for sorting the items)
member functions. The code for each of these will be shown in the sections that follow.

MeasureItem Member Function Code

Owner-draw list boxes can have two styles: fixed or variable. In the case
of variable-height items, the MeasureItem member function is called for
each item. In our case, each item is the same height, so we elected to
specify fixed-height entries in the Styles properties when the list box was

created. In this case, the MeasureItem member function is called by the framework only once. The code for MeasureItem is as follows:

```
void CAcctList::MeasureItem (LPMEASUREITEMSTRUCT lpMIS)
{
   lpMIS->itemWidth  = 429;    // width in pixels
   lpMIS->itemHeight =  30;    // height in pixels
}
```

The member function is called with a long pointer to a MEASUREITEM-STRUCT structure, which contains, among other things, fields that specify the item width and the item height in pixels. Once again, these values apply to a standard VGA display adapter. The foregoing code sets the contents of these fields to our empirically derived values.

DrawItem Member Function Code

The DrawItem member function is called by the framework whenever an owner-draw control needs to be redrawn. The single parameter passed to the member function is a long pointer to a DRAWITEMSTRUCT structure, which is defined as follows:

```
typedef struct tag DRAWITEMSTRUCT
{
   UINT    CtlType;       // type of control
   UINT    CtlID;         // control's resource ID
   UINT    itemID;        // item's ID
   UINT    itemAction;    // action to perform
   UINT    itemState;     // current state of item
   HWND    hwndItem;      // handle to window
   HDC     hDC;           // handle to device context
   RECT    rcItem;        // item's rectangle
   DWORD   itemData;      // data associated with item

} DRAWITEMSTRUCT;
```

The fields in this structure in which we are especially interested, for purposes of drawing the item, are `itemAction` and `itemState`. The `itemAction` field is defined to contain one of the following values:

❖ ODA_DRAWENTIRE – indicates that the entire entry is to be redrawn.

❖ ODA_FOCUS – indicates that the control has gained or lost focus.

❖ ODA_SELECT – indicates that the selection state has changed.

The ODA_FOCUS and ODA_SELECT actions are specified more fully by the value of the `itemState` field, which indicates one of the following states for the item:

❖ ODS_CHECKED – indicates that a menu item is checked.

❖ ODS_DISABLED – specifies that the item is to be drawn as disabled.

❖ ODS_FOCUS – specifies that the item has the input focus.

❖ ODS_GRAYED – specifies that a menu item is to be grayed.

❖ ODS_SELECTED – specifies that the item is selected.

In order to draw the list box item correctly, as specified by the lpDIS input argument, we must use the information in the LPDRAWSTRUCT's fields to prepare the drawing environment. The first part of the Draw-Item member function is as follows:

```
void CAcctList::DrawItem (LPDRAWITEMSTRUCT lpDIS)
{
   CDC* pDC = CDC::FromHandle (lpDIS->hDC);
   CAccount* pAccount = (CAccount *)GetParent();

   //
   // get the measurements of the current item
   //
   int nOrgLeft, nOrgTop, nWidth, nHeight;
   nOrgLeft = lpDIS->rcItem.left;
   nOrgTop  = lpDIS->rcItem.top;
   nWidth   = lpDIS->rcItem.right - lpDIS->rcItem.left;
   nHeight  = lpDIS->rcItem.bottom - lpDIS->rcItem.top;
```

The foregoing code creates a device context by using the FromHandle member function to create a temporary object to use for the drawing operations that follow. The code also accesses the parent (CAccount) view in order to access the view's DrawLines member function shown on page 85.

The foregoing code calculates the left and top points of the entry, as well as its width and height. The top and left coordinates are going to be converted into a point, which will be passed to the DrawLines member function to use as its origin. The next section of code determines what needs to be drawn and then performs the appropriate action, as follows:

```
   //
   // determine what we have to do
   //
   if (lpDIS->itemAction & ODA_DRAWENTIRE)
   {
      //
      // need to draw the item. First, we need to
      // draw the lines that delineate the fields.
      //
      CPen aPen (PS_SOLID, 0, RGB(192, 192, 192));
      CPen* oldPen = pDC->SelectObject (&aPen);
      CPoint p (nOrgLeft, nOrgTop);
      pAccount->DrawLines (p, pDC);
      pDC->SelectObject (oldPen);
      CBrush br (RGB(192, 192, 192));
```

```
            pDC->FrameRect (&lpDIS->rcItem, &br);

        //
        // next, we need to draw the contents of the
        // CListEntry object pertaining to this item,
        // but only if it's not empty.
        //
        CListEntry* pEntry;
        pEntry = (CListEntry *)GetItemDataPtr(lpDIS->itemID);
        if (pEntry->GetStatus() != E_EMPTY)
        {
            DrawEntry (pEntry, pDC, &lpDIS->rcItem);
        }
    }

    if ((lpDIS->itemAction & (ODA_SELECT | ODA_DRAWENTIRE))
    && (lpDIS->itemState & ODS_SELECTED))
    {
        //
        // item is selected, draw the black frame
        //
        CBrush br (RGB(0, 0, 0));
        pDC->FrameRect (&lpDIS->rcItem, &br);
    }

    if ((lpDIS->itemAction & ODA_SELECT)
    && !(lpDIS->itemState & ODS_SELECTED))
    {
        //
        // item is deselected, draw the gray frame
        //
        CBrush br (RGB(192, 192, 192));
        pDC->FrameRect (&lpDIS->rcItem, &br);
    }
}
```

In the foregoing, if the value of the `itemAction` field is to draw the entire item (ODA_DRAWENTIRE), then a gray pen is constructed and the DrawLines member function is called to draw the lines that separate the rows and fields of the entry. Then a gray brush is constructed and the item is framed by calling the FrameRect member function, using the rectangle specified in the `rcItem` field of the DRAWITEMSTRUCT. Finally, if the item status indicates that the item is not empty (E_EMPTY), the DrawEntry member function is called.

As execution of the DrawItem code continues, if it is determined that the `itemAction` field contains either the value ODA_SELECT or ODA_DRAWENTIRE, *and* the value of the `itemState` field is ODS_SELECTED, then the code constructs a black brush and frames the item's rectangle using the FrameRect member function.

Finally, the DrawItem code determines whether the value of the `itemAction` field is ODA_SELECT *and* the value of the `itemState` field is *not* ODS_SELECTED. If so, then the code constructs a gray brush and frames the item's rectangle using the FrameRect member function.

DrawEntry Member Function Code

The code to handle drawing the contents of the various fields into the
list box entry is contained in the DrawEntry member function for the
CAcctList class. The code is presented in several sections, as follows:

```
void CAcctList::DrawEntry (CListEntry* pEntry, CDC* pDC,
    LPCRECT  r)
{
  CRgn* pRgn   = new CRgn;
  int svDC = pDC->SaveDC();
  int length = 0;
  RECT rf;


  //
  // create a new font to use for drawing
  // the text of the entry.
  //
  CFont* pItemFont = new CFont;
  ASSERT (pItemFont != NULL);
  if (!pItemFont->CreateFont (-10, 0, 0, 0, FW_NORMAL, 0,
      0, 0, DEFAULT_CHARSET, OUT_DEFAULT_PRECIS,
      CLIP_DEFAULT_PRECIS, DEFAULT_QUALITY,
      DEFAULT_PITCH | FF_SWISS, "Arial"))
  {
    AfxMessageBox ("Can't Create Item Font");
    return;
  }
  CFont* oldFont = pDC->SelectObject (pItemFont);
```

The first section of the DrawEntry code constructs a font to be used in
drawing the contents of each of the fields. The new font is selected and
the old font is saved, to be restored before the member function returns.
The code to draw the contents of each item refers to an array of rectangle
specifications, which define the boundaries of each field within the item
(the values included in each array entry are specified in pixels, for a standard VGA display adapter). The array is specified separately as follows:

```
RECT __far fields[] =
{
    {  2,   3,   33, 16}, {  3, 19,   35, 31}, { 37, 19,   74, 31},
    { 78,   3, 215, 16}, { 78, 19, 140, 31}, {143, 19, 216, 31},
    {219, 19, 278, 31}, {281, 19, 345, 31}, {348, 19, 412, 31}
};
```

The code that follows draws the contents of each of the list entry's fields
by first accessing the `fields` array to get the boundaries of the specified
field in the item. This is to make sure that when each item is drawn, even
though it might overlap a succeeding field, its appearance will be clipped
to display only what will fit within the stated rectangle.

```cpp
//
// draw the contents of each field, if necessary.
//
pRgn->CreateRectRgnIndirect(r);
for (int i=0; i < 9; i++)
{
   pDC->SelectClipRgn (pRgn);
   rf.top    = r->top  + fields[i].top;
   rf.left   = r->left + fields[i].left;
   rf.right  = r->left + fields[i].right;
   rf.bottom = r->top  + fields[i].bottom;
   pDC->IntersectClipRect(&rf);

   switch (i)
   {
      case 0: // handle date mm/dd
      {
         CTime tim = pEntry->GetDate();
         CString szmmdd = tim.Format ("%m/%d");
         pDC->TextOut (rf.left, rf.top, szmmdd);
         break;
      }
      case 1: // handle date year
      {
         CTime tim = pEntry->GetDate();
         CString szyear = tim.Format ("%Y");
         pDC->TextOut (rf.left, rf.top, szyear);
         break;
      }
      case 2: // handle item number
      {
         CString szNum = pEntry->GetItem();
         length = szNum.GetLength();
         if (length > 0)
         {
            pDC->TextOut (rf.left, rf.top, szNum, length);
         }
         break;
      }
      case 3: // handle description
      {
         CString szDesc = pEntry->GetDescription();
         length = szDesc.GetLength();
         if (length > 0)
         {
            pDC->TextOut (rf.left, rf.top, szDesc, length);
         }
         break;
      }
      case 4: // handle info field
      {
         CString szInfo = pEntry->GetInfo();
         length = szInfo.GetLength();
         if (length > 0)
         {
            pDC->TextOut (rf.left, rf.top, szInfo, length);
         }
         break;
      }
      case 5: // handle category
      {
```

```
            CString szCat = pEntry->GetCategory();
            length = szCat.GetLength();
            if (length > 0)
            {
               pDC->TextOut (rf.left, rf.top, szCat, length);
            }
            break;
         }
         case 6: // handle payment (right justify)
         {
            if (pEntry->GetPaymentValue() != 0)
            {
               CString szPay = pEntry->GetPayment();
               length = szPay.GetLength();
               if (length > 0)
               {
                  CSize nPay = pDC->GetTextExtent (szPay,
                     length);
                  int nxc = rf.right - nPay.cx;
                  pDC->TextOut (nxc, rf.top, szPay, length);
               }
            }
            break;
         }
         case 7: // handle deposit (right justify)
         {
            if (pEntry->GetDepositValue() != 0)
            {
               CString szDep = pEntry->GetDeposit();
               length = szDep.GetLength();
               if (length > 0)
               {
                  CSize nDep = pDC->GetTextExtent (szDep,
                     length);
                  int nxc = rf.right - nDep.cx;
                  pDC->TextOut (nxc, rf.top, szDep, length);
               }
            }
            break;
         }
```

The foregoing code handles drawing each of the first eight fields. Each field is converted to a string equivalent, and the TextOut member function is used to output the field's contents. The clipping rectangle, computed just after the beginning of the loop, ensures that the display will be clipped to the field's boundaries.

The final case is the display of the current balance field for the entry. We have elected not to store the balance in the entries themselves, mainly because an entry could be easily sorted into a new position by changing its date or adding a new entry with an earlier date, and this would require that we recompute the balances of every entry at that time. Rather than try to keep up with the balances for each entry, as they are sorted, we have decided to compute the balance dynamically, as the entries are drawn. This requires that we iterate through the list of entries, beginning with the first, and calculate the balance for each. If it is determined that the entry is within the window's clipping region and its balance is non-zero, the value is displayed. The loop continues, calculating and displaying balances until either the end of the list or the first empty entry is found. The code to compute and display the balance fields is as follows:

```cpp
case 8: // handle balance (right justify)
{
    CRgn* pRegion = new CRgn;
    CRgn* pWReg = new CRgn;
    RECT  rI, rC, rW, rF = fields[8];
    CListEntry* pEntry;
    long balance;

    //
    // get the window RECT to use as a clipping
    // region for updating the balance values.
    //

    GetWindowRect (&rW);
    ScreenToClient(&rW);
    pWReg->CreateRectRgnIndirect(&rW);

    //
    // the balance for this item depends upon the
    // previous balances, which can dynamically
    // change, according to the positioning of the
    // items in the list. We need to recompute all
    // of the balances and draw them into the list.
    //
    CAccount* pAccount = (CAccount *)GetParent();
    balance = pAccount->m_nBalanceFwd;
    int nItems = GetCount();
    for (int index=0; index < nItems; index++)
    {
        //
        // create regions for the item and window
        // rectangles, then combine them into a
        // clipping region.
        //
        GetItemRect (index, &rI);
        pRegion->CreateRectRgnIndirect(&rI);
        pRegion->CombineRgn (pRegion, pWReg, RGN_AND);
        pDC->SelectClipRgn (pRegion);
        rC.top    = rI.top  + rF.top;
        rC.left   = rI.left + rF.left;
        rC.right  = rI.left + rF.right;
        rC.bottom = rI.top  + rF.bottom;

        //
        // calculate the new balance, unless the
        // current entry is empty.
        //
        pEntry = (CListEntry *)GetItemDataPtr (index);
        if (pEntry->GetStatus() == E_EMPTY)
        {
            //
            // stop on the first empty entry
            //
            pRegion->DeleteObject();
            break;
```

```
                              }
                              balance += pEntry->GetDepositValue();
                              balance -= pEntry->GetPaymentValue();
                              //
                              // if the intersection of the clipping region
                              // and the balance field is empty, we needn't
                              // draw the balance field for this item.
                              //
                              if (pDC->IntersectClipRect(&rC) == NULLREGION)
                              {
                                 pRegion->DeleteObject();
                                 continue;
                              }

                              if (balance != 0)
                              {
                                 CString szBal;
                                 int length;

                                 long dollars = balance / 100;
                                 long cents = balance - dollars * 100;
                                 if (cents < 0)
                                 {
                                    cents = -cents;
                                 }
                                 wsprintf (szBal.GetBuffer(14), "%ld.%02ld",
                                    dollars, cents);
                                 szBal.ReleaseBuffer();
                                 length = szBal.GetLength();
                                 CSize nBal = pDC->GetTextExtent (szBal,
                                    length);
                                 int nxc = rC.right - nBal.cx;
                                 pDC->TextOut (nxc, rC.top, szBal, length);
                              }
                           pRegion->DeleteObject();
                        }
                  pWReg->DeleteObject();
                  pAccount->UpdateBalance (balance);
               }
            }
         }
      pDC->SelectObject (oldFont);
      delete pItemFont;
      pRgn->DeleteObject();
      pDC->RestoreDC(svDC);
}
```

When the foregoing loop is complete, the balances for all of the visible
items in the list box will have been displayed. Notice the code just prior
to the beginning of the balance loop that calculates a rectangular region
for the list box window. Just after the beginning of the loop, another
rectangular region, representing the item's rectangle, is computed and
then is combined with the foregoing window's region to create an intersection of the two regions. If it is found that the intersection of these regions is empty, then the item is not in view and its balance value is thus
not displayed. Also notice that we must delete the clipping region object

when we are finished using it, so that we can construct a new region for the next item.

Near the end of the foregoing code, a member function named Update-Balance, which is contained in the code for the view class (CAccount), is called to write the new balance into the static text field at the bottom of the form. The code to convert the balance value for display in the static text field is as follows:

```
void CAccount::UpdateBalance (long balance)
{
   long dollars, cents;
   CString szBal;

   dollars = balance / 100;
   cents = balance - dollars * 100;
   if (cents < 0)
   {
      cents = -cents;
   }
   wsprintf (szBal.GetBuffer(14), "$ %ld.%02ld", dollars,
      cents);
   szBal.ReleaseBuffer();
   SetDlgItemText (IDC_BALANCE, szBal);
}
```

CompareItem Member Function Code

Just to complete the code that responds to the framework's requests to handle tasks concerning the individual list box entries, we present the code for comparing two items to determine their relative positions in the list. Each time we call member functions, inherited from the CListBox class, which would alter the position of an entry in the list (e.g., AddString), the framework will call our CompareItem member function. The code for this member function is as follows:

```
int  CAcctList::CompareItem (LPCOMPAREITEMSTRUCT lpCIS)
{
   CTime tim1;
   CTime tim2;
   int s1, s2;
   tim1 = (CTime)((CListEntry *)lpCIS->itemData1)->GetDate();
   tim2 = (CTime)((CListEntry *)lpCIS->itemData2)->GetDate();
   s1   = ((CListEntry *)lpCIS->itemData1)->GetStatus();
   s2   = ((CListEntry *)lpCIS->itemData2)->GetStatus();

   //
   // here's the rationale: If item s1 is empty, then we
   // are going to assume that it should be sorted later
   // in the list than item s2. If instead item s2 is empty,
   // then item s1 should be sorted before item s2. If
   // neither of the items is empty, then they are sorted
   // according to their dates.
   //
```

```
              if (s1 == E_EMPTY)
              {
                 return 1;
              }
              if (s2 == E_EMPTY)
              {
                 return -1;
              }
              if (tim1 < tim2)
              {
                 return -1;
              }
              else if (tim1 > tim2)
              {
                 return 1;
              }
              else
              {
                 if (lpCIS->itemID1 < lpCIS->itemID2)
                 {
                    return -1;
                 }
                 else
                 {
                    return 0;
                 }
              }
}
```

The rationale for sorting the entries is shown at the beginning of the code. We have decided that empty items should sort after any other entries. If neither of the two entries being compared is empty, then they sort according to the value of their dates.

Handling User Actions

User actions, in this regard, pertain to selection of list entries using the mouse and entering or changing the contents of any field. An entry is selected by clicking anywhere within the gray rectangle that delimits its boundaries. When an entry is selected, its date field will be highlighted and preparations will be made to allow keyboard entry of data into that field. The user will be allowed to move from one field to the next using either the TAB or arrow keys. The combination of SHIFT and TAB are honored to provide a backtab capability.

When an entry is complete, it can be saved by clicking the Save button at the bottom of the form, or by pressing the return (or enter) key. When an entry is saved, it is sorted into the proper position in the list and all of the visible entries are displayed, along with their balances, as described in the previous section.

The most difficult hurdle to overcome in providing the user with the means to enter data into our custom list box is the fact that the CListBox class does not allow keyboard entry of data into its entries. This could be an almost fatal limitation if there wasn't some way to get around the problem. Fortunately, we can fool users into believing that they are entering data directly into a list entry by creating an editable text window that overlays each field, exactly, as the user tabs to that position. When properly positioned, the editable text window (an object of the CListEdit class) will fill the current field completely. The current contents of the field in the CListEntry object are copied into the CListEdit window, and its text, if any, will be highlighted and ready for modification. When the user tabs to the next field, the contents of the CListEdit object are copied into the CListEntry object and redisplay of the item is requested. In this way, we give the appearance of allowing the user to type directly into the list box entries.

Accomplishing the foregoing actions is the topic of the remainder of this section. In the following, we will be discussing code in both the CListEdit and CAccount classes.

Processing Keystrokes

The main feature of the CListEdit class is that it overrides the message handlers for OnGetDlgCode, OnKeyDown, and OnChar, which allows it to process all keyboard input. This is important to our application because of the functionality we require when any of the TAB, arrow, or return keys are pressed.

OnGetDlgCode Member Function Code

We override the OnGetDlgCode member function to instruct the framework that we wish to process all keyboard input. We do this as follows:

```
UINT CListEdit::OnGetDlgCode()
{
    return CEdit::OnGetDlgCode() | DLGC_WANTALLKEYS;
}
```

The member function calls the base (CEdit) class member function and returns its value combined with the DLGC_WANTALLKEYS value, which indicates that we wish to process all keyboard input in our derived class.

OnKeyDown Member Function Code

When the user presses a nonsystem key (i.e., when ALT is not pressed), the framework calls the OnKeyDown handler. The usual function of this code is to display the character corresponding to the key in the edit control. In our case, we handle certain keys in a special manner. The code is as follows:

```cpp
void CListEdit::OnKeyDown(UINT nChar, UINT nRepCnt,
   UINT nFlags)
{
   if (nChar == VK_UP    || nChar == VK_DOWN ||
       nChar == VK_LEFT  || nChar == VK_RIGHT)
   {
     HandleKeys (nChar);
   }
   else
   {
     CEdit::OnKeyDown(nChar, nRepCnt, nFlags);
   }
}
```

The input arguments are the key's character code, the repeat count and a word containing flags that identify the type of key being pressed, and other status values. The incoming character is tested to determine whether it is one of the arrow keys and, if so, the HandleKeys member function is called; otherwise, the base (CEdit) class's OnKeyDown handler is called for the input key.

OnChar Member Function Code

The OnChar handler is called after the OnKeyDown handler, but before the OnKeyUp handler is called for a given key. The code for the OnChar member function is as follows:

```cpp
void CListEdit::OnChar(UINT nChar, UINT nRepCnt,
   UINT nFlags)
{
   UINT uChar = VkKeyScan (nChar) & 0xFF;
   if (uChar >= 0x30)
   {
     CAccount*pParent = (CAccount *)GetParent();
     CListEntry* pEntry = pParent->m_pCurEntry;

     //
     // all we do with normal keys is send them to
     // CEdit::OnChar for display and set the entry's
     // status to E_MODIFIED.
     //
     CEdit::OnChar (uChar, nRepCnt, nFlags);
     pEntry->SetStatus (E_MODIFIED);
     return;
   }
   if (!HandleKeys (nChar))
   {
     CEdit::OnChar(nChar, nRepCnt, nFlags);
   }
}
```

The code for the OnChar handler is also simple. It first calls the VKKey-Scan function to ascertain whether the keycode is for a normal, display-able, character. If so, it passes the translated keycode to the OnChar member function in the CEdit class; otherwise, it calls the HandleKeys member function, and if that member function returns a value of FALSE, the base (CEdit) class's OnChar member function is called for the key.

HandleKeys Member Function Code

The foregoing OnKeyDown handler calls the HandleKeys member function, depending upon the type of key that is pressed. The OnChar member function, on the other hand, arbitrarily calls the HandleKeys member function and tests the return value to determine whether the base class's OnChar member function should be called. The code for the HandleKeys member function is as follows:

```
BOOL CListEdit::HandleKeys (UINT nChar)
{
   CAccount* pParent = (CAccount *)GetParent();
   CAcctList* pAcct = pParent->m_pAcctList;
   CListEntry* pEntry = pParent->m_pCurEntry;
   int nOldField = pParent->m_nEditField;
   int nNewField = nOldField;
   RECT r = fields[nOldField];

   switch (nChar)
   {
     case VK_TAB:
     {
        if (GetKeyState (VK_SHIFT) & 0x8000)
        {
          // it's a back-TAB
          nNewField = (nOldField > 0) ? nOldField-1 : 7;
        }
        else
        {
          // it's a forward-TAB
          nNewField = (nOldField < 7) ? nOldField+1 : 0;
        }
        pParent->UpdateFields (nNewField, FALSE);
        break;
     }
     case VK_RETURN:
     {
        pParent->UpdateFields (nOldField, TRUE);
        break;
     }
     case VK_LEFT:
     {
        nNewField = (nOldField > 0) ? nOldField-1 : 7;
        pParent->UpdateFields (nNewField, FALSE);
        break;
     }
     case VK_RIGHT:
     {
        nNewField = (nOldField < 7) ? nOldField+1 : 0;
        pParent->UpdateFields (nNewField, FALSE);
        break;
     }
     case VK_UP:
     {
```

```
            if (nOldField == 1) nNewField = 0;
            else if (nOldField == 4 || nOldField == 5) nNewField = 3;
            if (nNewField != nOldField)
            {
                pParent->UpdateFields (nNewField, FALSE);
            }
            break;
        }
        case VK_DOWN:
        {
            if (nOldField == 0) nNewField = 1;
            if (nOldField == 3) nNewField = 4;
            if (nNewField != nOldField)
            {
                pParent->UpdateFields (nNewField, FALSE);
            }
            break;
        }
        default:
        {
            pEntry->SetStatus (E_MODIFIED);
            return FALSE;
        }
    }
    return TRUE;
}
```

The foregoing code determines what to do next, depending upon which key was pressed. We check the virtual-key code and determine whether it is one of the special keys that we use for navigation or saving the current entry. The member function keeps track of `nOldField` and `nNew-Field` values, the former of which is initialized to be the number of the field in which the CListEdit window is currently positioned (accessed from the CAccount class `m_nEditField` member variable).

Depending upon which, if any, of the navigation keys was pressed, the HandleKeys member function sets the `nNewField` variable to the next field to be edited, and then calls the UpdateFields member function in the CAccount class. If the virtual-key code passed to the member function is for a normal (nonnavigation) key, then the member function returns a FALSE result; otherwise, it returns a value of TRUE. When a normal key has been pressed, the SetStatus member function for the CListEntry class is called, indicating that the user has typed some information into the entry (setting the status to E_MODIFIED).

Navigating From Field to Field

When a navigation or return keystroke has been entered (as described in the foregoing section), the HandleKeys member function calls a member function in the primary view, called UpdateFields, which has the responsibility for storing and validating the contents of the CListEdit window into the field being currently edited, repositioning the CListEdit window to the next field, loading its contents into the window, and then high-lighting the text in the window.

UpdateFields Member Function Code

The UpdateFields member function is called when a navigation or return key has been pressed. The purpose of the member function is to validate the contents of the CListEdit object, store the field's contents into the CListEntry object, and then force the list box to be redrawn. The code is as follows:

```cpp
void CAccount::UpdateFields (int nNewField, BOOL bDone)
{
   RECT rE;

   //
   // update currently edited field & move to next
   //
   switch (m_nEditField)
   {
      case 0: // date mmdd
      {
         CTime tim = m_pCurEntry->GetDate ();
         int index = 0;
         int month = 0;
         int day = 0;
         CString mmdd;
         int year = tim.GetYear ();
         m_pListEdit->GetWindowText (mmdd);
         char *pBuf = mmdd.GetBuffer (5);
         if (Get2Nums (pBuf, index, month, '/'))
         {
            if (Get2Nums (pBuf, index, day, '\0'))
            {
               CTime t (year, month, day, 0, 0, 0);
               m_pCurEntry->SetDate (t);
            }
            else
            {
               mmdd.ReleaseBuffer ();
               return;
            }
         }
         else
         {
            mmdd.ReleaseBuffer ();
            return;
         }
         mmdd.ReleaseBuffer ();
         break;
      }
      case 1: // date year
      {
         CString yyyy;
         CTime tim = m_pCurEntry->GetDate ();
         int index = 0;
         int month = tim.GetMonth ();
         int day = tim.GetDay ();
         int year = 0;
```

```cpp
         m_pListEdit->GetWindowText (yyyy);
         char *pBuf = yyyy.GetBuffer(4);
         for (int i=0; i < 4; i++)
         {
            if (pBuf[i] < '0' || pBuf[i] > '9')
            {
               yyyy.ReleaseBuffer();
               return;
            }
            year *= 10;
            year += (pBuf[i] - '0');
         }
         yyyy.ReleaseBuffer();
         CTime t (year, month, day, 0, 0, 0);
         m_pCurEntry->SetDate (t);
         break;
      }
      case 2: // item number
      {
         CString item;
         m_pListEdit->GetWindowText(item);
         m_pCurEntry->SetItem(item);
         break;
      }
      case 3: // description
      {
         CString desc;
         m_pListEdit->GetWindowText(desc);
         m_pCurEntry->SetDescription (desc);
         break;
      }
      case 4: // info
      {
         CString info;
         m_pListEdit->GetWindowText (info);
         m_pCurEntry->SetInfo (info);
         break;
      }
      case 5: // category
      {
         CString category;
         m_pListEdit->GetWindowText (category);
         m_pCurEntry->SetCategory (category);
         break;
      }
      case 6: // payment
      {
         CString payment;
         m_pListEdit->GetWindowText (payment);
         if (!m_pCurEntry->SetPayment (payment))
         {
            m_pListEdit->SetFocus();
            m_pListEdit->SetSel (0, -1, TRUE);
            return;
         }
         break;
      }
      case 7: // deposit
      {
         CString deposit;
         m_pListEdit->GetWindowText (deposit);
         if (!m_pCurEntry->SetDeposit (deposit))
         {
```

```cpp
            m_pListEdit->SetFocus ();
            m_pListEdit->SetSel (0, -1, TRUE);
            return;
          }
          break;
      }
    case 8:// balance
      {
          break;
      }
  }
  m_pListEdit->SetSel (-1, -1, TRUE);
  m_pAcctList->GetItemRect (m_nCurSel, &rE);
  m_pAcctList->RedrawWindow (&rE);
  if (bDone)
  {
    //
    // done editing
    //
    if (m_pCurEntry->GetStatus () == E_SELECTED)
    {
        BOOL bDesc = ValidDescription (m_pCurEntry);
        BOOL bCat  = ValidCategory (m_pCurEntry);
        if (!bDesc || !bCat)
        {
            SetUpEditItem (nNewField);
            return;
        }
    }
    if (m_pCurEntry->GetStatus () == E_MODIFIED)
    {
        GetDocument ()->SetModifiedFlag (TRUE);
    }
    if (ValidEntry (m_pCurEntry))
    {
        m_pCurEntry->SetStatus (E_COMPLETE);
        m_pListEdit->ShowWindow (SW_HIDE);
        m_pAcctList->DeleteString (m_nCurSel);
        m_pAcctList->AddString ((LPCSTR)m_pCurEntry);
        SelectNextEntry ();
        SetUpEditItem (0);
        return;
    }
  }
  SetUpEditItem (nNewField);
}
```

The UpdateFields member function is called with the number of the new
field to be edited (nNewField) and a boolean indication of whether the
return key was pressed (bDone), indicating the user has completed data
entry. The field in which the CListEdit window is currently positioned is
specified by the m_nEditField member variable, which is used in the
switch statement to select the action to be performed. There is a case for
each possible field, with the exception of the balance field (in which data
entry is not possible). The validation for each field is different, and in
many fields is neither necessary nor performed. The two components of
the date field are interesting in that when the month-and-day field has

just been edited, we substitute the current year into the computation, so that a valid CTime object can be constructed. In a similar fashion, when the field containing the year has just been edited, the current month and day are used so that the CTime object will be valid.

The description, info, and category fields are not validated; however, before the entry is entirely acceptable (when the bDone parameter is TRUE), both of the description and category fields must not be empty. This is an arbitrary decision, but in looking toward the preparation of reports, we have decided that requiring that the user enter data into these fields is in their best interest.

Both the payment and deposit fields are validated in the CListEntry member functions SetPayment and SetDeposit, respectively. If either is invalid, the UpdateFields member function returns to the HandleKeys caller, after an appropriate error dialog has been displayed and acknowledged by the user.

After the current field has been validated (if necessary) and its contents have been stored into the CListEntry object, the UpdateFields member function removes any highlights from the current item, accesses the item's display rectangle, and then calls the framework's RedrawWindow member function, passing it the item rectangle to be redrawn. This causes the framework to call the DrawItem member function for the CAcctList class, which updates the list box with the current field's data.

If the UpdateFields member function was called with a bDone parameter value of TRUE, then it is necessary to perform some final validation of the entry and either display an error dialog and return to the Handle-Keys member function to allow editing of the current entry to proceed or prepare to select the next item in the list box and set up its first item for editing by the user.

The process of determining whether an entry is complete depends upon the status of the entry. If the user has been merely navigating through its fields and has not modified any data within a field, then we make sure that the entry contains values in its description and category fields, and if not, we select the field specified by nNewField and return to the Han-dleKeys member function. If the entry has been modified, we call the SetModifiedFlag member function for the document to ensure that the user will be prompted to save the document in case they decide to exit the program before doing so.

Whether the entry's status is E_MODIFIED, or E_SELECTED, if the entry is valid, its status is set to E_COMPLETE, the CListEdit window is hidden, and we call the CListBox member functions to delete the currently in-dexed list box item and then add back the CListEntry object as a new item in the list box (causing it to be sorted into its proper position in the list). We then call SelectNextEntry to select the next entry in the list box for editing and then call the SetUpEditItem member function to prepare the first field of the new item for editing by the user.

If the bDone parameter was FALSE, we need only call the SetUpEditItem to edit the next (nNewField) field in the current item.

ValidDescription Member Function Code

The code to validate the description field in the current list box item is as follows:

```
BOOL CAccount::ValidDescription (CListEntry* pEntry)
{
   CString s;

   s = pEntry->GetDescription();
   if (s.GetLength() == 0)
   {
      return FALSE;
   }
   return TRUE;
}
```

As is evident in the foregoing code, a valid description field need contain only one or more characters of data. The exact contents are not important in determining its validity.

ValidCategory Member Function Code

The code to validate the category field in the current list box item is as follows:

```
BOOL CAccount::ValidCategory (CListEntry* pEntry)
{
   CString s;

   s = pEntry->GetCategory();
   if (s.GetLength() == 0)
   {
      return FALSE;
   }
   return TRUE;
}
```

As was the case with the description field, we test the contents of the category field only to see whether it contains one or more characters of data. We anticipate that this member function will be enhanced in a later version of the application to accept only predefined category values.

ValidEntry Member Function Code

The ValidEntry member function combines the test for a valid description field and a valid category field and displays an appropriate error dialog if either field is found to be invalid. The code is as follows:

```
BOOL CAccount::ValidEntry (CListEntry* pEntry)
{
  CString s;
  //
  // verify that required fields are present
  //
  if (pEntry == NULL) return FALSE;
  if (!ValidDescription(pEntry))
  {
    AfxMessageBox ("Description field is required.");
    return FALSE;
  }
  if (!ValidCategory(pEntry))
  {
    AfxMessageBox ("Category field is required.");
    return FALSE;
  }
  return TRUE;
}
```

SetUpEditItem Member Function Code

The SetUpEditItem member function is responsible for disposing of the previous object of the CListEdit class, creating a new object of that class, storing the contents of the appropriate CListEntry field into the object, positioning the object's window on top of the CAcctList entry to give the appearance that the user is editing the field's data, and highlighting the window's contents in preparation for further user actions.

The SetUpEditItem member function is called in several places in the program. The first such call is in the OnDraw member function (shown on page 84), which calls the member function only if the first time switch (m_bFirstTime) is TRUE. This call allows us to get started, after the list box has been drawn, and before we expect any user inputs. The UpdateFields member function (shown on pages 101–103) also calls the SetUpEditItem member function when an entry is complete. We will also see shortly that this member function is called when the user clicks the mouse cursor on some other item in the list box. The code for the SetUpEditItem member function is as follows:

```
void CAccount::SetUpEditItem (int field)
{
  CString s = "";
  CTime tim;
  RECT rF, rE, rL, rW;
```

```
//
// save the field number.
//
m_nEditField = field;

//
// compute the location of the new CListEdit window
//
m_pAcctList->GetItemRect (m_nCurSel, &rE);
m_pAcctList->GetWindowRect (&rL);
ScreenToClient (&rL);
rF = fields[field];
rW.left   = rL.left + rE.left + rF.left;
rW.top    = rL.top  + rE.top  + rF.top;
rW.right  = rW.left + rF.right - rF.left;
rW.bottom = rW.top  + rF.bottom - rF.top;
```

The first section of the SetUpEditItem member function declares variables that will be referenced in the member function, saves the new field number into the m_nEditField member variable, and then calculates the bounding rectangle for the current entry in the list box, with respect to the view's origin. This is necessary because we need to position the CListEdit window with respect to the view and not just the list box.

```
//
// delete the current CListEdit object and create a
// new CListEdit object that is positioned at the
// new location.
//
delete m_pListEdit;
m_pListEdit = new CListEdit;
if (field < 6)
{
   m_pListEdit->Create (WS_VISIBLE | ES_AUTOHSCROLL |
      ES_LEFT, rW, this, 99);
}
else
{
   m_pListEdit->Create (WS_VISIBLE | ES_MULTILINE | ES_RIGHT,
      rW, this, 99);
   m_pListEdit->GetRect (&rF);
   rF.right = rW.right - rW.left;
   m_pListEdit->SetRect (&rF);
}
m_pListEdit->SetFont (m_pEditFont);
m_pListEdit->SetWindowText(s);
```

The foregoing code is responsible for deleting the current CListEdit window and then creating another object with the proper text justification parameters. With the exception of the payment and deposit fields, all of the data are left-justified, while the data in the payment and deposit fields are right-justified.

After the CListEdit object and its associated window have been created, the font is specified and the text for the specified field is written into the window.

```cpp
// get the current entry and store the string value for
// the current field into the CListEdit window.
//
if (m_pCurEntry->GetStatus() != E_EMPTY)
{
   switch (field)
   {
      case 0: // date month/day
      {
         tim = m_pCurEntry->GetDate();
         s = tim.Format("%m/%d");
         m_pListEdit->SetWindowText (s);
         break;
      }
      case 1: // date year
      {
         tim = m_pCurEntry->GetDate();
         s = tim.Format("%Y");
         m_pListEdit->SetWindowText (s);
         break;
      }
      case 2: // item number
      {
         m_pListEdit->SetWindowText (m_pCurEntry->GetItem());
         break;
      }
      case 3: // description
      {
         m_pListEdit->SetWindowText (m_pCurEntry
            ->GetDescription());
         break;
      }
      case 4: // info field
      {
         m_pListEdit->SetWindowText (m_pCurEntry->GetInfo());
         break;
      }
      case 5: // category
      {
         m_pListEdit->SetWindowText (m_pCurEntry
            ->GetCategory());
         break;
      }
      case 6: // payment
      {
         m_pListEdit->SetWindowText (m_pCurEntry
            ->GetPayment());
         break;
      }
      case 7: // deposit
      {
         m_pListEdit->SetWindowText (m_pCurEntry
            ->GetDeposit());
         break;
      }
   }
}
```

```
    m_pListEdit->ShowWindow (SW_SHOW);
    m_pListEdit->SetSel (0, -1, TRUE);
    m_pListEdit->SetFocus();
}
```

The foregoing code writes the text for the specified field into the CList-Edit window, makes the window visible, highlights all of the text and then sets the focus to the newly displayed window. The specified field is then ready to receive user inputs, which will appear to be reflected directly in the list box entry.

SelectNextEntry Member Function Code

When the user completes an entry and presses the return key, the Up-dateFields member function completes the validation of the entry, and then it calls the SelectNextEntry member function to select the appropriate next list box entry. The code for this member function is as follows:

```
void CAccount::SelectNextEntry(void)
{
   int nEntryCount = m_pAcctList->GetCount();
   if (++m_nCurSel >= nEntryCount)
   {
     m_pCurEntry = GetDocument()->NewListEntry();
     GetDocument()->AddListEntry (m_pCurEntry);
     m_pAcctList->InsertString (-1, (LPCSTR)m_pCurEntry);
   }
   m_pCurEntry = (CListEntry *)m_pAcctList
     ->GetItemDataPtr (m_nCurSel);
   m_pCurEntry->SetStatus(E_SELECTED);
   m_pAcctList->SetCurSel(m_nCurSel);
}
```

The foregoing code adds one to the current entry index (m_nCurSel) and tests whether its new value exceeds the number of entries in the list. If so, a new CListEntry object is created by calling NewListEntry, the new entry is added to the document's CObList list, and the entry is placed at the end of the list box by using the InsertString member function (which does not cause the list to be re-sorted).

Whether the code advances to a new list entry or the next list entry, it accesses the entry's item data pointer and stores it into the current entry pointer member variable (m_pCurEntry). The status of the entry is changed to E_SELECTED and the SetCurSel member function of the CListBox class is called to display the entry in its selected state.

OnSelChgAcctList Message Handler Code

When the user clicks the left mouse button, with the mouse cursor positioned on a different entry from the one currently selected, the application must first determine whether the current entry has been modified, and if so, the user must be given the chance to save the current entry, discard the current entry, or cancel the selection. The OnSelChgAcctList message handler processes the mouse click and handles the appropriate interaction with the user. The code for this handler is as follows:

```cpp
void CAccount::OnSelChgAcctList()
{
    if (m_pCurEntry->GetStatus() == E_MODIFIED)
    {
        if (!ValidEntry(m_pCurEntry))
        {
            m_pAcctList->SetCurSel (m_nCurSel);
            SetUpEditItem (m_nEditField);
            return;
        }
        int answer = AfxMessageBox (IDS_SAVE_ITEM,
            MB_YESNOCANCEL);
        if (answer == IDCANCEL)
        {
            m_pAcctList->SetSel (m_nCurSel);
            SetUpEditItem (m_nEditField);
            GetDocument()->SetModifiedFlag(TRUE);
            return;
        }
        else if (answer == IDYES)
        {
            m_pCurEntry->SetStatus(E_COMPLETE);
            m_pAcctList->DeleteString (m_nCurSel);
            m_pAcctList->AddString ((LPCSTR)m_pCurEntry);
            GetDocument()->SetModifiedFlag(TRUE);
        }
        else     // answer == IDNO
        {
            m_pAcctList->DeleteString (m_nCurSel);
            GetDocument()->DeleteListEntry (m_pCurEntry);
            GetDocument()->SetModifiedFlag(TRUE);
        }
    }
}
```

The foregoing section of the OnSelChgAcctList member function handles the interaction with the user if it is determined that the current selection has been modified (i.e., its status is E_MODIFIED). The first action is to determine whether the entry is valid as it currently exists. We call the ValidEntry member function to ascertain the entry's validity. If it is invalid, that member function will display an appropriate error dialog and when the dialog is dismissed, the OnSelChgAcctList will reselect the current entry, call the SetUpEditItem member function to highlight and prepare the entry for editing, and then return. This effectively nullifies the new selection click.

If the current entry is found to be valid, then the user must decide whether it should be saved or discarded, or whether the new selection should be ignored. This is accomplished by displaying a Yes-No-Cancel dialog, which explains the options to the user and solicits a choice.

If the user elects to cancel the selection, then the current selection is reselected, the SetUpEditItem member function is called to set it up to be edited, and the document's SetModifiedFlag member function is called to ensure that the document is marked to be saved if the user chooses to exit the application.

If the user elects to save the entry, its status is set to E_COMPLETE, the entry is deleted from the list box and is added back, causing it to sort into the correct position in the list. The document's SetModifiedFlag member function is called to indicate that the document has been changed.

If the user elects not to save the entry, the entry is deleted from the list box, and then it is deleted from the document's CObList list. The SetModifiedFlag member function is also called to indicate that the document has been changed.

```
if (m_pCurEntry->GetStatus() == E_SELECTED)
{
    BOOL bDesc = ValidDescription (m_pCurEntry);
    BOOL bCat  = ValidCategory (m_pCurEntry);
    if (bDesc && bCat)
    {
        m_pCurEntry->SetStatus (E_COMPLETE);
    }
    else
    {
        m_pCurEntry->SetStatus (E_EMPTY);
    }
}
```

The foregoing code handles the case where the current entry has not been modified, but is selected (i.e., its status is E_SELECTED). If the description and category fields are valid, the current selection's status is changed to E_COMPLETE. If either field is invalid, the current selection's status is changed to E_EMPTY.

```
m_nCurSel = m_pAcctList->GetCurSel();
m_pCurEntry = (CListEntry *)m_pAcctList
    ->GetItemDataPtr (m_nCurSel);
if (m_pCurEntry->GetStatus() == E_EMPTY)
{
    //
    // new selection is empty
    //
    CListEntry* pEntry;
    int prevEntry;

    prevEntry = m_nCurSel - 1;
    if (prevEntry >= 0)
```

```
                        {
                            pEntry = (CListEntry *)m_pAcctList
                                ->GetItemDataPtr (prevEntry);
                            if (pEntry->GetStatus() == E_EMPTY)
                            {
                                //
                                // the previous entry is empty, too. We
                                // need to reset the selection to the entry
                                // after the last non-empty selection.
                                //
                                int i, n = m_pAcctList->GetCount();
                                for (i=0; i < n; i++)
                                {
                                    pEntry = (CListEntry *)m_pAcctList
                                        ->GetItemDataPtr (i);
                                    if (pEntry->GetStatus() == E_EMPTY)
                                    {
                                        break;
                                    }
                                }
                                m_nCurSel = i-1;
                                SelectNextEntry();
                            }
                        }
                    }
    m_pCurEntry->SetStatus (E_SELECTED);
    SetUpEditItem (0);// select first field
}
```

The final section of the OnSelChgAcctList handler in the foregoing
code is responsible for selecting the entry on which the mouse was
clicked. This would be relatively straightforward were it not for the fact
that the list box could contain a number of empty entries, and the
mouse was clicked in other than the first of these. The code handles this
case by first determining whether the newly selected entry's status is
E_EMPTY. If so, the code checks whether the previous entry's status is
also E_EMPTY. In that case, the code loops through the list, from its beginning, to find the very first empty entry to select, and then chooses
that entry by calling the SelectNextEntry member function. Finally, the
newly selected entry's status is changed to E_SELECTED, and the SetU-
pEditItem member function is called to allow editing of the first
(month and day) field to commence.

Global Support Functions

Almost every application requires the use of one or more utility routines
to handle its various mundane tasks. This application is no exception.

Get2Nums Function Code

Validation of the date field in the UpdateFields member function requires that the month and day fields be specified by one or two digits,
followed by a delimiter character (which, in the case of the day value, can
be NULL). The code for the Get2Nums function is as follows:

```
BOOL Get2Nums (char* str, int& index, int& field, char
delim)
{
   int value;

   if (str[index] < '0' || str[index] > '9')
   {
      return FALSE;
   }
   value = str[index] - '0';
   index++;
   if (str[index] < '0' || str[index] > '9')
   {
      if (str[index] == delim)
      {
         index++;
         field = value;
         return TRUE;
      }
      return FALSE;
   }
   else
   {
      value *= 10;
      value += (str[index] - '0');
      index++;
      if (str[index] == delim)
      {
         index++;
         field = value;
         return TRUE;
      }
      return FALSE;
   }
}
```

Saving and Loading Account Data Files

In order for the application to be truly useful, it is necessary to be able to save all of the entries in the account list and then load them back into the list at a later date. The save and load functionality is quite simple to implement in Visual C++, using the many built-in features of the MFC. Everything is accomplished using the automatically provided "serialization" facilities for all objects that are derived from the CObject class. It is important to put serialization code into newly created objects so that they too can be written to or read from a file.

Serializing the Document

When the user chooses the Save command from the File menu, it is necessary to provide some means to serialize the document's data so that they can be written to the chosen file (if a file doesn't already exist, the framework will prompt the user to specify one—one that has a **kpd** extension, which we have specified as the unique extension for Keepit's data files. Our override of the Serialize member function handles this case.

Serialize Member Function Code

When the user chooses to either save or open a file, the framework calls the document's Serialize member function to handle the process of writing or reading the document's data. The Serialize member function is passed a reference to a CArchive object, which is much like the descriptors used for stream operations. The CArchive class allows you to store the contents of a complex collection of objects in a compact binary form, such that when the file is later read, the objects are re-created with their saved contents intact. This process of making objects persistent between runs of the program is called serialization. The CArchive class defines a couple of boolean member variables that we can use to determine whether to save or load the document's data when the Serialize member function is called. These are `IsLoading` and `IsStoring`. The code in the CKeepitDoc class Serialize member function is as follows:

```
void CKeepitDoc::Serialize(CArchive& ar)
{
    int count;

    m_ListEntries.Serialize (ar);
    if (ar.IsLoading)
    {
        count = m_ListEntries.GetCount();
        if (count < 7)
        {
        //
        // if we didn't load enough entries to
        // cause the vertical scroll bar to activate,
        // do so.
        //
        for (int i=count-1; i < 7; i++)
        {
         CListEntry* pEntry = NewListEntry();
         AddListEntry (pEntry);
        }
        }
    }
}
```

The foregoing code immediately calls the Serialize member function for the CObList object, `m_ListEntries`. CObList objects contain code in their Serialize member functions to determine the run-time class of the objects stored in the list and call their respective Serialize member functions for each entry in the list. When the document's serialization is complete, the foregoing code makes sure that there are at least seven entries in the list box, but only if the Serialize member function was called to load entries from a file.

Serializing the List Entries

The code to serialize a CListEntry object is called automatically by the framework during the serialization of the CObList object. The Serialize member function is passed a single parameter, which is a reference to an object of the CArchive class.

A CArchive object is similar to a stream object in that it implements the use of the << and >> operators for storing or loading data, respectively, from an archive file. The serialization operators support data of type BYTE, WORD, LONG, DWORD, float, double, or other objects that are capable of being serialized (this includes most any object that is derived from the CObject class).

CListEntry Serialize Member Function Code

In the case of the CListEntry class, the serialization member function is called directly by the Serialize member function in the CKeepitDoc class when a file is saved or loaded. When data are being stored (i.e., the IsStoring member variable is TRUE), the Serialize member function determines whether the entry is empty or contains valid data. Empty entries are not written to the archive. The code for the Serialize member function is as follows:

```
void CListEntry::Serialize (CArchive& ar)
{
  CObject::Serialize (ar);

  if (ar.IsStoring())
  {
    if (m_nStatus == E_EMPTY)
    {
      //
      // don't save any empty entries
      //
      return;
    }
    ar << m_nStatus;
    ar << m_EntryDate;
    ar << m_szItemNo;
    ar << m_szDescription;
    ar << m_szInfo;
    ar << m_szCategory;
    ar << m_nPayment;
    ar << m_nDeposit;
  }
  else
  {
    ar >> m_nStatus;
    ar >> m_EntryDate;
    ar >> m_szItemNo;
```

```
          ar >> m_szDescription;

          ar >> m_szInfo;

          ar >> m_szCategory;

          ar >> m_nPayment;

          ar >> m_nDeposit;

      }

  }
```

The foregoing code shows, depending upon whether the value contained in the `IsStoring` member variable is TRUE, how each member of the CListEntry object is either written to or read from the file, using the CArchive class object (`ar`) to address the output or input stream, respectively. The Serialize member function is called automatically for each member of the document's CObList class (`m_ListEntries`).

Summary of the Application's Features

At the present stage of its construction, the Keepit application implements quite a number of features. It provides the user with the ability to create one or more files of transactions, which, in turn, can be saved to or loaded from disk files.

The application also illustrates a method for providing what appears to be a custom form, using the standard Windows list box as its basis, and a derived class (CAcctList), which implements the custom appearance of the form.

In addition, a special class, which was derived from the standard CEdit class, provides the means for keystrokes to be captured and interpreted as either navigation or data entry characters. The CListEdit derived class, along with helper member functions in the CAccount (view) class, provides the user the ability to skip from field to field, either entering data or not, within a single transaction.

As a whole, the application's functions are complete, at least at this stage of its construction. It is useful as it exists as a stand-alone computerized checkbook program. In succeeding chapters, we will add new features that provide many more capabilities to this application. All the while, we will be showing how the various elements of both the MFC and the Windows application programming interface (API) contribute to provide a great deal of functionality, automatically. We will also be demonstrating new uses for the various tools that are bundled into the Visual C++ program development product.

Exercises

1. In the foregoing text, we have presented a class derived from the CListBox class. How is the association between this class and the list box control, which was created with the App Studio tool in the Account dialog, established?

2. What is the purpose of the framework's call to the CAcctList MeasureItem member function? How would the appearance of the application suffer if the member function was not called? Explain your answers in detail.

3. How do we ensure that an integral number of items only are displayed in the list box? (*Hint*: Examine the properties of the list box control in the App Studio screen shots. Do you see a property that would affect the appearance of the display?)

4. Rather than create the CListEdit window dynamically for each field, why didn't we create a single CEdit control in App Studio and then move it around, resizing it as needed?[1] What sort of overhead, if any, could be avoided by using a pair of permanently created windows for this purpose?

5. Modify the code to adopt the technique of using permanent Edit windows for displaying the contents of the list item fields.[2]

6. Microsoft Windows and the MFC do not support fully the existence of overlapped controls. In what situations might there be unresolved conflicts with regard to the CAcctList and CListEdit objects? Explain why this is not an issue for the Keepit application.

7. Describe how to implement a "Restore" button in the CAccount view so that the user who has modified the contents of an entry might decide to restore it to its original contents. Implement this feature.[3]

8. One of the shortcomings of the current application is that the name in the title bar does not reflect the account to which the transactions apply. What additional code would be necessary to provide this functionality? Implement this feature. (*Hint*: Achieving an under-

---

[1] Answering this question may require that you look carefully at the requirements of each field in the form and ascertain whether a single control could be used for the stated purpose.

[2] Performing this modification should be fairly straightforward; however, this task could be assigned as an extra credit project for the student.

[3] A Restore button is a worthwhile addition to the application. Creating it could be assigned as an extra credit project for the student. Because implementation of this feature will touch a number of the existing member functions, sufficient time should be given to complete this exercise.

standing of how the MFC is constructed is a worthwhile task. Please take the time to examine the relationship between the main frame, the child frame, the document, and the view. A detailed examination of the features of each of these components will enable you to complete the exercise.)[1]

9. Develop an approach for implementing multiple accounts within the context of a single document (i.e., a single document, multiple view architecture). Does the MFC lend itself to such an architecture? Explain your answer.[2]

10. The coordinates for positioning the labels and separator lines in both the heading and list entries were calculated heuristically for a standard VGA display adapter. What would be the result if the user has only an EGA display adapter? Can you think of a way in which these values could be defined in a device-independent manner? Explain your answer.

---

[1] Displaying the account name in the window title is so important that it will be addressed in a later chapter. Please don't look ahead to see how it has been accomplished. Develop your own approach, and then use the later material to verify your implementation.

[2] Handling multiple accounts is a fairly extensive project; however, it is worthy of study and could be a very worthwhile class project. A later chapter will show how this is accomplished for the Keepit application. Don't look ahead, but use the material concerning the book's implementation to verify your approach.

Chapter 5

Adding Accounts and Account Support

In this chapter, we are going to add support for multiple account views and also for creating and validating transaction categories. The process of adding these features includes further tutorials in the use of the *wizards*, App Studio and ClassWizard, as well as additions to the code previously shown. The main objective of incremental (or evolutionary) programming is to build upon what has already been created, attempting to use as much of the existing code as possible. In order to accomplish this objective, it is important to design your application prior to commencing its implementation. While the implementation can be easily accomplished in stages, as we show in this book, the design must be fixed at the outset; otherwise, you will find yourself rewriting a lot of the code each time you add a new feature.

The purpose of having transaction categories will become clear when we get to the part of the development where reports are to be prepared. Until then, it is necessary that we make provision for creating and saving a list of standard category names and settings, so that these can be used when the time comes to prepare reports. Building in features that will be used later is an important part of the incremental development process.

In the sections that follow, we will show how the user interface elements for handling the creation and editing of new accounts and categories are added to the application. In addition, we will describe the new structure of the application and how each piece relates to the MFC. The next chapter will focus on the custom code we have added to implement these new features.

Additions and Changes to the Menu Bars

The first step toward providing support for multiple accounts and a list of category names is to create new menus and associated commands that enable the user to choose the new features. The steps for creating the new user interface elements are as follows:

1. Assuming that Visual C++ is already running and the Keepit project has already been opened, choose App Studio from the Tools menu.

2. When App Studio has launched, you will see a list of resource types in the left-hand window. Choose the Menu resource by clicking on it or by navigating to it using the arrow keys.

3. After you have selected Menu as the resource type, you will see a list of the existing menu bars. Each menu bar is associated with a particular frame window type. The list should consist of only two menu bar names at this point. They are listed in alphabetical order. The first in the list is named IDR_KEEPITTYPE, which is the one in which we are interested. The other, IDR_MAINFRAME, applies only to the main frame window when no document is open. Choose the IDR_KEEPITTYPE menu bar by clicking on it with the mouse or by navigating with the arrow keys and pressing the Return key.

4. The menu bar for the IDR_KEEPITTYPE resource contains five menus, which are File, Edit, View, Window, and Help. You will also see an unnamed portion of the menu bar, to the right of the Help menu, that is enclosed by a dotted rectangle. Click on this rectangle, hold down the mouse button, and drag it to the immediate left of the Window menu. You will see that as you drag the rectangle to the left, a bar cursor indicates where the empty menu will be located on the menu bar. When the bar cursor is to the left of the Window menu, release the mouse button.

5. Name the new menu by double clicking on the blank rectangle in the menu bar. This will open up the Properties window for the menu. Change the properties to reflect the settings shown in Figure 5-1. Note in the figure that the only change we have made to the

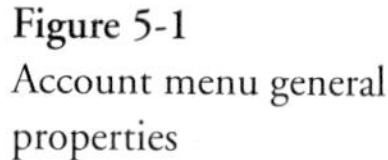
Figure 5-1
Account menu general
properties

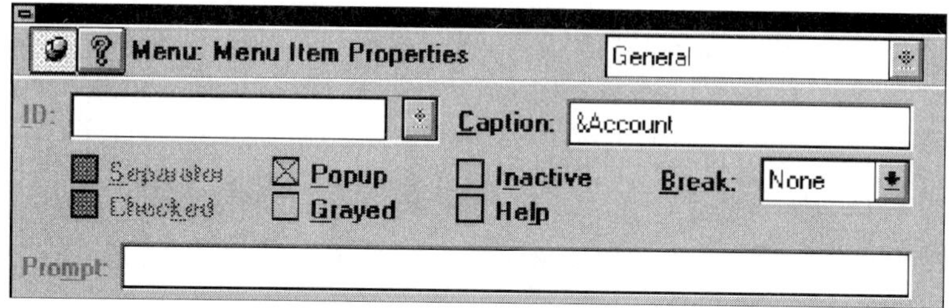

default properties is to enter the word Account in the Caption field, with a leading & character, which allows the menu to be dropped down by using the ALT-A shortcut. The Popup checkbox should be checked, but none of the other active checkboxes should be checked. You can move the Properties window to a more convenient location on your screen and pin it into place by clicking on the push-pin icon at the upper left of the window, or you can dismiss the Properties window by either clicking in the (rather tiny) close box or by pressing the return (or enter) key.

6. The next step is to click on the Account menu name, which should drop down the menu and display an empty menu item, enclosed by a dotted rectangle. Double click on the empty item to display its properties, and change these to correspond with the contents of the Properties window shown in Figure 5-2. Notice that we have entered the item name (Edit…) in the Caption field with three trailing dots (ellipses), indicating that a dialog will be displayed when this command is chosen. We have also provided a Prompt string,

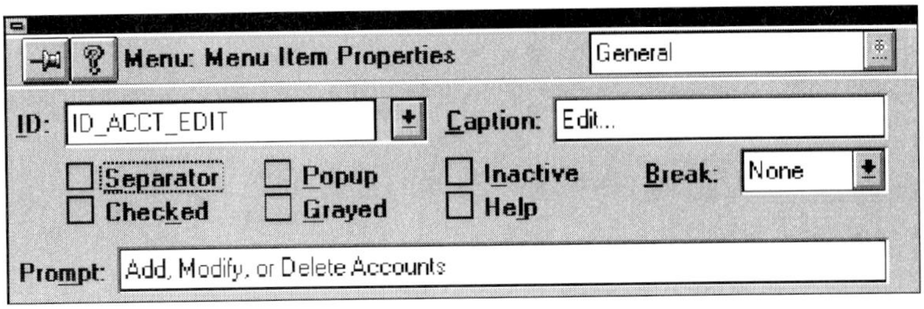

Figure 5-2
Edit menu item
properties

which will be displayed in the status bar when the user navigates to this menu item. Providing prompts aids the user in determining the purpose of a particular menu command.

7. The next step is to double click on the blank menu item entry just below the Edit command and fill in the fields of the Properties window, as shown in Figure 5-3. Note that because this is a separator item, no Caption has been entered, and the Separator checkbox has been checked. Separator items provide visual separation between groups of related commands.

Figure 5-3
Separator menu item
properties

8. Each time we create a new menu item, App Studio provides an empty item at the bottom of the menu, in anticipation that we will want to create another item. At this point, we are finished with the additions to the Account menu, but we don't have to worry about the extra empty item. It will disappear when we quit the App Studio program.

9. Click on the View menu name on the menu bar at this time. The menu will drop down and display the existing entries, which include Toolbar and Status Bar menu commands. There will also be

a blank, empty item, at the bottom of the menu. Add a Separator entry, as shown in the foregoing step 7.

10. Immediately below the separator added in the preceding step, double click on the empty item to show the Properties window and add the Categories item, as shown in Figure 5-4. Note the & in front of the word Categories in the caption. This allows the command to be easily chosen using an accelerator-key combination of ALT-C.

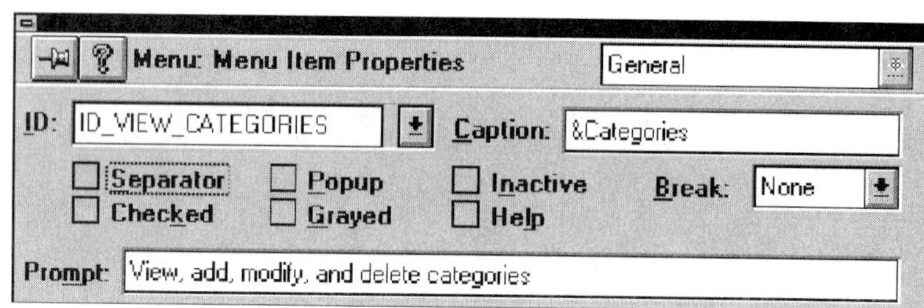

Figure 5-4
Categories menu item properties

This concludes the steps pertaining to the creation and modification of menu resources in the new version of the application. Note that in the final step, the Caption field for the Categories command did not contain the ellipsis (three dots) marking. This is because the Category command causes a new view to be created, which can remain on the screen while transactions are entered into an account.

Creating the Category View

The next series of steps shows how the Category view is created. Prior to commencing these steps, the menu editor should be closed. This can be accomplished by double clicking App Studio's child frame Document Control Icon, clicking the child frame's Document Control Icon and choosing the Close command, or by using the CTRL-F4 keyboard shortcut. In any case, after you have closed the menu editor, App Studio should still be running and you should see the list of resource types in the pane on the left and the highlighted IDR_KEEPITTYPE menu resource in the pane on the right. If you have quit App Studio inadvertently, you will probably have been asked if you want to save the changes you have made thus far. Choose Yes and then reinvoke App Studio from the Tools menu, as previously described. When App Studio is prepared for editing a new resource type, then continue with the tutorial. The steps for creating the Category view are as follows (you may wish to refer to Figure 5-7 while following this procedure):

1. Navigate in the left pane of App Studio's resource types to Dialog, and then click the New button at the bottom left of the window. This will display a Dialog showing the available resource types, with

the entry for Dialog highlighted. Make sure that the Dialog type is selected and then click the OK button. A default dialog window with OK and Cancel buttons will appear on the screen.

2. Click on the OK button, press the delete key to delete that button, and then click on the Cancel button and delete it also. Because the view is not a real dialog, we will not be needing the functionality these buttons provide. However, until we get to the point where the code to support the new view is to be generated, there is no distinction made by App Studio between editing a dialog or a form view.

3. Double click inside the view to show its Properties window and fill in the General properties as shown in Figure 5-5. Note that we have changed the ID for the view to IDD_CATEGORIES.

Figure 5-5
Categories view General properties

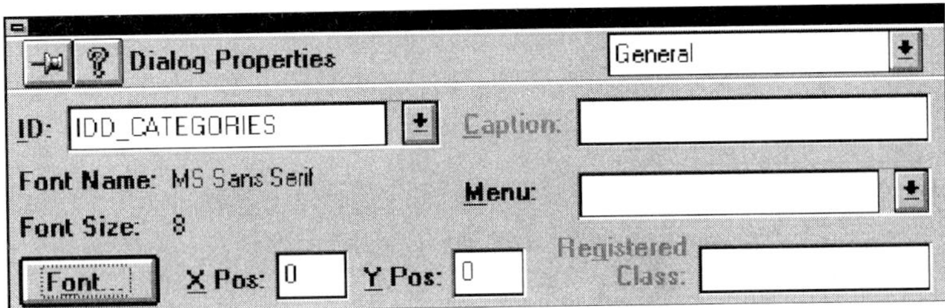

4. Next, without dismissing the Properties window for the new view, click on arrow at the right of the combo box displaying the word General and choose the Styles properties. Set the Styles properties so that they correspond to what is shown in Figure 5-6.

Figure 5-6
Categories view Styles properties

5. The final appearance of the Category view is shown in Figure 5-7. The first step in creating the contents of this view is to click on the static text tool in the dialog editor's control palette and drag a static text field onto the view, where the word **Category:** appears, at the upper left of the view shown in Figure 5-7. The location of this static text field is shown in the status bar of App Studio as 3, 5. The size of the field is shown also on the status bar, to the right of the location, as 32x10. These are dialog units (i.e., DLUs), which are not to be confused with pixels. Double click on the static text field and change its properties to those shown in Figure 5-8.

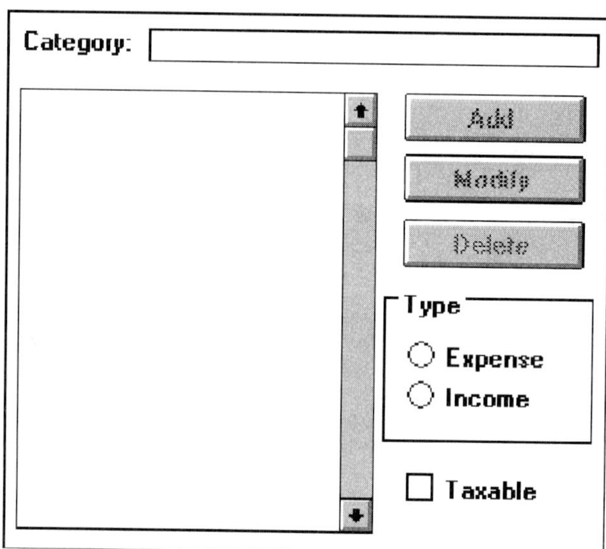

Figure 5-7
Appearance of completed
Category view

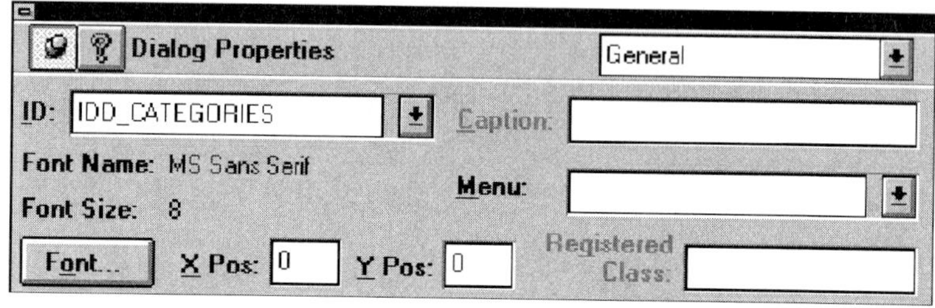

Figure 5-8
Category static text
General properties

6. Create an edit box by clicking and dragging the control from the control palette, and resize it so that it is located at coordinates of 39, 4, with a size of 121 x 12. This will allow a fairly long category name to be entered, without using the horizontal scroll feature of the control. Double click on the control to display its properties, change its General properties as shown in Figure 5-9, and change its Styles properties to correspond with those shown in Figure 5-10.

Figure 5-9
Category name edit text
General properties

7. The next control to be created is the List Box, which is selected by choosing that tool from App Studio's palette. Drag the list box con-

Figure 5-10
Category name edit text
styles properties

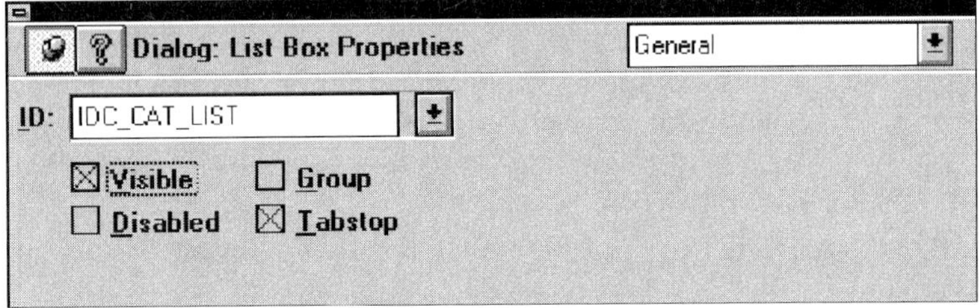

trol into place in the Category view. You should resize the list so that
it is located at the coordinates 3, 22 and with a size (in DLUs) of
100x130. Double click on the list and change its General properties
to those shown in Figure 5-11, and its Styles properties to those
shown in Figure 5-12. The list should appear in approximately the
same location and in the same size as shown in Figure 5-7. We do
not anticipate the need for a horizontal scroll bar at this point; however, should the category names become rather long, it could be
added later, with no effect to the code.

Figure 5-11
Category list General
properties

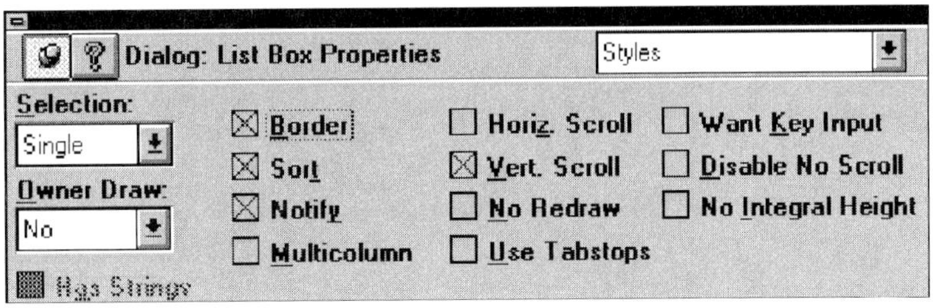

Figure 5-12
Category list Styles
properties

8. The next step is to create a group to contain the category type radio
   button controls. To do this, click on the group icon in the control
   palette and drag the group icon into its approximate position in the
   view. The coordinates of its location are 108, 78, and its size is
   approximately 54x46. Double click on the group control and
   change its properties to correspond to those shown in Figure 5-13.

9. After the Type group has been created in the foregoing step, the
   radio button controls can be placed inside the group. Begin by
   clicking on the radio button control in App Studio's control palette

Figure 5-13
Type group control
General properties

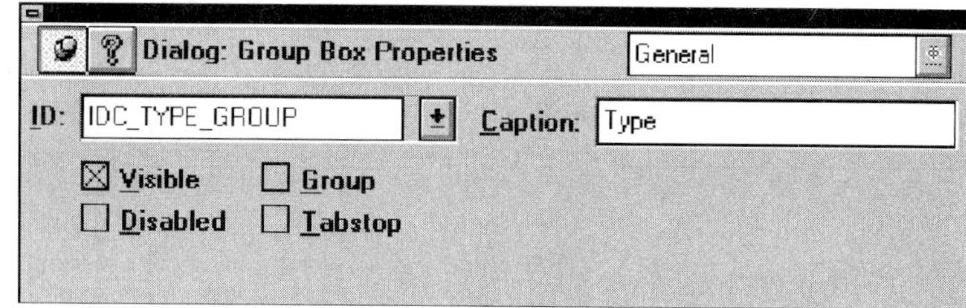

and dragging the first radio button onto the view. The approximate position of the control is at coordinates of 116, 93 with a size, to accommodate the caption, of 41 x 10. Double click the control to enter the parameters shown in Figure 5-14.

Figure 5-14
Expense radio button
General properties

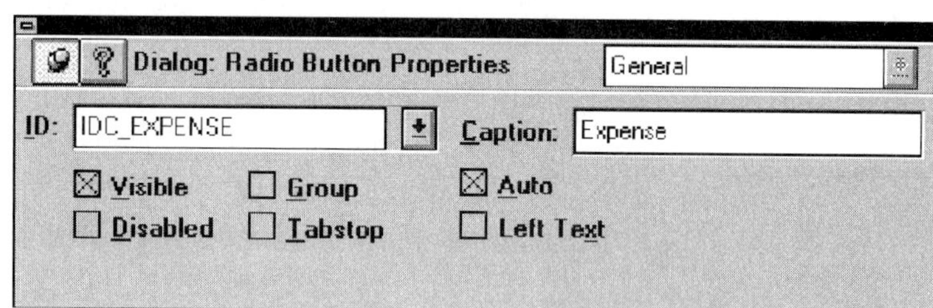

10. In a similar fashion to the foregoing step, drag a radio button from the control palette to coordinates 116, 105 with a field size of 35 x 10. Double click the control and change its properties to correspond to those shown in Figure 5-15.

Figure 5-15
Income radio button
General properties

11. Immediately below the radio button group is a single checkbox labeled "Taxable." Create this control by clicking the checkbox in the control palette and dragging it to the coordinates of 112, 133. Change its size to be approximately 41 x 10 and then double click the control to change its properties as shown in Figure 5-16.

12. The final step in creating the Category view is to create the Add, Modify and Delete buttons. They are all created with a disabled status. This will be changed by the program, as appropriate, when a category has been selected or entered. The Add button is positioned

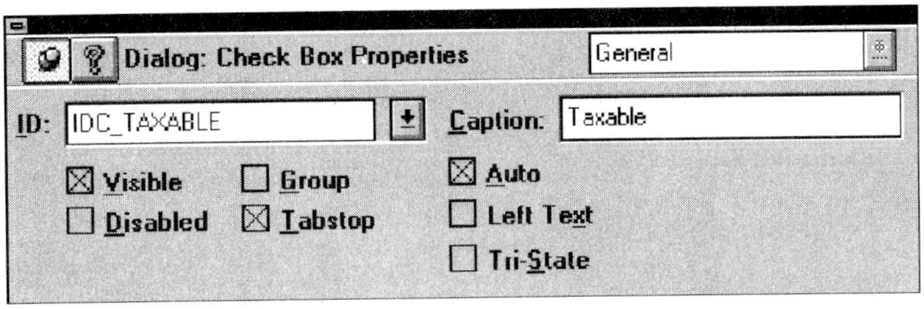

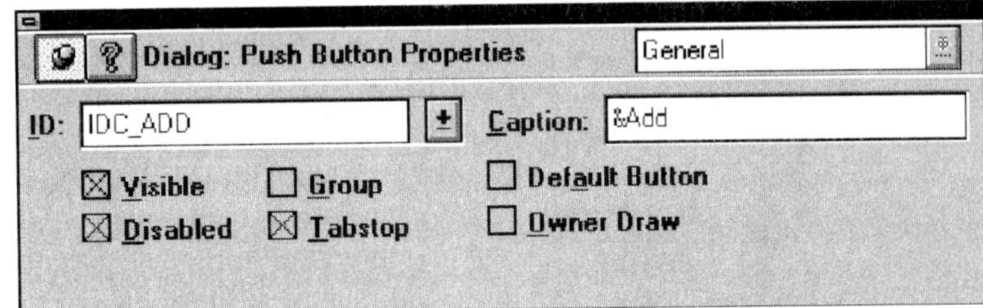

Figure 5-16
Taxable checkbox
General properties

at coordinates of 110, 22, with a size of 50×14. The General properties are shown in Figure 5-17.

Figure 5-17
Add button General
properties

13. The Modify button is located at coordinates of 110, 40, with a size of 50×14. Double click the button to change its properties to correspond to those shown in Figure 5-18.

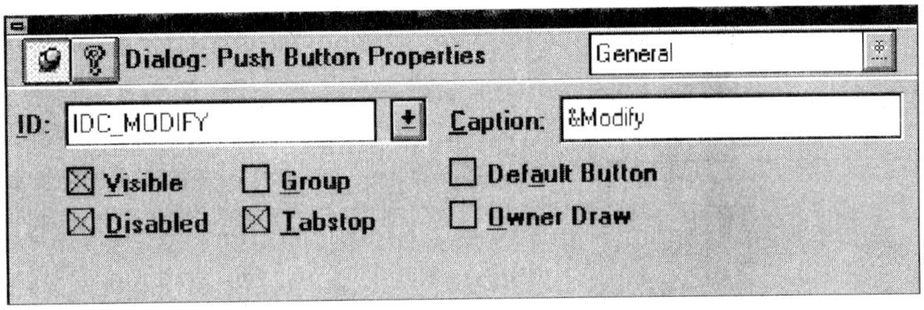

Figure 5-18
Modify button General
properties

14. Finally, the Delete button is located at coordinates of 110, 59, with a size of 50×14. Double click the button to change its properties to correspond to those shown in Figure 5-19.

Figure 5-19
Delete button General
properties

This concludes the steps for creating the Category view. You may wish to refer to Figure 5-7 to verify that you have positioned the elements in the same relative positions as in the figure, and also whether all of the controls have been placed onto the view. Once again, we would like to stress that it is not absolutely essential that you create the controls in the exact positions and with the exact sizes specified, although this is easy to accomplish if you use the arrow keys to position, and in combination with the Shift key to size, the controls. Take special care to ensure that the border is set to "None," as shown in the Styles properties depicted in Figure 5-6. The view will be bordered by the MDI child frame, within which the view will be created

Creating the Edit Account Dialog

This section will describe the creation of a dialog that will be invoked when the user chooses the Edit command from the Account menu. The properties of the Edit command are shown in Figure 5-2. The purpose of the Edit dialog is to permit the user to create new accounts and to modify the characteristics of existing accounts. The final appearance of the dialog is shown in Figure 5-20. The steps for creating the dialog are as follows:

Figure 5-20
Completed Edit Account
dialog

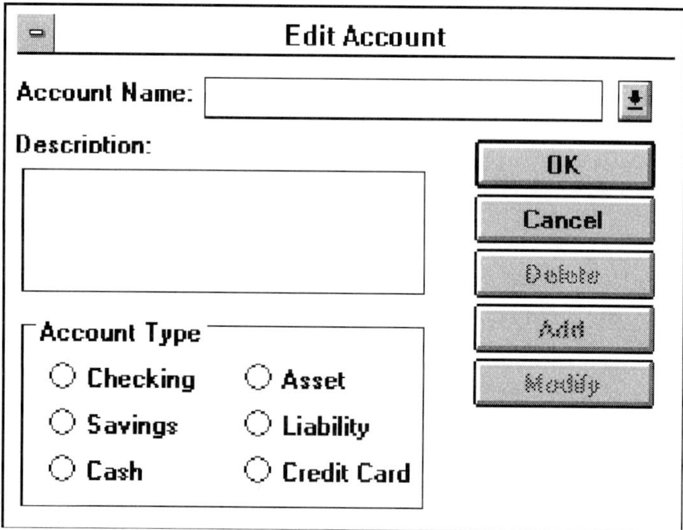

1. If the Category view is still showing on the screen, then close that view by double clicking on the document control icon for the view, or by using the Ctrl-F4 keyboard shortcut. App Studio should be running and you should see the list of resource types on the left and the available resources of the selected type on the right. Click the

New button at the bottom of the view to cause the resource type dialog to be displayed. Choose Dialog for the type to be newly created and then click OK.

2. When the new dialog is created, it will have OK and Cancel buttons and be of medium size. You'll want to resize it so that its new dimensions are 185x136.

3. Double click the dialog to show its properties. Make sure that the General properties are being displayed and change them to correspond to those shown in Figure 5-21. Select the Styles properties of the dialog and change them to conform with the properties shown in Figure 5-22.

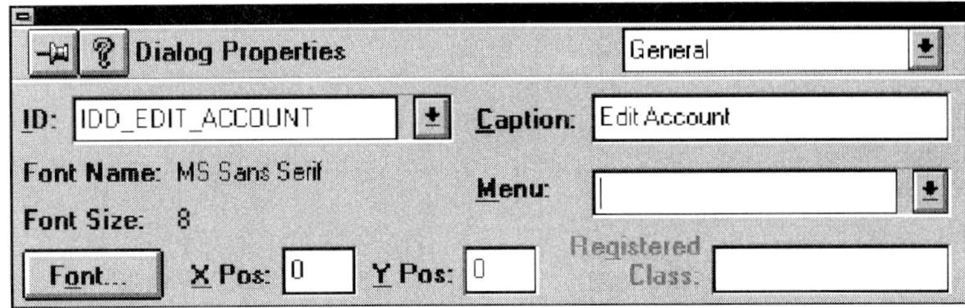

Figure 5-21
Account Edit dialog
General properties

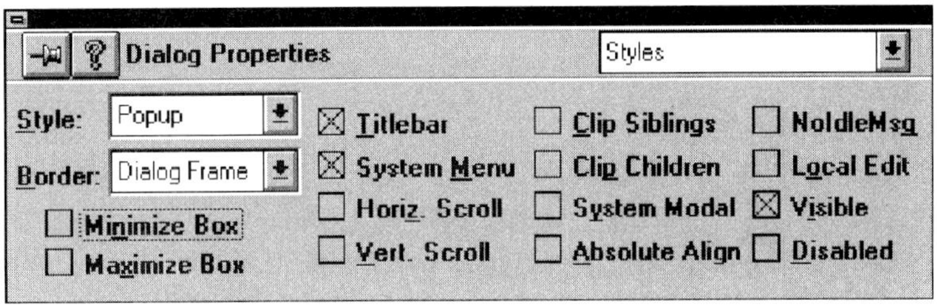

Figure 5-22
Account Edit dialog
Styles properties

4. Click on the static text tool in App Studio's control palette and drag a static text control onto the dialog at the coordinates 0, 7. Change the size of the control to approximately 51x7 DLUs. Then double click on the control and change its properties to correspond to those shown in Figure 5-23.

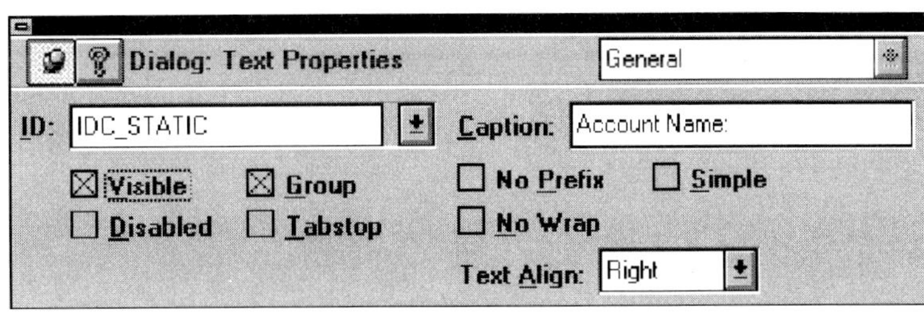

Figure 5-23
Account Name static text
control properties

5. Click on the combo box tool in the control palette and drag the control onto the dialog. Its coordinates should be approximately 53, 6, and its dimensions should be approximately 125 x 12. Double click on the control and change its General properties to correspond with those shown in Figure 5-24, and then change its Styles properties to correspond with those shown in Figure 5-25.

Figure 5-24
Account Name combo box General properties

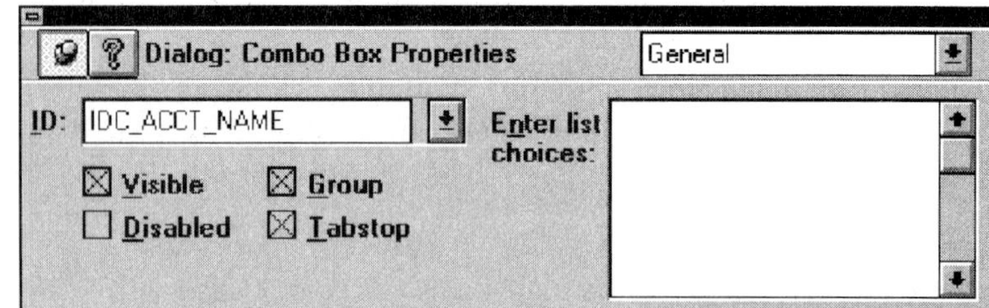

Figure 5-25
Account Name combo box Styles properties

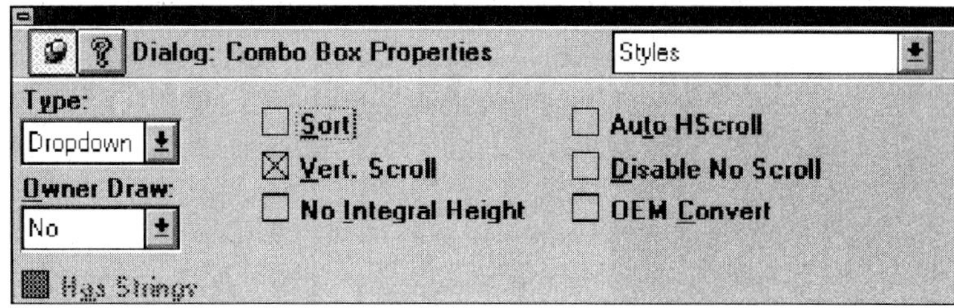

6. Click in the control palette and drag another static text control onto the dialog, at the approximate coordinates of 0, 22. Its size should be set to approximately 39 x 7 DLUs. After the control has been placed onto the dialog, double click on it to show its General properties and change these properties to correspond to the settings shown in Figure 5-26.

Figure 5-26
Description static text General properties

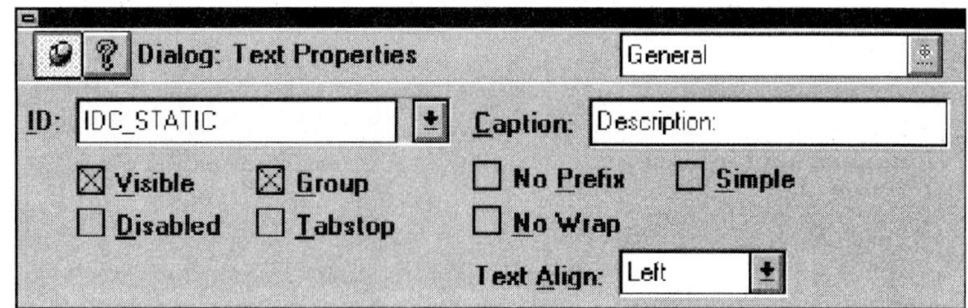

7. Create the edit text Description field in the dialog by clicking the edit text tool in the control palette and dragging a copy of this control to the dialog at coordinates 2, 33. Change the size of the control to approximately 113 x 36 DLUs. Then double click on the control and set its General properties to correspond to the settings

shown in Figure 5-27, and then select the Styles properties and change them to conform to those shown in Figure 5-28.

Figure 5-27
Description field General
properties

Figure 5-28
Description field Styles
properties

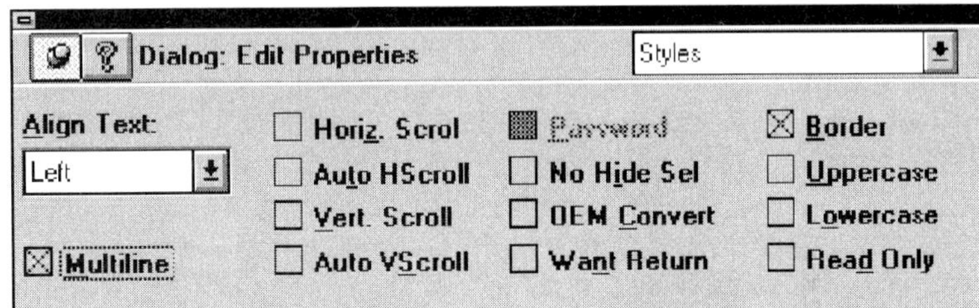

8. This and the following two steps create the Delete, Modify, and Add buttons in the Edit Account dialog. Each of these buttons is created with a disabled status. This will be changed at run time when an existing account is selected or a new account name is entered into the editable portion of the Account Name combo box. The first step is to create the Delete button. Click the button tool in App Studio's control palette and drag a button control to coordinates 129, 56. Check that the dimensions of the button are approximately 50x14 DLUs. Then double click the button and change its General properties to correspond with those shown in Figure 5-29.

Figure 5-29
Delete button General
properties

9. Drag another button to coordinate position 129, 72 and ensure that its dimensions are 50x14. Double click the button and change its properties to correspond to those shown in Figure 5-30.

10. Drag one last button to the dialog from the control palette and position it at coordinates 129, 88. Check to be sure that its dimen-

Figure 5-30
Add button General
properties

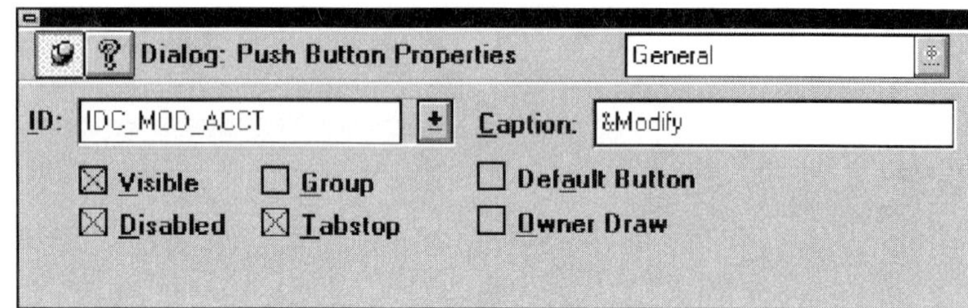

Figure 5-31
Modify button General
properties

sions are 50x14. Double click the button and change its properties
to correspond with those shown in Figure 5-31.

11. The final stage of construction of the dialog involves creation of the
group box to hold the radio buttons, which identify the type of
account, and then the placement of the radio buttons themselves.
The first step of this stage is to click on the group icon in the control palette and drag a group control onto the dialog. Change its
position to the coordinates 2, 75 and its dimensions to 113x57.
Then double click on the group and change its properties to correspond with those shown in Figure 5-32.

Figure 5-32
Account Type group
General properties

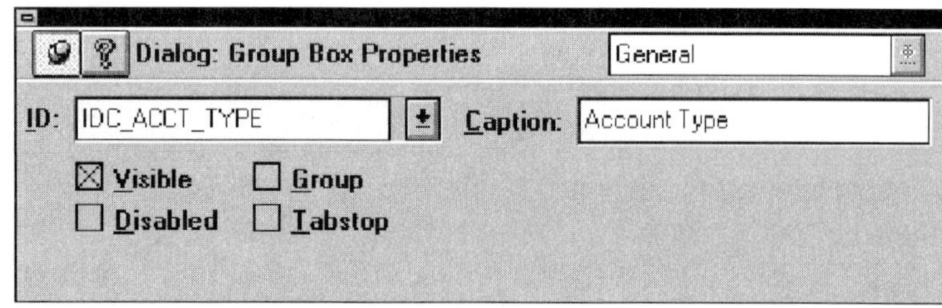

12. The next several steps place radio buttons into the Account Type
group described in the foregoing step. Each button is dragged from
the control palette and placed onto the dialog within the group's
borders. The first button is placed at coordinates 10, 89 with
dimensions of 46x10. The General properties for the Checking
button are shown in Figure 5-33.

Figure 5-33
Checking button
General properties

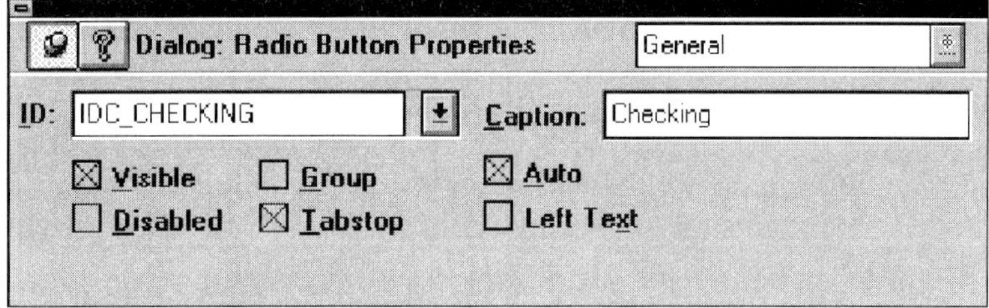

13. Drag another button from the control palette, place it at the coordinates of 10, 103, and change its dimensions to 42x10. Double click the button and change the properties to correspond to those shown in Figure 5-34.

Figure 5-34
Savings button General properties

14. Drag another button from the control palette, place it at the coordinates 10, 116, and then change its dimensions to 35x10. Double click the button to display its General properties and change the settings to correspond with what is shown in Figure 5-35.

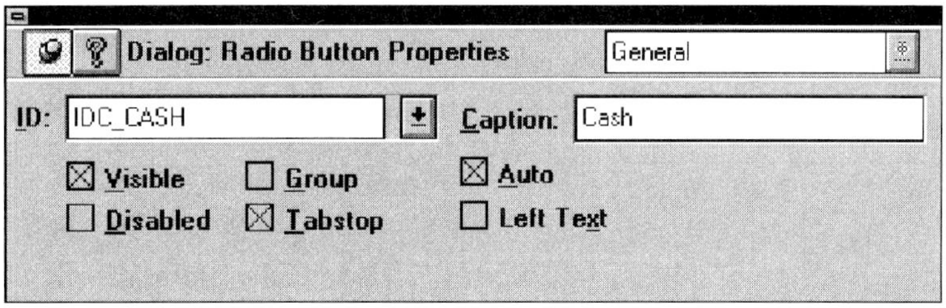

Figure 5-35
Cash button General properties

15. Drag another button from the control palette, place it at the coordinates 65, 89, and then change its dimensions to 35x10. Double click the button and change its properties to correspond with those shown in Figure 5-36.

16. Drag another button from the control palette and place it at the coordinates 65, 103, and then change its dimensions to 38x10. Double click the button and change its properties to correspond with those shown in Figure 5-37.

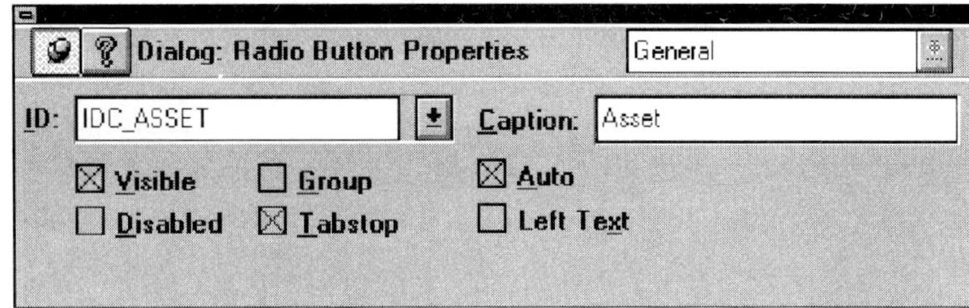

Figure 5-36
Asset button General
properties

Figure 5-37
Liability button General
properties

17. Drag the final button from the control palette, place it at the coordinates 65, 116, and then change its dimensions to 48x10. Double click the button to display its properties window and change the properties to correspond to those shown in Figure 5-38.

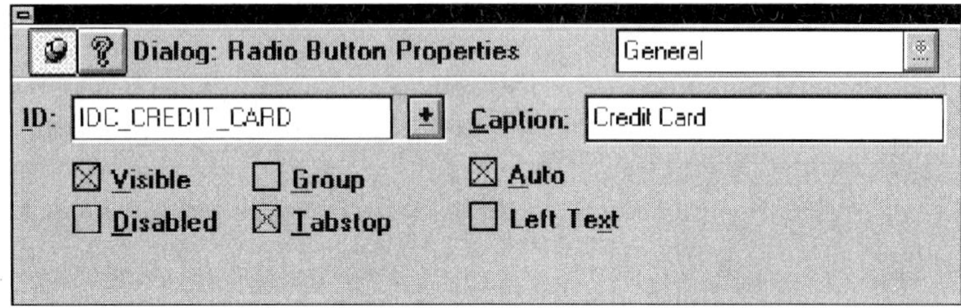

Figure 5-38
Credit Card button
General properties

This concludes the procedure for creating the Edit Account dialog. Save the changes to your resources so that you don't lose the results of any of the foregoing steps and close the dialog editor by using the Ctrl-F4 keyboard shortcut. The next series of sections focuses on the creation of classes and member functions to support message handling for the new Category view and Edit Account dialog. This is a very good time to take a break and review what has been accomplished so far in this series of additions to the Keepit project.

Resource Creation Recap

In the foregoing section, we created a new menu, called Account, which provides the means to invoke the Edit Account dialog, and serves as a menu from which individual account views can be chosen. The accounts will be added to the menu, dynamically, as the user defines them, from the Edit Account dialog. The account names for the new accounts will be entered into the menu, below the separator line.

We have also created a new command in the View menu, which when chosen will permit us to create the Category form view, in which transaction categories can be added, modified, and deleted.

In addition to the menus, we also created the Edit Account dialog and the Category view. The former of these is a true dialog and must be used and then dismissed before other actions can take place. In contrast to this, the Category view can remain open, once chosen, and the user will be able to add, modify, or delete category names at any time during execution of the Keepit application.

The addition of the menus, dialog, and view are preparatory to the addition of command message handlers and classes to support these elements. We will describe those additions in the next section. The custom code to implement the new features fully will be presented in Chapter 6.

Creating Support for the Category View

Whether you are continuing on from the previous steps or have taken a break and are now ready to proceed with the next phase, make sure that App Studio is still running and that you are looking at its main screen, which contains the list of resource types in the left pane and the list of resources of the selected type (if any) in the right pane. Choose Dialog as the resource type of interest by clicking on it or by navigating to it with the arrow keys on the keyboard. Next, double click on the dialog resource whose name is IDD_CATEGORIES. This will cause the Category view, shown in Figure 5-7, to be displayed. When the Category view is being displayed, you will be ready to commence the next tutorial.

Creating the New CCatList Class and Its Member Variables

Before beginning the tutorial, it will be worthwhile to explain what we intend to accomplish in the following steps. Although in the previous sections we have created the Category view, we have not yet written any code to implement its functions. The ClassWizard tool will be used to create the skeleton code for a new class, derived from the MFC CFormView base class, which will provide a lot of the functionality we require of the new view. In addition, while using the ClassWizard, we will create member variables in the new class, which will allow us to directly address the various controls in the view. The procedure for doing so is as follows:

1. With the Category view on the screen, while using the App Studio tool, pull down the Resource menu and choose the ClassWizard tool (or use the Ctrl-W keyboard shortcut). ClassWizard will begin execution and will display the Add Class dialog shown in Figure 5-39. Fill in the fields of the dialog, making sure to specify the class name as CCatList, and the names of the header and source code files as **catlist.h**, and **catlist.cpp**, respectively. Also, make sure that the base class for this new class is CFormView, and then click the Create Class button.

Figure 5-39
Add Class dialog for the
IDD_CATEGORIES

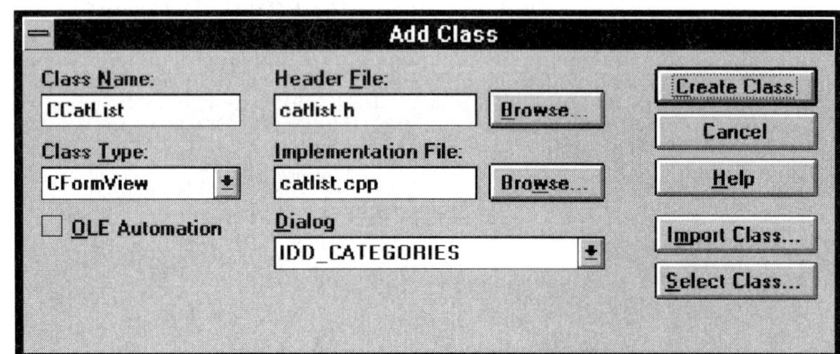

2. When the foregoing step is complete, the ClassWizard tool will have created skeleton source and header files for the new class. The next task is to define member variables for accessing the view's controls from within the program code. To begin this process, click the Member Variables tab in the ClassWizard's main window, click the IDC_CAT_LIST Control ID, then click the Add Variable button and fill in the fields of the Add Member Variable dialog as shown in Figure 5-40. This adds a member variable called m_CatList, which when loaded with the corresponding control's handle by the dynamic data exchange (DDE) facility, can be used to address the list box control directly. When the Add Member Variable dialog has been filled in as shown in the foregoing figure, you can click the OK button to dismiss the dialog.

3. Click to select the IDC_TAXABLE Object ID and then click the Add Variable button once again. This time you will be adding a member variable to address the Taxable checkbox in the view. Fill in the fields for the m_Taxable member variable as shown in Figure 5-41. Note that although this variable is a checkbox, it is described as type CButton for purposes of identifying the MFC class in which the characteristics of the control are implemented. (As an aside, push buttons, checkboxes, and radio buttons are all classified as buttons and are implemented in the CButton class.) Dismiss the dialog after you have filled in the fields, by clicking its OK button.

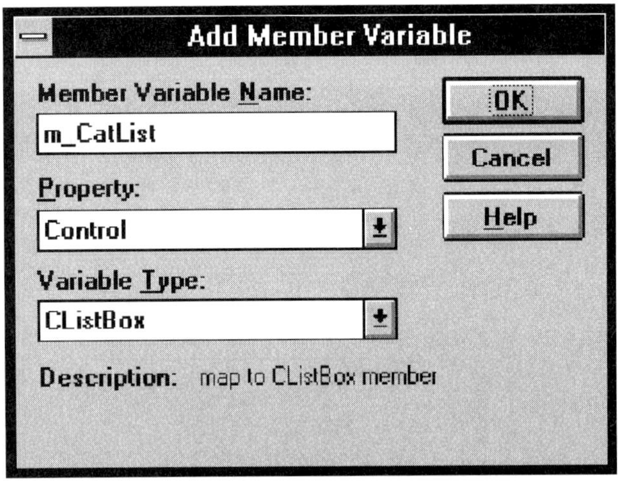

Figure 5-40
Adding the m_CatList
member variable

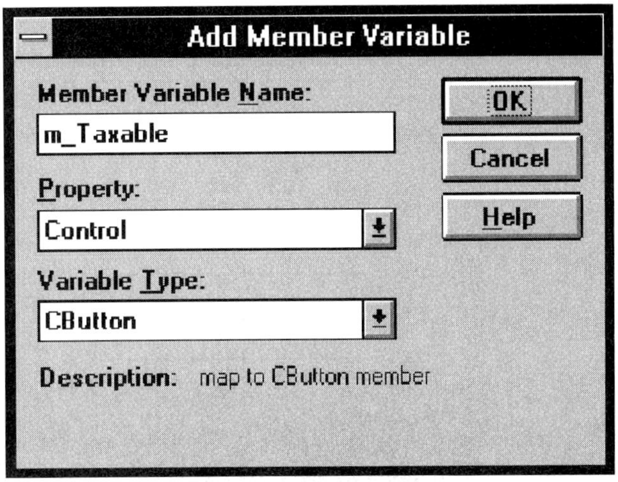

Figure 5-41
Adding the m_Taxable
member variable

4. Add another variable by selecting the IDC_ADD object and then clicking on the Add Variable button in the ClassWizard's main window. Change the settings to match those shown in Figure 5-42. Note that the m_AddButton member variable has a Control property and that its type is CButton. Click OK.

5. Create another variable by selecting the IDC_DELETE object and then click on the Add Variable button. Change the settings to correspond with those shown in Figure 5-43. The m_DeleteButton variable is also a CButton with a Control property. Click OK to dismiss the dialog.

6. Create another button by selecting the IDC_MODIFY object, clicking the Add Variable button, and then filling in the dialog with the set-

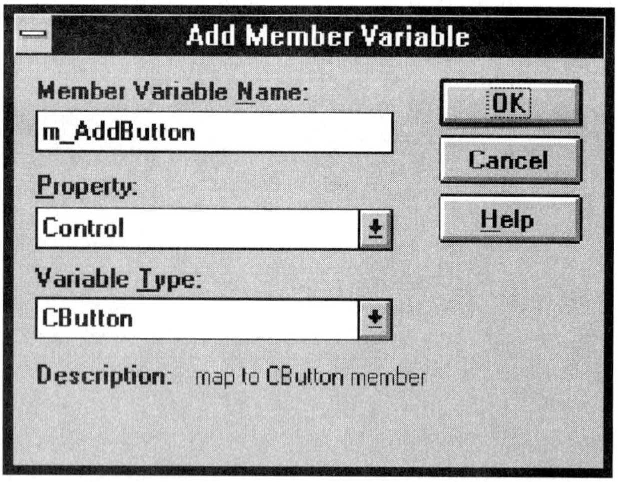

Figure 5-42
Creating the
m_AddButton member
variable

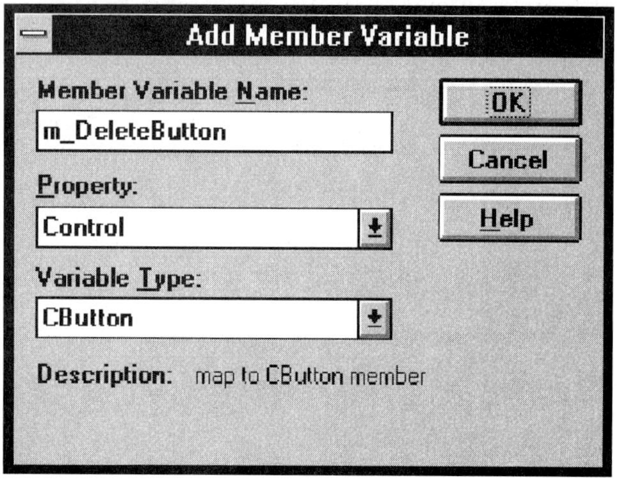

Figure 5-43
Creating the
m_DeleteButton
member variable

tings shown in Figure 5-44. This is the member variable called `m_ModifyButton`. It is also a CButton, with the Control property.

7. The final member variable provides access to the Category edit text control. Create this variable by selecting the IDC_CATEGORY object, clicking on the Add Variable button, and then changing the settings to correspond with those shown in Figure 5-45, and then click OK to dismiss the dialog. The `m_Category` variable allows us to read or write text from/to the control.

This concludes the addition of member variables to the newly created CCatList class. The final appearance of the ClassWizard's main window is shown in Figure 5-46.

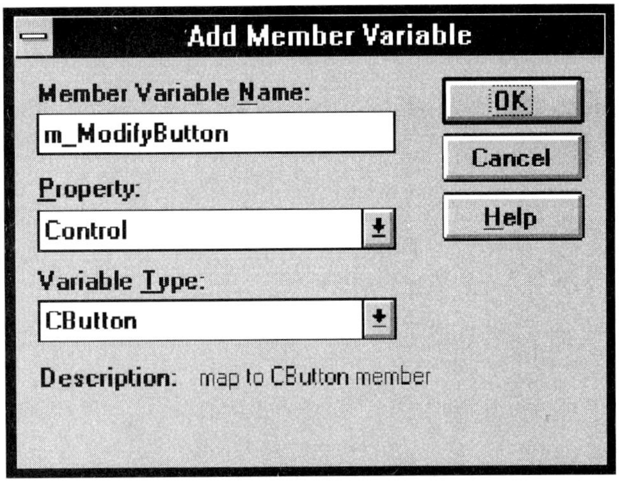

Figure 5-44
Adding the
m_ModifyButton
member variable

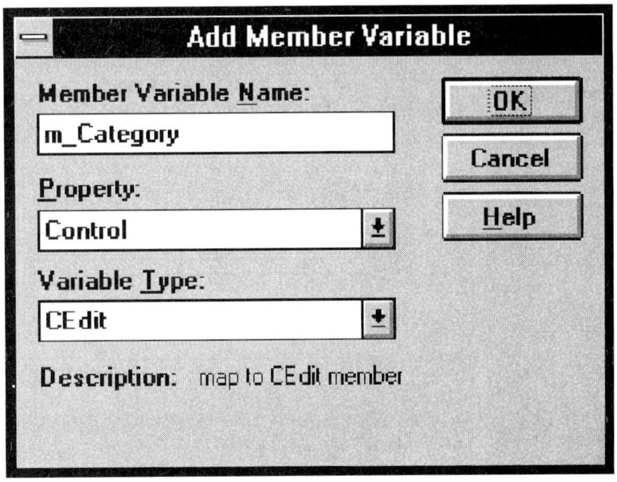

Figure 5-45
Adding the m_Category
member variable

The next series of steps focus on the addition of handlers for the various messages that can occur while the user is manipulating the controls in this view. For example, when the user selects an existing category, the view object will receive an LBN_SELCHANGE message from the framework. Similarly, when the user has entered a new category and tabs to the next control, an EN_KILLFOCUS message will be received. We will be adding handlers (member functions) for these and other messages pertinent to the operation of the new Category view.

Creating the CCatList Message Handler Functions

ClassWizard will be used to generate prototype handlers for the various messages that we will need to handle in the course of implementing the

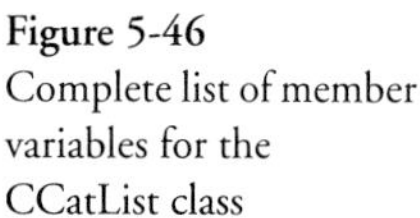

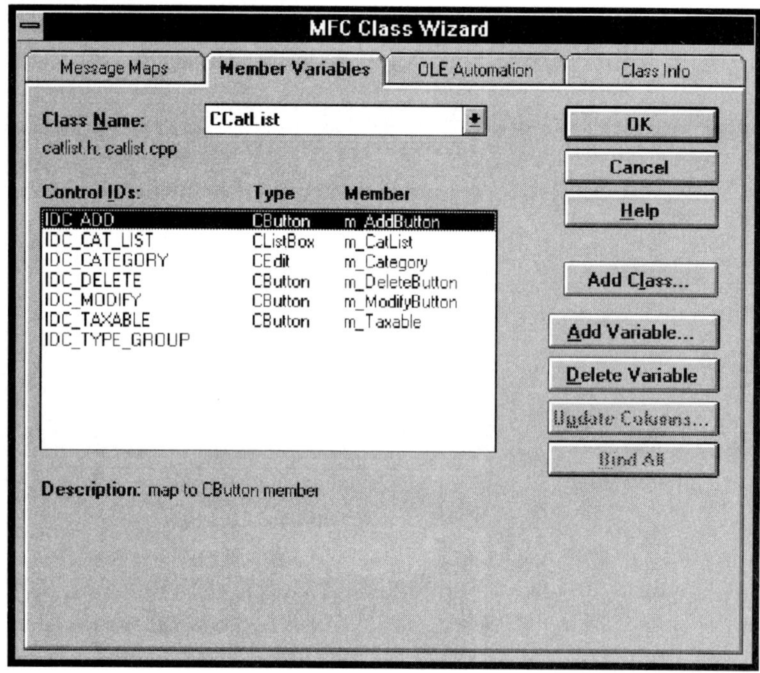

full functionality of the view. The procedure to create these new sections of code is as follows:

1. With the main ClassWizard window still in full view, click on the Message Maps tab and then click on the IDC_ADD entry in the "Object IDs" list (top left pane in the main ClassWizard window). You should now see two possible messages in the top right pane, either of which can be created by this control. Click once on the BN_CLICKED message in the "Messages" pane and then click the Add Function button, which should be enabled at this point. When doing so, you will be presented with a dialog that allows you to determine the name of the message handler member function to be inserted into your CCatList class's source code. Change the name to OnAdd, as shown in Figure 5-47. Click OK to dismiss the dialog. You'll note that the new OnAdd handler name has become associated with the ON_IDC_ADD:BN_CLICKED message in the bottom pane of the ClassWizard's main window.

2. Click on the IDC_DELETE object type in the top left pane, click on the BN_CLICKED message type, and then click the Add Function button. Change the name of this handler to OnDelete, as shown in Figure 5-48, and then click OK to dismiss the dialog.

3. Click on the IDC_MODIFY object type in the top left pane, click on the BN_CLICKED message type, and then click on the Add Function

Figure 5-47
Creating the OnAdd
message handler
member function

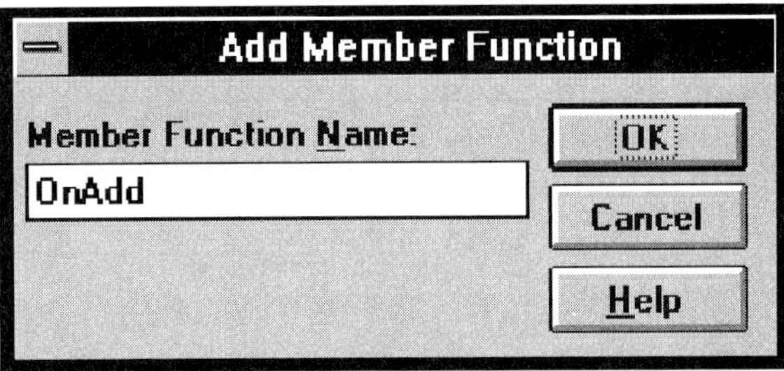

Figure 5-48
Adding the OnDelete
message handler
member function

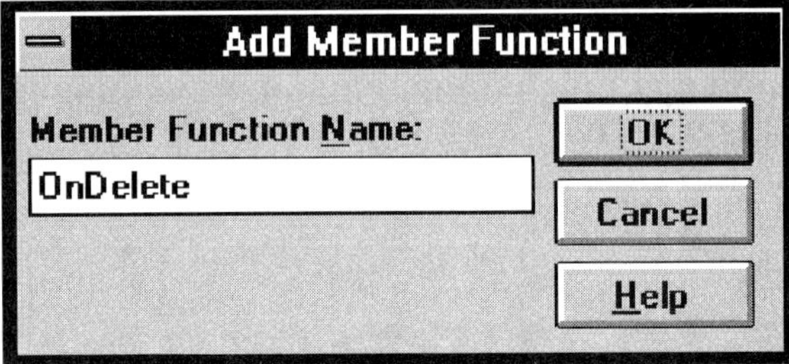

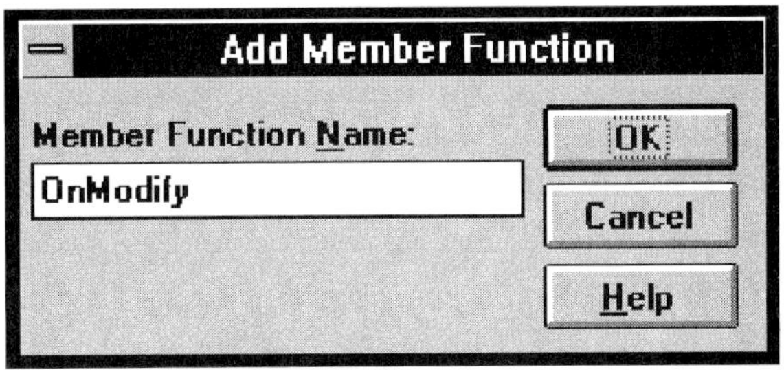

Figure 5-49
Adding the OnModify
message handler
member function

button. Change the name of this handler to OnModify, as shown in Figure 5-49, and then click OK to dismiss the dialog.

4. Click on the IDC_CATLIST object type in the top left pane of the Class Wizard's main window, click on the LBN_SELCHANGE message type in the right pane (indicating you want to be notified when the user makes a selection in the list box), click on the Add Function button to display the Add Member Function dialog and change the handler's name to OnSelectCat, as shown in Figure 5-50.

5. Finally, click on the IDC_CATEGORY object type in the left pane, click on the EN_KILLFOCUS message type, click the Add Function button and change the handler's name to OnKillfocusCategory, as shown in Figure 5-51.

This concludes the steps for creating handlers for the various messages that we wish to intercept in the newly created CCatList class. Note that whenever the ClassWizard has been called upon to create a member vari-

Figure 5-50
Adding the OnSelectCat
message handler
member function

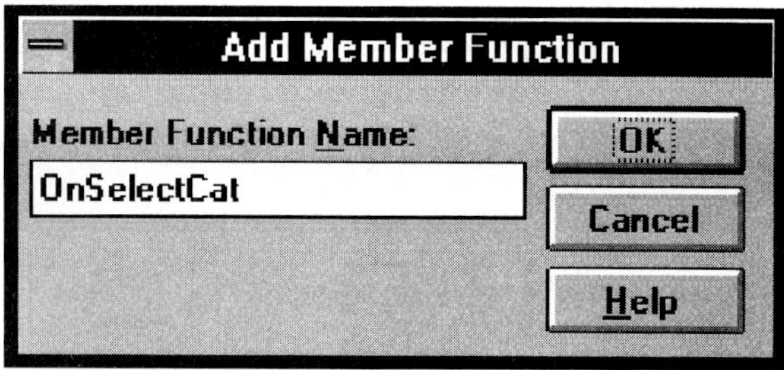

Figure 5-51
Adding the
OnKillfocusCategory
message handler
member function

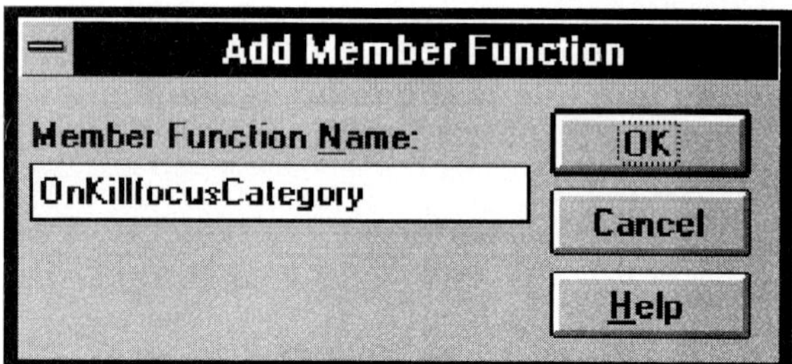

able or a handler member function, it has updated both the **catlist.h** header file and also the **catlist.cpp** source file to reflect these additions. Should you choose to remove a handler at some time in the future, ClassWizard will display a dialog indicating that although it will remove the handler from the message map, you will be responsible for manually deleting the code that comprises the handler itself. Before moving on to the next step, take a look at Figure 5-52, which shows all of the messages to which we have attached handlers (displayed in the bottom pane of the figure).

At this point in the tutorial, you may want to take a break to rest and review the results of your efforts. Although we will be examining the wizard-created code, you may want to look at the **catlist.h** header file and **catlist.cpp** source file to see what has been generated into these. The first step in doing so is to dismiss the ClassWizard by clicking the OK button at the top right of the main window. It is also a good idea to save the resource file at this time by pulling down the File menu in App Studio and choosing the Save command. You can then either exit from the App Studio application or switch to the Visual C++ workbench to open the aforementioned source and header files.

Creating Support for the Edit Account Dialog

The Edit Account dialog is shown in Figure 5-20. This is a true modal dialog, which is used to create new accounts, edit accounts, or modify existing accounts. Unlike the Category view, which the user may elect to

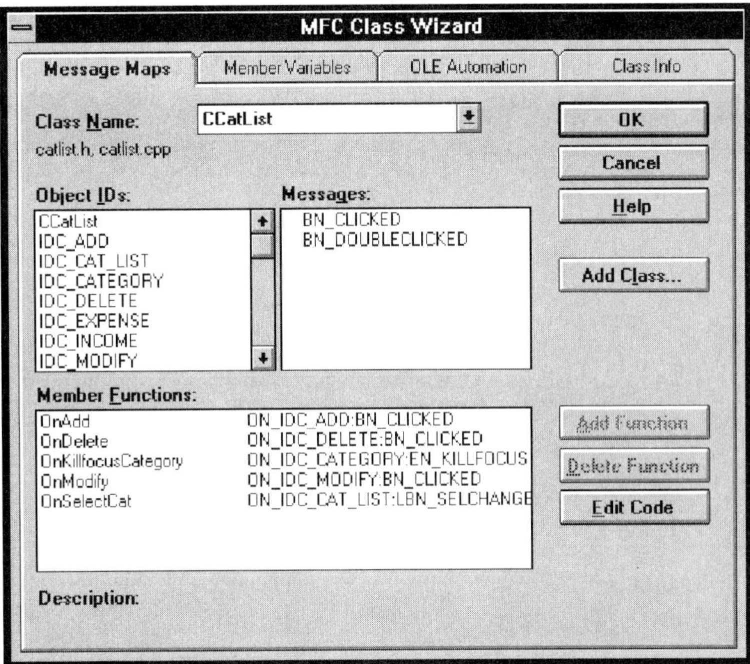

allow to remain on the screen, for reference to valid category names, the Account dialog is intended to be used and then dismissed. Because of this, we have created it as a modal dialog. This means that while the dialog is being displayed, the user is prevented from taking any other actions until the dialog has been dismissed by clicking either its OK or Cancel button. If the Cancel button has been clicked, the changes made to the accounts will not be applied. Only if the OK button has been clicked will the changes be applied to the list of accounts.

The custom code described in the next chapter will implement a list of accessible accounts, below the separator in the Account menu, from which list they can be chosen. The first step in providing support for the Edit Account dialog is to create a new class, member variables, and message handlers for the visual elements.

Creating the New CEditAcct Class and Its Member Variables

Prior to commencing the tutorial to create the new CEditAcct class and its member variables, you should invoke the App Studio tool, select Dialog as the resource type to edit, and then open the dialog resource by double clicking on the IDD_EDIT_ACCOUNT resource name in the right-hand pane of App Studio's main window. This will cause the Edit Account dialog to be displayed. You can now begin the tutorial to create member variables for the dialog, as follows:

1. With the Edit Account dialog on your screen, pull down the Resource menu and choose the ClassWizard command (or use the ALT-R W keyboard shortcut). This will cause the ClassWizard tool to be executed, displaying its main window on the screen.

2. The Add Class dialog should be displayed automatically by the ClassWizard tool. Fill in the fields in the dialog as shown in Figure 5-53. Note that the class name is CEditAcct and the header and source files are **editacct.h** and **editacct.cpp**, respectively. Click the Create Class button to dismiss the dialog.

Figure 5-53
Creating the CEditAcct class and its header and source files

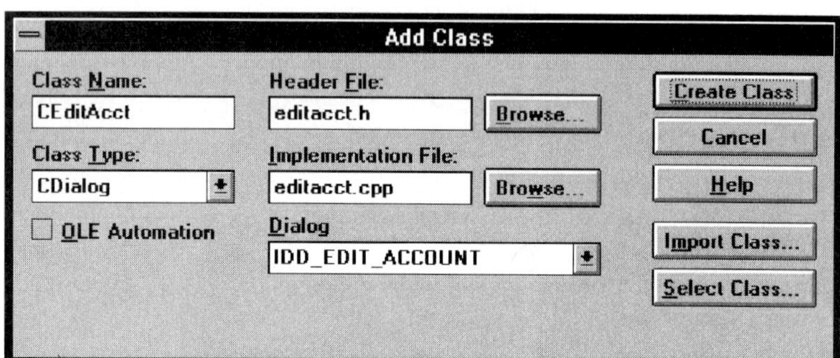

3. The next series of steps add member variables to the CEditAcct class so that we can access the controls in the dialog from within the CEditAcct's member functions. Display the member variables by clicking the Member Variables tab in the ClassWizard's main window. This will display a view of the ClassWizard's main window in which all of the controls are listed by their resource IDs. Click the object whose ID is IDC_ACCT_NAME, click the Add Variable button to display a new dialog, and then fill in its fields so that they correspond to what is shown in Figure 5-54. Note that we've created a variable called m_Accounts, which refers to the combo box and is of type Control. This will allow us to refer to the list of accounts directly. Click the OK button to dismiss the Add Variable dialog.

4. With the Edit Member Variables window still on the screen, select the IDC_DESCRIPTION object, click the Add Variable button once again, and then fill in the dialog's fields so that they correspond to what is shown in Figure 5-55. This variable is named m_szDescription and is a variable whose property is Value, and whose type is CString. Click the OK button to dismiss the Add Member Variable dialog.

5. The next several variables refer to button controls in the dialog. Select the IDC_ADD_ACCT object, click the Add Variable button, and then complete the entry to correspond with the values shown in Fig-

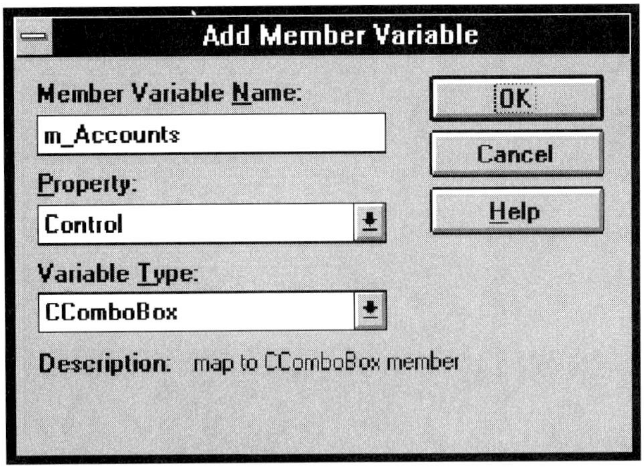

Figure 5-54
Adding the m_Accounts
member variable

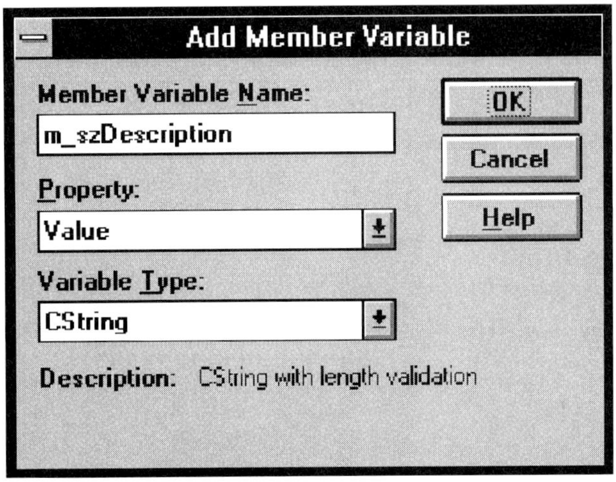

Figure 5-55
Adding the
m_szDescription
member variable

ure 5-56. This variable is named `m_Add`, and it allows us to access the Add control directly. Click the OK button to dismiss the dialog.

6. Select the IDC_MOD_ACCT object, click the Add Variable button once again, and then complete the Add Member Variable dialog so that its contents correspond to what is shown in Figure 5-57. This variable is named `m_Modify`, and it will allow us to manipulate the state of the Modify button in the dialog. Click the OK button to dismiss the dialog.

7. Select the IDC_DEL_ACCT object, click the Add Variable button, and then fill in the dialog's fields so that their contents correspond to what is shown in Figure 5-58. This variable is named `m_Delete`, and it will provide access to the Delete button in the dialog. Click the OK button to dismiss the Add Member Variable dialog.

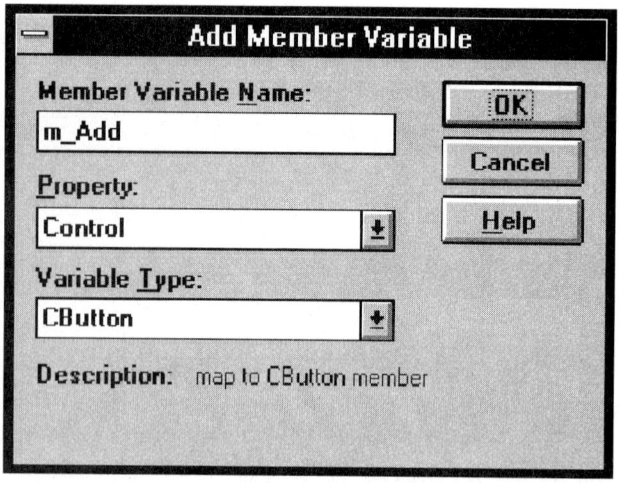

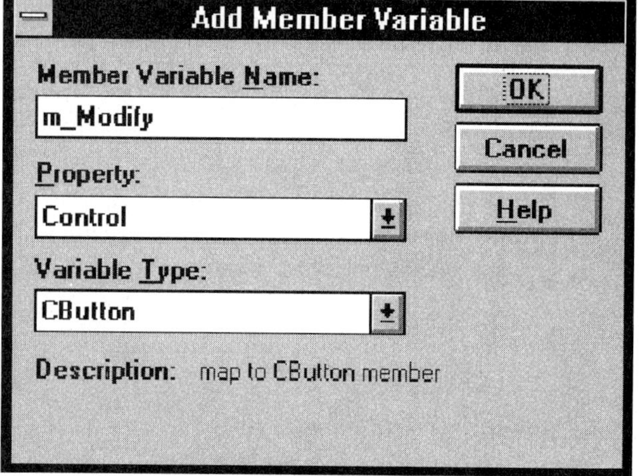

Figure 5-56
Adding the m_Add
member variable

Figure 5-57
Adding the m_Modify
member variable

8. Select the IDC_DESCRIPTION object, click the Add Variable button, and then fill in the fields so that their contents correspond to what is shown in Figure 5-59. This variable is named m_Description, and it provides access to the contents of the edit control whose resource ID is IDC_DESCRIPTION. This variable is not to be confused with the one named m_szDescription, which is a string variable intended to hold the contents of the Description field. The current variable (m_Description) has a Control property and is of type CEdit. Click the OK button to dismiss the dialog after you have completed the entry of the variable's definition.

9. Select the IDOK object and then click the Add Variable button one last time to add a member variable that references the OK button in the dialog. Fill in the fields to correspond with what is shown in Fig-

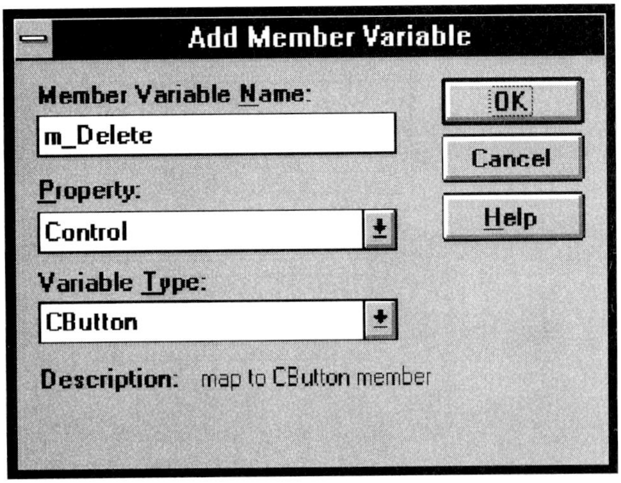

Figure 5-58
Adding the m_Delete
member variable

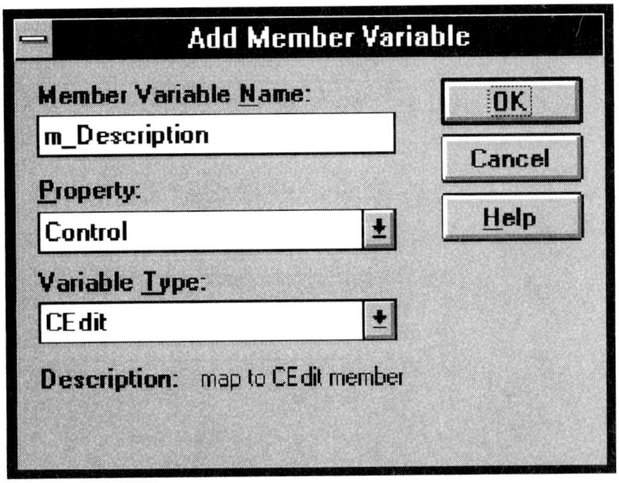

Figure 5-59
Adding the
m_Description member
variable

ure 5-60. We will use this control to change the state of the OK button, so as to disallow the entry of an illegal account entry or modification should the user attempt to make such an error. Click the OK button to dismiss the Add Member Variable dialog, click the Close button to dismiss the Edit Member Variables window. We will leave the ClassWizard's main window open for reference in the next series of steps.

This completes the steps to create member variables for the CEditAcct class. The complete list of variable assignments is shown in Figure 5-61. Note that all have the Control property, with the exception of the `m_szDescription` variable.

Now that this set of steps is complete, you may wish to take a break and review the variables we have created for the CEditAcct class and the ac-

Figure 5-60
Adding the m_OK
member variable

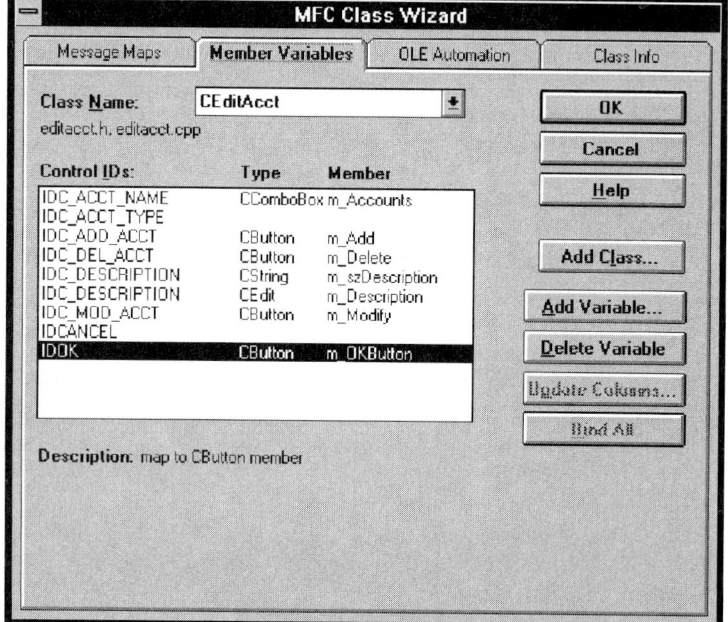

cess each of them provides. In the next tutorial, we will be creating handlers, for which skeleton code will be written, automatically, by the
ClassWizard tool. Whenever the ClassWizard makes changes to your
source or header files, it always saves the files. You are not required to do
this manually. You can dismiss the ClassWizard by clicking the OK button in its main window, or you can leave it running, in preparation for
the tutorial in the next section. You may also wish to exit the App Studio
tool. If so, you can do so by choosing Save from its File menu and then
choosing Exit. At that point, Visual C++ can be exited.

Creating the CEditAcct Message Handler Functions

This section describes the assignment of handlers for some of the messages sent by the Edit Account dialog to its CEditAcct object when the user interacts with the dialog's controls. We are interested in only five of the possible messages in this case. The procedure for creating the skeleton handlers and their association with the appropriate messages is accomplished using the ClassWizard tool. The steps for creating the message handlers are as follows:

1. We assume that the ClassWizard tool is still executing and that its main window is currently displayed on your screen. In case you are starting the program again after taking a break, launch the App Studio tool by choosing it from the Visual C++ Tools menu, choose Dialogs as the resource type to view, then open the dialog whose resource name is IDD_EDIT_ACCT. Then, to invoke the ClassWizard, pull down the Resource menu and choose the ClassWizard command (or use the ALT-R w keyboard shortcut).

2. When the ClassWizard's main window has opened, with the Message Maps tab selected, click on the object named IDC_ACCT_NAME, scroll in the list of messages in the right-hand pane to expose the CBN_SELCHANGE message, and then click on the Add Function button. Fill in the name of the handler to correspond with what is shown in Figure 5-62. Click the OK button to dismiss the Add Member Function dialog.

Figure 5-62
Adding the
OnSelchangeAcctName
message handler

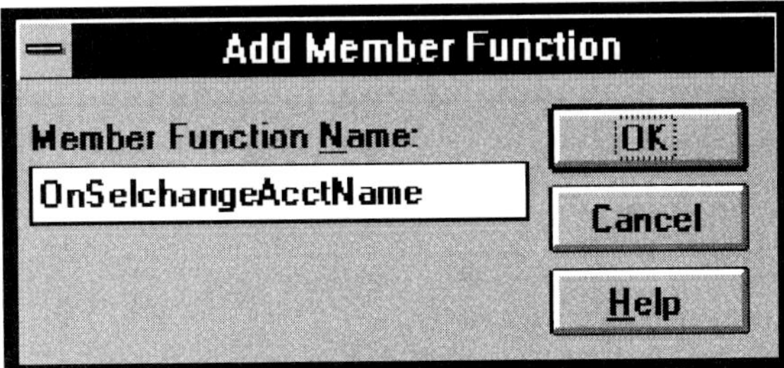

3. The next step is to add another handler for the IDC_ACCT_NAME object. In this case, it is for the CBN_KILLFOCUS message. Click on that message type and then click the Add Function button. Fill in the handler name as shown in Figure 5-63. Click the OK button to dismiss the Add Member Function dialog.

4. Next, scroll down the list of objects and click on the one named IDC_DEL_ACCT and then click on the BN_CLICKED message. Click the Add Function button, fill in the handler name in the Add Mem-

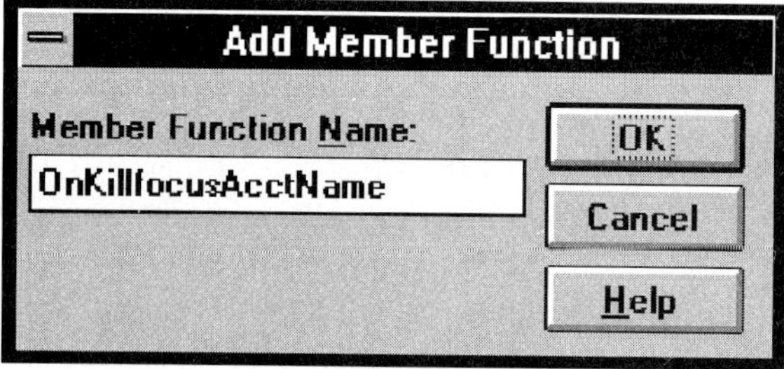

Figure 5-63
Adding the
OnKillfocusAcctName
message handler

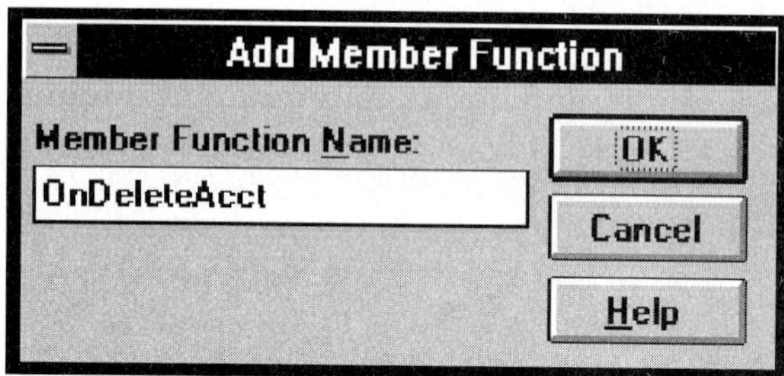

Figure 5-64
Adding the
OnDeleteAcct message
handler

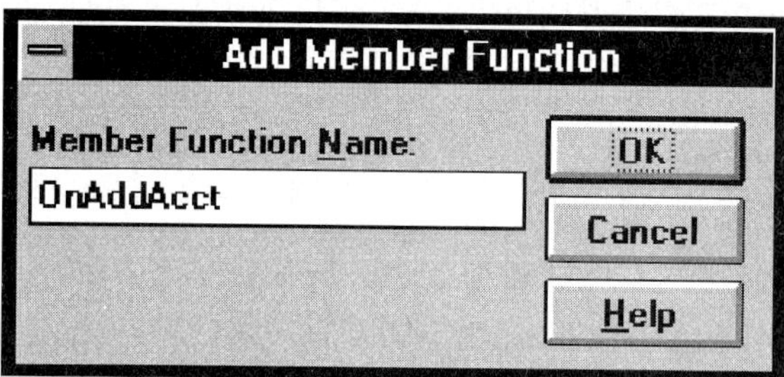

Figure 5-65
Adding the OnAddAcct
message handler

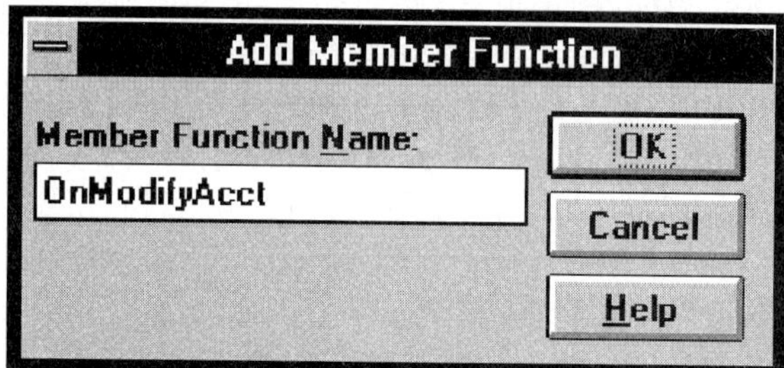

Figure 5-66
Adding the
OnModifyAcct message
handler

ber Function dialog, as shown in Figure 5-64, and then click OK to
dismiss the dialog.

5. Click on the IDC_ADD_ACCT object, click on the message named
BN_CLICKED, and then click the Add Function button. Change the
handler name to correspond with what is shown in Figure 5-65 and
then click OK to dismiss the dialog.

6. Finally, click on the IDC_MOD_ACCT object, click on the message
named BN_CLICKED, fill in the handler name as shown in Figure

5-66, and then click OK to dismiss the Add Member Function dialog. The bottom pane of the main ClassWizard window should now show all of the handler names and the messages to which they have been assigned.

This completes the steps to create handlers for the messages that we intend to accept from the Edit Account dialog. The final appearance of the ClassWizard's main window is shown in Figure 5-67. Click the OK button in the ClassWizard's main window to quit the tool, save the resources by choosing Save from the App Studio's File menu, and then exit the App Studio tool by choosing Exit from its File menu.

Figure 5-67
Completed list of message handler assignments

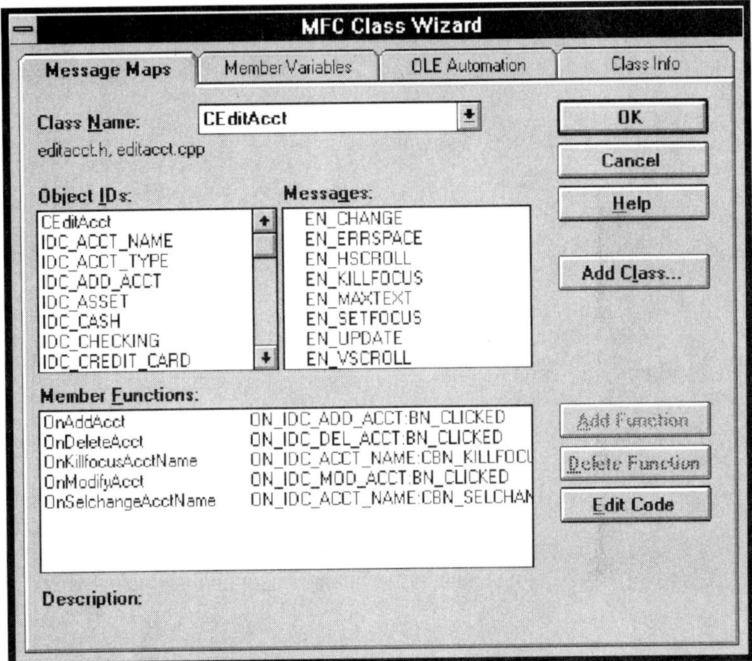

At this point, we are nearly finished with the assignment of message handlers for the new version of our application. The next section covers the creation of the final set of handlers.

Adding Command Handlers to the CKeepitDoc Class

As you may recall, in the first series of steps, we added the new Account menu with its Edit command and then added the Categories command to the View menu using the App Studio tool (see the section titled *Additions and Changes to the Menu Bars* on pages 119–122).

At this point we need to add handlers for the WM_COMMAND messages that are generated when the user chooses one of these commands. We wish for these message handlers to be located within the CKeepitDoc class, mainly because the document will be responsible for providing the data required in both the Category view and the Edit Account dialog. These objects will be created when the user chooses the corresponding command from either the View or Account menu. The steps for creating the new message handlers are as follows:

1. We are assuming that both the ClassWizard and App Studio tools have been exited, as indicated at the end of the previous procedure. The Keepit project window or one of the source files should be open at this point. Invoke the ClassWizard by pulling down the Browse menu and choosing the ClassWizard command (or by using the ALT-B w keyboard shortcut).

2. When the ClassWizard's main window is displayed, make sure that the Message Maps tab has been selected, click the arrow at the right of the Class Name combo box to drop it down, and then choose the CKeepitDoc class.

3. When the CKeepitDoc class has been chosen, all of the objects that are pertinent to that class will be shown in the Object IDs pane in the ClassWizard dialog. The first message handler we want to create should be associated with the ID_ACCT_EDIT object. Click on that object name, click on the COMMAND message in the right-hand pane, and then click the Add Function button and enter a handler name to correspond with what is shown in Figure 5-68.

Figure 5-68
Adding the OnAcctEdit
message handler

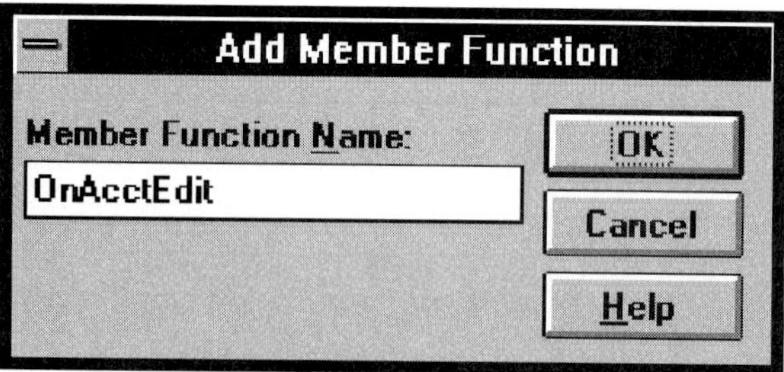

4. Next, scroll down the object list, click on the ID_VIEW_CATEGORIES object, click on the COMMAND message, click the Add Function button, and then enter the handler name in the Add Member Function dialog, as shown in Figure 5-69. Click OK to dismiss the dialog.

This completes the steps to define message handlers for the new menu commands. The final appearance of the ClassWizard's main window is shown in Figure 5-70. Note that only two message handlers have been

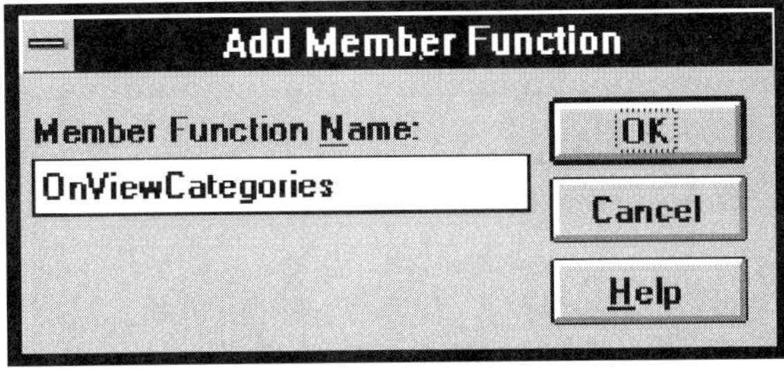

Figure 5-69
Adding the
OnViewCategories
message handler

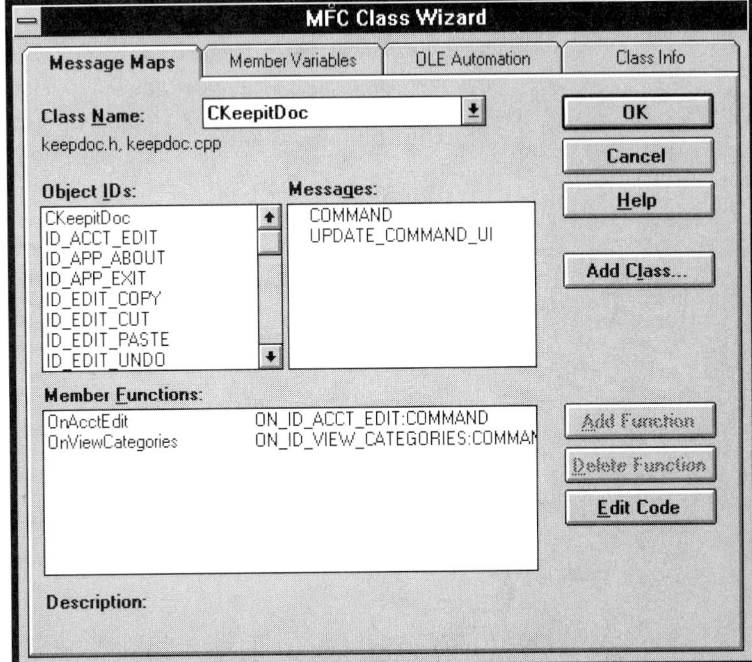

Figure 5-70
Complete list of message
handlers for the
CKeepitDoc class

added to this class. In later stages of construction, the Keepit application
will contain additional handlers to support the new features.

Examining the Newly Generated Code

We will be customizing the wizard-created code, which was produced by
following the foregoing procedures, in the next chapter; however, it will
be worthwhile to examine the skeleton code in the form in which it has
been generated automatically. The following sections will show the
header and source files of the two new classes we have created (CCatList
and CEditAcct), as well as the additions to the CKeepitDoc class. For
reference, the header and source files for the CCatList class are **catlist.h**
and **catlist.cpp**, while those for the CEditAcct class are **editacct.h** and

editacct.cpp, respectively. Of course, the files associated with the CKeep-itDoc class are **keepdoc.h** and **keepdoc.cpp**, for the header and sources, respectively.

Examining the CCatList Code

The CCatList class was created when we added the Category view to the project, using the Dialog editor in the App Studio tool. This procedure is described on pages 122–128. The result of following the procedure to create the new view and then following the procedures to add member variables and message handlers to the class (shown on pages 135–142) is the creation of a new header file named **catlist.h** and a new source file named **catlist.cpp**. The newly generated code for these files is as follows:

CatList.h Header File

The wizard-created code in the **catlist.h** header file is as follows:

```cpp
// catlist.h : header file
//
/////////////////////////////////////////////////////////////////
// CCatList form view

#ifndef __AFXEXT_H__
#include <afxext.h>
#endif

class CCatList : public CFormView
{
    DECLARE_DYNCREATE(CCatList)
protected:
    CCatList(); // protected constructor

// Form Data
public:
    //{{AFX_DATA(CCatList)
    enum { IDD = IDD_CATEGORIES };
    CEdit       m_Category;
    CButton     m_ModifyButton;
    CButton     m_DeleteButton;
    CButton     m_AddButton;
    CButton     m_Taxable;
    CListBox    m_CatList;
    //}}AFX_DATA

// Attributes
public:

// Operations
public:

// Implementation
protected:
    virtual ~CCatList();
    // DDX/DDV support
    virtual void DoDataExchange(CDataExchange* pDX);
    // Generated message map functions
    //{{AFX_MSG(CCatList)
    afx_msg void OnAdd();
```

```cpp
   afx_msg void OnDelete();
   afx_msg void OnModify();
   afx_msg void OnSelectCat();
   afx_msg void OnKillfocusCategory();
   //}}AFX_MSG
   DECLARE_MESSAGE_MAP()
};
```

In the foregoing, the member variables are declared within special Class-Wizard comments that indicate they are to be assigned values via the DDX/DDV dialog data exchange functions. The exchange of data between the controls in a dialog or form view takes place when the DoDataExchange member function is called by the framework.

The message handler member functions are similarly enclosed by the AFX_MSG comments in the foregoing code listing. The ClassWizard will manage all message handler entries, which are contained within those special comments. Make sure when you modify the code not to delete or change any of the statements within these special comment blocks.

CatList.cpp Source File

The wizard-created code for the **catlist.cpp** source file is as follows:

```cpp
// catlist.cpp : implementation file
//

#include "stdafx.h"
#include "keepit.h"
#include "catlist.h"

#ifdef _DEBUG
#undef THIS_FILE
static char BASED_CODE THIS_FILE[] = __FILE__;
#endif

/////////////////////////////////////////////////////////////////////
// CCatList
IMPLEMENT_DYNCREATE(CCatList, CFormView)
CCatList::CCatList()
    : CFormView(CCatList::IDD)
{
   //{{AFX_DATA_INIT(CCatList)
     // NOTE: the ClassWizard will add member
     //   initialization here
   //}}AFX_DATA_INIT
}

CCatList::~CCatList()
{
}

void CCatList::DoDataExchange(CDataExchange* pDX)
{
   CFormView::DoDataExchange(pDX);
   //{{AFX_DATA_MAP(CCatList)
   DDX_Control(pDX, IDC_CATEGORY, m_Category);
   DDX_Control(pDX, IDC_MODIFY, m_ModifyButton);
   DDX_Control(pDX, IDC_DELETE, m_DeleteButton);
```

```cpp
    DDX_Control(pDX, IDC_ADD, m_AddButton);
    DDX_Control(pDX, IDC_TAXABLE, m_Taxable);
    DDX_Control(pDX, IDC_CAT_LIST, m_CatList);
    //}}AFX_DATA_MAP
}

BEGIN_MESSAGE_MAP(CCatList, CFormView)
    //{{AFX_MSG_MAP(CCatList)
    ON_BN_CLICKED(IDC_ADD, OnAdd)
    ON_BN_CLICKED(IDC_DELETE, OnDelete)
    ON_BN_CLICKED(IDC_MODIFY, OnModify)
    ON_LBN_SELCHANGE(IDC_CAT_LIST, OnSelectCat)
    ON_EN_KILLFOCUS(IDC_CATEGORY, OnKillfocusCategory)
    //}}AFX_MSG_MAP
END_MESSAGE_MAP()

/////////////////////////////////////////////////////////////////////
// CCatList message handlers


void CCatList::OnAdd()
{
    // TODO: Add your control notification handler code here
}

void CCatList::OnDelete()
{
    // TODO: Add your control notification handler code here
}

void CCatList::OnModify()
{
    // TODO: Add your control notification handler code here
}

void CCatList::OnSelectCat()
{
    // TODO: Add your control notification handler code here
}

void CCatList::OnKillfocusCategory()
{
    // TODO: Add your control notification handler code here
}
```

The foregoing wizard-created code consists of preprocessor directives (such as the `#include` statements), constructor and destructor member functions (which are empty), a DoDataExchange member function for implementing the transfer of handles and data to or from the view's controls, message map definitions for associating messages with handlers, and the set of message handler member functions. Each of the handlers contains a "TO-DO" comment, generated by the ClassWizard tool, which indicates where you need to add additional code to implement the functionality of the member function.

Examining the CEditAcct Code

The wizard-created code for the CEditAcct class implements the Edit Account dialog, whose construction procedure is described on pages

128–134. In addition, the creation of member variables and message handler member functions is described on pages 142–151. The wizard-created code produced as a result of executing the ClassWizard tool and the foregoing procedures is written into the **editacct.h** and **editacct.cpp** header and source files. The newly generated code for these files is as follows:

EditAcct.h Header File

The wizard-created code for the **editacct.h** file is as follows:

```
// editacct.h : header file
//
//////////////////////////////////////////////////////////////////
// CEditAcct dialog

class CEditAcct : public CDialog
{
// Construction
public:
    CEditAcct(CWnd* pParent = NULL);  // standard constructor
// Dialog Data
    //{{AFX_DATA(CEditAcct)
    enum { IDD = IDD_EDIT_ACCOUNT };
    CButton    m_OKButton;
    CEdit      m_Description;
    CButton    m_Delete;
    CButton    m_Modify;
    CButton    m_Add;
    CComboBox m_Accounts;
    CString    m_szDescription;
    //}}AFX_DATA

// Implementation
protected:
    // DDX/DDV support
    virtual void DoDataExchange(CDataExchange* pDX);
    // Generated message map functions
    //{{AFX_MSG(CEditAcct)
    afx_msg void OnSelchangeAcctName();
    afx_msg void OnKillfocusAcctName();
    afx_msg void OnDeleteAcct();
    afx_msg void OnAddAcct();
    afx_msg void OnModifyAcct();
    //}}AFX_MSG
    DECLARE_MESSAGE_MAP()
};
```

In the foregoing class declaration, the CEditAcct class is specified to be derived from the CDialog base class. This relationship was established when the class was created by the ClassWizard tool. As in the header file for the CCatList class, the member variables for the CEditAcct class are contained within special AFX_DATA comments inserted by the ClassWizard tool. The declarations for message handler functions are similarly bracketed by the AFX_MSG comments. The ClassWizard is responsible for management of these declarations.

EditAcct.cpp Source File

The wizard-created code for the **editacct.cpp** source file is as follows:

```cpp
// editacct.cpp : implementation file
//

#include "stdafx.h"
#include "keepit.h"
#include "editacct.h"

#ifdef _DEBUG
#undef THIS_FILE
static char BASED_CODE THIS_FILE[] = __FILE__;
#endif

/////////////////////////////////////////////////////////////
// CEditAcct dialog

CEditAcct::CEditAcct(CWnd* pParent /*=NULL*/)
    : CDialog(CEditAcct::IDD, pParent)
{
    //{{AFX_DATA_INIT(CEditAcct)
    m_szDescription = "";
    //}}AFX_DATA_INIT
}

void CEditAcct::DoDataExchange(CDataExchange* pDX)
{
    CDialog::DoDataExchange(pDX);
    //{{AFX_DATA_MAP(CEditAcct)
    DDX_Control(pDX, IDOK, m_OKButton);
    DDX_Control(pDX, IDC_DESCRIPTION, m_Description);
    DDX_Control(pDX, IDC_DEL_ACCT, m_Delete);
    DDX_Control(pDX, IDC_MOD_ACCT, m_Modify);
    DDX_Control(pDX, IDC_ADD_ACCT, m_Add);
    DDX_Control(pDX, IDC_ACCT_NAME, m_Accounts);
    DDX_Text(pDX, IDC_DESCRIPTION, m_szDescription);
    //}}AFX_DATA_MAP
}

BEGIN_MESSAGE_MAP(CEditAcct, CDialog)
    //{{AFX_MSG_MAP(CEditAcct)
    ON_CBN_SELCHANGE(IDC_ACCT_NAME, OnSelchangeAcctName)
    ON_CBN_KILLFOCUS(IDC_ACCT_NAME, OnKillfocusAcctName)
    ON_BN_CLICKED(IDC_DEL_ACCT, OnDeleteAcct)
    ON_BN_CLICKED(IDC_ADD_ACCT, OnAddAcct)
    ON_BN_CLICKED(IDC_MOD_ACCT, OnModifyAcct)
    //}}AFX_MSG_MAP
END_MESSAGE_MAP()

/////////////////////////////////////////////////////////////
// CEditAcct message handlers

void CEditAcct::OnSelchangeAcctName()
{
    // TODO: Add your control notification handler code here
}
void CEditAcct::OnKillfocusAcctName()
{
    // TODO: Add your control notification handler code here
}

void CEditAcct::OnDeleteAcct()
{
```

```
    // TODO: Add your control notification handler code here
}

void CEditAcct::OnAddAcct()
{
    // TODO: Add your control notification handler code here
}

void CEditAcct::OnModifyAcct()
{
    // TODO: Add your control notification handler code here
}
```

As with the source file for the CCatList class, the wizard-created code for the CEditAcct class consists of preprocessor directives (such as the #include statements) and a constructor member function that, in this case, is not empty, but that initializes the m_szDescription variable to contain an empty string. The code also includes the DoDataExchange member function, which will be invoked by the framework to transfer handles to the dialog's controls into the corresponding member variables. Finally, the foregoing code contains the message map, with its mapping of message identifiers to handler names, followed by the handlers themselves. Also, as with the wizard-created handler member functions for the CCatList class, the ClassWizard has included a comment in each handler function, indicating where new code is to be added to complete the functionality of the member function.

Examining the Additions to the CKeepitDoc Class

When the ClassWizard was used to generate new message handlers into the CKeepitDoc class, to handle the newly added menu commands, it also generated code into the **keepdoc.h** and **keepdoc.cpp** header and source files. The procedure for adding the message handlers to these files is described on pages 151–153. The additions to these files are as follows:

KeepDoc.h Header File Additions

The additions to the **keepdoc.h** header file, to declare new message handler member functions for the menu commands are as follows:

```
// Generated message map functions
protected:
    //{{AFX_MSG(CKeepitDoc)
    afx_msg void OnAcctEdit();
    afx_msg void OnViewCategories();
    //}}AFX_MSG
```

In the foregoing code fragment, we have shown only the new message map member function declarations. A complete listing of the **keepdoc.h** file will be shown in the next chapter.

KeepDoc.cpp Source File Additions

The additions to the **keepdoc.cpp** source file, which correspond to the newly added message handlers, include the new message map definitions, which are as follows:

```
BEGIN_MESSAGE_MAP(CKeepitDoc, CDocument)
  //{{AFX_MSG_MAP(CKeepitDoc)
  ON_COMMAND(ID_ACCT_EDIT, OnAcctEdit)
  ON_COMMAND(ID_VIEW_CATEGORIES, OnViewCategories)
  //}}AFX_MSG_MAP
END_MESSAGE_MAP()
```

As with the other source files, the ClassWizard has also generated prototype message handler member functions, which, for the preceding message map entries, are as follows:

```
/////////////////////////////////////////////////////////////////////
// CKeepitDoc commands

void CKeepitDoc::OnAcctEdit()
{
    // TODO: Add your command handler code here
}

void CKeepitDoc::OnViewCategories()
{
    // TODO: Add your command handler code here
}
```

The wizard-created message handlers will be customized and described fully in the next chapter.

Exercises

1. Why did we choose to define the Category view as a form view, rather than as a modal dialog? Explain your answer.

2. What method could have been used to create the Category view, other than using the App Studio tool? What benefits, compared to other methods, does using the App Studio provide?

3. Why do you think that the Edit Account view was created to be a dialog, rather than a form view? Explain your answer.

4. When the Category view or Edit Account dialog is designed, where are the specifications for these stored? Is it possible to edit the specifications by hand, using the Visual C++ editor? Explain why performing manual edits of the information is sometimes useful.

5. What is the purpose of adding member variables to the Category view or Edit Account dialog using the ClassWizard tool? Explain why it isn't just as efficient to enter these declarations into the corresponding header files using the Visual C++ editor.

6. Describe how the message map is used by the MFC framework to determine whether a handler exists for a particular message. In what order are the various objects searched when a message is generated by clicking one of the buttons in the CCatList view, for example? Explain your answer.

7. When the user drops down the View menu and chooses the Categories command, in what sequence are the message maps for the various objects searched? Describe how the handling of COMMAND messages is different from the handling of windows messages.

8. Describe why you think the CKeepitDoc class was chosen to contain the handlers for the Categories command from the View menu and the Edit command from the Account menu.

9. Examine the construction of the Account menu and describe how you would proceed to add menu items for each new account as it is created. How is it possible to do so while the application is executing? Explain your answer.

10. Read the description in the *Class Library Reference Manual* concerning *Working with Menus and Commands* and hypothesize how newly added commands could be handled by the program's code.[1]

---

[1] A full description of this methodology is given in the next chapter; however, it would be a good exercise to give to a class, to test their reasoning power and understanding of the operation of the application framework. It will take some time to formulate this answer, so it could be assigned as an extra credit project.

Chapter 6
Customizing the Account Features Code

In the previous chapter, we included tutorials for creating a new view class (CCatList) and a new dialog class (CEditAcct). Along with the tutorials, we presented the wizard-created code for the header and source files for those classes. In addition, we showed the added declarations and code to handle two new command messages in the document-derived class (CKeepitDoc).

This chapter will be devoted to a discussion of the custom code required to fully implement the newly defined features of the Keepit application, including the following:

❖ Support for multiple account views, any or all of which can be visible, simultaneously, on the screen.

❖ Support for dynamically adding and removing account names from the Account menu, as well as new code to handle the WM_COMMAND message generated when the user chooses an account from the menu.

❖ Support for adding new accounts or editing the characteristics of existing accounts using the Edit Account dialog.

❖ Support for defining and editing transaction categories, which are used in validating the category fields in the account views.

❖ Support for saving and loading account descriptions, category descriptions, and account transactions in a single file and under the control of a single document object.

During the course of discussing these topics, we will present the definition of two new classes (CCategory and CAcctObj), which contain member variables and member functions for accessing the variables in category and account objects. This technique of defining new objects to encapsulate data and then provide functions to access these data is important in implementing robust object-oriented programs.

We will also make many additions to the existing application (CKeepit-App), document (CKeepitDoc), and account view (CAccount) classes to provide the aforementioned support. In addition, we will present the code to implement fully the newly defined CCatList view and CEdit-Acct dialog.

The structure of the application, when we have completed the custom code additions and modifications, will appear as shown in Figure 6-1. The figure illustrates how the various objects are created and also shows the messages that are handled by the various classes.

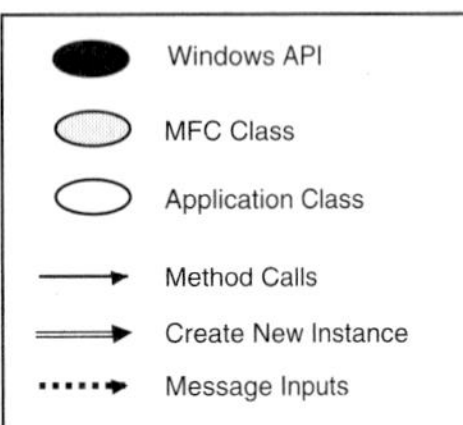

Figure 6-1
Structure and message handling in Keepit application after being customized

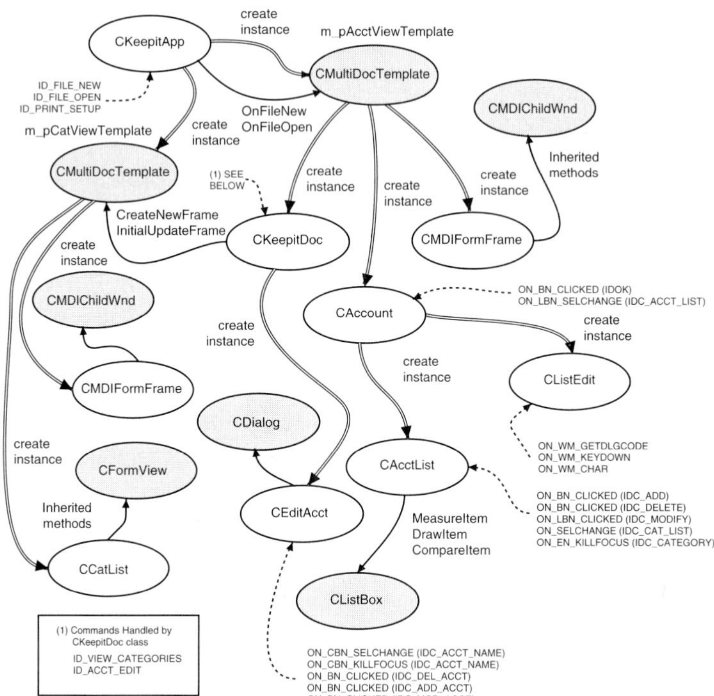

Adding New Object Classes

In the previous version of the Keepit application, we handled a single account view, and the category field in the account transactions was required, but not validated, input. In the new version of the application, we intend to provide support for handling a variety of accounts, and we intend to validate the category field in individual account entries to enforce the use of predefined category names. The latter feature will be of great use to us in a future version, when we implement the construction of reports using the transaction categories.

We have also elected to store the account, category, and transaction data in a single file so that a single document object can be used to access the data and provide reports (when these are implemented) that span the boundaries of individual accounts. In a sense, we are setting ourselves up for the next generation of the application in making these provisions. However, with the exception of the inability to provide hard copy output, the new version of the Keepit application will be very useful for a variety of record-keeping uses.

Implementing the CCategory Class

Because we want to store information concerning valid transaction categories, we have decided to create a separate class, member variables, and member functions to provide the necessary functionality. The features of the class are as follows:

❖ Member variables to contain the category name, type, and taxable status are defined.

❖ Member functions to get and set the value of each of the member variables have been provided.

❖ A Serialize member function has been defined to support loading and saving the category data from or to a data file.

The CCategory class encapsulates fully both the data and access member functions for interfacing with objects of the class. Other classes have full access to the public member functions, but are prevented from accessing the individual data items, other than by using the member functions provided for this purpose. This provides the insulation we require. Should we later decide to modify the data definitions, or the manner in which they are referenced, it will be a simple matter to modify the associated member functions and not have to worry about impacting any other parts of the application. Of particular value is the serialization code, which provides a completely transparent method of loading and storing the contents of a CCategory object.

CCategory Class Header File Code

We have created the code for the **category.h** header file using the Visual C++ editor. After the header file and its corresponding source file were created, we added the files to the project manually, by choosing the Edit command from the Project menu, selecting the **category.cpp** file in the list of available files in the Keepit directory, and then clicking the Add button. The code for the **category.h** header file is as follows:

```
//////////////////////////////////////////////////////////////////
// CCategory - category.h

class CCategory : public CObject
{
protected:
```

```cpp
   CString m_szCatName; // category name
   WORD    m_nCatType;  // 0=expense, 1=income
   WORD    m_nTaxable;  // 1 = taxable, 0 = non-taxable

   DECLARE_SERIAL (CCategory)
public:
   CCategory( );           // public constructor
   void    Serialize (CArchive& ar);

   CString GetCatName ();
   WORD    GetCatType ();
   WORD    GetTaxable ();

   void    SetCatName (CString& cat);
   void    SetCatType (WORD type);
   void    SetTaxable (WORD tax);
};
```

Note in the foregoing code that we have written the class description in much the same style as code created by the AppWizard and ClassWizard tools.

The member variables (m_szCatName, m_nCatType, and m_nTaxable) are declared as protected so that they aren't accessible to any but a derived or friend class of the CCategory class. The member functions are all declared with public accessibility. This allows us to reference them from within any other class in the application.

We used a storage type of WORD for the m_nCatType and m_nTaxable member variables for purposes of remaining compatible with the types of data for which serialize member functions are defined for the overloaded insertion (<<) and extraction (>>) operators. The DECLARE_SERIAL macro specifies that the class is compatible with dynamic (run-time) construction member functions.

The constructor having no arguments is defined to support both explicit and implicit (serialization) construction of the CCategory objects.

CCategory Class Source File Code

The source code for the CCategory class is contained in the **category.cpp** file and is as follows:

```cpp
////////////////////////////////////////////////////////////////////
// CCategory source file - category.cpp
#include "stdafx.h"
#include "category.h"

IMPLEMENT_SERIAL(CCategory, CObject, 2)

CCategory::CCategory ( )
{
   // empty
}
void CCategory::Serialize (CArchive& ar)
```

```
{
   CObject::Serialize (ar);
   if (ar.IsStoring())
   {
      ar << m_szCatName;
      ar << m_nCatType;
      ar << m_nTaxable;
   }
   else
   {
      ar >> m_szCatName;
      ar >> m_nCatType;
      ar >> m_nTaxable;
   }
}

CString CCategory::GetCatName ()
{
   return m_szCatName;
}

WORD CCategory::GetCatType ()
{
   return m_nCatType;
}

WORD CCategory::GetTaxable ()
{
   return m_nTaxable;
}

void CCategory::SetCatName (CString& cat)
{
   m_szCatName = cat;
}

void CCategory::SetCatType (WORD type)
{
   m_nCatType = type;
}

void CCategory::SetTaxable (WORD tax)
{
   m_nTaxable = tax;
}
```

The beginning of the foregoing code contains `#include` preprocessor directives, which are needed to input the standard Windows-defined types, as well as the declarations from the **category.h** header file.

The IMPLEMENT_SERIAL macro defines the name of the current class, its immediate base class, and a "schema" number for use by the serialization member functions. The schema allows the serialization member functions to make provision for different versions of data within the data file. Each object that is derived from the CObject class (which includes most of the classes in the MFC and the Keepit application) is associated with the CRuntimeClass. You can access the Runtime Class of a particular object by calling the GetRuntimeClass member function inherited by each class from the CObject class. The CRuntimeClass object contains such information as the class name, object size, schema number, pointer to the Runtime Class object for the base class, and member functions used to construct, load, and store data for the class.

The Serialize member function follows in the source file. The `IsStoring` member function of the CArchive class returns TRUE if the data in the class are to be inserted (written) into the archive; otherwise, the data are to be extracted (read) from the archive. The overloaded insertion and extraction operators (<< and >>) are used to serialize the individual member variables in the CCategory class.

The remaining member functions implement access to the individual member variables. While each of the member functions encloses a single statement to either return or store the corresponding member variable's value, the insulation provided by the access function greatly outweighs any loss in program efficiency.

Implementing the CAcctObj Class

The new version of the Keepit application supports the creation and use of more than one account. Because of this, and also because each account may be of a different type (checking, savings, asset, credit card, etc.), we need to retain the characteristics of each account so that it can be saved and later restored when the account is serialized. Much of the characteristic data will be pertinent when we provide the means to produce reports in a future version of the Keepit application.

We have created both the **acctobj.h** and **acctobj.cpp** header and source files using the Visual C++ editor and have written the code in the same style as is produced by the App Studio and ClassWizard tools. As with the CCategory class, the CAcctObj class fully encapsulates the member variables and access functions to interface with objects of the class.

CAcctObj Class Header File Code

The declaration for the CAcctObj class, its member variables, and member functions is contained in the **acctobj.h** header file. The code is as follows:

```
/////////////////////////////////////////////////////////////////
// CAcctObj header file - acctobj.h

#define    ACCT_UNCHANGED 0
#define    ACCT_ADDED     1
#define    ACCT_MODIFIED  2
#define    ACCT_DELETED   3

class CAcctObj : public CObject
{
protected:
    WORD    m_nAcctStatus; // account status
```

```
    CString m_szAcctName;    // account name
    CString m_szAcctDesc;    // account description
    WORD    m_nAcctType;     // account type
    WORD    m_nAcctID;       // account command ID

    DECLARE_SERIAL (CAcctObj)

public:
    CAcctObj ( );   // public constructor
    void Serialize (CArchive& ar);

    WORD    GetAcctStatus ();
    CString GetAcctName ();
    CString GetAcctDesc ();
    WORD    GetAcctType ();
    WORD    GetAcctID ();

    void    SetAcctStatus (WORD state);
    void    SetAcctName (CString& acct);
    void    SetAcctDesc (CString& desc);
    void    SetAcctType (WORD type);
    void    SetAcctID (WORD ID);

    CAcctObj(CAcctObj* pObj);// copy constructor
};
```

The foregoing code declares the member variables and member functions of the CAcctObj class. The first part of the file contains a number of #define statements, which specify names for the account status values. The status is relevant only when the application is executing; however, this information is saved and restored by the serialization process.

The CAcctObj class has five member variables to hold data that describes the characteristics of an object of the class. The variables are as follows:

❖ The m_nAcctStatus variable contains the current status of the account.

❖ The m_szAcctName variable contains the account name in the form of a string.

❖ The m_szAcctDesc variable contains a string that describes the account and which can include any information the user desires to provide, such as the account number, address, or other pertinent data.

❖ The m_nAcctType variable specifies the type of account, as defined by the App Studio tool when the Edit Account dialog was created, and which definitions are stored in the **resource.h** header file. We use the names of the resource definitions as a convenient means of referencing their associated values. The definitions are as follows:

  ■ IDC_CHECKING specifies a checking account.

  ■ IDC_SAVINGS specifies a savings account.

  ■ IDC_CASH specifies a cash on hand account.

- ■ IDC_ASSET specifies an asset account, such as would be used to track an investment, capital equipment, or the like.

- ■ IDC_LIABILITY specifies a liability account, which could be used to track a debt or the owner's equity.

- ■ IDC_CREDIT_CARD specifies a credit card account.

❖ The m_nAcctID variable specifies the command identifier for the account. This value is assigned at the time the account is created and will always be equal to or greater than the hexadecimal value 0x8400. (The MFC specifies that all command numbers must be equal to or greater than the hexadecimal value 0x8000, so we have arbitrarily decided to leave some space between the foundation-determined and our dynamically assigned account numbers.)

Following the declaration of the member variables, the header file contains the DECLARE_SERIAL macro, which declares the CAcctObj class as one that is capable of being constructed at run-time.

The default constructor function declaration and the declaration of the other member functions follow in the file. One departure from what was presented for the CCategory class declaration is the declaration of a second constructor member function. This additional member function is declared at the end of the file, just prior to the closing brace, and it specifies a constructor to be used when a new object of the class is constructed, given a pointer to another CAcctObj object as a parameter. This type of constructor is called a "copy constructor" and is used when we wish to create a copy of an existing object and transfer the contents of the member variables of the original object to the new object.

CAcctObj Class Source File Code

The source file for the CAcctObj was created using the Visual C++ text editor. The code is contained in the **acctobj.cpp** file and is as follows:

```
/////////////////////////////////////////////////////////////////
// CAcctObj member functions - acctobj.cpp
//
#include "stdafx.h"
#include "acctobj.h"

IMPLEMENT_SERIAL (CAcctObj, CObject, 2)

CAcctObj::CAcctObj ()
{
   // empty standard constructor
}

CAcctObj::CAcctObj (CAcctObj* pObj)
{
   m_nAcctStatus = pObj->m_nAcctStatus;
   m_szAcctName  = pObj->m_szAcctName;
   m_szAcctDesc  = pObj->m_szAcctDesc;
```

```cpp
    m_nAcctType    = pObj->m_nAcctType;
    m_nAcctID      = pObj->m_nAcctID;
}

void CAcctObj::Serialize (CArchive& ar)
{
   CObject::Serialize (ar);
   if (ar.IsStoring())
   {
      ar << m_nAcctStatus;
      ar << m_szAcctName;
      ar << m_szAcctDesc;
      ar << m_nAcctType;
      ar << m_nAcctID;
   }
   else
   {
      ar >> m_nAcctStatus;
      ar >> m_szAcctName;
      ar >> m_szAcctDesc;
      ar >> m_nAcctType;
      ar >> m_nAcctID;
   }
}

WORD CAcctObj::GetAcctStatus ()
{
   return m_nAcctStatus;
}

CString CAcctObj::GetAcctName ()
{
   return m_szAcctName;
}

CString CAcctObj::GetAcctDesc ()
{
   return m_szAcctDesc;
}

WORD CAcctObj::GetAcctType ()
{
   return m_nAcctType;
}

WORD CAcctObj::GetAcctID ()
{
   return m_nAcctID;
}

void CAcctObj::SetAcctStatus (WORD status)
{
   m_nAcctStatus = status;
}

void CAcctObj::SetAcctName (CString& acct)
{
   m_szAcctName = acct;
}

void CAcctObj::SetAcctDesc (CString& desc)
{
   m_szAcctDesc = desc;
}

void CAcctObj::SetAcctType (WORD type)
{
```

```
    m_nAcctType = type;
}

void CAcctObj::SetAcctID (WORD ID)
{
    m_nAcctID = ID;
}
```

The foregoing code begins with `#include` preprocessor statements, which permit the code to access standard Windows declarations as well as the declarations contained in the **acctobj.h** header file. Next, the file contains the IMPLEMENT_SERIAL macro, which allows objects of the class to be constructed at run-time. As with the CCategory class, the macro defines the name of the current class, the name of its immediate base class, and the schema number for this version of the code. (See page 167 for a description of the schema parameter.)

The default constructor and copy constructor member functions follow in the file. Note that the copy constructor transfers the contents of each of the specified object's member variables to the corresponding variables in the current (new) object.

The member functions for accessing the object's member variables follow the constructors in the source file.

Providing Support for Multiple Accounts

In order to support the creation and display of multiple account views, we have made changes to some of the existing classes, most notably member functions in the CKeepitApp, CKeepitDoc, and CAccount classes. Changes to existing code are minimal, however. We have been able to provide most of the required functionality by adding new code to what already exists. This is an important consideration when undertaking an evolutionary development approach. One must plan carefully, and only then commence the implementation of the plan. The sections that follow describe the changes that we have made to support viewing of multiple accounts. The Edit Account dialog and CCatList view will be described separately.

Enhancing the CKeepitApp Class

The CKeepitApp class implements the application-wide functions for the Keepit program. It inherits its behavior from the CWinApp class and includes all of the member functions that provide custom behavior for the application. In the course of adding new functionality to the Keepit application, we have added some new member functions and modified existing member functions in the code. In the sections that follow, we present the entire contents of the **keepit.h** header file. Following this, we present the member functions in the **keepit.cpp** source file that have been modified. Changes to existing code are indicated by "change bars" next to the corresponding lines in the source code listing.

CKeepitApp Class Header File Code

The header file for the CKeepitApp class is named **keepit.h** and its contents are as follows:

```
// keepit.h : main header file for the KEEPIT application
//

#ifndef __AFXWIN_H__
   #error include 'stdafx.h' before including this file for
PCH
#endif

#include "resource.h"  // main symbols

#define FIRST_ACCT_MENU_ID 0x8400

////////////////////////////////////////////////////////////
// CKeepitApp:
// See keepit.cpp for the implementation of this class
//

class CKeepitApp : public CWinApp
{
public:
   CKeepitApp();

// Attributes
   CMultiDocTemplate*  m_pAcctViewTemplate;// added
   CMultiDocTemplate*  m_pCatViewTemplate;  // added
   WORD                m_nNextMenuID;       // added

// Overrides
   virtual BOOL InitInstance();

// Implementation

   //{{AFX_MSG(CKeepitApp)
   afx_msg void OnAppAbout();
      // NOTE - the ClassWizard will add and remove member
      //    functions here.
      //     DO NOT EDIT what you see in these blocks of
      //     generated code !
   //}}AFX_MSG
   DECLARE_MESSAGE_MAP()
};
```

There are several features in the foregoing code that it is worthwhile to point out. We have defined a constant called FIRST_ACCT_MENU_ID, which is associated with the value 0x8400 (the value we have chosen to represent the first dynamically assigned account identifier and command code). We have also defined a member variable called m_nNextMenuID, in which we will store the next available menu (command) identifier value. The value will be increased monotonically for each newly defined account. This identifier is used to provide the means to recognize transactions belonging to an account and is also the command identifier sent to the document by the framework when the account name is chosen by the user from the Account menu.

Of additional interest is the definition of two new member variables, which are declared as pointers to objects of the CMultiDocTemplate class. These pointers are assigned values within the revised source code for the application, which will be shown shortly.

We have decided, as a design feature, to permit the user to choose multiple views of the data stored in the document. The Edit Account dialog is a view of an account description, and this view will be accessible by choosing the Edit command from the Account menu. Views of the individual accounts are be accessible from the Account menu, as dynamically created menu entries (and their dynamic nature is the reason for assigning a command identifier as the means to identify an individual account). The category view is chosen by means of the Category command in the View menu. All of the data to construct these views are saved in a single file (with the **kpd** extension) and are available via member variables and access functions in the CKeepitDoc class. Each of the views will be discussed later.

CKeepitApp Constructor Source Code

Most of the code in the **keepit.cpp** file was presented in Chapter 2. One new addition to the application is a small revision of the code in the CKeepitApp constructor, which we present as follows:

```
CKeepitApp::CKeepitApp()
{
    //
    // initialize the m_nNextMenuID variable
    //
    m_nNextMenuID = FIRST_ACCT_MENU_ID; // Dynamic account IDs
}
```

In the foregoing, we initialize the m_nNextMenuID member variable with the constant FIRST_ACCT_MENU_ID, when the constructor is invoked. The value is assigned to the first account we create. (If the user elects to open an existing file, the account identifiers will already have been assigned. In that case, we will set the m_nNextMenuID variable to the next available account identifier from within the serialization code.)

CKeepitApp InitInstance Source Code

We have made some changes to the InitInstance member function to support the ability to create both account and category views in this version of the application. The newly modified code is as follows:

```
BOOL CKeepitApp::InitInstance()
{
   // Standard initialization
   // If you are not using these features and wish to reduce
   // the size of your final executable, you should remove
   // from the following any specific initialization
   // routines you do not need.

   SetDialogBkColor();
   LoadStdProfileSettings();

   // Register the application's document templates.
   // Document templates serve as the connection between
   // the document, frame windows, and their views.

   m_pAcctViewTemplate = new CMultiDocTemplate(IDR_KEEPITTYPE,
         RUNTIME_CLASS(CKeepitDoc),
         RUNTIME_CLASS(CMDIFormFrame),// custom MDI form frame
         RUNTIME_CLASS(CAccount));
   AddDocTemplate (m_pAcctViewTemplate);

   m_pCatViewTemplate = new CMultiDocTemplate (IDR_CATVIEWTYPE,
         RUNTIME_CLASS(CKeepitDoc),
         RUNTIME_CLASS(CMDIFormFrame),// custom MDI form frame
         RUNTIME_CLASS(CCatList));
   AddDocTemplate (m_pCatViewTemplate);

   // create main MDI Frame window
   CMainFrame* pMainFrame = new CMainFrame;
   if (!pMainFrame->LoadFrame(IDR_MAINFRAME)) return FALSE;
   m_pMainWnd = pMainFrame;

   // enable file manager drag/drop and DDE Execute open
   EnableShellOpen();
   RegisterShellFileTypes();

   // simple command line parsing
   if (m_lpCmdLine[0] == '\0')
   {
      // don't call OnFileNew initially
   }
   else
   {
      // open an existing document
      OpenDocumentFile(m_lpCmdLine);
   }
   m_pMainWnd->DragAcceptFiles();
   pMainFrame->ShowWindow(m_nCmdShow);
   pMainFrame->UpdateWindow();
   return TRUE;
}
```

Most of the foregoing code is unchanged from what was presented in Chapter 2, with the exception of the creation of two document templates, and the storage of pointers to these in the member variables men-

tioned previously. The code for creation and registration of the templates
is shown, in isolation, as follows:

```
m_pAcctViewTemplate = new CMultiDocTemplate(IDR_KEEPITTYPE,
    RUNTIME_CLASS(CKeepitDoc),
    RUNTIME_CLASS(CMDIFormFrame),// custom MDI form frame
    RUNTIME_CLASS(CAccount));
AddDocTemplate (m_pAcctViewTemplate);

m_pCatViewTemplate = new CMultiDocTemplate (IDR_CATVIEWTYPE,
    RUNTIME_CLASS(CKeepitDoc),
    RUNTIME_CLASS(CMDIFormFrame),// custom MDI form frame
    RUNTIME_CLASS(CCatList));
AddDocTemplate (m_pCatViewTemplate);
```

If you compare the first five lines in the foregoing code with what is
shown in Chapter 2, on page 17, you will see that we have separated the
creation of the template from its addition to the application's list, have
assigned its pointer to the member variable, and then have added the
template to the list using the AddDocTemplate member function. We
follow the same procedure to create the new (IDR_CATVIEWTYPE) template, save its pointer in a member variable, and then add the template to
the application's list. One other difference in the foregoing code is the
reference to the CMDIFormFrame class, which is newly created and
based upon the CMDIChildWnd class. We will describe the purpose
and contents of this new class shortly.

Finally, in the overall code for the InitInstance member function, we
have deleted the call to OnFileNew, which has, previously, caused an
empty object of the CAccount View to be created and displayed. We
have chosen not to display an initial view, but instead allow the user to
either open an existing file or make the conscious decision to create a
new file. In most cases, the user will, after running the program the first
time, decide to open an existing file.

Document Template String Resources

In support of the framework's automatic association of file types with
document templates, the resource file for every new application includes
a string table entry for the primary document template, written into that
file when the application was first created by the App Studio wizard. In
the case of the Keepit application, the string table entry is called
IDR_KEEPITTYPE. Because we intend to support multiple views and also
make use of document templates to associate the document, main frame,
and its view, we must create an additional string table entry that contains
much of the same information as is generated automatically into the primary string table entry. Each string table entry contains seven fields, each
of which is accessible via a single member function in the CDocTem-
plate class (GetDocString). The fields are as follows:

❖ **windowTitle** — contains the name that appears in the frame window's title bar (for SDI applications only, empty for MDI applications).

❖ **docName** — contains the root of the current document's name (e.g., Keepit). The root plus a number form the name for a new document of this type (although we will be customizing this behavior to display the name of the account in an Account view).

❖ **fileNewName** — specifies the name of this document type. The name is also displayed in the New File dialog when the user creates a new document. *If this field is empty, the document type will not be accessible when using the File New command.*

❖ **filterName** — contains a description of the document type and a wild card filter matching documents of this type. This string is listed in the drop-down list of file types that the user is allowed to open for this application. The filter for the Keepit application is (`*.kpd`). *If this field is empty, the document type will not be accessible when using the File Open command.*

❖ **filterExt** — specifies the extension for files of this type (e.g., "`.kpd`"). *If this field is empty, the document type will not be accessible when using the File Open command.*

❖ **regFileTypeId** — contains the identifier that is stored in the Windows registration database. *If this field is empty, the document type cannot be registered with the Windows File Manager.*

❖ **regFileTypeName** — contains the name of the document type to be stored in the registration database.

What all of the foregoing boils down to is that each document type must have an associated string table entry that specifies the values for the various fields. The string table entries can be created or edited either with the App Studio tool (by choosing the String Table resource type and then double clicking the "String Segment 0" entry), or by editing the application's main resource file (e.g., **keepit.rc**). The contents of the string table entries for the IDR_KEEPITTYPE and the new IDR_CATVIEWTYPE document template resources are as follows:

```
IDR_KEEPITTYPE    "\nKeepit\nKEEPIT Document\nKEEPIT Files
(*.kpd)\n.kpd\nKeepitFileType\nKEEPIT File Type"

IDR_CATVIEWTYPE   "\nKeepit\n\n\n\nKeepitFileType\nKEEPIT
File Type"
```

Although each of the foregoing entries occupies two lines, each must be entered as a single line in the file. The name of the resource is listed first, followed by the quoted string containing the seven fields (in App Studio, the resource name is in a separate field and the quotation marks are not entered into the string). Each field is separated from the next with a new-line '\n' code. Note that because Keepit is an MDI application, the first field is empty in both entries (i.e., the string table entry begins with \n in both).

The string table entry for the primary document template contains data for each of the fields (except the first), while the IDR_CATVIEWTYPE entry leaves out the fileNewName, filterName, and filterExt fields, which causes the framework to disregard that entry when the New or Open command is chosen from the File menu. Creating the IDR_CATVIEWTYPE entry in this way causes the framework to bypass prompting for which document type is to be created or opened and assume that both views will share the same document object.

Creating a New Child Frame Window

In the previous version of the application, the child frame window had the appearance depicted in Figure 4-1. Some aspects of this appearance are not appropriate for our views. For example, there is no need for each MDI child window to have maximize and minimize buttons. In addition, there is no need for the user to be able to resize the window, which would serve only to expose blank space that the form view does not fill. Finally, because of the way the framework names each window, having each new account be named Keepit, with a trailing window number, is not acceptable.

What we desire is the ability to modify the style of the frame and gain complete control over its title bar's content. To accomplish this goal, we must create a new class, derived from the CMDIChildWnd class, and enter the new class name into the document templates for our views.

If you look at the new document template entries in the application's InitInstance member function (see page 175), you will observe that we have provided the name CMDIFormFrame as our new MDI child window frame's class name. We created both the header and source code files for this new class using the Visual C++ editor.

CMDIFormFrame Header File Code

The CMDIFormFrame header file is named **mdifmfrm.h** and the code contained in that file is as follows:

```
//////////////////////////////////////////////////////////////////////
// CMDIFormFrame Header File - mdifmfrm.h
//

class CMDIFormFrame : public CMDIChildWnd
{
```

```
   DECLARE_DYNCREATE(CMDIFormFrame)

public:
   CMDIFormFrame ();
   virtual ~CMDIFormFrame();

protected:
   BOOL PreCreateWindow(CREATESTRUCT& cs);
};
```

The foregoing class declaration specifies that the CMDIFormFrame class is a direct descendant of the CMDIChildWnd base class. The new class contains declarations of constructor and destructor functions, but, more importantly, it contains an override of the PreCreateWindow member function. This is the member function that directly affects the appearance and style of the frame window, before the window is displayed to the user.

CMDIFormFrame Source File Code

The source code for the CMDIFormFrame class is contained in the file named **mdifmfrm.cpp**. This file contains empty constructor and destructor member functions as well as the override of the PreCreateWindow member function, in which we are most interested. The source code for this new class is as follows:

```
//////////////////////////////////////////////////////////////////
// CMDIFormFrame Source File - mdifmfrm.cpp
//

#include "stdafx.h"
#include "keepdoc.h"
#include "acctobj.h"
#include "mdifmfrm.h"

IMPLEMENT_DYNCREATE(CMDIFormFrame, CMDIChildWnd)

BOOL CMDIFormFrame::PreCreateWindow (CREATESTRUCT& cs)
{
   //
   // set the style for the frame window
   //
   LONG ls = ~((LONG)WS_MAXIMIZEBOX
             | (LONG)WS_MINIMIZEBOX
             | (LONG)WS_THICKFRAME
             | (LONG)FWS_ADDTOTITLE);

   //
   // get rid of minimize, maximize buttons
   // and also the add-to-title style
   //
   cs.style &= ls;
   return CMDIChildWnd::PreCreateWindow (cs);
}

//////////////////////////////////////////////////////////////////
// CMDIFormFrame construction/destruction
```

```
CMDIFormFrame::CMDIFormFrame()
{
   // empty
}


CMDIFormFrame::~CMDIFormFrame()
{
   // empty
}
```

In the foregoing code, the PreCreateWindow member function is the most important. In order to modify the style and appearance of the window, we must change the settings in the `style` field of the CREATE-STRUCT variable (cs) passed to the member function. The modifications to the style include removal of many of the default settings, including the maximize (WS_MAXIMIZEBOX) and minimize (WS_MINIMIZEBOX) boxes, the standard thick frame style (WS_THICKFRAME), and also the "add to title" (FWS_ADDTOTITLE) feature (which directs the framework to compose the title of the frame from the document name and a new sequential number).

To remove these settings, we create a LONG value that contains the inverse of the logical conjunction of the style values and then AND that with the existing `style` field's contents. This simple change eliminates the maximize and minimize buttons, changes the frame style so that the user is not able to resize it, and causes the framework to leave the frame title blank (allowing us to write the Account name, or whatever text we wish, into the title bar).

After the foregoing changes have been made to the frame's style, the member function calls the PreCreateWindow member function of its base class (CMDIChildWnd), to perform additional verification of the frame's parameters. The result of calling the base class member function is returned to the framework to complete the creation of the frame window and its view.

Updating the CKeepitDoc Class

Support for multiple views is vested primarily in the CKeepitDoc class. In addition to making some rather simple changes to existing member functions, several new member functions have been added. In this section we will describe the modifications and additions that support the creation of new accounts; however, we will reserve the description of member functions that interact with the EditAccount dialog and CCatList views until later.

CKeepitDoc Header File Code

The complete code for the new version of the CKeepitDoc class is in the
file named **keepdoc.h**, and is as follows:

```
// keepdoc.h : interface of the CKeepitDoc class
//
/////////////////////////////////////////////////////////////

class CListEntry;
class CAcctList;
class CAcctObj;

#define ACCOUNT_MENU_POS    3    // fourth menu on menubar

class CKeepitDoc : public CDocument
{
protected: // create from serialization only

   CKeepitDoc();
   DECLARE_DYNCREATE(CKeepitDoc)
   BOOL OnCmdMsg (UINT nID, int nCode, void *pExtra,// added
      AFX_CMDHANDLERINFO* pHandlerInfo);

   void OnAccountName (UINT nID); // added
   void OnAccountNameUpdate (UINT nID, CCmdUI* pExtra);// added

// Attributes
public:

   CObList    m_ListEntries;      // list of account entries
   CObList    m_CatList;          // list of category objects
   CObList    m_AcctList;         // list of accounts
   BOOL       m_bFirstTime;       // first time switch
   CString    m_szCurAcctName;    // current account name
   WORD       m_nCurrentAccount;  // current account ID

// Operations
public:

   CListEntry* NewListEntry (void);
   void DeleteListEntry (CListEntry* anEntry);
   void AddListEntry (CListEntry* anEntry);
   void FillAcctList (CAcctList* pList);           // added

// Implementation
public:
   virtual ~CKeepitDoc();
   virtual void Serialize(CArchive& ar);           // override
   virtual void DeleteContents(void);              // override
   virtual BOOL CanCloseFrame(CFrameWnd* pFrame);// override
#ifdef _DEBUG
   virtual void AssertValid() const;
   virtual void Dump(CDumpContext& dc) const;
#endif

protected:
   BOOL OnNewDocument();     // create a new document
   void RemoveAcctMenu (CAcctObj* pAcct);// remove a menu item
   void RemoveTransactions (WORD nAcctID);// remove trans.
   void RemoveMDIFrame (CString& szName); // delete window

public:
   void AddAcctMenu (CAcctObj* pAcct);   // add a menu command
```

```
    void SetMenuNames(void);                    // set account names
                                                // in Account menu

// Generated message map functions
protected:
  //{{AFX_MSG(CKeepitDoc)
  afx_msg void OnViewCategories();
  afx_msg void OnAcctEdit();
  afx_msg void OnAcctPrint();
  //}}AFX_MSG
  DECLARE_MESSAGE_MAP()
};
```

We have added comments to many of the foregoing member variables and member functions in the foregoing class declaration to indicate that these are new additions to the class and for what purpose they were added. A listing of the variables and member functions associated with multiple view support is shown in Table 6-1.

Table 6-1

Variables and member functions in support of multiple views in the CKeepitDoc class

Name	Type	Description
m_ListEntries	variable	contains a list of transaction entries.
m_CatList	variable	contains a list of category entries.
m_AcctList	variable	contains a list of account entries.
m_bFirstTime	variable	serves as a first-time switch.
m_szCurAcctName	variable	contains the name of the current account.
m_nCurrentAccount	variable	contains the command ID of the current account.
FillAcctList	member function	fills the account list with empty entries.
Serialize	member function	serializes accounts, categories, and transactions.
OnNewDocument	member function	creates a new document and its frame and view.
AddAcctMenu	member function	adds the name of an account to the Account menu.
RemoveAcctMenu	member function	removes an account name from the Account menu.
SetMenuNames	member function	sets all the account names for a newly opened file.

There are member functions in the CKeepitDoc class, in addition to those shown in Table 6-1, which are relevant to the support of individual views, that we will describe later.

The CKeepitDoc member functions that support multiple views will be described individually, in the sections that follow.

CKeepitDoc Constructor Function Code

The constructor for the CKeepitDoc class was not mentioned in the foregoing table because it has only a minor role in support of multiple views. The code is as follows:

```
CKeepitDoc::CKeepitDoc()
{
   m_nCurrentAccount = 0;
   m_bFirstTime = TRUE;
}
```

The foregoing constructor initializes the m_nCurrentAccount identifier to 0 and then sets the m_bFirstTime variable to TRUE. The purpose of this initialization will be described shortly.

FillAcctList Member Function Code

The FillAcctList member function is responsible for making sure that the member variable m_AcctList contains at least seven entries for the current account. This is to ensure that the scroll bar is activated in the Account view's list box and that the visible portion of the box is filled with entries, even if they are empty. The code for this member function is as follows:

```
void CKeepitDoc::FillAcctList (CAcctList* pList)
{
   int nEntries = 0;
   POSITION pos = m_ListEntries.GetHeadPosition();
   while (pos != NULL)
   {
      CListEntry* pEntry;
      pEntry = (CListEntry *)m_ListEntries.GetNext (pos);
      if (pEntry->GetAccountID() == m_nCurrentAccount)
      {
         pList->AddString ((LPCSTR)pEntry);
         nEntries++;
      }
   }

   // if there are fewer than 7 entries in the list,
   // fill the remaining space in both the object
   // list and the Account view with empty entries.

   while (nEntries++ <= 7)
   {
      CListEntry* pEntry = NewListEntry();
      AddListEntry (pEntry);
      pList->AddString ((LPCSTR)pEntry);
   }
}
```

The foregoing member function iterates through the entire list of account transactions, counting those that correspond to the current account ID, and then adds new empty entries to the list, if necessary, so that the total number of entries for the current account is at least seven.

OnNewDocument Member Function Code

We have overridden the CDocument class's OnNewDocument member function so that we can provide support for multiple accounts and perform the initialization steps needed when a new document is created. The code for our override member function is as follows:

```
BOOL CKeepitDoc::OnNewDocument()
{
   if (!CDocument::OnNewDocument())
     return FALSE;

   //
   // create an untitled account entry for the first
   // account in a new document.
   //
   CString szAcctName = "(Untitled Account)";
   CString szAcctDesc = "";
   CAcctObj* pAcct = new CAcctObj;
   pAcct->SetAcctStatus (ACCT_UNCHANGED);
   pAcct->SetAcctName (szAcctName);
   pAcct->SetAcctDesc (szAcctDesc);
   pAcct->SetAcctType (IDC_CHECKING);
   m_nCurrentAccount = ((CKeepitApp *)AfxGetApp())
      ->m_nNextMenuID++;
   pAcct->SetAcctID (m_nCurrentAccount);
   m_AcctList.AddTail (pAcct);

   //
   // set the current account name.
   //
   m_szCurAcctName = szAcctName;// set current account name

   //
   // for a new document, we need to generate enough
   // empty entries in the m_ListEntries list to force
   // the list box to activate its vertical scroll bar.
   //
   for (int i=0; i < 7; i++)
   {
     CListEntry* pEntry = NewListEntry();
     AddListEntry (pEntry);
   }

   return TRUE;
}
```

The foregoing code calls its base class OnNewDocument member function first and then performs the additional initialization of the Account view. The steps for initializing a new account are as follows:

1. Create a new object of the CAcctObj class, setting its member variables (see the description of the CAcctObj class on pages 168–172) to default values as follows:

    a. Account status is set to ACCT_UNCHANGED.

    b. Account name is set to (Untitled Account).

    c. Account description is set to an empty string.

    d. Account type is set to IDC_CHECKING.

    e. The m_nCurrentAccount member variable in the CKeepit-Doc class is set to the value currently held in the application object's m_nNextMenuId variable, and that variable is incremented for use in the next new account.

    f. Account ID is set to the value in the m_nCurrentAccount member variable of the CKeepitDoc class.

2. Enter the new account's pointer into the m_AcctList list.

3. Set the document's m_szCurAcctName variable equal to the current account's name [i.e., "(Untitled Account)"].

4. Create seven entries for the account in the m_ListEntries list.

5. Return a TRUE result to the framework's OpenDocumentFile member function in the CMultiDocTemplate class.

The foregoing steps prepare the document's lists for handling a new document and its empty Account view.

Serialize Member Function Code

The Serialize member function is called automatically by the framework when the user chooses to open an existing file or save the contents of the document in a file. Note in the following that no distinction is made between reading or writing the file. The code is as follows:

```
void CKeepitDoc::Serialize(CArchive& ar)
{
  m_AcctList.Serialize (ar);      // serialize accounts
  m_CatList.Serialize (ar);       // serialize categories
  m_ListEntries.Serialize (ar);   // serialize transactions

  //
  // initialize the current account to be the first
  // one in the account list.
  //
  CAcctObj* pAcct = (CAcctObj *)m_AcctList.GetHead();
  m_nCurrentAccount = pAcct->GetAcctID();
  m_szCurAcctName = pAcct->GetAcctName();
}
```

The primary responsibility of the foregoing code is to call the Serialize member function for the list of accounts (m_AcctList), the list of categories (m_CatList), and the list of account transactions (m_ListEntries). Each of the lists is an object of the CObList class, which contains the necessary code for serializing objects read into or written out of the list. The input file contains a count of the number of entries in each list and the type of object that each represents. When each object is read, an object of that class is created automatically, the object is stored into the list, and its Serialize member function is called to input the values associated with its member variables. On output (when the document is being saved), the document's Serialize member function performs the reverse operations.

The code for the CAcctObj Serialize member function is shown on page 171. The code for the CCategory Serialize member function is shown on page 166. The code for the CListEntry Serialize member function was presented in Chapter 4, on page 115; however, since writing that code we have added the m_nAccountID member variable and have modified the Serialize code for that class as follows:

```
void CListEntry::Serialize (CArchive& ar)
{
    CObject::Serialize (ar);

    if (ar.IsStoring())
    {
        if (m_szDescription == "" || m_szCategory == "")
        {
            m_nStatus = E_EMPTY;
        }
        ar << m_nAccountID;
        ar << m_nStatus;
        ar << m_EntryDate;
        ar << m_szItemNo;
        ar << m_szDescription;
        ar << m_szInfo;
        ar << m_szCategory;
        ar << m_nPayment;
        ar << m_nDeposit;
    }
    else
    {
        ar >> m_nAccountID;
        ar >> m_nStatus;
        ar >> m_EntryDate;
        ar >> m_szItemNo;
        ar >> m_szDescription;
        ar >> m_szInfo;
        ar >> m_szCategory;
        ar >> m_nPayment;
        ar >> m_nDeposit;
        if (m_nStatus == E_EMPTY)
        {
            MakeToday (m_EntryDate);
        }
    }
}
```

Note in the foregoing that the m_nAccountID member variable is now being written and read as part of the serializing process. Also, when we write an entry whose description or category fields is blank, we change the status of the entry to E_EMPTY. For entries being read, whose status is E_EMPTY, we set the date to today's date.

AddAcctMenu Member Function Code

In support of the creation of new accounts (and multiple views), we have made provision for adding new account names to the Account menu, below the separator line. By placing each new account name into the menu, the user will be able to open the appropriate account window by choosing the corresponding command name from the menu. The code to add new account names to the menu is as follows:

```
void CKeepitDoc::AddAcctMenu (CAcctObj* pAcct)
{
    //
    // get the main menu bar pointer and find the Account menu
    //
    CWnd* pMainWnd = AfxGetApp()->m_pMainWnd;
    CMenu* pMenuBar = pMainWnd->GetMenu();
    CMenu* pMenu = pMenuBar->GetSubMenu (ACCOUNT_MENU_POS);
    ASSERT(pMenu != NULL);

    //
    // get the account ID and name, and then
    // add the the name to the Account menu.
    //
    WORD nID = pAcct->GetAcctID();
    CString szName = pAcct->GetAcctName();
    pMenu->AppendMenu(MF_STRING | MF_ENABLED, nID, szName);
    pMainWnd->DrawMenuBar();
}
```

The foregoing code adds the name of the account to the Account menu. The single argument to the member function is a pointer to the CAcct-Obj object. Before the account name can be added to the menu, the Account menu must be located in the menu bar. This is accomplished by getting the pointer to the main frame (m_pMainWnd), accessing the pointer to its menu by calling the GetMenu member function, and then retrieving the pointer to its submenu object by calling the GetSubMenu member function with the constant ACCOUNT_MENU_POS, which we have defined to be the value 3 (the fourth menu in the menu bar).

After the Account menu has been located (an object of the CMenu class), we can call the GetAcctID member function to access the account ID for the account object whose pointer is passed as input to the function. We also call the GetAcctName member function to access the account's name. These data are then used in the call to AppendMenu, for the Account submenu object.

RemoveAcctMenu Member Function Code

The code for renaming an account in the menu bar removes the old name and then adds back the new name. The code for removing an account name from the menu bar is as follows:

```
void CKeepitDoc::RemoveAcctMenu (CAcctObj* pAcct)
{
   // get the main menu bar pointer

   CWnd* pMainWnd = AfxGetApp()->m_pMainWnd;
   CMenu* pMenu = pMainWnd->GetMenu();

   // locate the Account popup menu and remove the item

   WORD nID = pAcct->GetAcctID();
   CMenu* pAcctMenu = pMenu->GetSubMenu (ACCOUNT_MENU_POS);
   ASSERT_VALID (pAcctMenu);
   pAcctMenu->RemoveMenu (nID, MF_BYCOMMAND);
   pMainWnd->DrawMenuBar();
}
```

As with the AddAcctMenu function, the foregoing code accesses the frame's menu bar, then accesses the Account submenu, and, finally, removes the specified account name from that submenu.

SetMenuNames Member Function Code

The purpose of the SetMenuNames member function is to add all of the account names to the Account menu when the very first view is opened. The code is as follows:

```
void CKeepitDoc::SetMenuNames()
{
   WORD nAcctID, nHighestID = 0;

   if (m_bFirstTime)
   {
      // add the names of all of the accounts to the
      // Account menu and set the application's next
      // menu ID (m_nNextMenuID).

      POSITION pos = m_AcctList.GetHeadPosition();
      while (pos != NULL)
      {
         CAcctObj* pAcct = (CAcctObj *)m_AcctList.GetNext(pos);
         AddAcctMenu (pAcct);
         nAcctID = pAcct->GetAcctID();
         if (nAcctID > nHighestID)
         {
            nHighestID = nAcctID;
         }
      }
      ((CKeepitApp *)AfxGetApp())->m_nNextMenuID = nHighestID+1;
      m_bFirstTime = FALSE;
   }
}
```

The foregoing code is executed only once for each document. When each Account view is created, its OnInitialUpdate member function is called. That member function calls the document's SetMenuNames member function, which tests whether the m_bFirstTime member variable has the value TRUE or FALSE. If the value is TRUE, then the code is executed. The code loops through all of the entries in the document's m_AcctList list, calling the AddAcctMenu member function for each account object, and then determining the value of the largest account ID. This value, plus one, is stored into the application's m_nNextMenuID member variable as the value to be assigned to the next new account. The last act of the SetMenuNames member function is to set the document's m_bFirstTime member variable's value to FALSE.

DeleteContents Member Function Code

The document's DeleteContents member function is called whenever the document is closed, allowing us to clean up before the document is deleted. The code for this override member function is as follows:

```cpp
void CKeepitDoc::DeleteContents()
{
   POSITION pos;

   // delete the CObList Entries for accounts, categories,
   // and list entries, and then remove all of the entries
   // from the list.

   pos = m_AcctList.GetHeadPosition();
   while (pos != NULL)
   {
      // while we're deleting accounts, make sure to
      // delete the menu entry for the account.

      CAcctObj* pAcct = (CAcctObj *)m_AcctList.GetNext(pos);
      RemoveAcctMenu (pAcct);
      delete pAcct;
   }
   m_AcctList.RemoveAll();

   pos = m_CatList.GetHeadPosition();
   while (pos != NULL)
   {
      CCategory* pCat = (CCategory *)m_CatList.GetNext(pos);
      delete pCat;
   }
   m_CatList.RemoveAll();

   pos = m_ListEntries.GetHeadPosition();
   while (pos != NULL)
   {
      CListEntry* pEntry;
      pEntry = (CListEntry *)m_ListEntries.GetNext(pos);
      delete pEntry;
   }
   m_ListEntries.RemoveAll();
}
```

After the foregoing member function executes, all of the objects that we have allocated have been deleted and we can safely close the file. Note that when the account objects are being deleted, their corresponding menu entries are also deleted. If they were not and we immediately opened another file, the menu items for the old accounts would still be in the Account menu, followed by the items for the new accounts.

Customizing and Supporting the Views

This section describes the new CCatList view, the CEditAcct dialog, and the changes to the existing CAccount view, to support multiple accounts. We will also discuss newly added code to the CKeepitDoc class to support the command messages generated when the user pulls down the Account or View menus and chooses one of the new views.

We will present the CCatList class and the CEditAcct class first, and then cover the additions to the CKeepitDoc class to support the creation and interaction with these views and their menu commands.

Customizing the CCatList View

The wizard-created code for the CCatList class was described in Chapter 5, on pages 154–156. We will expand upon this code to implement the full functionality of the CCatList view in this section.

CCatList Header File Code

The updated version of the header file for the CCatList class is contained in the **catlist.h** file whose contents are as follows:

```
// catlist.h : header file
//
///////////////////////////////////////////////////////////////////////
// CCatList form view

#ifndef __AFXEXT_H__
#include <afxext.h>
#endif

class CKeepitDoc;// forward reference

class CCatList : public CFormView
{
    DECLARE_DYNCREATE(CCatList)
protected:
    CCatList();// protected constructor used by dynamic
creation

public:
    CKeepitDoc*  GetDocument();    // copied from account.h
    void         OnInitialUpdate ();// copied from account.h

// Form Data
```

```
public:
  //{{AFX_DATA(CCatList)
  enum { IDD = IDD_CATEGORIES };
  CEdit     m_Category;
  CButton   m_ModifyButton;
  CButton   m_DeleteButton;
  CButton   m_AddButton;
  CButton   m_Taxable;
  CListBox  m_CatList;
  //}}AFX_DATA

// Attributes
public:
  int       m_nCurEntry;    // index of current category
  CString   m_szCurName;    // name of current entry
  WORD      m_nCurTaxable;  // 1 = taxable, 0=non-taxable
  WORD      m_nCurType;     // 0 = expense, 1 = income

// Operations
public:
  BOOL FindCategory (CString& szName);

// Implementation
protected:
  virtual ~CCatList();
  virtual void DoDataExchange(CDataExchange* pDX);// DDX/
DDV

  // Generated message map functions
  //{{AFX_MSG(CCatList)
  afx_msg void OnAdd();
  afx_msg void OnDelete();
  afx_msg void OnModify();
  afx_msg void OnSelectCat();
  afx_msg void OnKillfocusCategory();
  //}}AFX_MSG
  DECLARE_MESSAGE_MAP()
};

#ifndef _DEBUG// debug version in catlist.cpp
inline CKeepitDoc* CCatList::GetDocument()
  { return (CKeepitDoc*) m_pDocument; }
#endif
```

In the foregoing, we have copied two member function declarations from the CAccount class (GetDocument and OnInitialUpdate), for which we will include the necessary source code. As with the CAccount class, the GetDocument member function is defined as an in-line member function when the application is compiled as a non-debug (i.e., release) version. We have also added new member variables to the class to aid in keeping track of the settings for the currently active entry. Other than these additions, the header file is essentially the same as was generated by the ClassWizard tool.

The CCatList Source File Beginning Code

The source code for the CCatList class is contained in the **catlist.cpp** file. We have made a very few changes to the beginning of the source file.

The preprocessor statements, as modified, and the wizard-created constructor and destructor functions are as follows:

```cpp
// catlist.cpp : implementation file
//
#include "stdafx.h"
#include "keepit.h"
#include "keepdoc.h"    // added
#include "category.h"   // added
#include "catlist.h"
#ifdef _DEBUG
#undef THIS_FILE
static char BASED_CODE THIS_FILE[] = __FILE__;
#endif


/////////////////////////////////////////////////////////////////////
// CCatList

IMPLEMENT_DYNCREATE(CCatList, CFormView)

CCatList::CCatList()
    : CFormView(CCatList::IDD)
{
    //{{AFX_DATA_INIT(CCatList)
    //}}AFX_DATA_INIT
}


CCatList::~CCatList()
{
}
```

Note in the foregoing that we have added only the two `#include` statements, which import the declarations associated with the document and category objects to the source file. The constructor and destructor functions are unchanged.

Adding the CCatList GetDocument Member Function

We have added code to retrieve a pointer to the current document to the source file for the CCatList member function. It was copied from the CAccount class and modified to apply to the current class. The code is all newly added to the class and is as follows:

```cpp
#ifdef _DEBUG
CKeepitDoc* CCatList::GetDocument()// non-debug version is
                                   // inline
{
    ASSERT(m_pDocument->IsKindOf(RUNTIME_CLASS(CKeepitDoc)));
    return (CKeepitDoc*) m_pDocument;
}
#endif //_DEBUG
```

Note in the foregoing that the code is compiled only if the _DEBUG variable is defined (as is the case for a debug build of the application). If the release version of the application is being built, the in-line version of this member function is used.

OnInitialUpdate Member Function Code

The OnInitialUpdate member function is called by the framework prior to displaying the view. Making changes in this member function provides us with the opportunity to change the nature of the view and initialize any of the view's features before it is made visible to the user. We have added this member function to the wizard-created code for just these purposes. The code is all newly added and is as follows:

```
void CCatList::OnInitialUpdate()
{
   POSITION pos;

   CFormView::OnInitialUpdate();// call the ancestor first

   //
   // set the initial state for the Expense and Taxable
   // controls.
   //
   CheckRadioButton (IDC_EXPENSE, IDC_INCOME, IDC_EXPENSE);
   m_Taxable.SetCheck (0);// Taxable UnChecked

   //
   // resize the parent frame to fit the formview
   //
   GetParentFrame()->RecalcLayout ();
   ResizeParentToFit (FALSE);
   ResizeParentToFit (TRUE);

   //
   // set the window's name
   //
   CString szCat = "List Of Categories";
   GetParentFrame()->SetWindowText (szCat);
```

The first section of the OnInitialUpdate member function calls the CFormView (ancestor's) OnInitialUpdate member function to perform preliminary initialization of the view, perform the data exchange of control handles in the view to the CCatList object's corresponding member variables, and then checks the Expense radio button and unchecks the Taxable checkbox as the view's initial settings.

After performing the foregoing initialization, the MDI child frame window is resized to enclose the form view's boundaries, exactly. To accomplish this, we need to get the view's parent frame by calling the GetParentFrame member function and then call ResizeParentToFit twice in succession. The reason for the two calls is so that if the initial form view was created with scroll bars, the first call, with an argument of FALSE, will resize the frame to completely encompass the form view's dimensions. The second call, with an argument of TRUE, shrinks the frame, as necessary, for it to fit within the main MDI frame window. The OnInitialUpdate member function continues, as follows:

```
//
// load the category list with any existing
// categories, if any.
//
CKeepitDoc* pDoc = GetDocument ();
pos = pDoc->m_CatList.GetHeadPosition ();
while (pos != NULL)
{
   CCategory* pCat;
   pCat = (CCategory *)pDoc->m_CatList.GetNext (pos);
   m_CatList.AddString (pCat->GetCatName ());
}

// initialize the member variables

m_nCurEntry   = 0;            // first entry
m_szCurName   = "";           // blank name
m_nCurTaxable = 0;            // non-taxable
m_nCurType    = IDC_EXPENSE;// expense
```

The foregoing section of the OnInitialUpdate member function loads the names of the existing categories (if any) into the list box in the CCatList view. The code concludes, as follows:

```
// select the first entry in the ListBox and then
// look up its settings in the document's CObList.

if (m_CatList.GetCount () > 0)
{
   m_CatList.SetCurSel (m_nCurEntry);
   m_CatList.GetText (m_nCurEntry, m_szCurName);
   m_Category.SetWindowText (m_szCurName);
   m_Taxable.SetCheck (m_nCurTaxable);
   CheckRadioButton (IDC_EXPENSE, IDC_INCOME, m_nCurType);

   // set the buttons for a selected entry

   m_AddButton.EnableWindow (FALSE);
   m_ModifyButton.EnableWindow (TRUE);
   m_DeleteButton.EnableWindow (TRUE);
}
else
{
   // clear the edit text and set the status
   // of the buttons appropriately.

   m_Category.SetWindowText ("");
   m_Taxable.SetCheck (0);
   CheckRadioButton (IDC_EXPENSE, IDC_INCOME, IDC_EXPENSE);
   m_AddButton.EnableWindow (TRUE);
   m_ModifyButton.EnableWindow (FALSE);
   m_DeleteButton.EnableWindow (FALSE);
}
}
```

The final action of the foregoing OnInitialUpdate code determines whether the list box contains any entries, and if so, selects the first entry and sets the buttons and other controls to prepare for the user's interaction with that or another entry. If the list box is empty, then the controls are set to enable a new entry to be added to the list.

FindCategory Member Function Code

We have added a new member function to aid the various message handlers in determining whether a category name, specified as an input parameter, has already been defined. The code is as follows:

```
BOOL CCatList::FindCategory (CString& szName)
{
   CKeepitDoc* pDoc;
   POSITION pos;

   pDoc = GetDocument();
   pos = pDoc->m_CatList.GetHeadPosition();
   BOOL bFound = FALSE;
   while (pos != NULL)
   {
      CCategory* pCat;
      pCat = (CCategory *)pDoc->m_CatList.GetNext(pos);
      if (pCat->GetCatName() == szName)
      {
         bFound = TRUE;
         break;
      }
   }
   return bFound;
}
```

In the foregoing code, the member function is called with a reference to a CString object as an argument. The member function searches through the document's list of categories (contained in the m_CatList member variable's list) and returns a result value of TRUE if an entry with a matching string value is found; otherwise, a FALSE result is returned.

OnAdd Message Handler Code

The OnAdd message handler is invoked by the framework when the user clicks the Add button in the view. The OnAdd member function is the message handler defined to handle the "button click" message, as described in the tutorial in Chapter 5, on page 140, in step 1. The code for the handler is newly added and is as follows:

```
void CCatList::OnAdd()
{
   CString szText;
   WORD nTax, nType;
   int nEntry;

   // validate the new entry
```

```cpp
m_Category.GetWindowText(szText);
if (szText.GetLength() <= 0)
{
   AfxMessageBox ("Category text is required");
   return;
}
if (FindCategory (szText))
{
   AfxMessageBox ("Duplicate category name");
   return;
}
nType = GetCheckedRadioButton (IDC_EXPENSE, IDC_INCOME);
if (nType != IDC_EXPENSE && nType != IDC_INCOME)
{
   AfxMessageBox("Either Expense or Income must be selected");
   return;
}
nTax = m_Taxable.GetCheck();
```

The first section of the OnAdd message handler, shown in the foregoing code, is responsible for determining whether the category entry is valid. The user must enter a name in the Edit control, and the name must not duplicate an existing entry (determined by calling the FindCategory member function described previously). In addition, one of the account type radio buttons must be selected. After verifying these conditions, the handler concludes, as follows:

```cpp
//
// it looks good, so create a new CCategory object,
// add it to the document's list of categories, and
// then add its name to the category ListBox.
//
CCategory* pCat = new CCategory;
pCat->SetCatName (szText);
pCat->SetCatType (nType);
pCat->SetTaxable (nTax);
GetDocument()->m_CatList.AddTail(pCat);
m_CatList.AddString (szText);
nEntry = m_CatList.SelectString (-1, szText);

//
// change the current entry information
//
m_nCurEntry   = nEntry;
m_szCurName   = szText;
m_nCurTaxable = nTax;
m_nCurType    = nType;

//
// change the state of the buttons now that the
// new category has been entered.
//
m_AddButton.EnableWindow (FALSE);
m_ModifyButton.EnableWindow (TRUE);
m_DeleteButton.EnableWindow (TRUE);
m_Category.SetFocus();
m_Category.SetSel (0, -1, TRUE);
}
```

The final section of the OnAdd message handler creates a new object of the CCategory class, calls that object's access functions to set the category type, name, and taxable member variables to the settings specified by the user, adds the category to the document's list of CCategory objects, adds the category name to the list box in the view (which causes it to be sorted, alphabetically, into the proper position), and then selects the text in the Edit control, in anticipation that the user might want to modify or delete the newly added entry.

The handler concludes by setting the view's member variables to the settings for the current entry, disables the Add button, enables the Modify and Delete buttons, and then selects the category name in the list box.

OnDelete Message Handler Code

The OnDelete message handler was created with the ClassWizard in the tutorial in Chapter 5, on page page 140, in step 2. The handler is called by the framework when the user clicks the Delete button. The custom code for the handler is all newly added and is as follows:

```
void CCatList::OnDelete()
{
   CString szText;
   POSITION pos, pPos;

   //
   // get the entry text and validate it
   //
   m_Category.GetWindowText(szText);
   if (szText.GetLength() <= 0)
   {
      AfxMessageBox ("Category text is required");
      return;
   }
   if (!FindCategory (szText))
   {
      AfxMessageBox ("Category name does not match\
          an existing entry");
      return;
   }
```

The first section of the OnDelete message handler is responsible for determining whether the entry is valid, as shown in the foregoing code.

To be valid, the user must have entered a category name in the Edit control and the name must match the name of an existing category in the document's list of CCategory objects. If either of these conditions is not met, an appropriate error dialog is displayed and the member function terminates execution. If both of these conditions are met, the handler continues execution, as follows:

```
//
// delete the entry in the category list
// and also in the ListBox.
//
CKeepitDoc* pDoc = GetDocument();
pos = pDoc->m_CatList.GetHeadPosition();
while (pos != NULL)
{
   pPos = pos;
   CCategory* pCat;
   pCat = (CCategory *)pDoc->m_CatList.GetNext(pos);
   if (pCat->GetCatName() == szText)
   {
      pDoc->m_CatList.RemoveAt (pPos);
      break;
   }
}

int count = m_CatList.GetCount();
for (int index=0; index < count; index++)
{
   CString szName;
   m_CatList.GetText (index, szName);
   if (szName == szText)
   {
      m_CatList.DeleteString (index);
      break;
   }
}
//
// clear out the current selection information
// and update the view to correspond.
//
m_nCurEntry    = 0;            // first entry
m_szCurName    = "";           // blank name
m_nCurTaxable = 0;             // non-taxable
m_nCurType     = IDC_EXPENSE;// expense
if (m_CatList.GetCount() > 0)
{
   m_CatList.SetCurSel (m_nCurEntry);
   m_CatList.GetText (m_nCurEntry, m_szCurName);
   m_Taxable.SetCheck (m_nCurTaxable);
   CheckRadioButton (IDC_EXPENSE, IDC_INCOME, m_nCurType);
}

//
// disable the Modify and Delete buttons
// and enable the Add button.
//
m_ModifyButton.EnableWindow (FALSE);
m_DeleteButton.EnableWindow (FALSE);
m_AddButton.EnableWindow (TRUE);
m_Category.SetWindowText ("");
m_Category.SetFocus();
}
```

The foregoing code locates the category in the document's list of CCategory objects and deletes that entry. The code continues by deleting the category from the view's scrolling list box and then resetting the view's member variables to an initial state. If the scrolling list is found to contain one or more entries after the previous entry was deleted, then the first entry in the scrolling list is selected and the view's member variables are updated to reflect the settings associated with the entry. Finally, because an entry was newly deleted, both the Modify and Delete buttons are disabled and the AddButton is enabled. The handler concludes by setting the contents of the Edit control to an empty string and moving the focus to that control.

OnModify Message Handler Code

The OnModify message handler is invoked by the framework when the user clicks the Modify button in the view. The creation of this handler was discussed in Chapter 5, on page 141, in step 3. The custom code for this handler is as follows:

```
void CCatList::OnModify()
{
  CString szText;
  POSITION pos;
  WORD nType, nTax;

  m_Category.GetWindowText (szText);
  if (szText.GetLength() <= 0)
  {
    AfxMessageBox ("Category text is required");
    return;
  }
  if (!FindCategory (szText))
  {
    AfxMessageBox ("You can't change a category name using\
    Modify. You must first delete and then add the new name.");
    return;
  }
  nType = GetCheckedRadioButton (IDC_EXPENSE, IDC_INCOME);
  if (nType != IDC_EXPENSE && nType != IDC_INCOME)
  {
    AfxMessageBox ("Either Expense or Income must be\
      selected");
    return;
  }
  nTax = m_Taxable.GetCheck();
```

The first section of the OnModify message handler determines whether the user entered a valid category. To be valid, the Edit control must not be empty of text, the category name must exist in the document's list of CCategory objects, and either the Expense or Income radio button must be checked.

If any of the foregoing conditions is not met, an appropriate error dialog is presented to the user and the handler returns control to the framework. If all of the conditions are met, then the handler continues execution by locating the category object in the document's list and then changing the settings for the object, as follows:

```
    //
    // locate the entry in the category list and
    // change the settings.
    //
    CKeepitDoc* pDoc = GetDocument ();
    pos = pDoc->m_CatList.GetHeadPosition ();
    while (pos != NULL)
    {
       CCategory* pCat;
       pCat = (CCategory *)pDoc->m_CatList.GetNext (pos);
       if (pCat->GetCatName () == szText)
       {
          pCat->SetCatType (nType);
          pCat->SetTaxable (nTax);
          break;
       }
    }

    //
    // enable the Modify and Delete buttons, disable
    // the Add button, and set the focus to the category.
    //
    m_ModifyButton.EnableWindow (TRUE);
    m_DeleteButton.EnableWindow (TRUE);
    m_AddButton.EnableWindow (FALSE);
    m_Category.SetFocus ();
    m_Category.SetSel (0, -1, TRUE);
}
```

The foregoing code concludes by enabling the Modify and Delete buttons, disabling the Add button, setting the focus to the Edit control, and selecting the text in the control.

OnSelectCat Message Handler Code

The OnSelectCat message handler is executed by the framework when the user clicks the mouse on (or navigates using the keyboard to) one of the existing categories in the scrolling list box. This message handler was created in the ClassWizard tutorial in Chapter 5, on page 141, in step 4. The custom code for the handler is all newly added and is as follows:

```
void CCatList::OnSelectCat ()
{
    CString szText;
    POSITION pos;
    WORD nType, nTax;
    int nEntry;

    nEntry = m_CatList.GetCurSel ();
    m_CatList.GetText (nEntry, szText);
    CKeepitDoc* pDoc = GetDocument ();
    pos = pDoc->m_CatList.GetHeadPosition ();
    while (pos != NULL)
    {
       CCategory* pCat;
       pCat = (CCategory *)pDoc->m_CatList.GetNext (pos);
       if (pCat->GetCatName () == szText)
       {
          //
```

```
        // found the selected entry. set the controls
        // to the values in the category list.
        //
        m_Category.SetWindowText (szText);
        nType = pCat->GetCatType();
        nTax  = pCat->GetTaxable();
        m_Taxable.SetCheck (nTax);
        CheckRadioButton (IDC_EXPENSE, IDC_INCOME, nType);


        //
        // set the values for the current entry
        //
        m_nCurEntry   = nEntry;
        m_szCurName   = szText;
        m_nCurTaxable = nTax;
        m_nCurType    = nType;


        //
        // enable the Modify and Delete buttons and
        // disable the Add button.
        //
        m_ModifyButton.EnableWindow (TRUE);
        m_DeleteButton.EnableWindow (TRUE);
        m_AddButton.EnableWindow (FALSE);
        break;
    }
  }
}
```

The foregoing code performs the necessary functions for handling the
selection of a new category. The first step is to loop through the CCategory objects in the document's list until the selected category is found.
The settings for the category are then used to change the values in the
view's controls. After the settings have been changed, the view's member
variables are modified to reflect the new settings. The handler concludes
by enabling the Modify and Delete buttons and disabling the Add button in the view.

OnKillfocusCategory Message Handler Code

The OnKillfocusCategory message handler is invoked when the user
tabs from the Edit control to another control in the tab order or clicks
any other control with the mouse. The message handler was created, as
shown in the ClassWizard tutorial in Chapter 5, on page 141, in step 5.
The custom code for this handler is all newly added and is as follows:

```
void CCatList::OnKillfocusCategory()
{
  CString szText;

  m_Category.GetWindowText (szText);
  if (szText.GetLength() <= 0)
  {
    //
    // nothing has been entered, so we
    // need to disable all of the buttons.
    //
    m_ModifyButton.EnableWindow (FALSE);
```

```
            m_DeleteButton.EnableWindow (FALSE);
            m_AddButton.EnableWindow (FALSE);
            return;
        }

    if (FindCategory (szText))
    {
        //
        // entry matches an existing category,
        // so enable the Modify and Delete buttons
        // and disable the Add button.
        //
        m_ModifyButton.EnableWindow (TRUE);
        m_DeleteButton.EnableWindow (TRUE);
        m_AddButton.EnableWindow (FALSE);
    }
    else
    {
        //
        // it doesn't match an existing entry, so
        // the user must be trying to add a new
        // entry. disable the Modify and Delete
        // buttons and enable the Add button.
        //
        m_ModifyButton.EnableWindow (FALSE);
        m_DeleteButton.EnableWindow (FALSE);
        m_AddButton.EnableWindow (TRUE);
    }
}
```

The first action of the foregoing code is to check whether the Edit control is empty of text. If so, the handler disables all three of the buttons (Add, Delete, and Modify) and returns. If the control does contain some text and the text matches an existing category name, the handler enables both the Modify and Delete buttons and disables the Add button. If the text in the Edit control does not match an existing category, then the handler disables the Modify and Delete buttons and enables the Add button.

Customizing the CEditAcct Dialog

The CEditAcct class was created by the ClassWizard after the Edit Account dialog was designed using the App Studio tool. The process for creating both the dialog and then generating the default code is discussed in Chapter 5. The wizard-created code for the CEditAcct class is shown on pages 156–159. The sections that follow describe the custom code additions that make the dialog fully functional.

The Edit Account dialog is intended to provide the user with the means to create new accounts and edit existing accounts, mainly to change their type (e.g., Savings rather than Checking), but also to change their names. The default account name, when a new document is created, is preset to "(Untitled Account)." One of the first actions that a user will take is to rename that account using the Edit Account dialog. The Edit command is chosen from the Account menu.

CEditAcct Header File Code

The header file for the CEditAcct class is named **editacct.h**. The contents of this file, as modified for our use, are as follows:

```
// editacct.h : header file
//
/////////////////////////////////////////////////////////////////
// CEditAcct dialog

class CEditAcct : public CDialog
{
// Construction
public:
    CEditAcct(CWnd* pParent = NULL); // standard constructor

// Dialog Data
    //{{AFX_DATA(CEditAcct)
    enum { IDD = IDD_EDIT_ACCOUNT };
    CEdit       m_Description;
    CButton     m_OKButton;
    CButton     m_Delete;
    CButton     m_Modify;
    CButton     m_Add;
    CComboBox   m_Accounts;
    CString     m_szDescription;
    //}}AFX_DATA

    int         m_nEntry;      // added
    CObList     m_Accts;       // added
    CString     m_szName;      // added
    int         m_nType;       // added
    int         m_nStatus;     // added

// Implementation
protected:
    virtual void DoDataExchange(CDataExchange* pDX);

    virtual BOOL OnInitDialog(); // override added

    // Generated message map functions
    //{{AFX_MSG(CEditAcct)
    afx_msg void OnSelchangeAcctName();
    afx_msg void OnKillfocusAcctName();
    afx_msg void OnDeleteAcct();
    afx_msg void OnAddAcct();
    afx_msg void OnModifyAcct();
    //}}AFX_MSG
    DECLARE_MESSAGE_MAP()

    virtual void SetAcctInfo (void);    // added
    virtual void ClearSettings (void);  // added
};
```

In the foregoing code, the only changes are to the lines that contain change bars at their left. Other than these, the code remains as it was created by the ClassWizard. Note that the dialog's major controls are implemented as objects of the associated MFC classes, and handles to the actual dialog's controls are stored into these objects, automatically, by the use of the dialog data exchange (DDX) features of the application framework. Both data exchange and validation (DDV) functions are available; however, we will be using only the exchange features and will perform our own validation of the user's data entries.

CEditAcct Preprocessor Declarations

The first section of the source code in the **editacct.cpp** file contains the `#include` directives, which provide the dialog with access to declarations pertinent to its task. The declarations are as follows:

```
// editacct.cpp : implementation file
//

#include "stdafx.h"
#include "keepit.h"
#include "keepdoc.h"    // added
#include "acctobj.h"    // added
#include "editacct.h"

#ifdef _DEBUG
#undef THIS_FILE
static char BASED_CODE THIS_FILE[] = __FILE__;
#endif
```

As is evident in the foregoing code, we have added `#include` statements to provide the CEditAcct class with access to the declarations associated with the CKeepitDoc and CAcctObj classes.

OnInitDialog Member Function Code

The OnInitDialog member function is an override of the same member function in the CDialog class. We need to override this member function to perform additional initialization of the dialog, prior to its being displayed by the framework. The code is as follows:

```
BOOL CEditAcct::OnInitDialog()
{
    CDialog::OnInitDialog();

    //
    // set the initial control values
    //
    m_OKButton.EnableWindow (FALSE);
    m_Delete.EnableWindow (FALSE);
    m_Modify.EnableWindow (FALSE);
    m_Add.EnableWindow (TRUE);
    CheckRadioButton (IDC_CHECKING, IDC_CREDIT_CARD,
        IDC_CHECKING);

    // get the entries in the m_Accts list and
    // enter them into the m_Accounts CComboBox.
    POSITION pos = m_Accts.GetHeadPosition();
```

```
   while (pos != NULL)
   {
      CAcctObj* pAcct = (CAcctObj *)m_Accts.GetNext(pos);
      CString szName = pAcct->GetAcctName();
      pAcct->SetAcctStatus (ACCT_UNCHANGED);
      m_Accounts.AddString (szName.GetBuffer(20));
   }

   //
   // initialize the remaining variables
   //
   m_szName = "";
   m_szDescription = "";
   m_nEntry = -1;
   return TRUE;
}
```

In the foregoing code, the very first act is to call the CDialog (base class) OnInitDialog member function. After that, the member function sets each of the controls to its initial state. The code disables the OK, Delete, and Modify buttons, and enables the Add button. The account type is set to Checking. The next task is to loop through the CObList of CAcctObj objects and load the combo box with all of the existing account names and set their status to the constant ACCT_UNCHANGED value. How the dialog's m_Accts variable is loaded with the account entries will be described later, when we discuss invocation of the dialog in the section regarding CKeepitDoc support. Finally, the local member variables are preset to initial values.

SetAcctInfo Member Function Code

The SetAcctInfo member function is a newly added helper for some of the other message handler functions. The code is as follows:

```
void CEditAcct::SetAcctInfo (void)
{
   POSITION pos = m_Accts.GetHeadPosition();
   while (pos != NULL)
   {
      CAcctObj* pAcct = (CAcctObj *)m_Accts.GetNext(pos);
      CString szName = pAcct->GetAcctName();
      if (szName == m_szName)
      {
         // the account entry matches the current account.
         // so set the controls in the dialog to match the
         // settings inthe account.

         m_szDescription = pAcct->GetAcctDesc();
         m_nType = pAcct->GetAcctType();
         m_nStatus = pAcct->GetAcctStatus();
         m_Description.SetWindowText (m_szDescription);
         CheckRadioButton(IDC_CHECKING,IDC_CREDIT_CARD, m_nType);
         break;
      }
   }
}
```

The preceding code is used to set the controls in the Edit Account dialog to the values specified for the current account (whose name is stored in the member variable m_szName).

ClearSettings Member Function Code

The ClearSettings member function is also a newly added helper for the message handler functions. Its purpose is to reinitialize the member variables, clear the text in the Edit control portion of the combo box, reset the account status to ACCT_UNCHANGED, check the appropriate account type radio button, and then set the focus on the Edit control. The code is as follows:

```
void CEditAcct::ClearSettings (void)
{
   CString szS = "";
   m_Accounts.SetWindowText (szS);
   m_szDescription = szS;
   m_Description.SetWindowText (szS);
   m_nStatus = ACCT_UNCHANGED;
   CheckRadioButton(IDC_CHECKING, IDC_CREDIT_CARD,m_nType);
   m_Accounts.SetFocus();
}
```

OnSelchangeAcctName Message Handler Code

The OnSelchangeAcctName message handler is invoked by the framework when the user chooses one of the existing accounts in the combo box. The code is as follows:

```
void CEditAcct::OnSelchangeAcctName()
{
   //
   // the user selected one of the combo box entries, so we'll
   // let her either delete or modify this account entry,
   // but not add a duplicate entry, by enabling or disabling
   // the buttons,as is appropriate.
   //
   m_Add.EnableWindow (FALSE);
   m_Modify.EnableWindow (TRUE);
   m_Delete.EnableWindow (TRUE);

   //
   // set the type and description for the selected account.
   //
   m_nEntry = m_Accounts.GetCurSel();
   m_Accounts.GetLBText (m_nEntry, m_szName);
   SetAcctInfo();
}
```

The foregoing code disables the Add button and enables both the Modify and Delete buttons when an entry is selected. The code also saves the index and text corresponding to the selected entry and then calls the Set-AcctInfo member function to set up the account type and other variables.

OnKillfocusAcctName Message Handler Code

The OnKillfocusAcctName message handler is called by the framework when the user tabs away from the Edit control in the combo box (or clicks the mouse on some other control). The code is as follows:

```cpp
void CEditAcct::OnKillfocusAcctName()
{
    //
    // the user tabbed to another control
    //
    m_Accounts.GetWindowText (m_szName);
    if (m_szName.GetLength() <= 0)
    {
        //
        // the Edit control is empty, so disable all
        // of the buttons, invalidate the selection,
        // and return.
        //

        m_Add.EnableWindow (FALSE);
        m_Modify.EnableWindow (FALSE);
        m_Delete.EnableWindow (FALSE);
        m_OKButton.EnableWindow (FALSE);
        m_nEntry = -1;
        return;
    }
    //
    // something was selected or entered
    //
    int selected = m_Accounts.SelectString (-1, m_szName);
    if (selected == CB_ERR)
    {
        //
        // nothing was selected, so replace the text
        // in the Edit control because SelectString
        // clobbers it.
        //
        m_Accounts.SetWindowText (m_szName);

        //
        // an entry wasn't found, so enable the Add and
        // Modify buttons, disable the Delete button,
        // and disable the OK button.
        //
        m_Add.EnableWindow (TRUE);
        m_Modify.EnableWindow (TRUE);
        m_Delete.EnableWindow (FALSE);
        m_OKButton.EnableWindow (FALSE);
    }
    else
    {
        //
        // the entry was in the list, so enable the Modify
        // and Delete buttons and disable the Add button.
        // also, setup the current selection.
        //
        m_Modify.EnableWindow (TRUE);
        m_Delete.EnableWindow (TRUE);
        m_Add.EnableWindow (FALSE);
        m_nEntry = selected;

        //
        // set the account type and description
```

```
        // according to which account was selected.
        //
        SetAcctInfo();
    }
}
```

The foregoing OnKillfocusAcctName message handler has to contend
with a variety of potential conditions. The first of these is the case where
the user has cleared the contents of the Edit control and then has tabbed
to another control. In this case, the member function disables the Add,
Modify, Delete, and OK buttons and returns control to the framework.

The next condition is where the user has entered some text into the
Edit control, but that text doesn't match any existing entry. In this
case, the user is probably intending either to add a new account or
change the name of an existing account. In support of either of those
actions, the member function enables the Add and Modify buttons,
but disables the Delete and OK buttons. Only when the user chooses
to add or modify the entry is the OK button enabled.

The final condition occurs when the user has entered text that matches
one of the existing account names in the combo box. In this case, they
are probably intending to either delete or modify the account. In support of either of these actions, the member function enables the Modify
and Delete buttons, but disables the Add button, and then calls the Set-
AcctInfo member function to set the member variables and controls to
the values associated with the selected account.

OnDeleteAcct Message Handler Code

The OnDeleteAcct message handler is called by the framework when the
user clicks the Delete button in the dialog. The code to handle this condition is as follows:

```
void CEditAcct::OnDeleteAcct()
{
    CString szDel = "Do you really want to delete the account "
        "and all of its transactions?";
    int selected = m_Accounts.GetCurSel();

    if (selected != CB_ERR)
    {
        //
        // a valid entry was selected, so check whether
        // the user really wants to delete the account.
        //
        int response = AfxMessageBox (szDel, MB_YESNO);
        if (response == IDNO)
        {
            //
            // no, it was a mistake. Just return.
            //
            return;
        }
```

```cpp
    //
    // yes, the user really wanted to delete the account,
    // so get the index of the selected entry and then
    // delete it from the combo box.
    //
    m_Accounts.GetLBText (selected, m_szName);
    m_Accounts.DeleteString (selected);
    m_nEntry = -1;

    //
    // find the entry in the local list of accounts
    // and change its status.
    //
    POSITION pos = m_Accts.GetHeadPosition();
    BOOL bFound = FALSE;
    while (pos != NULL)
    {
        CAcctObj* pAcct = (CAcctObj *)m_Accts.GetNext(pos);
        CString szName = pAcct->GetAcctName();
        if (szName == m_szName)
        {
            pAcct->SetAcctStatus (ACCT_DELETED);
            bFound = TRUE;
            break;
        }
    }
    if (!bFound)
    {
        AfxMessageBox ("Existing Account Not Found! ERROR");
        return;
    }

    //
    // everything is okay, so clear the entry's
    // settings, disable all of the action buttons,
    // and then enable the OK button.
    //
    ClearSettings();
    m_Add.EnableWindow (FALSE);
    m_Modify.EnableWindow (FALSE);
    m_Delete.EnableWindow (FALSE);
    m_OKButton.EnableWindow (TRUE);
    }
}
```

In the foregoing code, the message handler checks whether an account was selected, in which case the `selected` variable would contain a value other than CB_ERR), and then continues execution only if an account had been selected. (Actually, the Delete button should not have been enabled unless an account had been selected, but we often take precautions not to do anything drastic if something has changed the environment.)

After it has been determined that an account has been selected for deletion, the message handler displays a dialog that offers the user the chance to recant the decision to delete the account *and* all of its transactions. Because this is a step that cannot be undone, it is important to make the user aware of the consequences of this action.

If the user decides not to delete the account, the message handler returns control to the framework. On the other hand, if the user answers in the affirmative that the deletion is intended, then the account name is deleted from the combo box, the status of the account in the local list is changed to ACCT_DELETED, and then the settings are cleared and all of the buttons are disabled with the exception of the OK button, which is enabled.

OnAddAcct Message Handler Code

The OnAddAcct message handler is called by the framework when the user clicks the Add button. The code is as follows:

```cpp
void CEditAcct::OnAddAcct()
{
  //
  // get the account name and the account type
  // and then add the name and description to the
  // ComboBox.
  //
  m_Accounts.GetWindowText (m_szName);
  m_nType = GetCheckedRadioButton (IDC_CHECKING,
      IDC_CREDIT_CARD);
  if (m_nType == 0)
  {
    AfxMessageBox ("An account type must be selected");
    return;
  }
  int selected = m_Accounts.AddString (m_szName);
  m_Description.GetWindowText(m_szDescription);
  m_Accounts.SetCurSel (selected);
  m_nEntry = selected;

  //
  // create an object of CAcctObj and put it into
  // the local list, along with the values of its
  // member objectvariables.
  //
  CAcctObj* pAcct = new CAcctObj;
  pAcct->SetAcctStatus (ACCT_ADDED);
  pAcct->SetAcctName (m_szName);
  pAcct->SetAcctDesc (m_szDescription);
  pAcct->SetAcctType (m_nType);
  pAcct->SetAcctID (((CKeepitApp *)AfxGetApp())
      ->m_nNextMenuID++);
  m_Accts.AddTail (pAcct);

  //
  // all is okay, so disable the Add button and
  // enable the Modify, Delete, and OK buttons.
  //
  m_Add.EnableWindow (FALSE);
  m_Modify.EnableWindow (TRUE);
  m_Delete.EnableWindow (TRUE);
  m_OKButton.EnableWindow (TRUE);
  m_Accounts.SetFocus();
}
```

In the foregoing code, the OnAddAcct message handler verifies that one of the account type radio buttons is selected and if so, it continues processing the request. In order to add a new account, a new object of CAcctObj must be created and its member variables must be initialized with the values associated with the current settings of the controls. The account's name is contained in the Edit control of the combo box, the account description is contained in the Edit control for that purpose, and the account type is specified by the radio button that is currently checked.

We assign an account identifier at this time by obtaining the current value of the `m_nNextMenuID` variable from the application object, incrementing the variable's value in the process, and then store the value into the new CAcctObj object. The new CAcctObj object is added to the document's list of accounts at this point. Finally, the Add button is disabled. The Modify, Delete, and OK buttons are enabled, and the focus is set to the Edit control of the combo box.

OnModifyAcct Message Handler Code

The OnModifyAcct message handler is called by the framework when the user clicks the Modify button in the Edit Account dialog. The code is as follows:

```cpp
void CEditAcct::OnModifyAcct()
{
    CString msg;
    CString szEName;
    m_Accounts.GetWindowText(szEName);
    msg = "Can't modify an entry which hasn't been selected"
        " previously.";
    int selected = m_Accounts.SelectString (-1, szEName);
    if (selected == CB_ERR)
    {
        //
        // the name in the Edit box doesn't match any
        // of the existing accounts, so the user must be
        // trying to change the account name.
        //
        m_Accounts.SetWindowText (szEName);
        if (m_nEntry < 0)
        {
            //
            // error---can't modify an entry which
            // hasn't been selected previously.
            //
            AfxMessageBox (msg);
            m_Modify.EnableWindow (FALSE);
            return;
        }
    }
    else
    {
        m_nEntry = selected;
    }
```

```cpp
//
// get the information we need for the account
// entry from the dialog.
//
m_Accounts.GetLBText (m_nEntry, m_szName);
m_nType = GetCheckedRadioButton (IDC_CHECKING,
   IDC_CREDIT_CARD);
m_Description.GetWindowText (m_szDescription);


//
// now, find the account that matches the selected
// entry and change its corresponding values.
//
POSITION pos = m_Accts.GetHeadPosition ();
BOOL bFound = FALSE;
while (pos != NULL)
{
   CAcctObj* pAcct = (CAcctObj *)m_Accts.GetNext (pos);
   CString szName = pAcct->GetAcctName ();
   if (szName == m_szName)
   {
      //
      // set the fields in the local account to
      // the values in the dialog.
      //
      pAcct->SetAcctName (szEName);
      pAcct->SetAcctType (m_nType);
      pAcct->SetAcctDesc (m_szDescription);
      pAcct->SetAcctStatus (ACCT_MODIFIED);
      bFound = TRUE;
      break;
   }
}
if (!bFound)
{
   AfxMessageBox ("Existing Account Not Found! ERROR2");
   return;
}


//
// if the name of the account was changed, we need
// to change the ComboBox name to match.
//
if (szEName != m_szName)
{
   m_szName = szEName;
   m_Accounts.DeleteString (m_nEntry);
   m_Accounts.InsertString (m_nEntry, szEName);
}


//
// finally, change the status of the buttons so that
// the action buttons are disabled and the OK button
// is enabled.
//
m_Add.EnableWindow (FALSE);
m_Modify.EnableWindow (FALSE);
m_Delete.EnableWindow (FALSE);
m_OKButton.EnableWindow (TRUE);
}
```

The foregoing OnModifyAcct message handler must contend with a number of situations. Unlike the Modify feature of the CCatList view, we can't allow the user to modify an account name by merely deleting the account and adding back a new one. The ramifications of deleting an account were discussed earlier, and it is important to make special provisions for an existing account name to be modified.

The first step is to determine whether the text in the Edit control matches an existing account. If not, then it is likely that the user is attempting to change the name of an existing account. To make sure, we check whether an account had been previously selected. If not, then an error dialog is displayed and the message handler returns. If a selection had previously been made then the message handler accesses the current contents of the various controls and stores these data into the member variables. The list of accounts is searched to find the entry to which the modification applies (using the previously selected account name to locate the account in the list, in the case where the name is being modified), and then the changes are applied to the list entry. If, for some reason, the list entry for the existing account isn't found, an error dialog is displayed and the message handler returns.

If the account name was changed, we also need to substitute the new name for the old one in the combo box's list. This is accomplished by deleting the old entry and adding the new one. It will be sorted into the correct alphabetic sequence automatically.

The final action after an account modification is to disable the Add, Modify, and Delete buttons and then enable the OK button.

Customizing the CAccount View

In order to support multiple accounts and make the CAccount view more robust, we have modified the OnInitialUpdate member function. In addition, we have added true validation of category names in the ValidCategory member function. Finally, to clean up the view when it is being closed, we have added an OnDestroy member function override. The sections that follow describe the new code.

OnInitialUpdate Member Function Code Changes

The OnInitialUpdate member function was presented originally in Chapter 4, on pages 80–83. The changes to that code are relatively minor and involve only the code that loads the transaction entries into the view's list box. The section of code affected by the modifications is as follows:

```
//
// fill the list box with all of the entries in the
// document's m_ListEntry list for the current account,
// and then select the first empty entry in the list.
//
GetDocument()->FillAcctList (m_pAcctList);
```

```
    int itemCount = m_pAcctList->GetCount();
    for (int index=0; index < itemCount; index++)
    {
      m_nCurSel = index;
      m_pCurEntry = (CListEntry *)m_pAcctList
        ->GetItemDataPtr (m_nCurSel);
      if (m_pCurEntry->GetStatus() == E_EMPTY)
      {
        break;
      }
    }
    m_pAcctList->SetCurSel (m_nCurSel);
```

Note in the foregoing code that we are calling the document's FillAcct-List member function, which was shown previously, on page 183. This member function fills the list box with entries which correspond to the current account number. After that has been accomplished, the code loops through the list of entries, looking for either the first empty entry or the last entry in the list. When the empty entry or the last entry is found, whichever is the case, that entry is selected as the first to be edited.

ValidCategory Member Function Code

The ValidCategory member function has been rewritten to perform validation of the category strings entered by the user. The code for the member function is all newly added and is as follows:

```
BOOL CAccount::ValidCategory (CListEntry* pEntry)
{
  CString szCatName;

  // first, verify that a category has been entered

  szCatName = pEntry->GetCategory();
  if (szCatName.GetLength() == 0)
  {
    return FALSE;
  }

  // next, search the document's category list for
  // a matching category name. If found, the category
  // is valid; otherwise, not.

  CKeepitDoc* pDoc = GetDocument();
  POSITION pos = pDoc->m_CatList.GetHeadPosition();
  while (pos != NULL)
  {
    CCategory* pCat;
    pCat = (CCategory *)pDoc->m_CatList.GetNext(pos);
    if (pCat->GetCatName() == szCatName)
    {
      return TRUE;
    }
  }
  return FALSE;
}
```

The foregoing code determines whether a category has been entered. If not, it immediately returns a FALSE result. If the string is not empty, then it is compared against the list of categories that the user has already defined. If a matching string is found, a TRUE result is returned; otherwise, a FALSE result is returned. The comparison is case sensitive.

OnDestroy Member Function Code

In this version of the application, we have taken pains to prevent memory leaks and make it more robust. The OnDestroy member function is called by the framework when a view is about to be destroyed. In our override of this member function, we take the precaution of deleting all of the objects created by the view. This includes the list itself, along with all of its entries. In addition, the special fonts and the label window are deleted. The code is newly added and is as follows:

```
void CAccount::OnDestroy()
{
    // get rid of all of the objects we've allocated
    // to clean up before the view is closed.

    CFormView::OnDestroy();            // call the ancestor
                                       // member function
    m_pAcctList->ResetContent();   // remove listbox entries
    delete m_pAcctList;               // and delete the object
    m_pAcctLabel->DestroyWindow();// destroy label window
    delete m_pAcctLabel;              // and delete the object
    delete m_pListEdit;               // delete the edit window
    delete m_pLabelFont;              // delete the label font
    delete m_pEditFont;               // delete the edit Wnd font
}
```

The comments in the foregoing code are self-explanatory. The cleanup of the allocated resources is limited mainly to the list itself and the fonts and label window that were allocated. The object pointers stored in the list refer to objects owned by the document, and will be destroyed by the DeleteContents member function (described beginning on page 189) when the document is disposed.

This concludes the changes and additions to member functions in the CAccount class. Very few changes were required to support the new requirements.

Changes to the CListEntry Class Member Functions

The CListEntry class implements the individual transaction objects. A list of these objects is kept in the document object, in the member variable named m_ListEntries. In this version of the Keepit application, we have added the m_nAccountID member variable to the CListEntry class and have modified the InitEntry member function shown in

Chapter 4 on page 72. In addition, we have added a new member function called MakeToday, which is referenced in the InitEntry member function and also in the Serialize member function shown in this chapter, on page 186.

InitEntry Member Function Code

The revised code for the InitEntry member function is as follows:

```
void CListEntry::InitEntry (int ID)
{
    CTime date;
    MakeToday (date);
    m_nStatus = E_EMPTY;
    CString szS = "";
    CString szN = "0.00";
    SetAccountID (ID);
    SetDate (date);
    SetItem (szS);
    SetDescription (szS);
    SetInfo (szS);
    SetCategory (szS);
    SetPayment (szN);
    SetDeposit (szN);
}
```

In the foregoing code, the MakeToday member function is called to store the current date into the CTime object called `date`.

MakeToday Member Function Code

The newly added MakeToday member function code is as follows:

```
void CListEntry::MakeToday (CTime& aDate)
{
    CTime tim = CTime::GetCurrentTime();
    int year  = tim.GetYear();
    int month = tim.GetMonth();
    int day   = tim.GetDay();
    CTime today (year, month, day, 0, 0, 0);
    aDate = today;
}
```

In the foregoing code, the newly created CTime object contains only the month, day, and year values. The time values have all been set to zeros so that successive list entries for the same date will compare as equals.

Customizing the CKeepitDoc Document Class Member Functions

Quite a number of member functions were changed and added to the CKeepitDoc class in support of multiple views (as described earlier in this chapter, on pages 180–190). This section covers the remaining additions to the CKeepitDoc class to support the COMMAND messages generated when the user chooses the Categories command from the View menu, the Edit command from the Account menu, or the choice of one of the account names from the Account menu. The support for these messages illustrates the best features of both the message map provisions in the MFC, as well as the ability to override the message map when it becomes necessary to do so.

OnViewCategories Message Handler Code

The OnViewCategories message handler is called by the framework when the user chooses the Categories command from the View menu. We used the ClassWizard to create a skeleton handler for this message in Chapter 5, the code for which is shown on page 160. The handler is invoked by the framework when the command is found in the document's message map. The customized code for this message handler is all newly added and is as follows:

```cpp
void CKeepitDoc::OnViewCategories()
{
   CKeepitApp* theApp = (CKeepitApp *)AfxGetApp();
   CMultiDocTemplate* pCatTmp = theApp->m_pCatViewTemplate;
   CFrameWnd* pCatFrame = pCatTmp->CreateNewFrame (this, NULL);
   pCatTmp->InitialUpdateFrame (pCatFrame, this);
}
```

The foregoing code makes good use of the template that we've constructed to support the new CCatList view. The message handler accesses the new template pointer (called `m_pCatViewTemplate`) by first acquiring a pointer to the application object and then accessing the template member variable. That variable is then used to create a new frame by calling the template's CreateNewFrame member function. If you recall, the template itself is a member of the CMultiDocTemplate class and is declared in the CKeepitApp header file on page 173. Once the CreateNewFrame member function is called, the CMDIFormFrame frame window and its enclosed CCatList view objects are created. The foregoing message handler then calls the template's InitialUpdateFrame member function, which makes the CCatList view the currently active view and sends the frame's descendents a WM_INITIALUPDATE message, which causes the OnInitialUpdate member function to be called for the view. Using the document template approach for creating new views makes the process quite easy, as is evidenced by the simplicity of the OnViewCategories member function code.

OnAcctEdit Message Handler Code

The OnAcctEdit message handler is called by the framework when the user chooses the Edit command from the Account menu. This message handler is responsible for displaying the Edit Account dialog and then processing the entries that result from the user's actions while the dialog is being displayed. Creating the dialog is quite easy. Processing the resulting entries is quite laborious, due mainly to the variety of actions that the user can take. In order to make the account editing (or creation) process more efficient, we don't limit the user to a single action with each invocation. Instead, the user is free to add new accounts or modify or delete existing accounts in a single invocation of the dialog. A complete description of the operation of the dialog, along with the source code for its various member functions and message handlers was presented earlier, in the description of the CEditAcct class on pages 202–213. The code for the document's OnAcctEdit message handler is newly added and is as follows:

```
void CKeepitDoc::OnAcctEdit()
{
    CEditAcct dlg;
    POSITION pos = m_AcctList.GetHeadPosition();

    while (pos != NULL)
    {
        // there are accounts in the list, so create copies
        // of them and store them into the dialog's list, so
        // that they can be modified.

        CAcctObj* pObj = (CAcctObj *)m_AcctList.GetNext(pos);
        CAcctObj* nObj = new CAcctObj (pObj);
        dlg.m_Accts.AddTail ((CObject *)nObj);
    }
```

The first section of the OnAcctEdit message handler builds a list of account entries into the dialog's local CObList object, called m_Accts. The reason for duplicating the account entries will soon become clear. Each CAcctObj object has a member variable called m_nAcctStatus. The value of this variable is ACCT_UNCHANGED in all of the document's account list entries.

During the course of interacting with the account list in the dialog, the local copies of the accounts are modified and the value in the m_nAcctStatus variable can change to ACCT_ADDED (for new account entries), ACCT_MODIFIED (for modified accounts), or to a value of ACCT_DELETED (for deleted accounts). Each of these status values has ramifications to the contents of the document, and if the user chooses to cancel the dialog rather than proceed with the changes that have been made, we need to ensure that the document isn't changed in any way. Therefore, the changes are honored only if the user dismisses the dialog by clicking the OK button. The code continues as follows:

```
    //
    // invoke the Edit Accounts dialog
```

```
if (dlg.DoModal() == IDOK)
{
   //
   // The user dismissed the dialog with the OK button,
   // so we can process the local list of accounts against
   // the ones in the document's account list to determine
   // what permanent changes need to be made.
   //
   POSITION lPos = dlg.m_Accts.GetHeadPosition();
   while (lPos != NULL)
   {
      CAcctObj* pL;
      pL = (CAcctObj *)dlg.m_Accts.GetNext(lPos);
      int stat = pL->GetAcctStatus();
      if (stat == ACCT_ADDED)
      {
         pL->SetAcctStatus (ACCT_UNCHANGED);
         SetModifiedFlag (TRUE);
         m_AcctList.AddTail (pL);
         AddAcctMenu (pL);
      }
```

The foregoing section of code begins a loop through the dialog's local list
of account entries. When the status of the entry indicates that a new account has been added, then the code calls the SetAcctStatus member
function to change the entry's status to ACCT_UNCHANGED, sets the document's modified flag to true, adds the new account to the document's
list of accounts, and then adds a menu item for the account into the Account menu. If the status is not ACCT_ADDED in the original entry, the
code continues as follows:

```
      else if (stat == ACCT_MODIFIED || stat == ACCT_DELETED)
      {
         SetModifiedFlag (TRUE);
         POSITION dPos = m_AcctList.GetHeadPosition();
         BOOL bFound = FALSE;
         WORD nAcctID = pL->GetAcctID();
         while (dPos != NULL)
         {
            POSITION pPos = dPos;
            CAcctObj* pD;
            pD = (CAcctObj *)m_AcctList.GetNext(dPos);
            if (pD->GetAcctID() == nAcctID)
            {
               //
               // found the matching entry
               //
               bFound = TRUE;
               if (stat == ACCT_DELETED)
               {
                  //
                  // remove the item from the document's
                  // account list, remove the menu command,
                  // and delete both copies of the object.
                  //
                  m_AcctList.RemoveAt(pPos);
                  RemoveAcctMenu (pD);
                  delete pD;
                  delete pL;
```

```
        //
        // the last task is to remove all of the
        // transactions matching this account from
        // the m_ListEntries list and then delete
        // the frame, if necessary.
        //
        RemoveTransactions (nAcctID);
        RemoveMDIFrame (szNewName);
        break;
    }
```

The foregoing section of the OnAcctEdit message handler checks
whether the status of the local entry is either ACCT_MODIFIED or
whether it is ACCT_DELETED. There is common code associated with
each of these cases. In either case, the matching entry must be found in
the document's list and then the appropriate actions must be taken, depending upon the entry's status.

The foregoing code singles out the deleted accounts as the first type to
handle. In that case, the matching entry is removed from the document's
list of accounts, the menu item associated with the account is removed,
both the local and document's CAcctObj objects are deleted, and, finally,
all of the transactions in the document's m_ListEntries list for the
account are removed by calling the RemoveTransactions member function (to be described shortly).

In case the account is currently being viewed, the code calls the RemoveMDIFrame member function to delete the frame and its view. If
the local account entry status is ACCT_MODIFIED, the message handler
continues as follows:

```
        //
        // stat must be == ACCT_MODIFIED
        // check to see whether the name has changed
        //
        CString szOldName = pD->GetAcctName();
        CString szNewName = pL->GetAcctName();
        if (szNewName != szOldName)
        {
            //
            // yes, the user changed the account
            // name, so change the name in the
            // document's account and also in
            // the menu title.
            //
            pD->SetAcctName (szNewName);
            RemoveAcctMenu (pD);
            AddAcctMenu (pL);

            //
            // we also need to update the frame title
            //
            POSITION vPos = GetFirstViewPosition();
            while (vPos != NULL)
            {
                CView* pView = GetNextView (vPos);
```

```
                              CFrameWnd* pFrame;
                              pFrame = pView->GetParentFrame();
                              CString szFrameName;
                              pFrame->GetWindowText(szFrameName);
                              if (szFrameName == szOldName)
                              {
                                  //
                                  // we've located the right frame, so
                                  // change its name.
                                  //
                                  pFrame->SetWindowText(szNewName);
                              }
                          }

                      }
```

In the case where the status was `ACCT_MODIFIED`, the foregoing code
checks whether the matching entry in the document's list of accounts
(using the account ID as the common variable value to compare) has the
same name as the local account entry. If the names are different, then the
user has chosen to change the account name and we must perform several operations to handle this situation. The new name must be entered
into document's copy of the account entry, the account's name in the
menu is changed by deleting the existing item and then adding back the
new item, and then the account name in the frame window (if shown)
must be changed to reflect the new name. The member function continues, handling the modified entry as follows:

```
                          //
                          // update the account entry and then
                          // delete the local object.
                          //
                          pD->SetAcctDesc (pL->GetAcctDesc());
                          pD->SetAcctType (pL->GetAcctType());
                          pD->SetAcctStatus (ACCT_UNCHANGED);
                          delete pL;
                          break;
                      }
                  }
                  if (!bFound)
                  {
                      AfxMessageBox ("No Matching Account. ERROR");
                      delete pL;
                  }
              }
              else
              {
                  //
                  // the status must == ACCT_UNCHANGED, so all we
                  // need to do is delete the local object.
                  //
                  delete pL;
              }
          }
      }
```

In addition to its account name being changed, the account's type or description might have been changed, so the foregoing code changes these fields in the document's version of the account entry by calling the object's member functions to do so, and then deletes the local account entry object.

In the event a matching entry isn't found in the document's list for the modified account (which event should never occur), an error dialog is displayed, the local entry is deleted, and the member function continues.

The final section of the OnAcctEdit message handler deals with the case where the user has dismissed the dialog by clicking its Cancel button. In this case, it is necessary only to delete the list of local account entries, and then conclude the process by falling into the code that removes all of the entries from the list. The code is as follows:

```
else
{
    //
    // the user has cancelled the dialog, so we must
    // simply delete all of the local account entries
    // and then delete the list.
    //

    POSITION lPos = dlg.m_Accts.GetHeadPosition();
    while (lPos != NULL)
    {
        CAcctObj* pL;
        pL = (CAcctObj *)dlg.m_Accts.GetNext(lPos);
        delete pL;
    }
}

//
// at last! Remove all of the entries from
// the dialog's list and we'll be finished.
//
dlg.m_Accts.RemoveAll();
}
```

As is evident in the foregoing code, when the user has canceled the dialog, the member function simply loops through the list of local entries and deletes each object. When this operation is complete, the code continues by executing the statement that calls the RemoveAll member function for the dialog's list, thereby removing all of the local account entries. This concludes the discussion of the OnAcctEdit message handler.

RemoveTransactions Member Function Code

The code for the RemoveTransactions member function is newly added and is as follows:

```
void CKeepitDoc::RemoveTransactions (WORD nAcctID)
{
   CListEntry* pEntry;
   POSITION pPos, nPos = m_ListEntries.GetHeadPosition();
   while (nPos != NULL)
   {
      pPos = nPos;
      pEntry = (CListEntry *)m_ListEntries.GetNext (nPos);
      if (pEntry->GetAccountID() == nAcctID)
      {
         m_ListEntries.RemoveAt (pPos);
         delete pEntry;
      }
   }
}
```

The foregoing code deletes all of the transactions for the account specified by the `nAcctID` argument by looping through the document list,
finding each entry that matches the account number, deleting the entry,
and then deleting the corresponding CListEntry object.

RemoveMDIFrame Member Function Code

The RemoveMDIFrame member function is called by the OnAcctEdit
message handler to delete a (possibly visible) view and its frame when the
account and all of its transactions have been deleted. The code is newly
added and is as follows:

```
void CKeepitDoc::RemoveMDIFrame (CString& szName)
{
   //
   // loop through the currently existing frames,
   // find the one that matches the specified name,
   // if any, and then delete it and its enclosed view.
   //
   POSITION vPos = GetFirstViewPosition();
   while (vPos != NULL)
   {
      CView* pView = GetNextView (vPos);
      CFrameWnd* pFrame = pView->GetParentFrame();
      CString szFrameName;
      pFrame->GetWindowText (szFrameName);
      if (szFrameName == szName)
      {
         pFrame->DestroyWindow();
         break;
      }
   }
}
```

The foregoing code calls the document's GetFirstViewPosition member
function to access the first view and then loops through each of the
views, accessing their parent frames to find the frame whose title bar
contains the name specified in the member function's argument. If a

frame with a matching name is found, the DestroyWindow member function is called to delete the frame and its enclosed view.

OnCmdMsg Member Function Code

The MFC message maps support the invocation of message handlers that are defined at the time the application is compiled. In the case where commands are created dynamically at run time, the message map methodology breaks down. Fortunately, the MFC makes provision for this case by allowing a given class to override the message map handler function, which allows the application to handle these dynamically created messages, according to its needs.

In the case of the Keepit application, we need to create menu commands for each of the accounts that the user defines. It is impossible to know how many of these may exist, or what command codes they will be assigned. When the user chooses one of the account name commands that were added to the Account menu, the framework sends a command message to the currently active child command-target object. If that object is unable to handle the command, it is routed to the window itself and, if the command is not handled, to the document.

In the case of the commands we have added to the Account menu, the document is the appropriate receiver for these commands. Choosing an account name is intended to cause a view for that account to be created or, if already created, brought into view and made active.

In the override of the OnCmdMsg member function, we will be concerned with only two types of messages. The CN_COMMAND message signals that a command has been chosen from one of the menus or a corresponding accelerator keystroke has been entered. The CN_UPDATE_COMMAND_UI message indicates that the framework requires the member function to update the status of any menu or toolbar commands with which it is concerned.

In our implementation of the OnCmdMsg member function, we first determine whether the command is applicable to our dynamic account items by testing the command code value. If the value is in the range between the first account identifier (FIRST_ACCT_MENU_ID) and the current value of the applications's m_nNextMenuID member variable, then the command is of interest; otherwise, the command is passed on to CDocument class's OnCmdMsg member function to handle. The code for this function is all newly added and is as follows:

```
BOOL CKeepitDoc::OnCmdMsg (UINT nID, int nCode, void
*pExtra,
    AFX_CMDHANDLERINFO* pHandlerInfo)
{
```

```
   if (pHandlerInfo == NULL)
   {
      // handle selection of Accounts

      UINT nNextAcctID
      nNextAcctID =((CKeepitApp *)AfxGetApp())->m_nNextMenuID;
      if (nID >= FIRST_ACCT_MENU_ID && nID < nNextAcctID)
      {
         // the command ID is for our menu items

         if (nCode == CN_COMMAND)
         {
            // handle selection of menu item

            OnAccountName(nID);
         }
         else if (nCode == CN_UPDATE_COMMAND_UI)
         {
            // handle UI update for menu item

            OnAccountNameUpdate (nID, (CCmdUI *)pExtra);
         }
         return TRUE;
      }
   }
   return CDocument::OnCmdMsg (nID, nCode, pExtra,
pHandlerInfo);
}
```

In the foregoing code, the first action is to test whether the value of the pointer to the handler information is NULL. If not, then the command is routed to the document to handle. If the pointer is NULL—which is usually the case—we test the command identifier (passed into the member function in the nID argument) to see whether it is in the range of commands in which we are interested. If not, then the command is passed to the document's handler to process.

You have probably realized by now that by assigning the various accounts ID numbers that double as their command numbers, we have solved two problems in a single stroke. Once the incoming command number is found to be within our range of interest, we need only test whether it is a CN_COMMAND or CN_UPDATE_COMMAND_UI command and then call the appropriate routine to handle it. If we handle the command, we return a result of TRUE to the framework. If the document's handler is called to handle the command, we return the result returned by that member function.

OnAccountName Member Function Code

The OnAccountName member function is called by our OnCmdMsg handler if the command type is CN_COMMAND and the command number is in the range of those assigned to existing accounts. The code for this function is newly added and is as follows:

```
void CKeepitDoc::OnAccountName (UINT nID)
{
  //
  // locate the account in the account list and
  // store its name and ID in the document's member
  // variables.
  //
  POSITION nPos = m_AcctList.GetHeadPosition();
  BOOL bAcctFound = FALSE;
  while (nPos != NULL)
  {
    CAcctObj* pAcct;
    pAcct = (CAcctObj *)m_AcctList.GetNext(nPos);
    WORD nAcctID = pAcct->GetAcctID();
    if (nAcctID == nID)
    {
      m_szCurAcctName = pAcct->GetAcctName();
      m_nCurrentAccount = pAcct->GetAcctID();
      bAcctFound = TRUE;
      break;
    }
  }
  if (!bAcctFound)
  {
    AfxMessageBox ("Account from Menu not in List");
    return;
  }
```

The first section of the OnAccountName member function locates the
entry in the document's account list that has an account number matching the one passed into the member function as its argument. If the account is found, as it should be, the document's member variables for the
current account are set to correspond to the settings for the entry. This is
to provide the means for the account view to access these variables to ascertain the account name and ID. In the event the matching account is
not found in the document's list, an error dialog is displayed and the
member function returns. The normal flow of the member function's
code is as follows:

```
  //
  // find a view whose frame matches the menu name
  // and activate its frame window.
  //
  POSITION pos = GetFirstViewPosition();
  while (pos != NULL)
  {
    CView* pView = GetNextView (pos);
    CFrameWnd* pFrame = pView->GetParentFrame();
    CString szFrameName;
    pFrame->GetWindowText(szFrameName);
    if (szFrameName == m_szCurAcctName)
    {
      //
      // we've located the right frame, so
      // activate it and return.
      //
      pFrame->ActivateFrame();
      return;
```

```
        }
    }

    //
    // at this point, it appears that the requested
    // view doesn't yet exist, so we need to create it.
    //
    CKeepitApp* pApp = (CKeepitApp *)AfxGetApp();
    CMultiDocTemplate* pTemp = pApp->m_pAcctViewTemplate;
    CFrameWnd* pFrame = pTemp->CreateNewFrame (this, NULL);
    ASSERT_VALID(pFrame);
    pTemp->InitialUpdateFrame (pFrame, this);
}
```

The last section of the OnAccountName member function's code searches for an existing frame whose name matches that of the newly chosen account. If a frame with a matching name is found, the member function calls the ActivateFrame member function to activate the frame and its view.

If a matching frame is not found, then the member function continues by creating a new frame, using the m_pAcctViewTemplate member variable to create the new child frame window and its view. After the creation of the new frame and its view is found to be valid, the InitialUpdateFrame member function is called to cause the view's OnInitialUpdate member function to be executed, initializing the frame's title bar with the chosen account name and performing the other initialization tasks shown in the code for that member function (described in Chapter 4, beginning on page 80, and slightly modified in this version of the application, as described beginning on page 213).

OnAccountNameUpdate Member Function Code

The OnAccountNameUpdate member function is called by our On-CmdMsg function when an CN_UPDATE_COMMAND_UI command is found to refer to one of the Account menu items.

The purpose of the OnAccountNameUpdate member function is to enable the menu item so that it can be selected. The framework automatically disables all menu items whenever the user drops down a menu and then enables the items for which there are message handlers defined in the message map. If there is no message map entry, as is the case for our dynamic account name items, it is necessary that we explicitly enable these items. The code to accomplish this task is as follows:

```
void CKeepitDoc::OnAccountNameUpdate (UINT nID, CCmdUI* pExtra)
{
    pExtra->Enable(TRUE);
}
```

The foregoing member function is called automatically for each menu item in the Account list for which there is no existing handler in the message map, when the user drops down the Account menu.

CanCloseFrame Member Function Code

We have added a final new member function to the CKeepitDoc class to override the document's CanCloseFrame member function. The code is all newly added and is as follows:

```
BOOL CKeepitDoc::CanCloseFrame(CFrameWnd* pFrame)
{
   int count = 0;

   if (CDocument::CanCloseFrame (pFrame))
   {
      //
      // count the views
      //
      POSITION pos;
      pos = GetFirstViewPosition();
      while (pos != NULL)
      {
         CView* pView = GetNextView (pos);
         count++;
      }

      //
      // if there is more than one view, OK.
      //
      if (count > 1)
      {
         return TRUE;
      }
   }
   return FALSE;
}
```

Our intention in the foregoing code is to prevent the user from closing the very last frame, and thereby causing the document to be closed. We don't really care whether the last frame contains a view of an account or is the CCatList view. In either case, preventing its closure allows the document to remain open. If the user desires to explicitly close the document by choosing either of the Close or Exit commands from the File menu, this function does not prevent that action from taking place.

Running the Keepit Application

When the Keepit application files are compiled and the application is run, you will be able to create multiple accounts, edit accounts, create new categories, edit categories, and view the accounts and categories on the screen. A view of an example set of accounts, the category view and the Edit Account dialog on the screen is shown in Figure 6-2.

Figure 6-2
View of the Keepit application in execution, with all of the elements showing

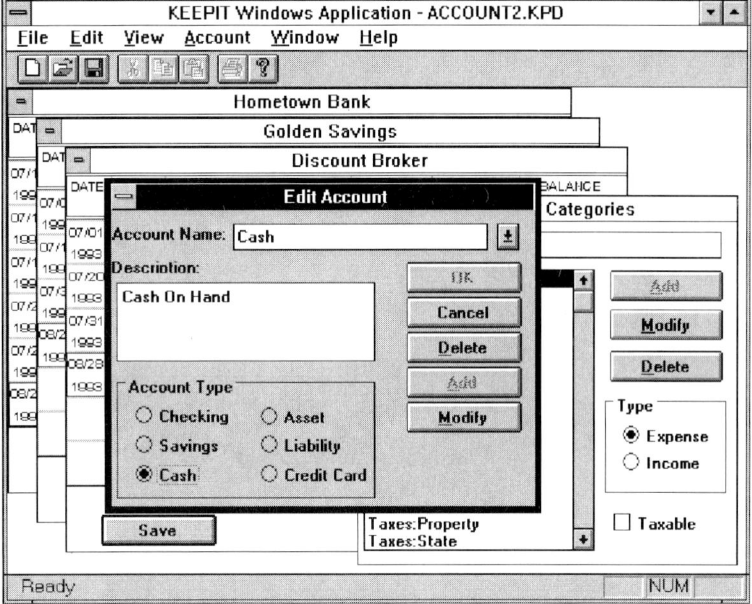

The best approach for creating a new set of accounts is as follows:

❖ Create a new document by choosing New from the File Menu.

❖ Create the list of transaction categories by choosing Categories from the View menu, adding the names you plan to use, along with their types (Expense or Income) and their Taxable status.

❖ Then you can change the name of the (Untitled Account) by choosing the Edit command from the Account menu. Enter a fairly short name that identifies the account (e.g., Hometown Bank).

❖ At the same time you change the name of the (Untitled Account), you can add new accounts by typing the name of each one into the Edit control, tabbing to the next control, selecting the account type, and then clicking the Add button.

❖ When you have finished entering new accounts, dismiss the Edit Account dialog by clicking the OK button.

At this point, you should see a list of the account names you have added by pulling down the Account menu. The accounts are listed in the order they are created. The only way to change the order is to rename an account, which causes the application to delete the old account name from the menu and add back the new name to the bottom of the list. No transactions will be lost in this process.

Experiment with the application in this stage of its development. It offers quite a number of features at this point. You can save a file of accounts and their corresponding transactions, exit the application, reinvoke the application, and then open the saved file. All of the accounts, transactions, and categories will be restored.

Exercises

1. Describe the differences between the two new windows in the current version of the Keepit application (Categories and Edit Account). Why were these implemented differently? Explain your answer.

2. The support for serialization of objects associated with the document includes a "schema" number in the IMPLEMENT_SERIAL macro. Describe how this number could be used in an application.

3. Why was the m_nNextMenuID member variable installed in the application class object? Elaborate on the ramifications of placing this variable in the document class (CKeepitDoc), for example.

4. The two document templates used in this version of the application have corresponding string resources in the resource file. The first is named IDR_KEEPITTYPE and the other is IDR_CATVIEWTYPE. describe the purpose and use of each of the fields in these resources. (*Hint*: The answer can be found in the material in this chapter.)

5. Describe the method that the framework uses to associate messages with the target objects to which they apply. In what way does the addition of the OnCmdMsg member function in the CKeepitDoc class enter this picture? Explain your answer by drawing a diagram that shows the path taken by a WM_COMMAND message (generated by the framework when the user chooses one of the account names in the Account menu) to its ultimate destination.[1]

6. In the OnAcctEdit message handler, the code constructs a new list of accounts in a member variable of the CEditAcct dialog object. Why was a separate list of accounts needed when there was an existing list in the CKeepitDoc object from which the dialog was invoked? Explain your answer.

7. When operating the Edit Account dialog, why doesn't the application permit an account name to be changed by allowing the user to

---

[1] This exercise will require quite a bit of time, reading both the reference material and the source code for the MFC classes involved in the routing of messages. It would be appropriate to assign this as an extra-credit project.

delete the existing account and add a new account? Explain your answer.

8. When the user enters a transaction, the new version of the Keepit application validates the category field to ensure that the string entered by the user matches an existing category exactly. The current technique uses a case-sensitive search. Modify the code to use a search technique that is not case sensitive.[1]

9. In the existing CEditAcct dialog code, there is nothing that restricts the user from modifying an account and then immediately deleting the account. Is this a valid methodology? Explain your answer.

10. Explain the purpose of the change to the CListEntry class to include a new member function called MakeToday. What purpose does this serve? In what way is the MakeToday member function valuable to the serialization code as well?

11. Describe the rationale behind adding the OnDestroy member function to the CAccount class and the addition of the DeleteContents member function to the CKeepitDoc class. Why were these member functions necessary? Explain your answer by providing a scenario where the absence of these member functions could lead to instability of the operating system.

---

[1] This exercise is not very time consuming and would enhance the current version of the application. However, keep in mind that the "official" list of category names is held in the list of categories. You might need to use these names in the future, so don't rely too heavily on the names in the transactions themselves if you implement this addition.

Chapter 7
Adding Support for Reports

In this chapter, we are going to add user interface elements to provide support for creating reports from the transactions stored in the various accounts. Tutorials will aid in the construction of two dialog boxes, a scrolling report view, and generation of the initial source files to support these elements.

The new user interface features support the creation of a single report, which is a listing of all of the transactions for selected accounts, within a specified time period. The creation of the dialogs and scrolling view will provide the basis for adding new reports in a subsequent phase of the program's construction.

In addition to providing a screen display of the selected data, the new code, after being customized (as described in the next chapter), will include provisions for the report to be printed on any Windows-compatible printer.

Creating the Report Menu and Its Items

In order to support the creation of reports, we have decided to add a new menu to the menu bar. This menu, called "Report," will contain command items for each of the reports we implement during the course of enhancing the Keepit application. The initial menu will contain a command to produce a single report. The steps for adding the Report menu and its single command item are as follows:

1. Make sure that the Visual C++ application has been launched and that the Keepit project (**keepit.mak**) is currently open.

2. Launch the App Studio resource editor by choosing App Studio from the Tools menu.

3. When the initial screen of App Studio appears, listing the types of available resources in the left portion of the view, click on the Menu resource type and then double click on the menu resource whose name is IDR_KEEPITTYPE. This will open that menu resource for editing.

4. Notice that there is a blank menu box immediately to the right of the Help menu. Click on that box and, holding down the mouse button, drag the box to the left, so that the cursor is between the menus labeled Account and Window. Release the mouse button.

5. Double click on the empty box and enter the string "&Report" into the Caption field of the properties window.

6. You will notice that there is now an empty item in the newly named Report menu. Double click on that item and enter its properties in that window, as follows:

   a. Enter ID_RPT_CASH_FLOW into the ID field.

   b. Enter "Cash Flow" into the Caption field.

   c. Enter "Creates a Cash Flow report" into the Prompt field.

7. Close the properties window by pressing the Enter key, and then close the resource window by double clicking in the window's document control icon (or use the Ctrl-F4 keyboard shortcut).

8. Open the menu resource named IDR_CATVIEWTYPE by double clicking on the name, and then repeat the foregoing steps 4 through 7 to duplicate the Report menu and its Cash Flow command in the category view's menu.

9. After the foregoing step 7 has been repeated, you should be looking once again at the main resource editor window, with the Menu resource selected in the left pane and the currently defined menus in the right pane. Duplicate the menu named IDR_KEEPITTYPE by clicking on it to select it, choose Copy from the Edit menu (or use the Ctrl-C keyboard shortcut), and then choose Paste from the Edit menu (or use the Ctrl-V keyboard shortcut). A copy of the menu should have been created and named IDR_KEEPITTYPE1.

10. Click on the newly created menu name to select it, and then click the Properties button at the bottom of the view. Change the menu's name in the properties window to IDR_REPORTTYPE. This will create a menu bar for use when any of the report views is being displayed.

11. Save the changes to the resource file by choosing the Save command from the File menu and then exit the App Studio tool by choosing the Exit command from the File menu.

This concludes the steps to create a new menu and also a new menu bar. The foregoing procedure has also added the new Report menu to the other existing menus.

Creating the Report Settings Dialog

When the Cash Flow command is chosen by the user from the Report menu, we want the user to be able to specify the accounts and the time period for which the report is to be prepared. To accomplish this goal, we will create a Settings dialog, which will be invoked automatically when the report command is chosen. The creation of the Settings dialog is a fairly involved procedure, you may wish to refer to Figure 7-18 while you are following the tutorial. Remember, the exact dimensions and co-ordinate values do not have to be duplicated; however, you may find that using the arrow keys to reposition controls, and the arrow keys, along with the Shift key, to resize the various controls will aid in the replication of these values. The steps to create the new dialog are as follows:

1. Launch the App Studio tool by choosing it from the Tools menu.

2. When App Studio's main window appears, with the resource types in the left pane, click on the Dialog type and then click on the New button at the bottom of the view. When the list of resource types appears, make sure Dialog is selected and then click OK. A new dialog, with the appearance shown in Figure 7-1, should now be on your screen.

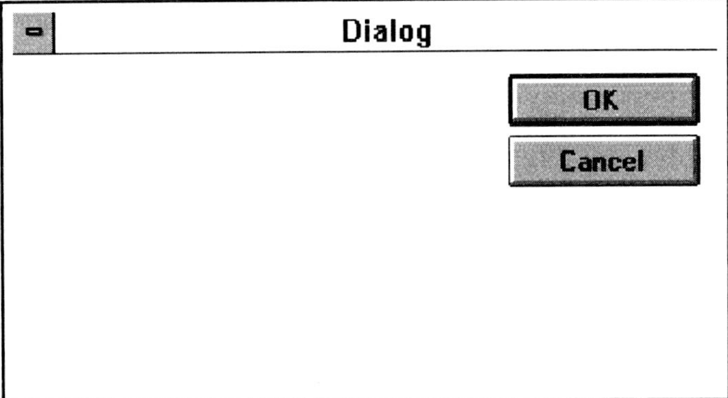

Figure 7-1
Appearance of new dialog in App Studio

3. Double click on the new dialog to cause the Properties window to appear. Make the General settings correspond with those shown in Figure 7-2.

4. Click the arrow at the right of the combo box whose contents are the word General and then select the Styles properties. Change these properties to correspond with those shown in Figure 7-3.

5. Change the size of the dialog by clicking on it to select it and then drag the lower right corner sizing handle until the dimensions of the dialog, as shown at the lower right corner of the dialog editor view,

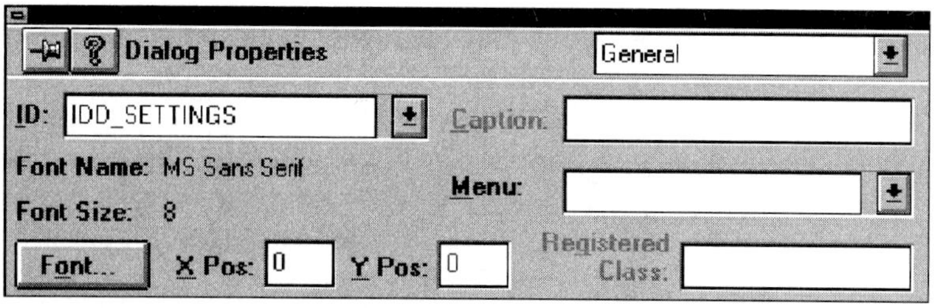

Figure 7-2
General properties for
Settings dialog

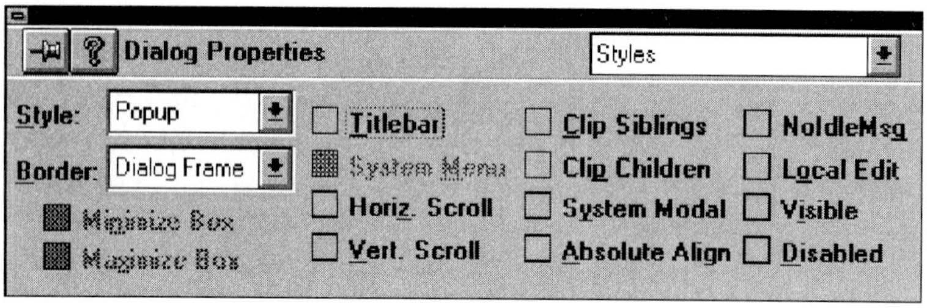

Figure 7-3
Style properties for the
Settings dialog

are 267 x 84. You will have to reposition the OK and Cancel buttons to the right side of the dialog, to make room for the remaining elements.

6. Choose the static text control from the dialog editor's control palette and drag the control onto the dialog at position 6,23 (as shown at the bottom right of the editor's view) and with dimensions of 19x8 (also shown at the bottom right corner of the dialog editor's view).

7. Double click the static text field and enter properties values that correspond with those shown in Figure 7-4.

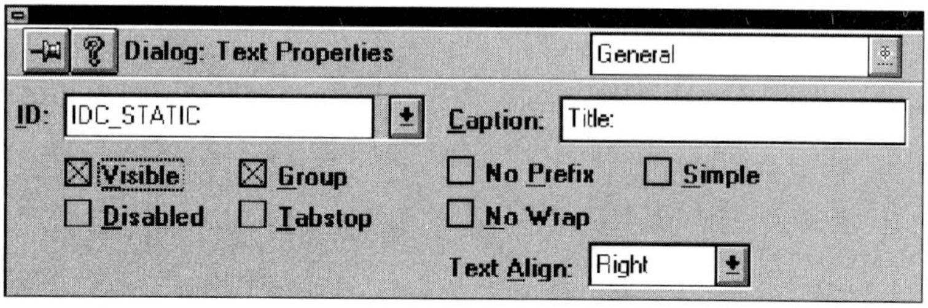

Figure 7-4
Static text Title field
properties

8. Click on the editable text control in the dialog editor's control palette and drag a copy of the control onto the dialog at position 27,22. Change the dimensions of the control to 174x11.

9. Double click on the editable text control just created and change its General properties to correspond with those shown in Figure 7-5.

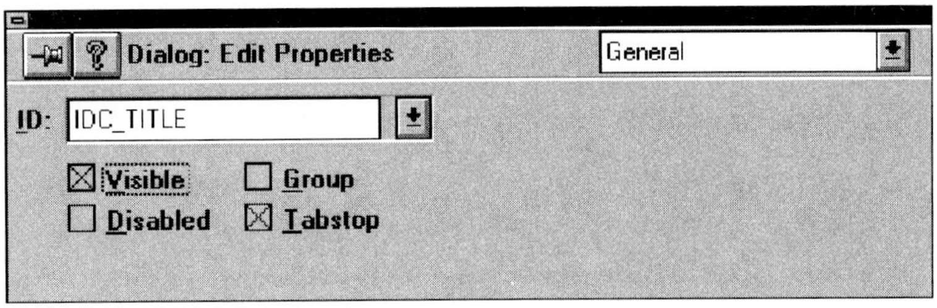

Figure 7-5
Editable text Title field's
General properties

Figure 7-6
Editable text Title field's
Styles properties

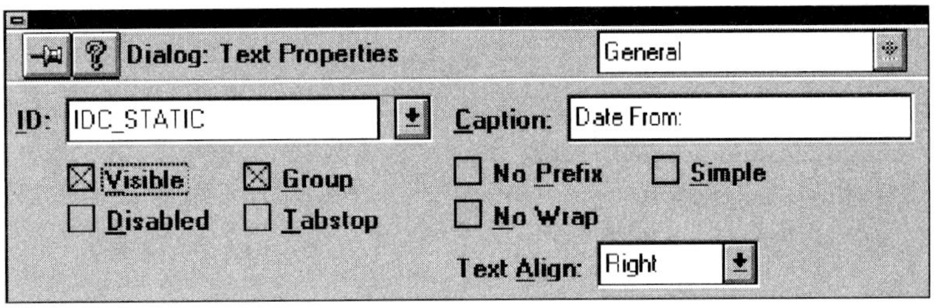

Figure 7-7
Static text From field's
properties

10. Click the arrow at the right of the combo box containing the word General and select the Styles properties. Change the settings in the dialog to match those shown in Figure 7-6.

11. Choose the static text control from the control palette and drag a static text control onto the dialog at position 7,46. Change the dimensions of the control to 39x8 and then double click and change the properties of the control to correspond with those shown in Figure 7-7. Note that the text alignment for this control is Right.

12. Choose the editable text control from the control palette and drag an editable text field onto the dialog at position 51,44. Change the measurements of the field to 41x11 and then double click on the field and change its General properties to correspond with those shown in Figure 7-8.

13. Change the Styles properties of the editable text control to correspond with those shown in Figure 7-9.

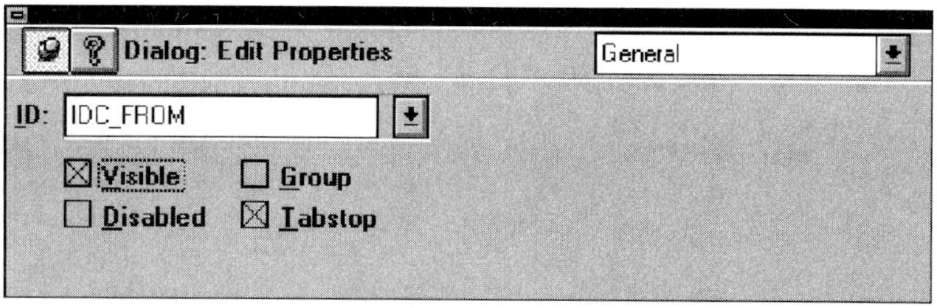

Figure 7-8
Editable text From date
field's General properties

Figure 7-9
Editable text From date
field's Styles properties

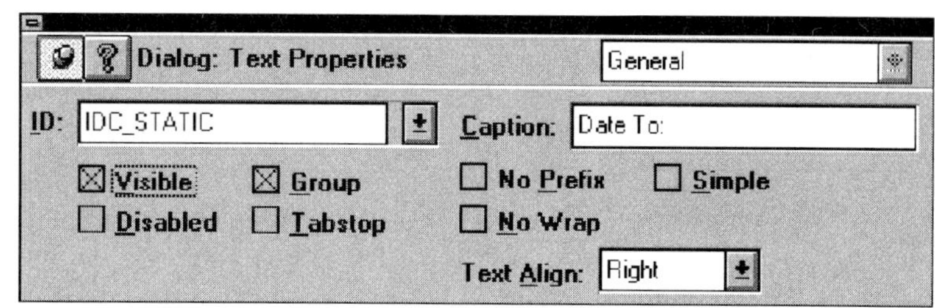

Figure 7-10
Static text To field's
properties

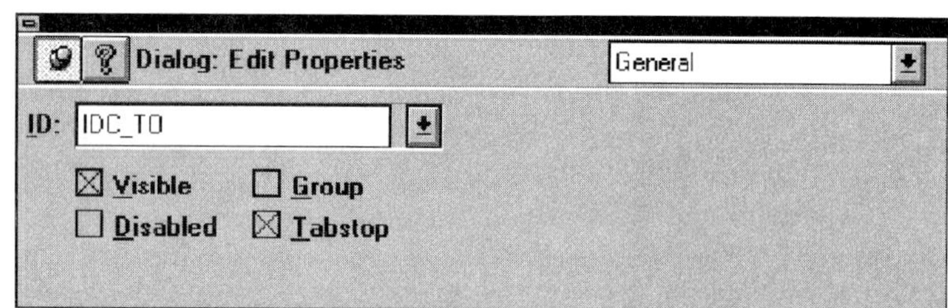

Figure 7-11
Editable text To field's
General properties

14. Choose the static text control and drag a copy of a static text field
    onto the dialog at position 123,46. Change the dimensions of the
    field to 31x8. Double click on the field and change its settings in
    the properties window to correspond with those shown in Figure
    7-10. Notice that the text alignment for this field is Right.

15. Choose the editable text control from the control palette and drag a
    copy of an editable text field to position 159,44 on the dialog.
    Change the field's dimensions to 41x11. Double click on the field
    and change its General settings to correspond with those shown in
    Figure 7-11.

Figure 7-12
Editable text To date
field's Styles properties

Figure 7-13
Accounts button General
properties

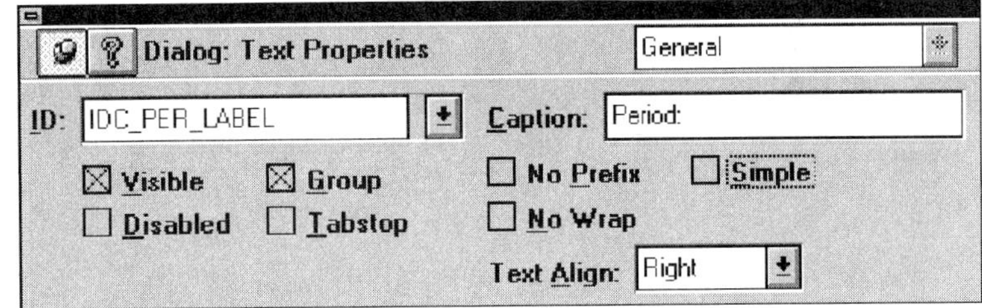

Figure 7-14
Static text Period field's
General properties

16. Choose the Styles properties in the combo box and change the settings for the editable text control to correspond with those shown in Figure 7-12.

17. Click on the button tool in the dialog editor's control palette and drag a button onto the dialog at position 27,62. Double click on the button and change its properties to correspond with those shown in Figure 7-13. The name of the button is followed by three "period" characters, indicating that when the button is clicked by the user, a dialog will be displayed. We will construct the "Accounts" dialog shortly.

18. Choose the static text tool from the dialog editor's control palette and drag a static text field onto the dialog at position 94,66. Change the field's dimensions to 30x7 and then double click on the field and change its General properties to correspond with those shown in Figure 7-14.

19. Choose the combo box control from the dialog editor's control palette and drag a combo box control onto the dialog at position

127,63. Change the dimensions of the visible portion of the combo box to 74x12 and then click on the arrow at the right of the combo box to drop down its list and change the overall measurements to 74x60.

20. Double click on the combo box in the dialog to display its properties. Change the General properties to correspond with those shown in Figure 7-15. Note that the figure does not show all of the entries in the "list choices" section of the properties window. The full set of choices is: Year-To-Date, Current Month, Current Quarter, Current Year, Last Month, Last Quarter, Last Year, and All Transactions.

Figure 7-15
Period combo box
General properties

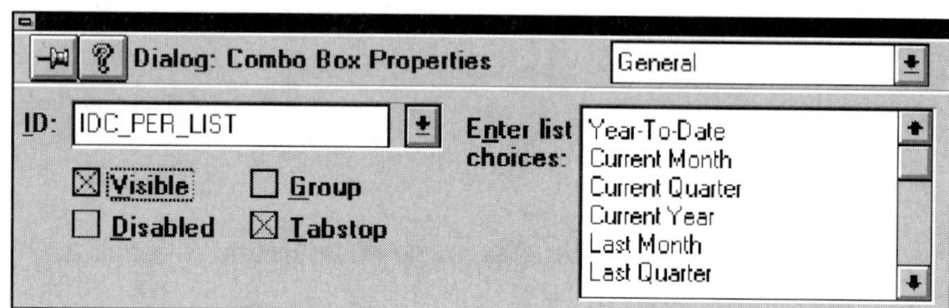

Enter each of the list choices, followed by a return. The return is entered by typing the Ctrl-Return (or Ctrl-Enter) key-combination. If you type just Return (or Enter), the dialog editor will assume that entry of the properties is complete.

21. Select the Styles properties for the Period combo box and change the settings to correspond with those shown in Figure 7-16. Note that the type of combo box is "Drop List," rather than "Drop-down." This type requires that the user choose one of the predetermined entries. The current choice is displayed in the top portion of the box when the list is closed.

Figure 7-16
Period combo box Styles
properties

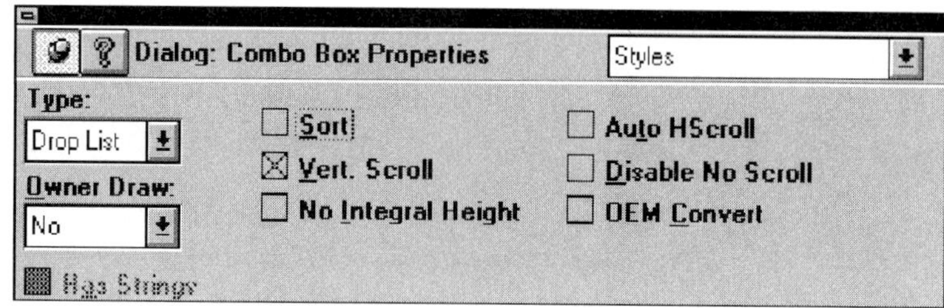

22. Choose the static text control from the control palette and drag a static text field onto the dialog at position 79,5. Change the dimensions of the field to 117x10 and then double click the field and change the settings to correspond with those shown in Figure 7-17. Note that the Text Align property is Center for this field.

Figure 7-17
Dialog title static text
General properties

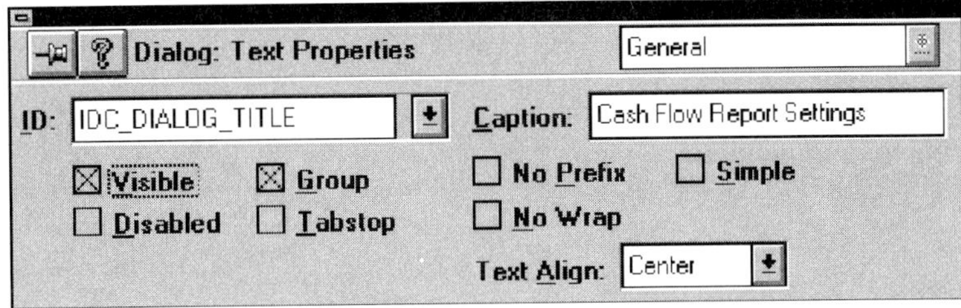

This completes the steps for creating the elements of the report settings dialog box. The resource file that we created positions the OK button at the coordinates 209,20. The Cancel button is positioned at 209,38. The completed dialog is shown in Figure 7-18 Save the resource file at this time by choosing Save from the File menu.

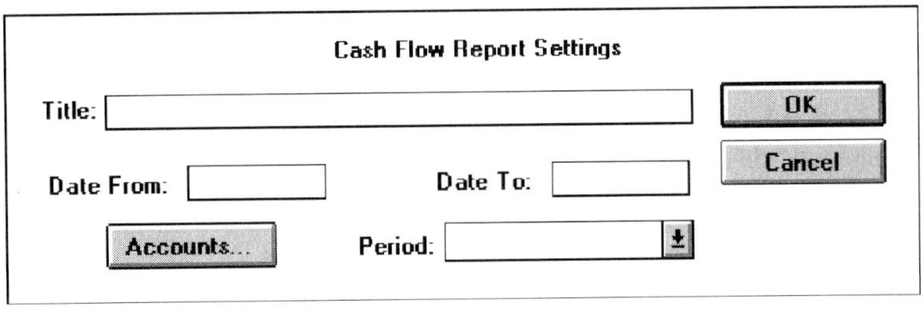

Figure 7-18
Completed Settings
dialog, as it appears in
the App Studio dialog
editor

Now, with the dialog still on the screen in App Studio, proceed to the next step, which is to create a new class, member variables, and accompanying member functions to manage the Settings dialog.

Creating the CSettings Class and Member Variables

New classes are created by the ClassWizard tool. It can be invoked either from the Visual C++ workbench environment or from within the App Studio environment. ClassWizard is implemented as a DLL, which enables it to be used within the context of multiple applications.

We will use the ClassWizard tool from within the App Studio dialog editor to create the CSettings class. The steps to do so assume that the dialog box shown in Figure 7-18 is still on the screen. The procedure is as follows:

1. Invoke ClassWizard by choosing it from the App Studio Resource menu. It will display a dialog requesting that you define a new class for the dialog that is currently being displayed. Fill in the fields of the dialog as shown in Figure 7-19. We have named the Class CSettings and its header and source files are named **settings.h** and **set-**

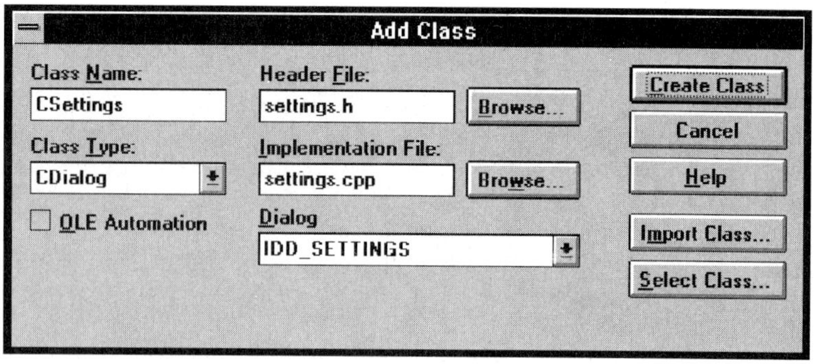

Figure 7-19
Add CSettings class
dialog in ClassWizard

tings.cpp, respectively. Note also that it references the dialog's identification, IDD_SETTINGS.

2. When the class and its associated file names have been entered, and after clicking the Create Class button, ClassWizard will display its main dialog, which contains the following elements:

   a. A combo box at the top of the dialog displays the currently selected class. In this case it contains CSettings.

   b. A row of tabs at the top, which provide the means to define Message Maps, Member Variables, OLE Automation, and view Class Info.

   c. With the Message Maps tab selected, a scroll pane on the top left portion of the dialog lists all of the available Object IDs.

   d. A scroll pane on the top right portion lists all of the available Messages for the selected objects.

   e. A text pane at the bottom shows the currently assigned message handlers for the class.

   f. On its right side, the dialog has a column of buttons, including OK, Cancel, Help (to access on-line help for the features provided by the ClassWizard tool), Add Class (for adding new classes), Add Function (which is active only when an object and message have been chosen, and then it becomes active—allowing message handler functions to be defined and entered into the class's files), Delete Function (which allows an existing message handler to be deleted), and, finally, Edit Code, which invokes the visual workbench editor with the source file for the current class preloaded and ready for editing.

With the ClassWizard's main dialog onscreen, click to select the Member Variables tab. Our first task will be to define member vari-

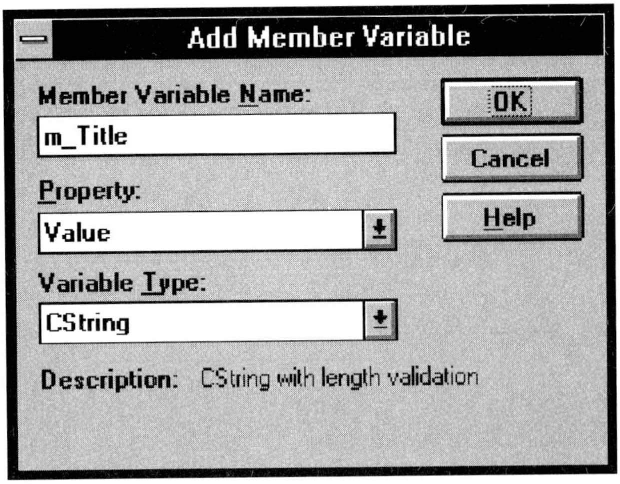

Figure 7-20
Adding the m_Title
member variable to the
CSettings class

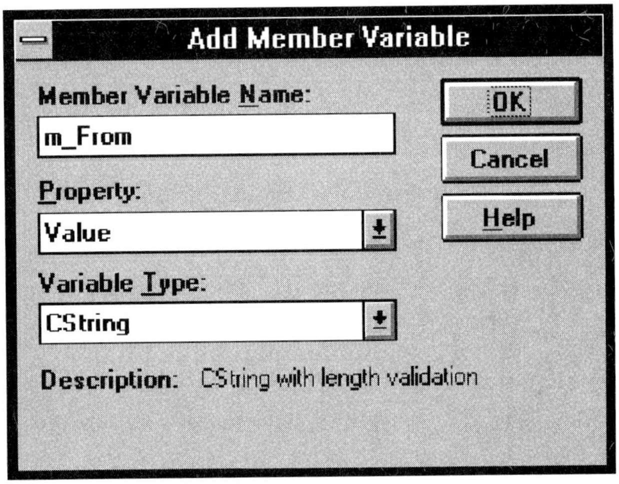

Figure 7-21
Adding the m_From
member variable to the
CSettings class

ables for some of the important controls in the dialog so that we can reference them directly in the code.

3. Click to select the IDC_TITLE control in the Control IDs pane and then click the Add Variable button in that dialog. The preceding action will cause the Add Member Variable dialog to be displayed. Fill in the fields of this dialog, as shown in Figure 7-20, and then click OK to accept the definition of the m_Title member variable. It is defined with a type of CString.

4. Select the IDC_FROM control, click the Add Variable button once again, and enter the values into the Add Member Variable dialog, as shown in Figure 7-21. Click OK to accept the definition of the m_From member variable. It is defined with a type of CString.

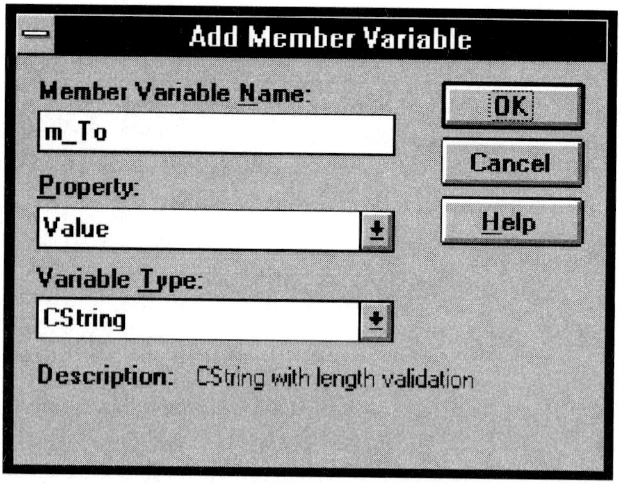

Figure 7-22
Adding the m_To
member variable to the
CSettings class

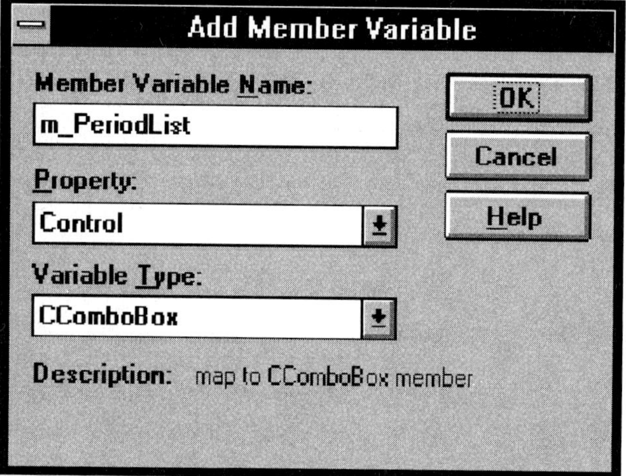

Figure 7-23
Adding the m_PeriodList
member variable to the
CSettings class

5. Select the IDC_TO control, click the Add Variable button, and enter
   the settings for the m_To member variable, as shown in Figure 7-22.
   Click OK to accept the settings and dismiss the dialog. It is defined
   with a type of CString.

6. Select the IDC_PER_LIST control, click the Add Variable button once
   again and enter the settings for the m_PeriodList member variable, as shown in Figure 7-23. Note that instead of this variable having a type of CString in the Add Member Variable dialog, it has a
   property of Control, rather than Value, and its Variable Type is
   CComboBox. When the dynamic data exchange code executes, we
   will gain direct access to this control through the handle that is
   stored in the member variable.

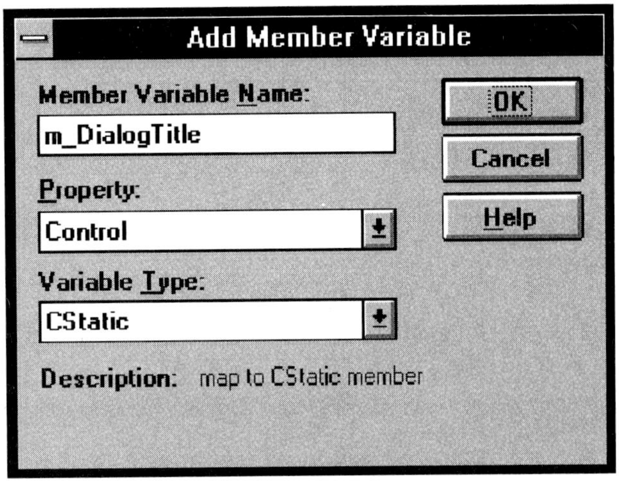

Figure 7-24
Adding the
m_DialogTitle member
variable to the CSettings
class

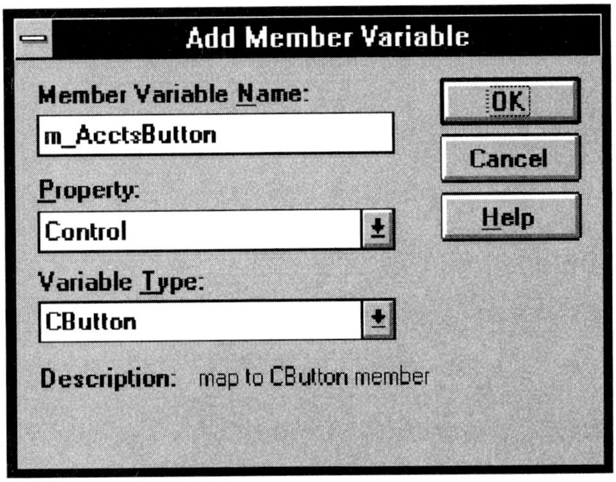

Figure 7-25
Adding the
m_AcctsButton member
variable to the CSettings
class

7. Select the IDC_DIALOG_TITLE control, click the Add Variable button, add the `m_DialogTitle` member variable, and then click OK to accept the definition. As with the previous member variable, this one has a property of Control and its Variable Type is CStatic, as shown in Figure 7-24.

8. Select the IDC_ACCTS_BUTTON control, click the Add Variable button one last time, and enter the settings for the `m_AcctsButton` member variable, as shown in Figure 7-25. This variable also has the Control property and is of type CButton.

This concludes the steps for creating the CSettings class, its header and source files, and the member variables for the class. We will examine the generated code, in detail, later in this chapter. The full list of member

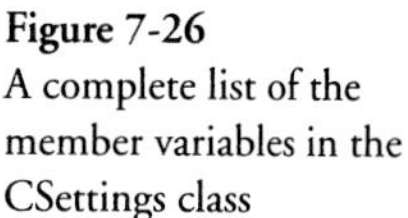

Figure 7-26

A complete list of the member variables in the CSettings class

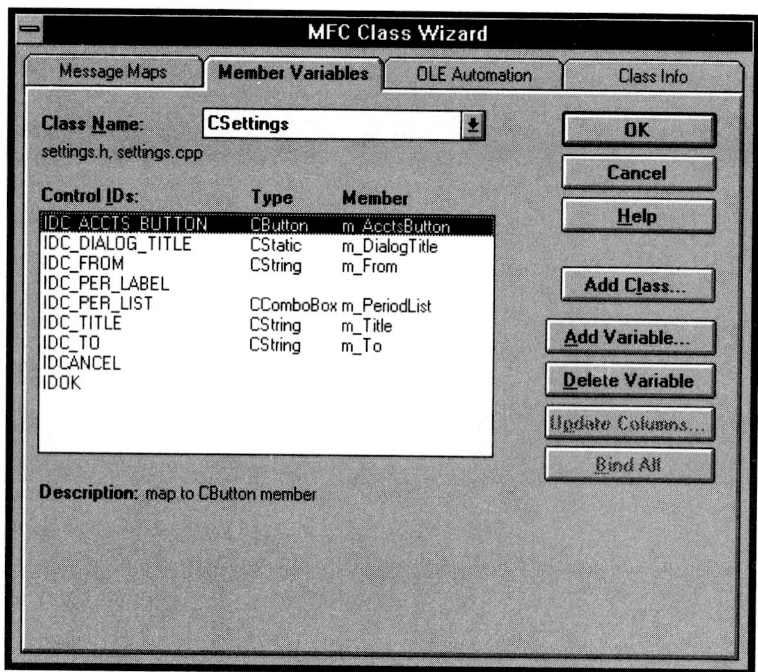

variables for the CSettings class is shown in Figure 7-26, as it appears in the ClassWizard's Member Variables window.

Defining Message Handlers for the CSettings Class

The ClassWizard tool is used to create the connection between various objects in the application, the messages that they generate, and the member functions that handle those messages. These functions are commonly called "handlers" or "message handlers" because their primary purpose is to handle messages.

To assign message handlers, we must first click the Message Maps tab at the top of the ClassWizard dialog to show the relevant Object IDs.

The Settings dialog contains two controls that generate messages that we wish to handle in the CSettings source code. The steps necessary to define the handlers for these messages are as follows:

1. Look in the list of "Object IDs" at the left side of the ClassWizard's dialog and locate the entry named IDC_ACCTS_BUTTON. Click on that entry and you will see that the list of "Messages" in the scrolling list on the right contains only two entries: BN_CLICKED (corresponding to the message sent when the button is clicked) and the message BN_DOUBLECLICKED (corresponding to the message sent when the button is double clicked).

2. Click on the BN_CLICKED entry in the right side pane and you will see that the Add Function button has now become active. This indicates that you can add a member function for this message.

3. Click the Add Function button and enter OnAcctsClicked as the name for the message handler in the Add Member Function dialog, as shown in Figure 7-27. Click OK to accept the handler name and to dismiss the dialog.

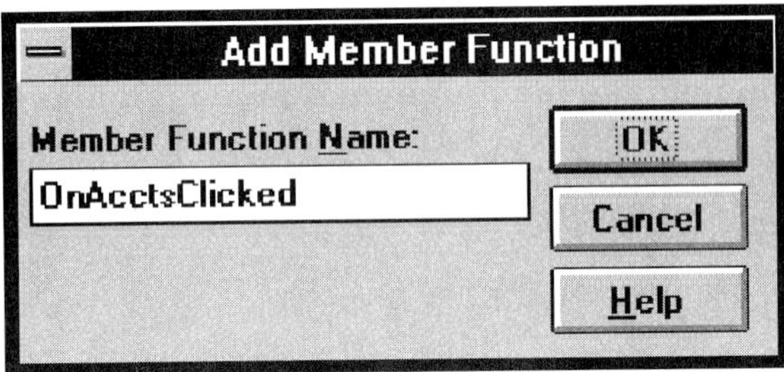

Figure 7-27
Adding the OnAcctsClicked message handler

4. Look in the list of "Object IDs" at the left side of the dialog, locate the entry named IDC_PER_LIST, and then click on that entry to select it. In this case, the period list, being a combo box, has quite a number of messages that it can send. Look in the list of "Messages" for the entry named CBN_SELCHANGE and then click on it to select that entry.

5. Click the Add Function button and enter OnPerListSelect for the name of the message handler in the Add Member Function dialog, as shown in Figure 7-28, and then click OK to accept the name and dismiss the dialog.

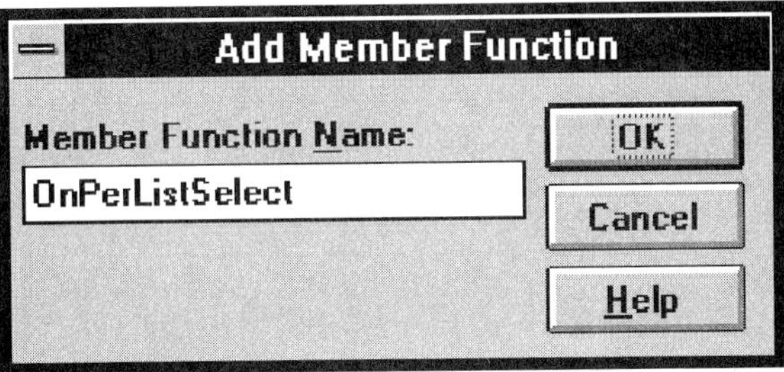

Figure 7-28
Adding the OnPerListSelect message handler

This completes the steps for adding message handlers to the CSettings class. The completed ClassWizard main dialog is shown in Figure 7-29. To see the member variables associated with the class, click the Member Variables tab at the top of the dialog.

To complete the procedures for using the ClassWizard to create the new CSettings class and its files, member variables, and message handlers, click the OK button at the top of the main window, as shown in Figure

Figure 7-29

Appearance of
ClassWizard dialog after
all member functions
have been added

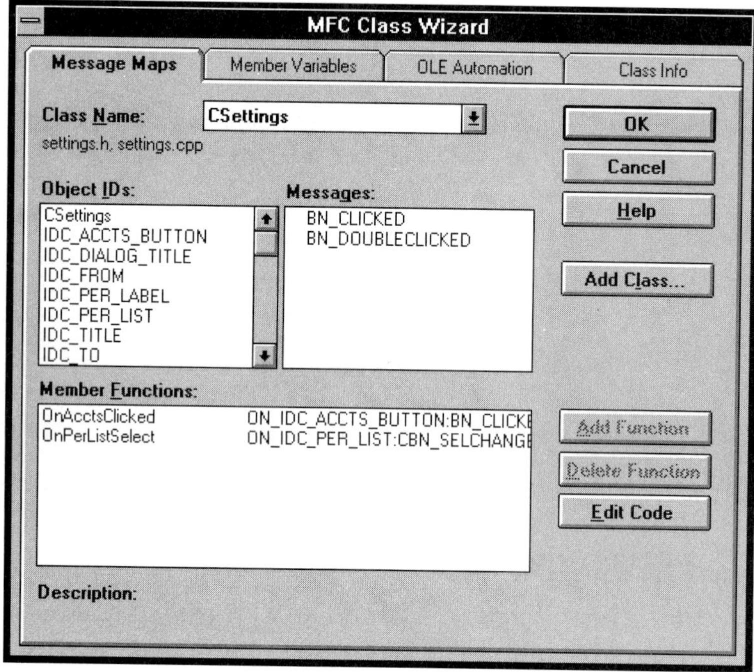

7-29. This will accept the additions, dismiss the dialog, and terminate
the ClassWizard tool's execution. The Settings dialog should still be on
your screen, in the App Studio's dialog editor. Close the window for the
Settings dialog by double clicking the document's control box, or by
pressing the Ctrl-F4 keyboard shortcut. You should now be looking at
App Studio's main window, which shows a list of the available resource
types and members of the selected type. (In this case, the selected type in
the left pane will be Dialog and the selected resource will be the one
named IDD_SETTINGS.)

Creating the List of Accounts Dialog

In the foregoing section, we added a message handler to the CSettings
class for the IDC_ACCTS_BUTTON, called OnAcctsClicked. Our intention
in doing so was to provide the means for the user to select from the list
of available accounts, the ones that should participate in the creation of
the current report. In order to provide this feature, we will design a new
dialog that displays the accounts and allows the user to select the ones of
interest by double clicking on the accounts in the list. The completed dialog is shown in Figure 7-30. Assuming that App Studio is running and
that its main window is on your screen, the steps to create the List of Accounts dialog are as follows:

Figure 7-30
Completed List of
Accounts dialog

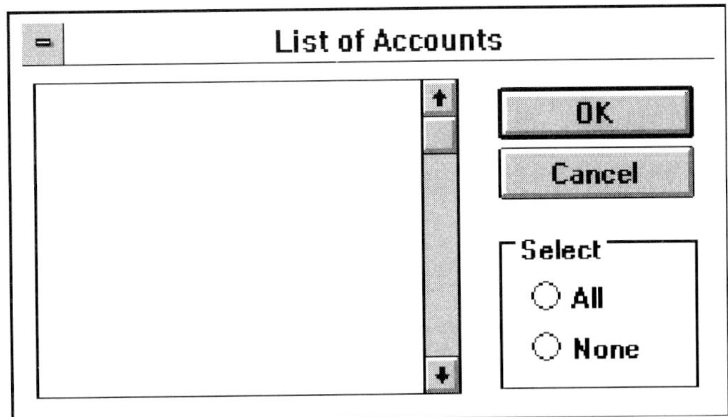

1. Click on the Dialog resource type in the left pane of App Studio's main window and then Click the New button at the bottom of the view. Make sure that the dialog that appears lists Dialog as the type of resource to be created and then click OK. The dialog editor for App Studio will be invoked and a default dialog with OK and Cancel buttons will be displayed on your screen. This dialog has the same appearance as the one shown in Figure 7-1. Resize the dialog so that its measurements are 177x92 and move the OK and Cancel buttons to the right side of the dialog, as shown in Figure 7-30.

2. Double click the default dialog to display its General properties window and change the settings to correspond with those shown in Figure 7-31.

Figure 7-31
List of Accounts dialog's
General properties

3. Click on the arrow next to the word General in the properties window and choose the Styles properties. Change the settings to correspond to those shown in Figure 7-32.

4. Click on the list box control in the control palette and drag a list box control onto the dialog at position 3,4. Change the measurements of the list box to 108x84 and then double click on the control to display its properties. Change the General properties to correspond with those shown in Figure 7-33.

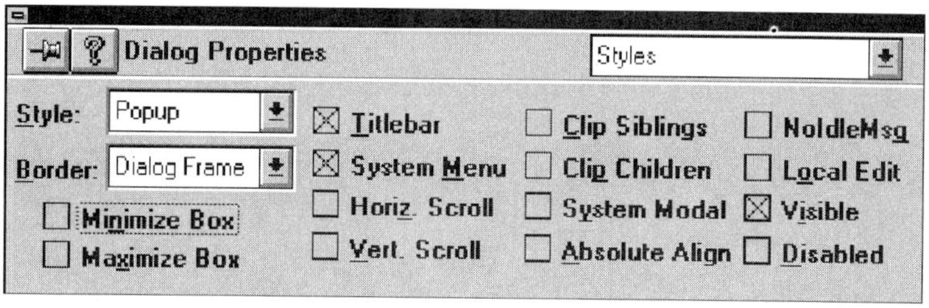

Figure 7-32
List of Accounts dialog's
Styles properties

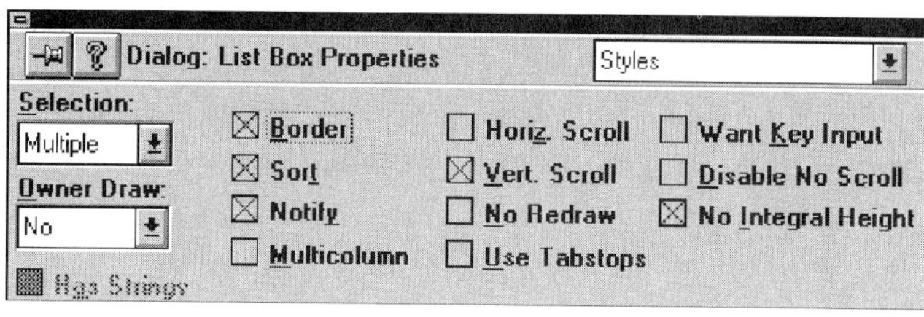

Figure 7-33
List box control General
properties

Figure 7-34
List box control Styles
properties

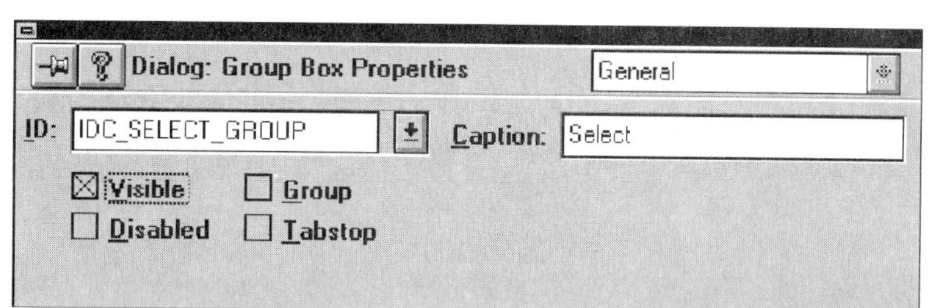

Figure 7-35
Group box General
properties

5. Select the Styles properties in the properties window combo box and change the list box control's Styles to correspond with those shown in Figure 7-34.

6. Select the group box control from the control palette and drag a group box onto the dialog at position 121,44. Change the dimensions of the control to 51x43 and then double click on the control to cause its General properties to be displayed. Change the properties to correspond with those shown in Figure 7-35. A group box is used to enclose related controls in a dialog.

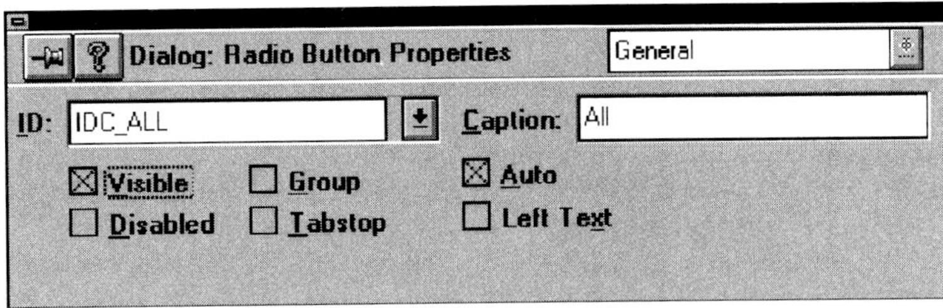

Figure 7-36
All radio button control's
General properties

Figure 7-37
None radio button
control's General
properties

7. Choose the radio button control from the control palette and drag a radio button onto the dialog at position 129,58. Change the dimensions of the control to 34x10 and then double click on the control to display its General properties. Change the properties to correspond with those shown in Figure 7-36.

8. Choose the radio button control once again and drag a radio button onto the dialog at position 129,71. Change the dimensions of the control to 34x10 and then double click on the control to cause its General properties to be displayed. Change the properties to correspond with those shown in Figure 7-37.

This concludes the steps for creating the List of Accounts dialog. When these steps are completed, the dialog should have the appearance shown in Figure 7-30. Leave App Studio running at this point, if you wish to continue with the following steps.

Creating the CSelectedAccts Class and Member Variables

If App Studio is not running currently, start it once again and open the dialog editor with the IDD_ACCOUNTS dialog showing on your screen

With the List of Accounts dialog being displayed, we must now create a class and its member variables, in order to provide the code to control the dialog. This is accomplished by using the ClassWizard tool, as was shown previously for creating the Settings dialog, beginning on page 235. The steps for creating the new CSelectedAccts class and its member variables are as follows:

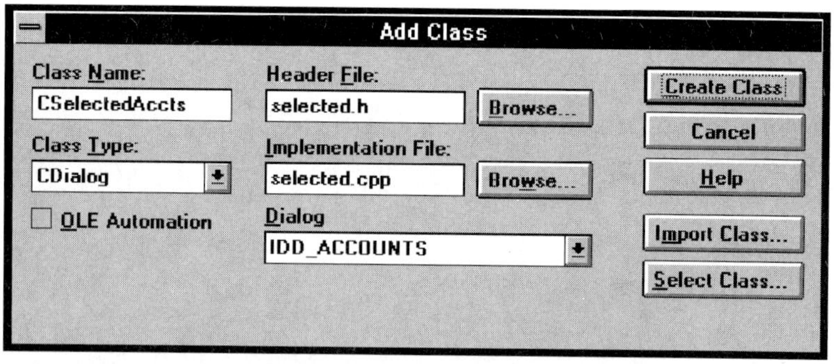

Figure 7-38
Creating the
CSelectedAccts class

Figure 7-39
Adding the m_AcctsList
member variable to the
CSelectedAccts class

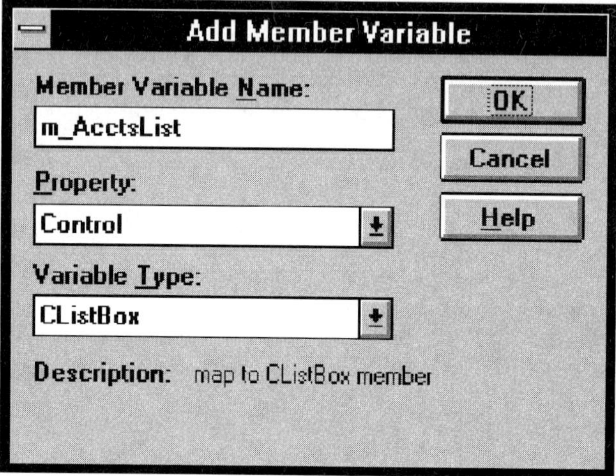

1. With the List of Accounts dialog still on your screen, invoke the ClassWizard tool by choosing it from App Studio's Resource menu. ClassWizard should display a dialog titled Add Class at this point. Fill in the fields in this dialog so that it corresponds to what is shown in Figure 7-38 and then click the Create Class button.

2. After the source and header files have been created automatically by the ClassWizard tool, we need to add member variables for the class. Click the Member Variables tab at the top of the main Class-Wizard window and then click to select the Control ID labeled IDC_ACCTS_SEL. Then click the Add Variable button and change the settings for the m_AcctsList variable to correspond with those shown in Figure 7-39. Click the OK button to accept the variable's definition. Note that we have defined this variable to have a property of Control, rather than Value, and a type of CListBox. When the Dynamic Data Exchange logic executes, a handle to the dialog's list box will be stored in the variable that we have defined.

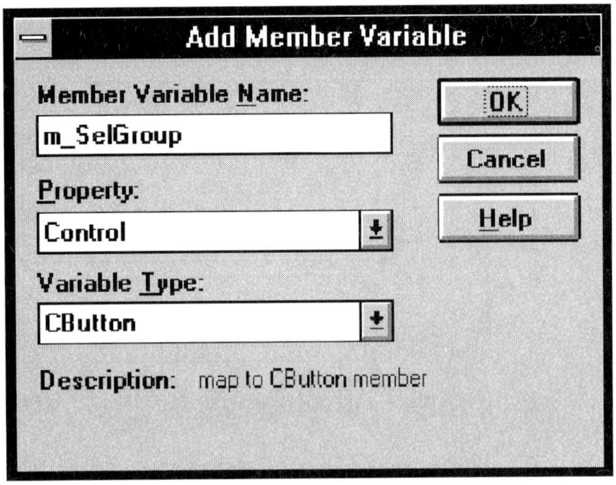

Figure 7-40
Adding the m_SelGroup
member variable to the
CSelectedAccts class

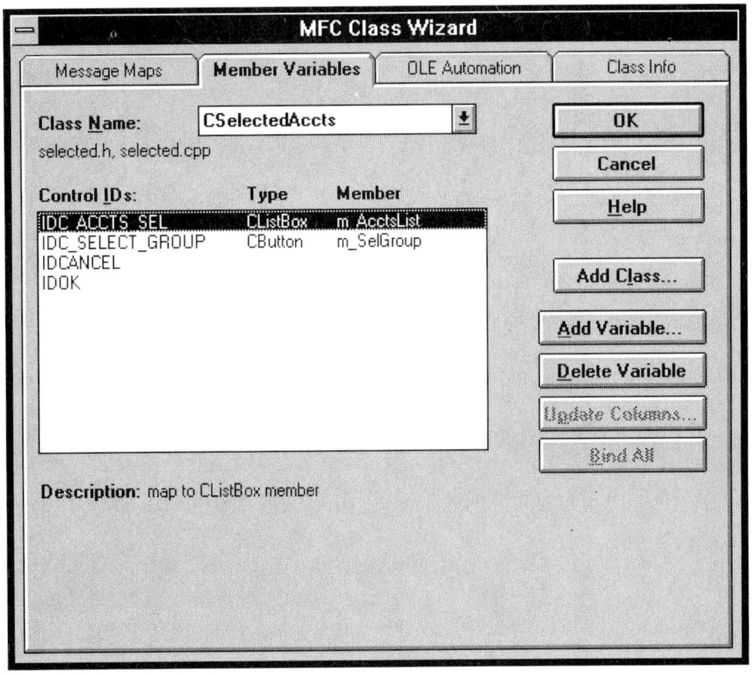

Figure 7-41
Complete list of member
variables for the
CSelectedAccts class

3. Click on the IDC_SELECT_GROUP Control ID and then click the Add Variable button once again. Create the m_SelGroup variable, according to the settings shown in Figure 7-40. Note that this variable has the Control property and is of type CButton.

This concludes the definition of the CSelectedAccts class and its member variables. The contents of the completed Edit Member Variables dialog are shown in Figure 7-41.

Figure 7-42
Creating the
OnSelectAccount
message handler

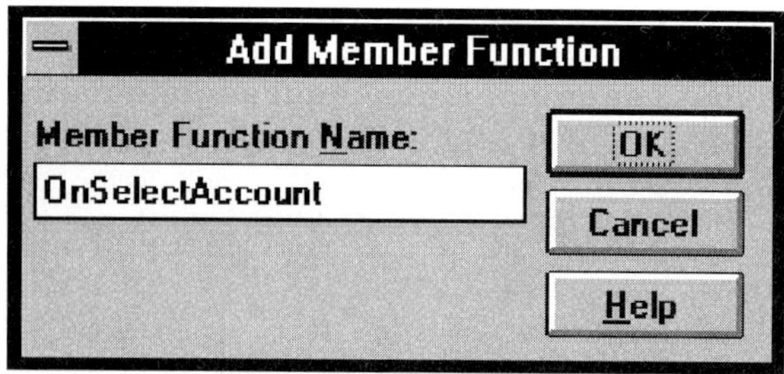

Figure 7-43
Creating the OnAll
message handler

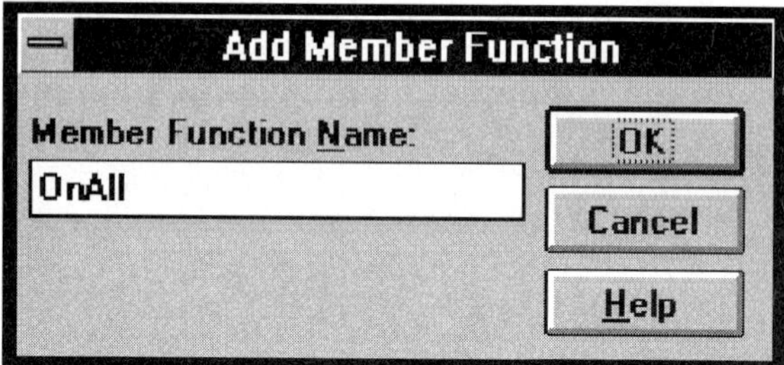

Defining Message Handlers for the CSelectedAccts Class

This section continues the development of the CSelectedAccts class by adding handlers for the messages that we are interested in processing. The definition of message handlers is carried out with the ClassWizard tool, as was shown previously with regard to the CSettings class, described beginning on page 246. The procedure for defining message handlers for the CSelectedAccts class is as follows:

1. With the ClassWizard's main window still on your screen, and with the class name of CSelectedAccts showing in the combo box at its top, click the Message Maps tab at the top of the dialog, click on the IDC_ACCTS_SEL object ID in the left pane, click on the LBN_DBLCLK message, and then click the Add Function button and fill in the message handler's name (OnSelectAccount), as shown in Figure 7-42. Click OK to accept the name and dismiss the dialog.

2. Click on the IDC_ALL control, click to select the BN_CLICKED message, click on the BN_CLICKED message, click the Add Function button, and then enter the message handler's name (OnAll), as shown in Figure 7-43. Click OK to accept the name and dismiss the dialog.

3. Click on the IDC_NONE control, then click to select the BN_CLICKED message, click the Add Function button, and then enter the message handler's name (OnNone), as shown in Figure 7-44. Click OK to accept the name and dismiss the dialog.

Figure 7-44
Creating the OnNone
message handler

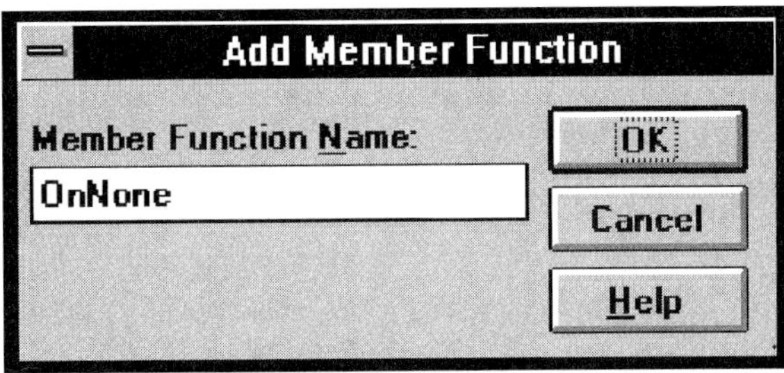

Figure 7-45
Appearance of the
ClassWizard's dialog
after adding the message
handlers

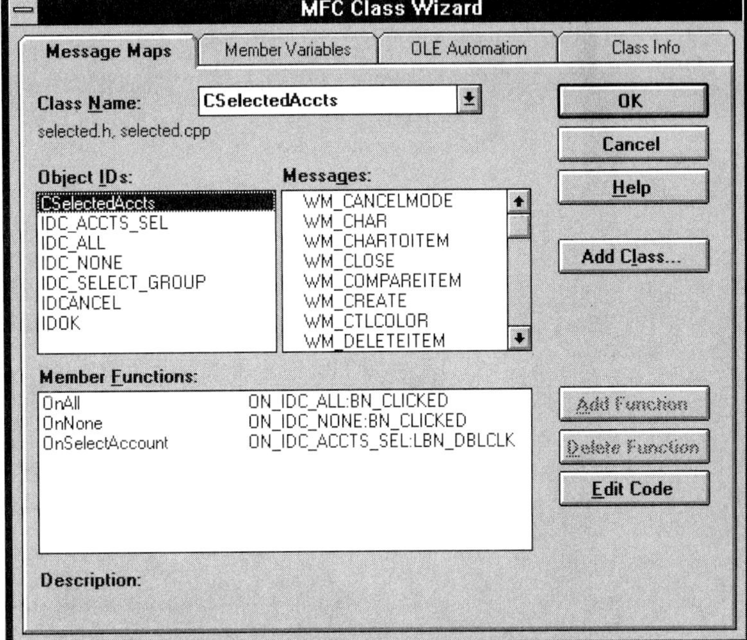

This concludes the procedure for adding message handlers to the CSelectedAccts class. The final appearance of the ClassWizard's main window for this class is shown in Figure 7-45. Dismiss the main window and terminate execution of the ClassWizard by clicking its OK button.

At this point, the List of Accounts dialog should still be on your screen. Save the resource file at this point by choosing the Save command from App Studio's File menu and then terminate execution of App Studio by choosing the Exit command from its File menu.

You may wish to take a break at this point; however, there are just a couple of simple tasks to perform. The next section describes the creation of the CReportView class and its message handlers. Unlike the involved dialog boxes created in the previous tutorials, the CReportView class is created entirely within the ClassWizard tool.

Creating the CReportView Class and Its Message Handlers

Now that we have created a dialog to allow the user to title a report, choose the accounts to be included in the report, and also select the time period for which the report is to be prepared, we need to create a new view in which our report will be displayed. Although the ClassWizard tool will be used to create our new class, we will not be using the App Studio tool to create the view.

The visual C++ workbench should be in execution for the next procedure. Its main window should display the title "Microsoft Visual C++ – KEEPIT.MAK." The procedure for creating the new view and its member variables is as follows:

1. Choose the ClassWizard command from the Browse menu. The main ClassWizard dialog window should appear. At this point, click the Add Class button and fill in the fields to correspond with what is shown in Figure 7-46. Click the Create Class button to accept the definition and dismiss the dialog.

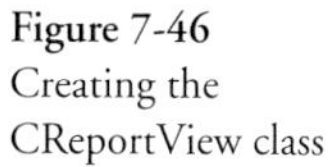

Figure 7-46
Creating the
CReportView class

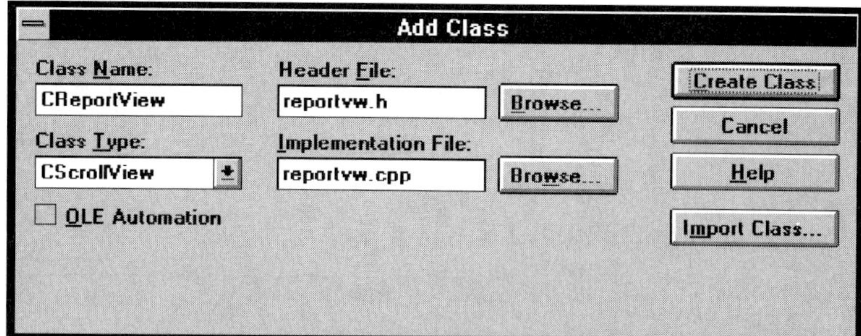

2. The ClassWizard's main window should show the new class name of CReportView in the combo box at its top, and with the Message Maps tab selected, a list of Object IDs should appear in the top left pane. Click on the CReportView object and then click on the WM_DESTROY message. When you click the Add Function button the name OnDestroy will be assigned to this handler, automatically.

3. With the CReportView object still selected, click on the message named WM_HSCROLL, click the Add Function button, and the name OnHScroll will be assigned to this message handler.

4. With the CReportView object still selected, click on the message named WM_VSCROLL, click the Add Function button, and the name OnVScroll will be assigned to this message handler.

5. Scroll down the list of Object IDs and select the one named ID_FILE_PRINT. Click the COMMAND message, click the Add func-

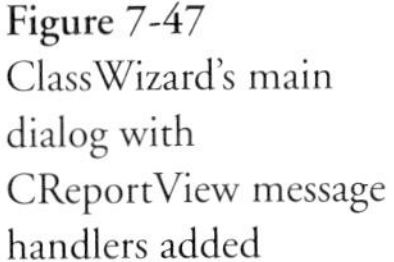

Figure 7-47
ClassWizard's main
dialog with
CReportView message
handlers added

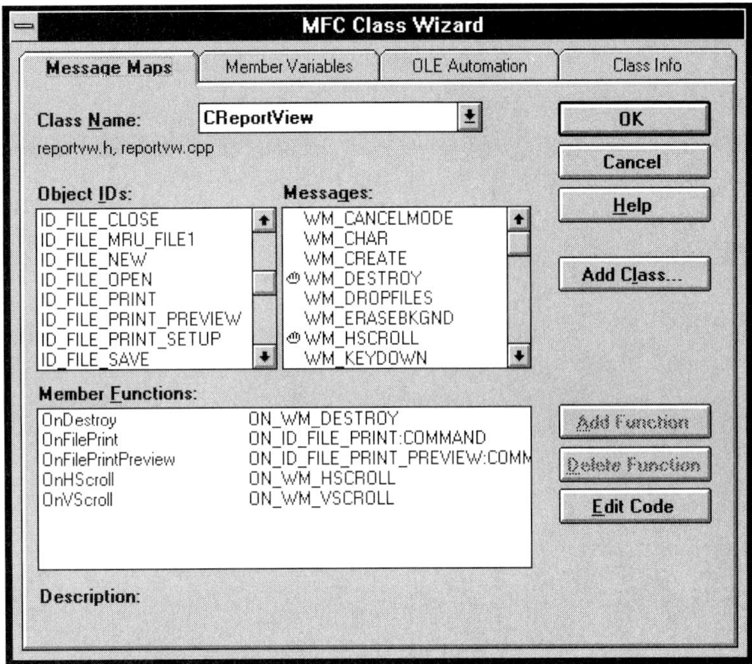

tion button, and then enter the name OnFilePrint for this message
handler. Click OK to dismiss the dialog.

6. Scroll down the list of Object IDs and select the one named
   ID_FILE_PRINT_PREVIEW. Click the COMMAND message, click the
   Add Function button, and then enter the name OnFilePrintPreview
   for this message handler. Click OK to dismiss the dialog.

This concludes the procedure to add the new CReportView class, which,
incidentally, inherits its behavior from the MFC CScrollView class. The
final appearance of the ClassWizard's main dialog, with all of the message handlers added, is shown in Figure 7-47.

Adding a Handler to the CKeepitDoc Class

Now that the CSettings, CSelectedAccts, and CReportView classes have
been defined, we need to create a handler for the COMMAND message that
is generated when the user chooses the Cash Flow command from the
application's Report menu.

Because all of the data for creating the report are already available in the
CKeepitDoc class, it seems natural for us to handle the Cash Flow command in that class. If you are continuing on from what was presented in
the preceding section, then the ClassWizard's main dialog will still be

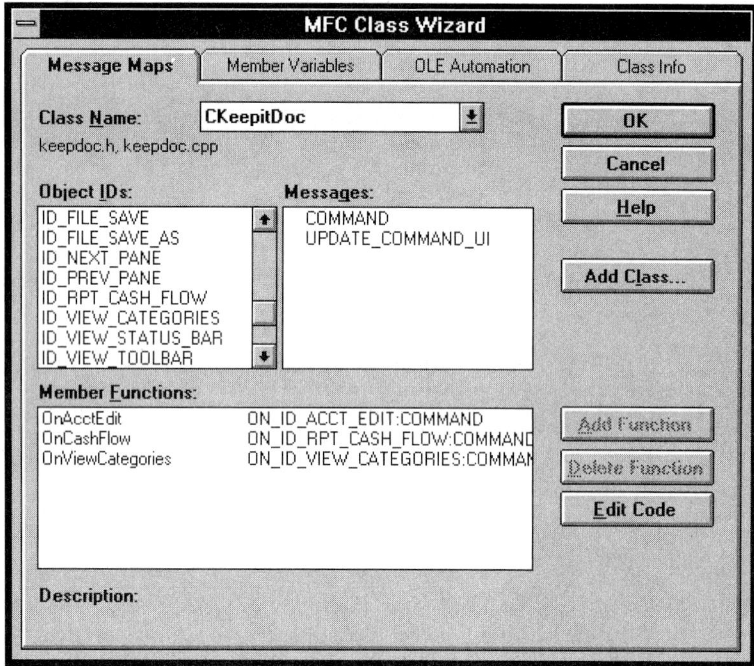

Figure 7-48
ClassWizard's main dialog with the OnCashFlow message handler added

showing on your screen. If not, then invoke the ClassWizard tool from within the Visual C++ workbench by choosing the ClassWizard tool from the Browse menu and make sure that the Message Maps tab is selected. The procedure for adding the new OnCashFlow message handler is as follows:

1. Locate the combo box at the top of the ClassWizard's main window, which lists the names of the classes currently defined for the Keepit application. Click on the arrow at its right to drop down the list and then click on the CKeepitDoc class name to choose that class. You should see quite a long list of Object IDs in the top left pane and, perhaps, you will see several messages in the top right pane. The bottom pane, which lists the currently defined message handlers, should contain entries for the OnAcctEdit and OnViewCategories message handlers.

2. Scroll down the list of Object IDs to locate the one whose name is ID_RPT_CASH_FLOW and click to select it. Click on the COMMAND message in the right pane, click the Add Function button, enter the name OnCashFlow into the dialog, and then click OK to accept the handler name and dismiss the dialog.

This concludes the steps for adding the OnCashFlow message handler. The revised appearance of the ClassWizard's main dialog is shown in Figure 7-48. Note that the new handler has been added to the list in the bottom pane of the dialog. Terminate execution of the ClassWizard at this time by clicking its OK button.

The additions to the user interface and the creation of new classes, member variables, and message handlers are now complete. The next section shows the results of these efforts by displaying and describing the wizard-created code for these elements. As with previous additions to the Keepit application, we describe the wizard-created code in the current chapter, and then in the following chapter we will describe the custom code we have added to make the new features fully functional.

Examining the Newly Generated Code

We will commence our description of the wizard-created code by showing you the changes to the CKeepitDoc class, which are a result of adding the OnCashFlow message handler.

The Settings dialog invokes the List of Accounts dialog and the wizard-created code for the corresponding CSelectedAccts class will also be presented in this section.

When the List of Accounts and the Settings dialogs have been dismissed by clicking their corresponding OK buttons, the CKeepitDoc class's On-CashFlow message handler will create the new CReportView object, whose wizard-created code will be shown at the end of this section.

Examining the Additions to the CKeepitDoc Class

The only addition to the CKeepitDoc header file (**keepdoc.h**), as a result of the wizard-created code, is the declaration of the message handler for the OnCashFlow command.

KeepDoc.h Header File Additions

The complete set of message handler declarations is as follows:

```
// Generated message map functions
protected:
  //{{AFX_MSG(CKeepitDoc)
  afx_msg void OnViewCategories();
  afx_msg void OnAcctEdit();
  afx_msg void OnCashFlow();
  //}}AFX_MSG
  DECLARE_MESSAGE_MAP()
```

The `afx_msg` entry for the OnCashFlow member function is the only new addition to the list of message handlers in the CKeepitDoc class, as indicated by the "change bar" at the left of the statement.

KeepDoc.cpp Source File Additions

The source file for the CKeepitDoc class (**keepdoc.cpp**) contains the wizard-created code for both the message map entry and the newly defined OnCashFlow handler as well as its skeleton code, which we will enhance in the next chapter. The complete, newly generated, message map for the CKeepitDoc class is as follows:

```
BEGIN_MESSAGE_MAP(CKeepitDoc, CDocument)
    //{{AFX_MSG_MAP(CKeepitDoc)
    ON_COMMAND(ID_VIEW_CATEGORIES, OnViewCategories)
    ON_COMMAND(ID_ACCT_EDIT, OnAcctEdit)
    ON_COMMAND(ID_RPT_CASH_FLOW, OnCashFlow)
    //}}AFX_MSG_MAP
END_MESSAGE_MAP()
```

Note that the OnCashFlow member function has been added to the message map and that it is associated with the ON_COMMAND message whose identification is ID_RPT_CASH_FLOW. When the user chooses the Cash Flow command from the application's Report menu, the OnCashFlow member function will be invoked, because of this message map entry. The wizard-created skeleton code for the OnCashFlow message handler is as follows:

```
void CKeepitDoc::OnCashFlow()
{
    // TODO: Add your command handler code here
}
```

Examining the CSettings Code

Earlier, we presented the procedures for creating the Settings dialog, its corresponding CSettings class, and the member variables and message handlers for the class. Bear in mind that when the user chooses the Cash Flow command from the application's Report menu, the OnCashFlow message handler in the CKeepitDoc class will execute. Our intention is for the Settings dialog to be invoked from within that message handler.

In this section, we will show the wizard-created code for the CSettings class, which should give us a good idea of what we need to do to fully implement the dialog.

Settings.h Header File Code

When we created the CSettings class, we specified that the header file for that class would be named **settings.h**. The wizard-created code for this file is as follows:

```cpp
// settings.h : header file
//
/////////////////////////////////////////////////////////////////
// CSettings dialog

class CSettings : public CDialog
{
// Construction
public:
   CSettings(CWnd* pParent = NULL); // standard constructor

// Dialog Data
   //{{AFX_DATA(CSettings)
   enum { IDD = IDD_SETTINGS };
   CComboBox m_PeriodList;
   CButton   m_AcctsButton;
   CStatic   m_DialogTitle;
   CString   m_From;
   CString   m_Title;
   CString   m_To;
   //}}AFX_DATA

// Implementation
protected:
   virtual void DoDataExchange(CDataExchange* pDX);

   // Generated message map functions
   //{{AFX_MSG(CSettings)
   afx_msg void OnPerListSelect();
   afx_msg void OnAcctsClicked();
   //}}AFX_MSG
   DECLARE_MESSAGE_MAP()
};
```

The foregoing header file code contains a standard default constructor, the set of member variables that we defined, and the two message handlers that we also defined.

Settings.cpp Source File Code

The source code for the CSettings class was generated into the source file we called **settings.cpp**. The wizard-created code is as follows:

```cpp
// settings.cpp : implementation file
//

#include "stdafx.h"
#include "keepit.h"
#include "settings.h"

#ifdef _DEBUG
#undef THIS_FILE
static char BASED_CODE THIS_FILE[] = __FILE__;
#endif

/////////////////////////////////////////////////////////////////
// CSettings dialog

CSettings::CSettings(CWnd* pParent /*=NULL*/)
   : CDialog(CSettings::IDD, pParent)
```

```
{
    //{{AFX_DATA_INIT(CSettings)
    m_From = "";
    m_Title = "";
    m_To = "";
    //}}AFX_DATA_INIT
}

void CSettings::DoDataExchange(CDataExchange* pDX)
{
    CDialog::DoDataExchange(pDX);
    //{{AFX_DATA_MAP(CSettings)
    DDX_Control(pDX, IDC_PER_LIST, m_PeriodList);
    DDX_Control(pDX, IDC_ACCTS_BUTTON, m_AcctsButton);
    DDX_Control(pDX, IDC_DIALOG_TITLE, m_DialogTitle);
    DDX_Text(pDX, IDC_FROM, m_From);
    DDX_Text(pDX, IDC_TITLE, m_Title);
    DDX_Text(pDX, IDC_TO, m_To);
    //}}AFX_DATA_MAP
}

BEGIN_MESSAGE_MAP(CSettings, CDialog)
    //{{AFX_MSG_MAP(CSettings)
    ON_CBN_SELCHANGE(IDC_PER_LIST, OnPerListSelect)
    ON_BN_CLICKED(IDC_ACCTS_BUTTON, OnAcctsClicked)
    //}}AFX_MSG_MAP
END_MESSAGE_MAP()

/////////////////////////////////////////////////////////////////
// CSettings message handlers

void CSettings::OnPerListSelect()
{
    // TODO: Add your control notification handler code here
}

void CSettings::OnAcctsClicked()
{
    // TODO: Add your control notification handler code here
}
```

The foregoing code includes the constructor for the Settings dialog, which invokes the constructor of its CDialog base class, to create the dialog object. The constructor initializes the `m_From`, `m_Title`, and `m_To` member variables with empty strings.

The DoDataExchange member function has been generated to call the CDialog's DoDataExchange member function and then execute the DDX/DDV (dialog data exchange/dialog data validation) routines for the control and data member variables we have defined. This member function is called, by default, by the CDialog's UpdateData member function, which, in turn, is called by the default version of the CDialog's OnInitDialog member function. We will be providing our own override of the OnInitDialog member function when we customize this code.

The message map is the next section of code in the source file. Entries for the OnPerListSelect and OnAcctsClicked handlers we defined are included in the map.

The final section of the wizard-created code contains the skeleton versions of the OnPerListSelect and OnAcctsClicked message handlers. These will be enhanced greatly in the next chapter.

Examining the CSelectedAccts Code

Procedures for creating the List of Accounts dialog, its CSelectedAccts class, and the member variables and message handlers were covered previously in this chapter. The wizard-created code consists of a new header file (**selected.h**) and a new source file (**selected.cpp**). The code in each of these files is shown in this section.

Selected.h Header File Code

The wizard-created code for the CSelectedAccts class header file (**selected.h**) is as follows:

```cpp
// selected.h : header file
//
/////////////////////////////////////////////////////////////////
// CSelectedAccts dialog

class CSelectedAccts : public CDialog
{
// Construction
public:
   CSelectedAccts(CWnd* pParent = NULL); // constructor

// Dialog Data
   //{{AFX_DATA(CSelectedAccts)
   enum { IDD = IDD_ACCOUNTS };
   CButton   m_SelGroup;
   CListBox  m_AcctsList;
   //}}AFX_DATA

// Implementation
protected:
   virtual void DoDataExchange(CDataExchange* pDX);

   // Generated message map functions
   //{{AFX_MSG(CSelectedAccts)
   afx_msg void OnSelectAccount();
   afx_msg void OnAll();
   afx_msg void OnNone();
   //}}AFX_MSG
   DECLARE_MESSAGE_MAP()
};
```

The foregoing header file code includes the declaration of the object constructor function (CSelectedAccts), declaration of the two control objects (m_SelGroup and m_AcctsList), declaration of the DoDataExchange member function, and then declaration of the message handlers that we created previously (OnSelectAccount, OnAll, and OnNone).

Selected.cpp Source File Code

The **selected.cpp** source file contains the wizard-created code for the List of Accounts dialog. The code is as follows:

```cpp
// selected.cpp : implementation file
//

#include "stdafx.h"
#include "keepit.h"
#include "selected.h"

#ifdef _DEBUG
#undef THIS_FILE
static char BASED_CODE THIS_FILE[] = __FILE__;
#endif

/////////////////////////////////////////////////////////////////////
// CSelectedAccts dialog

CSelectedAccts::CSelectedAccts(CWnd* pParent /*=NULL*/)
    : CDialog(CSelectedAccts::IDD, pParent)
{
    //{{AFX_DATA_INIT(CSelectedAccts)
        // NOTE: the ClassWizard will add member initialization
        // here.
    //}}AFX_DATA_INIT
}

void CSelectedAccts::DoDataExchange(CDataExchange* pDX)
{
    CDialog::DoDataExchange(pDX);
    //{{AFX_DATA_MAP(CSelectedAccts)
    DDX_Control(pDX, IDC_SELECT_GROUP, m_SelGroup);
    DDX_Control(pDX, IDC_ACCTS_SEL, m_AcctsList);
    //}}AFX_DATA_MAP
}

BEGIN_MESSAGE_MAP(CSelectedAccts, CDialog)
    //{{AFX_MSG_MAP(CSelectedAccts)
    ON_LBN_DBLCLK(IDC_ACCTS_SEL, OnSelectAccount)
    ON_BN_CLICKED(IDC_ALL, OnAll)
    ON_BN_CLICKED(IDC_NONE, OnNone)
    //}}AFX_MSG_MAP
END_MESSAGE_MAP()

/////////////////////////////////////////////////////////////////////
// CSelectedAccts message handlers

void CSelectedAccts::OnSelectAccount()
{
    // TODO: Add your control notification handler code here
}

void CSelectedAccts::OnAll()
{
    // TODO: Add your control notification handler code here
}

void CSelectedAccts::OnNone()
{
    // TODO: Add your control notification handler code here
}
```

The foregoing code begins with the preprocessor directives, followed by the definition of the CSelectedAccts constructor. In the case of the List of Accounts dialog, the constructor merely calls the CDialog class's constructor and does not perform any initialization functions.

The DoDataExchange member function calls the CDialog class's default member function and then executes the code to transfer the two control object handles (m_SelGroup and m_AcctsList) from the dialog's radio control group and list box, respectively, to the corresponding member variables.

The message map follows. Entries are provided to invoke the OnSelectAccount, OnAll, and OnNone message handlers when the appropriate messages arrive.

The final section of the source file contains the skeleton code for the OnSelectAccount, OnAll, and OnNone message handlers. Each of these will be enhanced in the customized version of the code, which is presented in the next chapter.

Examining the CReportView Code

The CReportView class was created with the ClassWizard and the generation of the header and source files and message handlers was presented earlier in this chapter. The wizard-created code consists of the header file (**reportvw.h**) and source file (**reportvw.cpp**). This class was generated to serve as the basis for displaying the Cash Flow report. The class will also contain "hooks" to enable printing the report to any Windows-compatible printer.

Reportvw.h Header File Code

The wizard-created code for the **reportvw.h** header file is as follows:

```
// reportvw.h : header file
//
/////////////////////////////////////////////////////////////////////
// CReportView view

class CReportView : public CScrollView
{
   DECLARE_DYNCREATE(CReportView)
protected:
   CReportView(); // protected constructor for dynamic
                  // creation

// Attributes
public:

// Operations
public:
```

```
// Implementation
protected:
   virtual ~CReportView();
   virtual void OnDraw(CDC* pDC);// overridden to draw this
view
   virtual void OnInitialUpdate();// first time after
construct

   // Generated message map functions
   //{{AFX_MSG(CReportView)
   afx_msg void OnFilePrint();
   afx_msg void OnFilePrintPreview();
   afx_msg void OnDestroy();
   afx_msg void OnHScroll(UINT nSBCode, UINT nPos,
      CScrollBar* pScrollBar);
   afx_msg void OnVScroll(UINT nSBCode, UINT nPos,
      CScrollBar* pScrollBar);
   //}}AFX_MSG
   DECLARE_MESSAGE_MAP()
};
```

The foregoing header file code declares the member functions for the
CReportView class. No member variables were defined when we created
the class with the ClassWizard tool. The class declaration contains the
constructor, destructor, and the OnDraw and OnInitialUpdate member
functions that are needed for almost every view. The final section of the
header file declares the message handler member functions for the class.

Reportvw.cpp Source File Code

The wizard-created code in the CReportView source file contains definitions of the member functions declared in the header file. The wizard-
created code is as follows:

```
// reportvw.cpp : implementation file
//

#include "stdafx.h"
#include "keepit.h"
#include "reportvw.h"
#ifdef _DEBUG
#undef THIS_FILE
static char BASED_CODE THIS_FILE[] = __FILE__;
#endif

/////////////////////////////////////////////////////////////
// CReportView

IMPLEMENT_DYNCREATE(CReportView, CScrollView)

CReportView::CReportView()
{
}

CReportView::~CReportView()
{
}

BEGIN_MESSAGE_MAP(CReportView, CScrollView)
   //{{AFX_MSG_MAP(CReportView)
```

```
   ON_COMMAND(ID_FILE_PRINT, OnFilePrint)
   ON_COMMAND(ID_FILE_PRINT_PREVIEW, OnFilePrintPreview)
   ON_WM_DESTROY()
   ON_WM_HSCROLL()
   ON_WM_VSCROLL()
   //}}AFX_MSG_MAP
END_MESSAGE_MAP()


/////////////////////////////////////////////////////////////////
// CReportView drawing

void CReportView::OnInitialUpdate()
{
   CScrollView::OnInitialUpdate();

   CSize sizeTotal;
   // TODO: calculate the total size of this view
   sizeTotal.cx = sizeTotal.cy = 100;
   SetScrollSizes(MM_TEXT, sizeTotal);
}

void CReportView::OnDraw(CDC* pDC)
{
   CDocument* pDoc = GetDocument();
   // TODO: add draw code here
}


/////////////////////////////////////////////////////////////////
// CReportView message handlers


void CReportView::OnFilePrint()
{
   // TODO: Add your command handler code here
}

void CReportView::OnFilePrintPreview()
{
   // TODO: Add your command handler code here
}

void CReportView::OnDestroy()
{
   // TODO: Add your command handler code here
}
void CReportView::OnHScroll(UINT nSBCode, UINT nPos,
   CScrollBar* pScrollBar)
{
   // TODO: Add your command handler code here
}

void CReportView::OnVScroll(UINT nSBCode, UINT nPos,
   CScrollBar* pScrollBar)
{
   // TODO: Add your command handler code here
}
```

The wizard-created code for the CReportView class is a bit longer than
that for the CSettings or CSelectedAccts classes we presented earlier in
this chapter. The main reason for this is that in addition to the constructor and destructor functions and the message handlers, ClassWizard is
programmed to generate OnInitialUpdate and OnDraw member functions for new classes based upon the CScrollView class.

The OnInitialUpdate member function is overridden so that the size of the view can be calculated and specified to the SetScrollSizes member function inherited from the CScrollView base class. Doing so defines the height and width of the view so that, when the user clicks in the scroll bars, the view can be scrolled appropriately. This member function is also the right place to add any other initialization that must be performed before the view is shown.

The OnDraw member function is called whenever the view's contents must be updated. In many cases, code in the document will call UpdateAllViews when a change to the document's data has occurred. This results in the OnDraw member function being called for each of the views. The OnDraw member function serves to render the view both for the display and the printer and we will describe this dual feature in the custom version of the code when it is presented in the next chapter.

The remainder of the source file contains the skeleton code for each of the message handlers we defined (OnFilePrint, OnFilePrintPreview, OnDestroy, OnHScroll, and OnVScroll).

Exercises

1. Instead of creating two dialogs, one of which merely lists the available account names, why wasn't a single dialog, containing the features of both the Settings and List of Accounts dialogs, created? Explain your answer.

2. Why is the Settings dialog intended to be invoked from the document class, rather than from the application class? What is unique about the document class that makes it a better choice for the invocation of this feature?

3. In the List of Accounts dialog, what is the purpose of the All and None radio buttons? Explain how these user interface features could be helpful to the user.

4. Both the Settings and List of Accounts dialogs were created by invoking the ClassWizard tool from inside the App Studio resource editor. Why was this done, and could the corresponding classes have been defined using any other method? Explain your answer.

5. The CReportView class was created to inherit the characteristics of the MFC's CScrollView base class. Why was this particular class chosen as the base class for the new view? Could some other class have been chosen for this purpose? What benefits does the CScrollView class provide? Explain your answers.

Chapter 8
Customizing the Reports Code

In this chapter, we will describe the custom code additions and modifications that implement fully the creation of the Cash Flow report and the Settings and List of Accounts dialogs. In addition, we will show the changes necessary to print the report to a Windows-compatible printer. The structure of the application (omitting some of the classes not involved in this customization) is shown in Figure 8-1. The Figure shows the messages handled by the various application classes. For an explanation of the line styles and shading, refer to the legend.

Figure 8-1
Structure of the portion of the Keepit application associated with creation of the Cash Flow report

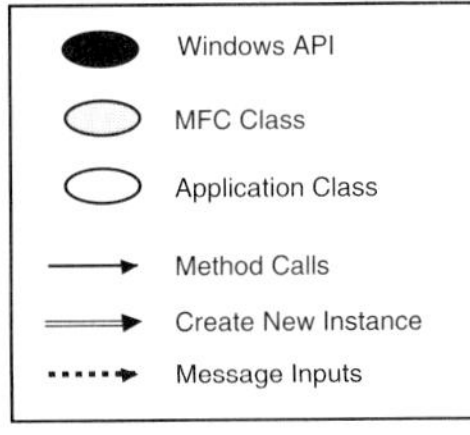

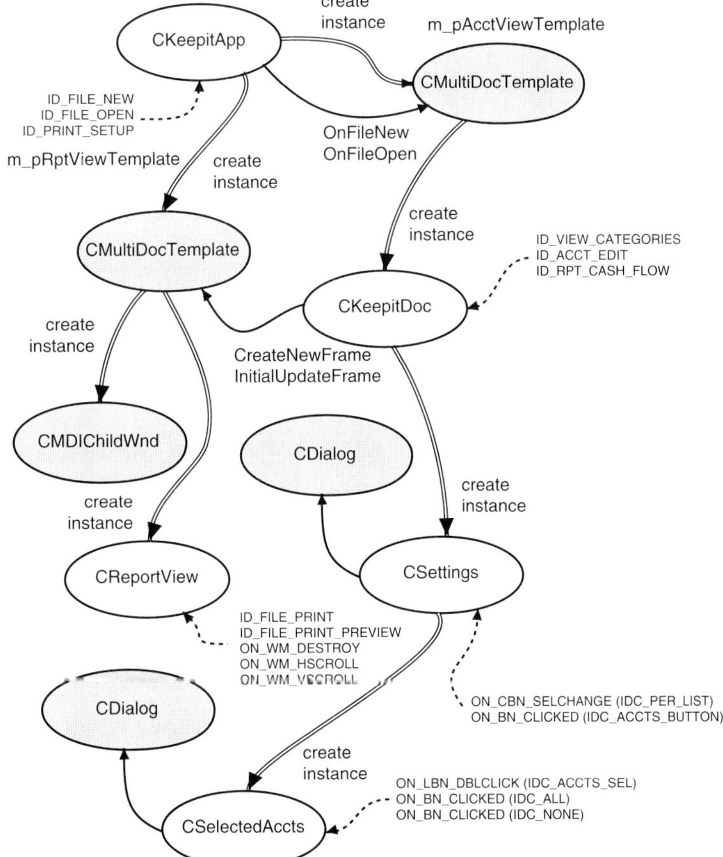

As is evident from Figure 8-1, a new CMultiDocTemplate object has been created by the CKeepitApp class (refer to Figure 6-1 for a view of the application's structure prior to the addition of the new classes and member functions) and the newly created CSettings and CSelectedAccts dialogs, as well as the newly created CReportView objects are shown. The sections that follow will describe all of these new elements fully.

Adding a New Document Template

The CKeepitApp class is the "keeper" of the document templates. In the case of the Keepit application, we have only one document at this point, but it contains multiple views. Each view is contained within a frame and the frame and its corresponding view and document are managed by the CMultiDocTemplate object. The single addition to the application's header file (**keepit.h**) to contain the new m_pRptViewTemplate template pointer is as follows:

```
CMultiDocTemplate  m_pRptViewTemplate; // added
```

The only change in the CKeepitApp source file (**keepit.cpp**) is in the InitInstance member function, where the new document template is created and added to the application's list. This code fragment is as follows:

```
m_pRptViewTemplate = new CMultiDocTemplate (IDR_REPORTTYPE,
    RUNTIME_CLASS(CKeepitDoc),
    RUNTIME_CLASS(CMDIChildWnd), // child window
    RUNTIME_CLASS(CReportView));
AddDocTemplate (m_pRptViewTemplate);
```

Note that the document class (CkeepitDoc) is the same as for the other views, but the MDI frame window class (CMDIChildWnd) is different from the CMDIFormFrame that we have been using previously.

In the case of the new view object, the standard frame is fine and we want the user to be able to minimize, maximize, and resize this window. The view managed by the new document template is implemented by the CReportView class.

In addition to the new application template, we have added a new string resource to the **keepit.rc** file. You can add this string to the file by editing the **keepit.rc** file (as we did), or by using the App Studio resource editor to do so. As it appears in the App Studio string resource editor, the new resource is as follows:

```
IDR_REPORTTYPE \nKeepit\n\n\n\nKeepitFileType\nKEEPIT File Type
```

The foregoing string resource is mentioned in the first argument in the code that creates the new CMultiDocTemplate object (m_pRptViewTemplate). The framework uses the information in the various fields of the string resource to determine whether to create a new document object, and whether to display a dialog for choosing one of several document types when a New or Open command is chosen from the File menu. By making several of the fields in the string resource "empty," we can ensure that the framework doesn't create a new document object or display a dialog for choosing a file type when one of those commands is chosen.

Document Support for the CReportView Creation

The CKeepitDoc object is the center of attention when the user chooses the Cash Flow command from the new Report menu. Because the document is responsible for keeping all of the data and providing member functions for other objects to access and store the data, it is natural to implement the invocation of the Cash Flow report from within the document class. This is accomplished by adding the ID_RPT_CASH_FLOW entry to the message map for the CKeepitDoc class (described in Chapter 7, beginning on page 257). When the user chooses the Cash Flow command from the Report menu, the document's OnCashFlow member function will be invoked.

CKeepitDoc Header File Additions

Several new statements have been added to the header file for the CKeepitDoc class (**keepdoc.h**), in support of the new additions to the application. The next few sections will show these additions.

New Definitions

The following forward declaration for the CSettings class and the new preprocessor definition are contained in the front of the updated header file. The code is as follows:

```
class CSettings; // added forward declaration

#define CASH_FLOW_REPORT   1 // added definition
```

New Member Variables

A set of new member variables to support the chosen report have been added to the header file. These are used to communicate data from the OnCashFlow message handler and the CSettings dialog to the new CReportView object when it is created and initialized. The newly added declarations are as follows:

```
// Attributes
public:
    int        m_nReportType;      // current report type
    CObList    m_ReportAccts;      // current report accounts
    CTime      m_FromDate;         // beginning of period
    CTime      m_ToDate;           // end of reporting period
```

Note in the foregoing that the report type is being stored into a member variable, even though only a single report is being prepared by the new custom code. By adding this variable, we are making advance preparations to store other report types into this variable. Also note that a CObList object and two objects of the CTime class are being created for use by the report view.

New DeleteDlgAccts Support Member Function

A new member function to support the OnCashFlow message handler was added to the CKeepitDoc class. The header file declaration for this member function is as follows:

```
protected:
    void DeleteDlgAccts(CSettings& dlg); // newly added
```

Message Map Function Declarations

A single new message handler (OnCashFlow) was added to the document class to process the Cash Flow command from the new Report menu. The complete set of message handler declarations is as follows:

```
// Generated message map functions
protected:
    //{{AFX_MSG(CKeepitDoc)
    afx_msg void OnViewCategories();
    afx_msg void OnAcctEdit();
    afx_msg void OnCashFlow(); // newly added
    //}}AFX_MSG
    DECLARE_MESSAGE_MAP()
};
```

CKeepitDoc Source File Additions

The additions to the source file for the CKeepitDoc class (**keepdoc.cpp**) consist of the member function to handle the newly added message handler for the Cash Flow command (OnCashFlow) and also the single newly defined helper member function (DeleteDlgAccts). The sections which follow describe the newly added code for these member functions.

New Preprocessor Directives

The additions to the CKeepitDoc class require that we import the header files for both the new Settings dialog, which is referenced directly in the OnCashFlow message handler, and also the header file for a new set of functions that perform dynamic data exchange and validation tasks (used by the Settings dialog). The **dattim.h** header file also declares a function that creates a CTime object from a date specified in a CString object (a function that we use in the new custom code in the OnCash-Flow member function). The added directives are as follows:

```
#include "settings.h"  // added
#include "dattim.h"    // added
```

Newly Generated Message Map

The message map for the CKeepitDoc class was modified by the Class-Wizard tool to include an entry for the ID_RPT_CASH_FLOW command. The complete message map is as follows:

```
BEGIN_MESSAGE_MAP(CKeepitDoc, CDocument)
  //{{AFX_MSG_MAP(CKeepitDoc)
  ON_COMMAND(ID_VIEW_CATEGORIES, OnViewCategories)
  ON_COMMAND(ID_ACCT_EDIT, OnAcctEdit)
  ON_COMMAND(ID_RPT_CASH_FLOW, OnCashFlow)
  //}}AFX_MSG_MAP
END_MESSAGE_MAP()
```

Note that the foregoing command is being mapped to the OnCashFlow member function in the CKeepitDoc class.

OnCashFlow Message Handler Code

The wizard-created code for the OnCashFlow message handler was shown in the previous chapter. The enhanced code to fully implement the new functionality is shown in several sections. The purpose of the following code is to display the Settings dialog to the user, allowing the characteristics of the report to be specified, and then create the CReport-View object to display the report. The code is all newly added and begins as follows:

```
void CKeepitDoc::OnCashFlow()
{
    int      nYr, nMo, nDy;
    CSettings dlg;

    // create a default cash flow report for year-to-date
    // income and expenses in all accounts.

    CTime curTime = CTime::GetCurrentTime();// current time
    nYr = curTime.GetYear();                 // current year
    nMo = curTime.GetMonth();                // current month
    nDy = curTime.GetDay();                  // current day
    CTime startTime (nYr, 1, 1, 0, 0, 0); // 01/01/year

    // set dialog member variables to their initial values

    dlg.m_szDialogTitle = "Cash Flow Report Settings";
    dlg.m_From = startTime.Format ("%m/%d/%y");// 01/01/yr
    dlg.m_To = curTime.Format ("%m/%d/%y");    // mm/dd/yr
    dlg.m_Title = "Cash Flow Report";          // title

    // create copies of the accounts and load them into the
    // dialog's list of accounts.

    POSITION pos = m_AcctList.GetHeadPosition();
    while (pos != NULL)
    {
        CAcctObj* pAcct = (CAcctObj *)m_AcctList.GetNext (pos);
        CAcctObj* nAcct = new CAcctObj (pAcct);
        dlg.m_Accounts.AddTail (nAcct);
    }
```

The foregoing (first) section of the OnCashFlow message handler creates
the CSettings dialog object on the stack, accesses the current date information from Windows, initializes the dialog's start time member variable
(m_From) to January 1 of the current year and the end time member
variable (m_To) to the current date, and then stores the report's title
(Cash Flow Report) into the m_Title member variable. Note that these
data are not written into the respective controls in the dialog, but are
merely stored into its member variables. The dialog's DDX/DDV code will
perform the transfer of these data to the dialog.

Following this, the foregoing code builds a list of the current accounts in
a separate CObList object in the dialog, which is addressed by its
m_Accounts member variable. The list-building loop creates a *copy* of
each CAcctObj object by using a newly defined *copy constructor,* which
was added to the CAcctObj class. The declaration of the CAcctObj constructor, newly added to the **acctobj.h** file, is as follows:

```
CAcctObj  (CAcctObj* pObj); // copy constructor
```

The definition of the copy constructor, newly added to the source file for the CAcctObj class (**acctobj.cpp**) is as follows:

```
CAcctObj::CAcctObj (CAcctObj* pObj)
{
   m_nAcctStatus = pObj->m_nAcctStatus;
   m_szAcctName  = pObj->m_szAcctName;
   m_szAcctDesc  = pObj->m_szAcctDesc;
   m_nAcctType   = pObj->m_nAcctType;
   m_nAcctID     = pObj->m_nAcctID;
}
```

The foregoing constructor copies the contents of each of the member variables in the argument to the corresponding member variables in the newly created object.

The code for the OnCashFlow message handler continues by invoking the DoModal member function to "run" the dialog and test the value it returns (i.e., whether the OK button was pressed). The code to perform these tasks is as follows:

```
//
// now we can invoke the dialog to get the settings
//
if (dlg.DoModal() == IDOK)
{
   //
   // convert the from and to dates to CTime objects
   // and verify that the from date is < the to date.
   //
   MakeDateObj (dlg.m_From, m_FromDate);
   MakeDateObj (dlg.m_To,   m_ToDate);
   if (m_FromDate > m_ToDate)
   {
      //
      // an invalid time span was given. Tell the user,
      // delete the dialog's account objects, and then
      // return.
      //
      AfxMessageBox ("End time must be greater "
         "than start time.");
      DeleteDlgAccts(dlg);
      return;
   }

   //
   // the settings are all good, so now we can
   // store them for use by the view.
   //
   m_nReportType = CASH_FLOW_REPORT;
   POSITION nPos = dlg.m_Accounts.GetHeadPosition();
   while (nPos != NULL)
   {
      CAcctObj* pObj;
      pObj = (CAcctObj *)dlg.m_Accounts.GetNext(nPos);
      if (pObj->GetAcctStatus() == ACCT_SELECTED)
      {
         CAcctObj* pRObj = new CAcctObj (pObj);
         m_ReportAccts.AddTail(pRObj);
```

```
            }
          }
          DeleteDlgAccts(dlg);

            //
            // make sure there's something to display, create
            // a new frame and view in which to display the
            // current report, and then let the view take over.
            //
            if (!m_ReportAccts.IsEmpty())
            {
            CKeepitApp* theApp = (CKeepitApp *)AfxGetApp();
            CMultiDocTemplate* pRptTmp;
            pRptTmp = theApp->m_pRptViewTemplate;
            CFrameWnd* pRptFrame = pRptTmp->CreateNewFrame (this,
                NULL);
            pRptTmp->InitialUpdateFrame (pRptFrame, this);
          }
        }
```

The foregoing code invokes the DoModal member function to "run" the dialog and then performs additional chores if the dialog is dismissed by clicking its OK button.

When the OK button has been clicked, the user has made the necessary changes to the settings and wishes for the report to be created. In order to accomplish this, we must first create objects of the CTime class for both the beginning and ending time periods and make sure that the ending time is later than the beginning time. We do this by using a function imported from the **dattim.cpp** source file (which will be shown shortly) called MakeDateObj. If the ending time is not later than the beginning time, we display an error dialog and return from the handler. We don't create the report in that case.

If the two dates define a valid period of time, we continue by looping through the (perhaps modified) list of accounts in the dialog and create new copies of the objects in a CObList object, which is addressed by the document's m_ReportAccts member variable. The reason we create new copies of the account objects is that the ones in the dialog's list are going to be deleted shortly. Immediately following the loop, we call the DeleteDlgAccts member function.

The final section of the foregoing code creates a new frame to contain the Cash Flow report view by calling the document template's CreateNewFrame member function and then calls the document template's InitialUpdateFrame member function, which causes the OnInitialUpdate member function for the CReportView class (the frame's view) to be called. This is all that is needed to initiate generation of the report.

In the event that the user dismissed the Settings dialog by clicking the Cancel button, we must delete the copies of the CAcctObj objects that were created previously. The final code in the OnCashFlow message handler performs this task, as follows:

```
    else
    {
      //
      // delete all of the dialog's account entries
      //
      DeleteDlgAccts(dlg);
    }
  }
```

DeleteDlgAccts Member Function Code

The DeleteDlgAccts member function is called to delete the contents of the dialog's m_Accounts list either after new copies have been made when the user has dismissed the Settings dialog with the OK button, or when the dialog is dismissed with the Cancel button. In either case, the member function must accomplish the same task. The code is newly added and is as follows:

```
void CKeepitDoc::DeleteDlgAccts(CSettings& dlg)
{
  POSITION pos = dlg.m_Accounts.GetHeadPosition();
  while (pos != NULL)
  {
    CAcctObj* pObj = (CAcctObj *)dlg.m_Accounts.GetNext (pos);
    delete pObj;
  }
  dlg.m_Accounts.RemoveAll();
}
```

The foregoing code consists of a simple loop, accessing each of the objects in the dialog's list, and then deleting the object. The code completes the process by removing all of the (deleted) object pointers from the list.

Customizing the Settings Dialog Code

The Settings dialog is invoked by the document's OnCashFlow message handler, in response to the user's choice of the Cash Flow command from the application's Report menu.

CSettings Header File Changes

The wizard-created code in the **settings.h** header file, for the CSettings class was shown in the previous chapter. We have added some additional preprocessor definitions, an override for the OnInitDialog member function, and some new member variables.

Newly Added Preprocessor Definitions

In order to be able to reference the various settings in the Period combo box, we had added the following definitions, which correspond directly to the entries we added when the combo box was added to the dialog in Chapter 7, on page 240, in step 20. The definitions are as follows:

```
#define YEAR_TO_DATE      0    // added
#define CURRENT_MONTH     1    // added
#define CURRENT_QUARTER   2    // added
#define CURRENT_YEAR      3    // added
#define LAST_MONTH        4    // added
#define LAST_QUARTER      5    // added
#define LAST_YEAR         6    // added
#define ALL_TRANSACTIONS  7    // added
```

OnInitDialog Override Declaration

In order to perform additional initialization of the dialog, prior to when it is displayed by the framework, we have added an override for the CDialog class's OnInitDialog member function. The new declaration is as follows:

```
virtual BOOL OnInitDialog(void); // override
```

Newly Added Member Variables

We have added new member variables to contain the list of selected accounts (which is initialized in the CKeepitDoc's OnCashFlow message handler) and also the dialog's title. The new declarations are as follows:

```
public:

// Local Member Variables
   CObList   m_Accounts;      // list of selected accounts
   CString   m_szDialogTitle; // dialog title string
```

CSettings Source Code Additions

We showed you the wizard-created source code for the CSettings class in the previous chapter. In this chapter we will show you newly added preprocessor statements, changes to the wizard-created DoDataExchange member function, the code for the newly added OnInitDialog override member function, and also the code for the OnPerListSelect and OnAcctsClicked message handlers.

Newly Added Preprocessor Statements

The custom code for the member functions in the CSettings class requires that we provide declarations of several of the member functions in other classes. The newly added `#include` statements are as follows:

```
#include "dattim.h"    // added
#include "acctobj.h"   // added
#include "selected.h"  // added
```

The foregoing statements provide the means for the code to reference the functions in the **dattim.cpp** file and member functions in the CAcctObj and CSelectedAccts classes.

DoDataExchange Member Function Code

In the course of implementing the code for the Settings dialog, we realized that we needed some code to validate and transfer strings that represented dates. Because the DDX/DDV (dynamic data exchange and dynamic data validation) code provides the means for user-specified exchange and validation routines, we have provided functions for performing this chore (to be described shortly). The modified code for the DoDataExchange member function is as follows:

```
void CSettings::DoDataExchange(CDataExchange* pDX)
{
   CDialog::DoDataExchange(pDX);
   //{{AFX_DATA_MAP(CSettings)
   DDX_Control(pDX, IDC_PER_LIST, m_PeriodList);
   DDX_Control(pDX, IDC_ACCTS_BUTTON, m_AcctsButton);
   DDX_Control(pDX, IDC_DIALOG_TITLE, m_DialogTitle);
   DDX_DateCheck(pDX, IDC_FROM, m_From);
   DDX_Text(pDX, IDC_TITLE, m_Title);
   DDX_DateCheck(pDX, IDC_TO, m_To);
   //}}AFX_DATA_MAP
}
```

The only changes from what was presented in the previous chapter, is the substitution of the word DDX_DateCheck instead of DDX_Text for the IDC_FROM and IDC_TO edit controls in the dialog.

Newly Added Validation Types

The newly specified transfer and validation type (DDX_DateCheck) is added to the ClassWizard information file (**keepit.clw**), in the section titled [General Info]. Alternatively, you can add new transfer and validation types to your **appstudio.ini** file, which allows them to be used by multiple projects. We have added the declarations to the **keepit.clw** file for use in this project only. The declarations are as follows:

```
[General Info]
ExtraDDXCount=1
ExtraDDX1=E;;Date;CString;"";DateCheck;mm/dd/yy
```

In the foregoing, the line beginning with `ExtraDDXCount` specifies the number of special transfer and validation declarations that follow. Each declaration is also numbered; the first one is called "`ExtraDDX1`," and succeeding entries would be named `ExtraDDX2`, `ExtraDDX3`, and so forth. Individual fields in the entry are separated by semicolon characters. The fields, reading from left to right, in these entries are defined as follows:

❖ Keys: This is a sequence of single-character identifiers for the type of dialog control to which the entry refers. The allowable characters for keys are as follows:

E	Edit control
C	Two-state checkbox control
c	Tri-state checkbox control
R	First radio button control in a group
L	Nonsorted list box control
l	Sorted list box control
M	Combo box control
N	Nonsorted drop list control
n	Sorted drop list control
V	VBX control
1	If the DDX insert should be added to the head of the list (the default is to add entries to the end of the list)

❖ VB Keys (Optional): This field is used only for VBX controls, and contains a sequence of single-character identifiers for VBX control properties. In our case, the field is empty, signaled by two consecutive semicolon characters. The allowable keys are as follows:

S	String property
I	Int property
L	Long property
B	Bool property
F	Float property
C	Color property
s	Read-only string property
i	Read-only int property

l   Read-only long property

b   Read-only bool property

f   Read-only float property

c   Read-only color property

❖ Prompt: This field contains a prompt string (without quotes) that is placed into the property combo box.

❖ Type: This field identifies the data type of the entry. The fields we wish to check are of type CString, so the field contains that type name.

❖ Initial Value: This field contains the initial value you wish for the control to contain. In the case of our string fields, this is specified as an empty string.

❖ DDX Proc: This field contains the name of the procedure to be used to transfer (and possibly validate, if a separate validation procedure is not specified) the value in the field to which the declaration pertains. In the case of the CString fields (`m_From` and `m_To`), which represent dates, the procedure name is given as DateCheck. The prefix "DDX_" is appended to the front of this name to construct the name of the procedure in the function calls included in the DoDataExchange member function, shown previously. The actual procedure name for the DateCheck function is `DDX_DateCheck`.

❖ Comment: This field contains a comment that is displayed in the ClassWizard's "Edit Member Variables" dialog, when the field name is selected. You can put any text you want in here. Do not include any quote or semicolon characters. In our case, we have entered a comment of "mm/dd/yy," to indicate the expected form of the date entry.

The next series of fields in the `ExtraDDX` entry is optional. They apply only if the field has a validation function that is separate from the data transfer function. The additional fields are as follows, beginning with a semicolon character:

❖ DDV Proc: This field contains the name of the procedure to be used to validate the associated control's contents. If the name of your validation routine is `DDV_CheckTime`, then you would enter Check-Time into this field.

❖ Prompt1: This field contains a string (without quotes), which is used as a prompt.

❖ Format1: This field contains the format of the first (of possibly two) DDV arguments. The allowed argument types are as follows:

d   Int

u   Unsigned

D   Long int (i.e., long)

U   Unsigned long (i.e., DWORD)

f   Float

F   Double

s   String

❖ Prompt-2: This field contains the prompt for an optional second DDV argument.

❖ Format2: This field contains the format for the optional second DDV argument and can contain any one of the formats described previously for the Format1 field.

The foregoing constitutes the complete description of an `ExtraDDX` entry in the ClassWizard's information file (i.e., **keepit.clw** in our case), or in App Studio's initialization file (**apstudio.ini**) in the Windows directory.

Looking back at the DoDataExchange member function, shown earlier, you will see that the data exchange task for the `m_From` and `m_To` date fields is being carried out by calling the `DDX_DateCheck` function. This function will be shown shortly.

OnInitDialog Member Function Code

The OnInitDialog member function in the CSettings class is called by the framework after the dialog has been created but just prior to its display. This member function is a perfect place to put initialization code that is executed only once, just prior to when the dialog is made visible. The code for this override of the OnInitDialog member function is as follows:

```
BOOL CSettings::OnInitDialog()
{
   CDialog::OnInitDialog();
   POSITION pos = m_Accounts.GetHeadPosition();
   while (pos != NULL)
   {
     //
     // all accounts are selected by default
     //
     CAcctObj* pAcct = (CAcctObj *)m_Accounts.GetNext(pos);
     pAcct->SetAcctStatus (ACCT_SELECTED);
   }
   m_DialogTitle.SetWindowText (m_szDialogTitle);
   m_PeriodList.SetCurSel (0);// select Year-To-Date
   return TRUE;
}
```

The foregoing code calls the CDialog's OnInitDialog member function first, which causes the DoDataExchange member function (described previously) to be called to transfer variables from the dialog's member variables to the corresponding controls in the dialog. Our override member function then proceeds to loop through the private list of accounts and set the status of each of these to ACCT_SELECTED, which status is used, in this case, to indicate that the account should be included in the specified report.

Following the loop, the title of the dialog window is set to the text contained in the `m_szDialogTitle` member variable, and the very first entry in the dialog's Period combo box (Year-To-Date) is selected. The code returns TRUE to indicate that the initialization was successful.

OnPerListSelect Message Handler Code

The OnPerListSelect message handler is invoked when the user chooses one of the selections from the Period combo box in the dialog. The selections were preset when the dialog was designed and the code handles the selection of any one of the items by setting the From and To date entries to values implied by the current selection. The code for the OnPerListSelect message handler is as follows:

```
void CSettings::OnPerListSelect()
{
   POINT cQtr[4] = {{1,3}, {4,6}, {7,9}, {10,12}};
   CTime curTime = CTime::GetCurrentTime();
   CTime fromTime, toTime;
   int nYr = curTime.GetYear();
   int nMo = curTime.GetMonth();
   int nDy = curTime.GetDay();
   int nSel = m_PeriodList.GetCurSel();
   switch (nSel)
   {
     case YEAR_TO_DATE:
     {
        fromTime = CTime(nYr, 1, 1, 0, 0, 0);
        toTime = curTime;
        break;
     }
     case CURRENT_MONTH:
     {
        fromTime = CTime(nYr, nMo, 1, 0, 0, 0);
        toTime = CTime(nYr, nMo, monthDays[nMo-1], 0, 0, 0);
        break;
     }
     case CURRENT_QUARTER:
     {
        int nQ = (nMo + 2)/3;
        fromTime = CTime(nYr, cQtr[nQ-1].x, 1, 0, 0, 0);
        toTime = CTime(nYr, cQtr[nQ-1].y,
           monthDays[cQtr[nQ-1].y-1], 0, 0, 0);
        break;
     }
     case CURRENT_YEAR:
     {
        fromTime = CTime(nYr, 1, 1, 0, 0, 0);
        toTime = CTime(nYr, 12, 31, 0, 0, 0);
        break;
     }
```

```cpp
      case LAST_MONTH:
      {
         nMo--;
         if (nMo == 0)
         {
            nMo = 12;
            nYr--;
         }
         fromTime = CTime(nYr, nMo, 1, 0, 0, 0);
         toTime = CTime(nYr, nMo, monthDays[nMo-1], 0, 0, 0);
         break;
      }
      case LAST_QUARTER:
      {
         int nQ = (nMo + 2) / 3 - 1;
         if (nQ == 0)
         {
            nQ = 4;
            nYr--;
         }
         fromTime = CTime(nYr, cQtr[nQ-1].x, 1, 0, 0, 0);
         toTime = CTime(nYr, cQtr[nQ-1].y,
            monthDays[cQtr[nQ-1].y-1], 0, 0, 0);
         break;
      }
      case LAST_YEAR:
      {
         nYr--;
         fromTime = CTime(nYr, 1, 1, 0, 0, 0);
         toTime = CTime(nYr, 12, 31, 0, 0, 0);
         break;
      }
      case ALL_TRANSACTIONS:
      {
         fromTime = CTime (1990, 1, 1, 0, 0, 0);
         toTime = CTime (1999, 12, 31, 0, 0, 0);
         break;
      }
   }
   m_From = fromTime.Format ("%m/%d/%y");
   m_To = toTime.Format ("%m/%d/%y");
   GetDlgItem (IDC_FROM)->SetWindowText (m_From);
   GetDlgItem (IDC_TO)->SetWindowText (m_To);
}
```

The preceding code uses the mnemonic definition of the selected item's index in the combo box to determine what values should be stored into the m_From and m_To member variables, and also what string values should be written into the corresponding edit controls in the dialog.

Because the contents of the edit controls can be altered by the user by simply tabbing into them and entering arbitrary date values, we have made provision for the DateCheck data validation function to be executed when the dialog is dismissed by clicking its OK button. In the case of an illegal date entry, the data validation code displays an appropriate error message and then highlights the text in the offending field.

OnAcctsClicked Message Handler Code

The OnAcctsClicked message handler is invoked by the framework when the user clicks the Accounts button in the Settings dialog. The purpose of this action is to specify which accounts should be included in the current report.

The main reason that we built a private list of accounts in the `m_Accounts` member variable of the CSettings class is so that the status of the account entries could be manipulated separately from the list used for the main account views. The code for the OnAcctsClicked message handler is as follows:

```cpp
void CSettings::OnAcctsClicked()
{
   CSelectedAccts dlg;

   //
   // store account objects in selected dialog's list
   //
   POSITION pos = m_Accounts.GetHeadPosition();
   while (pos != NULL)
   {
      CAcctObj* pAcct = (CAcctObj *)m_Accounts.GetNext(pos);
      CAcctObj* pObj  = new CAcctObj (pAcct);
      dlg.m_Selected.AddTail ((CObject *)pObj);
   }
   if (dlg.DoModal() == IDOK)
   {
      //
      // process list of modified selections
      //
      POSITION nPos1 = dlg.m_Selected.GetHeadPosition();
      while (nPos1 != NULL)
      {
         CAcctObj* pObj;
         pObj = (CAcctObj *)dlg.m_Selected.GetNext(nPos1);
         WORD nID = pObj->GetAcctID();
         POSITION nPos2 = m_Accounts.GetHeadPosition();
         while (nPos2 != NULL)
         {
            //
            // find matching account and change its status
            //
            CAcctObj* pAcct
            pAcct = (CAcctObj *)m_Accounts.GetNext (nPos2);
            if (pAcct->GetAcctID() == nID)
            {
               pAcct->SetAcctStatus (pObj->GetAcctStatus());
               break;
            }
         }
         delete pObj;
      }
      dlg.m_Selected.RemoveAll();
   }
   else
   {
      //
      // the user cancelled the dialog, so just delete
      // all of the copies of the account entries.
```

```
        //
        POSITION nPos3 = dlg.m_Selected.GetHeadPosition();
        while (nPos3 != NULL)
        {
            CAcctObj* pSel;
            pSel = (CAcctObj *)dlg.m_Selected.GetNext(nPos3);
            delete pSel;
        }
        dlg.m_Selected.RemoveAll();
    }
}
```

The foregoing code begins by creating the CSelectedAccts dialog. Following this, it creates copies of the CAcctObj objects listed in the m_Accounts member variable of the CSettings class (using the "copy constructor" mentioned previously). The reason for making yet another copy of the account objects is to provide support for restoration of the previous settings if the user decides to cancel the List of Accounts dialog. After the copies of the account entries have been stored in the dialog's m_Selected list, the DoModal member function is invoked to "run" the dialog. When the dialog is displayed, its "selected" entries reflect those that were selected in the previous invocation of this dialog (if any). On the first entry, if you recall, we elected for all accounts to be selected for inclusion in the Cash Flow report. However, the user has the ability to change these selections, dismiss the dialog with the OK button, reinvoke the dialog, and change them again, etc. If the List of Accounts dialog is dismissed with the Cancel button, then the previous selections will remain in effect.

After the List of Accounts dialog has been dismissed with the OK button, the foregoing code loops through the dialog's list of accounts, locates the matching entry in the list addressed by the m_Accounts variable, and changes the status in the m_Accounts list to match what is stored in the corresponding entry in the List of Accounts m_Selected list. After transferring the status of the account object from the List of Accounts dialog, the object is deleted. At the end of the loop, all of the (now invalid) object entries are removed from the list and the message handler returns control to the framework.

If the user dismisses the List of Accounts dialog by clicking its Cancel button, then the foregoing code loops through the dialog's account entries, deleting each one and then removing the entries from the list at the end of the loop. No further processing is necessary in this case, and the message handler returns control to the framework.

Data Exchange and Validation

We have described the data exchange and validation procedures previously, with regard to the DoDataExchange member function that the ClassWizard generates into each CDialog and CFormView-derived class. We have also explained that to check the dates in the CSettings dialog, we needed to create a custom validation routine, add definitions into the ClassWizard's information file (**keepit.clw**), and modify the DDX/DDV entries in the DoDataExchange member function.

Dattim Header File Declarations

A new pair of files has been created to hold special validation routines for the Settings (and perhaps other) dialogs. At present, the code in this file handles only the transfer and validation of date fields. The declarations in the **dattim.h** header file are as follows:

```
//
// dattim.h - header file for global routines that support
// the entry and validation of date fields in dialogs.
//

void AFXAPI DDX_DateCheck (CDataExchange* pDX, int nIDC,
    CString& szDat);
BOOL GetDate (HWND hWnd, CString& szDat);
void MakeDateObj (CString& szDateText, CTime& datObj);
```

The foregoing declarations include an entry for the dynamic data exchange and validation function (DDX_DateCheck), as well as two helper functions (GetDate and MakeDateObj).

Dattim Source File Code

The source file for the data exchange and validation code is **dattim.cpp**, and the functions declared in the foregoing header file are defined in this file. Note that the functions are global to the application and can be called from any other function.

Source File Definitions

The code in the **dattim.cpp** source file is all newly added. The source code begins with statements that include references to the declarations in the framework and other classes. Following this, a table of days in each month is defined. For the sake of simplicity, this table includes only 28 days for the month of February, but the validation code in the GetDate function compensates for the presence of a leap year. The code begins as follows:

```
//
// dattim.cpp - DDX/DDV routines to implement date checking
// and conversion of date strings to CTime structures.
//          (uses Get2Nums() from account.cpp file)
//

#include "stdafx.h"
#include "resource.h"
#include "account.h"
#include "dattim.h"
#include <string.h>

char __far monthDays[] =
{
   31, 28, 31, 30, 31, 30, 31, 31, 30, 31, 30, 31
};
```

DDX_DateCheck Function Code

The DDX_DateCheck function is called with three arguments. The first
is a pointer to an object of the CDataExchange class, which includes
member functions and variables that the function needs to reference.
The second argument is the identifier of which edit control is being addressed by the function. Data are either being transferred *into* or *from* the
specified control, depending on the state of a member variable in the
CDataExchange object. The code is as follows:

```
void AFXAPI DDX_DateCheck (CDataExchange* pDX, int nIDC,
   CString& szDat)
{
   HWND hWndCtrl = pDX->PrepareEditCtrl (nIDC);
   if (pDX->m_bSaveAndValidate)
   {
      if (!GetDate (hWndCtrl, szDat))
      {
         //
         // the date was invalid, so tell the user
         //
         AfxMessageBox (IDS_INVALID_DATE);
         pDX->Fail();
      }
   }
   else
   {
      ::SetWindowText (hWndCtrl, szDat.GetBufferSetLength(8));
   }
}
```

The foregoing code first acquires a handle to the edit control by calling
the PrepareEditCtrl member function pointed to by the pDX argument,
passing that member function the edit control's identifier. The function
then tests whether the m_bSaveAndValidate variable pointed to by
the pDX argument has a value of TRUE or FALSE. If TRUE, the variable indicates that the date string is to be transferred *from* the edit control and

validated before allowing the dialog to be dismissed. The foregoing code handles this case by calling a GetDate helper function with both the handle to the control and a reference to the CString variable into which the date is to be transferred. If the GetDate function returns a TRUE result, then the date is valid and the transfer has been accomplished. If the result from calling GetDate is FALSE, then an error message is displayed and the Fail member function addressed by the pDX pointer is called. This causes the dialog box to remain visible and the erroneous entry to be selected. No member function is called if the validation is successful. Note that the foregoing code makes reference to a "string resource" named IDS_INVALID_DATE, which has been entered into the application's resource file by using the App Studio string table editor. The contents of the entry are as follows (you do not enter the quotation marks that delimit the string if you are using the App Studio editor):

```
IDS_INVALID_DATE   "Please enter a date in the form: mm/dd/yy"
```

If the `m_bSaveAndValidate` member variable of the CDataExchange class is FALSE, then the DDX_DateCheck function is being called to transfer the contents of the date string from its corresponding member variable to the dialog's edit control. In this case, the date is assumed to be valid and no validation is necessary. The code calls the global function SetWindowText to store the string into the control and then exits the function.

GetDate Helper Function Code

The major portion of the validation task is handled by the GetDate function. Its purpose is to access the string in the edit control, validate it according to the specified format for dates (mm/dd/yy in our case), and if valid store the date into the CString variable passed as a reference in the argument list. The code for the GetDate function is as follows:

```
BOOL GetDate (HWND hWnd, CString& szDat)
{
   char szDateText[10];
   int  mo=0, dy=0, yr=0, index=0, days;

   ::GetWindowText (hWnd, szDateText, 9);
   if (strlen (szDateText) > 8)
   {
      return FALSE;
   }
   if (!Get2Nums (szDateText, index, mo, '/'))
   {
      return FALSE;
   }
   if (mo < 1 || mo > 12)
```

```
   {
      return FALSE;
   }
   if (!Get2Nums (szDateText, index, dy, '/'))
   {
      return FALSE;
   }
   if (dy < 1 || dy > 31)
   {
      return FALSE;
   }
   if (!Get2Nums (szDateText, index, yr, '\0'))
   {
      return FALSE;
   }
   if (yr < 90 || yr > 99)
   {
      return FALSE;
   }
   yr += 1900;
   days = monthDays [mo-1];
   if (mo == 2)
   {
      if (yr % 4 == 0)
      {
         days++;
      }
   }
   if (dy > days)
   {
      return FALSE;
   }
   szDat = szDateText;
   return TRUE;
}
```

The foregoing code accesses the text contained in the edit control and stores it into a local character array variable. The code makes use of a function called Get2Nums, which is defined in the **account.cpp** file and declared in the **account.h** header file, whose declarations we include in this file. (The Get2Nums function is described in Chapter 4, beginning on page 112.)

The code in the GetDate function tests to ensure that the length of the text entry is equal or less than eight characters and then begins accessing the month, day, and then year fields of the string. Each field can be one or two characters in length, and both the month and day must be followed by a forward slash character. The year field is tested to make sure that it is followed by a NULL character (indicating the end of the string) and that its value is between 90 and 99. The month and day fields are also validated, and if the month is February, the number of days in the month is adjusted if the specified year is a leap year. If all of the validation tests are passed, then the date is copied into the string referenced by the second argument to the function.

MakeDateObj Helper Function

Although the MakeDateObj function is not used during the validation task, it is used by the OnCashFlow message handler in the CKeepitDoc class. The code for the MakeDateObj function is as follows:

```
void MakeDateObj (CString& szDateText, CTime& datObj)
{
   char *szDat;
   int mo, dy, yr, index;

   szDat = szDateText.GetBuffer(8);
   index = 0;
   Get2Nums (szDat, index, mo, '/');
   Get2Nums (szDat, index, dy, '/');
   Get2Nums (szDat, index, yr, '\0');
   szDateText.ReleaseBuffer();
   CTime t (yr+1900, mo, dy, 0, 0, 0);
   datObj = t;
}
```

The foregoing code assumes that the string being passed by reference in the first argument is a valid date string. The Get2Nums function is called to convert the month, day, and then the year to numeric values, which are then used to construct a valid CTime object. After that object is created, it is stored in the variable passed as the second argument to the function (a reference to a CTime variable).

Customizing the CSelectedAccts Code

The CSelectedAccts class implements a dialog that is titled "List of Accounts" and which is used to provide the user with the means to select accounts for which the Cash Flow report is to be prepared. The header and source files for this class are **selected.h** and **selected.cpp**, respectively.

CSelectedAccts Header File Additions

We have added two lines to the ClassWizard-generated code for the CSelectedAccts class header file (**selected.h**). One is the declaration of the OnInitDialog override member function, and the other is the declaration of the m_Selected variable used to hold the list of selected accounts being displayed by the dialog. These two additions are both in a public section of the class definition and are as follows:

```
virtual BOOL OnInitDialog (void);// added
CObList m_Selected;             // added
```

CSelectedAccts Source File Additions

The additions to the source file include the custom code for the OnInit-Dialog override member function and the custom code for the OnSelect-Account, OnAll, and OnNone message handlers.

OnInitDialog Member Function Code

The override of the CDialog class's OnInitDialog member function provides the proper place to add code which is executed only once each time the dialog is invoked, and prior to when the dialog is made visible. The code for this member function is newly added and is as follows:

```
BOOL CSelectedAccts::OnInitDialog (void)
{
   CDialog::OnInitDialog();
   POSITION pos = m_Selected.GetHeadPosition();
   BOOL bAnyNotSelected = FALSE;
   while (pos != NULL)
   {
      //
      // load the ListBox with the strings in the m_Selected
      // list, selecting or deselecting them as we go.
      //
      CAcctObj* pObj = (CAcctObj *)m_Selected.GetNext (pos);
      WORD nStatus = pObj->GetAcctStatus();
      CString szName = pObj->GetAcctName();
      char* pBuf = szName.GetBuffer(20);
      m_AcctsList.AddString (pBuf);
      int index = m_AcctsList.FindString (-1, pBuf);
      szName.ReleaseBuffer();
      if (nStatus == ACCT_SELECTED)
      {
         //
         // select the string we just added
         //
         m_AcctsList.SetSel (index, TRUE);
      }
      else
      {
         //
         // indicate that one or more list entries
         // is not selected, and then deselect the
         // string in the ListBox.
         //
         bAnyNotSelected = TRUE;
         m_AcctsList.SetSel (index, FALSE);
      }
   }

   //
   // decide whether the "All" button should be checked
   //
   if (bAnyNotSelected)
   {
      //
      // uncheck both bottons
      //
      CheckRadioButton (IDC_ALL, IDC_NONE, 0);
   }
   else
```

```
   {
      // check "All" button
      CheckRadioButton (IDC_ALL, IDC_NONE, IDC_ALL);
   }
   return TRUE;
}
```

The foregoing code is concerned mainly with two tasks. The first is to loop through all of the entries in the `m_Selected` list (which was preloaded with entries by the Settings dialog prior to invoking the List of Accounts dialog), load each entry into the list box in the dialog, and then select the entry in the list if its status contains the value ACCT_SELECTED. The second task is to check either the All, None, or not either of the radio buttons in the dialog, depending on whether all, none, or some of the account entries were selected.

OnSelectAccount Message Handler Code

The OnSelectAccount message handler is invoked when the user double clicks on one of the entries in the list box. The double-click action may signal that the entry is to be selected, or deselected, according to its present status. The code for this message handler is as follows:

```
void CSelectedAccts::OnSelectAccount()
{
   CString szName;

   // get the index, selection state and name of
   // the item the user has double-clicked.

   int index = m_AcctsList.GetCaretIndex();
   int state = m_AcctsList.GetSel(index);
   m_AcctsList.GetText (index, szName);

   // locate the entry in the list of accounts
   // and change its selection status.

   POSITION pos = m_Selected.GetHeadPosition();
   while (pos != NULL)
   {
      CAcctObj* pObj = (CAcctObj *)m_Selected.GetNext (pos);
      CString szAcctName = pObj->GetAcctName();
      if (szAcctName == szName)
      {
         if (state > 0)
         {
            pObj->SetAcctStatus (ACCT_SELECTED);
         }
         else
         {
            pObj->SetAcctStatus (ACCT_UNCHANGED);
         }
         break;
      }
   }
}
```

The foregoing code determines the selection state of the entry on which the user double clicked, searches for that entry (by name) in the list of accounts (m_Selected), and then sets the entry's status to reflect the selection state.

OnAll Message Handler Code

The OnAll message handler is called when the user clicks on the radio button labeled All. The code is as follows:

```
void CSelectedAccts::OnAll()
{
   POSITION pos = m_Selected.GetHeadPosition();
   while (pos != NULL)
   {
      CAcctObj* pObj = (CAcctObj *)m_Selected.GetNext (pos);
      pObj->SetAcctStatus (ACCT_SELECTED);
      CString szName = pObj->GetAcctName();
      char* pBuf = szName.GetBuffer (20);
      int index = m_AcctsList.FindStringExact(-1, pBuf);
      szName.ReleaseBuffer();
      m_AcctsList.SetSel (index, TRUE);
   }
}
```

The foregoing message handler has the task of selecting all of the accounts in the list box and also setting the status of their corresponding m_Selected list entry to ACCT_SELECTED. It accomplishes both tasks in a loop through the m_Selected list, changing that entry's status, and then finding the corresponding entry in the list box and selecting it.

OnNone Message Handler Code

The OnNone message handler is called when the user selects the None radio button in the dialog. The task of this member function is to deselect all of the entries in the dialog's list box and change the status of the corresponding m_Selected list entry to ACCT_UNCHANGED. The code for this message handler is as follows:

```
void CSelectedAccts::OnNone()
{
   POSITION pos = m_Selected.GetHeadPosition();
   while (pos != NULL)
   {
      CAcctObj* pObj = (CAcctObj *)m_Selected.GetNext (pos);
      pObj->SetAcctStatus (ACCT_UNCHANGED);
      CString szName = pObj->GetAcctName();
      char* pBuf = szName.GetBuffer(20);
      int index = m_AcctsList.FindStringExact (-1, pBuf);
      szName.ReleaseBuffer();
      m_AcctsList.SetSel (index, FALSE);
   }
}
```

As with the OnAll message handler, the foregoing OnNone code loops through the entries in the `m_Selected` list of accounts and changes the status of each entry and then finds and deselects the corresponding entry in the dialog's list box.

Customizing the CReportView Code

The CReportView class was constructed by the ClassWizard tool to implement the Cash Flow (and possibly other) reports. The CReportView class is derived from the CScrollView class, which offers both horizontal and vertical scroll bars and handles scrolling the view automatically.

In addition to providing a blank canvas on which to display the Cash Flow report, we have also enabled the commands to print and can display a "preview" of the report, as it would appear on the selected printer.

One of the important considerations in producing reports that must be printed as well as displayed is how to handle the discrepancy between the resolutions of the two devices. Each device, whether it is a display screen or some other output device has a set of unique characteristics. The MFC supports the unique characteristics of each device by providing the drawing and drawing-related code with a pointer to the "device context," which specifies many parameters that describe the device. For example, the number of pixels per inch in both its horizontal and vertical dimensions are included in the device context. Another, very important set of parameters is established by the selected "Mapping Mode" of the device.

By default, each new device context (e.g., a display or printer) has a mapping mode of MM_TEXT, which is best for the display and printout of pure textual information. If the display or printout is to contain graphic figures, then one of the other mapping modes, such as MM_LOENGLISH or MM_TWIPS, would be more appropriate because these mapping modes convert measurements to the equivalent number of pixels on whatever device the output is written. The MM_TEXT mapping mode, on the other hand, uses a measurement unit of pixels, regardless of what output device is being used. That means that if you were to draw a line one inch in length on a display that offers 96-pixels-per-inch resolution in either dimension, that same line would be much shorter when printed on a 300-dots-per-inch (DPI) printer.

Nevertheless, it is convenient to use the MM_TEXT mapping mode and make appropriate adjustments for whether the output is written to the screen or to the printer. In fact, it is quite easy to use the MM_TEXT mapping mode if we make sure that we choose device-independent fonts for the text that we display or print. In the case of the Cash Flow report, we will be using the MM_TEXT mapping mode and TrueType® fonts.

To learn more about mapping modes you can examine the Scribble application in the *Class Library User's Guide* for the Microsoft Foundation Class Library, or you can refer to the member function descriptions in the CDC class in the *Class Library Reference* (or the corresponding online help files for that class). If you follow along the code in this section, we will show how the MM_TEXT mapping mode is used for the Cash Flow report and how the change in devices from display, to printer, and to the print preview display is handled.

CReportView Header File Additions

In order to implement the Cash Flow report, we have made a number of additions to the **reportvw.h** header file. Among these changes are the addition of declarations for new member functions and member variables. The contents of the modified header file are as follows:

```
// reportvw.h : header file
//
/////////////////////////////////////////////////////////////////
// CReportView view

class CReportView : public CScrollView
{
    DECLARE_DYNCREATE(CReportView)
protected:
    CReportView();                    // protected constructor
                                      // used by dynamic
creation

// Attributes
public:
    CObList m_RptEntries;             // report entries
    int     m_nReportType;            // type of report to
display
    CTime   m_FromDate;               // start of period
    CTime   m_ToDate;                 // end of period

// Operations
public:
    CKeepitDoc* GetDocument();        // copied from account.h
```

The first section of the file, shown in the foregoing declarations, contains the declaration of the standard constructor and also a set of new member variables that is made public and can be referenced from outside the class. The next section of the header file is specific to the current implementation and its contents are protected. The file continues, as follows:

```
// Implementation
protected:
    virtual ~CReportView();
    virtual void OnDraw(CDC* pDC); // overridden for this view
    virtual void OnInitialUpdate();// first time
    CSize  CashFlowViewSize ();   // compute Cash-Flow size
```

```
    void SortByDate (CObList& list);// sort by date

    void RectLPtoPositions (          // convert rect to positions
       CRect rectClip,                //  input CRect reference
       POSITION& nFirstEntry,         //  output POSITION reference
       POSITION& nLastEntry);         //  output POSITION reference

    void DrawRptLine (CDC* pDC,       // draw a report line
       CObject* pObj,                 //  object info to draw
       int& nYPos);                   //  position in viewport

    void OnPrepareDC (CDC* pDC,       // prepare the device
       CPrintInfo* pInfo = NULL);     // printer info == NULL

    void ComputeRptMetrics (CDC*pDC);// compute report metrics

// overridden member functions
   BOOL OnPreparePrinting (CPrintInfo* pInfo)
   void OnBeginPrinting (CDC* pDC, CPrintInfo* pInfo);
   void OnPrint (CDC* pDC, CPrintInfo* pInfo);

// print page header member function
   void PrintPageHeader (CDC* pDC, CPrintInfo* pInfo);
```

The foregoing declarations include overridden member functions and
newly defined member functions for implementing the Cash Flow report. It is possible that some of the member functions can be used (or
modified for use) in the preparation of other reports. The next section of
the header file contains the message map declarations. These statements
declare the message handlers that we have defined previously.

```
// Generated message map functions
//{{AFX_MSG(CReportView)
afx_msg void OnFilePrint();
afx_msg void OnFilePrintPreview();
afx_msg void OnDestroy();
afx_msg void OnHScroll(UINT nSBCode, UINT nPos,
   CScrollBar* pScrollBar);
afx_msg void OnVScroll(UINT nSBCode, UINT nPos,
   CScrollBar* pScrollBar);
//}}AFX_MSG
DECLARE_MESSAGE_MAP()
```

The next section of the header file contains declarations of member variables that are protected from access by other classes. They are apropos to
the preparation of the Cash Flow report, but may also be used for the
preparation of other reports in a future version of the application.

```
// new member variables for report preparation purposes
CString    m_szTitle;            // report title
CRgn       m_BlankLine;          // region for blank line
CSize      m_SizeTotal;          // total size of report
CSize      m_PageSize;           // amount to scroll for page
CSize      m_LineSize;           // amount to scroll for line
int        m_nTotalLines;        // total number of lines
int        m_nLinesPerPage;      // number of lines on a page
int        m_nLineHeight;        // height of one line
```

```
    int       m_nLineWidth;        // maximum width of one line
    int       m_nMinCharWidth;     // minimum character width
    int       m_nAvgCharWidth;     // average character width
    int       m_nMaxCharWidth;     // maximum character width
};
```

Finally, the last section of the header file contains a declaration for the nondebug version of the GetDocument member function. It was copied from the **account.h** header file and suitably modified to provide access to the document from within member functions in the CReportView class.

```
#ifndef _DEBUG    // debug version in reportvw.cpp
inline CKeepitDoc* CReportView::GetDocument()
    { return (CKeepitDoc*) m_pDocument; }
#endif
```

The comments in the foregoing header file provide a good idea of the function of each of the variables and member functions.

CReportView Source File Additions

The CReportView source file (**reportvw.cpp**) contains a fairly large number of member functions. Although all of the member functions are designed to support the display, printing, and printer preview of the Cash Flow report, many of these member functions can be modified easily, or used without change, for the preparation of other reports.

This section will be divided into subsections that contain the code that implements corresponding portions of the initialization, report generation, and report-printing tasks. Although there is some overlap between the functions associated with portions of the code, we will treat the screen display code as a separate section, and then its relationship to the task of outputting the report to the printer will be discussed. The printer preview feature comes almost for free, with the capabilities intrinsic to the MFC providing most of the functionality in this regard. Almost all of the code is newly added, so we will not be showing change bars in the definition of the various functions.

Report Initialization Code

Each report that you create will require that you perform a few initial steps to prepare the data for participation in the report and define the size of the report so that the range of travel of the scroll bars can be specified properly. In the case of our reports, these tasks are carried out by the OnInitialUpdate member function for the view.

OnInitialUpdate Member Function Code

The OnInitialUpdate member function is called by the framework, immediately after the view has been constructed and prior to execution of the OnUpdate member function. In fact, the default version of the OnInitialUpdate member function, found in the CView class, merely calls the OnUpdate member function. The code for our override of the OnInitialUpdate member function is as follows:

```
void CReportView::OnInitialUpdate()
{
   //
   // Get a pointer to the document and access
   // the variables that will be used to construct
   // the selected report.
   //
   CKeepitDoc* pDoc = GetDocument();
   m_nReportType = pDoc->m_nReportType;
   m_FromDate = pDoc->m_FromDate;
   m_ToDate = pDoc->m_ToDate;


   //
   // sort the entire list of transactions so that
   // we can compute the balance for each account.
   //
   SortByDate (pDoc->m_ListEntries);


   //
   // prepare the device context for sizing the report.
   //
   CClientDC aDC(this);
   ComputeRptMetrics (&aDC);
   m_BlankLine.CreateRectRgn (0, 0, m_nLineWidth, m_nLineHeight);


   //
   // calculate the size of the view, based upon the
   // values of the parameters and type of report.
   //
   switch (m_nReportType)
   {
      case CASH_FLOW_REPORT:
      {
         m_szTitle = "CASH FLOW DETAIL REPORT";
         m_SizeTotal = CashFlowViewSize ();
         break;
      }
      default:
      {
         return;
      }
   }
   SetScrollSizes(MM_TEXT, m_SizeTotal, m_PageSize, m_LineSize);
   Invalidate(TRUE);
}
```

The first section of the foregoing code accesses the document (via the GetDocument member function) to retrieve the values of several parameters whose values are important for defining the nature and scope of the report. The `m_nReportType`, `m_FromDate`, and `m_ToDate` member variables are accessed from the document object and are stored into member variables in the current object, with corresponding names. It is safe to do this because the code in the document's OnCashFlow message handler calls the InitialUpdateFrame member function of the document template class (`m_pRptViewTemplate`), which, in turn, sends the message WM_INITIALUPDATE to the view. Because this results in the On-InitialUpdate member function being called before any further processing takes place, the foregoing variables could not have been altered from the time that the OnCashFlow message handler begins execution, the OnInitialUpdate member function is called for the CReportView, and when the OnCashFlow message handler completes its execution.

The next section of code calls the SortByDate member function, which sorts all of the account transactions in the document's `m_ListEntries` list into date sequence. By doing so, we can ensure that, when we access the transactions for a given account, in the preparation of our Cash Flow report, the entries will be in proper date sequence. In addition to providing this sequence for the purpose of listing them in the report, the balance of the account can be computed properly for each transaction. If you recall, we do not generally keep the balance information updated when a transaction is made or modified. Instead, the DrawEntry member function in the CAcctList class (described in Chapter 4, beginning on page 90) computes the account balance "on the fly" when the account view is redrawn. This allows for entries to be re-sorted when they have been reentered, without requiring that the balance be constantly updated. However, in order to more easily support the preparation of the Cash Flow report, we have chosen to add a new member variable to the CListEntry class definition to hold the temporary balance value, and we have added three new access member functions to interface with the new member variable. The newly modified header file and its access member functions will be shown shortly.

The next section of the OnInitialUpdate member function's code creates a new device context object for the current view (the display screen device) and then proceeds to calculate various text metrics that are apropos to the display of the current report. The code also creates a pointer to a region that describes the height and width of a blank line for the current device context.

In the section of code that follows, we determine the type of report we are preparing and then execute a member function that computes the height and width of the report, based upon the text metrics for the current device. In this case, we have only one valid report from which to choose, but we have set up the code so that it can be used for other reports as well. It is possible, for reports with different organizations, that we may want to modify other portions of the foregoing code, based upon the requirements of the report. At present, the calculation of the report size will be unique to the Cash Flow report.

The final section of code calls the CScrollView's SetScrollSizes member function to set the mapping mode (MM_TEXT in our case), the total height and width of the report, in pixels (calculated by the CashFlow-ViewSize member function), the number of pixels to scroll, both horizontally and vertically when the user clicks the corresponding scroll bar arrow (for scrolling one line of the report), and the number of pixels to scroll, both horizontally and vertically when the user clicks in the body of the horizontal or vertical scroll bar, to effect a page-up or page-down scroll of the display. The SetScrollSizes member function uses these data to set the ranges and proper operation of the scroll bars for the view. Once we have provided these values, the operation of the scroll bars is handled automatically by the CScrollView class, with one exception.

The exception occurs when the user drags the "thumb" on the scroll bar to a different position. The default behavior in the CScrollView class is for the OnHScroll and OnVScroll message handlers to provide "live" scrolling of the display, where the display "moves" as the thumb is being dragged. Because we have to calculate the entries being displayed while the thumb is being dragged, it is not possible for us to provide "live" scrolling for this report. Instead, we have used the ClassWizard tool to create our own message handlers for the ON_WM_HSCROLL and ON_WM_VSCROLL messages and "fool" the CScrollView's OnScroll member function into scrolling the display only when the user has released the mouse button, after dragging the thumb to the desired final position. These handlers will be shown shortly.

The last act of the OnInitialUpdate member function is to call the view's Invalidate member function with an argument of TRUE. This invalidates the entire client area and causes Windows to erase the background (because of the TRUE argument) and, eventually, call the view's OnDraw member function to redraw the contents of the view.

SortByDate Member Function Code

The SortByDate member function is part of the report initialization code because it sorts the transactions in the document's `m_ListEntries` list into date order only once. When the entries are displayed, they will appear in strict chronological order. The description of this member function in the foregoing OnInitialUpdate member function also indicates that by presorting the entries, we can compute the running balance value for a given date range more easily. This is also important to the preparation of our report. The code for the SortByDate member function is as follows:

```
void CReportView::SortByDate (CObList& list)
{
   CListEntry *entry1, *entry2;
   POSITION pos1, pPos1, pos2, pPos2;

   //
   // sorts a list of CListEntry objects into order
   // by date using a simple linear scan algorithm.
   //
   pos1 = list.GetHeadPosition();
   while (pos1 != NULL)
   {
      pPos1 = pos1;
      entry1 = (CListEntry *)list.GetNext(pos1);
      pos2 = pos1;
      while (pos2 != NULL)
      {
         pPos2 = pos2;
         entry2 = (CListEntry *)list.GetNext (pos2);
         if (entry2->GetDate() < entry1->GetDate())
         {
            //
            // need to swap entries
            //
            list.SetAt (pPos1, entry2);
            list.SetAt (pPos2, entry1);
            entry1 = entry2;
         }
      }
   }
}
```

The foregoing code uses a simple N^2 sorting algorithm to put the entries into the proper order. It consists of two loops, one inside the other. The first loop commences by accessing the first entry in the list of transactions and then the second loop accesses each of the succeeding entries until the one with the earliest date is found. If the date in the first entry position is later than one of the entries in the remainder of the list, the two entries are "swapped." When the second loop completes a cycle through the entries, the entry associated with the first position value will contain the earliest date. The first loop continues by accessing the second entry in the list, and then the second loop tests each of the remaining entries against the first, swapping whenever an entry with an earlier date is found, until the end of the list is reached. This process continues until the entire list has been ordered from the earliest to latest date value. Note that the "swap" is handled by simply using the SetAt member function for the list, to change the object pointer held in the associated first or second list position. If we had thousands of entries to sort, we might be tempted to use a more efficient algorithm; however, in this case, it is unlikely that more than a few hundred entries would exist for any set of accounts during the course of a year, and the sort time is not perceptible.

ComputeRptMetrics Member Function Code

The ComputeRptMetrics member function is called by several other member functions in the code. Initially, in the OnInitialUpdate member function, it is called to calculate the text metrics for the display device, so that the CashFlowViewSize member function can compute properly the height and width of the report to be displayed. The member function is also referenced in the OnPrepareDC and OnBeginPrinting member functions. The code for this member function is as follows:

```
void CReportView::ComputeRptMetrics (CDC* pDC)
{
   TEXTMETRIC tm;
   CRect rectClient;
   int nPageHeight;

   CFont fRptFont;
   int nPtSz = MulDiv(8, pDC->GetDeviceCaps (LOGPIXELSY), 72);
   fRptFont.CreateFont (-nPtSz, 0, 0, 0, FW_NORMAL, 0, 0, 0,
      ANSI_CHARSET, OUT_TT_PRECIS, CLIP_DEFAULT_PRECIS,
      PROOF_QUALITY, DEFAULT_PITCH | FF_SWISS, "Arial");

   CFont* pOldFont = pDC->SelectObject (&fRptFont);
   if (!pDC->GetTextMetrics (&tm))
   {
      AfxMessageBox ("Can't get window's text metrics.");
      return;
   }
   m_nMinCharWidth = tm.tmAveCharWidth;
   m_nAvgCharWidth = (tm.tmAveCharWidth
      + tm.tmMaxCharWidth)/2;
   m_nMaxCharWidth = tm.tmMaxCharWidth;
   m_nLineHeight   = tm.tmHeight + tm.tmExternalLeading;
   m_nLineWidth    = m_nAvgCharWidth * 76;
   if (!pDC->IsPrinting())
   {
      GetClientRect (&rectClient);
      nPageHeight = rectClient.bottom - rectClient.top;
   }
   else
   {
      nPageHeight = pDC->GetDeviceCaps (VERTRES);
   }
   m_nLinesPerPage = (nPageHeight / m_nLineHeight);
   nPageHeight = m_nLinesPerPage * m_nLineHeight;
   m_PageSize.cx= m_nLineWidth/5;
   m_PageSize.cy = max (m_nLineHeight, nPageHeight);
   m_LineSize.cx= m_nLineWidth/20;
   m_LineSize.cy= m_nLineHeight;
   pDC->SelectObject (pOldFont);
}
```

The foregoing code begins by declaring several local variables that will be used during the calculation of the various report metrics. Our main purpose is to calculate values for the member variables that reference the report metrics. The member variables are as follows:

❖ `m_nMinCharWidth` is used as the measure of a minimum-width character in the current font. In actual fact, this value is assigned the value associated with the "average character width" in the TEXTMETRIC structure.

❖ `m_nAvgCharWidth` is used as the measure of the average character width in the current font. In our case, this value is computed by taking the average of the "average" and "maximum" character widths in the current font.

❖ `m_nMaxCharWidth` is used as the measure of the maximum character width in the font. In our case, the corresponding value from the TEXTMETRIC structure is used.

❖ `m_nLineHeight` is computed from information in the TEXTMETRIC structure for the current font. It is the sum of the height of the font (which includes the ascender height and the descender depth) and the external leading specified for the font.

❖ `m_nLineWidth` is the width of a line in the current font. It was computed heuristically by observing the appearance of the report on the display and then adjusting the value of the number of characters of "average" width (`m_nAvgCharWidth`) that can be displayed on a standard VGA display. As the report stands, the `m_nLineWidth` value permits the display to fill a maximized window on the screen. For other types of displays, the appearance will vary.

❖ `m_nLinesPerPage` is computed by dividing the value in the local `nPageHeight` variable by the value in the `m_nLineHeight` variable. The value in the `nPageHeight` variable is computed differently, depending on whether the ComputeRptMetrics member function is being called when printing is in progress, or not. In the case when printing is not in progress, the value of `nPageHeight` is taken from the height of the display's current client rectangle (by subtracting the top coordinate from the bottom in that measurement). When printing is in progress, then the `nPageHeight` value is taken from the vertical resolution of the device (by accessing the "device capabilities" and using the value of the VERTRES property, which specifies the total height, in raster lines, or pixels, of a page on the device). If the report is being displayed, then the ComputeRptMetrics member function will be called whenever the user changes the size of the window so that the display will always contain only the lines that will fit within the viewing area of the window. After the `m_nLinesPerPage` value is computed, then the `nPageHeight` value is recomputed by multiplying the value of `m_nLinesPerPage` by `m_nLineHeight` (in order for the page height to be a true multiple of the line height).

❖ `m_PageSize.cx` defines the number of pixels to scroll in the horizontal direction when the user clicks on the body of the horizontal scroll bar. It is computed to be one-fifth the width of a line so that it requires five "clicks" in the horizontal scroll bar to advance from one edge of the page to the other.

❖ `m_PageSize.cy` defines the number of pixels to scroll in the vertical direction when the user clicks on the body of the vertical scroll bar. It is computed as the maximum of either the height of a single line or the height of a page for the current device.

❖ `m_LineSize.cx` defines the number of pixels to scroll in the horizontal direction when the user clicks on one of the arrows at the ends of the horizontal scroll bar. It is computed to be the width of a line (`m_nLineWidth`) divided by 20, which means that it will require 20 "clicks" on the scroll arrow to scroll from one edge to the other on the display.

❖ `m_LineSize.cy` defines the number of pixels to scroll in the vertical direction when the user clicks on one of the arrows at the ends of the vertical scroll bar. It is assigned the value of the height of a single line (`m_nLineHeight`), which means that the display scrolls vertically one line each time a scroll bar arrow is clicked.

The foregoing variables are computed only after the ComputeRptMetrics member function has constructed an 8-point font for the current device. The 8-point device-dependent font is constructed by accessing the current device's capabilities for the property that defines the number of logical pixels-per-inch in the vertical direction (LOGPIXELSY), multiplying this property by the ratio 8/72 (by using the Windows MulDiv function), and then creating the font using the CreateFont member function for the CFont object. Actually, Windows doesn't actually "synthesize" a font with the desired characteristics; it "selects" one that most closely matches the parameters that we pass to the CreateFont member function. In the case of the 8-point font, we have specified the point size as a negative number. This indicates to Windows that we wish for that parameter (the height) to be transformed into device units and used to compare against the character height of the available fonts. We have also specified a number of other parameters that cause Windows to select a TrueType, rather than bitmapped, font, and also one that is in the Arial family, if possible. Because the Arial font ships with the Windows 3.1 environment, we feel sure that most users will have this font available for use with both their display and printer devices.

The next step is to access the metrics associated with the newly created font. Metrics simply means "measurements," and it is the height and width of characters in this font that make up part of the "metrics" that are stored in the TEXTMETRIC structure associated with the font. The full set of metrics includes the height of the tallest ascender, the depth of the longest descender, the overall height of the font, the amount of internal "leading"—or space above the individual characters to allow for the application of accents or other markings within the character cell, external leading, average character width, maximum character width, and a few other characteristics of the font.

After the device-dependent font has been constructed, we select it into the current device context by calling the SelectObject member function of the device context whose pointer is passed to the member function.

We are using only the average and maximum character widths, the external leading value, and the character height metric, from the newly created font, to compute all of the other measurements we require. Using the foregoing procedure ensures that we will create an 8-point font for whatever display or printer device the user chooses to use.

CashFlowViewSize Member Function Code

The CashFlowViewSize member function is used to compute the total height and width of the report, in pixels. These values are passed to the SetScrollSizes member function, inherited from the CScrollView class, as described previously. The code for this member function is as follows:

```
CSize CReportView::CashFlowViewSize()
{
    WORDnAccount;
    BOOLbFirstTime = TRUE;
    CSizedocSize (m_nLineWidth, 0);
    longnPayment, nDeposit, nBalance;

    CKeepitDoc* pDoc = GetDocument();
    POSITION pos = pDoc->m_ReportAccts.GetHeadPosition();
    m_nTotalLines = 0;
    while (pos != NULL)
    {
        //
        // iterate through accounts, selecting the transactions
        // which are within the date range, sorting them into
        // order by date and then placing them into the
        // m_RptEntries list.
        //
        if (!bFirstTime)
        {
            m_RptEntries.AddTail (&m_BlankLine);
            docSize.cy += m_nLineHeight;
            m_nTotalLines++;
        }
        bFirstTime = FALSE;
        CAcctObj* pAcct;
        pAcct = (CAcctObj *)pDoc->m_ReportAccts.GetNext(pos);
        m_RptEntries.AddTail (pAcct);
        docSize.cy += m_nLineHeight;
        m_nTotalLines++;
        nAccount = pAcct->GetAcctID();
```

```
nBalance = 0;
POSITION tPos = pDoc->m_ListEntries.GetHeadPosition();
while (tPos != NULL)
{
   CListEntry* pEntry;
   WORD nAcctID;
   CTimeeDate;

   //
   // get entries one at a time and check to see whether
   // they match the current account ID.
   //
   pEntry = (CListEntry *)pDoc
      ->m_ListEntries.GetNext (tPos);
   nAcctID = pEntry->GetAccountID();
   if (nAcctID != nAccount)
   {
      //
      // no match, continue the loop
      //
      continue;
   }

   if (pEntry->GetStatus() == E_EMPTY)
   {
      //
      // bypass empty entries
      //
      continue;
   }

   if (pEntry->GetStatus() == E_SELECTED)
   {
      if (pEntry->GetDescription().GetLength() == 0)
      {
         //
         // bypass selected but empty entries
         //
         continue;
      }
   }

   //
   // calculate the current balance for the account
   //
   nPayment = pEntry->GetPaymentValue();
   nDeposit = pEntry->GetDepositValue();
   nBalance = nBalance - nPayment + nDeposit;

   //
   // now, check to see whether the entry is within
   // the specified date range.
   //
   eDate = pEntry->GetDate();
   if (eDate < m_FromDate)
   {
      //
      // not yet in range, continue checking
      //
      continue;
   }
   else if (eDate > m_ToDate)
   {
      //
      // past the end of the period, quit.
      //
      break;
```

```
            }

            //
            // enter the balance value into the transaction,
            // add the transaction to the list, and then
            // increment the document size.
            //
            pEntry->SetBalanceValue (nBalance);
            m_RptEntries.AddTail (pEntry);
            docSize.cy += m_nLineHeight;
            m_nTotalLines++;
        }
    }
    return docSize;
}
```

The foregoing code accomplishes three important tasks, which must be completed before the view and its included report can be displayed. These are as follows:

❖ The total height and width of the report, as they will appear on the display monitor, are calculated.

❖ Only the entries that will participate in the report are selected to be stored into the local m_RptEntries list.

❖ The running balance of each account is calculated, as its entries are being processed. This eliminates the need to calculate these values when the display is scrolled.

The CashFlowViewSize member function accomplishes the foregoing tasks in a loop through all of the accounts in the document's list of accounts (m_ReportAccts). (Recall that the m_ReportAccts list is prepared during the execution of the OnCashFlow message handler in the CKeepitDoc class, which was described previously in this chapter, beginning on page 273.)

Prior to commencing the loop, a boolean variable, which acts as a "first time" switch, is set to TRUE, and the position of the first entry in the document's account list is accessed. In the first iteration of the loop, the bFirstTime variable is TRUE, causing the code that adds the m_BlankLine object to the m_RptEntries list to be bypassed. The value of the bFirstTime variable is set to FALSE immediately, so that the code will execute on the second and succeeding iterations of the loop. This ensures that there is an object that represents a blank line in the report between each account and the next, but not before the first account in the report. When this code executes, the total number of lines in the report (stored in the m_nTotalLines member variable) is incremented by one and the total document height is advanced by the height of one line.

As the main loop continues, the entry corresponding to the current position in the `m_ReportAccts` list is accessed and its pointer is stored in the `pAcct` variable. The number of lines is increased by one, and the document height is advanced by the height of one line to account for the display of the account title. The account object is also added to the tail of the `m_RptEntries` list. At this point, the account ID is accessed and stored in the `nAccount` variable, and the account balance is set to zero in the `nBalance` variable.

Then, the position of the first entry in the document's list of transactions (stored in its `m_ListEntries` variable) is accessed and stored into the `tPos` variable and a second loop is begun. The inner loop traverses the list of individual transactions, accessing each one, in turn, looking for those that have a matching account ID. If the transaction's account ID does not match the one stored in the `nAccount` variable, then the inner loop is continued from its beginning. If the account ID matches but the entry's status is set to E_EMPTY, or the status is set to E_SELECTED *and* the description field is empty, then the loop is continued from its beginning. The foregoing is the means to prevent the display of empty entries or the single selected entry in the account view being displayed currently, if any.

The inner loop continues after finding a qualifying entry, whose account ID matches the one for the entry in outer loop, and calculates the running balance of the account by adding the deposit and subtracting the payment amounts in the transaction entry's fields.

After the balance has been computed, the code tests whether the current transaction's date is within range of the beginning (`m_FromDate`) and ending (`m_ToDate`) dates. If the transaction's date is prior to the beginning date, then we must continue the loop from its beginning and access the next transaction. If, however, the transaction's date is later than the ending date for the report, we can terminate the inner loop, as the transactions were sorted previously into date sequence and we can be sure that there are no other entries for this account that fall within the date range for the Cash Flow report.

If the transaction's date is *within* the beginning and ending date period, then we set the transaction's balance value (by calling a newly added Set-BalanceValue access member function for the CListEntry object) and then add the transaction's object pointer to the list of report entries. At this point, we also advance the total document height by the height of one line. The count of the number of lines in the report is also increased by one.

The inner loop continues to traverse the list of transactions until either the end of the list or the ending date has been passed, whichever comes first, and then the outer loop is allowed to advance to the next account in the `m_ReportAccts` list.

During the course of executing the CashFlowViewSize member function, the entries that will be displayed (and printed) are stored into the CReportView's `m_RptEntries` list, the total height of the report is calculated, and the participating transaction entry balances are computed. Everything we need to produce the specified report, for the selected accounts, in the specified date range, is now available for the remainder of the member functions to use. The CashFlowViewSize member function returns a value of type CSize, which contains the horizontal width of the report (i.e., the width of a line) and the vertical height of the report in its `cx` and `cy` member variables, respectively. The CSize object is passed to the SetScrollSizes member function at the end of the OnInitialUpdate member function's execution.

Report-Drawing Code

When initialization of the report's metrics is complete and the entries to be included in the report have been stored into the list pointed to by the `m_RptEntries` member variable, the view is in the position to create the report. This is accomplished when the OnDraw message handler is invoked. The OnDraw handler is central to both the display and printing tasks and is responsible for writing the report to each of the devices (and also the print preview device, which happens also to be the display). Prior to the invocation of the OnDraw handler, the framework calls the OnPrepareDC member function. This member function prepares the device context environment for displaying or printing the report. We override this member function in order to call the ComputeRptMetrics member function, which changes the metrics for the report to be consistent with the current device on which the report is to be drawn. After the metrics have been recomputed and the OnPrepareDC member function has returned, the framework calls the OnDraw member function to render the visible area of the report. When we examine the member functions that are specific to printing, you will find that we will call the OnDraw member function directly within our OnPrint member function override, once for each page of the report.

OnPrepareDC Member Function Code

As mentioned previously, the framework is responsible for invoking the OnPrepareDC member function, immediately prior to its invocation of the OnDraw member function. We have overridden the OnPrepareDC member function to add code to recompute the device-specific metrics, before the OnDraw member function is called. The code is as follows:

```
void CReportView::OnPrepareDC (CDC* pDC, CPrintInfo* pInfo)
{
   CScrollView::OnPrepareDC (pDC, pInfo);
   ComputeRptMetrics (pDC);
}
```

The foregoing code is quite simple. The first step is to call the OnPrepareDC member function for the base class (CScrollView). When that step is complete, the code calls the ComputeRptMetrics member function (see page 303). After the ComputeRptMetrics member function has completed execution, the line height, page height, number of lines on the page, and other metrics have been computed.

OnDraw Message Handler Code

When the framework (or our OnPrint member function) calls the OnDraw member function, the device context passed to the member function accurately reflects the settings apropos to the current device context (whether display, printer, or print preview display). The function of the OnDraw member function is to draw the portion of the report that falls within the current "clipping region." You can think of the clipping region as being the portion of the display window, or the portion of a page that is currently visible, within which we wish the member function to draw.

Rather than draw the entire report, in one fell swoop, causing massive overhead if major portions of it are not currently visible, we draw only the portion defined by the current clipping region. This region is defined within the device context, a pointer to which is passed to the OnDraw member function as its only parameter.

Clearly, we have to make some adjustment of which report entries to draw into the visible region when the OnDraw member function is called. We can't begin displaying the report data from their beginning if the user has scrolled the display. Neither can we print more than one page at a time. So our task becomes one of identifying which report entries, out of the entire set, should be drawn each time the OnDraw handler is invoked. This is handled rather easily by the OnDraw code, as follows:

```
void CReportView::OnDraw(CDC* pDC)
{
   POSITION nFirstEntry, nLastEntry, pos;
   CRect rectClip;

   //
   // verify that there is something to draw
   //
   if (m_RptEntries.GetCount() == 0)
   {
      return;
```

```
    }

    if (pDC->GetClipBox(&rectClip) == NULLREGION)
    {
        return;
    }

    //
    // create a font with which to render the text
    //
    CFont fRptFont;
    int nPtSz = MulDiv(8, pDC->GetDeviceCaps (LOGPIXELSY), 72);
    fRptFont.CreateFont (-nPtSz, 0, 0, 0, FW_NORMAL, 0, 0, 0,
        ANSI_CHARSET, OUT_TT_PRECIS, CLIP_DEFAULT_PRECIS,
        PROOF_QUALITY, DEFAULT_PITCH | FF_SWISS, "Arial");

    //
    // display the contents of the clip region
    //
    CFont* pOldFont = pDC->SelectObject (&fRptFont);
    int nYPos = rectClip.top;
    RectLPtoPositions (rectClip, nFirstEntry, nLastEntry);
    pos = nFirstEntry;
    while (pos != nLastEntry)
    {
        CObject* pObj = m_RptEntries.GetNext(pos);
        DrawRptLine (pDC, pObj, nYPos);
    }
    pDC->SelectObject (pOldFont);
}
```

In the foregoing code, the first task is to determine whether there are any entries in the m_RptEntries list. It is possible for the user to choose a date range, for example, for which there are no entries in the selected list of accounts. In this case, the member function simply returns. The next major hurdle is crossed when it is determined that the current clipping region (accessed by calling the GetClipBox member function for the current device context) is not NULL. With those tests satisfied, the member function can continue to make preparations to draw the appropriate section of the report.

The first action is to create the device-specific font that we need to use for drawing the text. This font is created (or, actually, selected from those that are already available) on each entry to the member function, is selected into the device context prior to commencing any drawing operations, and then is deselected from the context when drawing is complete. The font is disposed when the member function exits and as the destructor for the CFont object is executed by the default code in the MFC. (As an aside, many of the Graphic Device Interface [GDI] objects that Windows supports have corresponding C++ "wrapper" classes, which contain default constructor and destructor member functions that ease the pain of using these objects, greatly.)

After the font has been created and selected into the device context, we initialize a variable (nYPos) to hold the current vertical position in the clipping region to the top of that region. Then we call a member function named RectLPtoPositions, which takes the clipping rectangle as input and returns the list-position values for the beginning and ending entries, in the list of those to be displayed, as its output. The nFirstEntry and nLastEntry values are of type POSITION, which allows us to use them directly to access the corresponding entries in the m_RptEntries list.

The next section of the OnDraw member function loops through the entries within the range specified previously and calls the DrawRptLine member function with a pointer to the device context, a pointer to the current entry, and the current vertical position, which is updated after drawing the entry. In this way, the DrawRptLine member function is responsible only for drawing a single line of the report (all other decisions having already been made).

The final statement in the OnDraw member function selects the previous font back into the device context so that the newly created font can be disposed. This allows other member functions that may use the device context to continue to operate properly.

Incidentally, when we wish to draw a number of different reports, it will be useful to select which member function to call and how to iterate through the list of report entries for that report. Because we have precluded the possibility of any other report to be drawn, by choosing to return from the OnInitialUpdate member function if the Cash Flow report was not selected, we have not added code to the OnDraw member function to provide for drawing any other report. It should be evident that such code, when needed, could be easily added to the current member function.

DrawRptLine Member Function Code

In reaching this point in the chapter, you have seen that the DrawRptLine member function is called by the OnDraw message handler, to render a single report line on the current device. This member function might more properly have been called DrawCashFlowLine because it is well and truly wedded to the format of that report. However, because the Cash Flow report is not the only one that we will implement eventually, we have chosen to give the member function a more generic name. This topic will be discussed in greater detail in a later chapter. For now, the sole task of the current member function is to draw a single line of the report, given a pointer to the device context, a pointer to the object whose data contents are to be drawn, and a reference to a variable holding the current vertical position within the device context in which to draw the object's contents. The code is as follows:

```cpp
void CReportView::DrawRptLine (CDC* pDC, CObject* pObj,
  int& nYPos)
{
  CAcctObj* pAcct;
  CListEntry* pEntry;
  CString szData;
  CTime eDate;
  CSize txSize;

  int nXPos = m_nAvgCharWidth, nWidth = 0, nDX = 0;
  if (pObj->IsKindOf (RUNTIME_CLASS (CAcctObj)))
  {
    pAcct = (CAcctObj *)pObj;
    szData = pAcct->GetAcctName ();
    pDC->TextOut (nXPos, nYPos, szData, szData.GetLength ());
    nYPos += m_nLineHeight;
  }
  else if (pObj->IsKindOf (RUNTIME_CLASS (CListEntry)))
  {
    nXPos += m_nAvgCharWidth * 1;
    pEntry = (CListEntry *)pObj;
    eDate = pEntry->GetDate ();
    szData = eDate.Format ("%m/%d/%y");
    pDC->TextOut (nXPos, nYPos, szData, szData.GetLength ());
    nXPos += m_nAvgCharWidth * 8;

    szData = pEntry->GetItem ();
    pDC->TextOut (nXPos, nYPos, szData, szData.GetLength ());
    nXPos += m_nAvgCharWidth * 6;

    szData = pEntry->GetDescription ();
    nWidth = min (szData.GetLength (), 25);
    pDC->TextOut (nXPos, nYPos, szData, nWidth);
    nXPos += m_nAvgCharWidth * 19;

    szData = pEntry->GetInfo ();
    nWidth = min (szData.GetLength (), 15);
    pDC->TextOut (nXPos, nYPos, szData, nWidth);
    nXPos += m_nAvgCharWidth * 10;

    szData = pEntry->GetCategory ();
    nWidth = min (szData.GetLength (), 15);
    pDC->TextOut (nXPos, nYPos, szData, nWidth);
    nXPos += m_nAvgCharWidth * 3;

    szData = pEntry->GetPayment ();
    txSize = pDC->GetTextExtent (szData, szData.GetLength ());
    nDX = nXPos + (12 * m_nAvgCharWidth - txSize.cx);
    pDC->TextOut (nDX, nYPos, szData, szData.GetLength ());
    nXPos += m_nAvgCharWidth * 8;

    szData = pEntry->GetDeposit ();
    txSize = pDC->GetTextExtent (szData, szData.GetLength ());
    nDX = nXPos + (12 * m_nAvgCharWidth - txSize.cx);
    pDC->TextOut (nDX, nYPos, szData, szData.GetLength ());
    nXPos += m_nAvgCharWidth * 8;

    szData = pEntry->GetBalance ();
    txSize = pDC->GetTextExtent (szData, szData.GetLength ());
    nDX = nXPos + (12 * m_nAvgCharWidth - txSize.cx);
    pDC->TextOut (nDX, nYPos, szData, szData.GetLength ());
    nXPos += m_nAvgCharWidth * 8;
    nYPos += m_nLineHeight;
  }
  else
```

```
  {
    RECT rectRgn;
    m_BlankLine.GetRgnBox (&rectRgn);
    nYPos += rectRgn.bottom;
  }
}
```

The foregoing code is rather straightforward. Given the input parameters described previously, the member function first determines what type of object is represented by the current entry. We use the IsKindOf member function, which is inherited by all objects based upon the CObject class, to ascertain whether the entry is a "kind of" CAcctObj or CListEntry object, or an object of some other kind (there being only one possibility for the latter case—a blank line region object).

If the entry is a member of the CAcctObj class, then we need only include its name on our report. The other information stored within that object is not essential to our purpose. The code to draw the entry's name uses the TextOut member function of the CDC (device context) class to draw the name text at the specified horizontal and vertical positions in the device context. The name in this case is the account name.

On the other hand, if the entry is a member of the CListEntry class, then we must render each of the entry's important fields. These entries are the individual transactions for the current account. The code to render the individual fields must position each one, in a device-dependent manner, so that it will be rendered appropriately on the display, printer, or print preview device. We accomplish this by using the `m_nAvgCharWidth` metric, which has been calculated previously by the ComputeRptMetrics member function. By advancing the horizontal position by multiples of the average character width metric, we can ensure that the report will be rendered in the same manner on each device and that the spacing between fields will be uniform on the device. In all honesty, the spacing was determined heuristically, by setting spacing values, checking the appearance of the report, adjusting the spacing, checking the appearance, and so forth. This repetitive process is necessary when creating any report that relies on proportional fonts for its creation—especially if the report contains columns of values that must align with one another.

The actual "drawing" of each field is, once again, handled by calling the TextOut member function in the device context object. In the case of the three numeric fields (payment, deposit, and balance), we also needed to justify these fields so that their decimals, and hence their rightmost characters, are aligned in the report. Right justification is handled by first calculating the width of the value's textual representation by calling the GetTextExtent member function of the device context object with the text string as its argument. When the width of the text is known, then the horizontal position in which to render its first character can be computed as the end position of the report field less the text width. With this, the TextOut member function can be called to output the text.

If the entry is neither a member of the CAcctObj nor the CListEntry class, then it must be, by definition, the blank line region that we defined. We chose to create a CRgn object to represent a blank line mainly because the CObject class is also its base class, and applying the IsKindOf member function to it works equally well as for the other object types (whose base class is also CObject).

RectLPtoPositions Member Function Code

The OnDraw member function determines which report entries to draw by passing the current clipping region parameters to the RectLPtoPositions member function, which determines the range of entries that fit within the vertical constraints of the clipping region. It sets the POSITION values that correspond to the beginning and ending entries in the m_RptEntries list. The code for this member function is as follows:

```cpp
void CReportView::RectLPtoPositions (CRect rectClip,
    POSITION& firstPosition, POSITION& lastPosition)
{
    // scan the m_ReportEntries list for entries which will
    // fit within the clipping region (rectClip) passed to the
    // member function, and then return the list-POSITION
    // values.

    int nViewHeight = 0;
    POSITION pos = m_RptEntries.GetHeadPosition();
    POSITION prevPos;
    BOOL bFirst=TRUE;
    firstPosition = pos;
    lastPosition = NULL;
    while (pos != NULL)
    {
        prevPos = pos;
        CObject *pObj = m_RptEntries.GetNext (pos);
        if (bFirst && nViewHeight >= rectClip.top)
        {
            bFirst = FALSE;
            firstPosition = prevPos;
        }
        nViewHeight += m_nLineHeight;
        if (nViewHeight >= rectClip.bottom)
        {
            lastPosition = pos;
            break;
        }
    }
    if (firstPosition == NULL)
    {
        lastPosition = NULL;
    }
}
```

The foregoing code is quite simple. After initializing a number of variables, including a first-time switch, the member function begins the process of determining which entries lie within the clipping region boundaries. Given the boundaries of the clipping region, the member function loops through the entries in the m_RptEntries list, accumulating the height of the view until it equals or exceeds the top of the clipping region. At that point, the position of the first entry to meet that criteria is saved in the firstPosition variable, and the first-time switch is set to FALSE. In this and succeeding iterations, the view height is advanced by the height of one line and is tested to determine whether it equals or exceeds the value of the bottom boundary of the clipping region. If so, then the entry's position is saved into the lastPosition variable, the loop is terminated, and the member function returns. If the bottom of the clipping region has not yet been reached, then the loop continues until that condition is met or the end of the list is reached.

OnHScroll Message Handler Code

Previously, we mentioned that the CScrollView class took care of all of the chores associated with scrolling the view, with the exception of the case where the user dragged the "thumb" in the scroll bar to reposition the display. Rather than implement the "live" scrolling that the CScrollView class assumes, we have chosen to provide our own message handlers for the OnHScroll and OnVScroll member functions. The code for the OnHScroll member function is as follows:

```cpp
void CReportView::OnHScroll(UINT nSBCode, UINT nPos,
   CScrollBar* pScrollBar)
{
   ASSERT (pScrollBar == GetScrollBarCtrl (SB_HORZ));
   if (nSBCode == SB_THUMBTRACK)
   {
      //
      // ignore thumbtrack messages
      //
      return;
   }
   if (nSBCode == SB_THUMBPOSITION)
   {
      //
      // fake thumbtrack message to OnScroll
      //
      nSBCode = SB_THUMBTRACK;
   }
   CScrollView::OnHScroll(nSBCode, nPos, pScrollBar);
}
```

The foregoing message handler is called for *all* horizontal scroll messages. The first action is ensure that it is being called for the horizontal scroll bar. If so, then the code tests whether the framework is calling it because the user is dragging the thumb. If so, rather than scroll to the new position and require the report to be updated instantly, we choose to ignore the SB_THUMBTRACK messages. When the user finally releases the mouse button, then the framework calls the member function with a SB_THUMBPOSITION message, and our handler changes it to a SB_THUMBTRACK message and passes it on to the OnHScroll member function of the CScrollView base class. All other horizontal scroll messages are passed directly to the OnHScroll member function of CScroll-View, without interpretation by our handler.

OnVScroll Message Handler Code

As for the OnHScroll message handler, described previously, the On-VScroll handler ignores the SB_THUMBTRACK messages and then passes on a SB_THUMBTRACK message only after the SB_THUMBPOSITION message has been received. All other vertical scroll messages are passed directly to the OnVScroll member function of the CScrollView base class.

```
void CReportView::OnVScroll(UINT nSBCode, UINT nPos,
   CScrollBar* pScrollBar)
{
   ASSERT (pScrollBar == GetScrollBarCtrl (SB_VERT));
   if (nSBCode == SB_THUMBTRACK)
   {
      //
      // ignore thumbtrack messages
      //
      return;
   }
   if (nSBCode == SB_THUMBPOSITION)
   {
      //
      // update thumb position to integral line height
      // and then fake a thumbtrack message to OnScroll
      //
      int nHt = m_nLineHeight;
      nPos = ((nPos + nHt - 1) / nHt) * nHt;
      nSBCode = SB_THUMBTRACK;
   }
   CScrollView::OnVScroll(nSBCode, nPos, pScrollBar);
}
```

Note in the foregoing that when the user drags the vertical thumb, we round the scroll position to an integral multiple of the line height before "faking" the SB_THUMBTRACK message.

Printing and Print Preview Code

While a report being displayed on the screen can be scrolled continuously, the same is not true for printed reports. They must be printed on a page-by-page basis, with headers and/or footers and other information more appropriate for long-term use of the data. Even in the halcyon days of computing, hard-copy reports were prepared with elaborate headings, for consumption by discriminating users. The same holds as true today as it did in the past. Our printed pages must now be prepared with more attention to their appearance and the position in the series within which they fall. The member functions in this section are related strictly to printing and print preview functions. Actually, the code is unaware of the print preview functionality. It appears to the code as though the report is being printed, when in fact it is being rendered in a special device context in which the characteristics of the current printer are being simulated on the display. Therefore, for all practical purposes, we will ignore the print preview function, although it is available after we implement these member functions, by simply choosing Print Preview from the File menu when the Cash Flow report is being displayed.

OnFilePrint Message Handler Code

The printing process is commenced when the user chooses the Print command from the File menu. This command is disabled unless the Cash Flow report is being displayed. Hard-copy output of the individual account transactions is accomplished by this report. The CAccount view is intended for display and data entry only.

When the user chooses Print from the File menu, the OnFilePrint message handler is invoked. The code for this handler is as follows:

```
void CReportView::OnFilePrint()
{
    CView::OnFilePrint();
}
```

As is evident from the foregoing code, the OnFilePrint message handler merely calls the corresponding member function in the CView class.

OnFilePrintPreview Message Handler Code

As with the OnFilePrint member function, we have chosen to merely call the corresponding member function in the CView class when the OnFilePrintPreview message handler is invoked. The code for this member function is as follows:

```
void CReportView::OnFilePrintPreview()
{
    CView::OnFilePrintPreview();
}
```

In both the OnFilePrint and OnFilePrintPreview member functions, it is necessary that we establish handlers for these, even though we are not adding any custom code, other than a single statement that calls the inherited member function. The necessity of providing the handlers is to ensure that the corresponding commands in the File menu are enabled when the CReportView object is created. The framework will disable any commands in the menubar for which no handlers currently exist, automatically. We specifically avoided the definition of handlers for the Print and Print Preview commands in earlier versions of the application, for just this reason.

OnPreparePrinting Member Function Code

The OnPreparePrinting member function is called by the framework (in the OnFilePrint member function of the CView class) prior to commencing the printing process. This member function can be used to perform initialization that is unique to that process. In our case, we have chosen to override this member function, in case we need to do something special in preparation for printing a report in the future. In this case, we call the DoPreparePrinting member function inherited from the CView base class. The DoPreparePrinting member function is the one that displays the standard print dialog and accepts the user's specification of which printer and what pages are to be printed. The code for the On-PreparePrinting member function is as follows:

```
BOOL CReportView::OnPreparePrinting (CPrintInfo* pInfo)
{
    return DoPreparePrinting (pInfo);
}
```

As is evident in the foregoing code, the value returned by the member function is whatever is returned by the DoPreparePrinting member function. This allows the user to cancel the printout by dismissing the standard print dialog with its Cancel button.

OnBeginPrinting Member Function Code

Immediately after the OnPreparePrinting member function is called by the framework and a TRUE result is returned, the OnFilePrint member function creates a print device context and attaches the currently selected printer to it. It also sets the `m_bPrinting` member variable of the device context to TRUE so that other member functions can test whether the view is being printed. Immediately after doing this, the OnFilePrint member function in the CView class calls the OnBeginPrinting member function.

We have overridden this member function, in order to perform some initialization tasks that require that the device context for the printer be established. The tasks include computation of the report metrics prior to rendering the pages. The code for this member function is as follows:

```
void CReportView::OnBeginPrinting (CDC* pDC, CPrintInfo* pInfo)
{
    ComputeRptMetrics(pDC);
    int nPageHeight = (m_nLinesPerPage - 7) * m_nLineHeight;
    int nSizeTotal = m_nTotalLines * m_nLineHeight;
    int nPageCount = (nSizeTotal + nPageHeight - 1) / nPageHeight;
    pInfo->SetMaxPage (nPageCount);
    pInfo->m_nCurPage = 1;
}
```

One of the purposes of the OnBeginPrinting member function is to determine for the framework how many printed pages will be produced for the report. This is similar to calculating the total size of the view, which we have already done for the display of the report, by calling the CashFlowViewSize member function to do so. Instead of going through this process once again, but for the printer, we can use the information in the device context (passed to the member function in its first parameter) to compute the metrics for the printer device by calling the ComputeRptMetrics member function to calculate the line height and then use the value in the `m_nTotalLines` variable, computed by the CashFlowViewSize member function to determine the number of pages needed for the report.

The foregoing code contains some other calculations that bear explanation. We compute the height of a page by subtracting the value 7 from the number of lines per page. The rationale for this is that we intend to leave one line blank at the top of each page, followed by two lines of page header information, and then a blank line prior to commencing the body of the page, for a total of four lines of heading information. In addition, we have decided to leave the equivalent of three blank lines of space at the bottom of the page so that the printed pages are balanced in appearance. The total height of the seven lines must be subtracted from the height of the page. Then the adjusted page height can be divided into the total height of the report to compute the number of pages that will need to be printed. Using the foregoing values, we call the SetMaxPage member function of the device context to specify the maximum number of pages to be printed. In addition, the member function sets the value of the `m_nCurPage` variable in the device context to 1.

After the OnBeginPrinting member function has been called, the framework displays the printing status dialog, which shows what document is being printed and which page is being rendered. This dialog is updated throughout the printing process. The OnFilePrint member function of the CView class commences the execution of a loop that begins with the value of the current page being set to the first page to be printed and ends with the last page to be printed. The user, through the print setup dialog is able to specify the starting and ending pages of the report and the framework will use these page numbers (subject to their being within the maximum number of pages in the report) to control the loop.

On each iteration of the loop, the OnPrepareDC member function is called and if the `m_bContinuePrinting` variable of the CPrintInfo object passed to that member function is still TRUE, the OnPrint member function is called to render the page, and then the page number is incremented and tested to determine whether the loop should continue. Also, during the loop, should an error occur, printing is terminated. After all of the pages have been printed, the OnEndPrinting member function is called so that any resources that might have been created in the OnPreparePrinting or OnBeginPrinting member functions can be disposed properly. We have chosen not to override the OnEndPrinting member function at this time. Perhaps it will be important to do so in a future version of the application.

The OnPrepareDC member function was described previously, with respect to the drawing member function code. (The description of the OnPrepareDC member function begins on page 310.)

OnPrint Member Function Code

As mentioned in the previous section, the OnFilePrint member function loops through the range of pages, selected by the user from the standard print dialog, and calls the OnPrepareDC and then the OnPrint member functions for each page. The function of the OnPrint member function is to perform any rendering that is special to the printing process and then call the OnDraw member function to print the body of the report entries for that page. In fact, it is not necessary to call the OnDraw member function at all, especially if the report, when printed, has completely different contents from when it is displayed on the screen. The entire rendering of each page of the printout can be done by the OnPrint member function. In our case, we need only to offset the viewport origin, render the page headings, set the new clipping rectangle, and then let the OnDraw member function render the remainder of each page. The code for the OnPrint member function is as follows:

```
void CReportView::OnPrint (CDC* pDC, CPrintInfo* pInfo)
{
    // get the printer's page size in pixels
    int nHRes = pDC->GetDeviceCaps (HORZRES);
    int nVRes = pDC->GetDeviceCaps (VERTRES);

    // create and select a new clipping region for use in
    // printing the page header, and then print the header.

    CRgn clipRgn;
    clipRgn.CreateRectRgn (0, 0, nHRes, nVRes);
    pDC->SelectClipRgn (&clipRgn);
    clipRgn.DeleteObject ();
```

```
    PrintPageHeader(pDC, pInfo);

    // now set up the viewport for printing the remainder
    // of the page and call the OnDraw routine to do it.

    int nDX = pDC->GetDeviceCaps (LOGPIXELSX)/2;
    int nDY = m_nLineHeight * 4;
    int nPageHeight = (m_nLinesPerPage - 7) * m_nLineHeight;
    int nPageWidth = nHRes;
    int yTopOfPage = (pInfo->m_nCurPage - 1) * nPageHeight;
    pDC->SetViewportOrg (nDX, -yTopOfPage + nDY);
    CRect rectClip = CRect (0, yTopOfPage, nPageWidth,
        yTopOfPage + nPageHeight);
    pDC->IntersectClipRect (&rectClip);
    OnDraw (pDC);
}
```

The foregoing code begins by accessing the device capabilities to get the horizontal and vertical resolution of the device. These values are the total size of a device page, in each dimension, in pixels. The foregoing code continues by creating a rectangular region that is the size of a device page, and then it selects this region as the current clipping region. This gives the succeeding code the ability to access the entire device page. After the clipping region has been selected, the rectangular region object is deleted. The member function then calls the PrintPageHeader member function with pointers to the device context and the print info objects.

After the page header has been printed, the OnPrint member function calculates offsets in the horizontal (nDX) and vertical (nDY) dimensions for moving the viewport origin, in preparation for rendering the body of the page. The horizontal offset is calculated to allow a one-half-inch space at the left edge of the report. This is accomplished by accessing the LOGPIXELSX property from the device context (which specifies the number of pixels per inch in the horizontal direction for the device) and then taking one-half of this value. The offset in the vertical direction is determined by first calculating the height of a page (in the same manner as was used in the OnBeginPrinting member function—subtracting the height of seven lines from the total page height) and then multiplying the page height by the value of the page number minus one. The preceding calculation results in a value of 0 for the first page, and then multiples of the page height for succeeding pages.

The viewport origin for the device context is then set to the coordinates, in the device space, corresponding to the horizontal offset (in the horizontal dimension) and the negation of the vertical offset plus the height of the four-line header. By setting the Y coordinate of the viewport origin to a negative value, the viewport is moved above the device page by the specified amount. The reason for this will become clear shortly. Once the viewport origin has been changed, the coordinates of the origin of the logical "window" into which the data are written are set to those coordinates. What the foregoing accomplishes is to move the logical coordinate system's origin "up" so that the coordinates of the clipping region become larger by the same amount. For the first page of the printout, the clipping region becomes (-156, -150, 3075, 2277) after execution of the SetViewportOrg member function. The negative top and left coordinates are caused by the fact that the window origin was shifted one-half inch to the right (-150 pixels on a 300 dpi printer device), and four lines (39 pixels/line height) down (-156) from the top of the page on the same device. For the second page, the clipping region after the viewport is repositioned becomes (2769, -150, 6000, 2277). Note that the vertical coordinates of the clipping region become more and more positive for each succeeding page.

Figure 8-2
Relationship of viewport, device origin, and clipping region for printout

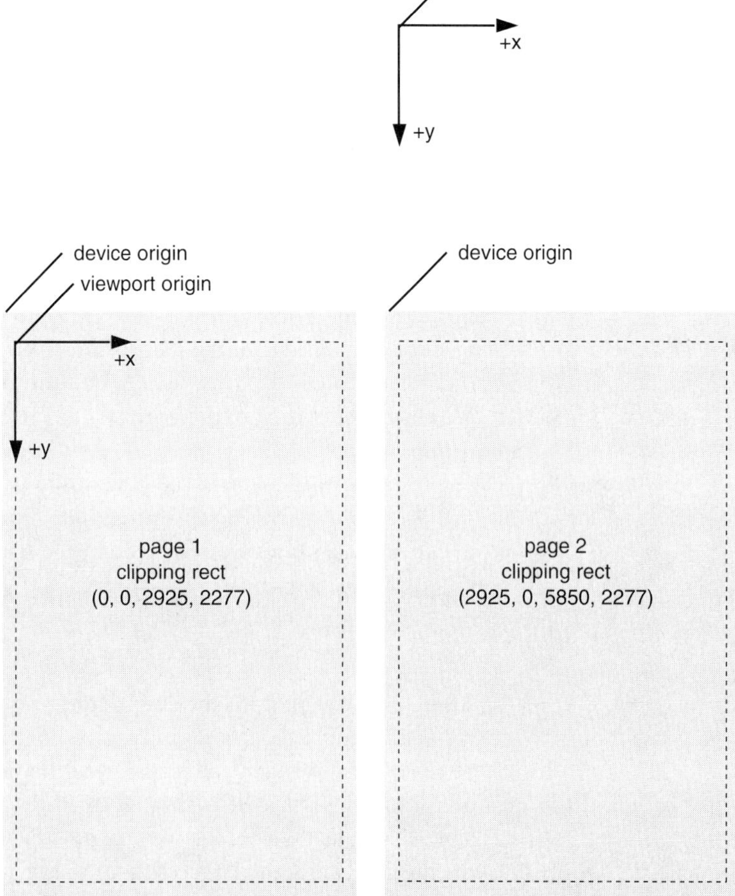

After the viewport has been adjusted, it is necessary to change the dimensions of the clipping region to include only the portion of the page in which text should be rendered by the OnDraw member function. We accomplish this by constructing a rectangle that has top and left coordinates that correspond to the adjusted position where the first body text line is to be rendered. The bottom and right coordinates correspond to the top and left coordinates, with the height and width of the body portion of the page added. By intersecting this rectangle (e.g., 0, 0, 2925, 2427 for the first page) with the existing clipping region, a new clipping region that includes only the overlap of the two regions is formed. (For the first page of the report, this region has the coordinates 0, 0, 2925, 2277.) These values apply only to a 300-dpi printer device. The coordinates for a printer of different resolution will vary from these values. The foregoing concept, for the first two pages of the report, is illustrated by Figure 8-2.

You may wonder why we have performed the foregoing operations. The rationale for this is that the OnDraw member function will render only the area of the report that is described by the clipping region. By creating an artificially increasing clipping region, we can cause the OnDraw member function to render successive portions of the report, in the same manner as new portions of the report come into view when the visual display is scrolled. There is one caveat to using this approach. Because the coordinate values become large rather quickly, and also because the 16-bit version of the Windows operating environment supports coordinate values that fall within the range of -32768 to +32767, this member function will fail if the printed report contains more than approximately ten pages of entries (or fewer if a printer of even higher resolution is used). A 600-dpi printer, for example, would halve the number of pages that we could print. Because we can fit approximately 750 entries on ten pages (using a 300-dpi printer), we have decided that, for this version of the application, we will continue to use the foregoing method. With the MM_TEXT mapping mode, both device and logical coordinate values are expressed in pixels. Be aware, however, that if you attempt something similar and use some mapping mode other than MM_TEXT, the process will fail.

PrintPageHeader Member Function Code

The PrintPageHeader member function is called by the OnPrint member function near the beginning of that member function. At the point at which the member function is called, the clipping region coordinates are set to (0, 0, 3231, 2427) for a 300-dpi printer. This allows the member function access to the entire scope of the device dimensions (as determined by accessing the device capabilities to acquire the HORZRES and

VERTRES values). The code for the PrintPageHeader member function is as follows:

```
void CReportView::PrintPageHeader (CDC* pDC, CPrintInfo*
pInfo)
{
  CFont fHdrFont;
  CString szLine, szPage;

  //
  // create a bold font for use in printing the
  // page header and then select it for use.
  //
  int nPtSz = MulDiv(8, pDC->GetDeviceCaps (LOGPIXELSY), 72);
  int nDX   = pDC->GetDeviceCaps (LOGPIXELSX)/2;
  fHdrFont.CreateFont (-nPtSz, 0, 0, 0, FW_BOLD, 0, 0, 0,
     ANSI_CHARSET, OUT_TT_PRECIS, CLIP_DEFAULT_PRECIS,
     PROOF_QUALITY, DEFAULT_PITCH | FF_SWISS, "Arial");
  CFont* pOldFont = pDC->SelectObject (&fHdrFont);

  //
  // format and print the two header lines and then
  // select the previous font.
  //
  wsprintf (szPage.GetBuffer(3), "%d", pInfo->m_nCurPage);
  szPage.ReleaseBuffer();
  szLine = " " + m_szTitle + "  Page " + szPage;
  pDC->TextOut (nDX, m_nLineHeight, szLine);
  szLine = " From: ";
  szLine = szLine + m_FromDate.Format ("%m/%d/%y");
  szLine = szLine + " To: ";
  szLine = szLine + m_ToDate.Format ("%m/%d/%y");
  pDC->TextOut (nDX, m_nLineHeight * 2, szLine);
  pDC->SelectObject (pOldFont);
}
```

In the foregoing, the first step is to calculate the logical height of an 8-point font in the current device context. This is accomplished by accessing the device capabilities to acquire the number of pixels per inch in the vertical dimension of the device (LOGPIXELSY) and then multiplying this value by the ratio 8/72 (knowing that there are approximately 72 printers points in one inch). We also access the LOGPIXELSX property and halve this value to arrive at a measurement that represents one-half inch in the horizontal direction, on the device. A temporary 8-point bold (FW_BOLD) font is created for the device and the font is selected into the device context, saving the previous font so that it can be restored before we return from the member function.

After the foregoing steps are complete, we create a string value that represents the current page number and then append the string to the end of the first line of the report title. The resulting string is then rendered on the device, beginning one-half inch from the left side of the page and one line-height measure down from the top of the page. We then construct the second line of the report, which uses the values in the m_FromDate and m_ToDate, to format strings that describe the period for which the report is being prepared. These strings are concatenated with other string constants to form the second line of the heading, which is then rendered at the one-half-inch left offset and two line-height measures down from the top of the page.

After the foregoing steps are complete, the original font, saved previously, is restored into the device context and the member function returns to the OnPrint member function to complete the rendering of the current page.

Final Cleanup When the Report Window Is Closed

When the report window is closed, we need to delete any persistent objects we have created previously. To accomplish this, we have defined a message handler to be invoked when the ON_WM_DESTROY message is sent to the view. This occurs when the user closes the window or quits the application.

OnDestroy Message Handler Code

The code for the OnDestroy message handler is as follows:

```
void CReportView::OnDestroy()
{
   CScrollView::OnDestroy();
   m_BlankLine.DeleteObject();
}
```

The foregoing code calls the OnDestroy member function for the CScrollView base class and then destroys the region addressed by the m_BlankLine pointer.

Exercises

1. Assume that the user has created or opened a second document while the first is still active. What is the effect on the document templates, if any, because of this action? Explain your answer.

2. Assume that the user has created a second copy of the application (multiple instances). What effect does this have on any of the elements of the application? In particular, what effect does a second instance have on the account identifiers associated with the second instance? Describe what you would do to solve the problem, if any.

3. Explain why we created *copies* of the account objects prior to invoking the Settings dialog. Was it necessary to do so? Explain how the code be modified to omit this step.

4. Just prior to the creation of the List of Accounts dialog, we again created copies of the account objects. Why was this necessary? Explain your answer.

5. Imagine that, instead of allowing the user to select from the available accounts, we wish to allow the user to choose from the available categories when the Accounts button is clicked in the Settings dialog. How would you go about reusing as much of the code and the List of Accounts dialog to accomplish this objective? Explain your answer. (*Hint*: Recall that we already have a handle to the Accounts button in the Settings dialog and that it is possible to change the title of a dialog by using the SetWindowText member function of the CWnd class.)

6. Although the validation of dates in the Settings dialog is fairly comprehensive, is there a flaw in the logic when dates are set automatically by choosing a period from the combo box? Explain your answer.

7. Assume that we have decided to add an Options button to the Settings dialog and then display entirely different report settings, such as the selection of individual transaction Categories or tax-related transactions. Describe how you would implement this feature. Implement your suggestions.[1]

8. Describe what changes to the existing code would be necessary to modify the report view window title to reflect the name of the current report and then implement your suggestions.[2]

9. Assume that a Net Worth report is to be prepared, where all assets (deposit values) will appear before all liabilities (payments) in the report. Also take into account the balance of any Asset, Credit Card, or Liability accounts in determining the report format. What changes to the existing code would be needed to implement this report? Design the report and then implement the changes.[3]

[1.] This is a fairly extensive project; however, it is one that will provide continued experience in the use of the App Studio and ClassWizard tools, as well as help to exercise the student's imagination of what options would be useful and how the selection of these could be accomplished within the framework of the existing code. It might be useful to assign this as an extra-credit project. A unique method of implementing this task is shown in the following two chapters, but don't peek. Check your approach and implementation with what we've done. It's possible that you can come up with an even better approach.

[2.] This is a fairly simple project, which can be accomplished by using techniques similar to those already being used for naming the individual account views. The student should be able to carry out this task in a very short time.

[3.] This is a fairly complex project and one that will require quite a bit of time to accomplish. One method of creating this report is shown in the course of the next two chapters. Don't peek, but take on this challenge as a class project and then compare your approach with what is shown in the book.

10. The limitations of 16-bit coordinate values was discussed in this chapter, in the section that describes the OnPrint member function. What different method could be used to render successive pages of a report so that the limitation of the size of the report is no longer a consideration? Explain your approach and then implement it using the current Cash Flow report to test your theory.[1] (*Hint:* The clipping region needn't change for successive pages of a printed report, but this will require that the OnDraw logic be modified when the report is being printed, versus when it is being displayed.)

---

[1] The limitations of 16-bit coordinates are overcome in the modified report code shown in Chapter 10. Determining what changes are needed to accomplish this and then implementing the changes, knowing what you do at this point, would be a very good class project. The 32-bit version of Visual C++ for Windows NT does not have these limitations. Using the foregoing methodology would work fine in that environment. If you are working in a 16-bit Visual C++ environment, as we were, then take on this challenge and compare your results with our solution (shown in Chapter 10).

Chapter 9

Adding Custom Report Features

This chapter sets the stage for adding new reports to the repertoire of the Keepit application. We will be modifying some existing resources, and we will also present a methodology for creating the design of custom dialogs, which will be implemented at run time by creating and disposing various controls programmatically. By customizing the existing "Settings" dialog to handle the requirements for individual reports, we can provide the user with an intuitive and easy-to-use interface for the creation of all future reports.

The previous chapter described the limitations of using the clipping region, expressed in device coordinates, for governing the printout of individual pages in long reports. In this chapter we will discuss an alternative approach that will then be implemented in the custom code described in Chapter 10.

Adding a New Report Command

New reports are implemented by first adding a new command to the application's Report menu. Each time a new report is desired, we will add a command that defines the type of report, provide a handler for it, and then customize the code in the handler. The methodology presented in this and succeeding chapters should make clear what steps are involved in this process. The steps for adding a new command are as follows:

1. With Visual C++ running and with the **keepit.mak** project file loaded, invoke the App Studio tool by choosing it from the Tools menu.

2. When App Studio begins execution, you will see the familiar split window display, with resource types on the left and resources of the selected type on the right. Select the Menu resource type by moving the cursor to that entry, or by clicking on the entry with the mouse.

3. When the Menu resource type is selected, the list of menus will appear in the right side of the split window. At the moment, we are interested in modifying the menu named IDR_KEEPITTYPE. Open that resource either by moving the cursor to it and then pressing the

Enter (or Return) key or by double clicking the entry with the mouse. In either case, App Studio should display the menu bar as it will appear when the main Keepit application account view is open.

4. Drop down the Report menu either by tabbing to that menu, or by clicking once on the Report menu title. This will expose the Cash Flow command that was created previously. Immediately below the existing Cash Flow command, you will see a blank placeholder for a new command. Use either the arrow keys or the mouse to select the blank placeholder and then press the Enter key (or double click the mouse on that space).

5. The property window for the new entry should now be on your screen. Fill in the fields of that window as shown in Figure 9-1. Note that we have added a command that when chosen will cause us to produce a Net Worth report.

<table>
<tr><td>

Figure 9-1

Properties of Net Worth report menu command

</td><td>

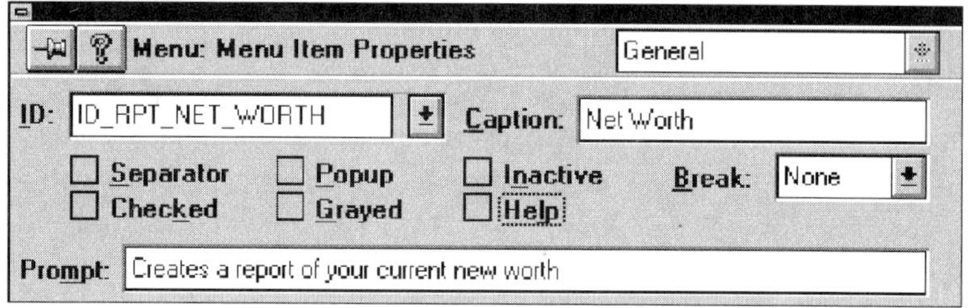

</td></tr>
</table>

6. After the foregoing step is complete, select the Net Worth entry in the Report menu, copy the entry to the clipboard either by choosing the Copy command from the Edit menu or by using the Ctrl-C keyboard shortcut.

7. Dismiss the IDR_KEEPITTYPE resource window by double clicking in the document's control menu, or by using the Ctrl-F4 keyboard shortcut. Make sure that you don't exit the App Studio application, by accident, at this point. If you do, you can reinvoke App Studio, select the IDR_KEEPITTYPE menu resource, open the Report menu, select the Net Worth entry, copy it once again to the clipboard, and then close the window.

8. After closing the IDR_KEEPITTYPE window, you should see App Studio's main split window view of the various resources, with the Menu resource selected in the left-hand pane and its various menu types shown in the right-hand pane. Open the menu whose name is IDR_CATVIEWTYPE, select the Report menu, select the empty placeholder entry, and then paste the Net Worth entry from the clipboard into that menu. You can do this either by choosing Paste from the Edit menu or by using the Ctrl-V keyboard shortcut. Close that menu resource window using one of the methods

described previously and repeat the procedure for the menu resource named IDR_REPORTTYPE. The menu resource named IDR_MAINFRAME is not modified. The menu associated with that frame is used only when no document is open. Choosing a report at that time is not appropriate.

9. Finally, when the foregoing steps are complete, save the resource file by choosing the Save command from the File menu, and then exit the App Studio tool by choosing Exit from the File menu.

This completes the procedure for installing the Net Worth command into the various menu bars, each of which is active at various times during the execution of the Keepit application.

The next series of steps concern the use of the ClassWizard tool for creating a message handler for the Net Worth command. The steps are as follows:

1. Invoke the ClassWizard tool by choosing that command from the Browse menu, making sure that the Message Maps tab is selected.

2. Select the CKeepitDoc class from the combo box at the top of the dialog, scroll down the list of Object IDs in the left-hand list box, and select the one named ID_RPT_NET_WORTH.

3. The list box at the right should contain two entries. Select the one named COMMAND, and then click the Add Function button at the right side of the window. This will cause another dialog to open, displaying a suggested name for the new command handler. Change the name to correspond with what is shown in Figure 9-2.

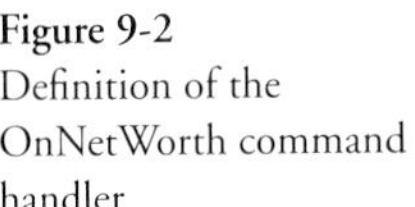

Figure 9-2
Definition of the
OnNetWorth command
handler

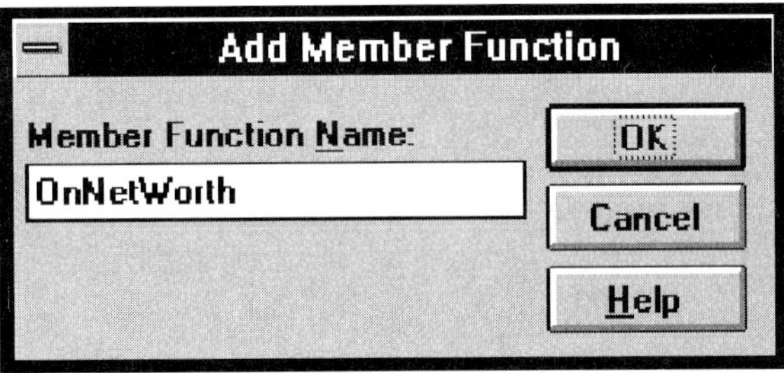

4. After entering the OnNetWorth handler name, click the OK button to return to the ClassWizard's main window. The final appearance of the main window should be as shown in Figure 9-3.

5. Click OK to dismiss the ClassWizard's main window and exit the tool.

This concludes the steps for adding a message handler for the Net Worth command. Commands for new reports and their respective message han-

Figure 9-3
ClassWizard's main
window after the
OnNetWorth command
is defined

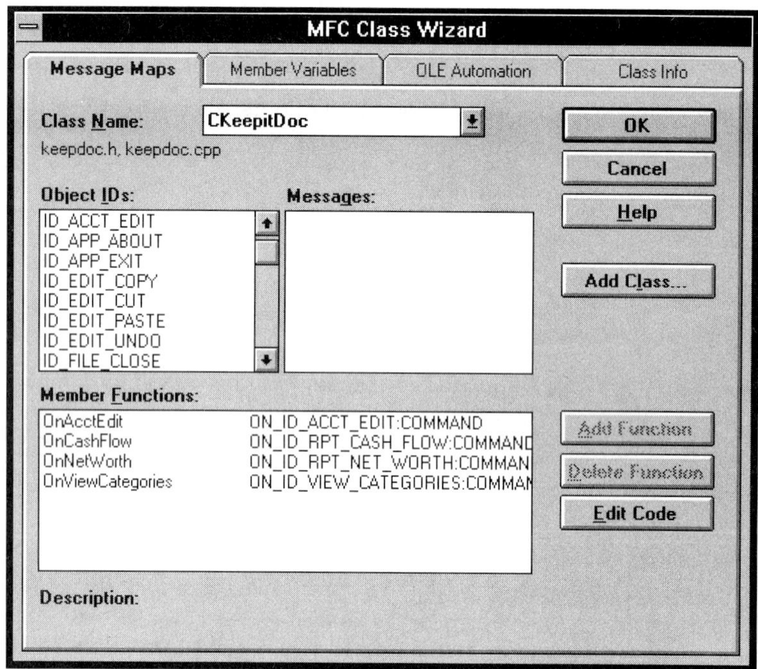

dlers can be added in this same manner. The seamless integration of the
Visual Workbench, App Studio, and ClassWizard tools makes the addition of new application features a simple and straightforward process.

Enhancing the Settings Dialog

The Settings dialog was introduced in Chapter 7 and its completed appearance, after having been designed with the App Studio dialog editor,
is shown in Figure 7-18, on page 241. The purpose of the original dialog
was to provide the user with the means to select the accounts and specify
the time period for which the Cash Flow report was to be created. Our
newly added Net Worth command requires us to either design a new dialog to handle the settings for that report or modify the existing dialog to
contain whatever options are appropriate to the new report.

We have chosen to modify the existing dialog for two important reasons,
which are as follows:

1. The settings for the Net Worth report don't require that we add any
   new controls to the dialog and any necessary changes can be made
   programmatically.

2. Because we want the Cash Flow report to offer new options so that
   the user can select specific categories of transactions to include in

the report, or select only the transactions whose Description or Info fields contain specified text strings to include in the report, we felt that the implementation of a dynamically changeable settings dialog would be more appropriate to the user's needs.

So, although no outward changes are necessary to support the options for the new Net Worth report, we want to provide a new set of options for the Cash Flow report. As evidenced by the size and contents of the existing dialog, shown in Figure 7-18, we need to solve the problem in a way that won't invalidate any of our existing code and that will allow us to add new reports and their options at any time.

The solution to the problem is to add an Options button to the existing dialog and then to make provision for the dialog to expand to display the additional options and also collapse again to hide the options. Although, to accomplish this feat, we need to perform most of the operations programmatically, we can use the existing App Studio dialog editor to great advantage in realizing our goal. The sections that follow will describe the addition of the Options button and its message handler, and then a member variable for accessing the Options button will be defined. Following this, the expanded Settings dialog will be shown.

Adding the Options Button

When you look at the existing Settings dialog, shown in Figure 7-18, you'll see that there is space for another button on the right side of the dialog, immediately below the Cancel button. This is where we intend to add the Options button. The procedure for doing so is as follows:

1. Launch the App Studio tool by choosing that command from the Tools menu. The main App Studio screen should display the list of resource types on the left and the resources of the currently selected type on the right.

2. Select the Dialog resource type in the left-hand list and you should see the resource corresponding to the Settings dialog in the right-hand list, named IDD_SETTINGS. Double click (or select and press the Enter or Return key) to open the App Studio dialog editor for that dialog.

3. Click on the Button tool in the dialog editor's control palette and, holding down the left mouse button, drag a button control onto the dialog at position 211,62. Double click on the button and change its properties to correspond with those shown in Figure 9-4.

4. The final appearance of the Settings dialog should be as shown in Figure 9-5.

Figure 9-4
Options button
properties

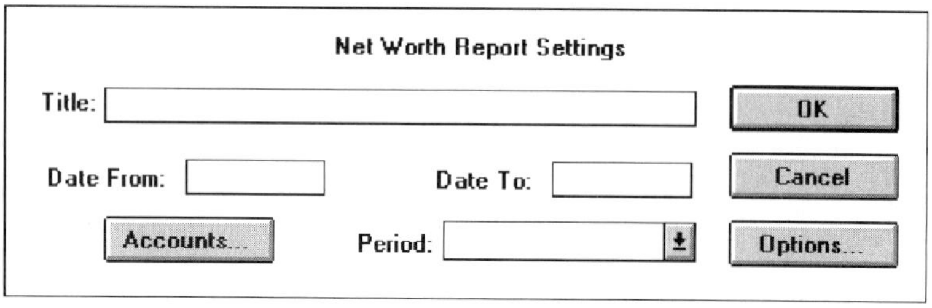

Figure 9-5
Final appearance of
Settings dialog

5. Save the resource file by choosing the Save command from the File menu, leave the App Studio tool running, and continue with the tutorial in the next section.

Adding the Message Handler and Member Variables

After the Options button has been added to the Settings dialog, we need to add a message handler function and also a member variable for the button. These elements are added by using the ClassWizard tool and we will invoke the ClassWizard from within the App Studio tool. Although the ClassWizard could just as easily be invoked, for this purpose, directly from the Visual Workbench, we will invoke it from within the App Studio environment because in so doing the ClassWizard will be prepared for making changes to the CSettings class, automatically, and also because we intend to return to the App Studio after making the necessary additions to that class. The procedure for adding the message handler and member variable for the Options button is as follows:

1. Invoke the ClassWizard tool from within the App Studio's dialog editor by choosing the ClassWizard command from the Resource menu. The main ClassWizard window should appear, with the CSettings class already specified in the combo box at the top of the window. Make sure that the Message Maps tab is selected.

2. Locate the Object ID in the left-hand list box named IDC_OPTIONS and select that entry.

3. Select the BN_CLICKED entry in the Messages list box and then click the Add Function button at the right side of the window. Change

the name of the message handler for the Options button in the Add Member Function dialog to OnOptions, and then click OK to dismiss the dialog and add the function.

4. The next step is to select the CSettings Object ID in the left-hand list box in the ClassWizard's main window, scroll the Messages list and select the entry named WM_DESTROY, and then click the Add Function button. This will add an OnDestroy handler to the Settings dialog code.

5. The main ClassWizard window should now appear as shown in Figure 9-6. Note that both the OnOptions and OnDestroy handlers are shown in the list box at the bottom of the dialog.

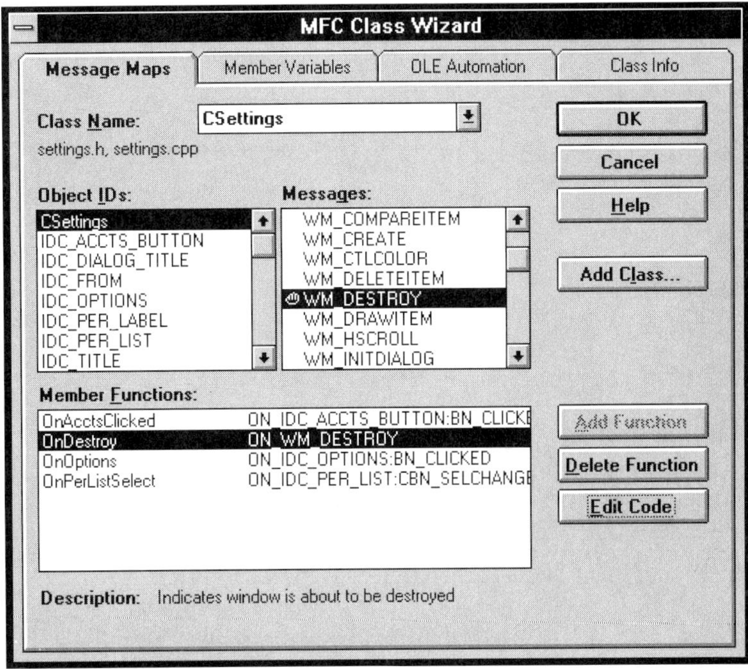

Figure 9-6
ClassWizard's main window after adding OnOptions and OnDestroy handles

The next series of steps concern the addition of a new member variable to the CSettings class. We have decided that we will need to address the Options button directly in order to change its title text from Options to Hide Options. To do so, we need only call the SetWindowText member function, inherited by the button from its CWnd ancestor, with the appropriate text. Having a member variable for the button object, which is initialized with a pointer to the object, automatically, by the dynamic data exchange (DDX) logic, offers the most straightforward approach to address this task. The procedure for adding the new member variable is as follows:

1. With the ClassWizard's main window still on your screen, click the Member Variables tab at the top of the dialog. This will display a list of all of the controls contained in the dialog in its main list box.

2. Click to select the control named IDC_OPTIONS, and then click the Add Variable button at the right side of the dialog. The Add Member Variable dialog should open. Change the settings to correspond with what is shown in Figure 9-7 and then click OK to dismiss the dialog.

Figure 9-7
m_Options member
variable added

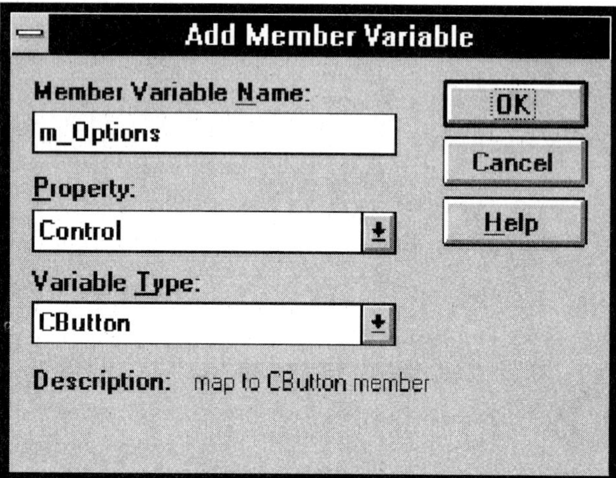

3. The final appearance of the Member Variables portion of the Class-Wizard's main window is shown in Figure 9-8. Click OK to accept these changes and dismiss the dialog, returning control to the App Studio tool.

Prototyping New Settings Dialog Options

Having made the decision to modify the Settings dialog to incorporate various controls and options programmatically, we are faced with the dilemma of potentially having to give up the wonderful WYSIWYG properties of the App Studio dialog editor. In the old days, when the only means for creating dialog controls was from within the program, getting them placed in the proper positions was a fairly major exercise in persistence and self-control. The App Studio's dialog editor has made this process very simple and makes us think twice before considering the loss of this marvelous tool. To lose it completely seems like a step backward in our growth as modern Windows application developers.

Fortunately, even though we intend to implement options for the Settings dialog via program statements, we can use the facilities of the App

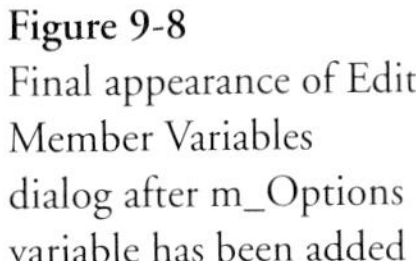

Figure 9-8

Final appearance of Edit Member Variables dialog after m_Options variable has been added

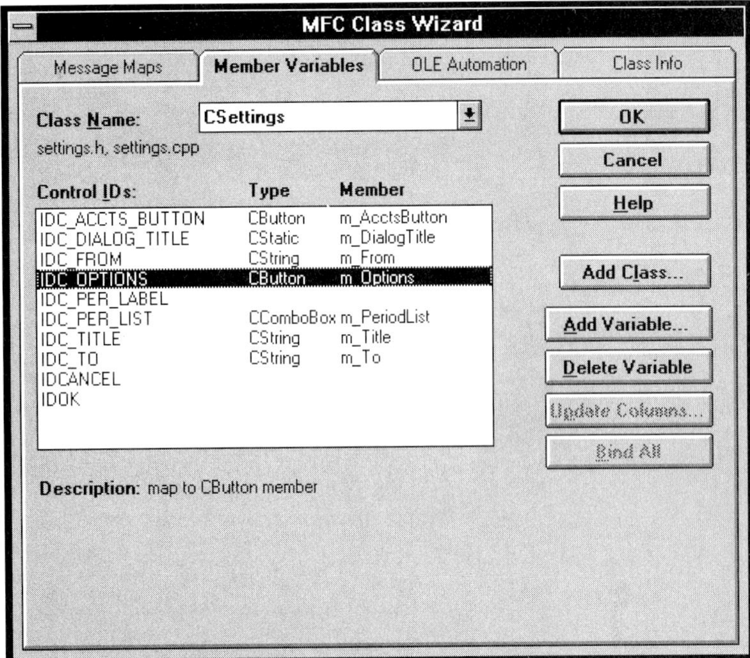

Studio dialog editor to prototype our designs and then translate its coordinates and size values directly to corresponding values in the program, without losing the device independent nature of the dialog editor.

The App Studio dialog editor operates with units called "dialog units," or DLUs. These bear no direct relationship to pixels or logical units, although it is possible to convert these units to either of those measures. Because all of the coordinates and dimensions used in the editor are in DLUs, we will use those values and perform the necessary translation at run time, as does Windows for dialogs we construct and store as resources. This will ensure that the coordinates and values we embed into our program will translate faithfully to displays of different types, with different horizontal and vertical resolutions, and with differing aspect ratios. The implementation of this technique will be discussed in the next chapter. The following sections describe the prototyping process and how the information gained by recording the DLU values can be applied during the implementation phase.

Prototyping the Categories Options

In order to make the Cash Flow report (which provides detailed transaction listings) more useful, we have decided to allow the user to specify which transactions should be included in the report by providing the ability to select from the list of expense or income categories defined previously. In addition, we have decided that providing for the selection of tax-related categories would be a useful option. In short, we envision having a list box in one portion of the expanded dialog and a set of radio buttons that allow the selection of All, None, or Tax-related categories only. Further, we envision that if None is selected, then individual categories could be chosen by double clicking on their entries in the list box. Finally, if the user chooses not to make option selections, we intend for all categories of transactions to be used.

To realize the appearance of the options we have just described, we must revise the appearance of the Settings dialog, but retain the original dialog to be invoked by the application, as it now stands. The procedure for prototyping the new options is as follows:

1. If the App Studio dialog editor is on your screen, with the Settings dialog being displayed, continue with this procedure. If you have just started up the App Studio tool, skip to step 3.

2. Close the Settings dialog window by choosing Close from the editor's Control menu, by double clicking in the document's Control menu box, or by using the Ctrl-F4 keyboard shortcut.

3. With App Studio's main window showing, with the resource types shown on the left side of the window, select the Dialog resource type and then select the Settings dialog, named IDD_SETTINGS in the right-hand list. Click just once to select the entry.

4. With the Settings dialog resource selected, choose the Copy command from the Edit menu (or use the Ctrl-C keyboard shortcut) and then immediately choose the Paste command from the Edit menu (or use the Ctrl-V keyboard shortcut). This will create a copy of the dialog, but with a new name of IDD_SETTINGS1.

5. The newly duplicated dialog name should be selected in the list. If not, select the dialog, and then open the dialog editor by typing the Enter or Return key (or just double click the name). You should see an exact copy of the existing Settings dialog on your screen.

6. The coordinates of the upper left corner of the dialog are 0,0 and the existing size of the dialog is 267x84 DLUs. Choose the pointer tool from the editor's control palette, and click on the dialog to select it if it isn't already selected. Move the pointer to the handle at the bottom and middle of the dialog, and drag down to increase the dialog's height until its dimensions are 267x169. As you can see, this will leave room for a variety of new controls to be added.

7. Choose the Group tool from the editor's control palette, and drag a copy of a group box control onto the dialog at position 6,82 (the

group box control is the one with a rectangular border and the letters **xyz** at its top). Choose the pointer tool, and resize the control so that its dimensions are 255x85. You will see that the group box will cover most of the lower portion of the dialog. Double click on the word "Static" to display the control's properties window, and change the caption to read "Options." This is not a necessary step, but it will give you a better idea of the final appearance of the dialog if you do so. All of the properties of the controls we are prototyping will be set via statements in the program, so whatever properties are chosen during this session are used only to enhance our perception of the dialog's final appearance, as it will exist at run time. By performing the procedures declared as *Optional,* you will be able to test the dialog by choosing the Test command from the Resource menu, and view its final appearance.

8. Choose the Static Text tool from the control palette, and drag a copy of a Static Text control onto the dialog at position 15,102. Change the dimensions of the control to 21x8, and then double click the control and change its caption to read "Type:" (*Optional:* Change the Text Align property to Right.)

9. Choose the Combo Box tool from the control palette and drag a copy of a combo box onto the dialog at position 40,100. Resize the closed combo box to the dimensions 73x12. Click on the arrow at the right side of the combo box to cause it to open, and change its open dimensions to 73x59. (*Optional:* Open the properties window and enter list choices of Categories, Description, and Info. Change the Style properties to Drop List, delete the Sort check, and make sure that Vert. Scroll is checked.)

10. Choose the List Box tool from the control palette, and drag a copy of a list box control onto the dialog at position 126,96. Drag the handle at the control's lower right corner to change the dimensions of the list box to 130x63. It isn't necessary to change any of its properties.

11. Choose the Radio Button tool from the control palette, and drag a radio button onto the dialog at position 40,121. Change the dimensions of the button to 68x10 and change its caption to read "All." Add additional radio buttons at positions 40,135 and 40,149. Change the dimensions of each to 68x10. Change the captions of the two additional buttons to "None" and "Tax-related Only."

This concludes the creation of a prototype for the expanded Settings dialog, when Categories is selected as the option type. You can test the dialog by choosing the Test command from the Resource menu and see how it is going to look and operate. Press the Escape key on the keyboard to return to the dialog editor. The dialog is shown in Figure 9-9.

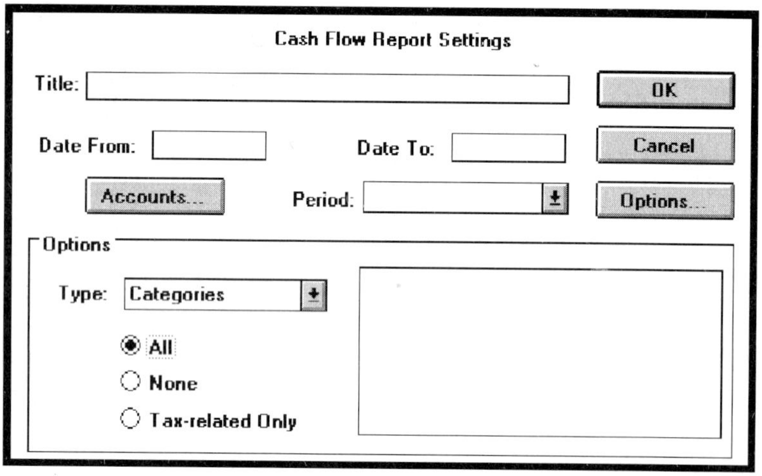

Figure 9-9
Appearance of Category options in the Settings dialog

Although the dialog we constructed in the foregoing steps will not be used in the application, the position coordinates and dimensions of the individual controls are important to preserve. The values for the controls, which we will be using in the next chapter, are shown in Table 9-1.

Table 9-1
Position and Dimension settings for Category options in Settings dialog

Control Name	Position	Dimensions
Overall Extended Dialog	0, 0	267 x 169
Options Group Box	6, 82	255 x 85
Type Static Text	15, 102	21 x 8
Type Combo Box	40, 100	73 x 59
Category List Box	126, 96	130 x 63
All Radio Button	40, 121	68 x 10
None Radio Button	40, 135	68 x 10
Tax-related Only Radio Button	40, 149	68 x 10

Prototyping the Description and Info Options

The foregoing prototype, which contains the controls for selecting from the list of available categories can be modified to provide options that allow the user to specify transactions for the Cash Flow report, based upon the contents of their Description and Info text fields. To prototype the new appearance of the lower portion of the Settings dialog, you can either create a new copy of the original Settings dialog (which is named IDD_SETTINGS) and repeat steps 1–9 in the foregoing procedure, or start with the completed dialog (shown in Figure 9-9) and delete the Category list box and the three radio buttons. In either case, the procedure for creating the controls to support entry of Description and Info text field constraints is as follows:

1. We assume that the App Studio dialog editor is running and that a copy of the Settings dialog, which has been expanded and has the controls common to both types of options already installed, as specified in steps 1–9 on pages 340–341, is on your screen.

2. Choose the Edit Box control and drag a copy of that control onto the dialog at position 124,100. Change the dimensions of the control to 129x12. No changes to the properties are necessary.

3. Choose the Radio Button control and drag a copy of that control onto the dialog at position 125,121. Change the dimensions of the control to 60x10, and then change the caption property of the control to "Starts With."

4. Create two additional radio button controls on the dialog at positions 125,135 and 125,149. Change the dimensions of each to 60x10. Change the captions of the two buttons to "Contains" and "Equals Exactly".

This concludes the procedure for prototyping the options that apply to the Description and Info text fields. Run the dialog by choosing the Test command from the Resource menu. You should see a dialog that has the appearance shown in Figure 9-10.

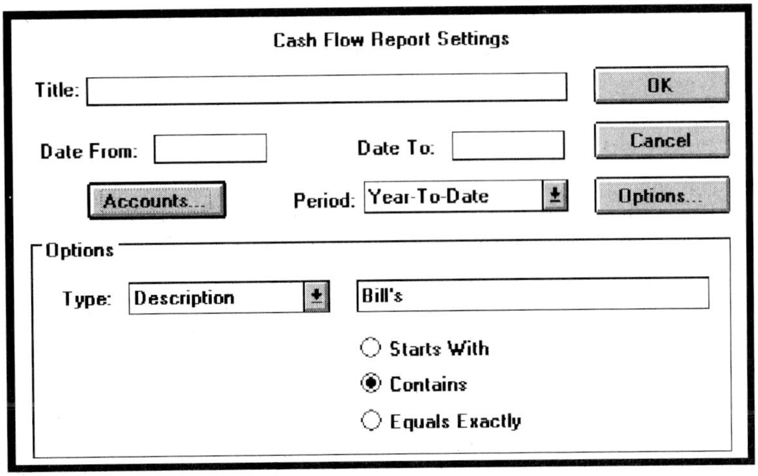

Figure 9-10
Appearance of Description and Info options in the Settings dialog

As with the Category options settings, we aren't interested in this dialog, but merely the position and dimensions of the various controls. We will use these values in the next chapter when we implement the controls programmatically. For your reference, we have reproduced the settings in tabular form, as shown in Table 9-1.

Table 9-2

Position and Dimension settings for Category options in Settings dialog

Control Name	Position	Dimensions
Overall Extended Dialog	0, 0	267 x 169
Options Group Box	6, 82	255 x 85
Type Static Text	15, 102	21 x 8
Type Combo Box	40, 100	73 x 59
Editable Text Box	124, 100	129 x 12
Starts With Radio Button	125, 121	60 x 10
Contains Radio Button	125, 135	60 x 10
Equals Exactly Radio Button	125, 149	60 x 10

The prototyping we have just completed illustrates techniques that can be used for future reports, or for prototyping other dynamic dialogs that you may choose to create. The program procedures to use the foregoing position and dimension values are described fully in the next chapter.

Now that we have completed the prototypes and are satisfied with the appearance of the individual controls, and we have recorded their position and dimension values, we can close the dialog's window by double clicking in its control box, or use the Ctrl-F4 keyboard shortcut to close the window. The dialog (or dialogs, if you chose to make two separate copies of the Settings dialog) can now be deleted. You may choose not to do so, in case you might want to make further adjustments or add additional options. If you choose not to delete the dialog, make sure that you do not delete the IDD_SETTINGS dialog, by mistake. Save the resource file by choosing Save from the File menu, and then exit the App Studio tool by choosing the Exit command from the File menu. The extra dialogs (if any) will remain in the resource file and will be compiled into the final application, but will not be referenced. If you choose to delete the dialog(s), then select the one (or both) in the list at the right side of App Studio's main window and press the Del (or delete) key on the keyboard. Then save the resource file and exit App Studio as described previously.

Examining the Newly Generated Code

The code generated by the ClassWizard tool as a result of following the foregoing procedures is confined to the CKeepitDoc class files (**keepdoc.h** and **keepdoc.cpp**) and the CSettings class files (**settings.h** and **settings.cpp**). Because only a few additions have been made to these files, we will show only the newly added declarations and corresponding member functions in this section.

Examining the Additions to the CKeepitDoc Class

The only addition to the CKeepitDoc class is the message handler function for the Net Worth report. This handler is invoked by the framework when the user chooses the Net Worth command from the Report menu.

KeepDoc.h Header File Additions

The only addition to the **keepdoc.h** header file is the declaration of the message handler for the Net Worth report. The code for the added declaration is shown, along with the other message handler declarations, as follows:

```
// Generated message map functions
protected:
  //{{AFX_MSG(CKeepitDoc)
  afx_msg void OnViewCategories();
  afx_msg void OnAcctEdit();
  afx_msg void OnCashFlow();
  afx_msg void OnNetWorth();
  //}}AFX_MSG
  DECLARE_MESSAGE_MAP()
```

KeepDoc.cpp Source File Additions

The newly generated skeleton code for the OnNetWorth message handler is as follows:

```
void CKeepitDoc::OnNetWorth()
{
    // TODO: Add your command handler code here
}
```

As is evident from the foregoing code, handling of the Net Worth command is going to require that we add the necessary code to create the report. This will be described fully in the next chapter.

Examining the Additions to the CSettings Class

We have made only a few additions to the CSettings class. We added the Options button to the dialog, and then we added a message handler and member variable for the button. In addition, we added a message handler for the WM_DESTROY message.

Settings.h Header File Additions

The additions to the **settings.h** header file consist of the declaration of new message handlers for OnOptions and OnDestroy, and the declaration of the m_Options member variable. The code for the message handler declarations is as follows:

```
// Generated message map functions
//{{AFX_MSG(CSettings)
afx_msg void OnPerListSelect();
afx_msg void OnAcctsClicked();
afx_msg void OnOptions();
afx_msg void OnDestroy();
//}}AFX_MSG
DECLARE_MESSAGE_MAP()
```

The declarations for all of the member variables that participate in the dynamic data exchange, when the dialog is created, is as follows:

```
//{{AFX_DATA(CSettings)
enum { IDD = IDD_SETTINGS };
CButton    m_Options;
CComboBox  m_PeriodList;
CButton    m_AcctsButton;
CStatic    m_DialogTitle;
CString    m_From;
CString    m_Title;
CString    m_To;
//}}AFX_DATA
```

Note in the foregoing that the m_Options variable is an object of the CButton class. When the dialog is invoked and the DDX/DDV code is executed, a handle to the Options button's window will be created and stored in the object. We will be able to change the name of the button simply by executing the SetWindowText member function inherited from the CWnd class.

Settings.cpp Source File Additions

The additions to the **settings.cpp** source file are limited to the generation of the skeleton code for the two new message handlers. The code for both the OnOptions and OnDestroy message handlers is newly added and is as follows:

```
void CSettings::OnOptions()
{
    // TODO: Add your command handler code here
}

void CSettings::OnDestroy()
{
    // TODO: Add your command handler code here
}
```

In addition to the foregoing, when the `m_Options` member variable was added to the class, a new statement was generated in the DoDataExchange member function. We therefore show the entire code for that function, as it now stands, after the ClassWizard has generated the new statement. The code is as follows:

```
void CSettings::DoDataExchange(CDataExchange* pDX)
{
  CDialog::DoDataExchange(pDX);
  //{{AFX_DATA_MAP(CSettings)
  DDX_Control(pDX, IDC_OPTIONS, m_Options);
  DDX_Control(pDX, IDC_PER_LIST, m_PeriodList);
  DDX_Control(pDX, IDC_ACCTS_BUTTON, m_AcctsButton);
  DDX_Control(pDX, IDC_DIALOG_TITLE, m_DialogTitle);
  DDX_DateCheck(pDX, IDC_FROM, m_From);
  DDX_Text(pDX, IDC_TITLE, m_Title);
  DDX_DateCheck(pDX, IDC_TO, m_To);
  //}}AFX_DATA_MAP
}
```

Exercises

1. We have included a new command named Net Worth in the Report menu. Describe why it was necessary to duplicate this command in several of the other menus. Why was this command left off of the menu named IDR_MAINFRAME? Explain your answer.

2. Other than the addition of the Net Worth command and its associated message handler to the code, why do you think that we have not made any other changes related to that command? Describe how you think that the Net Worth report will be created.

3. In the foregoing text, we created an expanded version of the Settings dialog in order to add new controls to it, but we didn't save the dialog resource. How do you think that we are going to create a larger dialog, given that the only one that exists in the resource file is what is shown in Figure 9-5? Explain your answer.

4. We prototyped two sets of controls in the foregoing text. Describe how you think that the dialog is going to operate. How will it be possible to have multiple sets of controls and manage to display one or the other and also save and restore settings, as the user requires?

5. We mentioned briefly that the dialogs designed within the App Studio dialog editor use dialog units (DLUs) as the unit of measure for the position and dimension values. Why aren't these values kept in pixels or some other convenient unit of measure? Explain why keeping measurements in pixels might affect the appearance of the dialog on various types of display monitors.

6. What is the relationship of a dialog unit to a measurement in pixels on any particular display? Explain your answer.

7. Using the same procedure described earlier in this chapter, prototype a set of options that will enable the user to select transactions for inclusion in the Cash Flow report, based upon the values in their Payment or Deposit fields. Provide for a range of values, or a value limit (either upper or lower) to be used in determining which transactions will be included in the report. Record the position and dimension values for each new control.[1]

---

[1] The student should be able to accomplish this task in a relatively short period of time. This would be a good extra-credit project or a useful classroom exercise.

Chapter 10

Additional Customizing of the Reports Code

This chapter covers a number of new topics. Chief among these are the descriptions of how to implement the dynamic dialogs, which were prototyped in the preceding chapter, and also how the printing member functions are modified to remove the limitations of using 16-bit clipping regions to specify the data to be printed.

This chapter also shows how the newly added Net Worth report is integrated into the existing code and provides insight into how subsequent reports could be implemented easily.

We have also created two new data types, which are referenced in multiple files, and have therefore elected to define these in a new header file that is precompiled along with the other standard data types and Windows declarations.

The modifications to support the newly defined Settings dialog options, the changes to enhance the inclusion criteria for the Cash Flow report, and the preparation of both the Cash Flow and Net Worth reports are all confined to the CKeepitDoc, CSettings, and CReportView classes. The remainder of this chapter discusses the changes to each of these classes (including header and source file modifications).

Because we have not added any classes in implementing the new features, the structure of the application is still as depicted in Chapter 8, shown in Figure 8-1.

Support for the Settings Dialog Options

If you look back in Chapter 9, you will see that we prototyped two new versions of the Settings dialog, which was first introduced in Chapter 7. The resource file description of the Settings dialog (IDD_SETTINGS) remains almost the same for this version of the application, but we have added an Options button and a message handler in the CSettings class to handle the case when the user clicks that button.

Our intention, in the case where the Options button is clicked, is to enlarge the Settings dialog, install a number of controls inside the enlarged area, and then handle the messages generated as a result of the user's interaction with the newly added controls. In fact, because we have prototyped two different arrangements of controls, depending upon which actions the user elects to take, we must switch dynamically between the two arrangements, with no impediments to the user's actions.

At this point we pause to review our design goals so that you will have a better understanding of why we have taken this approach in the design of the Settings dialog. Our rationale is as follows:

❖ When the user chooses a command from the Report menu, it is necessary to inquire which of the potential reporting options the user intends to use. We have chosen to display a dialog that offers the user a number of options, from which they are allowed to specify the ones of particular interest.

❖ Specification of the foregoing options should be a process that is as simple, yet comprehensive, as possible. Because of this, we have elected not to have unique dialogs for each new report, and particularly not for each option type in each report.

❖ Because the design of report options is a repeated task for each new report type, we wish to reuse as much of the existing code as possible and also minimize the depletion of system resources.

❖ By creating an "expandable" dialog whose option settings can vary from one type of option to another and from one type of report to another, we can make the most efficient use of our existing code, but at the expense of writing code to create and manage the dynamic dialog's controls programmatically.

As a result of the foregoing analysis, our new approach is confined to enhancements to the existing CSettings class, its associated header and source files, and some manual additions to the **resource.h** file.

Newly Defined Control Identifiers

Because we have elected to create a number of control resources programmatically, we need to define IDs for these that are unique. When AppStudio is used to create new controls, it writes `#define` statements into the **resource.h** file, which associates a control name with its numeric ID value. App Studio keeps track of the next available control value, as well as other values, in the **resource.h** file. Because the definitions in this file are available for use by any of the application's files, we have decided to assign names and associated control IDs for our dynamic controls by adding new `#define` statements to that file. In order to prevent any conflicts between the values we assign and any value App Studio assigns, we have begun our sequence of control IDs with the value 512. Following is a section of the end of our **resource.h** file, showing how the manually defined control identifiers have values that are well apart from what App Studio assigns for controls:

```
#define IDC_RADIO1                      161
#define IDC_RADIO2                      162
#define IDC_RADIO3                      163
#define IDC_FROM_LABEL                  164

#define IDC_OPTIONS_BOX                 512
#define IDC_TYPE_LABEL                  513
#define IDC_TYPE_COMBO                  514
#define IDC_ALL_RADIO                   515
#define IDC_NONE_RADIO                  516
#define IDC_TAX_RELATED_RADIO           517
#define IDC_CATEGORY_LIST               518
#define IDC_EDIT_TEXT_STRING            519
#define IDC_STARTS_RADIO                520
#define IDC_CONTAINS_RADIO              521
#define IDC_EXACT_RADIO                 522

#define ID_ACCT_EDIT                    32768
#define ID_VIEW_CATEGORIES              32769
#define ID_ACCT_PRINT                   32770
#define ID_RPT_CASH_FLOW                32771
#define ID_RPT_NET_WORTH                32772

// Next default values for new objects
//
#ifdef APSTUDIO_INVOKED
#ifndef APSTUDIO_READONLY_SYMBOLS

#define _APS_NEXT_RESOURCE_VALUE        111
#define _APS_NEXT_COMMAND_VALUE         32774
#define _APS_NEXT_CONTROL_VALUE         165
#define _APS_NEXT_SYMED_VALUE           101
#endif
#endif
```

As indicated previously, the foregoing is the final section of the **resource.h** file. Other definitions precede the ones shown. In any case, you can see that App Studio's control resources are still numbered well below the value of 512 we have chosen. The values above 32767 represent menu command numbers and will also not conflict with our assignments. By adding our values to the **resource.h** file, we can make sure that all control IDs are defined in one place and that they do not conflict with one another.

CSettings Class Header File Declarations

Because quite a number of new member variables and member functions have been added to the CSettings class, we have decided to show the entire contents of the new version of the **settings.h** header file. Also, because the file is becoming rather large, with sections that relate to various categories of declarations, we will present the file in sections so that it can be more easily described and understood. Changes to the file, from what was shown for previous versions, are indicated with change bars.

Settings.h Initial Section

The first section of the header file contains the definition of forward class references and also `#define` statements that associate numeric values with various reporting period options. The code is as follows:

```
// settings.h : header file
//

class CKeepitDoc;         // added forward reference

//////////////////////////////////////////////////////////////////////
// CSettings dialog

#define YEAR_TO_DATE       0
#define CURRENT_MONTH      1
#define CURRENT_QUARTER    2
#define CURRENT_YEAR       3
#define LAST_MONTH         4
#define LAST_QUARTER       5
#define LAST_YEAR          6
#define ALL_TRANSACTIONS   7
```

Dynamic (DDX) and General Variable Declarations

The next section of the **settings.h** header file contains the beginning of the class declaration, as well as the declaration of member variables which participate in the dynamic data exchange (DDX) actions when the dialog is created or dismissed. In addition, some general purpose member variables are also included in this section, which is as follows:

```
class CSettings : public CDialog
{
// Construction
public:
   CSettings(CWnd* pParent = NULL); // standard constructor

// Dialog Data
   //{{AFX_DATA(CSettings)
   enum { IDD = IDD_SETTINGS };
   CButton      m_Options;      // Options button
   CComboBox    m_PeriodList;   // Period list
   CButton      m_AcctsButton;  // Accounts button
   CStatic      m_DialogTitle;  // Dialog title
   CString      m_Title;        // Report title
   CString      m_From;         // Period begin date
   CString      m_To;           // Period end date
   //}}AFX_DATA

   virtual BOOL OnInitDialog(void);

public:
// Local Member Variables
```

```
CObList       m_Accounts;        // list of selected accounts
CString       m_szDialogTitle;   // dialog title string
CKeepitDoc*   m_pDoc;            // pointer to document
// Implementation
protected:
    virtual void DoDataExchange(CDataExchange* pDX);
```

Message Handler Function Declarations

The next section of the header file contains the declaration of message handler functions that were generated automatically by the ClassWizard tool when we chose to process the specified messages. Immediately following the generated function declarations, we have added message handler declarations for the controls that we will create dynamically.

```
// Generated message map functions
//{{AFX_MSG(CSettings)
afx_msg void OnPerListSelect();
afx_msg void OnAcctsClicked();
afx_msg void OnOptions();
afx_msg void OnDestroy();
//}}AFX_MSG

//
// dynamic message map functions to handle selected options
//
afx_msg void OnTypeSelect();    // select option type
afx_msg void OnCatSelect();     // category selected
afx_msg void OnCatRadio();      // category radio clicked
afx_msg void OnStringEntry();   // edit field entered
afx_msg void OnContentsRadio();// text contents radio

DECLARE_MESSAGE_MAP()
```

As is evident in the foregoing declarations, we do not require that many new message handlers be provided for the dynamically added controls. In any case, although the declarations for the new message handlers are outside those managed directly by the ClassWizard, they are declared in the same way and perform in exactly the same manner.

Standard Member Functions and Member Variables

The next section of the header file contains the declaration of member functions and member variables that are not related to the creation of specific report options. The code is as follows:

```
void Dlu2Pix (RECT& rd, RECT& rs);// RECT DLU's to Pixels
void RectAdd (RECT& rd, RECT& rs);// add rectangles
void RectSub (RECT& rd, RECT& rs);// subtract rectangles

void MakeStandardControls (void);// create standard controls
void DeleteStdControls (void);   // delete standard controls
void DeleteOptControls (void);   // delete optional controls

BOOL    m_bExpanded;    // settings dialog expanded?
```

```
RECT    m_rShortDialog;// short dialog position & size
RECT    m_rLongDialog; // long dialog position & size
RECT    m_rFrame;      // dialog frame position & size
RECT    m_rWindow;     // window RECT (current size)
int     m_nXUnits;     // X DLU's in pixels
int     m_nYUnits;     // Y DLU's in pixels
```

The first of the foregoing declarations pertains to a new member function that converts measurements expressed in dialog units (DLUs) to measurements in pixels for the current display adapter. This member function is key to the translation of the prototyped position and dimension values shown in the previous chapter. The member function will be described very shortly. The two declarations that follow pertain to new member functions that provide the ability to add and subtract one rectangle from another. These are not union or exclusion operations, such as are provided in the Windows API but, rather, involve arithmetic addition and subtraction of the corresponding elements in the RECT variables. They are used in calculating the client rectangle of the dialog.

The next three declarations are for new member functions that create the standard dynamic controls and delete both the standard and optional controls. The creation of controls specific to a report option is accomplished by report-specific member functions. At the present time member functions are needed only for the Cash Flow report, as the Net Worth report has no options.

Member Functions and Variables for the Cash Flow Report

The next section of the **settings.h** header file contains the declaration of member functions and member variables that are specific to settings for the Cash Flow report. The declarations are as follows:

```
///////////////////////////////////////////////////////////////
// Cash Flow Report Options

void MakeCashFlowControls (int t);// create default controls
void AddCategories (CListBox* p); // add categories to list
void SelectCategories (CListBox* p,// select categories
   int nWhich);                    // -- which category?
CCategory* FindCategory (         // find a category by name
   CObList& List,                 // -- object list
   CString& szName,               // -- name of category
   POSITION& pos);                // -- position if found
void MakeTextSettings(void);   // change text settings

//
// settings dialog specific font
//
CFont*       m_pSettingsFont;

//
// common options section controls
//
int          m_nPrevOptionType;// previous option type
```

```
        CButton*      m_pOptionsBox;        // options group box
        CStatic*      m_pTypeLabel;         // type label
        CComboBox*    m_pTypeCombo;         // combo box type list
        RECT          m_rOptionsBox;        // options box RECT
        RECT          m_rTypeLabel;         // type label RECT
        RECT          m_rTypeCombo;         // type combo RECT

        //
        // categories options controls
        //
        CButton*      m_pAllRadio;          // all categories radio
        CButton*      m_pNoneRadio;         // no categories radio
        CButton*      m_pTaxRelatedRadio;// tax-related radio
        CListBox*     m_pCategoryList;   // list of categories
        int           m_nPrevCatRadio;   // previous radio setting
        RECT          m_rAllRadio;          // all categories radio RECT
        RECT          m_rNoneRadio;         // no categories radio RECT
        RECT          m_rTaxRelatedRadio;// tax-related radio RECT
        RECT          m_rCategoryList;   // category list RECT

        //
        // text matching controls
        //
        CEdit*        m_pTextString;        // text string to be matched
        CButton*      m_pStartsRadio;       // starts with radio button
        CButton*      m_pContainsRadio;     // contains radio button
        CButton*      m_pExactRadio;        // exact match radio button
        int           m_nPrevDescRadio;     // previous descrip. radio
        int           m_nPrevInfoRadio;     // previous info radio
        RECT          m_rTextString;        // text string RECT
        RECT          m_rStartsRadio;       // starts with radio RECT
        RECT          m_rContainsRadio;     // contains radio RECT
        RECT          m_rExactRadio;        // exact match radio RECT
};
```

As mentioned previously, the foregoing section of the **settings.h** header file contains declarations that are specific to the creation and management of controls and settings for the Cash Flow report. The first group of declarations defines a number of member functions that create and operate on the various dynamic controls. Following these is the declaration of a pointer to a CFont object that will be created dynamically in the OnInitDialog member function to correspond to the properties of the user's display adapter. The properties of this font will be used in the translation of dialog units to pixels for display purposes.

The next group of declarations pertain to controls that are common to the two different arrangements we prototyped in the previous chapter. The m_nPrevOptionType variable is used to contain the option type previously selected, when a new type has been selected. This is to facilitate the disposal of the previous controls, before creating the new controls. The declarations that follow in that group consist of pointers to control objects, followed by RECT variables that will hold the translated position and dimensions of the corresponding controls.

The next group of declarations contains variables that are specific to the Categories option type, which are pointers to control objects and RECT variables that describe their positions and dimensions, including one that maintains the identifier for the radio button set previously.

The final set of declarations pertains to the Description and Info option types and contains pointers to the controls and RECT variables that describe their positions and dimensions. Two additional variables hold the previous radio button settings for the Description and Info option types.

Although a fairly large number of variables is involved, a similar number of controls and variables would be declared in a different implementation strategy, but they would be distributed among several different files. Although that might be an approach that is more modular in concept, the simplicity of the user interface would be diminished greatly.

CSettings Class Source File Definitions

Because we have reorganized the code in the CSettings class, to provide setting options, many of the member functions previously created have been modified, and a number of new member functions have been defined. We have elected to show the entire contents of the **settings.cpp** source file as it now exists. Although we have made some rather sweeping changes to the code in this class, we have not thrown away much of the previous code. Our plan, from the outset, was to evolve the Settings dialog to incorporate these changes, so the impact on the existing code to implement the new features is minimal. Each of the individual sections in the source code will be explained in detail.

Settings.cpp Initial Section

The initial section of the source file contains the #include declarations that enable us to reference member functions and declarations in other classes. The code is as follows:

```
// settings.cpp : implementation file
//
#include "stdafx.h"
#include "keepit.h"
#include "keepdoc.h"
#include "dattim.h"
#include "acctobj.h"
#include "selected.h"
#include "category.h"
#include "settings.h"
extern char __far monthDays[];

#ifdef _DEBUG
#undef THIS_FILE
static char BASED_CODE THIS_FILE[] = __FILE__;
#endif
```

As is usual for the first section of a source file, we have grouped all of the `#include` statements at the top, followed by the declaration of references to external variables (in this case, only the `monthDays` array from the **dattim.cpp** file is referenced), and ended by the declaration of the `THIS_FILE` variable (for use in debugging).

Dynamic Control Position Definitions

This next section of the source file contains the position and dimensions of the normal (short) and extended (long) dialogs, as well as the values for each of the possible controls. The values in the left, top, right, and bottom positions of the `RECT` structure are based upon the values that we recorded when prototyping the controls. The position coordinates are stored in the left and top positions of the structure and the dimensions of the controls have been added to these values to create the right and bottom values in the definitions. In all other respects, the values are all expressed in the same units of measure (DLUs) that we recorded in the prototyping process. The definitions are newly added, as follows:

```
///////////////////////////////////////////////////////////////
// Dynamic Control Positions
//
static RECT rShortDialog      = {  0,    0, 267,   84};
static RECT rLongDialog       = {  0,    0, 267,  172};
static RECT rOptionsBox       = {  6,   82, 261,  167};
static RECT rTypeLabel        = { 15,  102,  36,  110};
static RECT rTypeCombo        = { 40,  100, 113,  159};
static RECT rAllRadio         = { 40,  121, 108,  131};
static RECT rNoneRadio        = { 40,  135, 108,  145};
static RECT rTaxRelatedRadio  = { 40,  149, 108,  159};
static RECT rCategoryList      = {126,   96, 256,  159};
static RECT rTextString        = {124,  100, 253,  112};
static RECT rStartsRadio        = {125,  121, 185,  131};
static RECT rContainsRadio      = {125,  135, 185,  145};
static RECT rExactRadio         = {125,  149, 185,  159};
```

If you look back at the member variables for these controls, as declared in the **settings.h** file, you will discover that we have given them names similar to those shown in the foregoing code. For example, the member variable that holds the translated settings for the short dialog (called `rShortDialog` in the above list) is named `m_rShortDialog`. A similar convention is followed for the other names.

CSettings Constructor Member Function

The code for the constructor member function of the CSettings class is as follows:

```
///////////////////////////////////////////////////////////////
// CSettings dialog
//
```

```
CSettings::CSettings(CWnd* pParent /*=NULL*/)
    : CDialog(CSettings::IDD, pParent)
{
    //{{AFX_DATA_INIT(CSettings)
    m_From = "";
    m_Title = "";
    m_To = "";
    //}}AFX_DATA_INIT
}
```

You will note that the constructor code hasn't changed from what was presented in Chapter 8. The contents of the member variables related to the Edit Box controls are set to empty strings so that, when the dialog is initialized, those fields will be empty.

Dlu2Pix Member Function Code

The following member function is responsible for converting the measurements in a single RECT structure from dialog units to pixels. This member function depends upon the properties of the device context (specifically, the average character width and ascender height). The code for the Dlu2Pix member function is all newly added and is as follows:

```
void CSettings::Dlu2Pix (RECT& rd, RECT& rs)
{
    TEXTMETRIC tm;
    CClientDC client(this);
    client.GetTextMetrics (&tm);
    m_nXUnits = tm.tmAveCharWidth;
    m_nYUnits = tm.tmAscent;

    rd.left   = (rs.left   * m_nXUnits) / 4;
    rd.top    = (rs.top    * m_nYUnits) / 8;
    rd.right  = (rs.right  * m_nXUnits) / 4;
    rd.bottom = (rs.bottom * m_nYUnits) / 8;
}
```

RectAdd and RectSub Member Function Code

The code for adding and subtracting the corresponding fields of two rectangles is used in the OnInitDialog member function to convert back and forth between window and client coordinates in the dialog, by using the translated dialog position values. The code is all newly added and is as follows:

```
void CSettings::RectAdd (RECT& rd, RECT& rs)
{
    rd.left   += rs.left;
    rd.top    += rs.top;
    rd.right  += rs.right;
    rd.bottom += rs.bottom;
}
```

```
void CSettings::RectSub (RECT& rd, RECT& rs)
{
   rd.left    -= rs.left;
   rd.top     -= rs.top;
   rd.right   -= rs.right;
   rd.bottom  -= rs.bottom;
}
```

As is evident from the foregoing code, the corresponding fields of the source rectangle (rs) are added to or subtracted from the fields in the destination rectangle (rd). No attempt is made to validate the fields because we know that they contain proper values.

OnInitDialog Member Function Code

The OnInitDialog member function is called by the framework after the CSettings object has been created, its window handle has been attached, but before the dialog is displayed to the user. Most of the initialization pertinent to the dialog's controls (i.e., their initial settings) and the creation of any other objects (such as the settings dialog font) are performed in this member function. We also perform the translation of all of the measurements of the dynamic controls in this member function so that it is performed only once. The code for the OnInitDialog member function is as follows:

```
BOOL CSettings::OnInitDialog()
{
   //
   // compute the position and size of the
   // dialog window's border.
   //
   RECT rClient;
   GetWindowRect (&m_rFrame);
   GetClientRect (&rClient);
   RectSub (m_rFrame, rClient);

   //
   // select all of the accounts for this report
   //
   CDialog::OnInitDialog();
   POSITION pos = m_Accounts.GetHeadPosition();
   while (pos != NULL)
   {
      //
      // all accounts are selected by default
      //
      CAcctObj* pAcct = (CAcctObj *)m_Accounts.GetNext(pos);
      pAcct->SetAcctStatus (ACCT_SELECTED);
   }
   m_DialogTitle.SetWindowText (m_szDialogTitle);
   m_PeriodList.SetCurSel (0);// select Year-To-Date

   //
   // create a new font to use within the dialog
   //
   CClientDC* client = new CClientDC(this);
   int nHeight;
   nHeight = MulDiv (client->GetDeviceCaps (LOGPIXELSY), 8,72);
```

```cpp
    delete client;
    m_pSettingsFont = new CFont;
    m_pSettingsFont->CreateFont (-nHeight, 0, 0, 0, FW_BOLD,
        0, 0, 0, ANSI_CHARSET, OUT_DEFAULT_PRECIS,
        CLIP_DEFAULT_PRECIS, DEFAULT_QUALITY,
        DEFAULT_PITCH | FF_SWISS, "MS Sans Serif");

    //
    // convert ShortDialog and LongDialog to window coordinates.
    //
    Dlu2Pix (m_rShortDialog, rShortDialog);
    RectAdd (m_rShortDialog, m_rFrame);
    Dlu2Pix (m_rLongDialog, rLongDialog);
    RectAdd (m_rLongDialog, m_rFrame);

    //
    // set dialog as not expanded and convert all of the
    // DLU settings in the RECT variables to pixels.
    //
    m_bExpanded = FALSE;
    Dlu2Pix (m_rOptionsBox, rOptionsBox);
    Dlu2Pix (m_rTypeLabel, rTypeLabel);
    Dlu2Pix (m_rTypeCombo, rTypeCombo);
    Dlu2Pix (m_rAllRadio, rAllRadio);
    Dlu2Pix (m_rNoneRadio, rNoneRadio);
    Dlu2Pix (m_rTaxRelatedRadio, rTaxRelatedRadio);
    Dlu2Pix (m_rCategoryList, rCategoryList);
    Dlu2Pix (m_rTextString, rTextString);
    Dlu2Pix (m_rStartsRadio, rStartsRadio);
    Dlu2Pix (m_rContainsRadio, rContainsRadio);
    Dlu2Pix (m_rExactRadio, rExactRadio);

    //
    // now, resize the current dialog, just so that
    // when it's contracted once again it will be the
    // same size, and then set the initial options.
    //
    m_rWindow = m_rShortDialog;
    MoveWindow (&m_rWindow, FALSE);
    m_nPrevOptionType = -1; // no previous options
    m_nPrevCatRadio  = IDC_ALL_RADIO; // all categories
    m_nPrevDescRadio = IDC_STARTS_RADIO; // starts with radio
    m_nPrevInfoRadio = IDC_STARTS_RADIO; // starts with radio

    //
    // if report is "Net Worth Report", then hide the "Options"
    // button and also the "From Date" combo box and its label.
    //
    if (m_Title == "Net Worth Report")
    {
        m_Options.ShowWindow (SW_HIDE);
        GetDlgItem (IDC_FROM)->ShowWindow (SW_HIDE);
        GetDlgItem (IDC_FROM_LABEL)->ShowWindow (SW_HIDE);
    }

    //
    // return to Windows
    //
    return TRUE;
}
```

The foregoing code performs a number of functions, prior to the display
of the dialog to the user. The first section of code computes the width
and height of the dialog's border by accessing the position and dimen-

sions of the frame (which includes the border), accessing the position and dimensions of the client area of the dialog (which excludes the border) and then subtracting the client area from the frame area, leaving the position and dimensions of the border. The results of the subtraction are saved into the `m_rFrame` member variable.

The next section of code is essentially unchanged from the version presented in Chapter 8. All of the account entries currently defined are selected for inclusion in the report (no matter which report). Of course, the user can change this by clicking the Accounts button and then selecting the accounts he or she wishes to include.

Following the selection of accounts, the new font is created. This font is specified to be an 8-point bold MS Sans Serif font that is compatible with the user's display adapter. If you look at the properties of the Settings dialog in the App Studio editor, you will find that this is the same font used for defining the static controls in the dialog. Because we wish for the optional controls to have the same appearance as the others, we will use the font for any text associated with the new controls.

After the font has been created, we convert the measurements of the short and long dialogs to pixels and then add the position and dimensions of the border to each by using the RectAdd member function.

The next section in the OnInitDialog member function translates the measurements of all of the controls from dialog units to pixels, in preparation for placing those controls onto the dialog, when necessary.

The dialog is resized and repositioned according to the settings for the short dialog. Even though the dialog is in its shortened form when it is first created, we resize and reposition it so that any small differences in size or position won't be noticed by the user when the dialog is expanded or contracted during its use. The initial values of previous radio button settings are also defined.

The final section of code in the OnInitDialog member function, prior to returning control to the framework, is executed only in case the Net Worth report was requested. In that case, we wish to hide the Options button and the edit box control for the beginning of the reporting period, as well as its static text label. After this section of code, the member function returns a TRUE result to the framework.

DoDataExchange Member Function Code

The DoDataExchange member function is called by the framework when the OnInitDialog member function for the CDialog class is called, at the beginning of our override of that member function in the CSettings class. The base class member function creates the dialog, based upon the dialog template resource, and then calls the UpdateData member function with a FALSE argument (which causes the DoDataExchange member function to be called to transfer member variables from the CSettings object to the corresponding controls in the dialog).

The reverse procedure occurs when the user dismisses the dialog. The values of the controls are transferred back to the corresponding member variables (and are validated). The code for the DoDataExchange member function, as created by the ClassWizard, is as follows:

```
void CSettings::DoDataExchange(CDataExchange* pDX)
{
   CDialog::DoDataExchange(pDX);
   //{{AFX_DATA_MAP(CSettings)
   DDX_Control(pDX, IDC_OPTIONS, m_Options);
   DDX_Control(pDX, IDC_PER_LIST, m_PeriodList);
   DDX_Control(pDX, IDC_ACCTS_BUTTON, m_AcctsButton);
   DDX_Control(pDX, IDC_DIALOG_TITLE, m_DialogTitle);
   DDX_DateCheck(pDX, IDC_FROM, m_From);
   DDX_Text(pDX, IDC_TITLE, m_Title);
   DDX_DateCheck(pDX, IDC_TO, m_To);
   //}}AFX_DATA_MAP
}
```

Message Map Code

The code generated for the message map and for our own manually added message map entries is as follows:

```
BEGIN_MESSAGE_MAP(CSettings, CDialog)
   //{{AFX_MSG_MAP(CSettings)
   ON_CBN_SELCHANGE(IDC_PER_LIST, OnPerListSelect)
   ON_BN_CLICKED(IDC_ACCTS_BUTTON, OnAcctsClicked)
   ON_BN_CLICKED(IDC_OPTIONS, OnOptions)
   ON_WM_DESTROY()
   //}}AFX_MSG_MAP

   // standard control messages

   ON_CBN_SELCHANGE(IDC_TYPE_COMBO, OnTypeSelect)

   // category control messages

   ON_LBN_SELCHANGE(IDC_CATEGORY_LIST, OnCatSelect)
   ON_BN_CLICKED(IDC_ALL_RADIO, OnCatRadio)
   ON_BN_CLICKED(IDC_NONE_RADIO, OnCatRadio)
   ON_BN_CLICKED(IDC_TAX_RELATED_RADIO, OnCatRadio)

   // description & info control messages

   ON_EN_KILLFOCUS(IDC_EDIT_TEXT_STRING, OnStringEntry)
   ON_BN_CLICKED(IDC_STARTS_RADIO, OnContentsRadio)
   ON_BN_CLICKED(IDC_CONTAINS_RADIO, OnContentsRadio)
   ON_BN_CLICKED(IDC_EXACT_RADIO, OnContentsRadio)

END_MESSAGE_MAP()
```

In addition to the code within the section managed by the ClassWizard, we have included message map entries for each of the controls that can generate a message of interest. For ease of maintenance, we have placed the manually added message map entries into sections pertinent to the various option type control groupings.

The next section of the source file contains the message handler code and associated helper member functions. This section begins as follows:

```
//////////////////////////////////////////////////////////////////
// CSettings message handlers
```

OnPerListSelect Message Handler Code

The code for the OnPerListSelect message handler is identical to what was shown in Chapter 8. It is included here for sake of completeness only. The code is as follows:

```
void CSettings::OnPerListSelect()
{
   POINT cQtr[4] = {{1,3}, {4,6}, {7,9}, {10,12}};
   CTime curTime = CTime::GetCurrentTime();
   CTime fromTime, toTime;
   int nYr = curTime.GetYear();
   int nMo = curTime.GetMonth();
   int nDy = curTime.GetDay();
   int nSel = m_PeriodList.GetCurSel();
   switch (nSel)
   {
     case YEAR_TO_DATE:
     {
        fromTime = CTime(nYr, 1, 1, 0, 0, 0);
        toTime = curTime;
        break;
     }
     case CURRENT_MONTH:
     {
        fromTime = CTime(nYr, nMo, 1, 0, 0, 0);
        toTime = CTime(nYr, nMo, monthDays[nMo-1], 0, 0, 0);
        break;
     }
     case CURRENT_QUARTER:
     {
        int nQ = (nMo + 2)/3;
        fromTime = CTime(nYr, cQtr[nQ-1].x, 1, 0, 0, 0);
        toTime = CTime(nYr, cQtr[nQ-1].y,
           monthDays[cQtr[nQ-1].y-1], 0, 0, 0);
        break;
     }
     case CURRENT_YEAR:
     {
        fromTime = CTime(nYr, 1, 1, 0, 0, 0);
        toTime = CTime(nYr, 12, 31, 0, 0, 0);
        break;
     }
     case LAST_MONTH:
     {
        nMo--;
```

```
                    if (nMo == 0)
                    {
                       nMo = 12;
                       nYr--;
                    }
                    fromTime = CTime(nYr, nMo, 1, 0, 0, 0);
                    toTime = CTime(nYr, nMo, monthDays[nMo-1], 0, 0, 0);
                    break;
                }
                case LAST_QUARTER:
                {
                    int nQ = (nMo + 2) / 3 - 1;
                    if (nQ == 0)
                    {
                       nQ = 4;
                       nYr--;
                    }
                    fromTime = CTime(nYr, cQtr[nQ-1].x, 1, 0, 0, 0);
                    toTime = CTime(nYr, cQtr[nQ-1].y,
                       monthDays[cQtr[nQ-1].y-1], 0, 0, 0);
                    break;
                }
                case LAST_YEAR:
                {
                    nYr--;
                    fromTime = CTime(nYr, 1, 1, 0, 0, 0);
                    toTime = CTime(nYr, 12, 31, 0, 0, 0);
                    break;
                }
                case ALL_TRANSACTIONS:
                {
                    fromTime = CTime (1990, 1, 1, 0, 0, 0);
                    toTime = CTime (1999, 12, 31, 0, 0, 0);
                    break;
                }
         }
         m_From = fromTime.Format ("%m/%d/%y");
         m_To = toTime.Format ("%m/%d/%y");
         GetDlgItem (IDC_FROM)->SetWindowText (m_From);
         GetDlgItem (IDC_TO)->SetWindowText (m_To);
}
```

OnAcctsClicked Message Handler Code

The OnAcctsClicked message handler is identical to the code shown in
Chapter 8 and is included here for the sake of completeness only. The
code is as follows:

```
void CSettings::OnAcctsClicked()
{
   CSelectedAccts dlg;

   //
   // store account objects in selected dialog's list
   //
   POSITION pos = m_Accounts.GetHeadPosition();
   while (pos != NULL)
   {
      CAcctObj* pAcct = (CAcctObj *)m_Accounts.GetNext(pos);
      CAcctObj* pObj  = new CAcctObj (pAcct);
      dlg.m_Selected.AddTail ((CObject *)pObj);
   }
```

```cpp
    if (dlg.DoModal() == IDOK)
    {
      //
      // process list of modified selections
      //
      POSITION nPos1 = dlg.m_Selected.GetHeadPosition();
      while (nPos1 != NULL)
      {
        CAcctObj* pObj;
        pObj = (CAcctObj *)dlg.m_Selected.GetNext(nPos1);
        WORD nID = pObj->GetAcctID();
        POSITION nPos2 = m_Accounts.GetHeadPosition();
        while (nPos2 != NULL)
        {
          //
          // find matching account and change its status
          //
          CAcctObj* pAcct;
          pAcct = (CAcctObj *)m_Accounts.GetNext(nPos2);
          if (pAcct->GetAcctID() == nID)
          {
            pAcct->SetAcctStatus(pObj->GetAcctStatus());
            break;
          }
        }
        delete pObj;
      }
      dlg.m_Selected.RemoveAll();
    }
    else
    {
      //
      // the user cancelled the dialog, so just delete
      // all of the copies of the account entries.
      //
      POSITION nPos3 = dlg.m_Selected.GetHeadPosition();
      while (nPos3 != NULL)
      {
        CAcctObj* pSel;
        pSel = (CAcctObj *)dlg.m_Selected.GetNext(nPos3);
        delete pSel;
      }
      dlg.m_Selected.RemoveAll();
    }
}
```

The next section of code in the **settings.cpp** source file contains the helper routines for the various message handler member functions. The section begins as follows:

```cpp
//////////////////////////////////////////////////////////////
// Settings Options Helper Functions
//
```

DeleteStdControls Member Function Code

When the Settings dialog is expanded and the user clicks the Hide Options, OK, or Cancel buttons, we need to delete the controls that currently occupy the expanded area of the dialog. One set of these is what we term the "Standard Controls," which includes the Options group box, the Type label, and the Type combo box controls. These are deleted separately from the ones that are unique to a particular option type selection. The code for this member function is all newly added and is as follows:

```cpp
void CSettings::DeleteStdControls (void)
{
   if (m_Title == "Cash Flow Report")
   {
      //
      // delete the standard controls
      //
      delete m_pOptionsBox;
      delete m_pTypeLabel;
      m_pTypeCombo->ResetContent();
      delete m_pTypeCombo;
   }
}
```

In addition to deleting the group box and static text label controls, we also remove the contents of the combo box before deleting the control in the foregoing code.

DeleteOptControls Member Function Code

The optional controls are deleted by the DeleteOptControls member function. The code is all newly added and is as follows:

```cpp
void CSettings::DeleteOptControls (void)
{
   if (!m_bExpanded || m_nPrevOptionType == -1)
   {
      // if dialog isn't expanded or we haven't yet
      // installed controls, just return.

      return;
   }

   if (m_Title == "Cash Flow Report")
   {
      switch (m_nPrevOptionType)
      {
         case 0:// Categories Options
         {
            delete m_pAllRadio;
            delete m_pNoneRadio;
            delete m_pTaxRelatedRadio;
            m_pCategoryList->ResetContent();
            delete m_pCategoryList;
            break;
         }
         case 1:// Description Options
         case 2:// Info Options
         {
            delete m_pTextString;
            delete m_pStartsRadio;
            delete m_pContainsRadio;
```

```
            delete m_pExactRadio;
            break;
        }
    }
  }
}
```

Because the foregoing member function may be called when the dialog is not expanded, or when the dialog is first expanded and no previous controls occupy the expanded region, we must test these conditions before deleting nonexistent controls. Note that deletion of the two configurations of controls is handled by specifying the three cases within a switch statement. Because the same controls are used for both the Description and Info options, both of those cases are handled by a single section of code.

FindCategory Member Function Code

The FindCategory member function is used to locate the position of a CCategory object within the specified CObList object by comparing the name returned by the object's GetCatName member function with the name specified in the string variable argument. If a match is found, then the position of that value is stored into the pos variable and a pointer to the CCategory object is returned; otherwise, the position value is undefined and the return value is NULL. The code is newly added, as follows:

```
CCategory* CSettings::FindCategory (CObList& List,
  CString& szName, POSITION& pos)
{
  CCategory* pCat;
  POSITION nPos = List.GetHeadPosition();
  while (nPos != NULL)
  {
    pos = nPos;
    pCat = (CCategory *)List.GetNext (nPos);
    if (pCat->GetCatName() == szName)
    {
      return pCat;
    }
  }
  return NULL;
}
```

AddCategories Member Function Code

The AddCategories member function is used to initialize the dialog's list box with the names of all of the defined categories. The code is newly added and is as follows:

```
void CSettings::AddCategories (CListBox* pList)
{
  ASSERT (pList != NULL);
```

```
    POSITION pos = m_pDoc->m_CatList.GetHeadPosition();
    while (pos != NULL)
    {
       CCategory* pCat;
       pCat = (CCategory *)m_pDoc->m_CatList.GetNext(pos);
       pList->AddString (pCat->GetCatName());
    }
    SelectCategories (pList, m_nPrevCatRadio);
}
```

In addition to adding all of the category names to the dialog's list box,
the foregoing member function calls the SelectCategories member function, whose code is shown next.

SelectCategories Member Function Code

The SelectCategories member function is used to select the categories in
the dialog's list box that correspond to the current radio button setting.
The code is newly added and is as follows:

```
void CSettings::SelectCategories (CListBox* pList, int nWhich)
{
   ASSERT (pList != NULL);
   CString szName;
   POSITION pos;
   CCategory* pCat;
   m_pDoc->m_ReportCats.RemoveAll();
   int numEntries = pList->GetCount();
   for (int index=0; index < numEntries; index++)
   {
      switch (nWhich)
      {
         case IDC_ALL_RADIO:// select all
         {
            pList->SetSel (index, TRUE);
            pList->GetText (index, szName);
            pCat = FindCategory (m_pDoc->m_CatList, szName, pos);
            ASSERT (pCat != NULL);
            m_pDoc->m_ReportCats.AddTail (pCat);
            break;
         }
         case IDC_NONE_RADIO:// select none
         {
            pList->SetSel (index, FALSE);
            break;
         }
         case IDC_TAX_RELATED_RADIO:// tax-related only
         {
            CString szName;
            pList->GetText (index, szName);
            pCat = FindCategory (m_pDoc->m_CatList, szName, pos);
            ASSERT (pCat != NULL);
            if (pCat->GetTaxable() > 0)
            {
               m_pDoc->m_ReportCats.AddTail (pCat);
               pList->SetSel (index, TRUE);
            }
            else
            {
               pList->SetSel (index, FALSE);
            }
```

```
            break;
        }
    }
}
    pList->SetTopIndex (0);
}
```

The foregoing code handles three conditions, which correspond directly to the three radio buttons in the Category options view. When the appropriate categories have been selected, we reset the list box so that its first item is showing, by using the SetTopIndex member function.

MakeStandardControls Member Function Code

The MakeStandardControls member function is responsible for creating what we have termed the "Standard Controls" for the expanded area of the dialog. These consist of the Options group box, the Type label, and the Type combo box. The code is newly added and is as follows:

```cpp
void CSettings::MakeStandardControls(void)
{
    m_pOptionsBox = new CButton;
    m_pOptionsBox->Create ("Options", WS_CHILD | WS_VISIBLE
        | BS_GROUPBOX, m_rOptionsBox, this, IDC_OPTIONS_BOX);

    m_pTypeLabel = new CStatic;
    m_pTypeLabel->Create ("Type:", WS_CHILD | WS_VISIBLE
        | SS_RIGHT, m_rTypeLabel, this, IDC_TYPE_LABEL);

    m_pTypeCombo = new CComboBox;
    m_pTypeCombo->Create (WS_CHILD | WS_VISIBLE | WS_VSCROLL
        | CBS_DROPDOWNLIST, m_rTypeCombo, this, IDC_TYPE_COMBO);
    m_pTypeCombo->AddString ("Categories");
    m_pTypeCombo->AddString ("Description");
    m_pTypeCombo->AddString ("Info");
    m_pTypeCombo->SetCurSel (0);

    m_pOptionsBox->SetFont (m_pSettingsFont, TRUE);
    m_pTypeLabel->SetFont (m_pSettingsFont,TRUE);
    m_pTypeCombo->SetFont (m_pSettingsFont, TRUE);
}
```

The three controls mentioned previously are created by the foregoing code. We use the font we created to label the controls.[1] In addition to creating the combo box, we load it with entries describing the available options and then select the first option, which happens to be Categories.

---

[1] The font referenced in the SetFont function **must** outlive the existence of the controls. It is very important that the font be created such that it is available should the controls need to be updated by the framework. Windows does not make a copy of this font when it is specified in the member function call. The best approach is to create the font in the OnInitDialog (or in the case of a CFormView window, the OnInitialUpdate) member function and then destroy the font only when the window is being destroyed (e.g., in the OnDestroy member function or the destructor function for the window or dialog object).

After creating each of the controls, we call the SetFont function to cause the text font to be set to the one we created in the OnInitDialog member function (shown on page 359). This will ensure a consistent appearance in all of the controls in the dialog.

In the case of our dialog, the font referenced by the `m_pSettingsFont` variable is destroyed in the OnDestroy member function, which is executed *after* the CWnd object has been removed from the screen. Also, although the child window controls may exist at the time the OnDestroy member function is called, we make sure to delete any of these in the extended area of the dialog before we destroy the font.

MakeCashFlowControls Member Function Code

The code for the MakeCashFlowControls member function is newly added and is as follows:

```cpp
void CSettings::MakeCashFlowControls (int t)
{
   if (t == m_nPrevOptionType)
   {
      //
      // there was no change, so just return.
      //
      return;
   }

   //
   // delete the previous option's controls and
   // create new controls for this option.
   //
   DeleteOptControls ();
   switch (t)
   {
      case 0: // Categories Options
      {
         m_pAllRadio = new CButton;
         m_pAllRadio->Create ("All", WS_CHILD | WS_VISIBLE
            | BS_AUTORADIOBUTTON, m_rAllRadio, this,
            IDC_ALL_RADIO);

         m_pNoneRadio = new CButton;
         m_pNoneRadio->Create ("None", WS_CHILD | WS_VISIBLE
            | BS_AUTORADIOBUTTON, m_rNoneRadio, this,
            IDC_NONE_RADIO);

         m_pTaxRelatedRadio = new CButton;
         m_pTaxRelatedRadio->Create ("Tax-related Only",
            WS_CHILD | WS_VISIBLE | BS_AUTORADIOBUTTON,
            m_rTaxRelatedRadio, this, IDC_TAX_RELATED_RADIO);

         CheckRadioButton (IDC_ALL_RADIO, IDC_TAX_RELATED_RADIO,
            m_nPrevCatRadio);

         m_pCategoryList = new CListBox;
         m_pCategoryList->Create (WS_CHILD | WS_VISIBLE
            |WS_BORDER | WS_VSCROLL | WS_TABSTOP |LBS_NOTIFY
            | LBS_SORT | LBS_MULTIPLESEL, m_rCategoryList,
            this, IDC_CATEGORY_LIST);
         m_pAllRadio->SetFont (m_pSettingsFont, TRUE);
```

```cpp
      m_pNoneRadio->SetFont (m_pSettingsFont, TRUE);
      m_pTaxRelatedRadio->SetFont (m_pSettingsFont, TRUE);
      m_pCategoryList->SetFont (m_pSettingsFont, TRUE);

      AddCategories (m_pCategoryList);
      break;
   }

   case 1: // Description Options
   case 2: // Info Options
   {
      m_pTextString = new CEdit;
      m_pTextString->Create (WS_CHILD | WS_VISIBLE
         |WS_BORDER |ES_AUTOHSCROLL | ES_LEFT,
         m_rTextString, this, IDC_EDIT_TEXT_STRING);
      m_pStartsRadio = new CButton;
      m_pStartsRadio->Create ("Starts With", WS_CHILD
         | WS_VISIBLE | BS_AUTORADIOBUTTON,
         m_rStartsRadio, this, IDC_STARTS_RADIO);
      m_pContainsRadio = new CButton;
      m_pContainsRadio->Create ("Contains", WS_CHILD
         | WS_VISIBLE | BS_AUTORADIOBUTTON,
         m_rContainsRadio, this, IDC_CONTAINS_RADIO);
      m_pExactRadio = new CButton;
      m_pExactRadio->Create ("Equals Exactly", WS_CHILD
         | WS_VISIBLE | BS_AUTORADIOBUTTON, m_rExactRadio,
         this, IDC_EXACT_RADIO);

      m_pTextString->SetFont (m_pSettingsFont, TRUE);
      m_pStartsRadio->SetFont (m_pSettingsFont, TRUE);
      m_pContainsRadio->SetFont (m_pSettingsFont, TRUE);
      m_pExactRadio->SetFont (m_pSettingsFont, TRUE);

      if (t == 1)
      {
         CheckRadioButton (IDC_STARTS_RADIO,
            IDC_EXACT_RADIO, m_nPrevDescRadio);
         m_pTextString->SetWindowText(m_pDoc
            ->m_szDescription);
         m_pTextString->SetSel (0, -1, FALSE);
      }
      else
      {
         CheckRadioButton (IDC_STARTS_RADIO, IDC_EXACT_RADIO,
            m_nPrevInfoRadio);
         m_pTextString->SetWindowText (m_pDoc->m_szInfo);
         m_pTextString->SetSel (0, -1, FALSE);
      }
      break;
   }
   default:
   {
      ASSERT (FALSE);
      break;
   }
   }
   m_nPrevOptionType = t;
}
```

The foregoing code is divided into a case for each of the option types.
Controls are created and initialized, as required. When the creation of
controls is complete, the new option type, passed to the member function in the variable named t, is stored into the m_nPrevOptionType

member variable, from which it can be referenced by other member functions.

One of the first actions in the foregoing code is to test whether the new option type is the same as the previous option. In that case we needn't perform any operations and can return immediately. If the option type is different from the previous selection, we call the DeleteOptControls member function to delete the previously installed controls, and then we create controls that are appropriate to the new option type.

OnOptions Message Handler

The next section of code in the **settings.cpp** source file is the code for the OnOptions message handler function. This handler gains control when the user clicks the Options button (no matter whether its caption reads Options or Hide Options). The Options button, which we defined within the App Studio dialog editor as IDC_OPTIONS, sends the message ON_BN_CLICKED when the button is clicked. The handler receives control by virtue of the message map entry that specifies the OnOptions member function be invoked for that action. The code for this handler is newly added and is as follows:

```
void CSettings::OnOptions()
{
   if (!m_bExpanded)
   {
      //
      // window is not expanded, so change it back
      // to its long (expanded) form.
      //
      m_rWindow = m_rLongDialog;
      MoveWindow (&m_rWindow);

      //
      // determine which report type we're creating
      // and then set up the additional controls
      // for that report.
      //
      if (m_Title == "Cash Flow Report")
      {
         MakeStandardControls();
         MakeCashFlowControls(0);
      }

      //
      // change Options button to say "Hide Options"
      // and set expanded flag to TRUE.
      //
      m_Options.SetWindowText ("Hide Options");
      m_bExpanded = TRUE;
   }
   else
   {
      //
      // window is expanded, so delete the current
      // controls and then change the dialog back
      // to its short (contracted) form.
```

```
        if (m_Title == "Cash Flow Report")
    {
      DeleteStdControls();
      DeleteOptControls();
    }
    m_rWindow = m_rShortDialog;
    MoveWindow (&m_rWindow);

    //
    // change Options button to say "Options...",
    // set expanded flag to FALSE, and set the
    // previous option type to -1.
    //
    m_Options.SetWindowText ("Options...");
    m_bExpanded = FALSE;
    m_nPrevOptionType = -1;
  }
}
```

The foregoing OnOptions message handler code has two sections. The first section is executed if the dialog is not already expanded, and the second section is executed if the dialog is already expanded.

In the first case, we need to change the size of the dialog to the larger, expanded version. This is accomplished by setting the value of the `m_rWindow` member variable to the dimensions contained in the `m_rLongDialog` variable and then calling the MoveWindow member function to change the window's size. If you recall, we initialized both the `m_rLongDialog` and `m_rShortDialog` variables to the dimensions of the long and short dialogs, respectively, in the OnInitDialog member function. After expanding the dialog, we can call the MakeStandardControls and MakeCashFlowControls member functions if the current settings will apply to the creation of the Cash Flow report.

If some other report is being prepared, we do not create any controls in this section of the code. Just to refresh your memory, in the case of the Net Worth report, we have hidden the Options button, so we couldn't have received a message pertaining to that report in this handler, but the logic is set up to make provision for creating different sets of controls, to supply settings for report types that we might add in the future.

When the controls have been set up, we change the caption of the Options button from "Options..." to "Hide Options." Therefore, when the dialog is expanded, the user is provided with the feedback that when the button is clicked, the options section of the dialog will be deleted and the dialog will be reduced to its shorter dimensions.

In the second case, where the dialog is already expanded, we determine whether options were being set for the Cash Flow report, and if so, we call the DeleteStdControls and DeleteOptControls member functions to delete the controls. In any case, we change the size of the dialog to the dimensions held in the `m_rShortDialog` rectangle, and then change the caption of the button to read "Options..." We also set the value of the `m_nPrevOptionType` variable to -1, indicating that no options have been set.

In both of the foregoing cases, we set the value of the `m_bExpanded` variable to indicate whether the dialog has been expanded or shortened.

Settings Dialog OnDestroy Handler

When the user dismisses the dialog, by clicking either the OK or Cancel button, the framework calls the OnDestroy handler to dispose of any resources that were allocated while the dialog was running.

In our case, the dialog may have been expanded at the time the dialog is being dismissed, and so we need to delete the controls that occupy the expanded area of the dialog. Whether or not the dialog is expanded at this point, we also dispose of the font we created in the OnInitDialog member function. The code for the OnDestroy handler is newly added and is as follows:

```
void CSettings::OnDestroy()
{
   CDialog::OnDestroy();
   if (m_bExpanded)
   {
      //
      // first, delete the standard controls
      //
      DeleteStdControls();

      //
      // now, delete the controls that currently
      // occupy the options area of the expanded
      // dialog box.
      //
      DeleteOptControls();
   }
   delete m_pSettingsFont;
}
```

Settings Dialog Dynamic Message Handlers

In addition to the message handlers that we defined through the use of the ClassWizard tool, we also added message handler entries, manually, to the message map, in order to process messages associated with the various controls in the expanded options section of the Settings dialog. The additional message map entries are shown on page 362. The sections that follow show the code and describe the functions of each of the newly added message handlers.

OnTypeSelect Message Handler Code

When the user selects one of the options from the Type combo box, the
OnTypeSelect message handler gains control to perform whatever actions are appropriate to that selection. The code for this message handler
is newly added and is as follows:

```
void CSettings::OnTypeSelect()
{
    int nType = m_pTypeCombo->GetCurSel();
    MakeCashFlowControls (nType);
}
```

In the foregoing message handler, we need only access the index of the
current selection from the combo box and then call the MakeCashFlow-
Controls member function with that index value. As described previously (see page 370), the MakeCashFlowControls member function
deletes any currently installed controls in the expanded portion of the dialog, and then installs the controls appropriate to the new option type.
Because the Type combo box is standard to all of the Cash Flow report
options, it remains available to be used as long as the dialog is expanded.

OnCatSelect Message Handler Code

The OnCatSelect message handler is invoked when the Categories options are in effect and the user double clicks to select (or deselect) a specific category name in the list box. The code for this message handler is
newly added and is as follows:

```
void CSettings::OnCatSelect()
{
    CCategory* pCat;
    POSITION pos;

    // access the list box and get the current item,
    // determine whether it is selected, and get its
    // text string.

    CString szCategory;
    int nSel = m_pCategoryList->GetCurSel();
    int nSS  = m_pCategoryList->GetSel(nSel);
    ASSERT (nSS != LB_ERR);
    m_pCategoryList->GetText (nSel, szCategory);

    // search the document's "m_ReportCats" list for
    // a category object whose name matches and then
    // either add or remove the new selection.

    pCat = FindCategory (m_pDoc->m_ReportCats, szCategory, pos);
    if (nSS > 0)
    {
        // the item was newly selected, so it shouldn't
        // have been found in the setting's list. Find
        // it in the main category list.
```

```
        ASSERT (pCat == NULL);
        pCat = FindCategory (m_pDoc->m_CatList, szCategory, pos);
        ASSERT (pCat != NULL);
        m_pDoc->m_ReportCats.AddTail (pCat);
    }
    else
    {
        // item was deselected, so it should have
        // been found in the document's m_ReportCats
        // list. Delete it from that list.

        ASSERT (pCat != NULL);
        m_pDoc->m_ReportCats.RemoveAt (pos);
    }
}
```

The foregoing code obtains the index of the item that was double clicked (single clicks do not cause the selection status to change, although they do cause the highlight to appear or disappear) and then accesses the selection status of the item at the indexed position in the list box. The handler calls the FindCategory helper function to access the pointer to the CCategory object, as well as its position in the separate list of report-specific categories. (While the contents of the list box are sorted in alphabetic sequence, automatically, by the framework, the CCategory objects in the list are stored in the order in which the objects were created.) Depending upon the value of the selection status, the execution of the remainder of the member function takes one of two courses.

If the item is newly selected (i.e., the selection status is greater than 0), then we verify (via an assertion) that the object pointer returned by the FindCategory member function is NULL. The foregoing assertion being TRUE (otherwise a program error has occurred), the handler looks up the CCategory object in the document's list of categories, makes sure that the object pointer returned is not NULL, and then appends the pointer to the end of the list of report categories.

If the item is newly deselected, then the handler verifies that the pointer returned from the original search of report-specific categories is not NULL. The object is removed from that list by using the position value returned in the pos variable in a call to the CObList class's RemoveAt member function.

OnCatRadio Message Handler Code

The OnCatRadio handler is called when the Categories options are in effect and the user clicks any one of the All, None, or Tax-related Only radio buttons. The code for this handler is as follows:

```
void CSettings::OnCatRadio()
{
    int nWhich;
    nWhich = GetCheckedRadioButton (IDC_ALL_RADIO,
```

```
            IDC_TAX_RELATED_RADIO);
    SelectCategories (m_pCategoryList, nWhich);
    m_nPrevCatRadio = nWhich;
}
```

The foregoing code calls the CWnd class's GetCheckedRadioButton to ascertain which radio button was clicked and then calls the SelectCategories helper function with the radio button's identifier to select or deselect the appropriate categories.

If the All button was clicked, then the result is that all categories in the list box will be selected and all will be entered into the report categories list. If None was clicked, then all categories are deselected (and removed) from the report categories list. If the Tax-related Only button was clicked, then each of the document's category objects is examined to determine whether its tax-related status is nonzero, and if so, the category is added to the list of report categories.

In any case, the `m_nPrevCatRadio` member variable is updated with the currently selected button's identifier so that if some other set of options is selected and then the Categories option is reselected, the appropriate button and its implied list of categories can be restored.

MakeTextSettings Helper Member Function Code

When either the Description or Info option type is chosen, the actions taken, whether text has been entered into the text box control or any of the radio buttons (Starts With, Contains, or Equals Exactly) is clicked, are identical. Because of this, we have merged all of the code for the actions into a single helper function, which is called by both the OnString-Entry and OnContentsRadio message handlers. The code for this helper function is as follows:

```
void CSettings::MakeTextSettings()
{
   CString  szText;
   CString  szType;
   TInclude Include;
   int nWhich;

   //
   // determine which radio button is checked and then set
   // the "Include" variable to reflect the corresponding
   // inclusion setting.
   //
   nWhich = GetCheckedRadioButton (IDC_STARTS_RADIO,
      IDC_EXACT_RADIO);
   switch (nWhich)
   {
      case IDC_STARTS_RADIO:
      {
         Include = startsWith;
         break;
      }
```

```
         case IDC_CONTAINS_RADIO:
         {
            Include = contains;
            break;
         }
         case IDC_EXACT_RADIO:
         {
            Include = equals;
            break;
         }
         default:
         {
            Include = all;
            break;
         }
      }

      //
      // determine which field (Description or Info) is being
      // referenced, set the inclusion condition to "all" if
      // the text string is empty, or set the inclusion condition
      // to correspond to the radio button setting.
      // (Note: An empty string specifies inclusion of all values.)
      //
      m_pTextString->GetWindowText (szText);
      int index = m_pTypeCombo->GetCurSel();
      m_pTypeCombo->GetLBText (index, szType);
      if (szType == "Description")
      {
         if (szText == "")
         {
            m_pDoc->m_eDescInclude = all;
         }
         else
         {
            m_pDoc->m_eDescInclude = Include;
         }
         m_nPrevDescRadio = nWhich;
         m_pDoc->m_szDescription = szText;
      }
      else if (szType == "Info")
      {
         if (szText == "")
         {
            m_pDoc->m_eInfoInclude = all;
         }
         else
         {
            m_pDoc->m_eInfoInclude = Include;
         }
         m_nPrevInfoRadio = nWhich;
         m_pDoc->m_szInfo = szText;
      }
   }
```

The first step in handling either the completion of a text entry, which is
signaled by the text box control losing focus (i.e., the receipt of the
ON_KILLFOCUS message), or the receipt of the ON_BN_CLICKED message
from any of the three radio buttons, is to determine which radio button
is selected currently. Note that in the case statements that we set a variable called Include to the value startsWith, contains, equals,

or `all`. Each of these values is defined in an enumerated type definition that we will show you shortly.

After the current radio button selection has been determined, then the handler must determine whether the Description or Info option is selected currently.

In the case of the Description option, if the contents of the text box are empty, then we set the value of the document's `m_eDescInclude` variable to `all`; otherwise, the value in the local variable named `Include` is stored into the document's `m_eDescInclude` variable. This preserves the inclusion criteria as it currently stands so that the report can be prepared according to the user's wishes. In addition to setting the inclusion criteria into a member variable in the document, we also store the current radio button selection and the contents of the text box into member variables in the document. These are updated with each new selection so that the report will reflect the latest settings when the dialog is dismissed.

In the case of the Info option, we also determine whether the contents of the text box are empty, and if so, we set the document's inclusion status variable for the Info field (`m_eInfoInclude`) to `all`. If the text box contains some text, then the document's inclusion status is set to the value held in the local `Include` variable. In either case, the current radio button setting and the contents of the text box are written into the document's member variables for the Info option.

OnStringEntry Message Handler Code

As described previously, when the text box loses focus, then the message handler named OnStringEntry is invoked. The code for this handler is newly added and is as follows:

```
void CSettings::OnStringEntry()
{
    MakeTextSettings();
}
```

As is evident in the foregoing code, we handle the message by calling the MakeTextSettings helper function, described previously.

OnContentsRadio Message Handler Code

As with the OnStringEntry message handler, when any of the radio buttons associated with either the Description or Info text options is clicked, the OnContentsRadio handler is invoked via the message map entry. The code for this handler is newly added and is as follows:

```
void CSettings::OnContentsRadio()
{
   MakeTextSettings();
}
```

As with the OnStringEntry message handler, the foregoing code calls the MakeTextSettings helper function to perform all of the operations relevant to the selection of an inclusion criteria.

KeepType.h Header File Contents

In order to support the inclusion criteria expressed as mnemonic values that can be referenced by several different source files, we found that defining these in one of the normal header files didn't make the definitions sufficiently visible to all of the source files. In addition, because we wanted to define another new type, we decided to create a separate header file to contain these definitions and then import that file into the **stdafx.h** header file so that the definitions will be precompiled and available to all of the source files. If we decide to add other new data types, we will be able to do so easily, by adding them to the **keeptype.h** header file we have constructed. The contents of this header file are all newly created and are as follows:

```
//////////////////////////////////////////////////////////////////
// keeptype.h - type definitions unique to Keepit
//
//

// qualifiers for inclusion of transactions, based
// upon the strings specified in the Settings dialog.
//
enum TInclude
{
   all,
   startsWith,
   contains,
   equals
};

//
// new long RECT structure
//
typedef struct
{
   long left;
   long top;
   long right;
   long bottom;

} longRECT;
```

As is evident in the foregoing, we have defined the TInclude enumerated type to include values of `all`, `startsWith`, `contains`, and `equals`.

These are used in the Settings dialog, member functions in the CKeepit-Doc class, and also member functions in the CReportView class. The longRect structure is used only in the CReportView class, but it seemed convenient to define this along with the types that are specific to the Keepit application.

Just to be complete, the contents of our modified version of the **stdafx.h** header file are as follows:

```
// stdafx.h : include file for standard system include files,
// or project specific include files that are used frequently,
// but are changed infrequently

#include <afxwin.h>      // MFC core and standard components
#include <afxext.h>      // MFC extensions (including VB)
#include "keeptype.h" // types defined specifically for keepit
```

As is evident in the foregoing code, all of the standard MFC components and extensions are precompiled by the inclusion of this file. In addition, we have added our own **keeptype.h** file to be precompiled, as well.

Additions to the CKeepitDoc Class

The structure of the MFC framework includes the concept of the "Document View" architecture. We reiterate this because it is important to structure your applications so that the document is the central repository for your data. In addition to playing that role, the document class creates the various views requested by the user. Although views are sometimes global to an application as a whole, more often views are specific to the data associated with a particular document object. Because of this, we create all of the views for the Keepit application from member functions or message handlers in the CKeepitDoc class. You can have multiple document objects in the Keepit application, and each will be associated with a newly created, untitled account, or a file of data that represents the definition of various accounts, account categories, and the data transactions themselves. Using the foregoing data, we can create temporary sets (or lists) of these that represent the data relevant to a particular report. These data are episodic and remain valid only for the period of time in which the view to which they pertain is being initialized. The data stored for a specific report, in a temporary list, will not interfere with data stored in the same container for a different report.

In order to implement the transmission of data to and from the Settings dialog and the report views, we use variables and object lists in the document object to contain these data. Because the Settings dialog is modal during its execution, the contents of the document's variables and lists are updated during execution of the dialog. When the dialog has been dismissed, if the report is to be generated, the report view is created and the contents of these data are transferred immediately to corresponding member variables in the new view, and then the data are disposed. If the user cancels the dialog, then the data in the temporary variables and lists are disposed.

New views and, specifically, report views, are created by calling the framework's CreateNewFrame and InitialUpdateFrame member functions. The latter member function uses SendMessage to invoke the OnInitialUpdate member function for the new view, directly, thus avoiding any potential conflict that would disturb the contents of the temporary variables and lists.

Because only the report-oriented logic of the CKeepitDoc source file has been modified by the recent additions to the application, we present only those portions that have changed. In the case of the header file, we present the new version in its entirety.

KeepDoc.h Header File Contents

The **keepdoc.h** header file has been revised to include the temporary variables referenced in the foregoing section. In addition, member functions relevant to the creation of the Settings dialog and the various report views have been added. The contents of the **keepdoc.h** file are as follows:

```
// keepdoc.h : interface of the CKeepitDoc class
//
/////////////////////////////////////////////////////////////////////

class CListEntry;
class CAcctList;
class CAcctObj;
class CSettings;

#define ACCOUNT_MENU_POS 3      // fourth menu on menubar
#define CASH_FLOW_REPORT 1      // cash flow detail report
#define NET_WORTH_REPORT 2      // net worth summary report

class CKeepitDoc : public CDocument
{
protected:                      // create from serialization only
    CKeepitDoc();
    DECLARE_DYNCREATE(CKeepitDoc)
    BOOL OnCmdMsg (UINT nID, int nCode, void *pExtra,
        AFX_CMDHANDLERINFO* pHandlerInfo);

    void OnAccountName (UINT nID);
    void OnAccountNameUpdate (UINT nID, CCmdUI* pExtra);

    void DeleteDlgAccts(CSettings& dlg);

// Attributes
public:
```

```
    CObList      m_ListEntries;      // list of entries
    CObList      m_CatList;          // list of category objects
    CObList      m_AcctList;         // list of accounts
    BOOL         m_bFirstTime;       // first time switch
    CString      m_szCurAcctName;    // current account name
    WORD         m_nCurrentAccount;  // current account ID
    int          m_nReportType;      // current report type
    CObList      m_ReportAccts;      // current report accounts
    CTime        m_FromDate;         // beginning of period
    CTime        m_ToDate;           // end of reporting period
    CString      m_szDialogTitle;    // title for settings dialog

    //
    // declarations specific to Settings dialog options
    //
    CObList      m_ReportCats;       // current report catagories
    CString      m_szDescription;    // description qualifier
    TInclude     m_eDescInclude;     // description inclusion
    CString      m_szInfo;           // info qualifier
    TInclude     m_eInfoInclude;     // info inclusion

// Operations
public:

    CListEntry* NewListEntry (void);
    void DeleteListEntry (CListEntry* anEntry);
    void AddListEntry (CListEntry* anEntry);
    void FillAcctList (CAcctList* pList);

// Implementation
public:
    virtual ~CKeepitDoc();
    virtual void Serialize(CArchive& ar);// override
    virtual void DeleteContents(void); // override

    virtual BOOL CanCloseFrame(CFrameWnd* pFrame);// override

#ifdef _DEBUG
    virtual void AssertValid() const;
    virtual void Dump(CDumpContext& dc) const;
#endif

protected:
    BOOL OnNewDocument();// create a new document
    void RemoveAcctMenu (CAcctObj* pAcct);// remove menu command
    void RemoveTransactions (WORD nAcctID);// remove trans.
    void RemoveMDIFrame (CString& szName);// delete named frame

public:
    void AddAcctMenu (CAcctObj* pAcct);// add a menu command
    void SetMenuNames(void);// set account names

// Generated message map functions
protected:
    //{{AFX_MSG(CKeepitDoc)
    afx_msg void OnViewCategories();
    afx_msg void OnAcctEdit();
    afx_msg void OnCashFlow();
    afx_msg void OnNetWorth();
    //}}AFX_MSG
    DECLARE_MESSAGE_MAP()

// report helper member functions
    void ReportSetup (int nReportType);
};
```

The main differences in the foregoing from what was presented in Chapter 8 are the addition of the OnNetWorth message handler, the ReportSetup helper member function (shown at the end of the foregoing declarations), and the declarations specific to Settings dialog options. Other declarations related to the creation of reports were shown previously. We have indicated the changes to the version of the **keepdoc.h** file presented previously by placing change bars at the left of the newly added lines.

KeepDoc.cpp Source File Additions

As indicated previously, we are including only the member functions that have been modified or added to this version of the application in the following sections. Aside from these, all of the code and descriptions included in earlier chapters still apply (unless otherwise indicated). The source file changes are generally related to the invocation and postprocessing of data associated with the Settings dialog, and also the creation of both the Cash Flow and NetWorth report views.

CKeepitDoc Message Map Code

Due to the addition of the Net Worth command to the Report menu, the message map for the CKeepitDoc class has been expanded. The new contents of this map are as follows:

```
BEGIN_MESSAGE_MAP(CKeepitDoc, CDocument)
  //{{AFX_MSG_MAP(CKeepitDoc)
  ON_COMMAND(ID_VIEW_CATEGORIES, OnViewCategories)
  ON_COMMAND(ID_ACCT_EDIT, OnAcctEdit)
  ON_COMMAND(ID_RPT_CASH_FLOW, OnCashFlow)
  ON_COMMAND(ID_RPT_NET_WORTH, OnNetWorth)
  //}}AFX_MSG_MAP
END_MESSAGE_MAP()
```

The only difference in the foregoing from what was shown in Chapter 8 is the addition of the entry for the ID_RPT_NET_WORTH command.

DeleteDlgAccts Member Function Code

Because the DeleteDlgAccts member function is germane to the process of disposing the temporary account entries created during operation of the Settings dialog, and although it has been shown already in Chapter 8 (see page 277), we show it in its entirety, again, as follows:

```
void CKeepitDoc::DeleteDlgAccts(CSettings& dlg)
{
  POSITION pos = dlg.m_Accounts.GetHeadPosition();
  while (pos != NULL)
  {
    CAcctObj* pObj = (CAcctObj *)dlg.m_Accounts.GetNext (pos);
```

```
        delete pObj;
    }
    dlg.m_Accounts.RemoveAll();
}
```

ReportSetup Member Function Code

Because much of the code related to the Cash Flow and Net Worth reports is common to both, we have transferred much of the code that is shown in Chapter 8, in the OnCashFlow message handler, into a new member function called ReportSetup. If you like, you can refer to the earlier version of this code beginning on page 273.

The new ReportSetup member function discriminates between what must be executed for each report and what can be executed for either report. Because the code is rather lengthy, we will show it in sections. The code for the first section of this member function is as follows:

```
void CKeepitDoc::ReportSetup(int nReportType)
{
    int      nYr, nMo, nDy;
    CSettings    dlg;

    //
    // create a default cash flow report for year-to-date
    // income and expenses in all accounts.
    //
    CTime curTime = CTime::GetCurrentTime();// current time
    nYr = curTime.GetYear();   // current year
    nMo = curTime.GetMonth();  // current month
    nDy = curTime.GetDay();    // current day
    CTime startTime(nYr, 1, 1, 0, 0, 0);// 01/01/current year

    //
    // set dialog member variables to their initial values
    //
    if (nReportType == CASH_FLOW_REPORT)
    {
        dlg.m_szDialogTitle = "Cash Flow Report Settings";
        dlg.m_Title = "Cash Flow Report"; // title
    }
    else if (nReportType == NET_WORTH_REPORT)
    {
        dlg.m_szDialogTitle = "Net Worth Report Settings";
        dlg.m_Title = "Net Worth Report"; // title
    }
    else
    {
        dlg.m_szDialogTitle = "Unknown Report Settings";
        dlg.m_Title = "Unknown Report";
    }
    dlg.m_From = startTime.Format ("%m/%d/%y");// 01/01/yr
    dlg.m_To = curTime.Format ("%m/%d/%y");    // mm/dd/yr
    dlg.m_pDoc = this;
```

The first section of the ReportSetup member function creates the CSettings dialog object on the stack, sets the title appropriate to the report being requested into the dialog's m_Title variable, and then sets the report period dates for the initial appearance of the Settings dialog. The member function continues as follows:

```
//
// create copies of the accounts and load them into the
// dialog's list of accounts.
//
POSITION pos = m_AcctList.GetHeadPosition();
while (pos != NULL)
{
   CAcctObj* pAcct = (CAcctObj *)m_AcctList.GetNext (pos);
   CAcctObj* nAcct = new CAcctObj (pAcct);
   dlg.m_Accounts.AddTail (nAcct);
}
```

The foregoing code makes copies of each of the existing CAcctObj objects and stores the copies into the m_Accounts list in the Settings dialog. The member function continues as follows:

```
//
// initialize the report options variables by
// including all of the categories in the list
// and setting the inclusion criteria to "all"
// for both the Description and Info fields.
//
m_ReportCats.RemoveAll();
pos = m_CatList.GetHeadPosition();
while (pos != NULL)
{
   CCategory* pCat;
   pCat = (CCategory *)m_CatList.GetNext (pos);
   m_ReportCats.AddTail (pCat);
}
m_szDescription = "";
m_eDescInclude = all;
m_szInfo = "";
m_eInfoInclude = all;
```

When the foregoing code has executed, all of the initialization for the Settings dialog has been performed. At this point, the dialog is run and the results of its execution are analyzed, as follows:

```
//
// now we can invoke the dialog to get the settings
//
if (dlg.DoModal() == IDOK)
{
   // convert the from and to dates to CTime objects
   // and verify that the from date is < the to date.

   MakeDateObj (dlg.m_From, m_FromDate);
   MakeDateObj (dlg.m_To,   m_ToDate);
   if (m_FromDate > m_ToDate)
   {
       //
```

```
        // an invalid date span was given. Tell the user,
        // delete the dialog's account objects, and then return.
        //
        AfxMessageBox ("End date must be greater than\
            start date.");
        DeleteDlgAccts (dlg);
        return;
    }

    // the settings are all good, so now we can
    // store them for use by the view.

    m_nReportType = nReportType;
    POSITION nPos = dlg.m_Accounts.GetHeadPosition();
    while (nPos != NULL)
    {
        CAcctObj* pObj;
        pObj = (CAcctObj *)dlg.m_Accounts.GetNext(nPos);
        if (pObj->GetAcctStatus() == ACCT_SELECTED)
        {
            CAcctObj* pRObj = new CAcctObj (pObj);
            m_ReportAccts.AddTail(pRObj);
        }
    }
    DeleteDlgAccts (dlg);
```

The foregoing code runs the modal Settings dialog and then tests
whether the dialog was dismissed with the OK button. If so, then the
code validates the correspondence between the two dates in the reporting
period and if they are invalid issues an appropriate error message and returns without creating the requested report. If the report period is valid,
the code copies the account objects selected by the user into the document's m_ReportAccts list and then deletes all of the entries in the dialog's list by calling the DeleteDlgAccts member function. The code for
the ReportSetup member function continues as follows:

```
    //
    // make sure there's something to display, create
    // a new frame and view in which to display the
    // current report, and then let the view take over.
    //
    if (!m_ReportAccts.IsEmpty())
    {
        CKeepitApp* theApp = (CKeepitApp *)AfxGetApp();
        CMultiDocTemplate* pRptTmp = theApp->m_pRptViewTemplate;
        CFrameWnd* pRptFrame;
        pRptFrame = pRptTmp->CreateNewFrame (this, NULL);
        pRptTmp->InitialUpdateFrame (pRptFrame, this);
    }
}
```

After the settings have been validated, the member function tests
whether the list of accounts is empty. If so, then nothing more is done
and the member function returns without creating a report. If the list is
not empty, then the foregoing code creates a new frame and corresponding view, using a pointer to the document template stored in the

`m_pRptViewTemplate` variable in the CKeepitApp application object. When the creation of the new frame is complete, the view's OnInitial-Update member function is invoked via the call to the template's Initial-UpdateFrame member function. When that call is made and the OnInitialUpdate member function for the CReportView object is called, the specified report is created.

In the case where the user dismisses the Settings dialog by clicking its Cancel button, the ReportSetup member function needs only to delete the entries in the dialog's account list. This is accomplished as follows:

```
else
{
   //
   // delete all of the dialog's account entries
   //
   DeleteDlgAccts(dlg);
}
}
```

The foregoing code is the end of the ReportSetup member function. By combining the common code for both the Cash Flow and Net Worth reports, the message handlers for those two commands are very simple.

OnCashFlow Message Handler Code

The OnCashFlow message handler has been modified and is as follows:

```
void CKeepitDoc::OnCashFlow()
{
   //
   // we need only call the setup routine to get the
   // user's settings and then create the report.
   //
   ReportSetup (CASH_FLOW_REPORT);
}
```

OnNetWorth Message Handler Code

The OnNetWorth message handler is newly added and is as follows:

```
void CKeepitDoc::OnNetWorth()
{
   //
   // we need only call the setup routine to get the
   // user's settings and then create the report.
   //
   ReportSetup (NET_WORTH_REPORT);
}
```

CReportView Class Additions

Quite a number of changes have been made to the various member functions in the CReportView class. Most of the original code remains the same; however, we have added new code to prepare the Net Worth report and also to act upon the new options for the Cash Flow report.

As promised in Chapter 8, we have modified the OnPrint and OnDraw member functions so that printing a large number of pages, on a high-resolution output device, will not be a problem. The size of reports being displayed is still subject to the limitations of 16-bit coordinates; however, for normal 96-dpi vGA screens, reports which are up to 50 display pages can be shown. In order to circumvent the display limitation, the entire concept of the "clipping region" must be overridden with an entirely new design, which is outside the scope of our project.

Because quite a few changes have been made to both the header and source files in this version of the CReportView class, we will show all of the code for both of these files. Changes to previous code will be indicated by the addition of change bars to the affected statements.

ReportView.h Header File Contents

Quite a few new variables and a few new member functions have been added to the header file declarations in the **reportvw.h** file. The contents of this file are as follows:

```
// reportvw.h : header file
//
class CKeepitDoc;
class CListEntry;
class CAcctObj;

/////////////////////////////////////////////////////////////////
// CReportView view

class CReportView : public CScrollView
{
   DECLARE_DYNCREATE(CReportView)
protected:
   CReportView();// protected constructor
                       // used by dynamic creation

// Attributes
public:
   CObList       m_RptEntries;      // report entries
   int           m_nReportType;     // type of report to
display
   CTime         m_FromDate;        // start of period
   CTime         m_ToDate;          // end of period

   CObList       m_ReportCats;      // current report catagories
   CString       m_szDescription;   // description qualifier
   CString       m_szInfo;          // info qualifier
```

```cpp
    TInclude    m_eDescInclude;   // description inclusion
    TInclude    m_eInfoInclude;   // info inclusion type

// Operations
public:
  CKeepitDoc* GetDocument();   // copied from account.h

// Implementation
protected:
  virtual ~CReportView();
  virtual void OnDraw(CDC* pDC); // draw this view
  virtual void OnInitialUpdate();// after construction

  //
  // report view size computation member functions
  //
  CSize CashFlowViewSize ();// compute Cash-Flow view size
  CSize NetWorthViewSize ();// compute Net-Worth view size

  //
  // cash flow helper member functions
  //
  BOOL  MeetsRptCriteria (    // check if transaction meets
      CListEntry* pEntry);    // -- report criteria
  BOOL  MatchStrings (        // match using criteria
      CString szSrc,          // -- source string
      CString szPattern,      // -- pattern string
      TInclude criteria);     // -- inclusion criteria
                              // ---- startsWith
                              // ---- contains
                              // ---- equals
  //
  // net worth helper member functions
  //
  long  ComputeBalance (CAcctObj* p); // compute balance
  long  MakeAcctEntry (int n, int m); // make report entry
  CString MakeValueString (long v);   // return string
  void MakeRptListEntry (int nType,   // make report entry
    CString szLine);

  //
  // general purpose report member functions
  //
  void  SortByDate (CObList& list);   // sort by date

  void RectLPtoPositions (       // convert rect to pos.
    longRECT rectClip,           // -- input longRect
    POSITION& nFirstEntry,       // -- output POSITION
    POSITION& nLastEntry);       // -- output POSITION

  void DrawRptLine (CDC* pDC,    // draw a report line
    CObject* pObj,               // info to draw
    int& nYPos);                 // position in viewport

  void OnPrepareDC (CDC* pDC,    // prepare the device
    CPrintInfo* pInfo = NULL);   // printer info == NULL

  void ComputeRptMetrics (CDC*pDC);// compute report metrics

  //
  // printing-related member functions
  //
  BOOL OnPreparePrinting (CPrintInfo* pInfo);
  void OnBeginPrinting (CDC* pDC, CPrintInfo* pInfo);
  void OnPrint (CDC* pDC, CPrintInfo* pInfo);
  void PrintPageHeader (CDC* pDC, CPrintInfo* pInfo);
```

```cpp
    // Generated message map functions
    //{{AFX_MSG(CReportView)

      afx_msg void OnFilePrint();
      afx_msg void OnFilePrintPreview();
      afx_msg void OnDestroy();
      afx_msg void OnHScroll(UINT nSBCode, UINT nPos,
         CScrollBar* pScrollBar);
      afx_msg void OnVScroll(UINT nSBCode, UINT nPos,
         CScrollBar* pScrollBar);
    //}}AFX_MSG

    DECLARE_MESSAGE_MAP()

//
// report metrics
//
    CString       m_szTitle;          // report title
    CRgn          m_BlankLine;         // region for blank line
    CSize         m_SizeTotal;         // total size of report
    CSize         m_PageSize;          // amount to scroll for page
    CSize         m_LineSize;          // amount to scroll for line
    int           m_nTotalLines;       // total number of lines
    int           m_nLinesPerPage;     // number of lines on a page
    int           m_nLineHeight;       // height of one line
    int           m_nLineWidth;        // maximum width of one line
    int           m_nMinCharWidth;     // minimum character width
    int           m_nAvgCharWidth;     // average character width
    int           m_nMaxCharWidth;     // maximum character width
    int           m_nCurPage;          // current page number
};
////////////////////////////////////////////////////////////////
//
// the following statements were moved from the
// account.h header file, which also needs to
// access the document.
//
#ifndef _DEBUG  // debug version in reportvw.cpp
inline CKeepitDoc* CReportView::GetDocument()
   { return (CKeepitDoc*) m_pDocument; }
#endif
```

The major changes to the foregoing header file include the addition of
the public attributes that contain the current report categories, and the
Description and Info field inclusion types and qualifiers. These provide
access to the newly added options from the Settings dialog for the Cash
Flow report. In addition, we have added the MeetsRptCriteria and the
MatchStrings member functions to aid in the selection of transactions
that meet the report criteria for the Cash Flow report.

We have modified the prototype for the RectLPtoPositions member
function to require a variable of type `longRECT` as its first argument,
rather than the `RECT` that was specified previously. This enables us to
support very long printed reports. See page 380 for the definition of the
`longRECT` data type. All of the other changes are reflected in the source
code of the various member functions.

ReportView.cpp Source File Contents

Many of the member functions in the **reportvw.cpp** source file have been modified in some way, both to support the newly added options and printing methodology and also to implement the Net Worth report. Changes to existing member functions will be indicated by the addition of change bars to the affected statements. Entirely new member functions will be unmarked.

A short discussion of the new printing methodology is appropriate at this point. If you refer to Chapter 8, in the discussion that follows the definition of the OnPrint member function on page 322, you will see that in order to coerce the RectLPtoPositions member function to select the appropriate entries for each page, we moved the viewport origin up by successively larger negative values so that the clipping region passed to the OnDraw member function would reflect a correspondingly large positive value, thus causing the member function to select the appropriate records. This procedure is illustrated for the first two pages of a report by Figure 8-2.

Because the scope of the clipping region is limited by the precision of the 16-bit coordinate values in the `Windows API`,[1] the report size is limited to approximately ten pages on a 300-dpi printer. Although this would be entirely satisfactory for a sample program such as the Keepit application, we expect that you will be creating much more robust applications in the future, and so you will want to know how to circumvent the foregoing limitations. One approach, and the one we have chosen to implement, involves changing the OnPrint member function to use the same clipping region for every page. That is, we won't arbitrarily move the viewport to "fool" the OnDraw logic into passing larger values into the RectLPtoPositions member function. Instead, we will recognize that a report is being printed in the OnDraw member function and *compute* appropriate values to pass to the RectLPtoPositions member function, based upon the clipping `RECT`, the current page number, and the height of a page on the output device. The clipping region, from page to page, is illustrated in Figure 10-1.

As the Figure 10-1 illustrates, the value of the clipping `RECT` does not change from page to page, but the value passed in the `longRECT` argument to the RectLPtoPositions member function does. Because the definition of the `longRECT` data type specifies 32-bit values for the

---

[1]   Note that neither Windows NT, nor future versions of Windows will have this limitation, because the coordinate values used in the device context are stored in 32-bit variables. The 16-bit limitation that we describe is limited to Windows 3.1 and Visual C++ version 1.5, or earlier.

Figure 10-1
Clipping RECT values
for succeeding pages in
newly modified OnPrint
member function

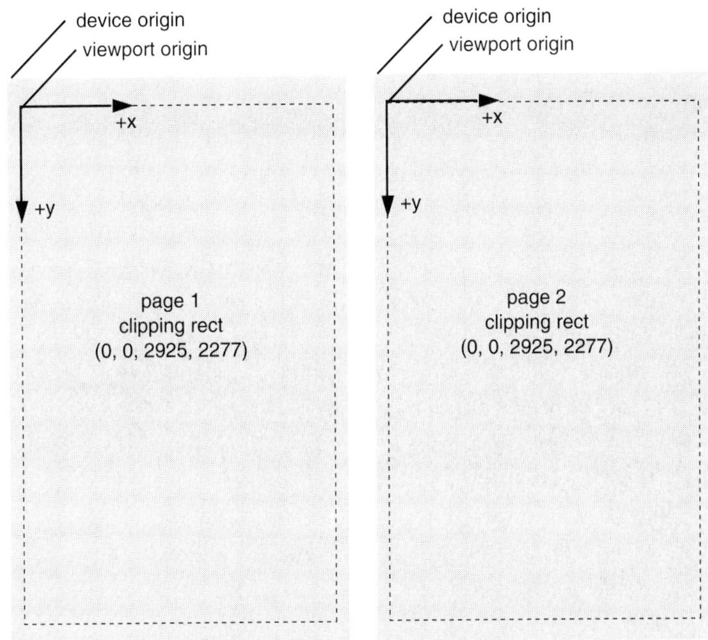

Although the clipping RECT does not change from page to page in the printing logic, we arbitrarily construct ever increasing top and bottom values in the longRECT that we pass to the RectLPtoPositions method, thereby selecting the transactions which are appropriate for output to the specified page.

components of the rectangle, the report size limitation for the same 300-dpi printer, using the new scheme, is over 700,000 pages.

CReportView Source File Beginning

The first section of the **reportvw.cpp** file contains the preprocessor definitions, constructor and destructor member functions, and the message map entries. The code is as follows:

```
// reportvw.cpp : implementation file
//

#include "stdafx.h"
#include "keepit.h"

#include "keepdoc.h"
#include "acctobj.h"
#include "listntry.h"
#include "category.h"    // added
#include "repline.h"     // added

#include "reportvw.h"

#ifdef _DEBUG
#undef THIS_FILE
```

```
static char BASED_CODE THIS_FILE[] = __FILE__;
#endif

/////////////////////////////////////////////////////////////////
// CReportView

IMPLEMENT_DYNCREATE(CReportView, CScrollView)

CReportView::CReportView()
{
}

CReportView::~CReportView()
{
}


BEGIN_MESSAGE_MAP(CReportView, CScrollView)
   //{{AFX_MSG_MAP(CReportView)
   ON_COMMAND(ID_FILE_PRINT, OnFilePrint)
   ON_COMMAND(ID_FILE_PRINT_PREVIEW, OnFilePrintPreview)
   ON_WM_DESTROY()
   ON_WM_HSCROLL()
   ON_WM_VSCROLL()
   //}}AFX_MSG_MAP
END_MESSAGE_MAP()
```

Notice in the foregoing code that two #include statements have been
added. Because the new version of the Cash Flow report must deal with
the selection of transactions based upon their category names, we have
imported the declarations from the **category.h** header file for those objects. In addition, we have added a new header file and an accompanying
source file, which describe report line objects for the Net Worth report.
We will describe the contents of these files shortly.

There are no new entries in the message map for this view. As in the previous version, we are handling the Print and Print Preview commands
from the File menu, and also the WM_DESTROY, WM_HSCROLL, and
WM_VSCROLL messages. The implementation of the foregoing three message handlers has not changed.

OnInitialUpdate Member Function Code

The OnInitialUpdate member function is called by the framework when
we call the InitialUpdateFrame member function within the Report-
Setup member function in the CKeepitDoc class, as shown on page 387.
The code for the OnInitialUpdate member function is as follows:

```
void CReportView::OnInitialUpdate()
{
   //
   // Get a pointer to the document and access
   // the variables that will be used to construct
   // the selected report.
   //
   CKeepitDoc* pDoc = GetDocument();
```

```cpp
m_nReportType = pDoc->m_nReportType;
m_FromDate = pDoc->m_FromDate;
m_ToDate = pDoc->m_ToDate;

switch (m_nReportType)
{
   case CASH_FLOW_REPORT:
   {
      //
      // get the cash flow report's specific
      // parameters from the document.
      //
      POSITION pos = pDoc->m_ReportCats.GetHeadPosition();
      while (pos != NULL)
      {
         CCategory* pCat;
         pCat = (CCategory *)pDoc->m_ReportCats.GetNext(pos);
         m_ReportCats.AddTail (pCat);
      }
      m_szDescription = pDoc->m_szDescription;
      m_szInfo = pDoc->m_szInfo;
      m_eDescInclude = pDoc->m_eDescInclude;
      m_eInfoInclude = pDoc->m_eInfoInclude;

      //
      // sort the transactions by date
      // for this report.
      //
      SortByDate (pDoc->m_ListEntries);

      //
      // prepare the device context for sizing the report.
      //
      CClientDC aDC(this);
      ComputeRptMetrics (&aDC);
      m_BlankLine.CreateRectRgn (0, 0, m_nLineWidth,
         m_nLineHeight);

      //
      // calculate the size of the view, based upon the
      // values of the parameters and type of report.
      //
      m_szTitle = "CASH FLOW DETAIL REPORT";
      m_SizeTotal = CashFlowViewSize ();
      SetScrollSizes(MM_TEXT, m_SizeTotal, m_PageSize,
         m_LineSize);
      Invalidate(TRUE);
      break;
   }

   case NET_WORTH_REPORT:
   {
      //
      // sort the transactions by date
      // for this report.
      //
      SortByDate (pDoc->m_ListEntries);

      //
      // prepare the device context for sizing the report.
      //
      CClientDC aDC(this);
      ComputeRptMetrics (&aDC);
      m_BlankLine.CreateRectRgn (0, 0, m_nLineWidth,
         m_nLineHeight);

      //
```

```
                        // calculate the size of the view, based upon the
                        // values of the parameters and type of report.
                        //
                        m_szTitle = "NET WORTH SUMMARY REPORT";
                        m_SizeTotal = NetWorthViewSize ();
                        SetScrollSizes(MM_TEXT, m_SizeTotal, m_PageSize,
                          m_LineSize);
                        Invalidate(TRUE);
                        break;
              }

          default:
          {
              return;
          }
        }
}
```

The foregoing code begins by transferring the values of the report type and the beginning and end of the report period to local member variables. After performing those transfers, execution continues according to the value in the m_nReportType variable through use of a switch statement that skips to the case corresponding to the current report.

The code for the CASH_FLOW_REPORT collects the categories that are applicable to the current report, transfers the values of the Description and Info field inclusion criteria and values to member variables, sorts the transactions into order by date, computes the initial metrics for the display device context, sets the title of the report into a member variable, computes the size of the view by calling the CashFlowViewSize member function, and then sets the scroll bar limits and invalidates the display region. When the Invalidate member function is called, the entire client rectangle is indicated to be invalid, which causes the framework to call the OnDraw member function, automatically, to redraw the contents of the window. The OnDraw member function is responsible for causing the transactions to be displayed.

The code for the NET_WORTH_REPORT is somewhat simpler than the initialization required for the Cash Flow report. In this code, the transactions are sorted by date, the initial report metrics are computed for the device context, the report title is stored into a member variable, the view size is computed by calling the NetWorthViewSize member function, and then the SetScrollSizes member function is called to set the scroll bar limits. As with the preceding code, the code for the Net Worth report invalidates the display region in order to force the OnDraw member function to be called to create the specified report.

OnPrepareDC Member Function Code

The new version of the OnPrepareDC member function calls the OnPrepareDC member function in the CScrollView base class, and then calls ComputeRptMetrics to set up the metrics for the current device context. Because the OnPrepareDC member function is called both for display and printing (including print preview) operations, we recompute the metrics each time it is called. In addition, if the IsPrinting member function in the CDC object indicates that printing (or print preview) is in progress, the second argument to the OnPrepareDC member function contains valid print information, including the current page number. In this case, we store the page number for reference by the drawing member functions. The code for the OnPrepareDC member function is as follows:

```
void CReportView::OnPrepareDC (CDC* pDC, CPrintInfo* pInfo)
{
   CScrollView::OnPrepareDC (pDC, pInfo);
   ComputeRptMetrics (pDC);
   if (pDC->IsPrinting())
   {
      m_nCurPage = pInfo->m_nCurPage;
   }
}
```

ComputeRptMetrics Member Function Code

As indicated previously, the ComputeRptMetrics member function is called in the OnInitialUpdate and OnPrepareDC member functions. The purpose of this member function is to acquire information about the current device context and compute dimensions that are used by the drawing function code.

In particular, we are interested in calculating values for the line height; line width; minimum, average, and maximum character widths; lines per page; page height in device units; and the page size and line size values. These are passed to the SetScrollSizes member function during initialization. The code for the ComputeRptMetrics member function is modified as shown and is as follows:

```
void CReportView::ComputeRptMetrics (CDC* pDC)
{
   TEXTMETRIC tm;
   CRect rectClient;
   int nPageHeight;

   CFont fRptFont;
   int nPtSz = MulDiv(8, pDC->GetDeviceCaps (LOGPIXELSY), 72);
   fRptFont.CreateFont ( nPtSz, 0, 0, 0, FW_NORMAL, 0, 0, 0,
      ANSI_CHARSET, OUT_TT_PRECIS, CLIP_DEFAULT_PRECIS,
      PROOF_QUALITY, DEFAULT_PITCH | FF_SWISS, "Arial");

   CFont* pOldFont = pDC->SelectObject (&fRptFont);
   if (!pDC->GetTextMetrics (&tm))
   {
      AfxMessageBox ("Can't get window's text metrics.");
      return;
   }
```

```
m_nMinCharWidth = tm.tmAveCharWidth;
m_nAvgCharWidth = (tm.tmAveCharWidth
   + tm.tmMaxCharWidth)/2;
m_nMaxCharWidth = tm.tmMaxCharWidth;
m_nLineHeight   = tm.tmHeight + tm.tmExternalLeading;
m_nLineWidth    = m_nAvgCharWidth * 76;
if (!pDC->IsPrinting())
{
   GetClientRect (&rectClient);
   nPageHeight = rectClient.bottom - rectClient.top;
}
else
{
   nPageHeight = pDC->GetDeviceCaps (VERTRES);
}
m_nLinesPerPage = (nPageHeight / m_nLineHeight);
nPageHeight = m_nLinesPerPage * m_nLineHeight;
m_PageSize.cx= m_nLineWidth/5;
m_PageSize.cy = max (m_nLineHeight, nPageHeight);
m_LineSize.cx= m_nLineWidth/20;
m_LineSize.cy= m_nLineHeight;
pDC->SelectObject (pOldFont);
}
```

OnDraw Member Function Code

The OnDraw member function is called by the framework, automatically, whenever any portion of the data in the current device context must be redrawn. This occurs initially when the Invalidate member function is called in the OnInitialUpdate member function, forcing the framework to refresh the entire client display area. In addition to this, however, if some other window or application causes a portion of the current window to be uncovered, the OnDraw member function will be called to update that region of the display.

When we are printing, the OnPrint member function calls the OnDraw member function directly, for each page of the report. While most of the logic of the OnDraw member function is common to both the display and printout of the report data, we must perform some additional tasks when we are printing. The new version of the OnDraw member function code is as follows:

```
void CReportView::OnDraw(CDC* pDC)
{
   POSITION nFirstEntry, nLastEntry, pos;
   CRect rectClip;
   longRECT posRect;

   //
   // verify that there is something to draw
   //
   if (m_RptEntries.GetCount() == 0)
   {
      return;
   }

   if (pDC->GetClipBox(&rectClip) == NULLREGION)
```

```
    {
        return;
    }


    //
    // create a font with which to render the text
    //
    CFont fRptFont;
    int nPtSz = MulDiv(8, pDC->GetDeviceCaps (LOGPIXELSY), 72);
    fRptFont.CreateFont (-nPtSz, 0, 0, 0, FW_NORMAL, 0, 0, 0,
        ANSI_CHARSET, OUT_TT_PRECIS, CLIP_DEFAULT_PRECIS,
        PROOF_QUALITY, DEFAULT_PITCH | FF_SWISS, "Arial");


    //
    // display the contents of the clip region
    //
    CFont* pOldFont = pDC->SelectObject (&fRptFont);
    posRect.left = (long)rectClip.left;
    posRect.right = (long)rectClip.right;
    if (pDC->IsPrinting())
    {
        long nPageHeight = (m_nLinesPerPage - 7) * m_nLineHeight;
        long nClipHeight = (long)rectClip.bottom
            - (long)rectClip.top;
        long nPageOffset = nPageHeight * (m_nCurPage - 1);
        posRect.top    = (long)rectClip.top + nPageOffset;
        posRect.bottom = posRect.top + nClipHeight;
    }
    else
    {
        posRect.top    = (long)rectClip.top;
        posRect.bottom = (long)rectClip.bottom;
    }
    RectLPtoPositions (posRect, nFirstEntry, nLastEntry);

    pos = nFirstEntry;
    int nYPos = rectClip.top;
    while (pos != nLastEntry)
    {
        CObject* pObj = m_RptEntries.GetNext(pos);
        DrawRptLine (pDC, pObj, nYPos);
    }
    pDC->SelectObject (pOldFont);
}
```

The foregoing code tests whether there are any report entries to draw
and also whether the current clipping region is NULL (in which case
nothing needs to be drawn). Once the member function has found that
there is information to be drawn and a region in which to do it, the standard report font is created and selected into the device context. The clipping rectangle is converted from short (16-bit) to long (32-bit)
coordinate values in the posRect variable.

If the OnDraw member function was called when printing is in progress,
then the value for the top of the page is computed by multiplying the
height of one page by the current page number (minus one) and then
adding the top of the clipping rectangle to that. The bottom of the page,
when printing, is computed to be the value of the top of the page plus
the height of the clipping region.

If the OnDraw member function is called to draw the report onto the display screen, then the top and bottom values from the clipping rectangle are transferred directly to the posRect variable in long coordinate form.

In either case, the posRect variable is passed as the first argument to the RectLPtoPositions member function, which determines which report entries are to be drawn by this invocation of the OnDraw member function. The final section of code uses the position values returned by the RectLPtoPositions member function to loop through the list of report entry objects and call the DrawRptLine member function for each of these. When drawing is complete, the previously saved font is restored in the device context and the member function returns.

DrawRptLine Member Function Code

The DrawRptLine member function is called to draw one line at a time of the currently specified report. The line to be drawn is determined by the type of object that is passed to the member function in the pObj object pointer. The vertical position in the current device context at which the line is drawn is specified by the nYPos argument. The first argument to the member function is a pointer to the device context, pDC. The code for the DrawRptLine member function is quite long and will be shown in several sections, beginning as follows:

```
void CReportView::DrawRptLine (CDC* pDC, CObject* pObj,
    int& nYPos)
{
    CAcctObj* pAcct;
    CListEntry* pEntry;
    CString szData;
    CTime eDate;
    CSize txSize;
    int nData;

    int nXPos = m_nAvgCharWidth;
    int nWidth = 0;
    int nDX = 0;
    int nDY = 0;
    if (pObj->IsKindOf (RUNTIME_CLASS (CAcctObj)))
    {
        pAcct = (CAcctObj *)pObj;
        szData = pAcct->GetAcctName ();
        pDC->TextOut (nXPos, nYPos, szData, szData.GetLength());
        nYPos += m_nLineHeight;
    }
    else if (pObj->IsKindOf (RUNTIME_CLASS (CListEntry)))
    {
        nXPos += m_nAvgCharWidth * 1;
        pEntry = (CListEntry *)pObj;
        eDate = pEntry->GetDate ();
        szData = eDate.Format ("%m/%d/%y");
        pDC->TextOut (nXPos, nYPos, szData, szData.GetLength());
        nXPos += m_nAvgCharWidth * 8;

        szData = pEntry->GetItem ();
```

```
    pDC->TextOut (nXPos, nYPos, szData, szData.GetLength());
    nXPos += m_nAvgCharWidth * 6;

    szData = pEntry->GetDescription();
    nWidth = min (szData.GetLength(), 25);
    pDC->TextOut (nXPos, nYPos, szData, nWidth);
    nXPos += m_nAvgCharWidth * 19;

    szData = pEntry->GetInfo();
    nWidth = min (szData.GetLength(), 15);
    pDC->TextOut (nXPos, nYPos, szData, nWidth);
    nXPos += m_nAvgCharWidth * 10;

    szData = pEntry->GetCategory();
    nWidth = min (szData.GetLength(), 15);
    pDC->TextOut (nXPos, nYPos, szData, nWidth);
    nXPos += m_nAvgCharWidth * 3;

    if (pEntry->GetPaymentValue() != 0)
    {
        szData = pEntry->GetPayment();
        txSize = pDC->GetTextExtent (szData,
          szData.GetLength());
        nDX = nXPos + (12 * m_nAvgCharWidth - txSize.cx);
        pDC->TextOut (nDX, nYPos, szData,
          szData.GetLength());
    }
    nXPos += m_nAvgCharWidth * 8;

    if (pEntry->GetDepositValue() != 0)
    {
        szData = pEntry->GetDeposit();
        txSize = pDC->GetTextExtent (szData,
          szData.GetLength());
        nDX = nXPos + (12 * m_nAvgCharWidth - txSize.cx);
        pDC->TextOut (nDX, nYPos, szData,
          szData.GetLength());
    }
    nXPos += m_nAvgCharWidth * 8;

    szData = pEntry->GetBalance();
    txSize = pDC->GetTextExtent (szData, szData.GetLength());
    nDX = nXPos + (12 * m_nAvgCharWidth - txSize.cx);
    pDC->TextOut (nDX, nYPos, szData, szData.GetLength());
    nXPos += m_nAvgCharWidth * 8;
    nYPos += m_nLineHeight;
}
```

The first section of code is unchanged from what was presented for the
DrawRptLine member function in Chapter 8. The foregoing code performs some initialization that is common to all of the object types and
then determines whether the object is of type CAcctObj or CListEntry.
If so, then the code draws the transaction lines for the Cash Flow report,
according to the contents of those objects. However, if the object is of
type CReportLine, then the data pertain to the Net Worth report (although, the member function is not written to distinguish between the
different report types). The Net Worth report has many different types
of report lines. It has several types of headings, detailed account summary lines, and several summary totals. Because of this, we have created
a new type of object to hold the data for these lines, called CReportLine

(to be described shortly), and have provided each object of this type with a member variable that specifies the type of data in the object as well as a variable that specifies the string to draw. The code to draw the various lines pertaining to the CReportLine objects is as follows:

```cpp
else if (pObj->IsKindOf (RUNTIME_CLASS (CReportLine)))
{
   CReportLine* pLine = (CReportLine *)pObj;
   CPen* oldPen = (CPen *)pDC->SelectStockObject (BLACK_PEN);
   szData = pLine->GetLine ();
   nData  = szData.GetLength ();
   txSize = pDC->GetTextExtent (szData, nData);
   switch (pLine->GetLineType ())
   {
      case FIRST_HEAD_LINE:
      {
         pDC->TextOut (1, nYPos, szData, nData);
         nYPos += m_nLineHeight;
         break;
      }

      case SECOND_HEAD_LINE:
      {
         nDX = m_nAvgCharWidth * 4;
         pDC->TextOut (nDX, nYPos, szData, nData);
         nYPos += m_nLineHeight;
         break;
      }

      case FIRST_SUBTOTAL_HEAD:
      {
         nDX = m_nAvgCharWidth * 12;
         pDC->TextOut (nDX, nYPos, szData, nData);
         break;
      }

      case FIRST_SUBTOTAL:
      {
         nDX = m_nAvgCharWidth * 36 - txSize.cx;
         nDY = nYPos + txSize.cy;
         pDC->TextOut (nDX, nYPos, szData, nData);
         pDC->MoveTo (nDX, nDY);
         pDC->LineTo (nDX+txSize.cx, nDY);
         nYPos += m_nLineHeight;
         break;
      }
      case SECOND_SUBTOTAL_HEAD:
      {
         nDX = m_nAvgCharWidth * 10;
         pDC->TextOut (nDX, nYPos, szData, nData);
         break;
      }

      case SECOND_SUBTOTAL:
      {
         nDX = m_nAvgCharWidth * 30 - txSize.cx;
         nDY = nYPos + txSize.cy;
         pDC->TextOut (nDX, nYPos, szData, nData);
         pDC->MoveTo (nDX, nDY);
         pDC->LineTo (nDX+txSize.cx, nDY);
         nYPos += m_nLineHeight;
         break;
      }
```

```
            case NAME_LINE:
            {
               nDX = m_nAvgCharWidth * 8;
               pDC->TextOut (nDX, nYPos, szData, nData);
               break;
            }

            case VALUE_LINE:
            {
               nDX = m_nAvgCharWidth * 30 - txSize.cx;
               pDC->TextOut (nDX, nYPos, szData, nData);
               nYPos += m_nLineHeight;
               break;
            }

            case GRAND_TOTAL_HEAD:
            {
               nDX = m_nAvgCharWidth * 14;
               pDC->TextOut (nDX, nYPos, szData, nData);
               break;
            }

            case GRAND_TOTAL:
            {
               nDX = m_nAvgCharWidth * 42 - txSize.cx;
               nDY = nYPos + txSize.cy;
               pDC->TextOut (nDX, nYPos, szData, nData);
               pDC->MoveTo (nDX, nDY);
               pDC->LineTo (nDX+txSize.cx, nDY);
               nYPos += m_nLineHeight;
               break;
            }

            default:
            {
               break;
            }
      }
      pDC->SelectObject (oldPen);
   }
```

The foregoing code shows that the Net Worth report contains ten different types of data. Each CReportLine object identifies the type of its data when we call the GetLineType member function. Individual cases contain the code to draw the appropriate report line types.

The final section of the DrawRptLine member function handles the case where the object passed to the member function is the blank line region. The code is as follows:

```
   else
   {
      RECT rectRgn;
      m_BlankLine.GetRgnBox (&rectRgn);
      nYPos += rectRgn.bottom;
   }
}
```

CashFlowViewSize Member Function Code

The CashFlowViewSize member function is responsible for calculating the total size of the Cash Flow report. It calculates both a display width and height (for use in setting the initial limits of the scroll bars and also determines the number of lines in the report. Because every line is the same height as any other, the line count can be used to calculate the report size for any device context. A detailed description of the logic of the member function is contained in Chapter 8, on pages 308–310. The code is as follows:

```
CSize CReportView::CashFlowViewSize()
{
    WORD    nAccount;
    BOOL    bFirstTime = TRUE;
    CSize   docSize (m_nLineWidth, 0);
    long    nPayment, nDeposit, nBalance;

    CKeepitDoc* pDoc = GetDocument();
    POSITION pos = pDoc->m_ReportAccts.GetHeadPosition();
    m_nTotalLines = 0;
    while (pos != NULL)
    {
        //
        // iterate through accounts, selecting the transactions
        // which are within the date range, sorting them into date
        // order and placing them into the m_RptEntries list.
        //
        if (!bFirstTime)
        {
            m_RptEntries.AddTail (&m_BlankLine);
            docSize.cy += m_nLineHeight;
            m_nTotalLines++;
        }
        bFirstTime = FALSE;
        CAcctObj* pAcct;
        pAcct = (CAcctObj *)pDoc->m_ReportAccts.GetNext(pos);
        m_RptEntries.AddTail (pAcct);
        docSize.cy += m_nLineHeight;
        m_nTotalLines++;
        nAccount = pAcct->GetAcctID();
        nBalance = 0;
        POSITION tPos = pDoc->m_ListEntries.GetHeadPosition();
        while (tPos != NULL)
        {
            CListEntry* pEntry;
            WORD nAcctID;
            CTimeeDate;

            //
            // get entries one at a time and check to see whether
            // they match the current account ID.
            //
            pEntry = (CListEntry *)pDoc->m_ListEntries.GetNext (tPos);
            nAcctID = pEntry->GetAccountID();
            if (nAcctID != nAccount)
            {
                //
                // no match, continue the loop
                //
                continue;
```

```cpp
        }

        if (pEntry->GetStatus() == E_EMPTY)
        {
          //
          // bypass empty entries
          //
          continue;
        }

        if (pEntry->GetStatus() == E_SELECTED)
        {
          if (pEntry->GetDescription().GetLength() == 0)
          {
            //
            // bypass selected but empty entries
            //
            continue;
          }
        }

        //
        // calculate the current balance for the account
        //
        nPayment = pEntry->GetPaymentValue();
        nDeposit = pEntry->GetDepositValue();
        nBalance = nBalance - nPayment + nDeposit;

        //
        // now, check to see whether the entry is within
        // the specified date range.
        //
        eDate = pEntry->GetDate();
        if (eDate < m_FromDate)
        {
          //
          // not yet in range, continue checking
          //
          continue;
        }
        else if (eDate > m_ToDate)
        {
          //
          // past the end of the period, quit.
          //
          break;
        }

        //
        // enter the balance value into the transaction,
        // check whether the additional reporting criteria
        // are met, add the transaction to the list, and
        // then increment the document size.
        //
        pEntry->SetBalanceValue (nBalance);
        if (MeetsRptCriteria (pEntry))
        {
          m_RptEntries AddTail (pEntry);
          docSize.cy += m_nLineHeight;
          m_nTotalLines++;
        }
      }
    }

    //
    // get rid of all of the accounts, now that
    // we're done with them, and then return the
```

```
   // document size to the caller.
   //
   pDoc->m_ReportAccts.RemoveAll();
   return docSize;
}
```

NetWorthViewSize Member Function Code

The NetWorthViewSize member function is new to this version of the CReportView class and is called by the OnInitialUpdate member function when the Net Worth report is to be prepared. The member function compiles the information for all of the accounts selected by the user and then creates objects of the CReportLine class for each summary line by calling the MakeRptListEntry member function for that line type. The code is as follows:

```
CSize CReportView::NetWorthViewSize ()
{
   CSize docSize (m_nLineWidth, 0);
   long nChecking, nAssets, nLiabilities;
   nChecking = nAssets = nLiabilities = 0;
   CKeepitDoc* pDoc = GetDocument();
   m_nTotalLines = 0;

   //
   // empty the list of report entries and then
   // enter the first heading line.
   //
   m_RptEntries.RemoveAll();
   MakeRptListEntry (FIRST_HEAD_LINE, "ASSETS");
   m_nTotalLines++;

   //
   // enter the heading for the next set, make
   // the entries for the Checking, Savings, and
   // Cash accounts in the report and then make
   // a subtotal entry.
   //
   MakeRptListEntry (SECOND_HEAD_LINE,
      "Checking & Cash Accounts");
   nChecking = MakeAcctEntry (IDC_CHECKING, IDC_CASH);
   MakeRptListEntry (SECOND_SUBTOTAL_HEAD,
      "Total Checking & Cash");
   MakeRptListEntry (SECOND_SUBTOTAL,
      MakeValueString (nChecking));
   m_RptEntries.AddTail (&m_BlankLine);
   m_nTotalLines += 3;

   // enter the heading for other assets, make the
   // entries for those accounts, and then make a
   // subtotal entry.
   //
   MakeRptListEntry (SECOND_HEAD_LINE,
      "Other Asset Accounts");
   nAssets = MakeAcctEntry (IDC_ASSET, IDC_ASSET);
   MakeRptListEntry (SECOND_SUBTOTAL_HEAD,
      "Total Other Assets");
   MakeRptListEntry (SECOND_SUBTOTAL,
      MakeValueString (nAssets));
   m_nTotalLines += 2;
```

```
//
// now, create a total of checking and other assets
// and make the report entry.
//
MakeRptListEntry (FIRST_SUBTOTAL_HEAD,
   "Total All Assets");
MakeRptListEntry (FIRST_SUBTOTAL,
   MakeValueString (nChecking+nAssets));
m_RptEntries.AddTail (&m_BlankLine);
m_nTotalLines += 2;

//
// enter the headings for liability accounts
// and then make the entries for those accounts.
//
MakeRptListEntry (FIRST_HEAD_LINE, "LIABILITIES");
MakeRptListEntry (SECOND_HEAD_LINE,
   "Liability & Credit Accounts");
nLiabilities = MakeAcctEntry (IDC_LIABILITY,IDC_CREDIT_CARD);
MakeRptListEntry (SECOND_SUBTOTAL_HEAD,
   "Total Liabilities");
MakeRptListEntry (SECOND_SUBTOTAL,
   MakeValueString (nLiabilities));
m_nTotalLines += 3;

//
// create the headings and value entries for all
// liabilities and enter these into the report list.
//
MakeRptListEntry (FIRST_SUBTOTAL_HEAD,
   "Total All Liabilities");
MakeRptListEntry (FIRST_SUBTOTAL,
   MakeValueString (nLiabilities));
m_nTotalLines++;

//
// finally, create the grand total heading and value entries.
//
long nGrandTotal = nChecking + nAssets - nLiabilities;
MakeRptListEntry (GRAND_TOTAL_HEAD, "Total Net Worth");
MakeRptListEntry (GRAND_TOTAL, MakeValueString (nGrandTotal));
m_nTotalLines++;

//
// compute the document size
//
docSize.cy = m_nTotalLines * m_nLineHeight;

//
// get rid of the document's report accounts, now
// that we've used them, and then return the document
// size to the caller.
//
pDoc->m_ReportAccts.RemoveAll();
return docSize;
}
```

The foregoing code begins by initializing a number of total counters and then makes entries into the report list for the "ASSETS" headline, and then the entry for the "Checking and Cash Accounts" headline. Following this, the MakeAcctEntry member function is called to make entries for the accounts whose ID fields contain values between and including those of IDC_CHECKING and IDC_CASH. The MakeAcctEntry member function also returns the total for the range of accounts, so we can immediately make an entry into the report list for the "Total Checking & Cash" subtotal heading, followed by an entry containing the string value of the total amount.

The member function continues by adding a blank line to the report list, calls MakeAcctEntry for accounts whose ID fields contain the IDC_ASSET identifier, makes entries for the "Total Other Assets" subtotal heading, and then an entry for the string value of the total amount.

The procedure continues with a main headline of "LIABILITIES," a secondary headline of "Liability and Credit Accounts," individual entries for each of the liability and credit accounts via a call to MakeAcctEntry for those accounts (IDC_LIABILITY through IDC_CREDIT_CARD), and then a subtotal header and subtotal value lines.

The member function completes its report entries with a "Total Net Worth" headline and the value of the sum of the checking and other assets minus the total liabilities.

When the member function is complete, the total size of the report is stored into the docSize variable, the total number of report lines has been accumulated into the m_nTotalLines variable, and all of the entries in the document's list of report accounts are removed.

MeetsRptCriteria Member Function Code

One of the first newly added "helper" member functions for the Cash Flow report is one that determines whether a given transaction in the list of overall transactions meets the criteria for being included in the report. Although this is listed as a helper for only the Cash Flow report, we have written it to be applicable to future reports when the logic for those reports is added. The code for the MeetsRptCriteria member function is as follows:

```
/////////////////////////////////////////////////////////////////
// cash flow report helper member functions
//
BOOL CReportView::MeetsRptCriteria (CListEntry* pEntry)
{
    //
    // determine whether pEntry object meets the criteria
    // for inclusion in the selected report.
    //
    switch (m_nReportType)
    {
      case CASH_FLOW_REPORT:
        {
            //
            // first, determine if the category matches
            // one in the m_ReportCats list.
            //
            CString szCategory = pEntry->GetCategory();
```

```cpp
      int nCategories = m_ReportCats.GetCount();
      if (nCategories == 0)
      {
         //
         // there aren't any valid categories
         //
         return FALSE;
      }
      POSITION pos = m_ReportCats.GetHeadPosition();
      BOOL bFound = FALSE;
      while (pos != NULL)
      {
         CCategory* pCat;
         CString szCatName;
         pCat = (CCategory *)m_ReportCats.GetNext (pos);
         szCatName = pCat->GetCatName();
         if (MatchStrings (szCatName, szCategory, equals))
         {
            bFound = TRUE;
            break;
         }
      }
      if (!bFound)
      {
         //
         // category wasn't found, so return FALSE
         //
         return FALSE;
      }

      //
      // now, determine whether the description or info
      // fields are to be examined for inclusion of the
      // transaction in the report.
      //
      if (m_eDescInclude != all)
      {
         CString szDescription = pEntry->GetDescription();
         if (!MatchStrings (szDescription, m_szDescription,
            m_eDescInclude))
         {
            //
            // description doesn't match, return FALSE.
            //
            return FALSE;
         }
      }
      if (m_eInfoInclude != all)
      {
         CString szInfo = pEntry->GetInfo();
         if (!MatchStrings (szInfo, m_szInfo, m_eInfoInclude))
         {
            //
            // info field doesn't match, return FALSE.
            //
            return FALSE;
         }
      }

      //
      // everything matches, so return TRUE.
      //
      return TRUE;
}

default:
{
```

```
              //
              // not one of our reports
              //
              return FALSE;
         }
    }
    return FALSE;
}
```

The foregoing code is written to enable code for other report types to be added, but at present only the code for the Cash Flow report is present. Because the Net Worth report has no optional criteria, other than the list of applicable accounts, we don't need to call this member function for that report.

The code consists of three sections. The first section determines whether the entry contains a category name that matches one of those specified for the report. If not, then the member function returns a FALSE result. If so, then the member function continues by calling the MatchStrings member function for each of the Description and Info fields in the entry, returning FALSE, immediately, if the field doesn't match the corresponding criteria and returning TRUE only if all of the criteria are met.

MatchStrings Member Function Code

The MatchStrings member function is used to determine whether the Description or Info string passed into the member function matches the pattern string, according to the specified criteria (starts with, contains, or equals exactly). The code for this member function is newly added and is as follows:

```
BOOL CReportView::MatchStrings (CString szSrc,
    CString szPattern, TInclude criteria)
{
    CString szS = szSrc;
    CString szP = szPattern;
    char* pString;
    int    nLength;

    //
    // matches szS with szP using criteria in a
    // case-insensitive manner. Start by converting both
    // strings to all lower-case characters.
    //
    pString = szS.GetBuffer (50);
    nLength = szS.GetLength();
    ::AnsiLowerBuff (pString, nLength);
    szS.ReleaseBuffer();

    pString = szP.GetBuffer (50);
    nLength = szP.GetLength();
    ::AnsiLowerBuff (pString, nLength);
    szP.ReleaseBuffer();

    //
    // now see if the szS string meets the criteria
```

```cpp
    //
    int index;
    int nSrc = szS.GetLength();
    int nPat = szP.GetLength();
    if (nSrc < nPat)
    {
        //
        // source must be at least as long as the pattern.
        //
        return FALSE;
    }
    switch (criteria)
    {
        case startsWith:
        {
            //
            // length of pattern string governs
            // the scope of the comparison.
            //
            for (index=0; index < nPat; index++)
            {
                if (szS[index] != szP[index])
                {
                    //
                    // source doesn't start with pattern
                    //
                    return FALSE;
                }
            }
            return TRUE;
        }

        case contains:
        {
            //
            // the entire pattern string must be contained
            // somewhere within the source string.
            //
            for (index=0; index < nSrc; index++)
            {
                BOOL bContains = FALSE;
                if (szS[index] == szP[0])
                {
                    //
                    // found the first matching character
                    // determine if the rest of the string
                    // matches the pattern.
                    //
                    bContains = TRUE;
                    for (int ix=0; ix < nPat; ix++)
                    {
                        if (index+ix >= nSrc)
                        {
                            //
                            // end of source reached
                            //
                            return FALSE;
                        }
                        if (szS[index+ix] != szP[ix])
                        {
                            bContains = FALSE;
                            break;
                        }
                    }
                    if (bContains)
                    {
                        return TRUE;
```

```
                    }
                }
            }

            //
            // we didn't find a match, so return FALSE.
            //
            return FALSE;
        }

        case equals:
        {
            if (nSrc != nPat)
            {
                //
                // lengths aren't equal, so return FALSE.
                //
                return FALSE;
            }
            for (index=0; index < nPat; index++)
            {
                if (szS[index] != szP[index])
                {
                    //
                    // found a mismatch, so return FALSE.
                    //
                    return FALSE;
                }
            }

            //
            // all characters matched, so return TRUE.
            //
            return TRUE;
        }

        default:
        {
            //
            // shouldn't occur
            //
            ASSERT (FALSE);
            return FALSE;// in case of Continue.
        }
    }
}
```

The input string is tested against the pattern string to determine whether it meets the criteria specified. If the criteria are that the string must start with the pattern string, then only the number of characters, starting at the source string's beginning, are compared with the pattern string. If, on the other hand, the criteria are that the source string only wholly contain the pattern string somewhere in its length, then we loop through the source string looking for a match with the pattern string, anywhere within its length. Finally, if the criteria are that the source string match the pattern string exactly, every character of the source is compared with the pattern and their lengths must also match exactly. None of the string comparisons is case-sensitive. The strings are converted to lower case prior to beginning the tests, using the Windows AnsiLowerBuff function.

ComputeBalance Member Function Code

The Net Worth report requires a number of "helper" member functions to facilitate the creation of the various report list entries. The first of these is the newly added ComputeBalance member function, whose code is as follows:

```
//////////////////////////////////////////////////////////////////
// net worth report helper member functions
//
long CReportView::ComputeBalance (CAcctObj* pAcct)
{
   long nPayment, nDeposit, nBalance;
   WORD nAccount = pAcct->GetAcctID();
   CKeepitDoc* pDoc = GetDocument();

   //
   // iterate through transaction list to find those
   // which match the account ID and then compute the
   // balance up 'til the end date specified by the user.
   //
   nBalance = 0;
   POSITION pos = pDoc->m_ListEntries.GetHeadPosition();
   while (pos != NULL)
   {
      CListEntry* pEntry;
      WORD nAcctID;
      CTimeeDate;

      //
      // get entries one at a time and check to see whether
      // they match the current account ID.
      //
      pEntry = (CListEntry *)pDoc->m_ListEntries.GetNext (pos);
      nAcctID = pEntry->GetAccountID();
      if (nAcctID != nAccount)
      {
         // no match, continue the loop
         //
         continue;
      }

      if (pEntry->GetStatus() == E_EMPTY)
      {
         //
         // bypass empty entries
         //
         continue;
      }

      if (pEntry->GetStatus() == E_SELECTED)
      {
         if (pEntry->GetDescription().GetLength() == 0)
         {
            //
            // bypass selected but empty entries
            //
            continue;
         }
      }

      //
      // calculate the current balance for the account
```

```
        //
        nPayment = pEntry->GetPaymentValue ();
        nDeposit = pEntry->GetDepositValue ();
        nBalance = nBalance - nPayment + nDeposit;

        //
        // now, check to see whether the entry is within
        // the specified date range.
        //
        eDate = pEntry->GetDate ();
        if (eDate < m_FromDate)
        {
          //
          // not yet in range, continue checking
          //
          continue;
        }
        else if (eDate > m_ToDate)
        {
          //
          // past the end of the period, quit.
          //
          break;
        }
    }
    return nBalance;
}
```

The foregoing member function loops through all of the individual
transactions, looking for those which match the specified account and
then computes the balance of the account, stopping only when the end
of the reporting period is reached (remember, all the transactions have
been sorted into date sequence, previously).

MakeValueString Member Function Code

One of the "helper" member functions for the Net Worth report is the
MakeValueString member function, which takes a long integer, representing a monetary value in cents, as input and then creates and returns a
string representation of that value. The code is newly added, as follows:

```
CString CReportView::MakeValueString (long nValue)
{
  CString szValue;
  long dollars, cents;

  dollars = nValue / 100;
  cents   = nValue - dollars * 100;
  wsprintf (szValue.GetBuffer (14), "%ld.%02ld", dollars,
    cents);
  szValue.ReleaseBuffer ();
  return szValue;
}
```

MakeRptListEntry Member Function Code

The MakeRptListEntry member function is used in the preparation of
the Net Worth report to create a new object of the CReportLine class, set
its member variables to the specified type and contents, and then enter
the object into the report entries list. The newly added code is as follows:

```cpp
void CReportView::MakeRptListEntry (int nType, CString szLine)
{
   CReportLine* pLine = new CReportLine;
   pLine->SetLineType (nType);
   pLine->SetLine (szLine);
   m_RptEntries.AddTail (pLine);
}
```

MakeAcctEntry Member Function Code

The MakeAcctEntry member function is used in the preparation of the
Net Worth report. The newly added code is as follows:

```cpp
long CReportView::MakeAcctEntry (int nTypeFrom, int nTypeTo)
{
   long nBalance;
   CString szBalance;
   long nTotalBalance = 0;
   CKeepitDoc* pDoc = GetDocument ();
   POSITION pos = pDoc->m_ReportAccts.GetHeadPosition ();
   while (pos != NULL)
   {
      //
      // iterate through the accounts, finding the accounts
      // in the list which match the specified type,
      //
      CAcctObj* pAcct;
      pAcct = (CAcctObj *)pDoc->m_ReportAccts.GetNext (pos);
      int nType = pAcct->GetAcctType ();
      if (nType >= nTypeFrom && nType <= nTypeTo)
      {
         CString szLine = pAcct->GetAcctName ();
         MakeRptListEntry (NAME_LINE, szLine);

         //
         // it's the right type of account, so compute
         // the balance of the account and then create
         // and make an entry in the report list.
         //
         nBalance = ComputeBalance (pAcct);
         szBalance = MakeValueString (nBalance);
         MakeRptListEntry (VALUE_LINE, szBalance);
         nTotalBalance += nBalance;
         //
         // advance the line count
         //
         m_nTotalLines++;
      }
   }
   return nTotalBalance;
}
```

The foregoing code loops through all of the accounts selected for inclusion in the report, finding ones that have an account type that is in the range of the `nTypeFrom` and `nTypeTo` input variables. When an account is found to qualify, then the ComputeBalance, MakeValueString, and MakeRptListEntry member functions are called to enter the computed account balance into the report entries list. The total number of report lines held in the `m_nTotalLines` member variable is advanced for each line that is added to the list. The overall balance for the series of accounts that fall within the type range is accumulated and returned when the member function completes execution.

SortByDate Member Function Code

The SortByDate member function sorts the specified list of transaction entries into chronological sequence. The code for this member function is unchanged from what was presented in Chapter 8. The code for this "helper" function is as follows:

```
//////////////////////////////////////////////////////////////////////
// general purpose helper member functions

void CReportView::SortByDate (CObList& list)
{
   CListEntry *entry1, *entry2;
   POSITION pos1, pPos1, pos2, pPos2;

   //
   // sorts a list of CListEntry objects into order
   // by date using a simple linear scan algorithm.
   //
   pos1 = list.GetHeadPosition();
   while (pos1 != NULL)
   {
      pPos1 = pos1;
      entry1 = (CListEntry *)list.GetNext(pos1);
      pos2 = pos1;
      while (pos2 != NULL)
      {
         pPos2 = pos2;
         entry2 = (CListEntry *)list.GetNext (pos2);
         if (entry2->GetDate() < entry1->GetDate())
         {
            //
            // need to swap entries
            //
            list.SetAt (pPos1, entry2);
            list.SetAt (pPos2, entry1);
            entry1 = entry2;
         }
      }
   }
}
```

The foregoing code consists of a pair of nested loops. It is not an efficient sort algorithm; however, for our purposes, because it is executed only once for each report, it will be suitable.

RectLPtoPositions Member Function Code

The RectLPtoPositions member function is called by the OnDraw member function to select report entries to be drawn. The code is as follows:

```
void CReportView::RectLPtoPositions (longRECT rectClip,
   POSITION& firstPosition, POSITION& lastPosition)
{
   // scan the m_ReportEntries list for entries within the
   // clipping region current passed to the OnDraw member
   // function, and then return their POSITION values.
   long nViewHeight = 0;
   POSITION pos = m_RptEntries.GetHeadPosition();
   POSITION prevPos;
   BOOL bFirst=TRUE;
   firstPosition = lastPosition = NULL;
   while (pos != NULL)
   {
      prevPos = pos;
      CObject *pObj = m_RptEntries.GetNext (pos);
      if (bFirst && nViewHeight >= rectClip.top)
      {
         bFirst = FALSE;
         firstPosition = prevPos;
      }
      if (m_nReportType == CASH_FLOW_REPORT)
      {
         nViewHeight += m_nLineHeight;
      }
      else if (m_nReportType == NET_WORTH_REPORT)
      {
         if (pObj->IsKindOf (RUNTIME_CLASS (CReportLine)))
         {
            CReportLine* pRObj = (CReportLine *)pObj;
            switch (pRObj->GetLineType())
            {
               case FIRST_HEAD_LINE:
               case SECOND_HEAD_LINE:
               case FIRST_SUBTOTAL:
               case SECOND_SUBTOTAL:
               case VALUE_LINE:
               case GRAND_TOTAL:
               {
                  nViewHeight += m_nLineHeight;
               }
            }
         }
         else
         {
            nViewHeight += m_nLineHeight;
         }
      }
      if (nViewHeight >= rectClip.bottom)
      {
         lastPosition = pos;
         break;
      }
   }
   if (firstPosition == NULL)
   {
      lastPosition = NULL;
   }
}
```

The only changes between the current version of the foregoing member function and the one presented in Chapter 8 (see page 417) are the change in the type of the first parameter from a short RECT to the newly defined longRect type, the change of the nViewHeight parameter to a longRECT, and the addition of code to handle the Net Worth report's objects. In all other respects the code is unchanged.

OnPreparePrinting Member Function Code

The OnPreparePrinting member function is called by the framework after the user chooses to print the current report, but before the printing process commences. One of the purposes of this member function is to display the print dialog, which enables the user to specify which printer is to be used and what range of pages should be printed. The code for the OnPreparePrinting member function is unchanged, as follows:

```
/////////////////////////////////////////////////////////////////
// CReportView printing support

BOOL CReportView::OnPreparePrinting (CPrintInfo* pInfo)
{
    return DoPreparePrinting (pInfo);
}
```

The foregoing code merely calls the DoPreparePrinting member function inherited from the CView class.

OnBeginPrinting Member Function Code

The OnBeginPrinting member function is responsible for performing any initialization that must be accomplished after a printer has been chosen, but before the process commences. The code is as follows:

```
void CReportView::OnBeginPrinting (CDC* pDC, CPrintInfo* pInfo)
{
    ComputeRptMetrics(pDC);
    int nPageHeight = (m_nLinesPerPage - 7) * m_nLineHeight;
    int nSizeTotal = m_nTotalLines * m_nLineHeight;
    int nPageCount = (nSizeTotal + nPageHeight - 1) / nPageHeight;
    pInfo->SetMaxPage (nPageCount);
    pInfo->m_nCurPage = 1;
}
```

The foregoing code computes the number of lines available on each page, based upon the report metrics computed by calling the ComputeRptMetrics member function. The number of lines is reduced by 7 (to compensate for the header lines and to leave some space at the bottom of the page), and then, based upon the total number of lines in the report, the page count is computed and stored into the print information structure. The initial page number is also set to 1.

OnPrint Member Function Code

The new version of the OnPrint member function is much simpler than the one presented in Chapter 8. The difference is that we do not have to continually move the viewport origin to force an arbitrarily large clipping rectangle to be computed. The clipping rectangle remains the same for every page of the report.

We use the SetViewportOrg member function to inset the window origin slightly from the top and left sides of the page, for appearance sake. Other than this, the code creates and selects an initial clipping rectangle that is as large as the full device resolution, calls PrintPageHeader to print the page header, sets the viewport origin for printing the body of the report, calls IntersectClipRect to ensure that only an integral number of lines is printed, and then calls the OnDraw member function to draw the body of the page. OnPrint is called by the framework once for each page to be printed. The newly modified code is as follows (no change bars are shown, because we have deleted code, not added code):

```
void CReportView::OnPrint (CDC* pDC, CPrintInfo* pInfo)
{
  //
  // get the printer's page size in pixels
  //
  int nHRes = pDC->GetDeviceCaps (HORZRES);
  int nVRes = pDC->GetDeviceCaps (VERTRES);

  //
  // create and select a new clipping region for use in
  // printing the page header, and then print the header.
  //
  CRgn clipRgn;
  clipRgn.CreateRectRgn (0, 0, nHRes, nVRes);
  pDC->SelectClipRgn (&clipRgn);
  clipRgn.DeleteObject();
  PrintPageHeader(pDC, pInfo);

  //
  // now set up the viewport for printing the remainder
  // of the page and call the OnDraw routine to do it.
  //
  int nDX = pDC->GetDeviceCaps (LOGPIXELSX)/2;
  int nDY = m_nLineHeight * 4;
  int nPageHeight = (m_nLinesPerPage - 7) * m_nLineHeight;
  int nPageWidth = nHRes;

  pDC->SetViewportOrg (nDX, nDY);
  CRect rectClip = CRect (0, 0, nPageWidth, nPageHeight);
  pDC->IntersectClipRect (rectClip);
  OnDraw (pDC);
}
```

PrintPageHeader Member Function Code

The PrintPageHeader member function is called by the OnPrint member function, once for each page of the report to be printed. The member function prints the report title and page number on the first line and then the reporting period for which the report applies. The code is unchanged, and is as follows:

```cpp
void CReportView::PrintPageHeader (CDC* pDC, CPrintInfo* pInfo)
{
  CFont fHdrFont;
  CString szLine, szPage;

  //
  // create a bold font for use in printing the
  // page header and then select it for use.
  //
  int nPtSz=MulDiv(8, pDC->GetDeviceCaps (LOGPIXELSY), 72);
  int nDX    = pDC->GetDeviceCaps (LOGPIXELSX)/2;
  fHdrFont.CreateFont (-nPtSz, 0, 0, 0, FW_BOLD, 0, 0, 0,
     ANSI_CHARSET, OUT_TT_PRECIS, CLIP_DEFAULT_PRECIS,
     PROOF_QUALITY, DEFAULT_PITCH | FF_SWISS, "Arial");
  CFont* pOldFont = pDC->SelectObject (&fHdrFont);

  //
  // format and print the two header lines and then
  // select the previous font.
  //
  wsprintf (szPage.GetBuffer(3), "%d", pInfo->m_nCurPage);
  szPage.ReleaseBuffer();
    szLine = " " + m_szTitle + "  Page " + szPage;
  pDC->TextOut (nDX, m_nLineHeight, szLine);
  szLine = " From: ";
  szLine = szLine + m_FromDate.Format ("%m/%d/%y");
  szLine = szLine + " To: ";
  szLine = szLine + m_ToDate.Format ("%m/%d/%y");
  pDC->TextOut (nDX, m_nLineHeight * 2, szLine);
  pDC->SelectObject (pOldFont);
}
```

The foregoing code creates a bold version of the Arial font to print the heading information. The normal version of this same font is used for the body of the report.

OnFilePrint Message Handler Code

The OnFilePrint message handler is called by the framework when the user chooses the Print command from the File menu. The version of this handler in our view simply calls the OnFilePrint member function of the CView base class. The code is as follows:

```cpp
////////////////////////////////////////////////////////////////
// CReportView message handlers

void CReportView::OnFilePrint()
{
  CView::OnFilePrint();
}
```

user finally releases the mouse button. The difference between the On-VScroll member function and the OnHScroll member function is that vertical scrolling must be limited to an integral number of display lines. This ensures that the display doesn't contain any partial line artifacts when the thumb is dragged. Clicking on the arrows or the body of the scroll bar will automatically cause a single line or partial page advance in the direction being scrolled. This handler makes sure that the vertical position being set is an integral multiple of the line height value. The code is as follows:

```
void CReportView::OnVScroll(UINT nSBCode, UINT nPos,
   CScrollBar* pScrollBar)
{
   ASSERT (pScrollBar == GetScrollBarCtrl (SB_VERT));
   if (nSBCode == SB_THUMBTRACK)
   {
      //
      // ignore thumbtrack messages
      //
      return;
   }
   if (nSBCode == SB_THUMBPOSITION)
   {
      //
      // update thumb position to integral line height
      // and then fake a thumbtrack message to OnScroll
      //
      int nHt = m_nLineHeight;
      nPos = ((nPos + nHt - 1) / nHt) * nHt;
      nSBCode = SB_THUMBTRACK;
   }
   CScrollView::OnVScroll(nSBCode, nPos, pScrollBar);
}
```

CReportLine Class Additions

When we designed the Net Worth report, it became clear that we needed to print and display a variety of line types, unlike the Cash Flow report, which had only account headers and then detail entries. The Net Worth report has main section headings, secondary headings, detail summary lines, subtotals, and a grand total. There are ten different type of information that we need to represent. In designing the new report, we decided that we needed a new type of object in which to store these data and then identify the type of data contained in each object when the report is being drawn.

One other consideration is that the preexisting DrawRptLine member function discriminates between the various objects passed to it according to their run-time class names. In order to create an object for which a run-time name is available, it has to be derived from the CObject base class.

These considerations convinced us to create a new type of object, based upon the CObject class, which could therefore be created dynamically, and whose class could be determined at run time by using the IsKindOf member function. Our initial thought was to store complete report lines in the object, including values as well as textual content. However, after considering the flexibility we would gain in being able to position the component parts of a line individually, we decided to create the ten categories of data that were presented in the DrawRptLine member function (see page 400). In addition to creating the new object type, we also created member functions to access the individual member variables in the object.

RepLine.h Header File Contents

The header file for the newly created CReportLine class is as follows:

```
/////////////////////////////////////////////////////////////////////
// repline.h
//
// line types
//
#define BLANK_REPORT_LINE        0
#define FIRST_HEAD_LINE          1
#define SECOND_HEAD_LINE         2
#define FIRST_SUBTOTAL_HEAD      3
#define FIRST_SUBTOTAL           4
#define SECOND_SUBTOTAL_HEAD     5
#define SECOND_SUBTOTAL          6
#define NAME_LINE               10
#define VALUE_LINE              11
#define GRAND_TOTAL_HEAD        98
#define GRAND_TOTAL             99

class CReportLine : public CObject
{
protected:
    int        m_nLineType;
    CString    m_szLine;

    DECLARE_DYNCREATE (CReportLine)

public:
    int        GetLineType();
    CString    GetLine();

    void       SetLineType (int nType);
    void       SetLine (CString szLine);

    CReportLine();
    virtual ~CReportLine();
};
```

The CReportLine object has only two member variables, currently. The first is an integer, which identifies the line type, and the second is a string, which holds the printable contents of the data. The assumption is that the drawing logic will determine how to place the contents of the various data on the display or the printed page.

RepLine.cpp Source File Contents

The implementation of the construction, destruction, and member functions for the CReportLine objects is contained in the **repline.cpp** file. Because each of the member functions is so simple, we have included them all in a single section, as follows:

```cpp
/////////////////////////////////////////////////////////////////
// repline.cpp
//
#include "stdafx.h"
#include "repline.h"

IMPLEMENT_DYNCREATE (CReportLine, CObject)

CReportLine::CReportLine()
{
    // empty
}

CReportLine::~CReportLine()
{
    // empty
}

int CReportLine::GetLineType()
{
    return m_nLineType;
}

CString CReportLine::GetLine()
{
    return m_szLine;
}

void CReportLine::SetLineType (int nType)
{
    m_nLineType = nType;
}

void CReportLine::SetLine (CString szLine)
{
    m_szLine = szLine;
}
```

The member functions in the foregoing code are very simple. Even so, we feel that it is important to insulate the user from the mechanics of accessing a particular piece of data from these objects. For this reason, looking back at the header file, you will see that the member variables are protected and not public. It is conceivable that we might change or add to these objects for future reporting needs. In that case, as long as we ensure that the interfaces to the existing member functions remain the same, we have the freedom to store the data and access them in any way we choose. This policy is called "Information Hiding" or "the Black Box Approach" to object-oriented programming. We firmly believe that it is a valid approach and encourage you to follow it, whenever it is possible to do so.

Viewing the Results of Our Work

This and the previous chapter presented a methodology for creating optional settings in the Settings dialog and then used the methodology for creating new versions of the Cash Flow and Net Worth reports. The Keepit application is nearly complete at this stage. A view of the screen, with one of the account windows, and both the Cash Flow and Net Worth report displays is shown in Figure 10-2.

Figure 10-2
View of screen with
Keepit application
running

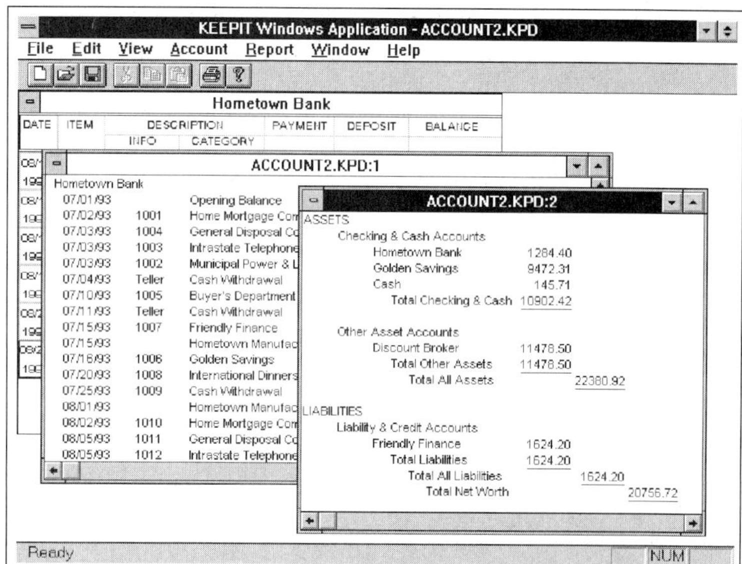

Exercises

1. In the Exercises section of Chapter 9, we suggested that you prototype a new set of Settings dialog options, which would provide the user with the ability to select transactions for inclusion in the Cash Flow report on the basis of the contents of their Payment and Deposit fields. We also suggested that you design the dialog options so that the user could specify values that were less than, greater than,

or within a range of values. If you have not already completed this exercise, please do so now.

2. Assuming that you have completed the former exercise, implement these new options, using both the information on prototyping the dialog (shown in the previous chapter) and the information on implementing the features of dynamic dialog options (shown in this chapter).[1]

3. Using the information on report preparation, design a new report, called the *Taxable Items Report*, and a corresponding Settings dialog. The report should contain only the transactions that match the accounts specified by the user, for the dates that describe the reporting period, and for the categories for which the Tax-related checkbox is checked. The transactions should be sorted by date and then alphabetically, according to category. The report should be prepared in category sequence, giving the user the ability to choose whether detailed transaction information or merely a summary total for each category should be included.[2]

4. Would it be possible for us to use the MM_TEXT mapping mode for the creation of graphics for display on any type of monitor, or to be printed on any printer? Explain your answer. (*Hint:* Mapping modes are merely predefined mathematical algorithms for transformations of coordinate values.)

5. Define the MM_ISOTROPIC and MM_ANISOTROPIC mapping modes. What characteristics distinguish these from the so-called Metric mapping modes? Explain your answer.

6. Design your own mapping mode, where the coordinate axes are located at the lower left corner of the display, positive horizontal values are to the right, and positive vertical values are toward the top of the display. With both horizontal and vertical coordinates ranging from 0 to 32767, make sure that both the horizontal and vertical axes have the same physical dimensions. (*Hint:* To create your own mapping mode, use the MM_ISOTROPIC or MM_ANISOTROPIC modes and change the window and viewport origins and extents to correspond to the desired results.)

[1.] The design and implementation of additional dialog options are quite straightforward, but a fairly extensive project. We suggest that this project be given either as an extra-credit project or be taken on as a classroom or computer lab exercise.

[2.] Creating a new report from scratch is going to be a rather lengthy project. The student will need to specify new report options for the Settings dialog, prototype the options section of the dialog, and then implement both the newly added settings and the report. This is a fairly major project, which would be a very good classroom or computer lab assignment.

7. Design an entirely new report, which, instead of text, describes the various account transaction data in the form of a bar graph. The abscissa of the bar graph should be time, with the ordinate showing the value of the items being plotted. Document your design concept, in enough detail so that it can be implemented from the specifications you provide.

8. Using the specifications created in the foregoing step, implement the new report. (*Hint*: You should not use the MM_TEXT mapping mode that we have used in the previous reports. Instead, either the MM_LOENGLISH or MM_HIENGLISH mapping mode is more appropriate for this purpose.)[1]

[1.] The design and implementation of a bar chart is a fairly straightforward, but time- consuming task. Be sure to allow enough time for the student to learn about mapping modes and how they apply to the creation of reports with graphic content. Prototyping and implementing a graph would be a good classroom project because these tasks embody all of the elements of the procedures described previously, as well as the new feature of drawing graphic objects, rather than text. The next two chapters should provide you with enough information on the use of the metric mapping modes and the drawing primitives for this project to be undertaken. You may wish to defer undertaking this assignment until you have read and understand the material in Chapters 11 and 12.

Chapter 11

Adding Support for Charts

This chapter describes the addition of the Net Worth Chart command to the Report menu and also the creation of new prototypes for the Options dialog to support creation of the chart. The newly generated code in support of the Net Worth Chart command is also shown.

We chose to add the production of a chart to the Keepit application because it gives us the opportunity to discuss the use of color and a different mapping mode for the display of the chart. The methodology presented in this and the next chapter can be extended to support the creation of other types of charts or the use of other mapping modes. Note, however, that the CReportView class that we have derived from the MFC's CScrollView class supports only the MM_TEXT and "metric" mapping modes (including MM_HIMETRIC, MM_TWIPS, MM_HIENGLISH, MM_LOMETRIC, and MM_LOENGLISH). The remaining mapping modes, MM_ISOTROPIC and MM_ANISOTROPIC, are not supported in the CScrollView class.

Adding the Net Worth Chart Command

The Net Worth Chart command is added to the Report menu using the App Studio resource editor. The procedure for adding this command is as follows:

1. Start the App Studio tool by choosing it from the Tools menu.

2. You should see App Studio's main window, which contains a list of resource types in the left pane and a list of resources of the selected type in the right pane. Click (or navigate using the keyboard) to select Menu resource type.

3. A list of four menus should appear in the pane on right side of App Studio's main window. Double click (or navigate to and press the Enter or Return key) the entry named IDR_REPORTTYPE.

4. You should see the menu bar that will be displayed when the report view is active. Click on the Report menu title to drop down the menu, showing its commands.

5. You will see that the Cash Flow and Net Worth commands are already present in the menu and an "empty" placeholder will be selected at the bottom of the menu. Double click on the empty placeholder to display the properties window (or select the empty placeholder and choose the Properties command from the Resource menu). Click the Separator checkbox and then press the Enter (or Return) key to dismiss the properties window. (If you like, you can click on the push-pin to force the properties window to remain on your screen. In that case, pressing Enter will simply cause the change to be accepted.)

6. You should see a separator line in the Report menu, immediately below the Net Worth command. A new empty placeholder will now be selected. Once again, double click the placeholder entry to show its properties. Change the properties as follows:

   a. Enter ID_CHRT_NET_WORTH in the ID field.

   b. Enter "Net Worth Chart" in the Caption field.

   c. Enter "Creates a chart based upon the Net Worth data" into the Prompt field.

   d. Press Enter (or Return) to accept the changes.

7. Close the resource editor window for the IDR_REPORTTYPE menu resource by double clicking the document's Control menu box (make sure it's the Control menu for the document and not for App Studio itself) or use the Ctrl-F4 keyboard shortcut.

8. You should now be looking at App Studio's main window once again. With the resource type of Menu still selected, open the menu resource named IDR_KEEPITTYPE, perform steps 5 and 6 for this menu bar, and then close the IDR_KEEPITTYPE resource editor window to once again reveal App Studio's main window.

9. Open the IDR_CATVIEWTYPE menu resource, perform steps 5 and 6 for that menu, and then close the IDR_CATVIEWTYPE resource editor window.

10. Save the resource file by choosing Save from the File menu and then choose Exit from the File menu to exit the App Studio editor.

After completing the foregoing steps, you will have created a Separator and Net Worth Chart command for the three main application menus. The next task is to add a message handler to the CKeepitDoc class for the new command.

Once again, it's important to emphasize that handling the commands in the Report menu within the document class is the proper approach. The document is the "keeper" of all of the data for the application, and it is the appropriate class from which report windows are created. Because Keepit is an MDI (multiple document interface) application, the user could choose to keep several sets of accounts in different files, each of which could be open, with its own CKeepitDoc object.

The creation of the message handler for the Net Worth Chart command is accomplished as follows:

1. Launch the ClassWizard from the main Visual C++ environment by choosing that command from the Browse menu (or use the Ctrl-W keyboard shortcut).

2. The main ClassWizard window should open. Make sure that the Class Name combo box shows CKeepitDoc as its selection and that the Message Maps tab is selected.

3. You should see an entry for the ID_CHRT_NET_WORTH resource in the Object IDs list (top left pane). Click to select that entry.

4. The list in the top right pane will show an entry for the COMMAND message. Select that entry and then click the Add Function button on the right side of the main window.

5. A dialog with a suggested name for the new message handler function will appear. Change the name to OnChrtNetWorth and then click the OK button to accept the name and close the window.

6. Following completion of the foregoing step, you should see the new message handler entry in the bottom pane of ClassWizard's main window. Click the OK button in the main window to accept the change, dismiss the window, and exit the ClassWizard tool.

If you open the **keepdoc.cpp** file, you will see that the ClassWizard has added the new skeleton code for the message handler at the end of the file, and it has also made an entry for the message in the Message Map at the beginning of that file.

Prototyping New Settings Dialog Options

In Chapter 9, we introduced the concept of using the App Studio tool to prototype the appearance of an expanded Settings dialog. In that chapter, we added a button called Options to the Settings dialog and then we prototyped the appearance of the dialog when the Options button was clicked for two different Cash Flow report options (Categories and Description). The Info option had the same appearance as Description. We decided not to create entirely new dialogs for each of the report options because doing so would consume additional program resources and fail to provide a seamless change of appearance when one of the options is chosen. Rather than close the dialog and open another, or open a secondary dialog for each set of options, we decided to dynamically enlarge the dialog vertically when the Options button was clicked and then alter the contents of the lower portion of the expanded dialog.

Alteration of the contents of the lower portion of the dialog consisted of adding a group box, with a caption of Options, a combo box to provide a choice of options, and then various other controls that were appropriate for the option choice.

In this chapter, we are going to continue the tradition of prototyping the appearance of the Settings dialog, with the addition of new options that are appropriate when executing the Net Worth Chart command. Three new sets of options will be shown. When each set of options is prototyped, we will record the coordinates and dimensions of each new control so that these may be installed into the program code to re-create the dialog's appearance.

Prototyping the Graph Type Options

The new Net Worth Chart report is going to consist of either a vertical bar chart or a line plot of the net worth value for each of a series of intervals. We are going to allow the user to choose which of the two types of graphs is desired. In addition, we will allow the user to specify the horizontal and vertical axis titles in this set of options. The process for prototyping the new appearance of the Settings dialog is as follows:

1. Launch the AppWizard tool by choosing that command from the Tools menu in the main Visual Workbench environment.

2. When App Studio's main window is displayed, select Dialog as the desired resource type in the left pane and then click to select (don't double click at this point) the IDD_SETTINGS dialog. The entry should be highlighted, indicating that it is selected.

3. Choose Copy from the Edit menu and then immediately choose Paste from the Edit menu. This will create a copy of the existing dialog in the list, but with the name IDD_SETTINGS1. The new copy will be selected.

4. Press the Enter (or Return) key to open the IDD_SETTINGS1 dialog editor. When you do so, you will see a view of the unexpanded Settings dialog, as shown in Chapter 9, Figure 9-5.

5. We need to enlarge this dialog, so click on the dialog to select it and then move the mouse to the handle at the bottom of the dialog and drag the handle down until the dimensions of the dialog (as shown

in the bottom right status bar pane) are 267 x 169. The blank area at the bottom of the expanded dialog is where we will add all of the new controls.

6. Choose the Group tool from the editor's control palette and drag a copy of the group box control onto the dialog at position 6, 82. Choose the pointer tool and resize the control so that its dimensions are 255 x 85. You will see that the group box will cover most of the lower portion of the dialog. Double click on the word "Static" to display the control's properties box and change the caption to read "Options." This is not a necessary step, but it will give you a better idea of the final appearance of the dialog if you do so. All of the properties of the controls we are prototyping will be set via statements in the program, so whatever properties are chosen during this session are used only to enhance our perception of the dialog's final appearance, as it will exist at run time. By performing the procedures declared as *Optional,* you will also be able to test the dialog by choosing the Test command from the Resource menu.

7. Choose the Static Text tool from the control palette and drag a copy of a Static Text control onto the dialog at position 15, 102. Change the dimensions of the control to 21 x 8, and then double click the control and change its caption to read "Type:" (*Optional:* Change the Text Align property to Right.)

8. Choose the Combo Box tool from the control palette and drag a copy of a combo box onto the dialog at position 40, 100. Resize the closed combo box to the dimensions 73 x 12. Click on the arrow at the right side of the combo box to cause it to open and change its open dimensions to 73 x 59. (*Optional:* Open the properties window and enter list choices of Graph Type, Interval, and Colors. Change the Style properties to Drop List, delete the Sort check, and make sure that Vert. Scroll is checked.)

9. At this point, we recommend that you save the resource file and close the current window by double clicking the document's control box (or use the Ctrl-F4 keyboard shortcut). The App Studio main window should be on your screen and the IDD_SETTINGS1 dialog should still be selected.

10. Duplicate this dialog by choosing the Copy and then Paste commands from the Edit menu. This action will cause another copy of the dialog to be created, named IDD_SETTINGS2 We will be using the IDD_SETTINGS1 dialog as a starting point for prototyping additional options. (If you see some number other than 1 following the dialog name, don't worry. Go ahead and use the new copy. There might still be some vestiges of earlier prototyping efforts remaining

in your resource file, causing App Studio to assign a dialog ID that doesn't conflict with any existing names. When we conclude these tutorials, we'll explain how to clean up your resource file and the **resource.h** header file.)

11. Open the IDD_SETTINGS2 (copy of IDD_SETTINGS1) dialog and begin adding the controls that pertain to the Graph Type option. To begin, choose the Group tool from the control palette and drag a group box onto the dialog at position 39,115. Choose the pointer tool and change the dimensions of the group box to 73x45.

12. Double click the word "Static" on the group box control to open its properties window and delete the word "Static" in the Caption property. This will cause the box to be untitled—an unbroken rectangle.

13. Choose the Radio Button tool from the control palette and drag a radio button on the dialog at position 45,127 and change its dimensions to 60x10. Double click the button and change its caption to "Vertical Bar." Create an additional radio button at position 45,142, change its dimensions to 60x10, and change its caption to "Line Plot."

14. Choose the Static Text tool from the control palette and drag a static text control onto the dialog at position 125,102. Change its dimensions to 130x8 and then change its caption to "Vertical Axis Title:" Drag another static text control onto the dialog at position 125,137 and change its dimensions to 130x8. Change its caption to read "Horizontal Axis Title:"

15. Choose the Edit Box tool from the control palette and drag an edit box control onto the dialog at position 125,116. Change its dimensions to 130x12. Drag another edit box control onto the dialog at position 125,149 and change its dimensions to 130x12.

When the foregoing steps are complete, the prototype for the Graph Type options is complete. You can test the operation of the dialog by choosing the Test command from the Resource menu. You should see a dialog that has the appearance shown in Figure 11-1.

Note in Figure 11-1 that we have entered example text into the axes titles, have selected the Vertical Bar graph type, and have entered dates for the interval for which the graph is to be drawn. When you have completed testing the dialog, press the Escape key to exit the test mode. Close the window for this dialog by double clicking in the document's control menu box (or use the Ctrl-F4 keyboard shortcut to do so).

As with the prototypes shown in Chapter 9, we aren't really interested in retaining the IDD_SETTINGS2 dialog, but are very interested in the posi-

Figure 11-1
Appearance of the Graph Type options in the Settings dialog

Net Worth Report Settings

Title: Net Worth for Calendar Year 1993   OK

Date From: 1/1/93   Date To: 12/31/93   Cancel

Accounts...   Period: Year-To-Date   Options...

Options

Type: Graph Type   Vertical Axis Title:

Net Worth in Dollars

Vertical Bar   Line Plot

Horizontal Axis Title:

Monthly Intervals

tion and dimension values for each of the controls. In order to make things easier for you to reproduce our results, we have created a table that describes the controls and their settings. You can refer to these settings in Table 11-1.

Table 11-1
Position and Dimension settings for Graph Type options in Settings dialog

Control Name	Position	Dimensions
Overall Extended Dialog	0, 0	267 x 169
Options Group Box	6, 82	255 x 85
Type Static Text	15, 102	21 x 8
Type Combo Box	40, 100	73 x 59
Graph Type Group Box	39, 115	73 x 45
Vertical Bar Radio Button	45, 127	60 x 10
Line Plot Radio Button	45, 142	60 x 10
Vertical Axis Static Text	125, 102	130 x 8
Vertical Axis Edit Box	125, 116	130 x 12
Horizontal Axis Static Text	125, 137	130 x 8
Horizontal Axis Edit Box	125, 149	130 x 12

Prototyping the Interval Options

The next set of options allow the user to specify an interval for which Net Worth values are to be graphed. For example, choices of monthly, quarterly, or annually are provided. The instructions for prototyping these new options are as follows:

1. If you are continuing to prototype the options for the Settings dialog from the point where the tutorial for creating the Graph Type options ended, then skip to Step 3 of this tutorial; otherwise, continue with the next step.

2. Launch App Studio from the Visual Workbench environment by choosing that command from the Tools menu. Select Dialog as the resource type to edit. You should see several dialogs, including ones named IDD_SETTINGS, IDD_SETTINGS1, and IDD_SETTINGS2 (if you have been following the prototyping tutorials). If the names for the copies of your Settings dialog are different from those mentioned, don't worry. Continue the tutorial with the dialog names that App Studio has assigned.

3. With App Studio's main window on your screen and with Dialog as the selected resource type, you should see three versions of the Settings dialog. Delete the one you constructed for the Graph Type options by clicking on it to select it (it should have a name of IDD_SETTINGS2, or some larger number at the end of the name), and then press the Delete key to delete the dialog resource.

4. Select the first copy of the Settings dialog resource that we created during the tutorial for creating the Graph Type options (see page 433, step 9). It should be named IDD_SETTINGS1 (or the version with the lowest number). This dialog is the expanded version, with only the Options group box, Type static text, and Type combo box controls added.

5. Create a duplicate of this dialog by choosing Copy and then Paste from App Studio's File menu. The dialog will probably not have the same name as the one you just deleted, but we will call it IDD_SETTINGS2 for purposes of this tutorial.[1]

6. Open the new duplicate dialog and add the controls for the Interval options. To do so, choose the Radio Button tool from App Studio's control palette and drag a radio button onto the dialog at position 42,123. Change the dimensions of the button to 66x10 and then double click on it to show the property window and enter a caption of "Monthly." Add two additional radio buttons to the dialog at positions 42,135 and 42,147, change their dimensions to 66x10, and then change their captions to "Quarterly" and "Annually," respectively.

---

[1] We indicated earlier that when you delete a resource, App Studio may leave some portions of the resource still defined in both the **keepit.rc** resource file and also in the **resource.h** header file. We will give you some guidelines for cleaning up these files later in this chapter.

After completing the foregoing steps, the dialog for the Interval options is complete. You can test the dialog by choosing the Test command from the Resource menu. The completed dialog should have the appearance shown in Figure 11-2.

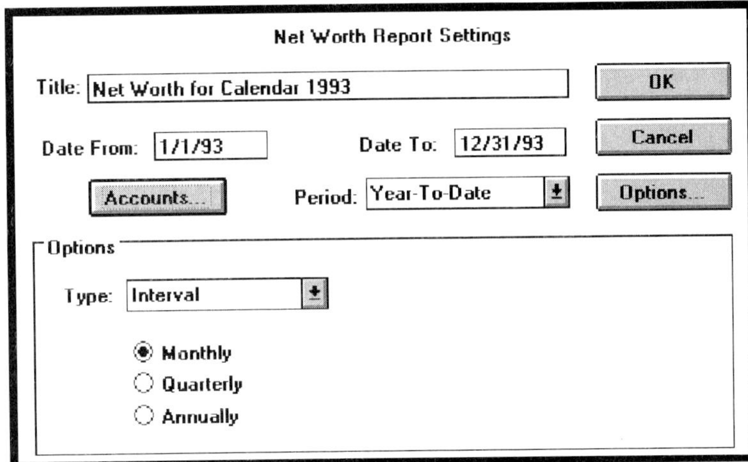

Figure 11-2
Appearance of completed Interval options in the Settings dialog

When you have completed the test, you can exit by pressing the Escape key. Close the dialog editor window by double clicking in the document's control box (or use the Ctrl-F4 keyboard shortcut). After recording the position and dimensions of each new control, you can delete the dialog by selecting it in App Studio's main window (if it isn't selected already) and then press the Delete key. The settings for the Interval options are shown in Table 11-2.

Table 11-2
Position and Dimension settings for Interval options in Settings dialog

Control Name	Position	Dimensions
Overall Extended Dialog	0, 0	267 x 169
Options Group Box	6, 82	255 x 85
Type Static Text	15, 102	21 x 8
Type Combo Box	40, 100	73 x 59
Monthly Radio Button	42, 123	66 x 10
Quarterly Radio Button	42, 135	66 x 10
Annually Radio Button	42, 147	66 x 10

Prototyping the Colors Options

We have decided that the user should have the ability to select the colors to be used for displaying various elements of the Net Worth Chart. In order to integrate the selection of colors along with other options in the Settings dialog, we have decided to create a palette of colors and a set of graph properties to which the color selections will apply. We have also decided to include a "Use Color" checkbox, to allow the user to elect for the application to use, or not use, color in its display of the chart. The instructions for creating the Colors options for the Settings dialog are as follows:

1. If you are prototyping the Colors options by following this tutorial, immediately after completing the tutorial for the creation of the Interval options in the foregoing section, then skip to step 3 of this tutorial; otherwise, proceed to the next step.

2. Launch App Studio from the Visual Workbench environment by choosing that command from the Tools menu. Select Dialog as the resource type to edit and you should see a list of several dialogs in the right hand pane of App Studio's main window.

3. There should be only two versions of the Settings dialog at this point. One should be named IDD_SETTINGS and the other should have a name such as IDD_SETTINGS1. If the second version has some other number as a suffix, that's all right. We want to use that version. Open the IDD_SETTINGS1 dialog (or equivalent) by double clicking on the name (or navigate with the keyboard to select the name and press the Enter key).

4. The dialog editor should show the expanded version of the Settings dialog, with only the Options group box, Type static text, and Type combo box controls included in the bottom portion of the dialog. Begin creating the Colors options by choosing the Check Box tool from App Studio's control palette and then drag a checkbox control onto the dialog at position 126,101. Change the dimensions of the control to 48x10 and then double click the control to set its Caption property to "Use Color."

5. Choose the Static Text tool from the control palette and drag a static text control onto the dialog at position 40,119. Change the dimensions of the control to 50x8 and change its caption to "Axis Color." Create three additional static text controls in the dialog at positions 40,131, 40,143, and 40,155. Change each of their dimensions to 50x8 and then change their captions to "Title Color," "Label Color," and "Graph Color," respectively.

6. Choose the User-defined tool from App Studio's control palette (it's the one with a picture of a person's head) and drag a user control onto the dialog at position 95,118. Change the dimensions of the control to 10x10. Drag three additional user controls onto the dia-

log at positions 95,130, 95,142, and 95,154. Change each of their dimensions to 10x10. These will all show up as grey squares on your screen. Each of these squares will contain a color button at run time, reflecting the color choice for that chart property.

7. Choose the Group Box tool from the control palette and drag a group box onto the dialog at position 183,89. Change the dimensions of the group box to 68x74 and then double click the word "Static" to open the properties window and change the caption text to read "Colors."

8. Choose the User-defined tool from the control palette and drag a number of user controls onto the dialog, in a 4x4 matrix of color samples. Each control should be sized to dimensions of 10x10 and the controls should be arranged so that controls 1–4 are in the first row, controls 5–8 are in the second row, controls 9–12 are in the third row, and controls 13–16 are in the fourth row. The controls correspond to color sample buttons, which will be displayed in various colors at run time and which can be chosen to set the color of a selected chart property. The positions of the color sample buttons are shown in Figure 11-3.

When the foregoing steps are complete, the dialog should appear as shown in Figure 11-3. The figure shows the dialog as it appears inside the App Studio dialog editor, with grey squares for the user controls. When the dialog is tested, as shown in Figure 11-4, the user controls do not appear. When you have finished testing the dialog, exit that mode by pressing the Escape key and then close the dialog editor window by double clicking in its control box (or use the Ctrl-F4 keyboard shortcut). Finally, you should delete the IDD_SETTINGS1 dialog, as it will no longer be needed. You should have only one Settings dialog at this point, whose name is IDD_SETTINGS.

The position and dimensions of each of the controls shown in Figure 11-3 are documented in Table 11-3 and Table 11-4. The user controls are named Color 1 through Color 16 and are numbered 1–4 in the first row, 5–8 in the second, 9–12 in the third, and 13–16 in the last. We will be creating each of the color samples as a user-draw button. Each button will be drawn with a custom color. The buttons in the first column will contain shades of grey, for users without color monitors.

Cleaning Up Your Resource Files

Earlier in this chapter we indicated that when you deleted a copy of the Settings dialog resource while inside App Studio and created a new copy of the dialog that it might not be named the same as the one that was deleted. This is because App Studio may leave some traces of the first copy's

Figure 11-3
Appearance of the Colors
options in the Settings
dialog, inside the App
Studio dialog editor

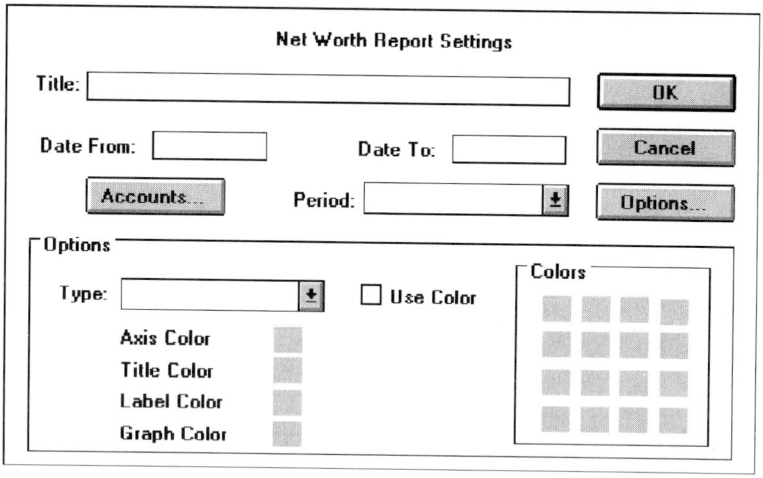

Figure 11-4
Appearance of the Colors
options in the Settings
dialog when being run in
test mode

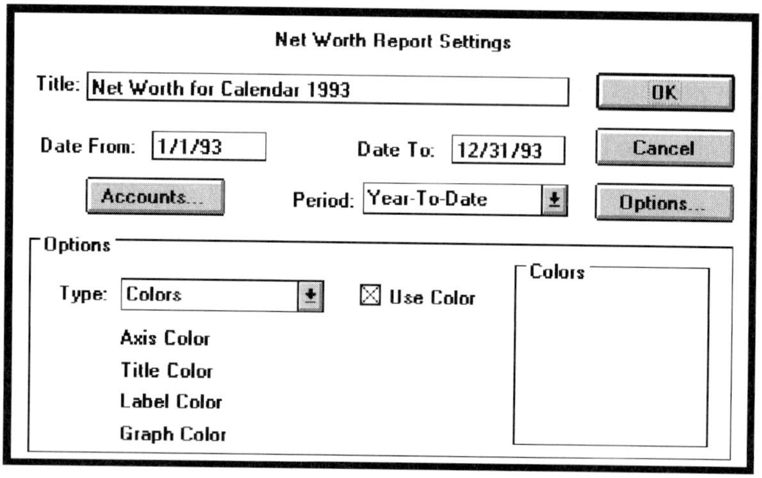

existence in the **keepit.rc** and **resource.h** files. It is possible to clean up
these files so that new dialogs will be numbered as indicated in the foregoing tutorials. However, you should understand that editing the resource and the corresponding header files is very prone to disaster if you
inadvertently delete any needed information. Therefore, BE VERY CARE-
FUL WHEN YOU ARE WORKING WITH EITHER OF THESE FILES. You are well
advised to make copies of the files in case you have problems later when
trying to use the versions you have cleaned up.

Cleaning Up the Keepit.rc Resource File

In order to clean up the **keepit.rc** resource file, you must first set the Editor Options (choose Editor from the Options menu) so that the check
box named "Open RC Files Using App Studio" is not checked. This will

Table 11-3

Position and Dimension settings for Colors options in Settings dialog

Control Name	Position	Dimensions
Overall Extended Dialog	0, 0	267 x 169
Options Group Box	6, 82	255 x 85
Type Static Text	15, 102	21 x 8
Type Combo Box	40, 100	73 x 59
Use Color Check Box	126, 101	48 x 10
Axis Color Static Text	40, 119	50 x 8
Title Color Static Text	40, 131	50 x 8
Label Color Static Text	40, 143	50 x 8
Graph Color Static Text	40, 155	50 x 8
Axis Color User Control	95, 118	10 x 10
Title Color User Control	95, 130	10 x 10
Label Color User Control	95, 142	10 x 10
Graph Color User Control	95, 154	10 x 10

Table 11-4

Position and Dimension settings for Color sample controls in Settings dialog

Control Name	Position	Dimensions
Color 1 User Control	192, 105	10 x 10
Color 2 User Control	206, 105	10 x 10
Color 3 User Control	220, 105	10 x 10
Color 4 User Control	234, 105	10 x 10
Color 5 User Control	192, 119	10 x 10
Color 6 User Control	206, 119	10 x 10
Color 7 User Control	220, 119	10 x 10
Color 8 User Control	234, 119	10 x 10
Color 9 User Control	192, 133	10 x 10
Color 10 User Control	206, 133	10 x 10
Color 11 User Control	220, 133	10 x 10
Color 12 User Control	234, 133	10 x 10
Color 13 User Control	192, 147	10 x 10
Color 14 User Control	206, 147	10 x 10
Color 15 User Control	220, 147	10 x 10
Color 16 User Control	234, 147	10 x 10

enable you to open the resource file as an ASCII text file with the Visual Workbench editor. The procedure for cleaning up this file is as follows:

1. Open the **keepit.rc** file by choosing Open from the Visual Workbench File menu and then choose that file.

2. Choose the Find command from the Edit menu (or use the Alt-F3 keyboard shortcut) and enter IDD_SETTINGS as the text to find. Click the Find Next button to locate the first occurrence of that text. You should find an entry for the original dialog, whose text description is as follows:

```
IDD_SETTINGS DIALOG DISCARDABLE  0, 0, 267, 84
STYLE DS_MODALFRAME | WS_POPUP
FONT 8, "MS Sans Serif"
BEGIN
    EDITTEXT        IDC_TITLE,27,22,174,11,ES_AUTOHSCROLL
    EDITTEXT        IDC_FROM,51,44,41,11,ES_AUTOHSCROLL
    EDITTEXT        IDC_TO,159,44,41,11,ES_AUTOHSCROLL
    PUSHBUTTON      "Accounts...",IDC_ACCTS_BUTTON,27,62,50,14
    COMBOBOX        IDC_PER_LIST,127,63,74,60,CBS_DROPDOWNLIST
                        | WS_VSCROLL | WS_TABSTOP
    DEFPUSHBUTTON    "OK",IDOK,211,20,50,14
    PUSHBUTTON      "Cancel",IDCANCEL,211,41,50,14
    PUSHBUTTON      "Options...",IDC_OPTIONS,211,62,50,14
    RTEXT           "Title:",IDC_STATIC,6,23,19,8
    RTEXT           "Date From:",IDC_FROM_LABEL,7,46,39,8
    RTEXT           "Date To:",IDC_STATIC,123,46,31,8
    RTEXT           "Period:",IDC_PER_LABEL,94,66,30,7
    CTEXT           "Net Worth Report Settings",
                    IDC_DIALOG_TITLE,79,5,117,10
END
```

The foregoing dialog description may not appear exactly as depicted, because we have had to wrap a few of the long lines onto succeeding lines in the book. However, don't change any of these lines. Now, search for another occurrence of the IDD_SETTINGS string. You may find something similar to the following:

```
IDD_SETTINGS DLGINIT
BEGIN
    143, 0x403, 13, 0
0x6559, 0x7261, 0x542d, 0x2d6f, 0x6144, 0x6574, "\000"
    143, 0x403, 14, 0
0x7543, 0x7272, 0x6e65, 0x2074, 0x6f4d, 0x746e, 0x0068,
    143, 0x403, 16, 0
0x7543, 0x7272, 0x6e65, 0x2074, 0x7551, 0x7261, 0x6574, 0x0072,
    143, 0x403, 13, 0
0x7543, 0x7272, 0x6e65, 0x2074, 0x6559, 0x7261, "\000"
    143, 0x403, 11, 0
0x614c, 0x7473, 0x4d20, 0x6e6f, 0x6874, "\000"
    143, 0x403, 13, 0
0x614c, 0x7473, 0x5120, 0x6175, 0x7472, 0x7265, "\000"
    143, 0x403, 10, 0
0x614c, 0x7473, 0x5920, 0x6165, 0x0072,
    143, 0x403, 17, 0
0x6c41, 0x206c, 0x7254, 0x6e61, 0x6173, 0x7463, 0x6f69, 0x736e,
"\000"
    0
END
```

The foregoing is the description of initialization values for the various controls in the dialog (once again, the long lines have been wrapped onto succeeding lines). This code should also be left intact. DO NOT DELETE EITHER OF THE FOREGOING TWO SECTIONS OF THE KEEPIT.RC FILE.

3. Next, search for another occurrence of the IDD_SETTINGS string. You may find a second copy of the initialization values, beginning with the name IDD_SETTINGS1 DLGINIT (or a similar numerical value at the end of the name). If so, then delete this entire section of the resource file, beginning with the line on which the new name occurs, the next line that contains the word BEGIN, and everything else, including the line containing the END statement for the initialization values.

4. Repeat the preceding step until no more occurrences of the string IDD_SETTINGS are found. There should be only one dialog description and associated set of initialization values for the IDD_SETTINGS dialog.

5. Save the **keepit.rc** file at this point and then close the file.

Cleaning Up the Resource.h Header File

The **keepit.rc** file inputs the **resource.h** header file to supply numerical values for the mnemonic names used for the various resources named in the resource file. During the course of prototyping various new versions of the Settings dialog, the **resource.h** header file may accumulate definitions for resources or dialogs that were deleted previously. The procedure for cleaning up this file is as follows:

1. Open the **resource.h** header file from within the Visual Workbench environment by choosing Open from the File menu, specify that file to be opened, and then click OK.

2. Choose the Find command from the Edit menu (or use the Alt-F3 keyboard shortcut) and specify the string IDD_SETTINGS as the text to be used in the search. Click the Find Next button to find the first occurrence of this string. You should find an entry whose text is somewhat like the following:

```
#define IDD_SETTINGS    105
```

You should leave the foregoing definition alone. Do not change or delete it.

3. Choose Find Next to find another occurrence of the string. You may find an entry that contains the following text:

```
#define IDD_SETTINGS1 106
```

Go ahead and delete the entry for the dialog that is no longer being used. Don't worry if the numbering is no longer sequential in the **resource.h** file.

4. Repeat the foregoing step until no more occurrences of the string IDD_SETTINGS are found. Save and then close the file at this time.

The foregoing steps will remove any traces of the additional versions of the Settings dialog that we have created in our prototyping efforts.

Examining the Newly Generated Code

The only newly generated code for this version of the application is the new message handler for the Net Worth Chart command, which was generated into the CKeepitDoc class.

Examining the Additions to the CKeepitDoc Class

The newly generated code for the Net Worth Chart features consists of a new message map declaration in the **keepdoc.h** header file and the message map entry and skeleton message handler function in the **keepdoc.cpp** source file.

KeepDoc.h Header File Additions

The entire group of message map declarations, including the newly generated declaration for OnChrtNetWorth, is as follows:

```
// Generated message map functions
protected:
    //{{AFX_MSG(CKeepitDoc)
    afx_msg void OnViewCategories();
    afx_msg void OnAcctEdit();
    afx_msg void OnCashFlow();
    afx_msg void OnNetWorth();
    afx_msg void OnChrtNetWorth();
    //}}AFX_MSG
    DECLARE_MESSAGE_MAP()
```

KeepDoc.cpp Source File Additions

The message map entries in the **keepdoc.cpp** file are as follows:

```
BEGIN_MESSAGE_MAP(CKeepitDoc, CDocument)
    //{{AFX_MSG_MAP(CKeepitDoc)
    ON_COMMAND(ID_VIEW_CATEGORIES, OnViewCategories)
```

```
      ON_COMMAND(ID_ACCT_EDIT, OnAcctEdit)
      ON_COMMAND(ID_RPT_CASH_FLOW, OnCashFlow)
      ON_COMMAND(ID_RPT_NET_WORTH, OnNetWorth)
      ON_COMMAND(ID_CHRT_NET_WORTH, OnChrtNetWorth)
      //}}AFX_MSG_MAP
END_MESSAGE_MAP()
```

The newly generated skeleton code for the OnChrtNetWorth message handler function is as follows:

```
void CKeepitDoc::OnChrtNetWorth()
{
    // TODO: Add your command handler code here
}
```

Exercises

1. When we created the new commands in the Report menu, we added a Separator item before adding the Net Worth Chart command. Explain why it was desirable to include the Separator.

2. Instead of including the Net Worth Chart command in the Report menu directly, what other means of selecting textual reports and graphic charts in the user interface would be useful? Explain your answer.

3. When creating the Colors options for the Settings dialog, we used a User-defined control as a placeholder for the color samples. Why was that done and could some other control have served the same purpose? Explain your answer.

4. Describe how you envision the Colors options to be handled by the user. How would a color choice be made for each of the properties of the graph? Describe in detail how you would implement the suggested behavior.

5. Define a new type of chart. Make it a pie chart. Determine what options would be needed to supply the information for creating this chart and then prototype the changes to the Settings dialog to provide the new options.[1]

---

[1] Creation of a pie chart is a nontrivial task. It is suggested that the design of its features and Settings options be the first phase of a two-phase project, either for extra credit or as a classroom project.

Chapter 12
Customizing the Chart Code

This chapter describes the custom code additions that fully implement the creation of vertical bar and line plot charts, whose settings were prototyped in Chapter 11.

The main features of this chapter are descriptions of code that uses the MM_LOENGLISH metric mapping mode, instead of the default MM_TEXT mapping mode, and also the use of color in the code that draws the charts on the display. Code for printout of charts, but in black-and-white mode only, is also provided.

Support for the New Settings Dialog Options

We prototyped three new options for the Settings dialog in Chapter 11. These options pertained to the creation of charts from data held in the document's individual account transaction lists.

As with the Settings dialog options that we created in support of the Cash Flow report, we have also prototyped the new chart options to occupy the expanded area of that dialog.

We described the method for prototyping the new options in Chapter 11 and we enumerated all of the newly defined controls, their positions, and their dimensions, in Tables 11-1 through 11-4. The next step is to create identifiers for the controls and then associate the identifiers with numeric values.

Newly Defined Control Identifiers

We have created quite a number of new controls in support of the chart options. As we indicated in Chapter 10, when we described our methodology for associating numeric values with the control identifiers, beginning on page 350, we have added the new entries to the **resource.h** header file. Each entry associates a mnemonic identifier with a numeric value. Also, in order not to conflict with the automatic resource numbering performed by the App Studio tool, we have numbered our controls beginning with the value 512. Chapter 10 illustrated the definition of a number of controls in this range. The newly added controls, in support of the chart options, are numbered beginning where the definitions in Chapter 10 left off. The full set of control definitions, including some prior to the ones we have defined, and also some important definitions in the **resource.h** header file, for use by the App Studio tool, following the ones we have defined are as follows:

```
// last portion of App Studio-defined resources
//
#define IDC_RADIO2                    162
#define IDC_RADIO3                    163
#define IDC_FROM_LABEL                164

// beginning of optional controls
//
#define IDC_OPTIONS_BOX               512
#define IDC_TYPE_LABEL                513
#define IDC_TYPE_COMBO                514
#define IDC_ALL_RADIO                 515
#define IDC_NONE_RADIO                516
#define IDC_TAX_RELATED_RADIO         517
#define IDC_CATEGORY_LIST             518
#define IDC_EDIT_TEXT_STRING          519
#define IDC_STARTS_RADIO              520
#define IDC_CONTAINS_RADIO            521
#define IDC_EXACT_RADIO               522

// newly added controls to support charts
//
#define IDC_GRAPH_BOX                 523
#define IDC_VERT_BAR                  524
#define IDC_LINE_PLOT                 525
#define IDC_VERT_LABEL                526
#define IDC_VERT_TITLE                527
#define IDC_HORZ_LABEL                528
#define IDC_HORZ_TITLE                529
#define IDC_MONTHLY                   530
#define IDC_QUARTERLY                 531
#define IDC_ANNUALLY                  532
#define IDC_USE_COLOR_CHECK           533
#define IDC_AXIS_COLOR                534
#define IDC_TITLE_COLOR               535
#define IDC_LABEL_COLOR               536
#define IDC_GRAPH_COLOR               537
#define IDC_AXIS_SAMPLE               538
#define IDC_TITLE_SAMPLE              539
#define IDC_LABEL_SAMPLE              540
#define IDC_GRAPH_SAMPLE              541
#define IDC_COLOR_1                   542
#define IDC_COLOR_2                   543
#define IDC_COLOR_3                   544
#define IDC_COLOR_4                   545
#define IDC_COLOR_5                   546
#define IDC_COLOR_6                   547
#define IDC_COLOR_7                   548
#define IDC_COLOR_8                   549
#define IDC_COLOR_9                   550
#define IDC_COLOR_10                  551
#define IDC_COLOR_11                  552
#define IDC_COLOR_12                  553
#define IDC_COLOR_13                  554
#define IDC_COLOR_14                  555
#define IDC_COLOR_15                  556
#define IDC_COLOR_16                  557
```

```
#define IDC_COLORS_BOX                              558

#define ID_ACCT_EDIT                                32768
#define ID_VIEW_CATEGORIES                          32769
#define ID_ACCT_PRINT                               32770
#define ID_RPT_CASH_FLOW                            32771
#define ID_RPT_NET_WORTH                            32772
#define ID_RPT_TAXABLE                              32773
#define ID_CHRT_NET_WORTH                           32774

// Next default values for new objects
//
#ifdef APSTUDIO_INVOKED
#ifndef APSTUDIO_READONLY_SYMBOLS

#define _APS_NEXT_RESOURCE_VALUE                    117
#define _APS_NEXT_COMMAND_VALUE                     32775
#define _APS_NEXT_CONTROL_VALUE                     165
#define _APS_NEXT_SYMED_VALUE                       101
#endif
#endif
```

As is evident in the foregoing, quite a number of controls have been added to the list in the **resource.h** header file. Keeping all of the control definitions in this one file will help to ensure that duplicate resources are not defined inadvertently.

CSettings Class Header File Declarations

Because we have added quite a number of new declarations to the header file for the CSettings class, we have decided to show you the entire contents of the file. Some portions of this file have been shown previously, but if you are re-creating the application step by step, by reading the tutorials in this book, you will appreciate being able to view the entire contents of the file. Because of the file's length, we have broken it up into sections that are easier to understand and explain.

Settings.h Initial Section

The first section of the **settings.h** header file contains the definitions of forward class references and report types that are used both in the settings dialog and report-generation code. The first section of the **settings.h** header file is as follows:

```
// settings.h : header file
//

class CKeepitDoc;         // added forward reference
class CCButton;           // added forward reference
class CCategory;          // added forward reference

/////////////////////////////////////////////////////////////////
// CSettings dialog

#define YEAR_TO_DATE      0
#define CURRENT_MONTH     1
```

```
#define CURRENT_QUARTER   2
#define CURRENT_YEAR      3
#define LAST_MONTH        4
#define LAST_QUARTER      5
#define LAST_YEAR         6
#define ALL_TRANSACTIONS  7
```

Dynamic (DDX) and General Variable Declarations

The next section of the **settings.h** header file contains the beginning of
the class declaration, as well as the declaration of member variables that
participate in the dynamic data exchange (DDX) actions when the dialog
is created or dismissed. In addition, some general-purpose member variables are also included in this section, which is as follows:

```
class CSettings : public CDialog
{
// Construction
public:
    CSettings(CWnd* pParent = NULL); // standard constructor

// Dialog Data
    //{{AFX_DATA(CSettings)
    enum { IDD = IDD_SETTINGS };
    CButton      m_Options;
    CComboBox    m_PeriodList;
    CButton      m_AcctsButton;
    CStatic      m_DialogTitle;
    CString      m_From;
    CString      m_Title;
    CString      m_To;
    //}}AFX_DATA

    virtual BOOL OnInitDialog(void);

public:
// Local Member Variables
    CObList      m_Accounts;      // list of selected accounts
    CString      m_szDialogTitle;// dialog title string
    CKeepitDoc*  m_pDoc;         // pointer to document (added)

// Implementation
protected:
    virtual void DoDataExchange(CDataExchange* pDX);
```

The foregoing declarations are accessible to any other class that has a
pointer to the current object. The only exception being the DoDataExchange member function, which has been declared to be protected.

Message Handler Function Declarations

The next section of the **settings.h** header file contains the message han-
dler declarations. Both the ones that are created automatically by the
App Studio tool and the ones that we have added to support the various
Settings dialog options are shown. These are as follows:

```
// Generated message map functions
//{{AFX_MSG(CSettings)
afx_msg void OnPerListSelect();
afx_msg void OnAcctsClicked();
afx_msg void OnOptions();
afx_msg void OnDestroy();
//}}AFX_MSG

// dynamic message map functions to handle selected options

afx_msg void OnTypeSelect();   // select option type
afx_msg void OnCatSelect();    // category selected
afx_msg void OnCatRadio();     // category radio clicked
afx_msg void OnStringEntry();  // edit field entered
afx_msg void OnContentsRadio();// text contents clicked

// dynamic message map functions for graph options

afx_msg void OnGraphTypeRadio();// select graph type
afx_msg void OnTitleEntry();   // graph title entered
afx_msg void OnIntervalRadio();// interval selected
afx_msg void OnUseColorCheck();// use color clicked
afx_msg void OnSampleClick();  // chart property clicked
afx_msg void OnColorClick();   // color sample clicked

DECLARE_MESSAGE_MAP()
```

Notice in the foregoing that we have been careful to segregate the message handler function declarations that pertain to the optional controls from the ones that are managed automatically by the ClassWizard tool. It is important to never modify any of the declarations between the special `//{{AFX_MSG` `//}}AFX_MSG` comments.

Standard Member Functions and Member Variables

The next section of the **settings.h** header file contains member function and variable declarations that are common to all of the optional controls. These are as follows:

```
//
// member functions related to dynamic options
//
void Dlu2Pix (RECT& rd, RECT& rs); // convert RECT DLU's
void RectAdd (RECT& rd, RECT& rs); // add rectangles
void RectSub (RECT& rd, RECT& rs); // subtract rectangles
void MakeStandardControls (void);  // create std controls
void DeleteStdControls (void);     // delete std controls
void DeleteOptControls (void);     // delete opt controls

BOOL    m_bExpanded;       // settings dialog expanded
RECT    m_rShortDialog;    // short dialog position & size
RECT    m_rLongDialog;     // long dialog position & size
RECT    m_rFrame;          // dialog frame position & size
RECT    m_rWindow;         // window RECT (current size)
int     m_nXUnits;         // X DLU's in pixels
int     m_nYUnits;         // Y DLU's in pixels
```

Member Functions and Variables for the Cash Flow Report

The next section of the **settings.h** header file contains the member function and member variable declarations that pertain to the Cash Flow report options. These are as follows:

```cpp
///////////////////////////////////////////////////////////////
// Cash Flow Report Options

void MakeCashFlowControls (int t);// create controls
void AddCategories (CListBox* p);// add categories
void SelectCategories (CListBox* p,// select categories
   int nWhich);
CCategory* FindCategory (          // find by name
   CObList& List,                  // -- list to search
   CString& szName,                // -- name of category
   POSITION& pos);                 // -- position if found
void MakeTextSettings(void);       // change settings
                                   // -- for text strings

//
// settings dialog specific font
//
CFont*      m_pSettingsFont;

//
// common options section controls
//
int         m_nPrevOptionType;    // previous option type
CButton*    m_pOptionsBox;        // options group box
CStatic*    m_pTypeLabel;         // type label
CComboBox*  m_pTypeCombo;         // combo box type list
RECT        m_rOptionsBox;        // options box RECT
RECT        m_rTypeLabel;         // type label RECT
RECT        m_rTypeCombo;         // type combo RECT

//
// categories options controls
//
CButton*    m_pAllRadio;          // all categories radio
CButton*    m_pNoneRadio;         // no categories radio
CButton*    m_pTaxRelatedRadio;   // tax-related radio
CListBox*   m_pCategoryList;      // list of categories
int         m_nPrevCatRadio;      // previous radio setting
RECT        m_rAllRadio;          // all categories RECT
RECT        m_rNoneRadio;         // no categories RECT
RECT        m_rTaxRelatedRadio;   // tax-related RECT
RECT        m_rCategoryList;      // category list RECT

//
// text matching controls
//
CEdit*      m_pTextString;        // text string matched
CButton*    m_pStartsRadio;       // starts with radio
CButton*    m_pContainsRadio;     // contains radio
CButton*    m_pExactRadio;        // exact match radio
int         m_nPrevDescRadio;     // prev. descrip. radio
int         m_nPrevInfoRadio;     // prev. info radio
RECT        m_rTextString;        // text string RECT
RECT        m_rStartsRadio;       // starts with radio RECT
RECT        m_rContainsRadio;     // contains radio RECT
RECT        m_rExactRadio;        // exact match radio RECT
```

Member Functions and Variables for the Net Worth Chart

The next (and final) section of the **settings.h** header file contains the declarations of member functions and variables that are associated with the creation of settings for the Net Worth chart. These are as follows:

```
///////////////////////////////////////////////////////////
// Net Worth Chart Options

CCButton* MakeColorButton (    // make color button
    int nID,                   // -- its control ID
    RECT& rBut);               // -- its RECT
void MakeChartControls (int t);// make controls for charts
void RedrawButton (int nID);   // redraw button nID

public:
    int GetSampleIndex (int nID); // get sample color

protected:

    //
    // graph type controls
    //
    int         m_nPrevGraphType;  // previous graph type radio
    CString     m_szPrevVertString;// previous vertical title
    CString     m_szPrevHorzString;// previous horizontal title
    CButton*    m_pGraphTypeBox;   // graph type group box
    CButton*    m_pVertBarRadio;   // vertical bar radio button
    CButton*    m_pLinePlotRadio;  // line plot radio button
    CStatic*    m_pVertLabel;      // vertical title label
    CEdit*      m_pVertString;     // vertical title string
    CStatic*    m_pHorzLabel;      // horizontal title label
    CEdit*      m_pHorzString;     // horizontal title string
    RECT        m_rGraphTypeBox;   // graph type box RECT
    RECT        m_rVertBarRadio;   // vertical bar radio RECT
    RECT        m_rLinePlotRadio;  // line plot radio RECT
    RECT        m_rVertLabel;      // vertical label RECT
    RECT        m_rVertString;     // vertical title RECT
    RECT        m_rHorzLabel;      // horizontal label RECT
    RECT        m_rHorzString;     // horizontal title RECT

    //
    // graph interval controls
    //
    int         m_nPrevInterval;   // previous interval radio
    CButton*    m_pMonthlyRadio;   // monthly interval radio
    CButton*    m_pQuarterlyRadio; // quarterly interval radio
    CButton*    m_pAnnuallyRadio;  // annual interval radio
    RECT        m_rMonthlyRadio;   // monthly interval RECT
    RECT        m_rQuarterlyRadio; // quarterly interval RECT
    RECT        m_rAnnuallyRadio;  // annual interval RECT

    //
    // graph color controls
    //
    int         m_nPrevUseColor;   // previous use color check
    int         m_nPrevSampleColors[4];  // previous colors
    int         m_nPrevSampleClick;// previous sample clicked
    int         m_nPrevColorClick; // previous color clicked
    CButton*    m_pUseColorCheck;  // use color check box
    CStatic*    m_pAxisColor;      // axis color label
    CStatic*    m_pTitleColor;     // title color label
    CStatic*    m_pLabelColor;     // label color label
    CStatic*    m_pGraphColor;     // graph color label
```

```
        CCButton*      m_pAxisSample;       // axis color sample button
        CCButton*      m_pTitleSample;      // title color sample button
        CCButton*      m_pLabelSample;      // label color sample button
        CCButton*      m_pGraphSample;      // graph color sample button
        CButton*       m_pColorsBox;        // color samples group box
        CCButton*      m_pColor_1;          // color sample #1
        CCButton*      m_pColor_2;          // color sample #2
        CCButton*      m_pColor_3;          // color sample #3
        CCButton*      m_pColor_4;          // color sample #4
        CCButton*      m_pColor_5;          // color sample #5
        CCButton*      m_pColor_6;          // color sample #6
        CCButton*      m_pColor_7;          // color sample #7
        CCButton*      m_pColor_8;          // color sample #8
        CCButton*      m_pColor_9;          // color sample #9
        CCButton*      m_pColor_10;         // color sample #10
        CCButton*      m_pColor_11;         // color sample #11
        CCButton*      m_pColor_12;         // color sample #12
        CCButton*      m_pColor_13;         // color sample #13
        CCButton*      m_pColor_14;         // color sample #14
        CCButton*      m_pColor_15;         // color sample #15
        CCButton*      m_pColor_16;         // color sample #16
        RECT           m_rUseColorCheck;    // use color check box RECT
        RECT           m_rAxisColor;        // axis color label RECT
        RECT           m_rTitleColor;       // title color label RECT
        RECT           m_rLabelColor;       // label color label RECT
        RECT           m_rGraphColor;       // graph color label RECT
        RECT           m_rAxisSample;       // axis color sample RECT
        RECT           m_rTitleSample;      // title color sample RECT
        RECT           m_rLabelSample;      // label color sample RECT
        RECT           m_rGraphSample;      // graph color sample RECT
        RECT           m_rColorsBox;        // color samples group RECT
        RECT           m_rColor_1;          // color sample #1 RECT
        RECT           m_rColor_2;          // color sample #2 RECT
        RECT           m_rColor_3;          // color sample #3 RECT
        RECT           m_rColor_4;          // color sample #4 RECT
        RECT           m_rColor_5;          // color sample #5 RECT
        RECT           m_rColor_6;          // color sample #6 RECT
        RECT           m_rColor_7;          // color sample #7 RECT
        RECT           m_rColor_8;          // color sample #8 RECT
        RECT           m_rColor_9;          // color sample #9 RECT
        RECT           m_rColor_10;         // color sample #10 RECT
        RECT           m_rColor_11;         // color sample #11 RECT
        RECT           m_rColor_12;         // color sample #12 RECT
        RECT           m_rColor_13;         // color sample #13 RECT
        RECT           m_rColor_14;         // color sample #14 RECT
        RECT           m_rColor_15;         // color sample #15 RECT
        RECT           m_rColor_16;         // color sample #16 RECT
};
```

All of the foregoing declarations are protected, except for the one access member function, GetSampleIndex, which must be referenced from outside the current object. Notice that all of the color samples have been declared as pointers to CCButton objects, a new class that we will introduce later in this chapter. The foregoing is the end of the **settings.h** header file.

CSettings Class Source File Definitions

The source file for the Settings dialog has been expanded greatly from what was presented in Chapter 10. This is to accommodate the newly added chart settings and the creation of the optional controls.

Settings.cpp Initial Section

As with the header file, we will present the entire contents of the **settings.cpp** source file so that you can see how the newly added code fits into that which has already been described. The first section of the file contains only the #include statements and other preliminary definitions. These are as follows:

```
// settings.cpp : implementation file
//

#include "stdafx.h"
#include "keepit.h"
#include "keepdoc.h"
#include "dattim.h"
#include "acctobj.h"
#include "selected.h"
#include "category.h"
#include "ccbutton.h"           // added
#include "settings.h"

extern char __far monthDays[];

#ifdef _DEBUG
#undef THIS_FILE
static char BASED_CODE THIS_FILE[] = __FILE__;
#endif
```

In the foregoing, we have added one new #include statement, for a new class that we call CCButton (for "color button"). That class will be described when we have finished the description of the CSettings class source file contents.

Dynamic Control Position Definitions

The next section of the **settings.cpp** source file contains the name of each of the controls and its position and size values (as shown in Chapter 11), expressed as the initial value of a RECT variable. These are as follows:

```
//////////////////////////////////////////////////////////////////
// Dynamic Control Positions
//
static RECT rShortDialog     = {  0,    0, 267,   84};
static RECT rLongDialog      = {  0,    0, 267,  172};
static RECT rOptionsBox      = {  6,   82, 261,  167};
static RECT rTypeLabel       = { 15,  102,  36,  110};
static RECT rTypeCombo       = { 40,  100, 113,  159};
```

```
static RECT rAllRadio         = {  40, 121, 108, 131};
static RECT rNoneRadio        = {  40, 135, 108, 145};
static RECT rTaxRelatedRadio  = {  40, 149, 108, 159};
static RECT rCategoryList      = {126,  96, 256, 159};
static RECT rTextString        = {124, 100, 253, 112};
static RECT rStartsRadio       = {125, 121, 185, 131};
static RECT rContainsRadio     = {125, 135, 185, 145};
static RECT rExactRadio        = {125, 149, 185, 159};

//
// dynamic controls for Net Worth Graph options
//
static RECT rGraphTypeBox     = {  39, 115, 112, 160};
static RECT rVertBarRadio     = {  45, 127, 105, 137};
static RECT rLinePlotRadio    = {  45, 142, 105, 152};
static RECT rVertLabel         = {125, 102, 255, 110};
static RECT rVertString        = {125, 116, 255, 128};
static RECT rHorzLabel         = {125, 137, 255, 145};
static RECT rHorzString        = {125, 149, 255, 161};
static RECT rMonthlyRadio     = {  42, 123, 108, 133};
static RECT rQuarterlyRadio   = {  42, 135, 108, 145};
static RECT rAnnuallyRadio    = {  42, 147, 108, 157};

static RECT rUseColorCheck     = {126, 101, 174, 111};
static RECT rAxisColor        = {  40, 119,  90, 127};
static RECT rTitleColor       = {  40, 131,  90, 139};
static RECT rLabelColor       = {  40, 143,  90, 151};
static RECT rGraphColor       = {  40, 155,  90, 163};
static RECT rAxisSample       = {  95, 118, 105, 128};
static RECT rTitleSample      = {  95, 130, 105, 140};
static RECT rLabelSample      = {  95, 142, 105, 152};
static RECT rGraphSample      = {  95, 154, 105, 164};
static RECT rColorsBox         = {183,  89, 251, 163};
static RECT rColor_1           = {192, 105, 202, 115};
static RECT rColor_2           = {206, 105, 216, 115};
static RECT rColor_3           = {220, 105, 230, 115};
static RECT rColor_4           = {234, 105, 244, 115};
static RECT rColor_5           = {192, 119, 202, 129};
static RECT rColor_6           = {206, 119, 216, 129};
static RECT rColor_7           = {220, 119, 230, 129};
static RECT rColor_8           = {234, 119, 244, 129};
static RECT rColor_9           = {192, 133, 202, 143};
static RECT rColor_10          = {206, 133, 216, 143};
static RECT rColor_11          = {220, 133, 230, 143};
static RECT rColor_12          = {234, 133, 244, 143};
static RECT rColor_13          = {192, 147, 202, 157};
static RECT rColor_14          = {206, 147, 216, 157};
static RECT rColor_15          = {220, 147, 230, 157};
static RECT rColor_16          = {234, 147, 244, 157};
```

If you refer back to the **settings.h** header file, you will see that we have adopted a standard naming convention for all of the optional control variables, their corresponding member RECT variables, and also the static control positions shown in the foregoing definitions. For example, we have named the member variable for the Use Color checkbox as m_pUseColorCheck, its corresponding RECT member variable is named m_rUseColorCheck, and its local static position rectangle definition is named rUseColorCheck. This same scheme is used for all of the optional controls.

Note that we expressed the local static RECT definition initializers in the form of dialog units (DLUs), as explained in Chapter 10. Rather than express the width and height as separate values, we have added these to the "left" and "top" fields of the RECT definition, giving valid "right" and "bottom" positions (but still expressed in DLUs). The dialog units are converted to pixels with the Dlu2Pix member function, which is shown later.

CSettings Constructor Member Function

The constructor for the CSettings object is defined next in the source file. It is as follows:

```
CSettings::CSettings(CWnd* pParent /*=NULL*/)
   : CDialog(CSettings::IDD, pParent)
{
   //{{AFX_DATA_INIT(CSettings)
   m_From = "";
   m_Title = "";
   m_To = "";
   //}}AFX_DATA_INIT
}
```

There is nothing special about the foregoing constructor code. It is shown just as it was generated automatically by the ClassWizard tool. The constructor initializes three of the member variables, which pertain to editable text fields in the Settings dialog.

Dlu2Pix Member Function Code

The Dlu2Pix member function is what we call a "helper member function," mainly because it is used by other member functions in the class. This particular member function performs the translation between the device-independent dialog units specified in the local RECT control position definitions to device-specific pixel values on the screen. The member function's code is as follows:

```
void CSettings::Dlu2Pix (RECT& rd, RECT& rs)
{
   TEXTMETRIC tm;
   CClientDC client(this);
   client.GetTextMetrics (&tm);
   m_nXUnits = tm.tmAveCharWidth;
   m_nYUnits = tm.tmAscent;

   rd.left   = (rs.left   * m_nXUnits) / 4;
   rd.top    = (rs.top    * m_nYUnits) / 8;
   rd.right  = (rs.right  * m_nXUnits) / 4;
   rd.bottom = (rs.bottom * m_nYUnits) / 8;
}
```

In the foregoing, the average character width and character ascent value of the dialog's standard font are used as the basis for determining the number of pixels associated with a dialog unit.

RectAdd Member Function Code

The RectAdd member function is used to add the corresponding fields of two RECT variables together and returning the sum in the first RECT passed to the member function. The code is as follows:

```
void CSettings::RectAdd (RECT& rd, RECT& rs)
{
   rd.left   += rs.left;
   rd.top    += rs.top;
   rd.right  += rs.right;
   rd.bottom += rs.bottom;
}
```

RectSub Member Function Code

The RectSub member function subtracts the corresponding fields of the second RECT argument to the member function from the first RECT argument and stores the results in the first argument. Unlike the SubtractRect member function for the CRect class, this member function makes no distinction between whether the two rectangles intersect or not. The code for this member function is as follows:

```
void CSettings::RectSub (RECT& rd, RECT& rs)
{
   rd.left   -= rs.left;
   rd.top    -= rs.top;
   rd.right  -= rs.right;
   rd.bottom -= rs.bottom;
}
```

MakeColorButton Member Function Code

The MakeColorButton member function is used to simplify the creation of a large number of CCButton objects. The code for this new class, which is a direct descendent of the CButton class, will be shown later. The code for the MakeColorButton member function is newly added and is as follows:

```
CCButton* CSettings::MakeColorButton (int nID, RECT& rBut)
{
   //
   // create an object of CCButton and then
   // call its Create member function to initialize it.
   //
   CCButton* pButton = new CCButton;
   ASSERT (pButton != NULL);
```

```
pButton->Create ("", WS_CHILD | WS_VISIBLE | BS_OWNERDRAW,
   rBut, this, nID);
return pButton;
}
```

The foregoing code creates an object of the CCButton class and then calls member function to create it as an "owner draw" button, inherited from the CButton base class. We have created the CCButton class so that we can override the DrawItem member function, which is responsible for drawing the button. By so doing, we can draw a custom button shape, with its own method for indicating its selection status, and, more importantly, for allowing us the liberty of drawing the button in a specified color.

GetSampleIndex Member Function Code

The GetSampleIndex member function is used to return the index of a color sample, within an array of COLORSPEC values, given the control ID to which the sample pertains. The code is newly added and is as follows:

```
int CSettings::GetSampleIndex (int nID)
{
   ASSERT (nID >= IDC_AXIS_SAMPLE && nID <= IDC_GRAPH_SAMPLE);
   return (m_nPrevSampleColors[nID-IDC_AXIS_SAMPLE]);
}
```

RedrawButton Member Function Code

The RedrawButton member function is used to force the redrawing of a specified chart property button, given the identifer of the control as input. The code accomplishes its objective by calling InvalidateRect for the specified control, thereby forcing Windows to call the DrawItem member function for the specific button. The code is newly added and is as follows:

```
void CSettings::RedrawButton (int nID)
{
   ASSERT (nID >= IDC_AXIS_SAMPLE && nID <= IDC_GRAPH_SAMPLE);
   int index = nID - IDC_AXIS_SAMPLE;
   switch (index)
   {
     case 0:// axis sample
     {
        InvalidateRect (&m_rAxisSample);
        break;
     }
     case 1: // title sample
     {
        InvalidateRect (&m_rTitleSample);
        break;
     }
     case 2: // label sample
     {
```

```
            InvalidateRect (&m_rLabelSample);
            break;
      }
      case 3: // graph sample
      {
            InvalidateRect (&m_rGraphSample);
            break;
      }
   }
}
```

OnInitDialog Member Function Code

One of the most important member functions in the CSettings class is
the OnInitDialog member function. This member function is responsible for performing all of the initialization prior to when Windows makes
the Settings dialog visible to the user. There are a great number of tasks
that must be performed before the dialog can be shown, not the least of
which are those that perform initialization of the RECT member variables that contain the various optional control position and dimension
values. The code for this member function will be presented in sections
so that each can be more easily described. Changes to the code are indicated with change bars. The first section of code is as follows:

```
BOOL CSettings::OnInitDialog()
{
   //
   // compute the position and size of the
   // dialog window's border.
   //
   RECT rClient;
   GetWindowRect(&m_rFrame);
   GetClientRect(&rClient);
   RectSub (m_rFrame, rClient);

   //
   // select all of the accounts for this report
   //
   CDialog::OnInitDialog();
   POSITION pos = m_Accounts.GetHeadPosition();
   while (pos != NULL)
   {
      //
      // all accounts are selected by default
      //
      CAcctObj* pAcct = (CAcctObj *)m_Accounts.GetNext(pos);
      pAcct->SetAcctStatus (ACCT_SELECTED);
   }
   m_DialogTitle.SetWindowText (m_szDialogTitle);
   m_PeriodList.SetCurSel (0);// select Year-To-Date

   //
   // create a new font to use within the dialog
   //
   CClientDC* client = new CClientDC(this);
   int nHeight=MulDiv (client->GetDeviceCaps(LOGPIXELSY),8,72);
   delete client;
   m_pSettingsFont = new CFont;
   m_pSettingsFont->CreateFont (-nHeight, 0, 0, 0, FW_BOLD,
```

```
0, 0, 0, ANSI_CHARSET, OUT_DEFAULT_PRECIS,
CLIP_DEFAULT_PRECIS, DEFAULT_QUALITY,
DEFAULT_PITCH | FF_SWISS, "MS Sans Serif");
```

The foregoing code begins by calculating the position of the dialog and also the height and width of the frame. The resulting rectangle is used to position and size both the short and expanded versions of the Settings dialog.

The code continues by looping through all of the accounts in the `m_Accounts` list and sets each of their status variables to `ACCT_SELECTED`. This presets the report or chart to include values from all of the accounts presently defined. The final section of the foregoing code creates an 8-point bold version of the MS sans serif typeface.

The code for the OnInitDialog member function continues, as follows:

```
//
// convert ShortDialog and LongDialog to window coordinates.
//
Dlu2Pix (m_rShortDialog, rShortDialog);
RectAdd (m_rShortDialog, m_rFrame);
Dlu2Pix (m_rLongDialog, rLongDialog);
RectAdd (m_rLongDialog, m_rFrame);

//
// set dialog not expanded and convert all of the
// DLU settings in the RECT variables to pixels.
//
m_bExpanded = FALSE;
Dlu2Pix (m_rOptionsBox, rOptionsBox);
Dlu2Pix (m_rTypeLabel, rTypeLabel);
Dlu2Pix (m_rTypeCombo, rTypeCombo);
Dlu2Pix (m_rAllRadio, rAllRadio);
Dlu2Pix (m_rNoneRadio, rNoneRadio);
Dlu2Pix (m_rTaxRelatedRadio, rTaxRelatedRadio);
Dlu2Pix (m_rCategoryList, rCategoryList);
Dlu2Pix (m_rTextString, rTextString);
Dlu2Pix (m_rStartsRadio, rStartsRadio);
Dlu2Pix (m_rContainsRadio, rContainsRadio);
Dlu2Pix (m_rExactRadio, rExactRadio);

//
// set the RECT variables for the graph options
//
Dlu2Pix (m_rGraphTypeBox, rGraphTypeBox);
Dlu2Pix (m_rVertBarRadio, rVertBarRadio);
Dlu2Pix (m_rLinePlotRadio, rLinePlotRadio);
Dlu2Pix (m_rVertLabel, rVertLabel);
Dlu2Pix (m_rVertString, rVertString);
Dlu2Pix (m_rHorzLabel, rHorzLabel);
Dlu2Pix (m_rHorzString, rHorzString);

Dlu2Pix (m_rMonthlyRadio, rMonthlyRadio);
Dlu2Pix (m_rQuarterlyRadio, rQuarterlyRadio);
Dlu2Pix (m_rAnnuallyRadio, rAnnuallyRadio);

Dlu2Pix (m_rUseColorCheck, rUseColorCheck);
Dlu2Pix (m_rAxisColor, rAxisColor);
Dlu2Pix (m_rTitleColor, rTitleColor);
```

```
Dlu2Pix (m_rLabelColor, rLabelColor);
Dlu2Pix (m_rGraphColor, rGraphColor);
Dlu2Pix (m_rAxisSample, rAxisSample);
Dlu2Pix (m_rTitleSample, rTitleSample);
Dlu2Pix (m_rLabelSample, rLabelSample);
Dlu2Pix (m_rGraphSample, rGraphSample);
Dlu2Pix (m_rColorsBox, rColorsBox);
Dlu2Pix (m_rColor_1, rColor_1);
Dlu2Pix (m_rColor_2, rColor_2);
Dlu2Pix (m_rColor_3, rColor_3);
Dlu2Pix (m_rColor_4, rColor_4);
Dlu2Pix (m_rColor_5, rColor_5);
Dlu2Pix (m_rColor_6, rColor_6);
Dlu2Pix (m_rColor_7, rColor_7);
Dlu2Pix (m_rColor_8, rColor_8);
Dlu2Pix (m_rColor_9, rColor_9);
Dlu2Pix (m_rColor_10, rColor_10);
Dlu2Pix (m_rColor_11, rColor_11);
Dlu2Pix (m_rColor_12, rColor_12);
Dlu2Pix (m_rColor_13, rColor_13);
Dlu2Pix (m_rColor_14, rColor_14);
Dlu2Pix (m_rColor_15, rColor_15);
Dlu2Pix (m_rColor_16, rColor_16);
```

The foregoing section of the OnInitDialog member function transforms all of the local static RECT definitions, given in DLUs, into pixel positions on the current display screen, and then stores the resulting RECT values into the specified member variables.

The OnInitDialog member function continues as follows:

```
// now, resize the current dialog, just so that
// when it's contracted once again it will be the
// same size, and then set the initial options.

m_rWindow = m_rShortDialog;
MoveWindow (&m_rWindow, FALSE);
m_nPrevOptionType = -1;            // no previous options
m_nPrevCatRadio  = IDC_ALL_RADIO;   // set to all categories
m_nPrevDescRadio = IDC_STARTS_RADIO;// starts with text
m_nPrevInfoRadio = IDC_STARTS_RADIO;// starts with text

// if report is "Net Worth Report", then hide the "Options"
// button and also the "From Date" combo box and its label.

if (m_Title == "Net Worth Report")
{
   m_Options.ShowWindow (SW_HIDE);
   GetDlgItem (IDC_FROM)->ShowWindow (SW_HIDE);
   GetDlgItem (IDC_FROM_LABEL)->ShowWindow (SW_HIDE);
}

// initialize settings for graph options

m_nPrevGraphType = IDC_VERT_BAR; // vertical bar graph
m_szPrevVertString = "";          // empty vertical title
m_szPrevHorzString = "";          // empty horizontal title
m_nPrevInterval = IDC_MONTHLY;   // monthly intervals
m_nPrevUseColor = 1;             // use color
for (int i=0; i < 4; i++)
{
   m_nPrevSampleColors[i] = i*4; // set shade of grey
```

```
    }
    m_nPrevSampleClick = IDC_AXIS_SAMPLE;// assume axis sample
    m_nPrevColorClick  = IDC_COLOR_1;   // assume black color

    //
    // return to Windows
    //
    return TRUE;
}
```

The final section of the OnInitDialog member function, shown in the foregoing code, resizes both the short and expanded (long) dialogs so that when the button labeled "Options" or "Hide Options," depending upon whether or not the dialog has been enlarged, is clicked, the user will see no repositioning of the dialog, simply the fact that it expands or contracts, whichever is the case. Following the repositioning and resizing code, the values of the member variables for various options and report types are initialized. If the Settings dialog is being shown for the Net Worth report, then the "Options" button is hidden. Each of the chart property color samples is set to a different shade of grey, initially. When all of the initialization is complete, the member function returns to the framework to make the dialog visible so that the user can operate it and change the default settings.

DoDataExchange Member Function Code

The DoDataExchange member function is called by the framework after the OnInitDialog member function calls the OnInitDialog member function in the CDialog base class. The code for the DoDataExchange member function for the CSettings class is as follows:

```
void CSettings::DoDataExchange(CDataExchange* pDX)
{
  CDialog::DoDataExchange(pDX);
  //{{AFX_DATA_MAP(CSettings)
  DDX_Control(pDX, IDC_OPTIONS, m_Options);
  DDX_Control(pDX, IDC_PER_LIST, m_PeriodList);
  DDX_Control(pDX, IDC_ACCTS_BUTTON, m_AcctsButton);
  DDX_Control(pDX, IDC_DIALOG_TITLE, m_DialogTitle);
  DDX_DateCheck(pDX, IDC_FROM, m_From);
  DDX_Text(pDX, IDC_TITLE, m_Title);
  DDX_DateCheck(pDX, IDC_TO, m_To);
  //}}AFX_DATA_MAP
}
```

Message Map Code

The code for the message map entries that are generated automatically by the ClassWizard tool and also the entries that we have added manually, to support processing of messages generated by the optional controls, are as follows:

```
BEGIN_MESSAGE_MAP(CSettings, CDialog)
  //{{AFX_MSG_MAP(CSettings)
  ON_CBN_SELCHANGE(IDC_PER_LIST, OnPerListSelect)
  ON_BN_CLICKED(IDC_ACCTS_BUTTON, OnAcctsClicked)
  ON_BN_CLICKED(IDC_OPTIONS, OnOptions)
  ON_WM_DESTROY()
  //}}AFX_MSG_MAP

  //
  // standard control messages
  //
  ON_CBN_SELCHANGE(IDC_TYPE_COMBO, OnTypeSelect)

  //
  // category control messages
  //
  ON_LBN_SELCHANGE(IDC_CATEGORY_LIST, OnCatSelect)
  ON_BN_CLICKED(IDC_ALL_RADIO, OnCatRadio)
  ON_BN_CLICKED(IDC_NONE_RADIO, OnCatRadio)
  ON_BN_CLICKED(IDC_TAX_RELATED_RADIO, OnCatRadio)

  //
  // description & info control messages
  //
  ON_EN_KILLFOCUS(IDC_EDIT_TEXT_STRING, OnStringEntry)
  ON_BN_CLICKED(IDC_STARTS_RADIO, OnContentsRadio)
  ON_BN_CLICKED(IDC_CONTAINS_RADIO, OnContentsRadio)
  ON_BN_CLICKED(IDC_EXACT_RADIO, OnContentsRadio)

  //
  // graph type control messages
  //
  ON_BN_CLICKED(IDC_VERT_BAR, OnGraphTypeRadio)
  ON_BN_CLICKED(IDC_LINE_PLOT, OnGraphTypeRadio)
  ON_EN_KILLFOCUS(IDC_VERT_TITLE, OnTitleEntry)
  ON_EN_KILLFOCUS(IDC_HORZ_TITLE, OnTitleEntry)

  //
  // interval control messages
  //
  ON_BN_CLICKED(IDC_MONTHLY, OnIntervalRadio)
  ON_BN_CLICKED(IDC_QUARTERLY, OnIntervalRadio)
  ON_BN_CLICKED(IDC_ANNUALLY, OnIntervalRadio)

  //
  // color selection messages
  //
  ON_BN_CLICKED(IDC_USE_COLOR_CHECK, OnUseColorCheck)
  ON_BN_CLICKED(IDC_AXIS_SAMPLE, OnSampleClick)
  ON_BN_CLICKED(IDC_TITLE_SAMPLE, OnSampleClick)
  ON_BN_CLICKED(IDC_LABEL_SAMPLE, OnSampleClick)
  ON_BN_CLICKED(IDC_GRAPH_SAMPLE, OnSampleClick)
  ON_BN_CLICKED(IDC_COLOR_1,  OnColorClick)
  ON_BN_CLICKED(IDC_COLOR_2,  OnColorClick)
  ON_BN_CLICKED(IDC_COLOR_3,  OnColorClick)
  ON_BN_CLICKED(IDC_COLOR_4,  OnColorClick)
  ON_BN_CLICKED(IDC_COLOR_5,  OnColorClick)
  ON_BN_CLICKED(IDC_COLOR_6,  OnColorClick)
  ON_BN_CLICKED(IDC_COLOR_7,  OnColorClick)
  ON_BN_CLICKED(IDC_COLOR_8,  OnColorClick)
  ON_BN_CLICKED(IDC_COLOR_9,  OnColorClick)
  ON_BN_CLICKED(IDC_COLOR_10, OnColorClick)
  ON_BN_CLICKED(IDC_COLOR_11, OnColorClick)
  ON_BN_CLICKED(IDC_COLOR_12, OnColorClick)
  ON_BN_CLICKED(IDC_COLOR_13, OnColorClick)
```

```
      ON_BN_CLICKED(IDC_COLOR_14, OnColorClick)
      ON_BN_CLICKED(IDC_COLOR_15, OnColorClick)
      ON_BN_CLICKED(IDC_COLOR_16, OnColorClick)

END_MESSAGE_MAP()
```

As is evident, we have economized in the use of unique message handlers
for the color sample buttons by referring all of the "button clicked" messages to the OnSampleClick member function. We have also economized for the individual color buttons by providing an OnColorClick
member function to handle clicks on any of the 16 buttons. There are
now many more message map entries for the optional controls than for
the standard controls in the unexpanded Settings dialog.

OnPerListSelect Message Handler Code

The OnPerListSelect handler is invoked whenever the user makes a selection in the Period list box. The code for this member function is unchanged and is as follows:

```
void CSettings::OnPerListSelect()
{
  POINT cQtr[4] = {{1,3}, {4,6}, {7,9}, {10,12}};
  CTime curTime = CTime::GetCurrentTime();
  CTime fromTime, toTime;
  int nYr = curTime.GetYear();
  int nMo = curTime.GetMonth();
  int nDy = curTime.GetDay();
  int nSel = m_PeriodList.GetCurSel();
  switch (nSel)
  {
    case YEAR_TO_DATE:
    {
      fromTime = CTime(nYr, 1, 1, 0, 0, 0);
      toTime = curTime;
      break;
    }
    case CURRENT_MONTH:
    {
      fromTime = CTime(nYr, nMo, 1, 0, 0, 0);
      toTime = CTime(nYr, nMo, monthDays[nMo-1], 0, 0, 0);
      break;
    }
    case CURRENT_QUARTER:
    {
      int nQ = (nMo + 2)/3;
      fromTime = CTime(nYr, cQtr[nQ-1].x, 1, 0, 0, 0);
      toTime = CTime(nYr, cQtr[nQ-1].y,
        monthDays[cQtr[nQ-1].y-1], 0, 0, 0);
      break;
    }
    case CURRENT_YEAR:
    {
      fromTime = CTime(nYr, 1, 1, 0, 0, 0);
      toTime = CTime(nYr, 12, 31, 0, 0, 0);
      break;
    }
    case LAST_MONTH:
    {
```

```
                nMo--;
                if (nMo == 0)
                {
                    nMo = 12;
                    nYr--;
                }
                fromTime = CTime(nYr, nMo, 1, 0, 0, 0);
                toTime = CTime(nYr, nMo, monthDays[nMo-1], 0, 0, 0);
                break;
            }
            case LAST_QUARTER:
            {
                int nQ = (nMo + 2) / 3 - 1;
                if (nQ == 0)
                {
                    nQ = 4;
                    nYr--;
                }
                fromTime = CTime(nYr, cQtr[nQ-1].x, 1, 0, 0, 0);
                toTime = CTime(nYr, cQtr[nQ-1].y,
                    monthDays[cQtr[nQ-1].y-1], 0, 0, 0);
                break;
            }
            case LAST_YEAR:
            {
                nYr--;
                fromTime = CTime(nYr, 1, 1, 0, 0, 0);
                toTime = CTime(nYr, 12, 31, 0, 0, 0);
                break;
            }
            case ALL_TRANSACTIONS:
            {
                fromTime = CTime (1990, 1, 1, 0, 0, 0);
                toTime = CTime (1999, 12, 31, 0, 0, 0);
                break;
            }
        }
        m_From = fromTime.Format ("%m/%d/%y");
        m_To = toTime.Format ("%m/%d/%y");
        GetDlgItem (IDC_FROM)->SetWindowText (m_From);
        GetDlgItem (IDC_TO)->SetWindowText (m_To);
    }
```

The function of various sections of the foregoing code is described in detail in Chapter 8.

OnAcctsClicked Message Handler Code

The OnAcctsClicked handler is invoked when the user clicks on the Accounts button in the Settings dialog. The code is unchanged and is as follows:

```
void CSettings::OnAcctsClicked()
{
    CSelectedAccts dlg;

    //
    // store account objects in selected dialog's list
    //
    POSITION pos = m_Accounts.GetHeadPosition();
    while (pos != NULL)
    {
```

```cpp
      CAcctObj* pAcct = (CAcctObj *)m_Accounts.GetNext(pos);
      CAcctObj* pObj  = new CAcctObj (pAcct);
      dlg.m_Selected.AddTail ((CObject *)pObj);
   }
   if (dlg.DoModal() == IDOK)
   {
      //
      // process list of modified selections
      //
      POSITION nPos1 = dlg.m_Selected.GetHeadPosition();
      while (nPos1 != NULL)
      {
         CAcctObj* pObj;
         pObj = (CAcctObj *)dlg.m_Selected.GetNext(nPos1);
         WORD nID = pObj->GetAcctID();
         POSITION nPos2 = m_Accounts.GetHeadPosition();
         while (nPos2 != NULL)
         {
            //
            // find matching account and change its status
            //
            CAcctObj* pAcct;
            pAcct = (CAcctObj *)m_Accounts.GetNext (nPos2);
            if (pAcct->GetAcctID() == nID)
            {
               pAcct->SetAcctStatus(pObj->GetAcctStatus());
               break;
            }
         }
         delete pObj;
      }
      dlg.m_Selected.RemoveAll();
   }
   else
   {
      //
      // the user cancelled the dialog, so just delete
      // all of the copies of the account entries.
      //
      POSITION nPos3 = dlg.m_Selected.GetHeadPosition();
      while (nPos3 != NULL)
      {
         CAcctObj* pSel;
         pSel = (CAcctObj *)dlg.m_Selected.GetNext(nPos3);
         delete pSel;
      }
      dlg.m_Selected.RemoveAll();
   }
}
```

The code for the OnAcctsClicked message handler was described in detail in Chapter 8 and is included here only for the sake of completeness.

DeleteStdControls Member Function Code

The DeleteStdControls member function is a "helper" for various of the message handlers. Specifically, when the user clicks the "Hide Options" button, the "standard" optional controls must be deleted, but only if we are preparing the Cash Flow or Net Worth Chart reports. The Net Worth report does not have any optional controls—in fact, the Options button is hidden—so it is not necessary to delete these controls for settings pertaining to that report. The revised code for the DeleteStdControls member function is as follows:

```cpp
void CSettings::DeleteStdControls (void)
{
   if (m_Title == "Cash Flow Report"
   || m_Title == "Net Worth Chart" )
   {
      //
      // delete the standard controls
      //
      delete m_pOptionsBox;
      delete m_pTypeLabel;
      m_pTypeCombo->ResetContent();
      delete m_pTypeCombo;
   }
}
```

Note in the foregoing that we test for both the Cash Flow Report and Net Worth Chart before deleting any of the standard controls (which are the Options group box, the Type static text label, and the Type list box.

DeleteOptControls Member Function Code

The DeleteOptControls member function is used to delete the controls that pertain to the currently selected option type. This member function has been expanded greatly, mainly to support the additional controls that are installed to implement the Net Worth Chart options. The revised code is as follows:

```cpp
void CSettings::DeleteOptControls (void)
{
   if (!m_bExpanded || m_nPrevOptionType == -1)
   {
      //
      // if dialog isn't expanded or we haven't yet
      // installed controls, just return.
      //
      return;
   }

   if (m_Title == "Cash Flow Report")
   {
      switch (m_nPrevOptionType)
      {
         case 0:// Categories Options
         {
            delete m_pAllRadio;
            delete m_pNoneRadio;
            delete m_pTaxRelatedRadio;
            m_pCategoryList->ResetContent();
            delete m_pCategoryList;
            break;
         }
         case 1: // Description Options
         case 2: // Info Options
         {
            delete m_pTextString;
```

```
                    delete m_pStartsRadio;
                    delete m_pContainsRadio;
                    delete m_pExactRadio;
                    break;
                }
            }
        }
        else if (m_Title == "Net Worth Chart")
        {
            switch (m_nPrevOptionType)
            {
                case 0:// Graph Type Options
                {
                    delete m_pVertBarRadio;
                    delete m_pLinePlotRadio;
                    delete m_pGraphTypeBox;
                    delete m_pVertLabel;
                    delete m_pVertString;
                    delete m_pHorzLabel;
                    delete m_pHorzString;
                    break;
                }
                case 1:// Interval Options
                {
                    delete m_pMonthlyRadio;
                    delete m_pQuarterlyRadio;
                    delete m_pAnnuallyRadio;
                    break;
                }
                case 2:// Colors Options
                {
                    delete m_pUseColorCheck;
                    delete m_pAxisColor;
                    delete m_pTitleColor;
                    delete m_pLabelColor;
                    delete m_pGraphColor;
                    delete m_pAxisSample;
                    delete m_pTitleSample;
                    delete m_pLabelSample;
                    delete m_pGraphSample;
                    delete m_pColorsBox;
                    delete m_pColor_1;
                    delete m_pColor_2;
                    delete m_pColor_3;
                    delete m_pColor_4;
                    delete m_pColor_5;
                    delete m_pColor_6;
                    delete m_pColor_7;
                    delete m_pColor_8;
                    delete m_pColor_9;
                    delete m_pColor_10;
                    delete m_pColor_11;
                    delete m_pColor_12;
                    delete m_pColor_13;
                    delete m_pColor_14;
                    delete m_pColor_15;
                    delete m_pColor_16;
                    break;
                }
            }
        }
}
```

In the foregoing, each option has a corresponding section of code. The `switch` statement provides the means to execute only the appropriate set of delete statements for each report type. Note that if the title of the current report is not Cash Flow Report or Net Worth Chart, then the member function simply returns. In addition, at the beginning of the member function, if no optional controls have been installed, the member function returns.

FindCategory Member Function Code

The FindCategory member function is one of a series of "helper" functions for the Category options in the Cash Flow report. The code is unchanged and is as follows:

```
CCategory* CSettings::FindCategory (CObList& List,
   CString& szName, POSITION& pos)
{
   CCategory* pCat;
   POSITION nPos = List.GetHeadPosition();
   while (nPos != NULL)
   {
      pos = nPos;
      pCat = (CCategory *)List.GetNext (nPos);
      if (pCat->GetCatName() == szName)
      {
         return pCat;
      }
   }
   return NULL;
}
```

AddCategories Member Function Code

The AddCategories member function is called to add a new entry to the list of categories to be included in the Cash Flow report. The code is unchanged and is as follows:

```
void CSettings::AddCategories (CListBox* pList)
{
   ASSERT (pList != NULL);
   POSITION pos = m_pDoc->m_CatList.GetHeadPosition();
   while (pos != NULL)
   {
      CCategory* pCat;
      pCat = (CCategory *)m_pDoc->m_CatList.GetNext(pos);
      pList->AddString (pCat->GetCatName());
   }
   SelectCategories (pList, m_nPrevCatRadio);
}
```

SelectCategories Member Function Code

The SelectCategories member function is called to select a particular entry in the Categories list box, in support of the Cash Flow report options. The code for this member function is unchanged and is as follows:

```cpp
void CSettings::SelectCategories (CListBox* pList, int nWhich)
{
  ASSERT (pList != NULL);
  CString szName;
  POSITION pos;
  CCategory* pCat;
  m_pDoc->m_ReportCats.RemoveAll();
  int numEntries = pList->GetCount();
  for (int index=0; index < numEntries; index++)
  {
    switch (nWhich)
    {
      case IDC_ALL_RADIO:// select all
      {
        pList->SetSel (index, TRUE);
        pList->GetText (index, szName);
        pCat = FindCategory (m_pDoc->m_CatList, szName, pos);
        ASSERT (pCat != NULL);
        m_pDoc->m_ReportCats.AddTail (pCat);
        break;
      }
      case IDC_NONE_RADIO:// select none
      {
        pList->SetSel (index, FALSE);
        break;
      }
      case IDC_TAX_RELATED_RADIO:// select tax-related only
      {
        CString szName;
        pList->GetText (index, szName);
        pCat = FindCategory (m_pDoc->m_CatList, szName, pos);
        ASSERT (pCat != NULL);
        if (pCat->GetTaxable() > 0)
        {
          m_pDoc->m_ReportCats.AddTail (pCat);
          pList->SetSel (index, TRUE);
        }
        else
        {
          pList->SetSel (index, FALSE);
        }
        break;
      }
    }
  }
  pList->SetTopIndex (0);
}
```

MakeStandardControls Member Function Code

The MakeStandardControls member function is called to create the
"standard" optional controls (which consist of the Options group box,
the Type static text label, and the Type list box). Although these controls
are the same for both the Cash Flow and Net Worth Chart reports, the
contents of the Type list box vary for the two different reports. We have
enhanced the previous version of this member function to handle the
new requirements. The code for this member function is as follows:

```cpp
void CSettings::MakeStandardControls(void)
{
   m_pOptionsBox = new CButton;
   m_pOptionsBox->Create ("Options", WS_CHILD | WS_VISIBLE
      | BS_GROUPBOX, m_rOptionsBox, this, IDC_OPTIONS_BOX);
   m_pTypeLabel = new CStatic;
   m_pTypeLabel->Create ("Type:", WS_CHILD | WS_VISIBLE
      | SS_RIGHT, m_rTypeLabel, this, IDC_TYPE_LABEL);
   m_pTypeCombo = new CComboBox;
   m_pTypeCombo->Create (WS_CHILD | WS_VISIBLE | WS_VSCROLL
      | CBS_DROPDOWNLIST, m_rTypeCombo, this, IDC_TYPE_COMBO);

   if (m_Title == "Cash Flow Report")
   {
      m_pTypeCombo->AddString ("Categories");
      m_pTypeCombo->AddString ("Description");
      m_pTypeCombo->AddString ("Info");
      m_pTypeCombo->SetCurSel (0);
   }
   else if (m_Title == "Net Worth Chart")
   {
      m_pTypeCombo->AddString ("Graph Type");
      m_pTypeCombo->AddString ("Interval");
      m_pTypeCombo->AddString ("Colors");
      m_pTypeCombo->SetCurSel (0);
   }

   m_pOptionsBox->SetFont (m_pSettingsFont, TRUE);
   m_pTypeLabel->SetFont (m_pSettingsFont,TRUE);
   m_pTypeCombo->SetFont (m_pSettingsFont, TRUE);
}
```

With the exception of the contents of the Type list box control, the controls themselves are the same for both types of reports.

MakeCashFlowControls Member Function Code

When the user clicks the Options button in the Settings dialog, the message handler for that event determines whether to create controls for the Cash Flow report or the Net Worth Chart report and then calls the appropriate member function to do so. The MakeCashFlowControls member function is called to make the appropriate optional controls for the Cash Flow report. The code is unchanged and is as follows:

```cpp
void CSettings::MakeCashFlowControls (int t)
{
   if (t == m_nPrevOptionType)
   {
      //
      // there was no change, so just return.
      //
      return;
   }

   //
   // delete the previous option's controls and
   // create new controls for this option.
   //
   DeleteOptControls();
```

```cpp
switch (t)
{
   case 0: // Categories Options
   {
      m_pAllRadio = new CButton;
      m_pAllRadio->Create ("All", WS_CHILD | WS_VISIBLE
         | BS_AUTORADIOBUTTON, m_rAllRadio, this,
         IDC_ALL_RADIO);
      m_pNoneRadio = new CButton;
      m_pNoneRadio->Create ("None", WS_CHILD | WS_VISIBLE
         | BS_AUTORADIOBUTTON, m_rNoneRadio, this,
         IDC_NONE_RADIO);
      m_pTaxRelatedRadio = new CButton;
      m_pTaxRelatedRadio->Create ("Tax-related Only",
         WS_CHILD | WS_VISIBLE | BS_AUTORADIOBUTTON,
         m_rTaxRelatedRadio, this, IDC_TAX_RELATED_RADIO);
      CheckRadioButton (IDC_ALL_RADIO, IDC_TAX_RELATED_RADIO,
         m_nPrevCatRadio);
      m_pCategoryList = new CListBox;
      m_pCategoryList->Create (WS_CHILD | WS_VISIBLE
         | WS_BORDER | WS_VSCROLL | WS_TABSTOP |LBS_NOTIFY
         | LBS_SORT | LBS_MULTIPLESEL, m_rCategoryList,
         this, IDC_CATEGORY_LIST);

      m_pAllRadio->SetFont (m_pSettingsFont, TRUE);
      m_pNoneRadio->SetFont (m_pSettingsFont, TRUE);
      m_pTaxRelatedRadio->SetFont (m_pSettingsFont, TRUE);
      m_pCategoryList->SetFont (m_pSettingsFont, TRUE);

      AddCategories (m_pCategoryList);
      break;
   }

   case 1: // Description Options
   case 2: // Info Options
   {
      m_pTextString = new CEdit;
      m_pTextString->Create (WS_CHILD | WS_VISIBLE
         | WS_BORDER | ES_AUTOHSCROLL | ES_LEFT,
         m_rTextString, this, IDC_EDIT_TEXT_STRING);
      m_pStartsRadio = new CButton;
      m_pStartsRadio->Create ("Starts With", WS_CHILD
         | WS_VISIBLE | BS_AUTORADIOBUTTON, m_rStartsRadio,
         this, IDC_STARTS_RADIO);
      m_pContainsRadio = new CButton;
      m_pContainsRadio->Create ("Contains", WS_CHILD
         | WS_VISIBLE | BS_AUTORADIOBUTTON, m_rContainsRadio,
         this, IDC_CONTAINS_RADIO);
      m_pExactRadio = new CButton;
      m_pExactRadio->Create ("Equals Exactly", WS_CHILD
         | WS_VISIBLE | BS_AUTORADIOBUTTON, m_rExactRadio,
         this, IDC_EXACT_RADIO);

      m_pTextString->SetFont (m_pSettingsFont, TRUE);
      m_pStartsRadio->SetFont (m_pSettingsFont, TRUE);
      m_pContainsRadio->SetFont (m_pSettingsFont, TRUE);
      m_pExactRadio->SetFont (m_pSettingsFont, TRUE);

      if (t == 1)
      {
         CheckRadioButton (IDC_STARTS_RADIO, IDC_EXACT_RADIO,
            m_nPrevDescRadio);
         m_pTextString->SetWindowText(m_pDoc
            ->m_szDescription);
         m_pTextString->SetSel (0, -1, FALSE);
      }
      else
```

```
        {
          CheckRadioButton (IDC_STARTS_RADIO, IDC_EXACT_RADIO,
            m_nPrevInfoRadio);
          m_pTextString->SetWindowText (m_pDoc->m_szInfo);
          m_pTextString->SetSel (0, -1, FALSE);
        }
        break;
      }
      default:
      {
        ASSERT (FALSE);
        break;
      }
    }
    m_nPrevOptionType = t;
}
```

At the conclusion of the foregoing code, the `m_nPrevOptionType`
variable is set to the option type for which the controls were just installed. This enables the DeleteOptControls member function to delete
the proper controls prior to installing those that pertain to the newly selected option.

MakeChartControls Member Function Code

MakeChartControls member function is used to create the optional controls for the Net Worth Chart report. Prior to creating the controls for
the newly selected option, the previous controls (if any) are deleted using
the DeleteOptControls member function. The code for the MakeChart-
Controls member function is newly added and is as follows:

```
void CSettings::MakeChartControls (int t)
{
   if (t == m_nPrevOptionType)
   {
      //
      // there was no change, so just return.
      //
      return;
   }

   //
   // delete the previous option's controls and
   // create new controls for this option.
   //
   DeleteOptControls();
   switch (t)
   {
      case 0:// Graph Type Options
      {
         m_pGraphTypeBox = new CButton;
         m_pGraphTypeBox->Create ("", WS_CHILD | WS_VISIBLE
            | BS_GROUPBOX, m_rGraphTypeBox, this,
            IDC_GRAPH_BOX);
         m_pVertBarRadio = new CButton;
         m_pVertBarRadio->Create ("Vertical Bar", WS_CHILD
            | WS_VISIBLE | WS_TABSTOP | BS_AUTORADIOBUTTON,
            m_rVertBarRadio, this, IDC_VERT_BAR);
         m_pLinePlotRadio = new CButton;
```

```cpp
   m_pLinePlotRadio->Create ("Line Plot", WS_CHILD
      | WS_VISIBLE | WS_TABSTOP | BS_AUTORADIOBUTTON,
      m_rLinePlotRadio, this, IDC_LINE_PLOT);
   m_pVertLabel = new CStatic;
   m_pVertLabel->Create ("Vertical Axis Title:",
      WS_CHILD | WS_VISIBLE | SS_LEFT,
      m_rVertLabel, this, IDC_VERT_LABEL);
   m_pVertString = new CEdit;
   m_pVertString->Create (WS_CHILD | WS_VISIBLE
      | WS_BORDER | WS_TABSTOP |ES_AUTOHSCROLL | ES_LEFT,
      m_rVertString, this, IDC_VERT_TITLE);
   m_pHorzLabel = new CStatic;
   m_pHorzLabel->Create ("Horizontal Axis Title:",
      WS_CHILD | WS_VISIBLE | SS_LEFT,
      m_rHorzLabel, this, IDC_HORZ_LABEL);
   m_pHorzString = new CEdit;
   m_pHorzString->Create (WS_CHILD | WS_VISIBLE
      | WS_BORDER | WS_TABSTOP |ES_AUTOHSCROLL
      | ES_LEFT, m_rHorzString, this, IDC_HORZ_TITLE);
   m_pOptionsBox->SetFont (m_pSettingsFont, TRUE);
   m_pVertBarRadio->SetFont (m_pSettingsFont, TRUE);
   m_pLinePlotRadio->SetFont (m_pSettingsFont, TRUE);
   m_pVertLabel->SetFont (m_pSettingsFont, TRUE);
   m_pVertString->SetFont (m_pSettingsFont, TRUE);
   m_pHorzLabel->SetFont (m_pSettingsFont, TRUE);
   m_pHorzString->SetFont (m_pSettingsFont, TRUE);

   CheckRadioButton (IDC_VERT_BAR, IDC_LINE_PLOT,
      m_nPrevGraphType);
   m_pVertString->SetWindowText (m_szPrevVertString);
   m_pHorzString->SetWindowText (m_szPrevHorzString);
   break;
}
case 1:// Interval Options
{
   m_pMonthlyRadio = new CButton;
   m_pMonthlyRadio->Create ("Monthly", WS_CHILD
      | WS_VISIBLE | WS_TABSTOP | BS_AUTORADIOBUTTON,
      m_rMonthlyRadio, this, IDC_MONTHLY);
   m_pQuarterlyRadio = new CButton;
   m_pQuarterlyRadio->Create ("Quarterly", WS_CHILD
      | WS_TABSTOP | WS_VISIBLE | BS_AUTORADIOBUTTON,
      m_rQuarterlyRadio, this, IDC_QUARTERLY);
   m_pAnnuallyRadio = new CButton;
   m_pAnnuallyRadio->Create ("Annually", WS_CHILD
      | WS_VISIBLE | WS_TABSTOP | BS_AUTORADIOBUTTON,
      m_rAnnuallyRadio, this, IDC_ANNUALLY);
   m_pMonthlyRadio->SetFont (m_pSettingsFont, TRUE);
   m_pQuarterlyRadio->SetFont (m_pSettingsFont, TRUE);
   m_pAnnuallyRadio->SetFont (m_pSettingsFont, TRUE);
   CheckRadioButton (IDC_MONTHLY, IDC_ANNUALLY,
      m_nPrevInterval);
   break;
}
case 2: // Colors Options
{
   m_pUseColorCheck = new CButton;
   m_pUseColorCheck->Create ("Use Color", WS_CHILD
      | WS_VISIBLE | BS_AUTOCHECKBOX, m_rUseColorCheck,
      this, IDC_USE_COLOR_CHECK);
   m_pUseColorCheck->SetCheck (m_nPrevUseColor);
   m_pAxisColor = new CStatic;
   m_pAxisColor->Create ("Axis Color", WS_CHILD
      | WS_VISIBLE | SS_LEFT, m_rAxisColor, this,
      IDC_AXIS_COLOR);
   m_pTitleColor = new CStatic;
   m_pTitleColor->Create ("Title Color", WS_CHILD
```

```
                   | WS_VISIBLE | SS_LEFT, m_rTitleColor, this,
                   IDC_TITLE_COLOR);
            m_pLabelColor = new CStatic;
            m_pLabelColor->Create ("Label Color", WS_CHILD
                   | WS_VISIBLE | SS_LEFT, m_rLabelColor, this,
                   IDC_LABEL_COLOR);
            m_pGraphColor = new CStatic;
            m_pGraphColor->Create ("Graph Color", WS_CHILD
                   | WS_VISIBLE | SS_LEFT, m_rGraphColor, this,
                   IDC_GRAPH_COLOR);
            m_pAxisSample = MakeColorButton (IDC_AXIS_SAMPLE,
                   m_rAxisSample);
            m_pTitleSample = MakeColorButton (IDC_TITLE_SAMPLE,
                   m_rTitleSample);
            m_pLabelSample = MakeColorButton (IDC_LABEL_SAMPLE,
                   m_rLabelSample);
            m_pGraphSample = MakeColorButton (IDC_GRAPH_SAMPLE,
                   m_rGraphSample);

            m_pColorsBox = new CButton;
            m_pColorsBox->Create ("Colors", WS_CHILD | WS_VISIBLE
                   | BS_GROUPBOX, m_rColorsBox, this, IDC_COLORS_BOX);
            m_pColor_1  = MakeColorButton (IDC_COLOR_1,  m_rColor_1);
            m_pColor_2  = MakeColorButton (IDC_COLOR_2,  m_rColor_2);
            m_pColor_3  = MakeColorButton (IDC_COLOR_3,  m_rColor_3);
            m_pColor_4  = MakeColorButton (IDC_COLOR_4,  m_rColor_4);
            m_pColor_5  = MakeColorButton (IDC_COLOR_5,  m_rColor_5);
            m_pColor_6  = MakeColorButton (IDC_COLOR_6,  m_rColor_6);
            m_pColor_7  = MakeColorButton (IDC_COLOR_7,  m_rColor_7);
            m_pColor_8  = MakeColorButton (IDC_COLOR_8,  m_rColor_8);
            m_pColor_9  = MakeColorButton (IDC_COLOR_9,  m_rColor_9);
            m_pColor_10= MakeColorButton (IDC_COLOR_10, m_rColor_10);
            m_pColor_11= MakeColorButton (IDC_COLOR_11, m_rColor_11);
            m_pColor_12= MakeColorButton (IDC_COLOR_12, m_rColor_12);
            m_pColor_13= MakeColorButton (IDC_COLOR_13, m_rColor_13);
            m_pColor_14= MakeColorButton (IDC_COLOR_14, m_rColor_14);
            m_pColor_15= MakeColorButton (IDC_COLOR_15, m_rColor_15);
            m_pColor_16= MakeColorButton (IDC_COLOR_16, m_rColor_16);

            m_pUseColorCheck->SetFont (m_pSettingsFont, TRUE);
            m_pAxisColor->SetFont (m_pSettingsFont, TRUE);
            m_pTitleColor->SetFont (m_pSettingsFont, TRUE);
            m_pLabelColor->SetFont (m_pSettingsFont, TRUE);
            m_pGraphColor->SetFont (m_pSettingsFont, TRUE);
            m_pColorsBox->SetFont (m_pSettingsFont, TRUE);
            break;
        }
      default:
      {
          ASSERT (FALSE);
          break;
      }
   }
   m_nPrevOptionType = t;
}
```

The foregoing code is structured the same as the MakeCashFlowControls member function and operates in the same manner. The member function returns if the current option type is the same as is currently set. That not being the case, the member function deletes all of the previously installed controls by calling the DeleteOptControls member function and then proceeds to install the controls for the newly selected option type. We use the special font that was constructed in the OnInit-Dialog member function to label each of the controls and we create special "color buttons" for each of the color samples. Code for the newly added CColorButton class, which implements the behavior of these new buttons, will be shown later.

OnOptions Message Handler Code

The OnOptions message handler is invoked when the user clicks the button labeled "Options" or "Hide Options." The button contains the former label when the Settings dialog is not yet expanded and the latter when it is. The function of the OnOptions handler is to expand or compress the size of the Settings dialog and, in addition, to install or delete option controls, as required. The revised code for this message handler function is as follows:

```cpp
void CSettings::OnOptions()
{
   if (!m_bExpanded)
   {
      //
      // window is not expanded, so change it back
      // to its long (expanded) form.
      //
      m_rWindow = m_rLongDialog;
      MoveWindow (&m_rWindow);

      //
      // check which report type we're creating
      // and then set up the additional controls
      // for that report.
      //
      if (m_Title == "Cash Flow Report")
      {
         MakeStandardControls();
         MakeCashFlowControls(0);
      }
      else if (m_Title == "Net Worth Chart")
      {
         MakeStandardControls();
         MakeChartControls(0);
      }

      //
      // change Options button to say "Hide Options"
      // and set expanded flag to TRUE.
      //
      m_Options.SetWindowText ("Hide Options");
      m_bExpanded = TRUE;
   }
   else
   {
      //
      // window is expanded, so delete the current
      // controls and then change the dialog back
      // to its short (contracted) form.
      //
      if (m_Title == "Cash Flow Report"
      || m_Title == "Net Worth Chart" )
```

```
        {
            DeleteStdControls ();
            DeleteOptControls ();
        }
        m_rWindow = m_rShortDialog;
        MoveWindow (&m_rWindow);

        //
        // change Options button to say "Options...",
        // set expanded flag to FALSE, and set the
        // previous option type to -1.
        //
        m_Options.SetWindowText ("Options...");
        m_bExpanded = FALSE;
        m_nPrevOptionType = -1;
    }
}
```

The comments in the foregoing code explain fairly well what the code intends to accomplish. The message handler has two fundamental parts. The first part deals with the situation where the dialog is not yet expanded and therefore must be made larger, according to the position and dimensions in the `m_rLongDialog` variable. After the dialog is expanded, the option controls are installed. In the expanded version of the dialog, the text of the Options button is changed to read "Hide Options."

In the event that the dialog is to be shortened, the second section of the foregoing code gains control. In that code, the option controls are deleted and then the dialog is made shorter, according to the position and dimensions in the `m_rShortDialog` variable. In the shortened version of the dialog, the text of the Options button is changed to read "Options." When the dialog is shortened, the `m_nPrevOptionType` variable is modified to contain -1 as its value. This indicates that no option controls are installed.

OnDestroy Message Handler Code

The OnDestroy message handler is called by the framework when the dialog is about to be disposed. By handling this message, we can get rid of any resources that were allocated for use by the dialog. In our case, the only resource we allocated was the special font which is used to label all of the controls; however, if the dialog is expanded at the time it is being destroyed, we need to delete all of the option controls as well. The code for the OnDestroy message handler is unchanged and is as follows:

```
void CSettings::OnDestroy()
{
    CDialog::OnDestroy();
    if (m_bExpanded)
    {
        //
        // first, delete the standard controls
```

```
   //
   DeleteStdControls();

   //
   // now, delete the controls that currently
   // occupy the options area of the expanded
   // dialog box.
   //
   DeleteOptControls();
   }
   delete m_pSettingsFont;
}
```

In the foregoing, the "standard controls" in the comment refers to the Options group box, the Type static text label, and the Type combo box control. Which other controls need to be deleted depends upon the value in the m_nPrevOptionType variable. Whether the dialog was expanded or not, the special font pointed to by the m_pSettingsFont variable is deleted.

OnTypeSelect Message Handler Code

The OnTypeSelect message handler is invoked by the framework when the user selects one of the options from the Type list box. Depending upon whether the list box holds the option types for the Cash Flow or Net Worth Chart reports, the code must call the appropriate member function to install the option controls for that selection. The revised code for the handler is as follows:

```
void CSettings::OnTypeSelect()
{
   int nType = m_pTypeCombo->GetCurSel();
   if (m_Title == "Cash Flow Report")
   {
      MakeCashFlowControls (nType);
   }
   else if (m_Title == "Net Worth Chart")
   {
      MakeChartControls (nType);
   }
}
```

OnCatSelect Message Handler Code

The OnCatSelect message handler is the first of several that process events that pertain to the Cash Flow report options. When the Categories option is selected, this message handler gets invoked by the framework when the user selects a particular category by double clicking on the category name in the list box. The code for this member function is unchanged and is as follows:

```
void CSettings::OnCatSelect()
{
   CCategory* pCat;
   POSITION pos;

   //
   // access the list box and get the current item,
   // determine whether it is selected, and get its
   // text string.
   //
   CString szCategory;
   int nSel = m_pCategoryList->GetCurSel();
   int nSS  = m_pCategoryList->GetSel(nSel);
   ASSERT (nSS != LB_ERR);
   m_pCategoryList->GetText (nSel, szCategory);

   //
   // search the document's "m_ReportCats" list for
   // a category object whose name matches and then
   // either add or remove the new selection.
   //
   pCat = FindCategory (m_pDoc->m_ReportCats, szCategory, pos);
   if (nSS > 0)
   {
      //
      // the item was newly selected, so it shouldn't
      // have been found in the setting's list. Find
      // it in the main category list.
      //
      ASSERT (pCat == NULL);
      pCat = FindCategory (m_pDoc->m_CatList, szCategory, pos);
      ASSERT (pCat != NULL);
      m_pDoc->m_ReportCats.AddTail (pCat);
   }
   else
   {
      //
      // item was deselected, so it should have
      // been found in the document's m_ReportCats
      // list. Delete it from that list.
      //
      ASSERT (pCat != NULL);
      m_pDoc->m_ReportCats.RemoveAt (pos);
   }
}
```

The functionality of the foregoing code was discussed in detail in Chapter 10, beginning on page 375. The code is included here only for the sake of completeness.

OnCatRadio Message Handler Code

As with the OnCatSelect member function, the OnCatRadio message handler is called only when the Categories options are in effect, for the Cash Flow report. The unchanged code is as follows:

```
void CSettings::OnCatRadio()
{
   int nWhich;
   nWhich = GetCheckedRadioButton (IDC_ALL_RADIO,
```

```
        IDC_TAX_RELATED_RADIO);
  SelectCategories (m_pCategoryList, nWhich);
  m_nPrevCatRadio = nWhich;
}
```

In the foregoing, the member function determines which of the All, None, or Tax-related radio buttons was clicked and then calls the Select-Categories member function to select (or deselect) the appropriate entries in the Category list box. This handler is discussed in Chapter 10, beginning on page 376.

MakeTextSettings Helper Member Function Code

The MakeTextSettings member function is used as a helper member function for both the OnStringEntry and OnContentsRadio message handlers. Both of those are associated with options for the Cash Flow report. The code for this "helper" member function is described in some detail in Chapter 10, beginning on page 377. The code is unchanged and is as follows:

```
void CSettings::MakeTextSettings()
{
  CString  szText;
  CString  szType;
  TInclude Include;
  int nWhich;

  //
  // determine which radio button is checked and then set
  // the "Include" variable to reflect the corresponding
  // inclusion setting.
  //
  nWhich = GetCheckedRadioButton (IDC_STARTS_RADIO,
    IDC_EXACT_RADIO);
  switch (nWhich)
  {
    case IDC_STARTS_RADIO:
    {
      Include = startsWith;
      break;
    }
    case IDC_CONTAINS_RADIO:
    {
      Include = contains;
      break;
    }
    case IDC_EXACT_RADIO:
    {
      Include = equals;
      break;
    }
    default:
    {
      Include = all;
      break;
    }
  }

  //
```

```cpp
   // determine which field (Description or Info) is being
   // referenced, set the inclusion condition to "all" if
   // the text string is empty, or set the inclusion condition
   // to correspond to the radio button setting.
   // (Note: An empty string specifies inclusion of all values.)
   //
   m_pTextString->GetWindowText (szText);
   int index = m_pTypeCombo->GetCurSel();
   m_pTypeCombo->GetLBText (index, szType);
   if (szType == "Description")
   {
      if (szText == "")
      {
         m_pDoc->m_eDescInclude = all;
      }
      else
      {
         m_pDoc->m_eDescInclude = Include;
      }
      m_nPrevDescRadio = nWhich;
      m_pDoc->m_szDescription = szText;
   }
   else if (szType == "Info")
   {
      if (szText == "")
      {
         m_pDoc->m_eInfoInclude = all;
      }
      else
      {
         m_pDoc->m_eInfoInclude = Include;
      }
      m_nPrevInfoRadio = nWhich;
      m_pDoc->m_szInfo = szText;
   }
}
```

OnStringEntry Message Handler Code

The OnStringEntry message handler is called by the framework when
the focus is switched away from the Description or Info editable text
field in the Cash Flow report options. The code for this handler merely
calls the MakeTextSettings member function to perform all of the necessary functions. The code for the handler is unchanged and is as follows:

```cpp
void CSettings::OnStringEntry()
{
   MakeTextSettings();
}
```

OnContentsRadio Message Handler Code

The OnContentsRadio message handler is called by the framework
when the user clicks one of the "Starts With," "Contains," or "Equals
Exactly" radio buttons associated with the Description or Info options of
the Cash Flow report. The code for this message handler is unchanged
and is as follows:

```
void CSettings::OnContentsRadio()
{
   MakeTextSettings();
}
```

As is evident, the foregoing code also makes use of the MakeTextSettings member function to do all of the work associated with any of the button selections. As mentioned previously, the functionality of the MakeText-Settings member function is discussed fully in Chapter 10, beginning on page 377.

The next series of message handlers is associated with the options for the newly created Net Worth Chart report.

OnGraphTypeRadio Message Handler Code

The OnGraphTypeRadio message handler receives control from the framework when the Graph Type options have been selected for the Net Worth Chart report and the user has clicked one of the "Vertical Bar" or "Line Plot" radio buttons. The newly added code is as follows:

```
void CSettings::OnGraphTypeRadio()
{
   int nWhich;
   nWhich = GetCheckedRadioButton (IDC_VERT_BAR, IDC_LINE_PLOT);
   m_nPrevGraphType = nWhich;
   m_pDoc->m_nGraphType = nWhich;
}
```

The foregoing code saves the identifier for the currently selected chart type into variables in the dialog and document objects.

OnTitleEntry Message Handler Code

The OnTitleEntry message handler is invoked by the framework when the focus is taken away from either the Vertical Axis Title or Horizontal Axis Title editable text field. Both of these fields are associated with the Graph Type options for the Net Worth Chart report. The code for the message handler is newly added and is as follows:

```
void CSettings::OnTitleEntry()
{
   m_pVertString->GetWindowText (m_szPrevVertString);
   m_pHorzString->GetWindowText (m_szPrevHorzString);
   m_pDoc->m_szVertTitle = m_szPrevVertString;
   m_pDoc->m_szHorzTitle = m_szPrevHorzString;
}
```

The foregoing code saves the text of both the Vertical Axis Title and Horizontal Axis Title CEdit controls into variables in the document object. This preserves these values for use by the report object, after the dialog has been dismissed.

OnIntervalRadio Message Handler Code

The OnIntervalRadio message handler is invoked by the framework when the user selects one of the "Monthly," "Quarterly," or "Annually" radio buttons associated with the Interval options of the Net Worth Chart report. The code for this handler is newly added and is as follows:

```
void CSettings::OnIntervalRadio()
{
    int nWhich;
    nWhich = GetCheckedRadioButton (IDC_MONTHLY, IDC_ANNUALLY);
    m_nPrevInterval = nWhich;
    m_pDoc->m_nInterval = nWhich;
}
```

The foregoing code saves the identifier of the radio button that was clicked, into member variables of the dialog and document objects.

OnUseColorCheck Message Handler Code

The OnUseColorCheck message handler is invoked by the framework when the user clicks in the Use Color checkbox associated with the Colors options of the Net Worth Chart report. The newly added code is as follows:

```
void CSettings::OnUseColorCheck()
{
    m_nPrevUseColor = m_pUseColorCheck->GetCheck();
    m_pDoc->m_nUseColor = m_nPrevUseColor;
}
```

The foregoing code saves the state of the Use Color checkbox into member variables associated with the dialog and document objects.

OnSampleClick Message Handler Code

The OnSampleClick message handler is invoked by the framework when the user clicks on any of the "Axis Color," "Title Color," "Label Color," or "Graph Color" color sample buttons, which are associated with the Colors options of the Net Worth Chart report. The newly added code for this message handler is as follows:

```
void CSettings::OnSampleClick()
{
    int control, index, nColor;
```

```
    BOOL found = FALSE;
    for (control=IDC_AXIS_SAMPLE; control <= IDC_GRAPH_SAMPLE;
      control++)
    {
      CButton* pBut;
      pBut = (CButton *)GetDlgItem (control);
      ASSERT (pBut != NULL);
      if (pBut->GetState() & 0x0008)
      {
        m_nPrevSampleClick = control;
        index = control - IDC_AXIS_SAMPLE;
        found = TRUE;
        break;
      }
    }
    if (!found)
    {
      AfxMessageBox ("Can't find which sample was clicked");
    }

    // set the sample to the specified color

    nColor = m_nPrevColorClick - IDC_COLOR_1;
    m_nPrevSampleColors[index] = nColor;
    m_pDoc->m_nColors[index] = nColor;
    RedrawButton(control);
}
```

The foregoing code loops through the four different control identifiers,
checking the state of each of the corresponding buttons. When the one
that has the current focus is found, the current (previously specified)
color selection is saved in member variables of the dialog and document
objects. The color selection is an index into an array of 16 colors, as will
be shown later, when the CCButton class is described. The code concludes by redrawing the button just clicked with the appropriate color
sample.

OnColorClick Message Handler Code

The OnColorClick message handler is invoked by the framework when
the user clicks on any of the 16 color sample buttons in the Colors options of the Net Worth Chart report. The code for this message handler
is newly added and is as follows:

```
void CSettings::OnColorClick()
{
  int control, index, nColor;
  BOOL found = FALSE;
  for (control=IDC_COLOR_1; control <= IDC_COLOR_16; control++)
  {
    CButton* pBut;
    pBut = (CButton *)GetDlgItem (control);
    ASSERT (pBut != NULL);
    if (pBut->GetState() & 0x0008)
    {
      m_nPrevColorClick = control;
      nColor = control - IDC_COLOR_1;
      found = TRUE;
```

```
                break;
        }
    }
    if (!found)
    {
        AfxMessageBox ("Can't find which color was clicked");
        return;
    }

    //
    // set the sample to the specified color
    //
    index = m_nPrevSampleClick - IDC_AXIS_SAMPLE;
    m_nPrevSampleColors[index] = nColor;
    m_pDoc->m_nColors[index] = nColor;
    RedrawButton(m_nPrevSampleClick);
}
```

In the foregoing code, the first section determines which of the 16 buttons has been clicked and then stores an index associated with the button into member variables for the dialog and document objects. The code then determines the latest chart property button that was clicked (Axis, Title, Label, or Graph Color) and redraws that button with the color sample just clicked.

Newly Added CCButton Class Code

When we decided to allow the user to select the colors to use for the Net Worth Chart properties, we determined that the user should be presented with a set of color samples from which to choose. Painting color samples in the dialog didn't seem to be too difficult a chore, and we soon realized that it would be even easier if we created buttons so that the user could see, through visual feedback, that a particular color sample had been clicked. Because we didn't want to create a bunch of bitmaps to represent the colors, and, instead, wanted to create these dynamically, as needed, we decided to create "owner draw" buttons for each of the colors and the chart properties. To do this properly, it was necessary to create a new class, based upon the CButton class, so that we could override the DrawItem member function to render our buttons the way we wanted. The result of these decisions is the creation of the CCButton class, which is a direct descendant of the CButton base class. CCButton inherits all of the member variables and member functions of the CButton class, but we have overridden the DrawItem member function.

CCButton Class Header File Declarations

We created the header file for the CCButton class manually, by choosing New from the Visual Workbench File menu and then entering the new class declaration.

CCButton.h Contents

The header file for the CCButton class (**ccbutton.h**) is quite small. The entire contents of the file are as follows:

```cpp
///////////////////////////////////////////////////////////
// ccbutton.h
//

class CCButton : public CButton
{
protected:

    DECLARE_DYNCREATE (CCButton)

public:
    virtual void DrawItem (LPDRAWITEMSTRUCT lpDIS);
    CCButton();
    virtual ~CCButton();
};

//
// global access function
//
    COLORREF RGBColor(int index);
```

In addition to the constructor and destructor declarations, the CCButton class has only one member function and that is the override of the DrawItem member function. In addition, however, we have defined a global function, called RGBColor, which can be referenced from anywhere in the application. This function takes the index (0–15) as input and returns a COLORREF result, which is an RGB color specification. The index corresponds to one of the 16 colors we support.

CCButton Source File Definitions

As is evident from the foregoing header file description, the contents of the source file for the CCButton class (**ccbutton.cpp**) is quite small. However, the class contains a static table of COLORREF values that are used by the RGBColor function to map an index to a color value.

In case you're interested in how we arrived at the individual RGB values, we'll share the secret. We launched the Adobe Illustrator application, selected colors that we thought would be appropriate for our purpose, and then copied down their individual RGB values so that they could be entered into the table. Any other table of RGB values, or any other application that displays colors and indicates their corresponding RGB values would suffice.

First Section of the CCButton.cpp Source File

The first section of the **ccbutton.cpp** source file is as follows:

```
//////////////////////////////////////////////////////////////////
// ccbutton.cpp
//
#include "stdafx.h"
#include "resource.h"
#include "settings.h"
#include "ccbutton.h"

//
// define color values for use in drawing buttons
// +---------+---------+---------+---------+
// | black   |   red   |  green  |  blue   |
// +---------+---------+---------+---------+
// | dk grey |  orange |lt green | purple  |
// +---------+---------+---------+---------+
// |  grey   |  gold   |sea green| magenta |
// +---------+---------+---------+---------+
// | lt grey | yellow  |turquoise|hot pink |
// +---------+---------+---------+---------+
//
static COLORREF __far colors[16] =
{
   RGB(  0,  0,  0), RGB(255,  0,0), RGB(0,255,  0),
      RGB(  0,0,255),
   RGB( 70, 70, 70), RGB(255, 85,0), RGB(0,255, 85),
      RGB( 85,0,255),
   RGB(140,140,140), RGB(255,171,0), RGB(0,255,171),
      RGB(171,0,255),
   RGB(210,210,210), RGB(255,255,0), RGB(0,255,255),
      RGB(255,0,255)
};
```

Constructor and Destructor Code

The constructor and destructor member functions are empty in this version of the code, but we have supplied them in case we want to add some code to them in the future. The code for this section of the **ccbutton.cpp** source file is as follows:

```
IMPLEMENT_DYNCREATE (CCButton, CButton)

CCButton::CCButton()
{
   // empty
}

CCButton::~CCButton()
{
   // empty
}
```

We used the IMPLEMENT_DYNCREATE macro so that objects of the class could be created dynamically, at run time.

DrawItem Member Function Code

The DrawItem member function override is the main feature of the CCButton class source code. This member function is called by the framework, automatically, whenever any of the buttons needs to be re-drawn. The member function is called with a pointer to a DRAWITEM-STRUCT structure, which holds quite a bit of information about the item to be drawn, including its position and size as well as its selection status. We use the information in the structure to draw the specified button, with the appearance that is appropriate to its selection state. The code for the DrawItem member function is as follows:

```
void CCButton::DrawItem (LPDRAWITEMSTRUCT lpDIS)
{
   CDC* pDC = CDC::FromHandle (lpDIS->hDC);
   CSettings* pParent = (CSettings *)GetParent();
   CRgn rButton;

   //
   // get the info we need for drawing the button
   //
   int nLeft, nTop, nRight, nBottom, index, cID;
   nLeft    = lpDIS->rcItem.left;
   nTop     = lpDIS->rcItem.top;
   nRight   = lpDIS->rcItem.right;
   nBottom  = lpDIS->rcItem.bottom;
   rButton.CreateRectRgn (nLeft, nTop, nRight, nBottom);
   cID = lpDIS->CtlID;
   if (cID >= IDC_AXIS_SAMPLE && cID <= IDC_GRAPH_SAMPLE)
   {
      index = pParent->GetSampleIndex(cID);
   }
   else
   {
      index = cID - IDC_COLOR_1;
   }

   //
   // determine what we have to do
   //
   if (lpDIS->itemAction & ODA_DRAWENTIRE)
   {
      //
      // need to draw the entire item
      //
      CBrush aBrush (colors[index]);
      pDC->FillRgn (&rButton, &aBrush);
      CBrush br (RGB(192, 192, 192));
      pDC->FrameRect (&lpDIS->rcItem, &br);
   }

   if ((lpDIS->itemAction & (ODA_SELECT | ODA_DRAWENTIRE))
   && (lpDIS->itemState & ODS_SELECTED))
   {
      //
      // item is selected, draw the black frame
      //
      CBrush br (RGB(0, 0, 0));
      pDC->FrameRect (&lpDIS->rcItem, &br);
   }
```

```
if ((lpDIS->itemAction & ODA_SELECT) &&
    !(lpDIS->itemState & ODS_SELECTED))
{
    //
    // item is deselected, draw the gray frame
    //
    CBrush br (RGB(192, 192, 192));
    pDC->FrameRect (&lpDIS->rcItem, &br);
}
}
```

One of the first acts of the DrawItem member function is to create a rectangular region from the button's coordinates so that we can use the FillRgn function to paint the button with its associated color. The next action in the code is to determine whether one of the chart properties buttons or one of the 16 color sample buttons was clicked. In either case, the appropriate index into the table of COLORREF values is calculated and the member function continues by determining whether to draw the entire button, draw just the selection rectangle, or draw the button as being deselected.

RGBColor Global Function Code

The RGBColor function returns a COLORREF value from the table of colors when supplied with an index value of 0–15 as input. The code for this function is as follows:

```
COLORREF RGBColor (int index)
{
    return colors[index];
}
```

Additions to the CKeepitDoc Class

We added a new message handler to the CKeepitDoc class to process the OnNetWorthChart command. In addition, we have also added a few new member variables that we will use to hold various selections from the Settings dialog, temporarily, until the CReportView object is created and its OnInitialUpdate member function is called by the framework.

If the user chooses to dismiss the Settings dialog with its Cancel button, then the CKeepitDoc class does nothing further with the OnNetWorth Chart command. If, however, the dialog is dismissed with its OK button, then the CReportView object is created and initialized.

KeepitDoc.h Header File Additions

As mentioned previously, the additions to the **keepdoc.h** header file consist mainly of the addition of the new message handler declaration and the declaration of member variables to hold various selections from the Setttings dialog that bear upon the creation of the Net Worth Chart report. As is our custom, the entire contents of the **keepdoc.h** header file are shown, as follows:

```
// keepdoc.h : interface of the CKeepitDoc class
//
/////////////////////////////////////////////////////////////////

class CListEntry;
class CAcctList;
class CAcctObj;
class CSettings;

#define ACCOUNT_MENU_POS 3  // fourth menu on menubar
#define CASH_FLOW_REPORT 1  // cash flow detail report
#define NET_WORTH_REPORT 2  // net worth summary report
#define NET_WORTH_CHART  3  // net worth chart

class CKeepitDoc : public CDocument
{
protected: // create from serialization only
   CKeepitDoc();
   DECLARE_DYNCREATE(CKeepitDoc)
   BOOL OnCmdMsg (UINT nID, int nCode, void *pExtra,
      AFX_CMDHANDLERINFO* pHandlerInfo);

   void OnAccountName (UINT nID);
   void OnAccountNameUpdate (UINT nID, CCmdUI* pExtra);

   void DeleteDlgAccts(CSettings& dlg);

// Attributes
public:

   CObList    m_ListEntries;      // list of entries
   CObList    m_CatList;          // list of category objects
   CObList    m_AcctList;         // list of accounts
   BOOL       m_bFirstTime;       // first time switch
   CString    m_szCurAcctName;    // current account name
   WORD       m_nCurrentAccount;  // current account ID

   int        m_nReportType;      // current report type
   CObList    m_ReportAccts;      // current report accounts
   CTime      m_FromDate;         // beginning of period
   CTime      m_ToDate;           // end of reporting period
   CString    m_szDialogTitle;    // title for settings dialog

   //
   // declarations specific to Settings dialog options
   //
   CObList    m_ReportCats;       // current report catagories
   CString    m_szDescription;    // description qualifier
   TInclude   m_eDescInclude;     // description inclusion type
   CString    m_szInfo;           // info qualifier
   TInclude   m_eInfoInclude;     // info inclusion type
```

```cpp
    int         m_nGraphType;       // selected graph type
    CString     m_szVertTitle;      // vertical axis title
    CString     m_szHorzTitle;      // horizontal axis title
    int         m_nInterval;        // charting interval
    int         m_nUseColor;        // use color?
    int         m_nColors[4];       // axis, title, label, graph
                                    // -- color index

// Operations
public:

    CListEntry* NewListEntry (void);
    void DeleteListEntry (CListEntry* anEntry);
    void AddListEntry (CListEntry* anEntry);
    void FillAcctList (CAcctList* pList);

// Implementation
public:
  virtual ~CKeepitDoc();
  virtual void Serialize(CArchive& ar);// overridden
  virtual void DeleteContents(void); // overridden
  virtual BOOL CanCloseFrame(CFrameWnd* pFrame);//
override

#ifdef _DEBUG
  virtual void AssertValid() const;
  virtual void Dump(CDumpContext& dc) const;
#endif

protected:
  BOOL OnNewDocument();// create a new document
  void RemoveAcctMenu (CAcctObj* pAcct);// remove menu command
  void RemoveTransactions (WORD nAcctID);// remove transactions;
  void RemoveMDIFrame (CString& szName);// delete named frame

public:
  void AddAcctMenu (CAcctObj* pAcct);// add a menu command
  void SetMenuNames(void);              // set account names in
                                        // -- Account menu

// Generated message map functions
protected:
  //{{AFX_MSG(CKeepitDoc)
  afx_msg void OnViewCategories();
  afx_msg void OnAcctEdit();
  afx_msg void OnCashFlow();
  afx_msg void OnNetWorth();
  afx_msg void OnChrtNetWorth();
  //}}AFX_MSG
  DECLARE_MESSAGE_MAP()

//
// report helper member functions
//
void ReportSetup (int nReportType);

};
```

Although we could have presented only the changed lines in the foregoing file, we feel that it is better for you see these in the context in which
they have been entered. Therefore, to help you see the small number of
changes to the **keepdoc.h** header file, we have placed change bars to the
left of the added declarations in this file.

KeepDoc.cpp Source File Additions

Rather than show the entire source file for the CKeepitDoc class, we will show you only the member functions which affect the creation of the NetWorth Chart report.

Message Map Code

The only change to the Message Map is the addition of the entry for the OnChrtNetWorth command. The newly updated message map code is as follows:

```
BEGIN_MESSAGE_MAP(CKeepitDoc, CDocument)
  //{{AFX_MSG_MAP(CKeepitDoc)
  ON_COMMAND(ID_VIEW_CATEGORIES, OnViewCategories)
  ON_COMMAND(ID_ACCT_EDIT, OnAcctEdit)
  ON_COMMAND(ID_RPT_CASH_FLOW, OnCashFlow)
  ON_COMMAND(ID_RPT_NET_WORTH, OnNetWorth)
  ON_COMMAND(ID_CHRT_NET_WORTH, OnChrtNetWorth)
  //}}AFX_MSG_MAP
END_MESSAGE_MAP()
```

OnChrtNetWorth Message Handler Code

The OnChrtNetWorth message handler is invoked by the framework when the user chooses the Net Worth Chart command from the Report menu. The revised code for the OnChrtNetWorth message handler is as follows:

```
void CKeepitDoc::OnChrtNetWorth()
{
  //
  // we need only call the setup routine to get the
  // user's settings and then create the chart.
  //
  ReportSetup (NET_WORTH_CHART);
}
```

When the handler gains control, it calls the ReportSetup member function to perform all of the functions related to the invocation of the Settings dialog, and the creation of the CReportView object and its initialization prior to creation of the chart.

ReportSetup Helper Member Function Code

The ReportSetup member function performs all of the work associated with any of the Report menu command choices. The revised code for this member function is as follows:

```cpp
void CKeepitDoc::ReportSetup(int nReportType)
{
   int     nYr, nMo, nDy;
   CSettingsdlg;

   //
   // create a default cash flow report for year-to-date
   // income and expenses in all accounts.
   //
   CTime curTime = CTime::GetCurrentTime();// current time
   nYr = curTime.GetYear();                    // current year
   nMo = curTime.GetMonth();                   // current month
   nDy = curTime.GetDay();                     // current day
   CTime startTime (nYr, 1, 1, 0, 0, 0); // 1/1/current year

   //
   // set dialog member variables to their initial values
   //
   if (nReportType == CASH_FLOW_REPORT)
   {
      dlg.m_szDialogTitle = "Cash Flow Report Settings";
      dlg.m_Title = "Cash Flow Report";   // title
   }
   else if (nReportType == NET_WORTH_REPORT)
   {
      dlg.m_szDialogTitle = "Net Worth Report Settings";
      dlg.m_Title = "Net Worth Report";   // title
   }
   else if (nReportType == NET_WORTH_CHART)
   {
      dlg.m_szDialogTitle = "Net Worth Chart Settings";
      dlg.m_Title = "Net Worth Chart";    // title
   }
   else
   {
      dlg.m_szDialogTitle = "Unknown Report Settings";
      dlg.m_Title = "Unknown Report";
   }
   dlg.m_From = startTime.Format ("%m/%d/%y"); // 01/01/yr
   dlg.m_To = curTime.Format ("%m/%d/%y");     // mm/dd/yr
   dlg.m_pDoc = this; // document pointer

   //
   // create copies of the accounts and load them into the
   // dialog's list of accounts.
   //
   POSITION pos = m_AcctList.GetHeadPosition();
   while (pos != NULL)
   {
      CAcctObj* pAcct = (CAcctObj *)m_AcctList.GetNext (pos);
      CAcctObj* nAcct = new CAcctObj (pAcct);
      dlg.m_Accounts.AddTail (nAcct);
   }

   //
   // initialize the report option variables by including all
   // of the categories in the list and setting the inclusion
   // criteria to "all" for both the Description and Info fields.
   //
   m_ReportCats.RemoveAll();
   pos = m_CatList.GetHeadPosition();
   while (pos != NULL)
   {
      CCategory* pCat;
      pCat = (CCategory *)m_CatList.GetNext (pos);
```

```cpp
        m_ReportCats.AddTail (pCat);
    }
    m_szDescription = "";
    m_eDescInclude = all;
    m_szInfo = "";
    m_eInfoInclude = all;


    //
    // include initialization for chart settings
    //
    m_nGraphType = IDC_VERT_BAR;// vertical bar graph
    m_szVertTitle = "";         // empty vertical title
    m_szHorzTitle = "";         // empty horizontal title
    m_nInterval = IDC_MONTHLY;  // monthly intervals
    m_nUseColor = 1;            // use color
    for (int i=0; i < 4; i++)
    {
       m_nColors[i] = i*4;// set shade of grey
    }


    //
    // now we can invoke the dialog to get the settings
    //
    if (dlg.DoModal() == IDOK)
    {
       //
       // convert the from and to dates to CTime objects
       // and verify that the from date is < the to date.
       //
       MakeDateObj (dlg.m_From, m_FromDate);
       MakeDateObj (dlg.m_To,   m_ToDate);
       if (m_FromDate > m_ToDate)
       {
          //
          // an invalid date span was given. Tell the user,
          // delete the dialog's account objects, and then
          // return.
          //
          AfxMessageBox ("End date must be greater "
                      "than start date.");
          DeleteDlgAccts(dlg);
          return;
       }


       //
       // the settings are all good, so now we can
       // store them for use by the view.
       //
       m_nReportType = nReportType;
       POSITION nPos = dlg.m_Accounts.GetHeadPosition();
       while (nPos != NULL)
       {
          CAcctObj* pObj;
          pObj = (CAcctObj *)dlg.m_Accounts.GetNext(nPos);
          if (pObj->GetAcctStatus() == ACCT_SELECTED)
          {
             CAcctObj* pRObj = new CAcctObj (pObj);
             m_ReportAccts.AddTail(pRObj);
          }
       }
       DeleteDlgAccts(dlg);

          //
          // make sure there's something to display, create
          // a new frame and view in which to display the
          // current report, and then let the view take over.
          //
```

```
                    if (!m_ReportAccts.IsEmpty())
                    {
                    CKeepitApp* theApp = (CKeepitApp *)AfxGetApp();
                    CMultiDocTemplate* pRptTmp;
                    pRptTmp = theApp->m_pRptViewTemplate;
                    CFrameWnd* pRptFrame;
                    pRptFrame = pRptTmp->CreateNewFrame (this, NULL);
                    pRptTmp->InitialUpdateFrame (pRptFrame, this);
                }
            }
        else
        {
            //
            // delete all of the dialog's account entries
            //
            DeleteDlgAccts(dlg);
        }
    }
```

The ReportSetup member function code was described in Chapter 10, in great detail, beginning on page 385. The sections of the member function that have been revised to provide support for the Net Worth Chart command are indicated by change bars at the left of the corresponding statements in the foregoing code.

The most important section of the code is the one that verifies that there is something to display in the report and then creates the new frame, using the m_pRptViewTemplate pointer from the CKeepitApp object. After creating the frame, we call InitialUpdateFrame member function, which calls the view's OnInitialUpdate member function by using the SendMessage function. This ensures that the OnInitialUpdate member function is executed prior to when the ReportSetup member function completes execution. This is important because we have stored values from the Settings dialog, temporarily, in member variables of the document object. If these settings were not copied into the CReportView object by its OnInitialUpdate member function, then the user's choice of a different report could wipe out the previous settings. Fortunately, this cannot occur.

Newly Added CReportView Code

The CReportView class is used for all of our reports. In the case of the Net Worth Chart report, we are not going to display textual information (except for axis annotations and titles); however, the CScrollView base class, from which the CReportView class inherits most of its behavior, is still important to the creation of the new chart. It is possible that the chart that the user has specified may not fit within the confines of the default window, and therefore, the ability to scroll the contents of the window is important.

Whether text or graphics are to be rendered should affect your choice of which mapping mode to use. The MM_TEXT mapping mode is the default for new views, but this can be changed easily by using the SetMap-Mode member function for a CDC-class object, or by specifying the mapping mode in the call to SetScrollSizes in the OnInitialUpdate member function. The CScrollView class supports the "metric" mapping modes, such as MM_HIMETRIC, MM_TWIPS, MM_HIENGLISH, MM_LOMETRIC, and MM_LOENGLISH, as well as the MM_TEXT mode. Each of these modes "maps" logical units to device units. In the case of the MM_TEXT mapping mode, both the logical and device units are assumed to be in pixels. When using the MM_TEXT mapping mode, positive vertical movements are downward, while with the other mapping modes, positive vertical movements are upward.

There are good reasons to choose one mapping mode over another. If you are going to render text only, the MM_TEXT mapping mode is the best choice. If, however, you plan to draw graphics and want them to be the same size and in the same perspective on all the devices on which they are rendered, then one of the metric mapping modes is more appropriate. The MM_LOENGLISH mapping mode assumes that each logical unit represents $\frac{1}{100}$ inch, whereas the MM_HIENGLISH mapping mode assumes that each logical unit represents $\frac{1}{1000}$ inch. In the same manner, in the MM_LOMETRIC mapping mode, one logical unit represents $\frac{1}{10}$ millimeter, whereas in the MM_HIMETRIC mapping mode, each logical unit represents $\frac{1}{100}$ millimeter. The final mapping mode, MM_TWIPS, is more oriented toward typographic resolution and, with it, logical units represent $\frac{1}{20}$ point (where one printer's point is approximately $\frac{1}{72}$ inch). Therefore one "twip" is approximately equal to $\frac{1}{1440}$ inch. This provides high enough resolution to position typographic elements for most imagesetting needs.

We have chosen to use the MM_LOENGLISH mapping mode for the creation of the Net Worth Chart report. This offers sufficient resolution for our needs and the units are independent of the device on which the chart is drawn. This makes it unnecessary for us to convert from logical units to pixels for drawing the chart, depending upon which device type it is rendered. The one negative aspect (no pun intended) of choosing this mapping mode is that when we draw elements from the top down to the bottom of the page, we will have to use increasingly negative Y values in our drawing instructions. It is possible to transform the origin of the co-ordinate system to the lower left corner and use positive Y values; however, for the relatively simple chart types we are drawing, it is not necessary to do so.

CReportView Header File Additions

We have added a number of new member variables and member functions to the **reportvw.h** header file. As is our custom, we will present the entire file, but we will mark the newly added statements with change bars at their left. The contents of the **reportvw.h** header file is as follows:

Reportvw.h First Section

The first section of the **reportvw.h** header file contains the forward class reference declarations and the class constructor member function. The code is as follows:

```
// reportvw.h : header file
//

class CKeepitDoc;
class CListEntry;
class CAcctObj;

/////////////////////////////////////////////////////////////////////
// CReportView view

class CReportView : public CScrollView
{
   DECLARE_DYNCREATE(CReportView)
protected:
   CReportView();          // protected constructor
                           // used by dynamic creation
```

Public Attribute Declarations

The next section of the header file contains the declaration of public attributes. The code is as follows:

```
// Attributes
public:
   CObList       m_RptEntries;    // report entries
   int           m_nReportType;   // type of report to display
   CTime         m_FromDate;      // start of period
   CTime         m_ToDate;        // end of period
   CObList       m_ReportCats;    // current report catagories
   CString       m_szDescription; // description qualifier
   CString       m_szInfo;        // info qualifier
   TInclude      m_eDescInclude;  // description inclusion type
   TInclude      m_eInfoInclude;  // info inclusion type
   int           m_nGraphType;    // chart type
   CString       m_szVertTitle;   // vertical chart title
   CString       m_szHorzTitle;   // horizontal chart title
   int           m_nInterval;     // interval type
   int           m_nUseColor;     // use color?
   COLORREF      m_cAxis;         // axis color
   COLORREF      m_cTitle;        // title color
   COLORREF      m_cLabel;        // label color
   COLORREF      m_cGraph;        // graph color
```

Member Function Declarations

Following are the declarations of the public member functions and all of the protected member functions used only for creating the various reports in the CReportView class. The code is as follows:

```
// Operations
public:
    CKeepitDoc* GetDocument();// copied from account.h

// Implementation
protected:
    virtual ~CReportView();
    virtual void OnDraw(CDC* pDC); // overridden for this view
    virtual void OnInitialUpdate();// first time

    //
    // report view size computation member functions
    //
    CSize CashFlowViewSize ();        // Cash-Flow view size
    CSize NetWorthViewSize ();        // Net-Worth view size
    CSize NetWorthChartSize(CDC& aDC);// Net-Worth chart size

    //
    // cash flow helper member functions
    //
    BOOL   MeetsRptCriteria (    // check if transaction meets
         CListEntry* pEntry);   // -- report criteria
    BOOL   MatchStrings (        // match using criteria
         CString szSrc,          // -- source string
         CString szPattern,      // -- pattern string
         TInclude criteria);     // -- inclusion criteria
                                 // ---- startsWith
                                 // ---- contains
                                 // ---- equals

    //
    // net worth helper member functions
    //
    long  ComputeBalance (CAcctObj* p,// account balance
      CTime tTo);                     // -- at the ending date
    long  MakeAcctEntry (int n, int m);// make report entry
    CString MakeValueString (long v);// value as string
    void MakeRptListEntry (int nType,  // make report list entry
      CString szLine);

    //
    // net worth chart helper member functions
    //
    long IntervalNetWorth(CTime tEnd);// net worth until tEnd
    CTime NextMonth (CTime tStart);  // date of next month
    CTime NextQuarter (CTime tStart);// date of next quarter
    CTime NextYear (CTime tStart);   // date of next year
    void  MakeChartEntry (int nType, // make chart entry
         long nValue,
         CString& szLabel);
    void DrawChart(CDC* pDC);        // draw the chart

    //
    // general purpose report member functions
    //
    void SortByDate (CObList& list); // sort transactions
    void RectLPtoPositions (         // rect to entry pos.
      longRECT rectClip,             // input longRect
```

```
            POSITION& nFirstEntry,          // output POSITION
            POSITION& nLastEntry);          // output POSITION

    void DrawRptLine (CDC* pDC,         // draw a report line
      . CObject* pObj,                  // object info to draw
        int& nYPos);                    // position in viewport

    void OnPrepareDC (CDC* pDC,         // prepare the device
        CPrintInfo* pInfo = NULL);      // default printer info

    void ComputeRptMetrics (CDC*pDC);  // compute report metrics

    //
    // printing-related member functions
    //
    BOOL OnPreparePrinting (CPrintInfo* pInfo); // override
    void OnBeginPrinting (CDC* pDC, CPrintInfo* pInfo);
    void OnPrint (CDC* pDC, CPrintInfo* pInfo); // override
    void PrintPageHeader (CDC* pDC, CPrintInfo* pInfo);
```

Message Map Declarations

The message map declarations are as follows:

```
    // Generated message map functions
    //{{AFX_MSG(CReportView)
    afx_msg void OnFilePrint();
    afx_msg void OnFilePrintPreview();
    afx_msg void OnDestroy();
    afx_msg void OnHScroll(UINT nSBCode, UINT nPos,
        CScrollBar* pScrollBar);
    afx_msg void OnVScroll(UINT nSBCode, UINT nPos,
        CScrollBar* pScrollBar);
    //}}AFX_MSG
    DECLARE_MESSAGE_MAP()
```

Protected Member Variable Declarations

The member variables that specify values used only in the preparation of
the various reports are declared as follows:

```
//
// report metrics
//
  CString    m_szTitle;          // report title
  CRgn       m_BlankLine;        // region for blank line
  CSize      m_SizeTotal;        // total size of report
  CSize      m_PageSize;         // amount to scroll for page
  CSize      m_LineSize;         // amount to scroll for line
  int        m_nTotalLines;      // total number of lines
  int        m_nLinesPerPage;    // number of lines on a page
  int        m_nLineHeight;      // height of one line
  int        m_nLineWidth;       // maximum width of one line
  int        m_nMinCharWidth;    // minimum character width
  int        m_nAvgCharWidth;    // average character width
  int        m_nMaxCharWidth;    // maximum character width
  int        m_nCurPage;         // current page number

//
// graph metrics
```

```
//
  long      m_nValPerInc;       // dollars / increment on chart
  double    m_dUnitsPerDollar;// logical units per dollar
  int       m_nBarDivHt;        // height of Y division
  int       m_nBarWidth;        // width of one bar
  int       m_nChartHeight;     // height of chart
  int       m_nChartWidth;      // width of chart
};
```

In-line GetDocument Member Function for Nondebug Version

The version of the GetDocument member function that is used when the application is generated for release is as follows:

```
/////////////////////////////////////////////////////////////////////
////
//
// the following statements were copied from the
// account.h header file, which also needs to
// access the document.
//
#ifndef _DEBUG// debug version in reportvw.cpp
inline CKeepitDoc* CReportView::GetDocument()
    { return (CKeepitDoc*) m_pDocument; }
#endif
```

Reportvw.cpp Source File Additions

We have made changes to quite a few of the member functions in the CReportView class and, in addition, have added new member functions for drawing the Net Worth Chart report. Because quite a number of existing member functions have been modified, we have decided to show the entire contents of the **reportvw.cpp** source file in the sections that follow.

Immediately after the frame and its view are created, the code in the CKeepitDoc object calls the InitialUpdateFrame member function, which causes that member function to send the WM_INITIALUPDATE message which causes the OnInitialUpdate member function in the CReportView object to be executed. After OnInitialUpdate initializes the important member variables, the size of the view is computed, the SetScrollSizes member function is called to set the height and width of the total report, and then the Invalidate member function is called to force the view to be drawn. From that point forward, all of the drawing or redrawing of the view depends upon actions taken by the user (e.g., scrolling the view or choosing to view the print-preview version of the report). The contents of the **reportvw.cpp** source file are as follows:

Initial Definitions

The first section of the source file contains the #include preprocessor statements and the definition of several constants and strings used in titling the charts. The code is as follows:

```cpp
// reportvw.cpp : implementation file
//

#include "stdafx.h"
#include "keepit.h"

#include "ccbutton.h"  // for color references
#include "keepdoc.h"
#include "acctobj.h"
#include "listntry.h"
#include "category.h"
#include "repline.h"

#include "reportvw.h"

#ifdef _DEBUG
#undef THIS_FILE
static char BASED_CODE THIS_FILE[] = __FILE__;
#endif

//
// define metrics for chart elements (logical units)
//
#define MIN_BAR_WID        25
#define MAX_BAR_WID        50
#define MIN_BAR_INC        40
#define MAX_BAR_INC        80
#define TITLE_GAP_HT       10
#define TITLE_HEIGHT       18
#define X_LABEL_HEIGHT     12
#define HORZ_TITLE_HT      18
#define Y_LABEL_WIDTH     100
#define Y_LABEL_GAP        25
#define Y_TIC_WIDTH        10
#define X_TIC_HEIGHT       10
#define BAR_SPACER_WID     12

//
// define month and quarter name strings
//
char* monthNames[] =
{
    "Jan", "Feb", "Mar", "Apr", "May", "Jun",
    "Jul", "Aug", "Sep", "Oct", "Nov", "Dec"
};

char* qtrNames[] =
{
    "1st Qtr.", "2nd Qtr.", "3rd Qtr", "4th Qtr."
};
```

Constructor and Destructor Member Functions

The code for the constructor and destructor member functions in the CReportView class is as follows:

```
//////////////////////////////////////////////////////////////
// CReportView

IMPLEMENT_DYNCREATE(CReportView, CScrollView)

CReportView::CReportView()
{
}

CReportView::~CReportView()
{
}
```

Message Map Entries

The message map entries for the CReportView class have not changed.
The code is as follows:

```
BEGIN_MESSAGE_MAP(CReportView, CScrollView)
   //{{AFX_MSG_MAP(CReportView)
   ON_COMMAND(ID_FILE_PRINT, OnFilePrint)
   ON_COMMAND(ID_FILE_PRINT_PREVIEW, OnFilePrintPreview)
   ON_WM_DESTROY()
   ON_WM_HSCROLL()
   ON_WM_VSCROLL()
   //}}AFX_MSG_MAP
END_MESSAGE_MAP()
```

OnInitialUpdate Member Function Code

As indicated previously, the OnInitialUpdate member function is executed before the view is first made visible to the user. It is in this member
function that we have the opportunity to perform any initialization that
applies to the creation of all of the various reports. Much of the code is
general, but certain portions are specific to the individual report types.
The revised code for this member function is as follows:

```
void CReportView::OnInitialUpdate()
{
   //
   // Get a pointer to the document and access
   // the variables that will be used to construct
   // the selected report.
   //
   CKeepitDoc* pDoc = GetDocument();
   m_nReportType = pDoc->m_nReportType;
   m_FromDate = pDoc->m_FromDate;
   m_ToDate  = pDoc->m_ToDate;

   switch (m_nReportType)
   {
      case CASH_FLOW_REPORT:
      {
         //
```

```cpp
    // get the cash flow report's specific
    // parameters from the document.
    //
    POSITION pos = pDoc->m_ReportCats.GetHeadPosition ();
    while (pos != NULL)
    {
      CCategory* pCat;
      pCat = (CCategory *)pDoc->m_ReportCats.GetNext(pos);
      m_ReportCats.AddTail (pCat);
    }
    m_szDescription = pDoc->m_szDescription;
    m_szInfo = pDoc->m_szInfo;
    m_eDescInclude = pDoc->m_eDescInclude;
    m_eInfoInclude = pDoc->m_eInfoInclude;

    //
    // sort the transactions by date
    // for this report.
    //
    SortByDate (pDoc->m_ListEntries);

    //
    // prepare the device context for sizing the report.
    //
    CClientDC aDC(this);
    ComputeRptMetrics (&aDC);
    m_BlankLine.CreateRectRgn (0, 0, m_nLineWidth,
      m_nLineHeight);

    //
    // calculate the size of the view, based upon the
    // values of the parameters and type of report.
    //
    m_szTitle = "CASH FLOW DETAIL REPORT";
    m_SizeTotal = CashFlowViewSize ();
    SetScrollSizes(MM_TEXT, m_SizeTotal, m_PageSize,
      m_LineSize);
    Invalidate(TRUE);
    break;
}

case NET_WORTH_REPORT:
{
    //
    // sort the transactions by date
    // for this report.
    //
    SortByDate (pDoc->m_ListEntries);

    //
    // prepare the device context for sizing the report.
    //
    CClientDC aDC(this);
    ComputeRptMetrics (&aDC);
    m_BlankLine.CreateRectRgn (0, 0, m_nLineWidth,
      m_nLineHeight);

    //
    // calculate the size of the view, based upon the
    // values of the parameters and type of report.
    //
    m_szTitle = "NET WORTH SUMMARY REPORT";
    m_SizeTotal = NetWorthViewSize ();
    SetScrollSizes(MM_TEXT, m_SizeTotal, m_PageSize,
      m_LineSize);
    Invalidate(TRUE);
    break;
```

```cpp
        }
      case NET_WORTH_CHART:
      {
         //
         // get the parameters specific to the chart
         //
         m_nGraphType   = pDoc->m_nGraphType;
         m_szVertTitle = pDoc->m_szVertTitle;
         m_szHorzTitle = pDoc->m_szHorzTitle;
         m_nInterval    = pDoc->m_nInterval;
         m_nUseColor    = pDoc->m_nUseColor;

         //
         // handle the color selections
         //
         if (m_nUseColor > 0)
         {
            m_cAxis        = RGBColor (pDoc->m_nColors[0]);
            m_cTitle       = RGBColor (pDoc->m_nColors[1]);
            m_cLabel       = RGBColor (pDoc->m_nColors[2]);
            m_cGraph       = RGBColor (pDoc->m_nColors[3]);
         }
         else
         {
            m_cAxis = m_cTitle = m_cLabel = m_cGraph
               = RGBColor(0);// black color
         }

         //
         // sort the transactions by date
         // for this report.
         //
         SortByDate (pDoc->m_ListEntries);

         //
         // prepare the device context for sizing the report.
         //
         CClientDC aDC(this);
         aDC.SetMapMode (MM_LOENGLISH);
         ComputeRptMetrics (&aDC);

         //
         // calculate the size of the view, based upon the
         // values of the parameters and type of report.
         //
         m_szTitle = "NET WORTH SUMMARY CHART";
         m_SizeTotal = NetWorthChartSize (aDC);
         SetScrollSizes(MM_LOENGLISH, m_SizeTotal,
            m_PageSize, m_LineSize);
         Invalidate(TRUE);
         break;
      }

   default:
   {
      return;
   }
   }
}
```

In the foregoing OnInitialUpdate member function, the part that applies directly to the initialization for the Net Worth Chart report is marked by change bars at the left side of the statements. The code in that section initializes the member variables with the values stored in the document object, sorts the transactions for all of the accounts into strict chronological sequence, computes the report metrics (many of which are of no particular value to the preparation of the chart), calls the NetWorthChartSize member function to compute the height and width of the chart (in logical units), calls the SetScrollSizes member function with the mapping mode and chart dimension parameters, and then calls Invalidate to cause the entire view to be drawn. The actual drawing of the view is accomplished by the OnDraw member function, which is called whenever any portion of the view needs to be redrawn. It is good programming practice to perform all of the drawing of a view such as this in the OnDraw member function, unless the drawing has to take place in "real time," as would be the case in an illustration or painting program.

OnPrepareDC Member Function Code

Prior to calling the OnDraw member function, the framework calls the OnPrepareDC member function to prepare the device context. The revised code for this member function is as follows:

```
void CReportView::OnPrepareDC (CDC* pDC, CPrintInfo* pInfo)
{
   CScrollView::OnPrepareDC (pDC, pInfo);
   if (pDC->IsPrinting())
   {
      m_nCurPage = pInfo->m_nCurPage;
      if (m_nReportType == NET_WORTH_CHART)
      {
         pDC->SetMapMode (MM_LOENGLISH);
      }
   }
   ComputeRptMetrics (pDC);
}
```

ComputeRptMetrics Member Function Code

The ComputeRptMetrics code is called to calculate the metrics associated with text (and also graph-oriented) measurements for the current report. The major change from what was being done for the Cash Flow and Net Worth text reports is that the Net Worth Chart reports requires that the font being used be sized according to the requirements of the MM_LOENGLISH logical unit, which requires that measurements be expressed in 1/100 inch increments, rather than pixels (as is the case for the MM_TEXT mapping mode). Therefore, all of the measurements that are based upon elements of the TEXTMETRIC structure's contents must use the newly created font. The revised code for the new member function is as follows:

```
void CReportView::ComputeRptMetrics (CDC* pDC)
{
   TEXTMETRIC tm;
```

```
   CRect rectClient;
   int nPageHeight, nPtSz;

   CFont fRptFont;
   if (m_nReportType == NET_WORTH_CHART)
   {
      nPtSz = MulDiv(8, 100, 72);
   }
   else
   {
      nPtSz = MulDiv(8, pDC->GetDeviceCaps (LOGPIXELSY), 72);
   }
   fRptFont.CreateFont (-nPtSz, 0, 0, 0, FW_NORMAL, 0, 0, 0,
      ANSI_CHARSET, OUT_TT_PRECIS, CLIP_DEFAULT_PRECIS,
      PROOF_QUALITY, DEFAULT_PITCH | FF_SWISS, "Arial");

   CFont* pOldFont = pDC->SelectObject (&fRptFont);
   if (!pDC->GetTextMetrics (&tm))
   {
      AfxMessageBox ("Can't get window's text metrics.");
      return;
   }
   m_nMinCharWidth = tm.tmAveCharWidth;
   m_nAvgCharWidth = (tm.tmAveCharWidth + tm.tmMaxCharWidth)/2;
   m_nMaxCharWidth = tm.tmMaxCharWidth;
   m_nLineHeight   = tm.tmHeight + tm.tmExternalLeading;
   m_nLineWidth    = m_nAvgCharWidth * 76;
   if (!pDC->IsPrinting())
   {
      GetClientRect (&rectClient);
      nPageHeight = rectClient.bottom - rectClient.top;
   }
   else
   {
      nPageHeight = pDC->GetDeviceCaps (VERTRES);
   }
   m_nLinesPerPage = (nPageHeight / m_nLineHeight);
   nPageHeight = m_nLinesPerPage * m_nLineHeight;
   m_PageSize.cx= m_nLineWidth/5;
   m_PageSize.cy = max (m_nLineHeight, nPageHeight);
   m_LineSize.cx= m_nLineWidth/20;
   m_LineSize.cy= m_nLineHeight;
   pDC->SelectObject (pOldFont);
}
```

OnDraw Member Function Code

The OnDraw member function must also create the text font to be used,
based upon the definition of the logical unit for the current mapping
mode. In the case of the Net Worth Chart report, the MM_LOENGLISH
mapping mode requires that logical units be expressed in integral multiples of $\frac{1}{100}$ inch, so the font is created with that in mind.

In addition to the difference in sizing the font to be used, the Net Worth
Chart report doesn't need to determine what portion of the report is currently within the update area and redraw only that portion. Instead, the
entire chart is redrawn by the DrawChart member function, whenever it
is called by the OnDraw code. The revised code for the OnDraw member function is as follows:

```cpp
void CReportView::OnDraw(CDC* pDC)
{
   POSITION nFirstEntry, nLastEntry, pos;
   CRect rectClip;
   longRECT posRect;
   int nPtSz;

   //
   // verify that there is something to draw
   //
   if (m_RptEntries.GetCount() == 0)
   {
      return;
   }

   if (pDC->GetClipBox(&rectClip) == NULLREGION)
   {
      return;
   }

   //
   // create a font with which to render the text
   //
   CFont fRptFont;
   if (m_nReportType == NET_WORTH_CHART)
   {
      nPtSz = MulDiv(8, 100, 72);
   }
   else
   {
      nPtSz = MulDiv(8, pDC->GetDeviceCaps (LOGPIXELSY), 72);
   }
   fRptFont.CreateFont (-nPtSz, 0, 0, 0, FW_NORMAL, 0, 0, 0,
      ANSI_CHARSET, OUT_TT_PRECIS, CLIP_DEFAULT_PRECIS,
      PROOF_QUALITY, DEFAULT_PITCH | FF_SWISS, "Arial");
   CFont* pOldFont = pDC->SelectObject (&fRptFont);

   //
   // if we're drawing the chart, then draw the whole
   // thing each time we're called. There really isn't
   // a good way to draw a partial chart.
   //
   if (m_nReportType == NET_WORTH_CHART)
   {
      DrawChart (pDC);
      pDC->SelectObject (pOldFont);
      return;
   }

   //
   // if we're not drawing a chart, then display
   // the contents of the clip region
   //
   posRect.left = (long)rectClip.left;
   posRect.right = (long)rectClip.right;
   if (pDC->IsPrinting())
   {
      long nPageHeight = (m_nLinesPerPage - 7) * m_nLineHeight;
      long nClipHeight = (long)rectClip.bottom
         - (long)rectClip.top;
      long nPageOffset = nPageHeight * (m_nCurPage - 1);
      posRect.top    = (long)rectClip.top + nPageOffset;
      posRect.bottom = posRect.top + nClipHeight;
   }
   else
```

```
      {
        posRect.top    = (long)rectClip.top;
        posRect.bottom = (long)rectClip.bottom;
      }
      RectLPtoPositions (posRect, nFirstEntry, nLastEntry);

      pos = nFirstEntry;
      int nYPos = rectClip.top;
      while (pos != nLastEntry)
      {
        CObject* pObj = m_RptEntries.GetNext(pos);
        DrawRptLine (pDC, pObj, nYPos);
      }
      pDC->SelectObject (pOldFont);
}
```

DrawRptLine Member Function Code

The DrawRptLine member function is used only for drawing the Cash
Flow and Net Worth reports. The code for these is unchanged and is as
follows:

```
void CReportView::DrawRptLine (CDC* pDC, CObject* pObj,
    int& nYPos)
{
  CAcctObj* pAcct;
  CListEntry* pEntry;
  CString szData;
  CTime eDate;
  CSize txSize;
  int nData;

  int nXPos = m_nAvgCharWidth;
  int nWidth = 0;
  int nDX = 0;
  int nDY = 0;
  if (pObj->IsKindOf (RUNTIME_CLASS (CAcctObj)))
  {
    pAcct = (CAcctObj *)pObj;
    szData = pAcct->GetAcctName();
    pDC->TextOut (nXPos, nYPos, szData, szData.GetLength());
    nYPos += m_nLineHeight;
  }
  else if (pObj->IsKindOf (RUNTIME_CLASS (CListEntry)))
  {
    nXPos += m_nAvgCharWidth * 1;
    pEntry = (CListEntry *)pObj;
    eDate = pEntry->GetDate();
    szData = eDate.Format ("%m/%d/%y");
    pDC->TextOut (nXPos, nYPos, szData, szData.GetLength());
    nXPos += m_nAvgCharWidth * 8;

    szData = pEntry->GetItem();
    pDC->TextOut (nXPos, nYPos, szData, szData.GetLength());
    nXPos += m_nAvgCharWidth * 6;

    szData = pEntry->GetDescription();
    nWidth = min (szData.GetLength(), 25);
    pDC->TextOut (nXPos, nYPos, szData, nWidth);
    nXPos += m_nAvgCharWidth * 19;

    szData = pEntry->GetInfo();
```

```cpp
      nWidth = min (szData.GetLength(), 15);
      pDC->TextOut (nXPos, nYPos, szData, nWidth);
      nXPos += m_nAvgCharWidth * 10;

      szData = pEntry->GetCategory();
      nWidth = min (szData.GetLength(), 15);
      pDC->TextOut (nXPos, nYPos, szData, nWidth);
      nXPos += m_nAvgCharWidth * 3;

      if (pEntry->GetPaymentValue() != 0)
      {
         szData = pEntry->GetPayment();
         txSize = pDC->GetTextExtent (szData, szData.GetLength());
         nDX = nXPos + (12 * m_nAvgCharWidth - txSize.cx);
         pDC->TextOut (nDX, nYPos, szData, szData.GetLength());
      }
      nXPos += m_nAvgCharWidth * 8;

      if (pEntry->GetDepositValue() != 0)
      {
         szData = pEntry->GetDeposit();
         txSize = pDC->GetTextExteMnt (szData, szData.GetLength());
         nDX = nXPos + (12 * m_nAvgCharWidth - txSize.cx);
         pDC->TextOut (nDX, nYPos, szData, szData.GetLength());
      }
      nXPos += m_nAvgCharWidth * 8;

      szData = pEntry->GetBalance();
      txSize = pDC->GetTextExtent (szData, szData.GetLength());
      nDX = nXPos + (12 * m_nAvgCharWidth - txSize.cx);
      pDC->TextOut (nDX, nYPos, szData, szData.GetLength());
      nXPos += m_nAvgCharWidth * 8;
      nYPos += m_nLineHeight;
   }
   else if (pObj->IsKindOf (RUNTIME_CLASS (CReportLine)))
   {
      CReportLine* pLine = (CReportLine *)pObj;
      CPen* oldPen = (CPen *)pDC->SelectStockObject (BLACK_PEN);
      szData = pLine->GetLine();
      nData  = szData.GetLength();
      txSize = pDC->GetTextExtent (szData, nData);
      switch (pLine->GetLineType())
      {
         case FIRST_HEAD_LINE:
         {
            pDC->TextOut (1, nYPos, szData, nData);
            nYPos += m_nLineHeight;
            break;
         }

         case SECOND_HEAD_LINE:
         {
            nDX = m_nAvgCharWidth * 4;
            pDC->TextOut (nDX, nYPos, szData, nData);
            nYPos += m_nLineHeight;
            break;
         }

         case FIRST_SUBTOTAL_HEAD:
         {
            nDX = m_nAvgCharWidth * 12;
            pDC->TextOut (nDX, nYPos, szData, nData);
            break;
         }

         case FIRST_SUBTOTAL:
         {
```

```cpp
            nDX = m_nAvgCharWidth * 36 - txSize.cx;
            nDY = nYPos + txSize.cy;
            pDC->TextOut (nDX, nYPos, szData, nData);
            pDC->MoveTo (nDX, nDY);
            pDC->LineTo (nDX+txSize.cx, nDY);
            nYPos += m_nLineHeight;
            break;
        }

        case SECOND_SUBTOTAL_HEAD:
        {
            nDX = m_nAvgCharWidth * 10;
            pDC->TextOut (nDX, nYPos, szData, nData);
            break;
        }

        case SECOND_SUBTOTAL:
        {
            nDX = m_nAvgCharWidth * 30 - txSize.cx;
            nDY = nYPos + txSize.cy;
            pDC->TextOut (nDX, nYPos, szData, nData);
            pDC->MoveTo (nDX, nDY);
            pDC->LineTo (nDX+txSize.cx, nDY);
            nYPos += m_nLineHeight;
            break;
        }

        case NAME_LINE:
        {
            nDX = m_nAvgCharWidth * 8;
            pDC->TextOut (nDX, nYPos, szData, nData);
            break;
        }

        case VALUE_LINE:
        {
            nDX = m_nAvgCharWidth * 30 - txSize.cx;
            pDC->TextOut (nDX, nYPos, szData, nData);
            nYPos += m_nLineHeight;
            break;
        }

        case GRAND_TOTAL_HEAD:
        {
            nDX = m_nAvgCharWidth * 14;
            pDC->TextOut (nDX, nYPos, szData, nData);
            break;
        }

        case GRAND_TOTAL:
        {
            nDX = m_nAvgCharWidth * 42 - txSize.cx;
            nDY = nYPos + txSize.cy;
            pDC->TextOut (nDX, nYPos, szData, nData);
            pDC->MoveTo (nDX, nDY);
            pDC->LineTo (nDX+txSize.cx, nDY);
            nYPos += m_nLineHeight;
            break;
        }

        default:
        {
            break;
        }
    }
    pDC->SelectObject (oldPen);
}
```

```
      else
      {
        RECT rectRgn;
        m_BlankLine.GetRgnBox (&rectRgn);
        nYPos += rectRgn.bottom;
      }
}
```

DrawChart Member Function Code

The DrawChart member function is used to draw the Net Worth Chart report. All of the code in this member function is associated with that task and is entirely new. There are four main properties of the chart. These are its main title, the axis labels, the axes themselves, and the chart (bars or line segments). Each of these properties may have a different color, or the entire chart may be drawn in monochrome only. That depends upon the setting of the UseColor checkbox in the Settings dialog, whose value is saved and tested in this code, or whether the chart is being printed. The DrawChart member function is presented in several sections to make it more readable. No "change bars" are associated with this code, mainly because it is entirely new to this version of the application. The code for the first section is as follows:

```
void CReportView::DrawChart (CDC* pDC)
{
   CSize sTitle;
   int nLength, nXPos, nYPos, index;
   int nNumEntries = m_RptEntries.GetCount ();
   int onePoint=MulDiv (1, pDC->GetDeviceCaps (LOGPIXELSX),72);

   //
   // create the pens & brushes
   //
   COLORREF oldText;
   CPen* pOldPen;
   CBrush* pOldBrush;
   CPen* pAxisPen = new CPen (PS_SOLID, onePoint, m_cAxis);
   CPen* pChartPen = new CPen (PS_SOLID, onePoint, m_cGraph);
   CBrush* pBarBrush = new CBrush (m_cGraph);
```

The foregoing section of code reserves variables to hold the previous text color, pen color, and brush color. In addition, new variables for the pen to draw the axis, the pen for the chart outline, and also the brush for filling in bars in the vertical bar chart are defined and initialized. The code continues as follows:

```
   //
   // the first action is to draw the title
   //
   nLength = m_szTitle.GetLength ();
   sTitle = pDC->GetTextExtent (m_szTitle, nLength);
   nXPos = m_nChartWidth / 2 - sTitle.cx / 2 + Y_LABEL_WIDTH;
   nYPos = - (TITLE_GAP_HT + TITLE_HEIGHT - sTitle.cy);
```

```cpp
if (m_nUseColor && !pDC->IsPrinting())
{
   oldText = pDC->SetTextColor (m_cTitle);
   pDC->TextOut (nXPos, nYPos, m_szTitle);
   pDC->SetTextColor (oldText);
}
else
{
   pDC->TextOut (nXPos, nYPos, m_szTitle);
}
```

The foregoing code draws the overall chart title. Note that the nYPos variable in the foregoing is given a negative offset. This is because the title is drawn below the top of the window (or page). Recall that as we advance down the page when using the MM_LOENGLISH mapping mode, Y coordinates become more and more negative. The code for the Draw-Chart member function continues as follows:

```cpp
//
// now we draw the horizontal axis title
//
nLength = m_szHorzTitle.GetLength();
CSize sHTitle = pDC->GetTextExtent (m_szHorzTitle, nLength);
nXPos = m_nChartWidth / 2 - sHTitle.cx / 2 + Y_LABEL_WIDTH;
nYPos = - (TITLE_GAP_HT + TITLE_HEIGHT + TITLE_GAP_HT
   + m_nChartHeight + TITLE_GAP_HT + X_LABEL_HEIGHT
   + TITLE_GAP_HT);
if (m_nUseColor && !pDC->IsPrinting())
{
   oldText = pDC->SetTextColor (m_cTitle);
   pDC->TextOut (nXPos, nYPos, m_szHorzTitle);
   pDC->SetTextColor (oldText);
}
else
{
   pDC->TextOut (nXPos, nYPos, m_szHorzTitle);
}

//
// next, we draw the vertical axis title, vertically!
//
nLength = m_szVertTitle.GetLength();
nXPos = Y_LABEL_GAP;
nYPos = - (TITLE_HEIGHT + TITLE_GAP_HT * 2
   + (m_nChartHeight - m_nLineHeight * nLength) / 2);
if (m_nUseColor && !pDC->IsPrinting())
{
   oldText = pDC->SetTextColor (m_cTitle);
}
for (index = 0; index < nLength; index++)
{
   CString szCh = m_szVertTitle[index];
   CSize sCh = pDC->GetTextExtent (szCh, 1);
   pDC->TextOut (nXPos - sCh.cx/2, nYPos, szCh);
   nYPos -= m_nLineHeight;
}
if (m_nUseColor && !pDC->IsPrinting())
{
   pDC->SetTextColor (oldText);
}
```

The foregoing section of code draws the horizontal and vertical axis titles. The vertical axis title is drawn, one character at a time, one on top of the other; however, each is centered with respect to the others. Rather than attempt to write the code to rotate the text, we have chosen to draw it upright in this case. In each section of the foregoing and the following code, you will see that we are consulting the value of the `m_nUseColor` variable, checking the IsPrinting status of the device context and are either rendering the associated element in the chosen color or rendering it in black. This applies to each of the four main properties of the chart. The code continues as follows:

```
//
// the next task is to draw the vertical axis with its
// numerical labels and tic marks, denoting the major
// divisions in the axis.
//
nXPos = Y_LABEL_WIDTH;
nYPos = - (TITLE_HEIGHT + TITLE_GAP_HT * 2 + m_nChartHeight);
pDC->MoveTo (nXPos, nYPos);
long nLabel = 0;
CString szLabel;
for (index = 0; index <= 5; index++)
{
    //
    // do what is necessary to print the axis label
    // and then increment to the next value
    //
    wsprintf (szLabel.GetBuffer(6), "%ld", nLabel);
    szLabel.ReleaseBuffer();
    int nLength = szLabel.GetLength();
    CSize nLabSize = pDC->GetTextExtent (szLabel, nLength);
    int nNewY = nYPos + index * m_nBarDivHt;
    if (m_nUseColor && !pDC->IsPrinting())
    {
        pOldPen = pDC->SelectObject (pAxisPen);
        pDC->LineTo (nXPos, nNewY);
        oldText = pDC->SetTextColor (m_cLabel);
        pDC->TextOut(nXPos - Y_TIC_WIDTH - nLabSize.cx,
            nNewY + nLabSize.cy/2, szLabel);
        pDC->SelectObject (pOldPen);
        pDC->SetTextColor (oldText);
    }
    else
    {
        pDC->LineTo (nXPos, nNewY);
        pDC->TextOut(nXPos - Y_TIC_WIDTH - nLabSize.cx,
            nNewY + nLabSize.cy/2, szLabel);
    }
    nLabel += m_nValPerInc;

    //
    // now, draw the tic mark on the vertical axis
    //
    pDC->MoveTo (nXPos - Y_TIC_WIDTH/2, nNewY);
    if (m_nUseColor && !pDC->IsPrinting())
    {
        pOldPen = pDC->SelectObject (pAxisPen);
        pDC->LineTo (nXPos + Y_TIC_WIDTH, nNewY);
        pDC->SelectObject (pOldPen);
    }
```

```
            else
            {
               pDC->LineTo (nXPos + Y_TIC_WIDTH, nNewY);
            }
            pDC->MoveTo (nXPos, nNewY);
   }
   pDC->MoveTo (nXPos, nYPos);
   if (m_nUseColor && !pDC->IsPrinting())
   {
      pOldPen = pDC->SelectObject (pAxisPen);
      pDC->LineTo (nXPos + m_nChartWidth, nYPos);
      pDC->SelectObject (pOldPen);
   }
   else
   {
      pDC->LineTo (nXPos + m_nChartWidth, nYPos);
   }
```

The foregoing section of code is concerned with drawing the vertical
axis, the "tic-marks" that establish the five divisions which we have decided to provide, and also the numeric value (in dollars) associated with
the top of each division. The code for the DrawChart member function
continues as follows:

```
//
// the final task is to draw the individual chart entries,
//  including their horizontal axis labels
//
CReportLine* pLine;
index = 0;
POSITION pos = m_RptEntries.GetHeadPosition();
if (m_nUseColor && !pDC->IsPrinting())
{
   pOldBrush = pDC->SelectObject (pBarBrush);
   pOldPen = pDC->SelectObject (pChartPen);
   oldText = pDC->SetTextColor (m_cLabel);
}
while (pos != NULL)
{
   pLine = (CReportLine *)m_RptEntries.GetNext (pos);
   long nVal = (pLine->GetValue() + 99L) / 100L;
   int nBarHeight = (int)(nVal * m_dUnitsPerDollar);

   //
   // move over to draw the first (or next) bar or point
   //
   nXPos += (BAR_SPACER_WID + m_nBarWidth/2);
   if (m_nGraphType == IDC_LINE_PLOT)
   {
      if (index == 0)
      {
         pDC->MoveTo (nXPos, nYPos + nBarHeight);
      }
      else
      {
         pDC->LineTo (nXPos, nYPos + nBarHeight);
      }
      index++;
   }
   else
   {
      pDC->Rectangle (nXPos - m_nBarWidth/2, nYPos+nBarHeight,
```

```
            nXPos + m_nBarWidth/2, nYPos);
    }

    //
    // draw the horizontal label
    //
    CString szLbl = pLine->GetLine();
    int nLblWid = szLbl.GetLength();
    CSize nLblSize = pDC->GetTextExtent (szLbl, nLblWid);
    pDC->TextOut(nXPos - nLblSize.cx/2,
       nYPos - TITLE_GAP_HT - X_LABEL_HEIGHT
       + nLblSize.cy, szLbl);
    nXPos += m_nBarWidth/2;
  }
  if (m_nUseColor && !pDC->IsPrinting())
  {
     pDC->SelectObject (pOldBrush);
     pDC->SelectObject (pOldPen);
     pDC->SetTextColor (oldText);
  }
```

The foregoing section of the DrawChart member function is responsible
for drawing the chart entries (whether vertical bars or a line plot) and
then drawing the horizontal axis label associated with the entry. The
code for the DrawChart member function is concluded as follows:

```
  //
  // delete the colored pens
  //
  delete pAxisPen;
  delete pChartPen;
  delete pBarBrush;
}
```

The last action of the DrawChart member function is to delete the pens
and the brush that were created at the beginning of the member function. This ensures that the application doesn't use up new resources on
each invocation, causing a "memory leak."

GetDocument Member Function Code

The debug version of the GetDocument member function is included as
a normal virtual function whose code is as follows:

```
#ifdef _DEBUG
CKeepitDoc* CReportView::GetDocument() // non-debug version
is inline
{
   ASSERT(m_pDocument->IsKindOf(RUNTIME_CLASS(CKeepitDoc)));
   return (CKeepitDoc*) m_pDocument;
}
#endif //_DEBUG
```

CashFlowViewSize Member Function Code

The code for the CashFlowViewSize member function has not changed
from what was presented in Chapter 10. The code is as follows:

```cpp
CSize CReportView::CashFlowViewSize()
{
   WORD    nAccount;
   BOOL    bFirstTime = TRUE;
   CSize   docSize (m_nLineWidth, 0);
   long    nPayment, nDeposit, nBalance;

   CKeepitDoc* pDoc = GetDocument();
   POSITION pos = pDoc->m_ReportAccts.GetHeadPosition();
   m_nTotalLines = 0;
   while (pos != NULL)
   {
      //
      // iterate through accounts, selecting the transactions
      // which are within the date range, sorting them into date
      // order and placing them into the m_RptEntries list.
      //
      if (!bFirstTime)
      {
         m_RptEntries.AddTail (&m_BlankLine);
         docSize.cy += m_nLineHeight;
         m_nTotalLines++;
      }
      bFirstTime = FALSE;
      CAcctObj* pAcct;
      pAcct = (CAcctObj *)pDoc->m_ReportAccts.GetNext(pos);
      m_RptEntries.AddTail (pAcct);
      docSize.cy += m_nLineHeight;
      m_nTotalLines++;
      nAccount = pAcct->GetAcctID();
      nBalance = 0;
      POSITION tPos;
      tPos = pDoc->m_ListEntries.GetHeadPosition();
      while (tPos != NULL)
      {
         CListEntry* pEntry;
         WORD nAcctID;
         CTimeeDate;

         //
         // get entries one at a time and check to see whether
         // they match the current account ID.
         //
         pEntry = (CListEntry *)pDoc->m_ListEntries.GetNext (tPos);
         nAcctID = pEntry->GetAccountID();
         if (nAcctID != nAccount)
         {
            //
            // no match, continue the loop
            //
            continue;
         }

         if (pEntry->GetStatus() == E_EMPTY)
         {
            //
            // bypass empty entries
            //
            continue;
```

```cpp
      }

      if (pEntry->GetStatus() == E_SELECTED)
      {
        if (pEntry->GetDescription().GetLength() == 0)
        {
          //
          // bypass selected but empty entries
          //
          continue;
        }
      }

      //
      // calculate the current balance for the account
      //
      nPayment = pEntry->GetPaymentValue();
      nDeposit = pEntry->GetDepositValue();
      nBalance = nBalance - nPayment + nDeposit;

      //
      // now, check to see whether the entry is within
      // the specified date range.
      //
      eDate = pEntry->GetDate();
      if (eDate < m_FromDate)
      {
        //
        // not yet in range, continue checking
        //
        continue;
      }
      else if (eDate > m_ToDate)
      {
        //
        // past the end of the period, quit.
        //
        break;
      }

      //
      // enter the balance value into the transaction,
      // check whether the additional reporting criteria
      // are met, add the transaction to the list, and
      // then increment the document size.
      //
      pEntry->SetBalanceValue (nBalance);
      if (MeetsRptCriteria (pEntry))
      {
        m_RptEntries.AddTail (pEntry);
        docSize.cy += m_nLineHeight;
        m_nTotalLines++;
      }
    }
  }

  //
  // get rid of all of the accounts, now that
  // we're done with them, and then return the
  // document size to the caller.
  //
  pDoc->m_ReportAccts.RemoveAll();
  return docSize;
}
```

NetWorthViewSize Member Function Code

The NetWorthViewSize member function is used to size the Net Worth
textual report, and the code for this member function has not changed
from what was presented in Chapter 10. The code is as follows:

```
CSize CReportView::NetWorthViewSize ()
{
  CSize   docSize (m_nLineWidth, 0);
  long    nChecking, nAssets, nLiabilities;
  nChecking = nAssets = nLiabilities = 0;
  CKeepitDoc* pDoc = GetDocument();
  m_nTotalLines = 0;

  //
  // empty the list of report entries and then
  // enter the first heading line.
  //
  m_RptEntries.RemoveAll();
  MakeRptListEntry (FIRST_HEAD_LINE, "ASSETS");
  m_nTotalLines++;

  //
  // enter the heading for the next set, make
  // the entries for the Checking, Savings, and
  // Cash accounts in the report and then make
  // a subtotal entry.
  //
  MakeRptListEntry (SECOND_HEAD_LINE,
    "Checking & Cash Accounts");
  nChecking = MakeAcctEntry (IDC_CHECKING, IDC_CASH);
   MakeRptListEntry (SECOND_SUBTOTAL_HEAD,
    "Total Checking & Cash");
  MakeRptListEntry (SECOND_SUBTOTAL,
    MakeValueString (nChecking));
  m_RptEntries.AddTail (&m_BlankLine);
  m_nTotalLines += 3;

  //
  // enter the heading for other assets, make the
  // entries for those accounts, and then make a
  // subtotal entry.
  //
  MakeRptListEntry (SECOND_HEAD_LINE, "Other Asset Accounts");
  nAssets = MakeAcctEntry (IDC_ASSET, IDC_ASSET);
  MakeRptListEntry (SECOND_SUBTOTAL_HEAD,
    "Total Other Assets");
  MakeRptListEntry (SECOND_SUBTOTAL,
    MakeValueString (nAssets));
  m_nTotalLines += 2;

  //
  // now, create a total of checking and other assets
  // and make the report entry.
  //
  MakeRptListEntry (FIRST_SUBTOTAL_HEAD, "Total All Assets");
  MakeRptListEntry (FIRST_SUBTOTAL,
    MakeValueString (nChecking+nAssets));
  m_RptEntries.AddTail (&m_BlankLine);
  m_nTotalLines += 2;

  //
  // enter the headings for liability accounts
  // and then make the entries for those accounts.
```

```
        //
        MakeRptListEntry (FIRST_HEAD_LINE, "LIABILITIES");
        MakeRptListEntry (SECOND_HEAD_LINE,
          "Liability & Credit Accounts");
        nLiabilities = MakeAcctEntry (IDC_LIABILITY, IDC_CREDIT_CARD);
        MakeRptListEntry (SECOND_SUBTOTAL_HEAD, "Total Liabilities");
        MakeRptListEntry (SECOND_SUBTOTAL,
          MakeValueString (nLiabilities));
        m_nTotalLines += 3;

        //
        // create the headings and value entries for all
        // liabilities and enter these into the report list.
        //
        MakeRptListEntry (FIRST_SUBTOTAL_HEAD,
          "Total All Liabilities");
        MakeRptListEntry (FIRST_SUBTOTAL,
          MakeValueString (nLiabilities));
        m_nTotalLines++;

        //
        // finally, create the grand total heading and value entries.
        //
        long nGrandTotal = nChecking + nAssets - nLiabilities;
        MakeRptListEntry (GRAND_TOTAL_HEAD, "Total Net Worth");
        MakeRptListEntry (GRAND_TOTAL,
          MakeValueString (nGrandTotal));
        m_nTotalLines++;

        //
        // compute the document size
        //
        docSize.cy = m_nTotalLines * m_nLineHeight;

        //
        // get rid of the document's report accounts, now
        // that we've used them, and then return the document
        // size to the caller.
        //
        pDoc->m_ReportAccts.RemoveAll ();
        return docSize;
}
```

NetWorthChartSize Member Function Code

The NetWorthChartSize member function is called by the OnInitalUp-
date member function (as are the other report sizing member functions),
and its purpose is to determine the size of the completed chart. In performing this action, it creates entries in a list of report entries using the
MakeChartEntry member function. The DrawChart member function
uses the data in this list to draw the various elements of the chart itself,
thus speeding up the drawing process. The code for the newly created
NetWorthChartSize member function begins as follows:

```
CSize CReportView::NetWorthChartSize (CDC& aDC)
{
  CSize docSize (0, 0);
  long nNetWorth;
  int nMonth, nQtr=0, nYr;
  CString szLabel;
```

```
CTime tStart, tEnd;
tStart = m_FromDate;
tEnd = tStart;
m_nTotalLines = 0;

//
// loop through the transactions for all accounts to
// be included in the report and make entries into
// the m_RptEntries list for each specified interval.
//
while (tEnd <= m_ToDate)
{
   switch (m_nInterval)
   {
      case IDC_MONTHLY:
      {
         nMonth = tStart.GetMonth();
         szLabel = monthNames[nMonth-1];
         tEnd = NextMonth (tStart);
         break;
      }
      case IDC_QUARTERLY:
      {
         nQtr = (tStart.GetMonth() + 2) / 3;
         szLabel = qtrNames[nQtr-1];
         tEnd = NextQuarter (tStart);
         break;
      }
      case IDC_ANNUALLY:
      {
         nYr = tStart.GetYear();
         wsprintf (szLabel.GetBuffer (4), "%d", nYr);
         szLabel.ReleaseBuffer();
         tEnd = NextYear (tStart);
         break;
      }
   }
   nNetWorth = IntervalNetWorth (tEnd);
   MakeChartEntry (GRAPH_VALUE, nNetWorth, szLabel);
   tStart = tEnd;
}

//
// get rid of all of the accounts, now that we're
// done with them
//
CKeepitDoc* pDoc = GetDocument();
pDoc->m_ReportAccts.RemoveAll();
```

The first portion of the NetWorthChartSize member function is responsible for making entries into the m_ReportEntries list. The number of entries to be made depends upon the total time span and the reporting interval chosen by the user.

For monthly intervals, one value is plotted for each month in the time span. For quarterly intervals, four values are plotted for each year, and for annual intervals, only one value is plotted for each year in the time span. After creating the entries, the code continues as follows:

```
//
// now that we know how many entries there will be,
// we can size the graph view, depending upon the type of
// graph and entry parameters. First, compute the max value.
//
int nEntries = m_RptEntries.GetCount();
long nMaxValue = -1000000000;
long nMinValue = 0;  // make 0 the min value
POSITION pos = m_RptEntries.GetHeadPosition();
while (pos != NULL)
{
   CReportLine* pLine;
   pLine = (CReportLine *)m_RptEntries.GetNext (pos);
   long nValue = pLine->GetValue();
   if (nValue > nMaxValue)
   {
      nMaxValue = nValue;
   }
   if (nValue < nMinValue)
   {
      pLine->SetValue (nMinValue);
   }
}
```

In the foregoing, we determine the maximum numeric value in the report entries made previously. We have arbitrarily decided to disallow any negative net worth values, so we set a minimum value of zero and do not allow any of the entries to be less than that value. If you want to support negative net worth values, it would be possible to do so by saving the most negative value and then allowing the chart to have both a positive and negative vertical axis. After computing the range of values represented by the data, the code continues as follows:

```
//
// the next step is to compute the range of values and then
// determine the preferred dimensions of the view. We
// intend to provide 5 divisions on the Y-Axis.
//
long nRange = ((nMaxValue - nMinValue + 99999) / 100000) * 1000;
CSize nWinSize = aDC.GetWindowExt();
int nHeight = nWinSize.cy / 5;
int nBarInc = MAX_BAR_INC;
if (nHeight < nBarInc)
{
   nBarInc = MIN_BAR_INC;
}
m_nBarDivHt = nBarInc;
int nBarWidth= nWinSize.cx / nEntries;
if (nBarWidth < MIN_BAR_WID + BAR_SPACER_WID)
{
   nBarWidth = MIN_BAR_WID;
}
else if (nBarWidth > MAX_BAR_WID)
{
   nBarWidth = MAX_BAR_WID;
}
m_nBarWidth = nBarWidth;
m_nValPerInc = nRange / 5;
m_nChartHeight = nBarInc * 5;
```

```
m_nChartWidth  = nEntries * (nBarWidth + BAR_SPACER_WID);
m_dUnitsPerDollar=((double)m_nChartHeight)/((double)nRange);
docSize.cx = m_nChartWidth;
docSize.cy = TITLE_GAP_HT + TITLE_HEIGHT + TITLE_GAP_HT
    + m_nChartHeight + TITLE_GAP_HT + X_LABEL_HEIGHT
    + TITLE_GAP_HT + HORZ_TITLE_HT + TITLE_GAP_HT;
return docSize;
}
```

The foregoing code completes the sizing of the Net Worth Chart report. Note that we have chosen the Y axis (ordinate) of the chart to be divided into five sections. This is an arbitrary decision. The number of divisions is something that could be determined, based upon the range of values in the data, or could be some other arbitrary value.

MeetsRptCriteria Member Function Code

The MeetsRptCriteria member function is a helper member function for the Cash Flow report. The code is unchanged from what was presented previously. The code for this member function is as follows:

```
BOOL CReportView::MeetsRptCriteria (CListEntry* pEntry)
{
   //
   // determine whether pEntry object meets the criteria
   // for inclusion in the selected report.
   //
   switch (m_nReportType)
   {
     case CASH_FLOW_REPORT:
     {
        //
        // first, determine if the category matches
        // one in the m_ReportCats list.
        //
        CString szCategory = pEntry->GetCategory();
        int nCategories = m_ReportCats.GetCount();
        if (nCategories == 0)
        {
           //
           // there aren't any valid categories
           //
           return FALSE;
        }
        POSITION pos = m_ReportCats.GetHeadPosition();
        BOOL bFound = FALSE;
        while (pos != NULL)
        {
           CCategory* pCat;
           CString szCatName;
           pCat = (CCategory *)m_ReportCats.GetNext (pos);
           szCatName = pCat->GetCatName();
           if (MatchStrings (szCatName, szCategory, equals))
           {
              bFound = TRUE;
              break;
           }
        }
        if (!bFound)
        {
```

```
                    //
                    // category wasn't found, so return FALSE
                    //
                    return FALSE;
                }

                //
                // now, determine whether the description or info
                // fields are to be examined for inclusion of the
                // transaction in the report.
                //
                if (m_eDescInclude != all)
                {
                    CString szDescription = pEntry->GetDescription();
                    if (!MatchStrings (szDescription, m_szDescription,
                      m_eDescInclude))
                    {
                        //
                        // description doesn't match, return FALSE.
                        //
                        return FALSE;
                    }
                }

                if (m_eInfoInclude != all)
                {
                    CString szInfo = pEntry->GetInfo();
                    if (!MatchStrings (szInfo, m_szInfo, m_eInfoInclude))
                    {
                        //
                        // info field doesn't match, return FALSE.
                        //
                        return FALSE;
                    }
                }

                //
                // everything matches, so return TRUE.
                //
                return TRUE;
            }

        default:
            {
                //
                // not one of our reports
                //
                return FALSE;
            }
    }
    return FALSE;
}
```

MatchStrings Member Function Code

The MatchStrings member function is a helper function for the Cash
Flow report. The code is unchanged and is as follows:

```
BOOL CReportView::MatchStrings (CString szSrc,
   CString szPattern, TInclude criteria)
{
   CString szS = szSrc;
   CString szP = szPattern;
```

```
char* pString;
int   nLength;

//
// matches szS with szP using criteria in a
// case-insensitive manner. Start by converting both
// strings to all lower-case characters.
//
pString = szS.GetBuffer (50);
nLength = szS.GetLength();
::AnsiLowerBuff (pString, nLength);
szS.ReleaseBuffer();
pString = szP.GetBuffer (50);
nLength = szP.GetLength();
::AnsiLowerBuff (pString, nLength);
szP.ReleaseBuffer();

//
// now see if the szS string meets the criteria
//
int index;
int nSrc = szS.GetLength();
int nPat = szP.GetLength();
if (nSrc < nPat)
{
   //
   // source must be at least as long as the pattern.
   //
   return FALSE;
}
switch (criteria)
{
   case startsWith:
   {
      //
      // length of pattern string governs
      // the scope of the comparison.
      //
      for (index=0; index < nPat; index++)
      {
         if (szS[index] != szP[index])
         {
            //
            // source doesn't start with pattern
            //
            return FALSE;
         }
      }
      return TRUE;
   }

   case contains:
   {
      //
      // the entire pattern string must be contained
      // somewhere within the source string.
      //
      for (index=0; index < nSrc; index++)
      {
         BOOL bContains = FALSE;
         if (szS[index] == szP[0])
         {
            //
            // found the first matching character
            // determine if the rest of the string
            // matches the pattern.
            //
```

```cpp
                    bContains = TRUE;
                    for (int ix=0; ix < nPat; ix++)
                    {
                        if (index+ix >= nSrc)
                        {
                            //
                            // end of source reached
                            //
                            return FALSE;
                        }
                        if (szS[index+ix] != szP[ix])
                        {
                            bContains = FALSE;
                            break;
                        }
                    }
                    if (bContains)
                    {
                        return TRUE;
                    }
                }
            }

            //
            // we didn't find a match, so return FALSE.
            //
            return FALSE;
        }

        case equals:
        {
            if (nSrc != nPat)
            {
                //
                // lengths aren't equal, so return FALSE.
                //
                return FALSE;
            }
            for (index=0; index < nPat; index++)
            {
                if (szS[index] != szP[index])
                {
                    //
                    // found a mismatch, so return FALSE.
                    //
                    return FALSE;
                }
            }

            //
            // all characters matched, so return TRUE.
            //
            return TRUE;
        }

        default:
        {
            //
            // shouldn't occur
            //
            ASSERT (FALSE);
            return FALSE;// in case of Continue.
        }
    }
}
```

ComputeBalance Member Function Code

The ComputeBalance member function is a helper function, originally created for use with the Net Worth textual report, and is also used to determine the account balance values needed by the Net Worth Chart report. This member function differs from the original implementation by the fact that it contains a second argument, which specifies the end of the period for which the balance is to be computed. The earlier version used the m_From and m_To member variables; however, for this version, it was convenient to pass the ending date into the member function (to support the monthly, quarterly, and annual intervals for which the chart is to be prepared). The revised code for this member function is as follows:

```
long CReportView::ComputeBalance (CAcctObj* pAcct, CTime tTo)
{
   long nPayment, nDeposit, nBalance;
   WORD nAccount = pAcct->GetAcctID();
   CKeepitDoc* pDoc = GetDocument();

   //
   // iterate through transaction list to find those
   // which match the account ID and then compute the
   // balance up 'til the end date specified by the user.
   //
   nBalance = 0;
   POSITION pos = pDoc->m_ListEntries.GetHeadPosition();
   while (pos != NULL)
   {
      CListEntry* pEntry;
      WORD nAcctID;
      CTimeeDate;

      //
      // get entries one at a time and check to see whether
      // they match the current account ID.
      //
      pEntry = (CListEntry *)pDoc->m_ListEntries.GetNext (pos);
      nAcctID = pEntry->GetAccountID();
      if (nAcctID != nAccount)
      {
         //
         // no match, continue the loop
         //
         continue;
      }

      if (pEntry->GetStatus() == E_EMPTY)
      {
         //
         // bypass empty entries
         //
         continue;
      }

      if (pEntry->GetStatus() == E_SELECTED)
      {
         if (pEntry->GetDescription().GetLength() == 0)
         {
            //
            // bypass selected but empty entries
```

```
                //
                continue;
            }
        }

        //
        // now, check to see whether the entry is dated
        // after the specified end date.
        //
        eDate = pEntry->GetDate();
        if (eDate >= tTo)
        {
            //
            // past the end of the period, quit.
            //
            break;
        }

        //
        // calculate the current balance for the account
        //
        nPayment = pEntry->GetPaymentValue();
        nDeposit = pEntry->GetDepositValue();
        nBalance = nBalance + nDeposit - nPayment;
    }
    return nBalance;
}
```

MakeValueString Member Function Code

The MakeValueString member function takes a numeric value (in cents)
and converts it to a string, with an embedded decimal between the dollars and cents components. The code is unchanged and is as follows:

```
CString CReportView::MakeValueString (long nValue)
{
    CString szValue;
    long dollars, cents;

    dollars = nValue / 100;
    cents   = nValue - dollars * 100;
    wsprintf (szValue.GetBuffer (14), "%ld.%02ld",
      dollars, cents);
    szValue.ReleaseBuffer();
    return szValue;
}
```

MakeRptListEntry Member Function Code

The MakeRptListEntry member function is used by the Net Worth textual report to create a new report entry in the m_RptEntries list. The
code for this member function is unchanged and is as follows:

```
void CReportView::MakeRptListEntry (int nType, CString
szLine)
{
    CReportLine* pLine = new CReportLine;
    pLine->SetLineType (nType);
```

```
    pLine->SetLine (szLine);
    m_RptEntries.AddTail (pLine);
}
```

We have not made any changes to the preceding member function, even though we have changed the CReportLine class to include a value field, in addition to the value string. We have revised the constructor of that member function to set the value field to zero so that none of the previously written code needs to change. We will present the newly modified CReportLine class later in this chapter.

MakeAcctEntry Member Function Code

The MakeAcctEntry member function is used to make report entries for the Net Worth textual report. Balances are summarized for the accounts whose identifiers fall within the `nTypeFrom` and `nTypeTo` input parameters. The member function has been modified slightly, to pass the contents of the `m_To` variable into the ComputeBalance member function. The revised code is as follows:

```
long CReportView::MakeAcctEntry (int nTypeFrom, int nTypeTo)
{
    long nBalance;
    CString szBalance;
    long nTotalBalance = 0;
    CKeepitDoc* pDoc = GetDocument ();
    POSITION pos = pDoc->m_ReportAccts.GetHeadPosition ();
    while (pos != NULL)
    {
        // iterate through the accounts, finding the accounts
        // in the list which match the specified type,

        CAcctObj* pAcct;
        pAcct = (CAcctObj *)pDoc->m_ReportAccts.GetNext (pos);
        int nType = pAcct->GetAcctType ();
        if (nType >= nTypeFrom && nType <= nTypeTo)
        {
            CString szLine = pAcct->GetAcctName ();
            MakeRptListEntry (NAME_LINE, szLine);

            // it's the right type of account, so compute
            // the balance of the account and then create
            // and make an entry in the report list.

            nBalance = ComputeBalance (pAcct, m_ToDate);
            szBalance = MakeValueString (nBalance);
            MakeRptListEntry (VALUE_LINE, szBalance);
            nTotalBalance += nBalance;

            // advance the line count

            m_nTotalLines++;
        }
    }
    return nTotalBalance;
}
```

NextMonth Member Function Code

The NextMonth member function is a newly added helper function for the Net Worth Chart report. Given an input month as a CTime value, it returns the following month as a CTime value. The code is as follows:

```
CTime CReportView::NextMonth (CTime tStart)
{
   int year  = tStart.GetYear();
   int month = tStart.GetMonth() + 1;
   int day   = 1;
   if (month > 12)
   {
      month = 1;
      year++;
   }
   CTime tRet (year, month, day, 0, 0, 0);
   return (tRet);
}
```

NextQuarter Member Function Code

The NextQuarter member function performs the same function as the NextMonth member function, except that it returns the date for the beginning of the next quarter in the year. The newly added code for this function is as follows:

```
CTime CReportView::NextQuarter (CTime tStart)
{
   int year  = tStart.GetYear();
   int month = ((tStart.GetMonth()+2)/3)*3+1;
   int day = 1;
   if (month > 12)
   {
      month = 1;
      year++;
   }
   CTime tRet(year, month, day, 0, 0, 0);
   return (tRet);
}
```

NextYear Member Function Code

The NextYear member function returns a CTime value that represents January 1st of the following year. The newly added code is as follows:

```
CTime CReportView::NextYear (CTime tStart)
{
   int year = tStart.GetYear() + 1;
   int month = 1;
   int day = 1;
   CTime tRet(year, month, day, 0, 0, 0);
   return (tRet);
}
```

IntervalNetWorth Member Function Code

The IntervalNetWorth member function is responsible for calculating the net worth value for all of the selected accounts in the interval up to the specified ending date, for use by the Net Worth Chart report. The newly added member function is as follows:

```
long CReportView::IntervalNetWorth (CTime tEnd)
{
   long nNetWorth = 0;// initialize net worth for period
   long nBalance;
   WORD nAcctType;

   CKeepitDoc* pDoc = GetDocument();
   POSITION pos = pDoc->m_ReportAccts.GetHeadPosition();
   while (pos != NULL)
   {
      CAcctObj* pAcct;
      pAcct = (CAcctObj *)pDoc->m_ReportAccts.GetNext(pos);
      nBalance = ComputeBalance (pAcct, tEnd);
      nAcctType = pAcct->GetAcctType();
      if (nAcctType >= IDC_CHECKING && nAcctType <= IDC_ASSET)
      {
         nNetWorth += nBalance;
      }
      else
      {
         nNetWorth -= nBalance;
      }
   }
   return nNetWorth;
}
```

MakeChartEntry Member Function Code

The MakeChartEntry member function is called to make entries into the `m_RptEntries` list for each of the intervals to be charted. The member function relies upon a new member function for the CReport-Line class named SetValue. The newly added MakeChartEntry member function is as follows:

```
void CReportView::MakeChartEntry (int nType, long nValue,
   CString& szLabel)
{
   CReportLine* pLine = new CReportLine;
   pLine->SetLineType(nType);
   pLine->SetValue(nValue);
   pLine->SetLine (szLabel);
   m_RptEntries.AddTail (pLine);
}
```

SortByDate Member Function Code

The SortByDate member function is the first of a series of general-purpose helper functions used by various of the reports. The code is unchanged from what was presented previously and is as follows:

```cpp
void CReportView::SortByDate (CObList& list)
{
   CListEntry *entry1, *entry2;
   POSITION pos1, pPos1, pos2, pPos2;

   //
   // sorts a list of CListEntry objects into order
   // by date using a simple linear scan algorithm.
   //
   pos1 = list.GetHeadPosition();
   while (pos1 != NULL)
   {
      pPos1 = pos1;
      entry1 = (CListEntry *)list.GetNext(pos1);
      pos2 = pos1;
      while (pos2 != NULL)
      {
         pPos2 = pos2;
         entry2 = (CListEntry *)list.GetNext (pos2);
         if (entry2->GetDate() < entry1->GetDate())
         {
            //
            // need to swap entries
            //
            list.SetAt (pPos1, entry2);
            list.SetAt (pPos2, entry1);
            entry1 = entry2;
         }
      }
   }
}
```

RectLPtoPositions Member Function Code

The RectLPtoPositions member function is used by both the Cash Flow and Net Worth textual reports. The code is unchanged from what was presented previously and is as follows:

```cpp
void CReportView::RectLPtoPositions (longRECT rectClip,
   POSITION& firstPosition, POSITION& lastPosition)
{
   //
   // scan the m_ReportEntries list for entries which will fit
   // within the clipping region current passed to the OnDraw
   // member function, and then return their POSITION values
   // in the list.
   //
   long nViewHeight = 0;
   POSITION pos = m_RptEntries.GetHeadPosition();
   POSITION prevPos;
   BOOL bFirst=TRUE;
   firstPosition = lastPosition = NULL;
   while (pos != NULL)
   {
```

```
        prevPos = pos;
        CObject *pObj = m_RptEntries.GetNext (pos);
        if (bFirst && nViewHeight >= rectClip.top)
        {
           bFirst = FALSE;
           firstPosition = prevPos;
        }
        if (m_nReportType == CASH_FLOW_REPORT)
        {
           nViewHeight += m_nLineHeight;
        }
        else if (m_nReportType == NET_WORTH_REPORT)
        {
           if (pObj->IsKindOf (RUNTIME_CLASS (CReportLine)))
           {
              CReportLine* pRObj = (CReportLine *)pObj;
              switch (pRObj->GetLineType())
              {
                 case FIRST_HEAD_LINE:
                 case SECOND_HEAD_LINE:
                 case FIRST_SUBTOTAL:
                 case SECOND_SUBTOTAL:
                 case VALUE_LINE:
                 case GRAND_TOTAL:
                 {
                    nViewHeight += m_nLineHeight;
                 }
              }
           }
           else
           {
              nViewHeight += m_nLineHeight;
           }
        }
        if (nViewHeight >= rectClip.bottom)
        {
           lastPosition = pos;
           break;
        }
     }
     if (firstPosition == NULL)
     {
        lastPosition = NULL;
     }
}
```

OnPreparePrinting Member Function Code

The Net Worth Chart report can be printed and the OnPreparePrinting
member function is called by the framework prior to commencing the
print operation. The code is unchanged from what was presented previously and is as follows:

```
BOOL CReportView::OnPreparePrinting (CPrintInfo* pInfo)
{
   return DoPreparePrinting (pInfo);
}
```

OnBeginPrinting Member Function Code

The OnBeginPrinting member function is called by the framework immediately prior to commencing the print operation. A small change to the code presented previously changes the maximum number of pages in the report to one page for the Net Worth Chart. Otherwise, the code is unchanged and is as follows:

```
void CReportView::OnBeginPrinting (CDC* pDC, CPrintInfo* pInfo)
{
   ComputeRptMetrics (pDC);

   //
   // if this is the net worth chart, then there's only
   // one page to print.
   //
   if (m_nReportType == NET_WORTH_CHART)
   {
      pInfo->SetMaxPage (1);
      pInfo->m_nCurPage = 1;
      return;
   }

   //
   // otherwise, compute the number of pages to print
   //
   int nPageHeight = (m_nLinesPerPage - 7) * m_nLineHeight;
   int nSizeTotal = m_nTotalLines * m_nLineHeight;
   int nPageCount = (nSizeTotal + nPageHeight - 1) / nPageHeight;
   pInfo->SetMaxPage (nPageCount);
   pInfo->m_nCurPage = 1;
}
```

OnPrint Member Function Code

The OnPrint member function has been simplified for the case where the Net Worth Chart report is to be printed. In that case, we do not have to print page headers or perform gyrations with the clipping region. The code has been modified to treat the Net Worth Chart report as a special case. The revised code is as follows:

```
void CReportView::OnPrint (CDC* pDC, CPrintInfo* pInfo)
{
   //
   // get the printer's page size in pixels
   //
   int nHRes = pDC->GetDeviceCaps (HORZRES);
   int nVRes = pDC->GetDeviceCaps (VERTRES);

   //
   // create and select a new clipping region for use in
   // printing the page header, and then print the header.
   //
   CRgn clipRgn;
   clipRgn.CreateRectRgn (0, 0, nHRes, nVRes);
   pDC->SelectClipRgn (&clipRgn);
   clipRgn.DeleteObject ();
```

```cpp
    //
    // if we're printing the net worth chart, then there's
    // only one page and no need to print a page header.
    //
    if (m_nReportType == NET_WORTH_CHART)
    {
       int nDX = pDC->GetDeviceCaps (LOGPIXELSX) / 2;
       int nDY = pDC->GetDeviceCaps (LOGPIXELSY);
       pDC->SetViewportOrg (nDX, nDY);
       OnDraw (pDC);
       return;
    }

    // otherwise, print the page header.
    //
    PrintPageHeader(pDC, pInfo);

    //
    // now set up the viewport for printing the remainder
    // of the page and call the OnDraw routine to do it.
    //
    int nDX = pDC->GetDeviceCaps (LOGPIXELSX)/2;
    int nDY = m_nLineHeight * 4;
    int nPageHeight = (m_nLinesPerPage - 7) * m_nLineHeight;
    int nPageWidth = nHRes;

    pDC->SetViewportOrg (nDX, nDY);
    CRect rectClip = CRect (0, 0, nPageWidth, nPageHeight);
    pDC->IntersectClipRect (rectClip);
    OnDraw (pDC);
}
```

PrintPageHeader Member Function Code

The PrintPageHeader member function is used by both the Cash Flow
and Net Worth textual reports. The code is unchanged from what was
presented in Chapter 10. The code is as follows:

```cpp
void CReportView::PrintPageHeader (CDC* pDC, CPrintInfo* pInfo)
{
   CFont fHdrFont;
   CString szLine, szPage;

   // create a bold font for use in printing the
   // page header and then select it for use.

   int nPtSz = MulDiv(8, pDC->GetDeviceCaps (LOGPIXELSY), 72);
   int nDX   = pDC->GetDeviceCaps (LOGPIXELSX)/2;
   fHdrFont.CreateFont (-nPtSz, 0, 0, 0, FW_BOLD, 0, 0, 0,
      ANSI_CHARSET, OUT_TT_PRECIS, CLIP_DEFAULT_PRECIS,
      PROOF_QUALITY, DEFAULT_PITCH | FF_SWISS, "Arial");
   CFont* pOldFont = pDC->SelectObject (&fHdrFont);

   // format and print the two header lines and then
   // select the previous font.

   wsprintf (szPage.GetBuffer(3), "%d", pInfo->m_nCurPage);
   szPage.ReleaseBuffer();
     szLine = " " + m_szTitle + "  Page " + szPage;
   pDC->TextOut (nDX, m_nLineHeight, szLine);
   szLine = " From: ";
   szLine = szLine + m_FromDate.Format ("%m/%d/%y");
```

```
        szLine = szLine + " To: ";
        szLine = szLine + m_ToDate.Format ("%m/%d/%y");
        pDC->TextOut (nDX, m_nLineHeight * 2, szLine);
        pDC->SelectObject (pOldFont);
}
```

OnFilePrint Message Handler Code

The message handler for the OnFilePrint command is as follows:

```
void CReportView::OnFilePrint()
{
    CView::OnFilePrint();
}
```

OnFilePrintPreview Message Handler Code

The message handler for the OnFilePrintPreview command is unchanged from the version presented previously. The code is as follows:

```
void CReportView::OnFilePrintPreview()
{
    CView::OnFilePrintPreview();
}
```

OnDestroy Message Handler Code

The OnDestroy message handler is unchanged from the version shown
in Chapter 10. The code is as follows:

```
void CReportView::OnDestroy()
{
    CScrollView::OnDestroy();

    switch (m_nReportType)
    {
        case CASH_FLOW_REPORT:
        {
            m_BlankLine.DeleteObject();
            m_ReportCats.RemoveAll();
            m_RptEntries.RemoveAll();
            break;
        }
        case NET_WORTH_REPORT:
        {
            POSITION pos = m_RptEntries.GetHeadPosition();
            while (pos != NULL)
            {
                CObject* pObj = m_RptEntries.GetNext (pos);
                if (pObj->IsKindOf (RUNTIME_CLASS (CReportLine)))
                {
                    delete pObj;
                }
            }
            m_BlankLine.DeleteObject();
            m_RptEntries.RemoveAll();
```

```
         break;
      }
   }
}
```

OnHScroll Message Handler Code

The OnHScroll message handler is called when the display is scrolled in the horizontal direction. The code is unchanged from what was presented in Chapter 10 and is as follows:

```
void CReportView::OnHScroll(UINT nSBCode, UINT nPos,
CScrollBar* pScrollBar)
{
   ASSERT (pScrollBar == GetScrollBarCtrl (SB_HORZ));
   if (nSBCode == SB_THUMBTRACK)
   {
     // ignore thumbtrack messages
     return;
   }
   if (nSBCode == SB_THUMBPOSITION)
   {
     // fake thumbtrack message to OnScroll

     nSBCode = SB_THUMBTRACK;
   }
   CScrollView::OnHScroll(nSBCode, nPos, pScrollBar);
}
```

OnVScroll Message Handler Code

The OnVScroll message handler is called when the view is scrolled in the vertical direction. The code is unchanged from what was presented in Chapter 10 and is as follows:

```
void CReportView::OnVScroll(UINT nSBCode, UINT nPos,
CScrollBar* pScrollBar)
{
   ASSERT (pScrollBar == GetScrollBarCtrl (SB_VERT));
   if (nSBCode == SB_THUMBTRACK)
   {
     // ignore thumbtrack messages
     return;
   }
   if (nSBCode == SB_THUMBPOSITION)
   {
     // update thumb position to integral line height
     // and then fake a thumbtrack message to OnScroll

     int nHt = m_nLineHeight;
     nPos = ((nPos + nHt - 1) / nHt) * nHt;
     nSBCode = SB_THUMBTRACK;
   }
   CScrollView::OnVScroll(nSBCode, nPos, pScrollBar);
}
```

Additions to the CReportLine Class

As indicated in the foregoing sections, we elected to add a new member variable to the CReportLine class so that we could store a numeric value in the object, which could be used for computational purposes. We have modified the constructor for the class to store a zero value in that member variable when an object is created. To simplify access to the new numeric member variable, we have added two new member functions.

RepLine.h Header File Additions

The header file for the CReportLine class has been modified to provide the definition of a new entry type and the new member variable and its access member functions have been added to the class declaration. The new contents of the header file are as follows:

```
///////////////////////////////////////////////////////////////
// repline.h
//
// line types
//
#define BLANK_REPORT_LINE       0
#define FIRST_HEAD_LINE         1
#define SECOND_HEAD_LINE        2
#define FIRST_SUBTOTAL_HEAD     3
#define FIRST_SUBTOTAL          4
#define SECOND_SUBTOTAL_HEAD    5
#define SECOND_SUBTOTAL         6
#define NAME_LINE               10
#define VALUE_LINE              11

#define GRAPH_VALUE             20

#define GRAND_TOTAL_HEAD        98
#define GRAND_TOTAL             99

class CReportLine : public CObject
{
protected:
    int         m_nLineType;
    long        m_nValue;
    CString     m_szLine;

    DECLARE_DYNCREATE (CReportLine)

public:
    int         GetLineType();
    CString     GetLine();
    long        GetValue();

    void        SetLineType (int nType);
    void        SetLine (CString szLine);
    void        SetValue (long nValue);

    CReportLine();
    virtual ~CReportLine();
};
```

RepLine.cpp Source File Additions

The source file of the CReportLine class has been modified to support the Net Worth Chart report's requirements by modifying the constructor member function and also by adding the two new access member functions, GetValue and SetValue. The entire contents of the **repline.cpp** source file is as follows:

```cpp
//////////////////////////////////////////////////////////////////
// repline.cpp
//
#include "stdafx.h"
#include "repline.h"

IMPLEMENT_DYNCREATE (CReportLine, CObject)

CReportLine::CReportLine()
{
   m_nValue = 0;
   m_szLine = "";
}

CReportLine::~CReportLine()
{
   // empty
}

int CReportLine::GetLineType()
{
   return m_nLineType;
}

CString CReportLine::GetLine()
{
   return m_szLine;
}

long CReportLine::GetValue()
{
   return m_nValue;
}

void CReportLine::SetLineType (int nType)
{
   m_nLineType = nType;
}

void CReportLine::SetLine (CString szLine)
{
   m_szLine = szLine;
}

void CReportLine::SetValue (long nValue)
{
   m_nValue = nValue;
}
```

Changes to what was presented previously, in Chapter 10, are indicated by change bars in the foregoing code. In all other respects, the code for this class is unchanged.

Application Summary

The foregoing chapters have presented the evolutionary design and implementation of a comprehensive application, which is useful as it stands for household record keeping and report generation.

The application was begun with the creation of its initial skeleton by using the AppWizard tool supplied with the Visual C++ product. Further additions to the skeleton were made through the use of the App Studio and ClassWizard tools. The addition of custom code implemented each new feature fully.

In every case, when new features were added, we presented and described the custom code in its entirety. By doing so, we hope that we have given you a good head start in learning how to implement useful features of your own applications. We believe that the variety of user interface elements, the use of different mapping modes, implementation of printing, and fully documented custom code for the creation of both textual and graphic reports should be a good resource upon which to draw for your own needs. More than anything else, we hope that you have gained a more thorough understanding of the workings of the Microsoft Foundation Classes and how they can be used to great advantage in the creation of complex applications in record time.

Exercises

1. In the exercises in Chapter 11, we suggested that you prototype the settings for the creation of a pie chart. Assuming that you have accomplished this task, we now ask you to implement that chart in the context of the code presented in this chapter.[1]

2. When charts are printed, why doesn't the code print the various properties in color? Explain how the code could be modified to provide more graphical sophistication in a monochrome printout.

3. If you examine the code for the production of the Net Worth Chart carefully, you will notice that we make no special provision for tiling charts that extend beyond the boundaries of a printed page. Modify

---

[1] Implementing a pie chart will be a rather sizable effort. This should be undertaken as either an extra-credit task or a classroom project.

the code so that multiple segments of a wide chart are printed on successive pages, so that they may be pasted together.[1]

4. Now that the main body of the code is complete, we have some suggestions for modifying it to be more applicable to real-life accounting problems. Each of these suggestions is a separate task, which could be undertaken as a special project. The tasks are as follows:

   a. Change the headings on the account views, according to the type of account being viewed. For example, Payment and Deposit are not really appropriate for Credit Card accounts. The headings could be Payment and Charge, instead. For Asset accounts, Increase and Decrease might be more appropriate.

   b. Change the method of handling Liability account entries. Either define a special account to accumulate the principal and interest amounts separately so that the interest could be taken as a tax deductible item, or create two accounts that are linked in some manner to handle the principal and interest amounts separately. Also, change the headings for the Liability accounts to be more appropriate. When payments are made, the portions attributable to interest and principal should be handled automatically.

   c. Provide an "Amortization" report for selected liability accounts. Provide a separate listing of the loan payment schedule, and a summary of the principal and interest paid to date, remaining principal amount, and number of remaining payments.

   d. Provide the means for the user to select a category in the list of categories view and have that category name be transferred automatically to the account entry being revised.

   e. Consider providing the means to output a tab-delimited file, containing the information in the Keepit transaction file, in the form in which a tax preparation program could use the data.

5. The final suggested task is to provide context-sensitive help for all of the elements of the Keepit application. The reason this was not done from the outset is that doing so requires the use of a word processor that can edit help files in "Rich Text Format," and we could not presume that such a program was available to you in the construction of the application.

[1.] Paginating the chart so that it is printed in sections will require a fair number of changes to the existing DrawChart member function logic. We suggest that this project be assigned as an optional task, for extra credit. It could also be undertaken as a classroom project.

Index